OFFSHORE FINANCE

It is estimated that up to 60 per cent of the world's money may be located offshore, where half of all financial transactions are said to take place. Meanwhile, there is a perception that secrecy about offshore is encouraged to obfuscate tax evasion and money laundering. Depending upon the criteria used to identify them, there are between forty and eighty offshore finance centres spread around the world. The tax rules that apply in these jurisdictions are determined by the jurisdictions themselves and often are more benign than comparative rules that apply in the larger financial centres globally. This gives rise to potential for the development of tax mitigation strategies. McCann provides a detailed analysis of the global offshore environment, outlining the extent of the information available and how that information might be used in assessing the quality of individual jurisdictions, as well as examining whether some of the perceptions about 'Offshore' are valid. He analyses the ongoing work of what have become known as the 'standard setters' – including the Financial Stability Forum, the Financial Action Task Force, the International Monetary Fund, the World Bank and the Organization for Economic Co-operation and Development. The book also offers some suggestions as to what the future might hold for offshore finance.

HILTON MCCANN was the Acting Chief Executive of the Financial Services Commission, Mauritius. He has held senior positions in the respective regulatory authorities in the Isle of Man, Malta and Mauritius. Having trained as a banker, he began his regulatory career supervising banks in the Isle of Man. In Malta, his focus was on investment business, and in Mauritius his focus was on the establishment and strategic development of the recently created FSC.

OFFSHORE FINANCE

HILTON McCANN

CAMBRIDGE
UNIVERSITY PRESS

CAMBRIDGE UNIVERSITY PRESS
Cambridge, New York, Melbourne, Madrid, Cape Town, Singapore, São Paulo

CAMBRIDGE UNIVERSITY PRESS
The Edinburgh Building, Cambridge CB2 2RU, UK

Published in the United States of America by Cambridge University Press, New York

www.cambridge.org
Information on this title: www.cambridge.org/9780521862332

© Hilton McCann 2006

First published 2006

Printed in the United Kingdom at the University Press, Cambridge

A catalogue record for this publication is available from the British Library

ISBN-13 978-0-521-86233-2 hardback
ISBN-10 0-521-86233-7 hardback

CONTENTS

List of figures   *page* vii

List of tables   viii

Preface   xi

List of abbreviations   xix

PART I   **The past**   1

1   Linkages   3

2   The 'Offshore' environment   10

3   The service providers and the consumer (1)   37

4   The service providers and the consumer (2)   58

5   The significance of taxation   82

6   A description of regulatory and supervisory
     processes   116

7   The regulator and the regulatory authority   177

8   Money laundering   202

9   Some international organisations and groupings   230

PART II   **The present**   259

10   Supranational focus (1): the Financial Stability Forum and the
      International Monetary Fund   261

11 Supranational focus (2): the Financial Action Task Force 287

12 Supranational focus (3): the Organization for Economic Cooperation and Development 307

PART III **The future** 331

13 Some problems 'Offshore' 333

14 Some problems 'Onshore' 345

15 Small islands and 'Offshore' 359

16 Some information on particular centres 373

17 The UK and 'Offshore' 388

18 The USA and 'Offshore' 400

19 Can the problems be identified? 422

20 Offshore's Future 433

21 How to assess an 'Offshore Finance Centre' 465

22 Conclusion 479

Appendix 1 491

Appendix 2 531

Index 534

FIGURES

6.1   Regulation: problem/impact analysis   *page* 120
6.2   Regulation: cost/benefit analysis   121
21.1   The success paradigm   472

vii

TABLES

1 Participation in the Information Framework   *page* 491
2 Services 'Offshore'   491
3 The medical paradigm   492
4 Financial services regulatory tools   492
5 Number of registered companies   492
6 Regulatory structures worldwide   493
7 External factors versus regulatory factors   493
8 Examples of punitive measures that may be imposed by
   supervisory authorities   494
9 The evolutionary process describing the maturation
   of an international financial services centre   494
10 Members of the Basel Committee   495
11 Analysis as at end 2003 of the number of jurisdictions
    assessed under the Financial Sector Assessment Program   496
12 Analysis as at February 2005 showing the number of
    jurisdictions assessed under the Financial Sector
    Assessment Program   496
13 The general framework of the Forty Recommendations   497
14 The general framework of the Nine Special
    Recommendations   497
15 Population, land area and population density of
    selected OFCs   498
16 Global statistics: foreign direct investment, assets under
    management and world exports   498
17 The FSF's categorisation of OFCs (as at March 2000)   498
18 FATF Members and Observers   500
19 Tax havens, as defined by the OECD (as at June 2000)   501
20 The OECD's 'potential by uncooperative tax havens'   503
21 The OECD's 'uncooperative tax havens'   504
22 The FATF's 'First Set of Jurisdictions'   504

23 Ongoing changes to the FATF's list of Non-Cooperative
    Countries and Territories   506
24 Members of the Egmont Group   508
25 Members of the European Union   509
26 OECD/FATF/FSF reports summarised   510
27 Analysis of FSAP and Module 2 assessment reports
    (as at 12 March 2004)   516
28 Members of IOSCO (as at 30 April 2005)   518
29 OFCs, summary status   521
30 IMF assessment status summarised   524
31 Analysis of total assets held in OFCs   527

PREFACE

It has been estimated that up to 60 per cent of the world's money may be located 'Offshore' – which is the home of US$6.5 trillion of assets. Some 50 per cent of all financial transactions take place 'Offshore'. According to an IMF report dated March 2005, in respect of the Cayman Islands alone, 'the total international assets and liabilities held by Banks in the Cayman Islands were US$1.04 trillion'.[1] It has been suggested that 'the various offshore jurisdictions play a role in over US$1000bn of business annually . . . [and that] . . . off balance sheet transactions now account for a growing portion of offshore business, so that the true scale of the uses to which sophisticated businesses make of the offshore centres is not apparent from their public documents'.[2]

Even allowing for a material margin of inaccuracy in the estimates, the figures quoted indicate that the global economic potency of the composite 'Offshore' environment is significant. The potential may be positive or negative; for example, 'Offshore' centres clearly perform a useful function which the volume of financial trade reflects. The quantum makes 'Offshore' a factor in, and therefore a potential opportunity in respect of, global financial stability. The text describes in detail why 'Offshore' centres add so much value. However, there is a potential threat also. It has been stated that '[t]he potential for financial system instability in an offshore country underscores the need to better understand the nature of OFC [offshore finance centre] activities and inter-linkages with the global financial system'.[3] This text attempts to contribute to that understanding.

---

[1] Cayman Islands: Assessment of the Supervision and Regulation of the Financial Sector, March 2005, Vol. II; *Detailed Assessment of Observance of Standards and Codes*, para. 7, p. 6.

[2] D. P. Kempe and G. Wood, *The Bermuda International Business Guide 2003*, ISI Publications Ltd, p. 5.

[3] *Offshore Financial Centres – The Role of the IMF*, 23 June 2000, p. 3.

The increasing competition for good quality business, mainland jurisdictions' concerns about how they will continue to finance budget
deficits, the increasing frequency and extent of financial fraud and the
overriding concerns about global money laundering and the financing of
terrorism have all focused attention on financial environments and how
they operate. The 'Offshore' financial environment is no exception. In
the words of one commentator, '[i]t would be hard not to notice that
something is going on offshore, even if the public do not know much
about it, or whether it is a good thing or a bad thing'.[4]

Insofar as 'Offshore' is concerned, the focus culminated in three far-
reaching and fundamentally significant reports by the Organization for
Economic Cooperation and Development (OECD), the Financial Stability Forum (FSF) and the Financial Action Task Force (FATF) respectively.
(Subsequently, the International Monetary Fund (IMF), the United
Nations (UN) and the World Bank became involved also.) The reports
underscored the quantum of business transacted 'Offshore' and
prompted substantial further thought and action on the potential of
the 'Offshore' environment. Without doubt, the 'Offshore Environment'
has changed as a result of these reports and will change further as
'Offshore' attempts to optimise its potential in the global economic
environment. The profile of 'Offshore' was raised significantly as a result
of the amount of attention focused on it by the supranational bodies –
but care should be taken to avoid any misunderstandings. Without a
general awareness of the 'Offshore Environment', the rationale for such
attention may be misinterpreted to mean something negative.

In fact, it is a positive development that currently more attention is
being paid to 'Offshore' than ever before, and this book examines why
that should be the case. The image and credibility of 'Offshore' is
improving rapidly as jurisdictions understand their respective part in
the global economy. The text attempts to place this increased interest
into a meaningful perspective – but what is that perspective? Even those
who are aware of 'Offshore' may not know a great deal about it – for
example how might people in general – and financially oriented people
in particular – define 'Offshore'?

While it would be convenient to begin with a definition of 'Offshore',
it is not possible to do so – because there is some uncertainty about the
meaning of 'Offshore'. According to some, this uncertainty is the direct

---

[4] Milton Grundy, Introduction, The OFC Report 2003, *Offshore Legislation 2003*.

result of the shroud of secrecy that envelops everything to do with 'Offshore'. However, the breadth and depth of information produced in this text suggests that the 'Offshore' environment is generally speaking not opaque. The absence of definitions need not thwart any attempt to find out what 'Offshore' means. In this respect, to enable some sort of framework to be established, some 'working definitions' are suggested in the chapters that follow. To underline the fact that the definitions suggested are merely means to an end (and not generally agreed), other than where it appears as part of a quotation, the word 'Offshore' will be shown within inverted commas in this text.

Despite the reasons, in the absence of factual information about 'Offshore', people are likely to default to anecdotal evidence, assumptions and estimates and will rely on 'secondary information' to form opinions, to make assessments and to draw conclusions. Such opinions and assessments are unreliable because they are based on perceptions that may or may not conform to reality. In fact, perceptions are an integral part of the 'Offshore' environment and sometimes they give rise to bizarre impressions – which in turn can lead to pejorative attitudes towards 'Offshore'. Frequently, perceptions combine fact and fiction and are often subjective – having been influenced disproportionately by extraneous factors that have little real bearing on the true scheme of things. The progression begins with a classification of a jurisdiction as an 'Offshore Centre'. Although it ought not, to some this infers some type of stigma – the reasons for which are explored in the text. Naturally, jurisdictions that might otherwise not object to being referred to as 'Offshore Finance Centres' (OFCs,) are not willing to be regarded or classified as such if that stigma attaches.

Perceptions can be insidious in many aspects of life, but, in respect of financial matters, they have a nasty habit of becoming reality. For example, if, in error, customers perceive their bank to be in financial difficulties, they might anticipate a run on the bank. As one nervous depositor reveals his anxiety to another, the probability of the actual collapse of the bank increases – to the extent that it might even become a reality. In short, wrong perceptions can potentially lead to disastrous consequences. In respect of 'Offshore', the perception is likely to gain momentum if there is no contrary action and message that are coherently presented to demonstrate otherwise. Those who are unwilling or unable to undertake appropriate research themselves or who – for whatever reason – do not know any different will assume that whatever they hear is true. The momentum gathers pace – and the negative stigma becomes a reality.

In the context of 'Offshore', there are ways in which facts are mixed with fiction. For example, it is generally true that many 'Offshore Finance Centres' are sparsely populated, tropical islands – where the main enterprises are finance and tourism. It is also frequently true that financial institutions in general and banks in particular which are located in such jurisdictions proliferate. There are likely to be many more banks than necessary for the business of the local community – which is almost certain to be small. Further, it is probable that the quantum of financial transactions processed through such centres will be extremely large both in value and in number. Probably, very large amounts of money will be held on deposit.

Having presented some of the facts, here is some of the fiction:

- 'Offshore' centres have more banks per head of population than other financial centres. Not true – for example, compare Lugano in Switzerland;
- there is no meaningful regulation 'Offshore', which means that virtually anything is possible there;
- the few rules that exist are benign, and even those are not really enforced;
- the unwritten rule is that few (if any) questions are asked;
- the only purpose that 'Offshore' serves is to help very wealthy people evade tax;
- the reason why everything to do with 'Offshore' is so secret is because all the business transacted has to do with tax evasion;
- 'Offshore' does not discourage money laundering; in fact, it is argued that the lack of rigour there encourages wrongdoing;
- money laundering is only possible because 'Offshore' jurisdictions will do anything to attract new business, so 'funny money' is acceptable 'Offshore';
- opening a bank account 'Offshore' is a mere formality;
- cash transactions are likely to be commonplace 'Offshore';
- 'brass plate operations' proliferate 'Offshore' (i.e. entities that are present only in legal form but without any physical presence or real substance);
- financial institutions operating 'Offshore' knowingly open accounts for money launderers and other criminals.

Here are some reasons why 'Offshore' is an enigma. First, it is axiomatic that 'Offshore Finance' is conducted in an island jurisdiction – referred to as an 'Offshore Finance Centre' – but even this is not always the case (e.g. the International Financial Services Centre in Dublin has been referred to as 'Offshore – Onshore'). It is irrelevant per se whether a person's bank is on the island of Manhattan or on the island of Mauritius. The quality and security of the financial environment is more important than whether the jurisdiction is an island or not.

Secondly, the 'quality' of the business that is conducted within the 'Offshore' environment is the key to its future. One commentator has said that '[i]n a world of 24 hour-a-day global markets and of integrated financial systems, having a mass of dirty money floating around the world threatens not just the markets but also western democracy'.[5] Subsequent chapters will examine this global phenomenon and indicate the extent to which financial institutions in both mainland and 'Offshore' jurisdictions have been used to warehouse 'dirty money' (the proceeds of crime – including tax evasion – or representing terrorist finance).

Tax evasion should be distinguished from tax avoidance. It is the legitimate right of every person to pay no more tax than is due. Fundamentally, 'Offshore Centres' provide efficient opportunities for taxpayers to arrange their affairs in such a way as to minimise their tax bills. Business 'Offshore' revolves around tax. 'Offshore Centres' have been successful but this has aroused strong suspicions in larger mainland jurisdictions that their success infers that it is not legitimately achieved. Other citizens – for whom the 'Offshore' route is not an option – have no sympathy because they are not prepared to condone someone else being able to enjoy an advantage which they cannot. 'Offshore' is a whipping boy – often disparaged and always mistrusted. The text tries to treat such suspicions objectively by enabling readers to compare like with like.

Thirdly, 'Offshore' is vulnerable – but perversely its vulnerabilities are exactly what make 'Offshore' attractive in the first place. They include: autonomy, confidentiality offered to investors, benign tax structures, and a tailored regulatory environment that is frequently less prescriptive than might be applied in mainland jurisdictions. These attributes are precisely what tax-sensitive corporations and individuals are looking for.

[5] J. Robinson, *The Laundrymen*, Simon & Schuster UK Ltd, 1998, p. 394.

Regrettably, fraudsters, crooks, money launderers, tax evaders and financers of terrorism are looking for exactly the same things – for other purposes. When something wrongful happens 'Offshore', it often attracts a great deal of attention but surprises no one because the general opinion is that 'Offshore' infers dubious business at best. When something wrongful happens in a mainland jurisdiction, it seems to receive less attention. Is this because it is regarded as commonplace and not newsworthy? No financial environment is safe from those who would exploit its advantages for wrongful purposes – so why should the same type of wrongdoing attract such diverse responses?

It is hardly surprising that, thus far, all attempts to define 'Offshore' or to suggest what it comprises, or which jurisdictions are 'Offshore' jurisdictions, and what particular traits or characteristics make them fall within the definition, have proved problematic. The reasons for all this uncertainty are explored in the text.

Meanwhile, in the words of Blaise Pascal, 'Let it not be said that I have said nothing new. The arrangement of the material is new.' In fact, much of the information presented is not new per se – but the construct in which it is presented is different to what has gone before – and it is hoped that a composite presentation of the information contained in the text may be of use in particular to those who work 'Offshore'. It is hoped also that, simultaneously, the construct adopted will not dissuade the casual reader while attempting to stimulate the interests of researchers to probe further. This might be achieved in a number of ways – but the optimum use to which this text might be directed is as a platform for subsequent study and research.

While there is a substantial amount of information available about 'Offshore', it is in myriad forms, and to a large extent it is unclassified and disjointed. The source of most information that is available is likely to be an article in a journal or in a newspaper. The footnotes aptly demonstrate this point.

At best, newspaper articles (and, to a lesser extent, articles in journals) about 'Offshore' are often helpful – but their publication is in response to a matter of current public interest. Matters arising are discussed in an uncoordinated fashion and, most often, the context is unclear. Books about 'Offshore' that combine related matters in a coherent and co-ordinated framework are not common. Often, the books that are available are promotional in nature – they combine advertising with information that is sometimes superficial. Many are written with a view to persuading readers to contact the author (or related persons) for advice on tax planning or fiduciary services. This text attempts to collate some of that information and to show some of the synergies arising from having done so.

The difficulties in researching 'Offshore' arise not only because existing information is not collated in any cohesive or coordinated or easily managed form, but also because there is a dearth of statistical information in particular. In this respect, the IMF has said that '[a]ll examinations of the role of OFCs in the international financial system have been hampered by a lack of adequate data'.[6] This means that we are less than totally aware than we should be of the potential benefits (and dangers) that characterise this part of the global economy. By extension, sub-optimisation of the environment's positive potential is likely, and, at worst, the extent to which 'Offshore' is or might be used for wrongful purposes will not be understood properly. For example, it is only with the publication of a paper on Best Practice for Corporate Services Providers (CSPs) in 2002 that there has been any real emphasis on setting standards in what is an increasingly significant area of 'Offshore' activity. Even though the services provided by CSPs have been a staple part of the 'Offshore' menu for many years (some jurisdictions have hundreds of thousands of entities incorporated therein), they have received scant attention until recently. However, the advances made have allowed some of the more progressive jurisdictions to adopt a regulatory response that leaves much bigger mainland centres (such as the UK) far behind.

A clearer perspective of 'Offshore' may contribute to the general store of knowledge and to our understanding of this integral part of the global economy. Ultimately, this enhanced level of understanding may lend something positive to the possible future uses to which the 'Offshore Environment' might be put. 'There is a need for a better understanding of the operations of OFCs and surrounding risks.'[7] Contrarily, unless the problems that exist are analysed correctly, the remedies suggested may not be appropriate. In short, it is suggested that any attempt to understand 'Offshore' is a valuable endeavour.

In respect of structure, the book is divided into three parts. The first third of the book (Chapters 1 to 9) sets the scene. It describes the context of 'Offshore' and identifies some of the problems that arise because of the lack of satisfactory definitions. Three different interest groups are

---

[6] *Offshore Financial Centres – The Role of the IMF*, 23 June 2000, p. 20.
[7] *Offshore Financial Centres – The Role of the IMF*, 23 June 2000, p. 7.

identified – the marketplace, service providers and consumers. Tax and regulation – the two factors that are at the very core of 'Offshore' – are examined in detail.

The middle third of the book (Chapters 10 to 12) focuses on the extent to which 'Offshore' has been criticised, and explores whether it is fair to blame 'Offshore Centres' for not doing more to disenable criminals from exploiting their jurisdictions by laundering the proceeds of crime 'Offshore'. Some of the problems that affect the global financial services network are considered. The extent to which the 'Offshore' environment has become the focus of global attention is perhaps best understood by reference to work undertaken at the end of the 1990s by the FSF, the FATF and the OECD. An analysis of the work of these three organisations is spread over three chapters. Whether there is any correlation between 'Offshore' and small island jurisdictions is considered briefly.

The last third of the book (Chapters 13 to 22) begins with a synopsis of how things stand currently. There is a comparison of two of the world's largest – and most respected – financial services centres – the USA and the UK. This leads to consideration as to whether 'Offshore' is really the cause of so many global woes or whether it is somewhat a scapegoat. This section attempts to summarise the problems and to identify some options for the future – after the FSF, FATF, OECD and the catastrophic events of 11 September 2001 in the USA. Finally, the book provides a checklist that consumers might use in deciding where to transact 'Offshore', and ends with some recommendations for the future.

ABBREVIATIONS

AML/CFT	Anti-Money Laundering and Combating the Financing of Terrorism
APG	Asia/Pacific Group on Money Laundering
ATS	Alternative Trading Systems
BCP	Basel Core Principles
BIS	Bank for International Settlements
CAD	Capital Adequacy Directive
CARICOM	Caribbean Community and Common Market
CCJ	Caribbean Court of Justice
CDD	Customer Due Diligence
CFATF	Caribbean Financial Action Task Force
COSE	Committee of South African Stock Exchanges
CPIS	Coordinated Portfolio Investment Survey
CSME	Caribbean Single Market and Economy
CSP	Corporate Service Provider
CTAG	Counter Terrorism Action Group
EBRD	European Bank for Reconstruction and Development
ECB	European Central Bank
ECOFIN	Council for Economic and Financial Affairs (of the EU)
EEA	European Economic Area (EU countries plus Norway, Iceland and Liechtenstein)
EIB	European Investment Bank
ESAAMLG	Eastern and Southern Africa Anti-Money Laundering Group
FATF	Financial Action Task Force
FINTRAC	Financial Transactions and Reports Analysis Centre (of Canada)
FIU	Financial Intelligence Unit
FSA	Financial Services Authority (of the UK)
FSAP	Financial Sector Assessment Program
FSF	Financial Stability Forum

FSR	Financial Strength Rating
FSRB	FATF Style Regional Body
FSSA	Financial System Stability Assessment
G7	Canada, France, Germany, Italy, Japan, the United Kingdom and the United States
G8	Canada, France, Germany, Italy, Japan, Russia, the United Kingdom and the United States
GAFISUD	Financial Action Task Force on Money Laundering in South America
GCC	Gulf Cooperation Council
GIABA	Intergovernmental Group of Action Against Money Laundering in West Africa
GPML	Global Programme against Money Laundering (UN)
IAIS	International Association of Insurance Supervisors
IDB	Inter-American Development Bank
IFI	International Financial Institution
IMF	International Monetary Fund
IMoLIN	International Money Laundering Information Network
IMVT	Informal Money or Value Transfer System
IOSCO	International Organization of Securities Commissions
IRB	Internal Ratings Based
ISD	Investment Services Directive
ISMA	International Securities Market Association
ITIO	International Trade and Investment Organization
JMLSG	Joint Money Laundering Steering Group
KYC	Know Your Customer
MLAT	Money Laundering Assistance Treaties
MONEYVAL	Council of Europe Select Committee of Experts on the Evaluation of Anti-Money Laundering Measures
MOU	Memorandum of Understanding
NCCT	Non-Cooperative Countries and Territories
NCIS	National Criminal Intelligence Service (of the UK)
NPO	non-profit organisation
ODCCP	Office for Drug Control and Crime Prevention
OECD	Organization for Economic Cooperation and Development
OECS	Organization of Eastern Caribbean States
OFC	Offshore Financial Centre
OFSI	Office of the Superintendent of Financial Institutions
OGBS	Offshore Group of Banking Supervisors

OGIS	Offshore Group of Insurance Supervisors
PC-R-EV	See MONEYVAL
PEP	politically exposed person
ROSC	Report on Observance of Standards and Codes
SADC	South African Development Community
SAR	Suspicious Activity Report
SDE	Small and Developing Economies
SIB	Securities and Investment Board (of the UK)
SIE	Small Island Economies
SRO	self-regulatory organisation
STR	Suspicious Transaction Report
SWIFT	Society for Worldwide Inter-bank Financial Telecommunication
TA	Technical Assistance
TIEA	Tax Information Exchange Agreement
UCITS	Undertakings for Collective Investment in Transferable Securities
UNODCCP	United Nations Office for Drug Control and Crime Prevention
VAR	value at risk
VOI	verification of identity
WCO	World Customs Organization
WTO	World Trade Organization

PART I

The past

Part I comprises the first third of the text, embracing nine chapters. The timespan is from the beginnings of 'Offshore' (say, the 1930s) until the late 1990s (say, 1998). Chapter 1 provides an overview and a brief analysis of each of the chapters that follow. More generally, this Part sets the scene, by describing the context in which 'Offshore' exists, and identifies why the lack of relevant information is problematic. Three different interest groups are identified – the marketplace, the service providers and consumers. The two factors that are at the very core of 'Offshore' (tax and regulation) are examined in detail.

1

Linkages

Not many people will defend tax havens . . . They make fine whipping boys.[1]

1.1 The structure of the book

The three sections into which the book is divided equate roughly to the natural division between the past, the present and the future. Some licence is taken with this arbitrary division – but not to the extent that it will detract from the purposes described in the Preface.

Each chapter begins with a brief summary of its content. Many of the chapters 'stand alone', and can be read independently of other chapters. The object of Chapter 1 is not only to show the linkages between chapters but also to describe the core themes that run through the text.

1.2 What does 'Offshore' mean?

Chapter 2 quotes some technical definitions, and some 'working definitions' are suggested. The contributions of the OECD and of the IMF are noted in this respect. Some background information is provided on the origins of 'Offshore', and its development is traced. The world's 'Tax Havens' (as defined by the OECD) are identified. Whether Tax Havens are the same as 'Offshore Centres' is a debate that is left until later, but section 2.7 shows that some writers see clear distinctions between the two.

---

[1] 'The Mystery of the Vanishing Taxpayer', 29 January 2000, Special Supplement, *The Economist*, p. 6.

1.3 The market, the buyers and the sellers

Chapters 3 and 4 identify three different interest groups that exist in respect of 'Offshore'. Chapter 3 focuses on the marketplace, that is to say the 'Offshore Centre' per se. Comment is provided on some features of 'Offshore' jurisdictions and on the legitimacy of such centres, as described by the IMF. Reference is made to the three attributes that are the hallmarks of all 'Offshore' jurisdictions – tax, regulation and confidentiality. A brief comment is provided on confidentiality in Chapter 3. A subsequent chapter is devoted to tax and regulation. Chapter 3 ends with a description of some of the characteristics of 'Offshore Finance Centres', and a comparison with some of the characteristics of mainland finance centres.

Chapter 4 considers the remaining two interest groups – the service providers and the consumers. The range of products offered by the service providers is examined in detail. The FSF's description of why OFCs are used is quoted. The consumer and his or her expectations are considered at the end of the chapter.

1.4 Three fundamental criteria for 'Offshore Finance Centres'

The three key attributes of 'Offshore Finance Centres' have already been mentioned. Chapter 5 concentrates on the second of these (tax) and Chapter 6 is devoted to regulation.

Insofar as tax is concerned, 'Offshore' infers either no tax at all or low tax (see the OECD's definition of a tax haven in section 12.3 below). On this basis, it can be no surprise that the 'Offshore' environment is a factor in many tax mitigation strategies. Chapter 5 begins with a discussion of the differences between avoidance and evasion. The chapter includes consideration of tax competition and tax harmonisation before describing the importance of 'Offshore' in tax planning. The OECD's approach to tax and 'Offshore' is described. The rest of the chapter is given over to a description of the EU's Savings Tax Directive and its implications for 'Offshore'.

It is suggested that regulation is one of the most critical components for success within any 'Offshore' arena – and the reasons for this are teased out in a description of the 'success paradigm' (see section 21.7 below). In the meantime, regulation is the last of the criteria mentioned above. It is described in Chapter 6. In the main, the people who use 'Offshore' do not live in the jurisdiction where they conduct their business. Such people not only want to minimise their tax burden but also want to ensure that their assets are safe. This is why regulation is described as a 'critical success factor'. Chapter 6 provides the rationale for regulation, and explains its functions by reference to a clinical analogy. As an adjunct to a commentary on the role of the regulator and supervisor, some of the components of regulation, including licensing, fit and proper, compliance and 'Know Your Customer', are described in detail. Reference is made to different regulatory models (e.g. Twin Peaks) and techniques (e.g. consolidated supervision). Some differences between regulation and supervision are described.

Chapter 7 expands the theme of regulation – but does so with the emphasis on the role of the regulator and the regulatory authority – within the context of evolving financial services. A number of operational matters are considered – such as training and experience, communications, boards – and some of the advantages and disadvantages of a single unified regulatory authority.

1.5 The 'Offshore' enigma

Much has been said and written about money laundering. It is frequently the case that 'Offshore Centres' are blamed for not doing more to frustrate the attempts of criminals in laundering the proceeds of their crimes and to prevent terrorists from financing their illegal activities through 'Offshore Finance Centres'. Chapter 8 explores the extent to which this accusation is justified. The FATF and its work are considered at some length. The crime of money laundering is defined, and some of the factors that contribute to its insidious nature are described. The implications for 'Offshore Finance Centres' are considered before an analysis of the fight against money laundering is provided. The chapter introduces 'Financial Intelligence Units' and includes a description of their role and that of the Egmont Group. Reference is made to the Wolfsberg Principles. The chapter ends with some comments on the Basel Committee's paper entitled 'Customer Due Diligence for Banks'. Comments on the threats imposed by terrorist financing are mentioned.

1.6 'Offshore' in context

The global financial environment impinges upon 'Offshore' in many ways – not least through the myriad organisations whose operations bring them into close proximity with that environment. Some of these organisations are described in Chapter 9.

1.7 The supranational focus

The extent to which the 'Offshore' environment has become the focus of global attention is perhaps best understood by reference to work undertaken at the end of the 1990s by three supranational organisations.

The respective reports of the FSF, the FATF and the OECD are analysed in Chapters 10, 11 and 12, respectively. These reports are fundamentally significant because their influence on the 'Offshore' environment is direct. The involvement of the IMF and of the World Bank is also described.

The OECD published a report in 1998 entitled 'Harmful Tax Competition – An Emerging Global Issue'. The OECD believed that the development of tax systems encouraged by the globalisation of business enabled 'tax havens' to develop. The OECD's report proceeded to define a 'tax haven' and has led to substantial changes in the 'Offshore' industry.

Meanwhile, in February 2000, in order to identify anti-money laundering weaknesses generally, the FATF published a report entitled 'Report on Non-Cooperative Countries and Territories' that focused on (unnamed) countries and territories that were described as 'uncooperative' in the war against money laundering. This was to set the scene for what turned out to be a 'name and shame' exercise.

The FSF created a Working Group on 'Offshore Finance Centres'. The Group was asked to research and assess certain jurisdictions. The Group's work was completed in March 2000, and its conclusions were published in the 'Report of the Working Group on Offshore Financial Centres'. A survey (of both mainland and 'Offshore Finance Centres') was undertaken to obtain appropriate information. The results of the survey were used to classify those jurisdictions that were considered to have significant 'Offshore' activities into three categories according to their perceived quality of supervision and degree of co-operation.

1.8 Problems associated with some financial environments

Chapters 13 and 14 are a mirror image of each other. They describe some of the problems that affect the global financial services network.

Chapter 13 focuses on 'Offshore' and Chapter 14 looks at mainland jurisdictions – sometimes called 'Onshore'. There are many reasons for problems in financial services jurisdictions and it is naïve to suggest that merely tightening the rules will eradicate all weaknesses. Some of the examples cited will indicate why this is so. It is also the case that any jurisdiction that wants to continue in business as a financial services centre in the longer term cannot tolerate weak regulation and control. To do so would weaken the foundations on which meaningful growth will depend.

The following quote gives food for thought: 'It is often suggested that markets push governments into complying with international standards . . . At most . . . markets will encourage countries to claim to implement international standards, but will not encourage them to implement standards properly.'[2]

1.9 'Offshore' and small island jurisdictions

Chapter 15 presents some (brief) comments on the correlation between 'Offshore' finance and small island jurisdictions. The chapter indicates some of the tensions that exist in such environments and also describes some characteristics that make small islands ideal for the conduct of financial services – but at a price!

1.10 An overview of some financial centres

In order to 'globalise' the matters under discussion, Chapter 16 presents some information and figures that indicate the size of the 'Offshore' environment. However, there are problems in trying to do so because the statistics available are limited and because 'Offshore' centres are in a period of continuous change. Within limitations, the chapter provides a snapshot of how things stand currently in some jurisdictions. The information is not comprehensive – this is not the purpose of the text.

[2] J. Ward, 'Is Basel II Voluntary for Developing Countries', December 2002, *The Financial Regulator*, Vol. 7, No. 3, p. 54.

1.11 The extent to which 'Offshore' business is restricted to 'Offshore' centres

Chapters 17 and 18 present some information on two of the world's largest – and most respected – financial services centres. A closer look at what happens in the United States and in the United Kingdom indicates that what might be described as 'Offshore' business is carried on in centres other than small islands located off a mainland. The chapter further indicates that even the largest financial services jurisdictions face challenges.

1.12 'Offshore' and financial stability, money laundering and tax evasion

'Directors [of the IMF] recognised that OFCs could pose risks, associated with prudential and financial integrity concerns, to the international financial system.'[3] This is so, despite the fact that 'only limited evidence was available that far on the direct risks posed by OFCs for the global financial systems'.[4] There are at least three areas in which 'Offshore' impinges upon the global economy – financial stability, money laundering and tax evasion. Chapter 19 considers the extent to which 'Offshore' is the cause of difficulties in respect of each.

1.13 'Offshore' and the future

Chapter 20 attempts to tease out some options for the future of 'Offshore' post FSF, FATF, OECD and the catastrophic events of 11 September 2001 in the USA. There may be a direct correlation between the general public's perception of finance centres and their ultimate survival. The question is whether in fact there are really any options at all.

1.14 Assessment criteria

The penultimate chapter of the book, Chapter 21, is a practical chapter – in that it provides some suggestions that users and potential users of

---

[3] *IMF Executive Board Reviews the Assessment Program on Offshore Financial Centres,* 24 November 2003, IMF.
[4] *Offshore Financial Centres – The Assessment Program – A Progress Report and the Future of the Program,* 31 July 2003, International Monetary Fund, p. 5.

'Offshore Centres' might consider in deciding whether to use offshore centres at all, and if so which, jurisdiction they might use.

1.15 Conclusion

By way of a brief recap, the last chapter, Chapter 22, draws together some of the themes that have been examined in the previous chapters. The chapter concludes with some crystal ball gazing.

2

The 'Offshore' environment

> The demonstrated success of most of these [Offshore] centres and their
> liberalised financial regimes has to an extent rewritten the geography of
> world finance.[1]

2.1 Introduction

Jurisdictions that provide financial services can be broadly categorised
as being 'Onshore' or 'Offshore'. These two financial environments co-
exist within the global economic environment. This chapter starts with
a brief explanation of the origin of the 'Offshore' environment and
then proceeds to identify jurisdictions that might be described as
'Offshore Finance Centres'. The growth of the sector is described in
terms of available statistics.

2.2 Geographical dispersion

There are many ways in which the geographical dispersion of the
'Offshore' environment can be analysed. Here are two examples. First,
Johns[2] believes that 'Offshore Centres' fall within the following four
regions:

- the Caribbean Basin (e.g. Bermuda, the Bahamas, the Cayman Islands, the Netherlands Antilles and Panama);
- Europe (e.g. Switzerland and Luxembourg);
- the Middle East (e.g. Bahrain and the UAE); and

---

[1] C. F. Kerr and P. Donald, 'Some Aspects of the Geography of Finance in Canada', in *Readings in Canadian Geography*, ed. Robert M. Irving, Toronto, Holt, Rinehart and Winston, 1965, as quoted in R. A. Johns, 'A Study of Trans-national Economic Development', *Tax Havens and Offshore Finance*, Frances Pinter (Publishers) Ltd, 1983, p. 34.

[2] R. A. Johns, *Tax Havens and Offshore Finance – A Study of Transnational Economic Development*, Frances Pinter (Publishers) Ltd, 1983, p. 191.

- the Far East (e.g. Hong Kong, Singapore and Vanuatu).

Elsewhere, five regions have been identified as follows:

- Africa (e.g. Mauritius, Seychelles);
- Asia and the Pacific (e.g. the Cook Islands, Labuan, Nauru, Niue, Samoa etc.);
- the Caribbean (e.g. Anguilla, Antigua, Aruba, the Bahamas, Barbados, the Cayman Islands etc.);
- Europe (e.g. Cyprus, Gibraltar, Guernsey, the Isle of Man, Jersey etc.); and
- the Middle East (e.g. Bahrain, Dubai, the Lebanon).

Whether either of these categorisations is precise, or even whether any other is more precise, is not the most significant point. The most important point is that, despite how such jurisdictions are dispersed, they are not represented by a single global organisation. It might be argued that this is not surprising in light of this sort of dispersion – but, precisely because of their dispersion, there is an even greater need to be identified by a collective grouping within a sole forum. Each jurisdiction is relatively small so the potential synergies arising from combining forces seem worth considering. The implications of not having done so remain to be seen.

In the meantime, the geographical spread might have something to do with the intrinsic secretiveness that is or was the hallmark of every member of the 'Offshore' community – and which prevented the interdependence that a single forum infers. This individualism has been counter-productive generally, not least when it came to negotiating with the supranational organisations about issues that are common to all (see Chapters 10 to 12). The implication is that it has been easier for the supranational organisations to impose their will on individual jurisdictions than it might have been if the supranational organisations had to deal with a composite, representative body. The Offshore Group of Banking Supervisors (see section 9.21 below) comes closest to being that representative – but, since 'Offshore' comprises much more than banking, the OGBS's focus, while significant, is not comprehensive. There have been some suggestions about how best to tackle representation, but at this moment, there are no firm plans for change. Historically, when Americans want to use an 'Offshore Centre', they have tended to use the jurisdictions located in the Caribbean. By way of contrast, the Isle of Man and the Channel Islands (Jersey and Guernsey) have been used by

UK and Irish residents. Europeans favour Switzerland. There has always been a tendency for people onshore to use an 'Offshore' centre that is closest to where they themselves live – the comments above on the global dispersion of 'Offshore Centres' refer.

2.3 What does 'Offshore' mean?

It is not easy to say succinctly what 'Offshore' means because it can be interpreted to mean so many things that limiting its scope seems almost impossible. One observer has suggested that '[O]ffshore is a concept more appropriately defined not by whether a financial centre is large or small but rather by whether the client resides outside the jurisdiction providing the particular financial service'.[3] It is often said that elephants are hard to describe but, once seen, they are easily recognised. The same might be said of 'Offshore'. The boundaries of 'Offshore' are not fixed and its shape does not conform to any particular model or style that is readily identifiable – in fact one of its characteristics is its ability to change shape in adapting to new circumstances.

It has been said that:

> the terms onshore and offshore work often as an oppositional dualism. In this formulation they may be seen as exhaustive: that is, every space economy in the world fits into one of these two mutually exclusive categories. However, when observers and analysts have attempted to define the categories 'Onshore' and 'Offshore', and when places have been slotted into one or other of these categories, it becomes clear that while the terms are, by their very nature, oppositional, they may be better understood as relational. That is, the very idea of such a thing as offshore only makes sense in reference to its 'other', an onshore, and vice versa. Moreover, each term, each space, 'contains' the meaning of the other in its definition.[4]

In the report of the Working Group on 'Offshore Centres' published in April 2000, the Financial Stability Forum (FSF) acknowledged the

---

[3] R. Hay, 'International Financial Centres: Back on the Front Foot', in *The 2005 Guide to International Financial Centres*, Euromoney Institutional Investor plc, February 2005, p. 3.

[4] S. M. Roberts, 'Confidence Men: Offshore Finance and Citizenship', as quoted in *Offshore Finance Centres and Tax Havens – The Rise of Global Capital*, ed. Mark P. Hampton and Jason P. Abbott, Macmillan Press Ltd. 1999, Chapter 5, p. 132.

absence of a precise definition. It may be that trying to create a definition proved to be such a difficult task that this induced the Working Group to change its focus to describing the characteristics of 'Offshore Finance Centres' instead.

It is not that there are no definitions – because there are. However, existing definitions are disparate and inadequate to describe precisely all the concepts that are wrapped up in what is not only a word, but also a term. Perhaps the best way forward is akin to that adopted by the FSF. So, for the time being, the focus will be on exploring the concepts that lie behind the term rather than on the term itself.

The ninth edition of the *Concise Oxford Dictionary* defines 'Offshore' as 'situated at sea some distance from the shore . . . made or registered abroad'. Clearly, an island is envisaged. Not surprisingly, the word 'Offshore' is most commonly used to describe a geographical location. For example, an oil rig might be described as being located 'Offshore'. While this is a step forward in semantics, it is not progress in the direction intended because the context of our focus is financial, not geographical.

In this respect, the *Collins English Dictionary* sheds a little more light. There the word 'Offshore' is said to mean, among other things, 'based or operating abroad in places where the tax system is more advantageous than that of the home country'. So, when used in the context of 'finance', the latter dictionary says that the word 'Offshore' has more than geographic significance – although geography is relevant to its financial meaning. The definition includes a tax element, a comparative advantage element and a 'home country' element.

As it stands, the absence of a satisfactory definition coupled with vague references to comparative tax advantages somewhere other than at home is enough to prompt those who do not know any better (and sometimes those who do) to speculate that, although they cannot say precisely why, the word 'Offshore' has negative connotations. In the absence of a technical definition, the meaning of the word will be inferred rather than stated, thereby increasing the latitude for speculation and confusion. Confusion not only derives from the word per se, but also from the financial environment that the word is used to describe. Amidst all this confusion, there is at least one point that is clear – which is that, while the word 'Offshore' frequently conjures up images about its meaning, generally speaking the real meaning is not well understood.

That being so, there may be some value in clarifying that, for the purposes of this text, the terms 'Offshore Finance' (which includes 'Offshore banking', 'Offshore collective investment schemes (funds)', 'Offshore trusts' etc.)may be taken to include financial transactions conducted in a jurisdiction whose location is somewhere other than on the mainland ('Onshore').

It is not surprising that any location where finance is conducted is referred to as a finance centre. By extension, an 'Offshore Finance Centre' is a jurisdiction whose location is 'situated at sea some distance from the shore' where finance is conducted. Surely there must be more to it than that? Well, yes – because the word 'Offshore' not only infers that the location from which the service or product is offered is 'situated at sea some distance from the shore', it also infers that, because the service or product is provided 'some distance from the shore', certain attributes attach which would not or may not apply if the service or product were not offered 'Offshore'. These attributes are considered elsewhere in this text, but the *Collins English Dictionary* definition quoted above provides a strong hint of what is to follow.

In the meantime, the absence of an agreed definition of an 'Offshore Finance Centre' has a number of implications. For example, the lack of an agreed definition means that it is more difficult to determine with any accuracy how many 'Offshore Finance Centres' exist and what precisely is meant by the global 'Offshore Environment' or what its total quantum of business may be.

A further complication is that the word 'Offshore' is often used to mean different things in different contexts. Thus, many countries may be regarded as 'Offshore' by other countries in the context of specific transactions. For example, the United Kingdom might be considered as 'Offshore' in certain circumstances, although it is not usually referred to as an 'Offshore Centre' in the same way as, say, the Cayman Islands. Not all 'Offshore Finance Centres' regard themselves as such (see section 2.4 below).

Lastly in this respect, the distinctions between 'Onshore' and 'Offshore' are more blurred than they once were, and the range of people transacting business 'Offshore' is now much wider than ever before (although in light of developments such as the EU Savings Directive – which will be discussed later – the number of users is not continuing to grow at the same pace).

2.4 Some working definitions

Consider the following working definitions. First, 'Offshore Finance' may be regarded as a multidimensional, global concept, which involves consumers in a mainland 'home jurisdiction' ('Onshore') using financial services offered from an ('Offshore') 'host jurisdiction' (frequently an island) where the consumer will probably not reside.

The terms 'home' and 'host' are borrowed from regulatory terminology, where 'home jurisdiction' is used to refer to the country where a financial services company has its registered office. This might be on the mainland (i.e. 'Onshore'). In this example, the home jurisdiction is the consumer's country of residence. 'Host jurisdiction' in regulatory terminology means a country (other than the country of incorporation) where a financial services company is represented (by, say, a subsidiary or a branch). In this case, the host jurisdiction is where the consumer has chosen to transact his business (see section 5.4 below). 'Onshore' (the corollary of 'Offshore') should be interpreted to mean any mainland jurisdiction. Note that an 'Offshore' jurisdiction may be a 'home' jurisdiction, but is more likely to be a 'host' jurisdiction.

Secondly, the 'Offshore Environment' means the global population of 'Offshore Finance Centres'.

Thirdly, an 'Offshore Finance Centre' – commonly referred to as an 'OFC' – means a jurisdiction (which may be an island) that holds itself out as a financial services centre that enables financial services companies to conduct financial transactions – mainly with non-residents. The identity and the business of clients will be regarded as confidential. The infrastructure of the jurisdiction is likely to include a benign fiscal regime that is underpinned by a tailored legislative, financial and regulatory environment.

Whenever, the word 'Offshore' or any derivation of it appears subsequently in this text, its meaning should be interpreted by reference to the definitions provided above. The term will appear in the text within inverted commas to show that its interpretation should be that set out above and also to indicate that this definition is peculiar to this text and may not be universally acceptable. Where the word does not appear within inverted commas, this means that it has been used by a different author and so its meaning may be different to the working definition suggested above.

Note that, while an OFC may be an island, it need not be so. For example, the International Financial Services Centre in Dublin (IFSC), a

designated zone in the city of Dublin, has been dubbed by some as
'Offshore, Onshore' because all the benefits of locating 'Offshore' were
provided to promoters establishing in that zone – even though it is
located onshore. In this respect, it has been said that:

> there are several examples of deliberate regulatory changes designed to
> create onshore offshore. Selective de- (or re-)regulation in established
> onshore financial centres such as London and New York permitted the
> development of defined regulatory spaces within these centres in which
> various 'Offshore' services could take place. In fact, Ireland has been seen
> as something of an innovator in this regard with the development of
> Dublin's International Financial Services Centre (IFSC since 1987) . . .
> Dublin's IFSC has itself come under fire, especially from German author-
> ities, for being in effect a tax haven within the European Union.[5]

   However, Dublin does not regard itself as a tax haven. The IFSC was
established in the late 1980s. The IFSC is home to more than 400
financial institutions which employ around 4,000 people. This has been
possible (inter alia) because firms located there pay only 10 per cent
corporation tax as opposed to 37 per cent which is/was the average rate
applying in the EU. EU members approved this tax rate on the understanding that the IFSC would discontinue when it had achieved its goals.
Accordingly, in 1999, a new arrangement was established under which
Ireland imposed a 12.5 per cent corporate tax from 1 January 2003.
Naturally, this type of situation is frustrating for OFCs who might argue
that the EU has extended more flexibility to one of its own members
than it was willing to concede to OFCs (at least at one stage). Whether
this means that the Dublin IFSC is an 'Offshore Finance Centre' will be
left to the reader to judge.

2.5 Examples of some other definitions

Reference was made above to some technical definitions applied to
'Offshore'. Consider, for example, the definition provided by Johns.
R. A. Johns, *The British Isles 'Offshore Financial Centres'*, Pinter Publishers,

---

[5] L. Murphy, 'Financial Engine or Glorified Back Office? Dublin's International Financial
Services Centre Going Global', Vol. 30, No. 2, *Area*, 1998, pp. 157–65, as qoted by
S. M. Roberts, 'Confidence Men: Offshore Finance and Citizenship', in *Offshore Finance
Centres and Tax Havens – The Rise of Global Capital*, ed. Mark P. Hampton and Jason
P. Abbott, 1999, Macmillan Press Ltd, Chapter 5, p. 132.

1982. He suggested that an OFC will probably be a (geographically) small state that may be an inland enclave state, a coastal enclave or an island state. In any event, there will be an opportunity for mainland exploitation. The same author believes that OFCs will be located in 'economies which have made a deliberate attempt to attract thereto international trade-oriented activities by the minimisation of taxes and the reduction or elimination of other restrictions on business operations, such that, within the jurisdiction of the centre, aggregate economic activity is substantially geared to the special global invisible trade needs of external enterprises and investors'. So far as growth is concerned, Johns believes that 'more often than not their growth momentum in the first instance derived, and derives still in many cases, from a particular historical tax haven relationship with an onshore economy or continent in near proximity'.[6]

In this respect, it has been noted that '[m]ost OFCs are either dependencies, ex-dependencies or colonies of a major power or are in some form of relationship with a mainland or larger onshore country'.[7] (See section 2.7 below.)

It has been suggested elsewhere that an OFC is 'a centre that hosts financial activities that are separated from major regulating units (states) by geography and/or by legislation . . . [with] . . . no, or, at best, low, direct and indirect tax rates'.[8]

Another definition says that an OFC is 'a small territory in which the conduct of international banking business is facilitated by favourable and/or flexibly administered tax, exchange control and banking laws, and in which the volume of banking business is totally unrelated to the size and needs of the domestic market'.[9]

In his 1998 report on the British Crown Dependencies (see section 17.3 below), its author, Mr Edwards, said that:

> The terms 'Offshore Centre' or 'Offshore business' tend now to be used in several different senses. They always include the business of: small island finance centres, constitutionally independent at least as regards their domestic affairs, which have developed legislation, regulation and tax vehicles to attract non-resident business, mostly denominated in foreign currencies. But they are also sometimes used to include, by analogy, the non-resident business of some or all of the following types of centre, all of

[6] R. A. Johns, *The British Isles 'Offshore Finance Centres'*, Pinter Publishers, 1982.
[7] M. P. Hampton, *The Offshore Interface*, Macmillan Press Ltd, 1996, p. 69.
[8] M. P. Hampton, *The Offshore Interface*, Macmillan Press Ltd, 1996, p. 10.
[9] R. B. Johnston, *The Economics of the Euro-markets*, Macmillan Press Ltd, 1983.

which have seen rapid growth in recent years: similar centres which are coastal or inland enclaves; special tax and/or regulation zones established by larger countries within their own borders; any finance centre including the large world centres, with a large volume of non-resident clients.[10]

The IMF has suggested that:

Offshore Finance is, at its simplest, the provision of financial services by banks and other agents to non-residents . . . [T]he definition of an OFC is far less straightforward. At its broadest, an OFC can be defined as any financial centre where 'Offshore' activity takes place. This definition would include all the major financial centres in the world. In such centres, there may be little distinction between on- and offshore business . . . A more practical definition of an OFC is a centre where the bulk of financial sector activity is offshore on both sides of the balance sheet . . . where the transactions are initiated elsewhere, and where the majority of the institutions involved are controlled by non-residents. Thus, OFCs are usually referred to as:

- Jurisdictions that have relatively large numbers of financial institutions engaged primarily in business with non-residents;
- Financial systems with external assets and liabilities out of proportion to domestic financial intermediation designed to finance domestic economies; and
- More popularly, centres which provide some or all of the following services: low or zero taxation; moderate or light financial regulation; banking secrecy and anonymity.

However, the distinction is by no means clear cut . . . [T]he definition of an OFC depends on the use to which it is to be put.[11]

2.6 The origins and development of 'Offshore'

As human beings, we have many needs that are common and which are not peculiar to the age in which we live. One such need is to preserve safely whatever we consider to be valuable. This need has spawned more than one industry – including insurance, security, tax planning and custodial services – and not surprisingly that which is loosely referred to as 'Offshore'.

---

[10] M. Edwards, *Review of Financial Regulation in the Crown Dependencies*, 1998, Part 1, para. 2.2.
[11] 'Offshore Financial Centres', IMF Background Paper, 23 June 2000.

In respect of the latter, it seems that[12] many, many years ago, some wealthy people handed over their valuables to the inhabitants of Delos (an island off the coast of Greece) for protection. If this is correct, then the concept of moving assets 'Offshore' is far from being new – or even recent. Nevertheless, the sea is relevant:

> [T]he concept of 'Offshore' is founded upon the concept of 'Onshore', whereas the concept of 'Onshore' is independent of 'Offshore' – that is, it depends only on other 'Onshore(s)'. The concept of offshore therefore is a logical derivation of onshore, thus sovereignty defines both realms . . . 'Offshore' therefore is not a statement about the delimitation of sovereignty, but a statement about the relationship between a state and its territory, a statement encapsulated by the metaphor of the *new shores*. The metaphor of the 'shore' echoes the legal principles which gave rise to offshore, namely the Law of the Sea.[13]

In this respect, it has been said that:

> [W]hile sovereignty plays an enabling role in the evolution of offshore, it equally plays a constraining or a distortionary role. The significance of offshore and what sets it aside from other aspects of international deregulation is that it drives economic activities into jurisdictions they should not have been in in the first place. Strictly speaking, it does not make economic sense for the Cayman Islands to serve as the world's fifth largest financial centre; it does not make sense for the Marshall Islands, Vanuatu or Liberia to be the world's giant shipping nations. There is no obvious economic reason why small Pacific islands are at the forefront of the telecommunications revolution, nor why Guyana and Niue are the central re-routing areas for internet porn. In direct contradiction to the theory of comparative advantage which assumes that economic activities tend to gravitate towards geographically relevant areas, offshore has the opposite effect. Offshore is therefore a form by which political and regulatory policies distort the relocation policies of international capital . . . Offshore . . . is not about economic efficiency but perversely, in strict economic terms, about economic inefficacy; the most perfect market is in fact a distortionary mechanism, dispersing economic activities away from their 'natural' location and grouping them where they would not otherwise be.[14]

[12] T. L. Neal, 'The Tax Haven', in *The Offshore Advantage Newsletter*, 2001, Issue 10, p. 1.
[13] Ronen Palan, 'Offshore and the Structural Enablement of Sovereignty', in *Offshore Finance Centres and Tax Havens – The Rise of Global Capital*, ed. Mark P. Hampton and Jason P. Abbott, Macmillan Press Ltd, 1999, Chapter 2, pp. 27 and 28.
[14] Ronen Palan, 'Offshore and the Structural Enablement of Sovereignty' in *Offshore Finance Centres and Tax Havens – The Rise of Global Capital*, ed. Mark P. Hampton and Jason P. Abbott, Macmillan Press Ltd, 1999, Chapter 2, p. 35.

In one article, the author traced the development of 'Offshore' back to the 1930s.[15] The author, Mr Dwyer, referred to the end of the First World War, when tax rates increased (to 90 per cent in the USA), and the USA and the UK tried to discourage the transfer of assets abroad – although this affected only the very wealthy. Inevitably, the assets left the higher tax areas, bound for 'Offshore'.

The imposition of death duty and high rates of tax after the Second World War enhanced the attractiveness of 'Offshore' to an even wider range of 'consumers', and, in response to growing demands for the services and features that were available 'Offshore', their supply increased. Former British colonies with their Anglo-Saxon common law heritage were particularly well placed to develop this type of business – which, together with the need for increased revenue, encouraged the development of 'Offshore Sectors' in small islands whose main industry had previously been agriculture or tourism.

Interestingly, the OECD has said that, in respect of offshore banking, '[t]he need originated originally from inward looking anti-competitive, overregulated onshore financial markets, the unreformed organisation of which significantly frustrated the particular requirements of clients for national and external financial intermediation'.[16]

It has been said that: 'The Eurodollar market originated in the 1940s and 1950s when the Soviet Union and China decided to deposit their dollar holdings in Paris and London as they feared that these revenues might otherwise be frozen (as the US had done with Yugoslavia's gold held in New York). One of the bank's chosen for this purpose, Banque Commerciale pour l'Europe du Nord, had the telex address EURBANK; thus the term eurodollars.'[17] The strategy gained momentum, and growth was rapid, encouraged by the stability resulting from the fixed exchange rate mechanism that formed part of the Bretton Woods system. It allowed those using it to avoid exchange control regulations and to exploit 'interest arbitrage (avoiding the US regulation Q, which set a ceiling on interest paid by banks on their deposits and avoiding

---

[15] Terry Dwyer, 'Harmful Tax Competition and the Future of Offshore Financial Centres', *Journal of Money Laundering Control*, Vol. 5, No. 4.

[16] OECD Committee on Fiscal Affairs and Committee on Financial Markets in the OECD, *Offshore Financial Centres*, February 1996.

[17] Mattias Levin, 'The Prospects for Offshore Financial Centres in Europe', August 2002, Box 1, *CEPS Research Report*, p. 51.

minimum reserve requirements)'.[18] The involvement of an increasing number of participants, and the highly regulated nature of the financial markets in Europe, contributed to the establishment of an 'Offshore' market – in dollars – in London, as opposed to New York. The placement of deposits denominated in a currency other than the pound sterling (frequently US dollars) in the UK contributed to the development of the 'Offshore Environment'. Although the origins of the Eurodollar market are not absolutely clear, the earliest loans are dated around the late 1950s. Walker makes the point that 'the significance of this development was that the source of capital was separated from its place of trading and the currency of the debt from its country of issuance. This was the beginning of the development of a separate single or global financial market fundamentally separated from the earlier mercantile or trade related economies on which finance had traditionally been based'.[19]

The concept of 'Offshore' is said to have British roots. Those within the UK who were wealthy faced not only very high tax burdens but also an exchange control environment. However, since exchange controls did not apply to every jurisdiction, the transfer of capital to 'Offshore' jurisdictions became a very expedient way for the very wealthy to retain as much of their wealth as possible. The growth of this migration of capital was encouraged by the British Government. Meanwhile, UK fund managers have been described as 'leading pioneers' of the 'Offshore' industry because in the late 1960s they started to establish collective investment schemes ('schemes') in Hong Kong, Bermuda and the Channel Islands for sale to expatriates. Expatriates used these vehicles to protect themselves from high marginal tax in the UK on unearned income. The trend developed.[20] Hampton quotes one way that collective investment schemes were used to bypass exchange controls. He says that sterling feeder funds were established 'Offshore' to collect sterling investments which were used to acquire dollar denominated assets, 'avoiding both the dollar premium and the 25 per cent surrender clause'.[21] Other commentators have said that:

[18] Mattias Levin, 'The Prospects for Offshore Financial Centres in Europe', August 2002, Box 1, *CEPS Research Report*, p. 51.
[19] George Alexander Walker, *International Banking Regulation Law, Policy and Practice*, 2001, Kluwer Law international, p. 20.
[20] 'What Future for Offshore Financial Centres?', July/August 2000, *Compliance Monitor*, p. 246.
[21] Mark Hampton, *The Offshore Interface*, Macmillan Press Ltd, 1996, p. 27.

[t]he growth of offshore centres can be traced back to the restrictive regulatory regimes in many advanced countries in the 1960s and 1970s. These regimes blocked the flow of capital to and from other countries (excluding trade financing), or imposed restrictions on the interest banks could offer, or raised banks' funding costs in domestic markets (for example through the imposition of high non-interest bearing reserve requirements). These restrictions which, in many cases, were intended to provide governments with more control over monetary policy, encouraged a shift of deposits and borrowing to less regulated institutions, including banks in jurisdictions not subject to such restrictions.[22]

The Chief Executive of the International Securities Market Association, John Langton, said that: 'It was regulation in the form of President John F. Kennedy's introduction of the interest equalisation tax in 1963, together with Overseas Foreign Direct Investment Controls which forced a wholesale shift of US dollar denominated business to Europe.'[23]

Johns uses a concept that he calls the 'friction matrix' to describe government activity that interferes with markets and therefore prompts practitioners to contemplate operating offshore – where that friction does not exist – or exists to a lesser degree.[24] Hampton refers to Theobald's assertion that '[b]anks did not invent the Euromarket. Governments created it by seeking to control the natural flow of money'.[25] This is a good example of an Onshore friction matrix at work – resulting in funds going 'Offshore' – which in turn has led to the growth and use of such centres. Further, 'US domestic, or Onshore, regulation was a significant factor encouraging banks to relocate offshore (in the Regulatory sense) in the new Euromarkets in the 1960s'.[26]

'Improvements in communications and the greater sophistication of both tax planning and commercial structures resulted in the transformation of OFCs. . . .'.[27] However, it is arguably the case that tax and

[22] Salim M. Darbar, R. Barry Johnston, Mary G. Zephirin, *Assessing Offshore Financial Centres: Filling a Gap in Global Surveillance, Finance and Development*, September 2003, p. 32.

[23] Edward Russell-Walling, *A Necessary Autonomy, International Securities*, 2004/5, p. 130.

[24] Richard Anthony Johns, *A Study of Transnational Economic Development, Tax Havens and Offshore Finance*, Frances Pinter (Publishers) Ltd, 1983, p. 18.

[25] T. C. Theobald, 'Offshore Branches and Global Banking – One Bank's View', *Columbia Journal of World Business*, Vol. 16, Part 4, Winter, pp. 19–20 as quoted in *The Offshore Interface*, ed. Mark Hampton, Macmillan Press Ltd, 1996, p. 38.

[26] Mark Hampton, *The Offshore Interface*, Macmillan Press Ltd, 1996, p. 66.

[27] Bob Harland, 'Tax Competition, The OECD and the Offshore Industry', *Offshore Finance Yearbook*, 2001/2, p. 6.

regulation were the main drivers behind business relocating 'Offshore' in the 1960s.

According to Johns, development of 'Offshore' is consequent upon:

A. High tax, restrictive policies and regulation together with transnationalisation of national money and capital markets;
B. OFCs have become 'international invisible production interfaces' linked but yet separate from onshore world trade and capital markets – evolving as 'shelters for income';
C. Development has been made possible by advances in telecommunications allowing rapid access to relevant information;
D. The creation of the Eurocurrency markets was a crucial factor; and
E. OFCs 'constitute a global secondary trading system' – supporting the world's capital systems.[28]

In the 1960s, the USA imposed an interest equalisation tax on the Euro-dollar market. This prompted that market to move 'Offshore', thereby further stimulating the 'Offshore Environment'. It has been said that:

> The main contributing factor identified for the historical growth of 'Offshore' banking and OFCs was the imposition of increased regulations (reserve requirements, interest rate ceilings, restrictions on the range of financial products capital controls, financial disclosure requirements, high effective tax rates) in the financial sectors of industrial countries during the 1960s and 1970s. . . .. For example the growth of London as the largest offshore banking centre has been linked directly to regulations imposed on the US banking sector; capital controls implemented through the Interest Equalisation Tax of 1964, the Foreign Credit and Exchange Act of 1965, cash reserve requirements on deposits imposed in 1977 and a ceiling on time deposits in 1979. By establishing foreign branches to which these regulations did not apply, US Banks were able to operate in more cost attractive environments.[29]

In referring to a 'two phased offshore financial services revolution', Johns and Le Marchant suggest that phase one

> emerged as a result of the transformation in the 1960s and 1970s of certain 'old' and a number of comparatively 'new' tax havens into 'Offshore Finance Centres' as a result of local inward direct foreign investment by

---

[28] R. A. Johns, *A Study of Transnational Economic Development, Tax Havens and Offshore Finance*, Frances Pinter (Publishers) Ltd, 1983, p. 39.
[29] 'Report of the Working Group on Offshore Financial Centres', April 2000, p. 8.

non-resident financial institutions. Their raison d'être was the offering of 'Offshore banking', and its associated niche products, customised under conditions of relative local operational freedom, for the trans-nationalising private and corporate sectors emerging in largely protectionist, anti-competitive, anti-trade over-regulated onshore nationalistic financial centres and markets.[30]

Another observer has said that:

> By the late 1960s to early 1970s many US banks had set up branches in Caribbean tax havens as Eurocurrency booking offices. The early 1970s also saw the spectacular rise and fall of offshore funds . . . Further boosts to offshore development were given by two pieces of UK legislation, the 1972 changes to the Sterling Area and the 1979 lifting of Exchange Controls.[31]

In respect of the first, Hampton points out that the redesignation of the Sterling Area encouraged banks to set up in 'Offshore' centres within that Area (such as the Channel Islands), but the Caribbean area was outside it. The implication of the abolition of exchange controls was that capital movements were facilitated, which prompted the development of multi-currency activity, which in turn attracted a wider range of clients.

> The maintenance of historic and distortionary regulations on the financial sectors of industrial countries during the 1960s and 1970s was a major contributing factor in the growth of offshore banking and the proliferation of OFCs. Specifically, the emergence of the offshore inter-bank market during the 1960s and 1970s mainly in Europe – hence the Eurodollar – can be traced to the imposition of reserve requirements, interest rate ceilings, restrictions on the range of financial products that supervised institutions could offer, capital controls, and high effective taxation in many OECD countries.[32]

A further factor was that 'as compared with the late 1960s, the 1970s was a period in which there was an overwhelmingly general increase in domestic taxation pressure in OECD countries'.[33]

Luxembourg was popular in the early 1970s with the residents of Germany, France and Belgium because it offered low rates of tax,

---

[30] R. A. Johns and C. M. Le Marchant, Offshore Britain, 'The British Isles Finance Centre Since the Abolition of UK Exchange Controls', May 1993, *National Westminster Bank Quarterly Review*, p. 54.

[31] Mark Hampton, *The Offshore Interface*, Macmillan Press Ltd, 1996, p. 17.

[32] 'Offshore Finance Centres', IMF Background Paper, 23 June 2000.

[33] R. A. Johns, *A Study of Trans-national Economic Development, Tax Havens and Offshore Finance*, Frances Pinter (Publishers) Ltd, 1983, p. 5.

banking secrecy and no withholding tax for non-residents. Similar factors increased the attractiveness of Guernsey, the Isle of Man and Jersey, not to mention the Cayman Islands and the Bahamas. Around the same time, oil surpluses in the Middle East increased the popularity of Bahrain, and 'forays into offshore business led American and Canadian banks to develop neighbouring tax havens in the Caribbean'.[34] Many of these havens were introduced to the business by fugitive criminals. Others emulated their successful brethren. The Caribbean havens developed phenomenally fast during the 1970s with strong links to both London and New York.'[35]

Meanwhile

> in the tax havens sat a growing cache of unregulated, anonymous money seeking a quick buck. The offshore centres of London and Switzerland and the tax havens of Liechtenstein and the Channel Islands fed each other, generating a massive liquidity in search of investment opportunities. The Swiss banks were soon very active in London. Combined with the Channel Islands, London effectively emerged as the leader of a closely integrated system of European Financial Centres. This Centre was not only able to successfully challenge New York, but was in danger of displacing New York altogether.[36]

The type of consumer seems to have changed towards the end of the 1990s. The benefits of 'Offshore' for financial institutions from larger, more industrialised nations diminished – not least because of relaxed capital controls. However, corporate customers and individuals became more interested in 'Offshore' as a means of reducing taxes on capital and inheritance tax. 'Offshore' fund management business, trusts and private companies became highly significant services. Opportunities to maximise profit in a low tax jurisdiction is always appealing for international companies. 'By 1990, OFCs were the location for over 18 per cent of the world's total international lending.'[37]

---

[34] R. T. Naylor, *Hot Money and the Politics of Debt*, Unwin Hyman, 1987.

[35] Ronen Palan, *Offshore and the Structural Enablement of Sovereignty*, as quoted in *Offshore Finance Centres and Tax Havens – The Rise of Global Capital*, ed. Mark P. Hampton and Jason P. Abbott, Macmillan Press Ltd, 1999, Chapter 2, p. 34.

[36] Ronen Palan, *Offshore and the Structural Enablement of Sovereignty*, as quoted in *Offshore Finance Centres and Tax Havens – The Rise of Global Capital*, ed. Mark P. Hampton and Jason P. Abbott, Macmillan Press Ltd, 1999, Chapter 2, p. 35.

[37] *Bank of England Quarterly Bulletin*, Vol. 31, No. 3, p. 237, May, as reported in *The Offshore Interface*, Mark Hampton, p. 40, Macmillan Press Ltd. 1996.

It has been said that:

> The offshore industry as we know it today is in part a product of the
> political upheaval and social and economic changes which occurred
> during the 20th century which led to:
>
> 1. increased reliance upon higher direct rather than indirect taxes;
> 2. the desire by both private individuals and commercial organisations to
>   reduce effective rates of direct taxation to more acceptable levels by
>   appropriate structuring of their affairs;
> 3. the recognition that OFCs had a valuable role to play in both tax
>   efficient structuring of wealth and protecting it from political unrest
>   and exchange controls; and
> 4. a desire on the part of the island OFCs to diversify their economies
>   away from agriculture as their principal source of employment.

However, in the course of time, more people have accumulated wealth
and, as might be expected, have turned their attention to retaining as
much of it as possible. As tax burdens increased 'Onshore', greater
numbers of people became interested in the potential offered by
'Offshore' to mitigate such tax. In turn, the 'Offshore' market developed,
and, as word spread, more attention was focused on the level of direct tax
that applied 'Onshore'. In this sense, the momentum of the 'Offshore'
environment is not likely to have grown if (inter alia) the tax rates in
larger centres had not dropped to the levels that obtain 'Offshore'.
Perversely, however, the momentum of the 'Offshore Environment' is
likely to be adversely affected by other developments – in the form of
high tax charging nations preventing their citizens from using 'Offshore
Centres' by other means – such as the European Savings Directive (see
section 5.14 below).

Now the emphasis has changed, and the 'Offshore Centres' do not
like the change, as the following quote demonstrates: 'Those in opposition to the OECD actions argued that twenty years ago they were
encouraged by Britain and other countries to establish financial services
industries to build self-sustaining economies.'[38] In fact, the pressures
being put on some governments currently are so severe that some of
them are going out of the 'Offshore' business. By way of contrast, one

---

[38] 'Caribbean Tax Havens in Spotlight', *Caribbean Update*, 1 February 2001 as quoted in *The
Death of Tax Havens*, Akiko Hishikawa, Student Publications homepage, www.bc.edu/
bc_org/avp/law/lwsch/journals/bciclr/25_2/10_TXT.htm 20 June 2002.

commentator has noted that 'the history of offshore financial centres reflects the historical evolution of the tax systems of major countries, notably the USA and UK'.[39]

The appeal of 'Offshore' was not restricted to individuals. Multinational companies found that some of the tax complications associated with international transactions (e.g. taxation in more than one jurisdiction) were eradicated if they used jurisdictions 'Offshore'. The 'Offshore Environment' had obvious attractions then – and in this respect still does. For example, some companies incorporated in the USA have been migrating 'Offshore', especially to Bermuda (see section 18.14 below). This has caused major disruptions, and, in the post-11 September environment, the companies proposing to migrate have been branded by some as unpatriotic. The commercial rationale is clear and corporations that have been forced not to set up an associated company 'Offshore' have suffered the economic consequences (e.g. Stanley, which was forced to lay off 1,000 workers in May 2003: see section 18.14 below).

2.7 Tax havens identified

Originally, 'Offshore Finance Centres' were called 'tax havens', and, at the time, this terminology may have been acceptable if it referred to a jurisdiction where the tax rate was zero and where little or no real economic activity took place. There may have been a hint of subterfuge in the terminology but any negative inference was frequently treated with benign disregard – especially by those who felt that tax avoidance was what every right thinking person ought to be doing. The fashion changed as the hint of wrongdoing took on a more sinister guise and so the term 'tax haven' took on a different nuance. It implied something that was becoming increasingly less acceptable. That said, not all jurisdictions see it this way. For example, according to promotional material published by Vanuatu, 'Vanuatu is a tax haven. As such, there are no income taxes, withholding taxes, capital gains taxes, gift death, estate or succession duties applying to companies, trusts or individuals. There are also no tax treaties with other countries and thus no exchange of information with foreign governments.'[40] Further, in its promotional

---

[39] Terry Dwyer, 'Harmful Tax Competition and the Future of Offshore Financial Centres', Vol. 5, No. 4, *Journal of Money Laundering Control*, p. 302.
[40] Vanuatu Offshore Financial Services, www.financial.com.vu/vanuatu.htm.

material, Turks and Caicos says that 'Turks and Caicos is unique among those jurisdictions commonly called "tax havens" in that its development as an offshore centre was a considered decision by Britain.'[41]

One commentator sees it as follows:

> Offshore centres and tax havens have both evolved alongside the increasing liberalisation and globalisation of the financial markets. Despite this they are distinct from each other. The former can be identified as a centre where operators are permitted to raise funds from non-residents and invest or lend that money free from regulations or taxes . . . [T]he use of the term 'Offshore' denotes a regulatory space and consequently does not have to be physically offshore. What essentially distinguishes a tax haven from an offshore financial centre is that tax havens are: economies that have made a deliberate attempt to attract thereto international trade-oriented activities by minimisation of taxes and the reduction or elimination of other restrictions on business operations, such that, within the jurisdiction of the centre, aggregated economic activity is substantially geared to the special needs of external enterprises and investors . . . Subsequently the archetypal tax haven has either no taxation or a minimal level of taxation. Established tax havens such as the Channel Islands, Liechtenstein and Switzerland are merely vestiges of dukedoms and fiefdoms of a bygone age.[42]

Elsewhere, it has been said that 'the growth of international financial markets has more generally been characterised by the larger processes of globalisation, deregulation and integration.'[43] Globalisation of financial services – which gives rise to cross-border transactions – causes a fundamental problem in regulation in that financial responsibility for national markets is under local control. The question arises as to how to blend local and global control simultaneously (this matter will be pursued later when the work of the 'supranational' authorities is considered).

If the views of the tax partner of PriceWaterhouseCoopers reflect those of the whole population, the Irish certainly do not believe they operate a

[41] 'Turks and Caicos as a Financial Centre', www.savory-co.com/financial.htm.
[42] R. A. Johns, *Tax Havens and Offshore Finance, A Study of Transnational Economic Development*, Pinter, 1983, p. 20, as quoted by Jason P. Abbott, 'Mahathir, Malaysia and the Labuan International Offshore Financial Centre: Treasure Island, Pet Project or Ghost Town?' in *Offshore Finance Centres and Tax Havens: The Rise of Global Capital*, ed. Mark P. Hampton and Jason P. Abbott, 1999, Macmillan Press Ltd, Chapter 8, p. 194.
[43] George Alexander Walker, *International Banking Regulation Law, Policy and Practice*, Kluwer Law International, 2001, p. 7.

tax haven – as the following example aptly illustrates. According to the *Irish Independent*, he said that '[W]e are a legitimate low-tax jurisdiction, not a tax haven and we need to challenge any country that seeks to paint us as being anywhere near the wrong side of that divide'.[44] (The context was a circular issued by the UK's Inland Revenue at the end of July 2002. The circular identified Ireland as a 'tax haven' for the purposes of 'controlled foreign company' legislation (see section 5.25 below). The implication is that, for any UK company that has an Irish subsidiary, a series of tests must be satisfied if the profit arising in Ireland is not to suffer UK tax as well as Irish tax.) The Irish Government announced its intention to take the UK Government to court over this – so the issue was not treated lightly. It is not clear whether, or to what extent, PriceWaterhouseCoopers would have objected if the term 'tax haven' had been replaced by 'Offshore Finance Centre'.

The term 'Offshore Finance Centre' seemed like an improvement – although the latter terminology has never totally replaced the former. That said, the problems concerning what should or could be called an 'Offshore Finance Centre' made it difficult to know which jurisdiction fell into which category. As one observer has pointed out, 'although OFCs are usually tax havens, not all tax havens are also OFCs'.[45] Whether this is the cause or the effect remains to be seen, but, in any event, there has always been a great deal of speculation about what constitutes and what does not constitute an 'Offshore Finance Centre'. The debate continues, and, as the Irish example cited above indicates, this is not just a matter of semantics.

Frequently, the products and services offered by jurisdictions remain constant regardless of what the jurisdiction is called or from where the services are offered. Perhaps this explains why, at one stage, the term 'Offshore Finance Centre' was a description that many jurisdictions accepted. Whether this means they merely put up with it or whether they found it reasonable depends on which jurisdiction one addresses. As it turned out, much of the stigma that attached to the former 'tax haven' tag stuck – at least in part – also to the term 'Offshore Finance Centre'. The situation worsened with every consequent spate of adverse publicity – to the extent that the term 'Offshore Finance Centre' was, more often than not, used pejoratively. So, in due course, it became no

---

[44] Jason Gorringe, 'Brits Classify Ireland as a Tax Haven', Tax-News.com, 30 July 2002.
[45] Mark Hampton, *The Offshore Interface*, Macmillan Press Ltd, 1996, p. 15.

more preferable to be referred to as an 'Offshore Finance Centre' than it had been previously to be referred to as a 'tax haven'.

One of the difficulties is that, with usage, many people have developed some sort of impression about the meaning of the term 'Offshore Finance Centre'. That is to say, many people have a good idea of what it means even though they cannot explain it – but they are often quick to point out that the one thing about which they are sure is that it is not good! Given that it has not been possible to explain the meaning of the term satisfactorily, it will be obvious that trying to replace a term that cannot be explained with something else that properly conveys all that needs to be conveyed is no mean task. On this basis, it is likely that the terms 'tax haven' and 'Offshore Finance Centre' are likely to be in use for some time to come, however unsatisfactory the implications are. For example, it is said that '[t]here are several international lists of tax havens such as in the US Government's 1981 Gordon Report, the BIS Listing, The Banker's Offshore Surveys and The Economist Intelligence Unit's Report'.[46]

However, with the publication in 2000 of work undertaken by the OECD, the FATF and the FSF, there is now some 'official' focus on matters 'Offshore'. These reports will be analysed in some detail in Chapters 10 to 12 – but, in summary, they have had fundamental and far-reaching effects on the 'Offshore' environment and wider. The OECD's report entitled 'Harmful Tax Competition – An Emerging Global Issue', published in 1998, is significant in many respects but not least because it provides a definition of a 'tax haven'.

The OECD's work (inter alia) developed certain criteria which the OECD said indicated whether or not a jurisdiction was a 'tax haven'. Needless to say, and based on the comments above, no jurisdiction wanted to be categorised in this way. In any event, the OECD classified thirty-seven jurisdictions as 'tax havens'. So, at that stage, a definition of a 'tax haven' had been compiled, committed to paper and been published by a supranational authority. This implies that the definition has inherent credibility.

Meanwhile, the FATF identified certain jurisdictions which they de-scribed as 'non cooperative in the fight against money laundering'.

---

[46] C. Doggart, *Tax Havens and Their Uses*, 1981 (revised edition), Economist Intelligence Unit, as quoted in *The 'Offshore' Interface*, Mark P. Hampton, Macmillan Press Ltd, 1996, p. 10.

Further, the FSF identified the jurisdictions with the best (and worst) legal infrastructures and supervisory practices.

The results of all three exercises show that eight jurisdictions (the Bahamas, the Cook Islands, Liechtenstein, the Marshall Islands, Nauru, Niue, Panama and St Vincent and the Grenadines) were graded worst in all three reports (see Table 26 in Appendix 1). Inevitably, a poor categorisation is likely to affect reputation and credibility – the latter factors perhaps being the two most important factors which depositors/investors and other customers take into account in deciding where to transact their business. Further, the threat of 'sanctions' imposed on those with the lowest ratings added insult to injury.

Interestingly, the FSF counselled readers of their report against using its conclusions to assess centres, but inevitably, this will be one of the prime purposes to which these reports will be put. The advice may have been well intended, but there was never any likelihood that it would be heeded.

More than a few of the jurisdictions involved did not accept the classification they had been allocated, because they looked upon themselves quite differently, despite what the criteria suggest. A list now exists that classifies certain jurisdictions as 'tax havens'. It should also be noted that the criteria for being an 'Offshore Centre' have not been defined. In fact, a few jurisdictions, not otherwise regarded as 'Offshore Centres', demonstrate characteristics that are not unlike the characteristics which are generally attributed to 'Offshore Centres'. For example, according to the Financial System Stability Assessment (FSSA) carried out by the IMF on Switzerland in May 2002:

- Switzerland is a major international financial centre . . . A substantial share of financial centre activities is international; . . .
- the system consists of a small number of global players in banking and insurance; . . .
- professionalism, reliability, and client confidentiality have been the basis for private banking in Switzerland; . . .
- financial services account for about 11per cent of GDP (more than twice as much as in the United States, France, or Germany); . . .
- there were 375 banks operating in Switzerland at end 2000 . . . down from 625 in 1990 . . . Foreign banks account for 7.5 per cent of total assets and more than 50 per cent of fiduciary assets; . . .
- Swiss supervisory authorities do little on-site work; . . .

- the Swiss economy . . . is populated by a disproportionately large (for its size) number of international enterprises (large banks and insurance companies have more employees and assets abroad than domestically).

The FSSA goes on to say that 'recently the private banking sector, which is an important provider of cross-border financial services, has been faced with increasing competition from onshore providers of financial products'. This implies that Switzerland is an 'Offshore' service provider – which is in line with the FSF's original inclusion of Switzerland as a Category 1 Offshore Financial Centre. The Swiss vehemently oppose any suggestion that Switzerland is an 'Offshore Centre'.

The same might be said of Luxembourg – a member of the European Union – but which was classified as an OFC in the FSF's categorisation (Luxembourg is a member of the FATF). According to the FSSA on Luxembourg which was completed by the IMF and the World Bank in May 2002:

- [Despite the smallness of the country,] "[b]y end 2001, Luxembourg had 189 banks, mostly subsidiaries and branches of European banks, and was the second largest financial centre in the world in terms of assets managed by UCITS; . . .
- [Luxembourg is] a banking centre that operates largely with accounts of non-residents; . . .
- The absence of withholding taxes on interest income on all accounts;
- In the banking and investment areas, most activity derives from non-Luxembourg residents; . . .
- No distinctions are made in the legislation and regulations between onshore and offshore activities; . . .
- Luxembourg is a significant international financial centre with a legal mandate for bank secrecy that obliges a strict duty of confidentiality on the banks and financial professionals.

All this gives rise to more questions, such as whether or not tax havens are 'Offshore Finance Centres', or (perhaps the emphasis should be the other way around) are 'Offshore Finance Centres' tax havens? (This matter is pursued elsewhere.) It is also the case that some jurisdictions are 'Offshore Centres' under a different name.

Section 20.7 below includes a discussion of some jurisdictions that are aspiring to be 'Offshore Centres', but there are also some jurisdictions that no longer want to be 'Offshore Centres' for reasons best left to them to explain. For example, the following titles were published in July 2002: 'New-Look Bahamas to Shed "Offshore" Tag' and 'Malta Began the Move from "Offshore" to Onshore in 1994'.[47] Some centres are no longer in business. For example: 'The Government of Niue has made a policy decision to cease operations of its International Business Companies Offshore registration by the end of 2006 . . . However, the jurisdiction has been under pressure by the FATF and the OECD to prevent money laundering and end "harmful tax practices". The result has been the closure of the jurisdiction as an offshore centre.'[48] Some jurisdictions have an uncertain future. For example, in respect of the recommendations made by the IMF on Vanuatu, one observer said that: 'The recommendations if implemented will have the effect of eliminating Vanuatu's "Offshore" business and whatever may be left would be integrated into a society where all income would be taxed at UK rates (or similar).'[49]

2.8 Quantification of the size of the market

As mentioned in the Preface, only estimates of the size of the 'Offshore Environment' are available. In this respect, it has been said that 'the sheer amount of capital residing in or passing through OFCs and tax havens is now so great that it is beyond the ability of any single government to – in Mrs Thatcher's famous words "buck the market"'.[50] However:

> the Bank for International Settlements' (BIS) locational banking statistics show that reporting jurisdictions recorded $2.8 trillion in claims on [assets located in] OFCs at end 2002 . . . representing 20.9 per cent of total cross-border claims, and $2.5 trillion at end 2001. For banking, a more useful measure of risk exposure is provided by the BIS consolidated banking statistics which net out intra-group lending, and also identify ultimate risk. The consolidated banking statistics show net claims on OFCs of $1.8 trillion at end 2002, which reduces to $1.7 trillion in claims on OFCs on

---

[47] 'New-Look Bahamas to Shed "Offshore" Tag' and 'Malta Began the Move from Offshore to Onshore in 1994', *Portfolio International*, July 2002, pp. 3 and 7, respectively.

[48] Ciara Fitzpatrick, 'Who Is Regulating the Regulators?', *Offshore Investment*, March 2005, p. 14.

[49] Lindsay D. Barrett, '"Big Brother" Prevails and Vanuatu Reluctantly Succumbs', July/August 2003, Issue 138, *Offshore Investment.com*, p. 35.

[50] Mark P. Hampton, Jason P. Abbott, 'The Rise (and Fall?) of Offshore Finance in the Global Economy: Editors' Introduction', in *Offshore Finance Centres and Tax Havens – The Rise of Global Capital*, ed. Mark P. Hampton and Jason P. Abbott, 1999, Macmillan Press Ltd, Chapter 1, p. 13.

an ultimate risk basis (or 5.3 per cent of world output). The reduction in consolidated claims reflects the fact that the business in OFCs is largely conducted by affiliates of banks headquartered elsewhere.[51]

It has been reported recently that '[s]ome $10 million per day flows from Australia to identified tax havens'.[52]

It has been said also that '[t]ax havens have attracted an astounding $6.5 trillion in assets'.[53] (Please refer to the comments above concerning the implications arising from the absence of definitions – which inter alia make it difficult to determine whether 'tax havens' are 'Offshore Finance Centres' – and what criteria were used by those who compiled the figures just quoted.)

By the end of the second quarter of 2003, the level of total deposits in 'Offshore Centres' had reached $1.8 trillion according to the BIS's quarterly report. 'US Banks alone accounted for $601 billion, or one third of all offshore claims, with most of the money going to the Cayman Islands and Jersey'.[54]

The OECD's estimate of the amount held in 'Offshore' funds amounts to $1 trillion.[55] Putting this into context, while 'the world's roughly 70 OFCs only make up 1.2 per cent of the world's population and 3.1 per cent of the world's GDP, they are managing one quarter of the world's assets. At the end of 1997, OFCs' share of cross border assets stood at 54.2 per cent growing at an annual rate of over 6 per cent'.[56]

One commentator has noted that 'New York, London and Tokyo control between them nearly 60 per cent of the global market for offshore banking and capital markets services . . . OECD jurisdictions already

[51] 'Offshore Financial Centres – The Assessment Program – A Progress Report and the Future of the Program', International Monetary Fund, 31 July 2003, p. 6.
[52] 'Tide Begins to Turn as Cash from Tax Havens Returns to Australia', *Offshore Red*, March 2004, p. 8.
[53] Richard M. Salsman, *Capital on Strike: The Tax Haven Controversy*, The Capitalist Advisor, 21 May 2002, p. 3.
[54] BIS Quarterly Report, December 2003, as quoted in 'BIS Says US Banks Are the Biggest Users of OFCs', February 2002, *Offshore Red*, p. 219.
[55] Astrid Wendtlandt, 'Guernsey Stands Alone in the Face of Economic Sanctions', 27 July 2000, *Financial Times*.
[56] Ingo Walter, 'Globalisation of Markets and Financial-Centre Competition', 1998, and 'Offshore Banking: An Analysis of Micro- and Macro-Prudential Issues', IMF Working Paper, January 1999, WP/99/5, as quoted by Mattias Levin, 'The Prospects for Offshore Financial Centres in Europe', CEPS Research Report, August 2002, p. i.

control 80 per cent of the international market for offshore financial services.'[57]

If these estimates are anything to go by, it makes a lot of sense not to overlook what constitutes 'Offshore' because its size clearly makes it a material component of the world's economy, as the Directors of the IMF have recognised (see section 10.4 below). Everyone knows this. For example, the Directors of the IMF, in reviewing the assessment pro-gramme for OFCs at the end of 2003, 'encouraged jurisdictions to work with the Fund to develop data on OFCs for general dissemination.'[58] The next stage is to get something done about it – and work is under way; for example, there has been considerable encouragement given to OFCs to participate in the Coordinated Portfolio Investment Survey, which is a supplement to the BIS's international banking statistics quoted above (see also below). This increases the potential for more meaningful informa-tion about how the work of OFCs impinges upon international banking and securities markets. Meanwhile, it has been said that 'it is evident that the offshore financial markets are increasingly dominating finance'.[59]

2.9 The IMF's Coordinated Portfolio Investment Survey (CPIS)

The CPIS derives from the IMF's Committee on Balance of Payments – which established a task force in 1994 and charged it with developing a survey of portfolio investment assets. The first CPIS was conducted in 1997, and involved twenty-nine economies. The survey has been con-ducted annually since 2001 (sixty-seven economies). The intention is to improve global statistics on portfolio investment assets. The survey collects information on cross-border holdings of equities and of long- and short-term debt securities. The instruments are valued at the pre-vailing market price and the analysis is based on the residence of the issuer.[60] The CPIS data shows US$1.8 trillion in cross-border investment claims (equity and debt securities, excluding securities that comprise

---

[57] Richard Hay, 'International Financial Centres: Back on the Front Foot', February 2005, *The 2005 Guide to International Financial Centres*, Euromoney Institutional Investor plc, p. 3.

[58] 'IMF Executive Board Reviews the Assessment Program on Offshore Financial Centres', IMF, 24 November 2003.

[59] *Offshore Finance Centres and Tax Havens – The Rise of Global Capital*, ed. Mark P. Hampton and Jason P. Abbott, 1999, Macmillan Press Ltd, Chapter 2, 'Offshore and the Structural Enablement of Sovereignty', Ronen Palan, p. 27.

[60] More information is available at www.imf.org/external/np/sta/pi/cpis.htm.

direct investment) against OFCs at end of 2001, representing 14 per cent
of total cross-border holdings of securities reported in the survey.

2.10 The IMF's Information Framework

The IMF has said that the Information Framework evolved from discussions at their board meeting in November 2003, and represents part of
the IMF's response to 'jurisdictions' requests that the Fund assist in their
dissemination efforts'.[61] The core objective is the improvement of transparency by providing a common template for jurisdictions to use in
disseminating information. The IMF will use the project to collate information regularly as part of the process of monitoring financial centres –
whose involvement is voluntary. Where the quantum falls below a certain
threshold, more limited information may be submitted (e.g. banking –
total assets below US$5 billion; insurance – annual gross premiums
below US$100 million; and collective investment schemes – total value
of assets below US$5 billion). There are a number of options. For
example in respect of additional information and in respect of how
information is transmitted (for example, where information is already
provided to the BIS, the jurisdiction can authorise the BIS to transmit it
to the IMF). This project began with data in respect of the end of the
calendar year 2004, which had to be submitted by end June 2005.

  According to an IMF progress report dated February 2005, 'the final
version of the Information Framework was forwarded in December 2004
to the 46 jurisdictions listed in Tables 7.2 and 7.3 inviting their participation'.[62] The response is summarised in Table 1 in Appendix 1 below.

---

[61] 'Offshore Financial Centres, The Assessment Program – A Progress Report, Supplementary Information, Information Framework – Financial Activities in International and
Offshore Financial Centres', 24 February 2005, IMF, p. 8.
[62] 'Offshore Financial Centres – Progress Report', para. 16, 25 February 2005, IMF.

3

The service providers and the consumer (1)

Both the thinkers of the Enlightenment and their successors proved unable to agree as to precisely what those principles were which would be found undeniable by all rational persons . . . [N]or has subsequent history diminished the extent of such disagreement.[1]

3.1 Introduction

In any discussion about 'Offshore', there are at least three interest groups to be considered. First, there is the 'Offshore Finance Centre' itself – the marketplace where the 'sellers' and 'buyers' trade. The second group are the 'sellers' or the service providers which are those organisations that sell their services to the final consumers. Examples range from large banks to small trust and corporate services companies. The third group – the 'buyers' – are the ultimate users of the services. These are the clients of the service providers, for example the person who establishes a trust offshore.

This chapter describes the marketplace, i.e. the 'Offshore Centre' per se, and the next chapter focuses on the consumers and service providers.

3.2 Why should a jurisdiction want to be a marketplace?

First, the word 'jurisdiction' should be interpreted to include countries. In general, the smaller the jurisdiction, the more difficult it is to develop and to maintain a diversified economy. (Chapter 15 describes some of the difficulties that are faced by small island economies in particular.) Smaller 'Offshore' jurisdictions are islands, mainly because islands frequently do not have diversified economies, and imports represent a

---

[1] Alastair MacIntyre, *Whose Justice? Which Rationality?*, University of Notre Dame Press, 1989.

substantial portion of the balance of payments. Islands, like all other
jurisdictions, need to be able to pay for what they consume, and to do
this they need to generate revenue. Revenue might arise from selling
services or by the imposition of taxes.

Traditionally, the revenue-generating services of many island economies include (inter alia) agriculture, fishing and tourism. Naturally, if
the quantum of the revenue is insufficient to pay for what the jurisdiction consumes, the balance has to come from somewhere else. The
source may be tax, but not necessarily so because some jurisdictions levy
no direct tax (e.g. the Cayman Islands) and some levy only minimal
amounts of tax. In such cases, can they survive? Some jurisdictions
generate enough revenue to balance their books without charging direct
tax (although indirect taxes may be imposed, for example on imported
goods). Their needs are less than the needs of other countries and so they
do not need to impose tax to pay for those needs. Other jurisdictions
forego tax because, by doing so, they believe that they can generate more
revenue.

At one stage, the OECD regarded low or no tax as a negative sign –
and Chapter 12 will describe this view in detail and the context in which
it once prevailed. By way of summary, the OECD believed that no or low
tax was one of the characteristics of a 'tax haven'. Subsequently, the
OECD changed its view completely and now says that low or no taxation
is no longer considered to be a 'badge' of a tax haven. The cases of the
Isle of Man and Gibraltar show the extent to which things have changed.
In August 2002, both jurisdictions proposed to create a zero-rated tax
regime (which is described in section 5.22 below). Since then, other
jurisdictions have followed a similar strategy.

No or low tax provides the means to attract and/or to maintain
capital. So what is the source of the revenue if it is neither from tourism
etc. nor from tax? One source is the fees and charges that arise from
a developed 'Offshore Finance Centre's' infrastructure. The aspiration
is that more service providers will establish and the progression is that
they will require professional lawyers, accountants, bankers and staff. In
turn, this increases the need for buildings and other fixed assets, and so
on. The spin-off is that more people will be employed, and all these
factors will contribute to GDP, the infrastructure will develop and more
business will be attracted.

Thus, some governments consider it to be in the very best interests of
their constituents to make the jurisdiction as attractive as possible to
providers of financial services (and thereby to the clients of those service

providers). Why? The answer is to attract/maintain capital, to generate revenue and to minimise unemployment.

It has to be said that not everyone agrees that 'Offshore Finance Centres' have been established for positive purposes. For example, one author has said that 'reforms in the offshore banking centres, established as tax and regulatory avoidance havens, only took on momentum after September 11. This should not come as a surprise; these facilities exist as a result of deliberate policies in the advanced industrial countries, pushed by financial markets and the wealthy.'[2] This type of comment is at variance with those of some of the supranational bodies regarding the work and standards of regulators in some 'Offshore' jurisdictions (see sections 19.2 and 19.3 below).

3.3 The creation of a market

If it is accepted that the main rationale for regulation is to prevent market failure, then it follows that it is important to know what might give rise to such failure. Carmichael cites four causes: anti-competitive behaviour, market misconduct, information asymmetry and systemic instability (see section 6.2 below). To attract buyers and sellers, the marketplace must satisfy the needs of these two groups simultaneously. 'Offshore Finance Centres' represent markets, but there are many 'Offshore Finance Centres'/markets and the object of each jurisdiction is to attract appropriate business. Therefore, there is competition for the business. Generally speaking, competition is a good thing (because of the potential benefits for the economy), but, when supply (of jurisdictions offering such business) exceeds demand, potential problems arise, including the potential for lowering the threshold of acceptable standards for new business – just to win that business.

Considered from the perspective of the marketplace (the 'Offshore Centre'), the objective is – as has just been said – to attract international capital, generate revenue and create employment opportunities. It has been said of OFCs that: 'In the more successful cases, financial services account for a significant proportion of the local GDP... [G]overnments have seen them [OFCs] as a fast way of boosting tax and local employment.'[3] To an extent, this is true. The provision of financial services may

---

[2] Joseph Stiglitz, *Globalisation and its Discontents*, Penguin Books, 2002, p. 236.
[3] 'What Future for "Offshore Financial Centres"?', *Compliance Monitor*, July/August 2000, p. 246.

boost tax and employment – which satisfies at least some of the demands described above. All seems well – but this is not necessarily so. For example, in jurisdictions such as Jersey, Guernsey and the Isle of Man, the financial services sector contributes more to GDP than any other sector. (Some 'Offshore Finance Centres' (whether so called or not) generate more than 50 per cent of GDP from 'Offshore Finance'.) In one sense, this is positive, but, in another sense, dependency on only one product represents an exposed economic position. A downturn in demand for the products of 'Offshore Centres' (arising perhaps through less tolerance of 'Offshore' or some economic change) is liable to have a disproportionately negative effect.

While it is preferable for an island's economy to be diversified – and to offer a 'portfolio' of products and services – this is frequently easier said than done. One exception is Mauritius – a newer breed of centre that is growing quickly. In Mauritius, there are four pillars to the economy – sugar, textiles, tourism and financial services. The latter generated a modest (10 per cent in 2005) but growing contribution to GDP.

According to a United Nations report,[4] the principal stimulants to the establishment of an 'Offshore' (banking) sector are: consumers' aspirations to avoid tax and interest rate regulations, to tap long-term sources of funds and to establish sovereign lending.

In the main, 'Offshore Centres' are not homogeneous (although there are many common features). In fact, since the supply of 'Offshore Finance Centres' exceeds the demand for them, the extent to which one centre can differentiate itself from another may be a factor that contributes to its longevity.

3.4 Legitimacy

It has been said that 'tax havens and OFCs are regarded as central to the operation of the contemporary financial markets . . . [and that] . . . they have facilitated the rise of global capital, increased the velocity and volatility of the global financial markets, and have contributed to world-wide economic liberalisation'.[5] The IMF considers that the legitimate reasons for which OFCs can be used include:

---

[4] 'Financial Havens, Banking Secrecy and Money Laundering', United Nations Office for Drug Control and Crime Prevention, Issue 8 of the UNDCP Technical Series, Double Issue 34 and 35 of the *Crime Prevention and Criminal Justice Newsletter*, 1998, p. 22.

[5] Mark P. Hampton and Jason P. Abbott, 'The Rise (and Fall?) of Offshore Finance in the Global Economy, Editors' Introduction', in *Offshore Finance Centres and Tax Havens – The*

1. lower explicit taxation and consequently increased after tax profit;
2. simpler prudential regulatory frameworks that reduce implicit taxation;
3. minimum formalities for incorporation;
4. the existence of adequate legal frameworks that safeguard the integrity of principal–agent relations;
5. the proximity to major economies, or to countries attracting capital inflows;
6. the reputation of specific OFCs, and the specialist services provided;
7. freedom from exchange controls; and
8. means for safeguarding assets from the impact of litigation etc.[6]

It is important to remember that OFCs serve legitimate purposes – and this quote from the IMF is significant in that it demonstrates that fact so unambiguously. Their legitimacy derives from not only the type of factor described above, but also because they provide a means to exploit niche market opportunities to which they sometimes bring particular skills and experience, such as in the area of trusts. Further, generally speaking, decisions are made faster in OFCs.

According to the Edwards report,[7] the main reasons cited as to why business was attracted to Jersey included:

- stability;
- respectability;
- security;
- fiscal;
- flexibility; and
- quality.

None of these appear to be negative.

3.5 Tax, regulation and confidentiality

It is probable that confidentiality, tax and regulation give rise to most (external) criticism about the 'Offshore Environment'. Confidentiality will be dealt with in this chapter, but subsequent chapters have been

---

Rise of Global Capital, ed. Mark P. Hampton and Jason P. Abbott, 1999, Macmillan Press Ltd, Chapter 1, pp. 13 and 15.

[6] 'Offshore Financial Centres', IMF Background Paper, 23 June 2000.

[7] Michael Edwards, 'Review of Financial Regulation in the Crown Dependencies', Part 2, para. 3.7, 1998.

devoted to tax (Chapter 5) and regulation (Chapter 6) respectively, so their significance will only be mentioned briefly at this stage.

3.6 Tax

'Offshore Finance Centres' play an important role in tax optimisation strategies. 'Tax optimisation' is a euphemism for paying no more tax than necessary. The 'Offshore Environment' offers opportunities to mitigate the tax that consumers would suffer if their transactions were processed through their home environment. These comments apply to the avoidance of tax (see section 5.3 below), not to the evasion of tax (see section 5.5 below). The significance of OFCs arises in no small measure as a result of the potential they create to mitigate tax.

Those who believe they suffer too much tax in their home country have a right to look for a fiscal environment that is more benign provided they do not defraud their home country of tax due. 'Tax advantages are generally perceived as the single biggest reason for the use of OFCs.'[8] For example, deposit accounts 'Offshore' are basically the same as deposit accounts offered 'Onshore', except that, for the time being, interest earned 'Offshore' will only be assessed for tax some time after it is declared by the depositor to the tax authorities in the home jurisdiction. It will not be declared until it is credited to the account, so some time will pass before tax is paid on interest received (but see section 5.15 below in respect of changes resulting from the application of the EU Savings Directive). Meanwhile, interest earned on accounts 'Onshore' will (ordinarily) suffer tax at the time the interest is credited (e.g. the UK).

Further, a consumer may attempt to mitigate a tax burden by establishing an 'Offshore' company (which may be tax exempt 'Offshore'). However, it should be pointed out that merely establishing a company 'Offshore' does not mean (per se) that an individual's tax liability is lessened. 'Offshore Finance Centres' are used to avoid tax – but there are many other media that offer the same potential, and which are sometimes more efficient, in achieving the same objective. Note that it is unlawful in some countries to conduct financial transactions privately – and so the use of 'Offshore' vehicles or an 'Offshore Centre' is not allowed. In some ('Onshore') countries, reports of transactions in such circumstances must be declared to the government.

---

[8] 'Offshore Financial Centres – The Role of the IMF', 23 June 2000, p. 8.

The acceptability of using tax rules and rates as competitive factors is a matter of some debate, not least at the OECD. (Because this topic is dealt with at length in Chapter 5, the arguments that appear there will not be replicated here.)

3.7 Regulation

It has been said that: 'The process of regulation consists of two basic activities: the provision of guidance and the imposition of constraints . . . [I]t follows that the ultimate objective of regulation should be to achieve a high degree of economic efficiency and consumer protection in the economy.'[9] It is important to note that, to an extent, regulators are facilitators. Elsewhere, it has been suggested that: 'The risks that regulation is there to cover are those of sharp practice, or that your money will be stolen when under someone else's care. Regulation is not there to eliminate market risks.'[10] All that said, it remains to be seen whether everyone would go along with the suggestion that '[i]t is commonly agreed that the main purpose of regulation is to deal with market failures'.[11]

The need for financial regulation is probably beyond dispute. For example, one commentator suggests that: 'Although the supervision and regulation of financial markets has traditionally been considered to be a matter of concern only to central bankers and the relevant authorities in each particular national sector, this has subsequently received much wider political attention especially at the G7 heads of state and government level. This new focus on financial stability began with the collapse of Barings in February 1995 and has been further strengthened following the more recent crises in Mexico, Russia, East Asia, and elsewhere.'[12] (See below.) It has been said that '[i]t is, above all, their alleged susceptibility to contagious disturbances that distinguishes financial institutions from non-financial firms'.[13] The implications of not

---

[9] Hans Falkena, Roy Bamber, David Llewellyn, Tim Store, *Financial Regulation in South Africa*, Financial Sector Forum, 2001, p. 2.

[10] T. Walmsley, 'Financial Regulation Report', *Financial Times*, 17 May 1993.

[11] J. Franks and S, Schaefer, *The Costs and Effectiveness of the UK Financial Regulatory System*, The City Research Project, 1993.

[12] George Alexander Walker, *International Banking Regulation Law, Policy and Practice*, Kluwer Law International, 2001, pp. 7–8.

[13] R. Dale and S. Wolfe, 'The UK Financial Services Authority: Unified Regulation in the New Market Environment', 2003, Vol. 4, No. 3, *Journal of Banking Regulation*, p. 201.

having appropriate regulation are generally well understood. For example: 'The Asia financial crisis was brought on by a lack of adequate regulation of the financial sector.'[14] This text deals with regulation in some detail in Chapter 6, but for the purposes of the present section, 'regulation' may be regarded simply as the rules that apply to the conduct of financial services. Llewellyn[15] believes that regulators' basic functions are universal, covering ten main areas:

- prudential regulation for the safety and soundness of financial institutions;
- stability and integrity of the payments system;
- prudential supervision of financial institutions;
- conduct of business regulation (that is, rules about how firms conduct business with their customers);
- conduct of business supervision;
- safety net arrangements such as deposit insurance and the lender of last resort role performed by the central bank;
- liquidity assistance for systemic stability, that is, liquidity assistance for solvent institutions;
- the handling of insolvent institutions;
- crisis resolution; and
- issues related to market integrity.

It has been said that: 'Because regulation and enforcement, by their nature, elevate broad public purposes above the interests of private parties, one should expect regulatory practice to carry with it irreducible conflicts. Regulators inhabit, and are obliged to navigate, a landscape of conflicting and shifting interests.'[16]

Financial regulation 'Offshore' is likely to be less prescriptive than 'Onshore'. This does not mean weaker regulation – it means that the prevailing regulation will probably be tailored to meet particular circumstances. It is worth remembering that the distinction between 'Offshore' and 'Onshore' is a distinction that arises from the treatment of non-resident and resident source business. So, 'tailored' means that the

---

[14] Joseph Stiglitz, *Globalisation and its Discontents*, Penguin Books, 2002, p. 220.
[15] David Llewellyn, 'Institutional Structure of Financial Regulation and Supervision', as quoted by Alexander Fleming and David Llewellyn, *Aligning Financial Supervisory Structures with Country Needs*, ed. Jeffrey Carmichael, World Bank Institute, September 2004, p. 24.
[16] Malcolm K. Sparrow, *The Regulatory Craft*, Brookings Institution Press, 2000, p. 17.

regulatory requirements satisfy prudential norms in such a way that creativity and entrepreneurial flair are not discouraged. Simultaneously, this enhances flexibility whilst maintaining standards that are appropriate in the context in which they are being offered. The degree of flexibility available 'Offshore' is far greater than is evidenced in larger centres where the regulatory processes have to be standardised to a larger degree – an example of the 'one size fits all' approach. The application of the distinction arises in the philosophy involved in controlling licensees within one's own jurisdiction and controlling business that arises from outside the jurisdiction. As is often the case, the devil is in the detail because, irrespective of the philosophy and the inherent difficulties, '[a]ll the tools – from the gentlest persuasion to the harshest enforcement campaigns – should be melded within coherent strategies for producing broad compliance.'[17]

3.8 Voluntary compliance

There is always likely to be a dichotomy between the extent to which a regulated business will want to be sufficiently free to carry on its commercial activity without external interference from a regulator and the perceived need of the regulator to be involved. The ideal solution is to discover where the line between these two aspirations falls and to tread that line carefully. Voluntary compliance by those conducting financial services activities that are licensable ('licensees') will always be preferable to the imposition of rules backed up by threats and ultimately regulatory action. For this to work, a substantial paradigm shift is required from those persons conducting financial services activities that are licensable and who are used to working only in response to demands – and from whom cooperation cannot be assumed. Note that licensable activity differs between jurisdictions. (This matter is taken up in Chapter 22, where it is suggested that ethics will become increasingly important in future for 'Offshore' centres.)

Meanwhile, it must be remembered that, for some, regulatory intervention is unnecessary, unhelpful and merely a cost factor providing little or no added value to anyone. It has been suggested that:

> [I]t is unreasonable to imagine that regulatory and enforcement agencies find their justification in the satisfactions of those whom they compel to

[17] Malcolm K. Sparrow, *The Regulatory Craft*, Brookings Institution Press, 2000, p. 64.

contribute to public purposes . . . [and that] . . [f]ailure to enforce the law
swiftly and effectively against deliberate or persistent offenders undermines the incentives for compliance in the rest of the community and
may bring a regulatory regime into disrepute . . . corporate behaviour
moves swiftly to take advantage of any perceived softening.[18]

As in any other system, the scope of the rules, and the extent to which
they are applied, affect the flow of business. As described above, there is
potential that, by relaxing the rules, a jurisdiction can affect the business
it generates.

'Regulatory arbitrage' means competition on the basis of regulatory
requirements. This strategy is fundamentally dangerous for OFCs because some businesses will default to the jurisdiction whose rules are
easiest to satisfy – the line of least resistance (see section 6.26 below).

One commentator has offered the following counsel to regulators: '[A]s
you carefully pick and choose what to do and how to do it, reconcile your
pursuit of effectiveness with the values of justice and equity.'[19]

3.9 Confidentiality

'Offshore Finance Centres' offer attributes other than tax advantages. For
example, consumers who believe that they may be exposed in some way
in their home country may want to reduce or eradicate that exposure by
investing in an external jurisdiction which offers (inter alia) privacy. If an
individual believes that his assets are at risk or are likely to be seized in
his home jurisdiction, he may consider establishing some form of trust
'Offshore' to protect the value of those assets – or even the assets
themselves – from being seized by the government of the country of
residence. This is sometimes referred to as 'capital flight' (see section 3.16
below).

Individuals are required to declare their income in their home country, but in some countries, by so doing, they may draw the attention of
criminals to the extent of their wealth – if information submitted to the
authorities is not maintained securely. In turn, this might make him or a
family member susceptible to kidnapping. In an attempt to prevent this,

[18] Mark H. Moore, *Creating Public Value: Strategic Management in Government*, Harvard
University Press, 1995, p. 37, as reported in *The Regulatory Craft*, Malcolm K. Sparrow,
Brookings Institution Press, 2000, p. 63.
[19] Malcolm K. Sparrow, *The Regulatory Craft*, Brookings Institution Press, 2000, p. 28.

the individual might transfer his assets 'Offshore' to take advantage of any privacy that might be available there. (There is no suggestion that, in such circumstances, the evasion of tax is acceptable – it is not!)

In some cases, privacy is needed to protect strategies from exploitation by competitors.

Privacy – and a desire to minimise tax – give rise to the need for confidentiality – and 'confidentiality' is problematic. 'Scepticism concerning the ability of governments to resist the temptation to access information for unauthorised purposes is rife, particularly as there is, by definition, no opportunity to monitor unauthorised access. Affluent tax payers in at least one major OECD country also fear that tax data is routinely sold to criminal gangs seeking targets for kidnapping. Global sharing of information means that criminal access can occur at the weakest point of entry, multiplying the risks associated with unauthorised disclosure.'[20]

Arguably, the most important characteristic that an 'Offshore Finance Centre' must be able to offer is confidentiality. At the same time, confidentiality is perhaps the characteristic that renders 'Offshore Finance Centres' most vulnerable.

Generally, a banker has a duty to preserve the confidentiality of the affairs of his client. This concept applies in many countries. In the UK, the principle derives from the decision in *Tournier* v. *National Provincial and Union Bank of England* [1924] 1 KB 461. By extension, the public at large has a right to expect that each individual's financial affairs will be treated confidentially by the providers of financial services. The problem arises when the degree of confidentiality required of a service provider or of a financial services centre goes beyond the norm. What is the norm? It is not easy to be precise but, generally speaking, it can be taken to be the point where confidentiality and secrecy merge. The line between the two is a fine one, making it difficult to know where one ends and where the other begins. For the purposes of this text, 'confidentiality' is interpreted to mean 'privacy', and 'secrecy' is interpreted to mean 'withholding information'. In fact, these two words ('secrecy' and 'confidentiality') are often used as if they were synonyms, as the following quote demonstrates: 'Secrecy is what "Offshore banking" is all about.'[21] The potential for confusion is obvious.

---

[20] Richard Hay, 'International Financial Centrres and Information Exchange', Issue 157, June 2005, *Offshore Investment*, p. 2.

[21] Matthew Lynn, 'Time to End Banking Secrecy', 10 February 2001, www.bloomberg.com.

One commentator has said in respect of anti-money laundering, that banking secrecy should be lifted under the Vienna UN Convention, the Strasbourg Convention and the Palermo UN Convention, 'that is in the course of confiscation and international cooperation procedures; the other is under the FATF Recommendations and the EC Directive that is in the course of due diligence of financial institutions'.[22]

Those who oppose the 'Offshore' concept often cite the potential for harm created by excessive 'secrecy'. It has been argued that, in light of the terrorist attacks on the USA on 11 September 2001 (see Chapter 11), there is no longer any tolerance towards secrecy.

A distinction should be made between civil and criminal matters (see section 18.3 below). Although there may be different definitions of what constitutes criminal activity, there can be few (if any) jurisdictions that defend confidentiality/secrecy when it comes to criminal matters.

3.10 Dual criminality/mutual legal assistance

Frequently, there are agreements (such as Mutual Legal Assistance Treaties) which provide for cooperation between two countries to investigate an offence and to prosecute the wrongdoers where the offence breaks the law in both countries (dual criminality). This overrides the normal confidentiality provisions that otherwise apply in financial transactions. This means that, if the circumstances dictate that it is justifiable (e.g. where criminal activity is suspected), governments are able to gain access to financial records. So, in general, 'Offshore Finance Centres' do not prevent action to investigate and deal with terrorists – in fact information obtained in the manner described above can be used to prosecute criminal activity.

3.11 What else besides tax and confidentiality?

The attributes of 'Offshore Finance Centres' extend beyond confidentiality and tax mitigation potential. For example, 'Offshore' jurisdictions will probably have lower levels of costs than 'Onshore' jurisdictions. That said, in some centres, the potential for new business is limited because of the physical size of the landmass. (See section 16.5 below for

---

[22] He Ping, 'Banking Secrecy and Money Laundering', Vol. 7, No. 4, 2004, *Journal of Money Laundering Control*, p. 378.

an analysis of the landmass of some jurisdictions.) The size of an 'Offshore Centre's' landmass might be a factor that affects its potential for future growth and development. The connection is that new business inevitably brings with it the need for experienced people and these people have to be accommodated. In one sense, this is positive, but, if the housing stock is insufficient, the jurisdiction is likely to impose a cap on how many people will be able to live and work there. In turn, this will raise prices.

The employment of staff also becomes difficult because demand exceeds supply and the supply is probably at or near saturation point. This means that members of staff move from one organization to another at a premium over their previous salary – although it is all very artificial because the employee may not be worth the additional amount that he will earn in the new post. If this is so, the same service is costing more to provide. Increased costs make profitability harder to achieve, which makes the jurisdiction less competitive.

3.12 Standards 'Offshore'

The importance of credibility is described below (see section 21.4 below) – but, with respect to financial services, credibility is a basic requirement.

Credible jurisdictions will seek to demonstrate that they have in place appropriate regulatory and supervisory standards for financial services activity. The extent to which an OFC adheres to the standards published by the international regulatory organisations described below (see Chapter 8) may be amongst the criteria that can be used to assess its credibility.

The problem is that every jurisdiction will describe itself as being in the forefront of those that promote the highest standards and adherence to what is frequently described as 'international best practice' – whatever that means. In short, it is sometimes difficult to separate the desirable from the undesirable. However, the important thing is not the range of legislation that a jurisdiction has on its statute books but rather the extent to which this legislation is enforced. The recent efforts to placate the OECD and the other international standard setters has produced a raft of legislation in 'Offshore Centres' around the world – but substance over form applies.

It has been said that it is now more difficult to open a bank account in an 'Offshore' jurisdiction than elsewhere. Apart from that, it should be

pointed out that at least in respect of fiduciary business the trend
'Offshore' is that this type of business will become licensable. This is
the case in Gibraltar, Guernsey, the Isle of Man, Jersey and Mauritius.
Ordinarily, fiduciary business is not licensable in 'Onshore' jurisdictions –
not even in the UK or the US.

A growing trend is for jurisdictions to enter into a Mutual Legal
Assistance Treaty (see section 3.10 above) with other jurisdictions. These
usually cover criminal, non-tax-based investigations. Where one of the
parties is an OFC, this should provide substantial comfort because it
demonstrates transparency and a willingness to cooperate where criminality is involved. In fact, '[t]he United Nations has even acknowledged
that criminals avoid so-called tax havens because they are a "red flag" for
law enforcement'.[23]

3.13 Some characteristics of OFCs

3.13.1

The jurisdiction will probably be a (small) island with a small local
population. Therefore, on the face of it, few service providers should
be necessary, but in fact the number of service providers (e.g. the number
of banks) is likely to be far greater than needed to service the local
population. (The Cayman Islands is a case in point. The population is
38,000 but at one stage there were nearly 600 banks. The volume of
business conducted makes the Cayman Islands the fifth-largest banking
centre in the world.)

3.13.2

The finance industry makes a material contribution to Gross Domestic
Product, and in some centres the economy is dependant upon the
financial services industry.

3.13.3

The volume of business transacted is large in absolute terms.

---

[23] *Financial Havens, Banking Secrecy and Money Laundering*, United Nations, 1998, as
quoted by Daniel J. Mitchell, 'US Government Agencies Confirm that Low-Tax Jurisdictions Are Not Money Laundering Havens', *Journal of Financial Crime*, Vol. 11, No. 2,
October 2003, p. 128.

3.13.4

Even though not every OFC offers every service, the range and sophistication of the services offered by service providers is greatly in excess of
the needs of the local population. (A recent article summed up the
situation concisely when it said: '[E]very possible user of offshore finance
facilities, has a different reason for needing a haven.'[24]) Frequently,
expertise is accumulated in niche areas of activity. Some OFCs are linked
with particular services or industries because the size, location and
development of the respective centres lend themselves to different spe-
cialisms such as banking, insurance or trusts.

3.13.5

Most users of the services are likely to live outside the jurisdiction. The
main users of OFCs are expatriates, but other users include those whose
home tax regime imposes (comparatively) high rates of tax and also
those who are taxed on worldwide income and gains. (One estimate
suggests that there are as many as 9 million professional expatriates
around the world.[25]) Further, people whose home is in a jurisdiction that
is politically or economically unstable may use an OFC to protect their
assets from inflation – or worse! An article published in *Investment
International*[26] described the main uses of OFCs as holding 'assets in a
low tax or nil tax environment, secretly and safely in a variety of savings
and investment structures like bank or building society accounts,
offshore funds, life policies, trusts and offshore companies. Held offshore,
these various investments can assist greatly in the avoidance of income
and capital gains taxes and often inheritance tax as well.' 'Offshore'
products enable higher rate taxpayers 'Onshore' to 'roll up' gains on
investments – which means that tax is not deducted as the value of the
investment increases year by year – but only upon repatriation after
redemption or distribution (deemed or actual) and then possibly at the
marginal rate.

---

[24] 'In the Mainstream', June 1996, *Investment International*, p. 61.
[25] Geoff Cook, 'Financial Services Catering for the Needs of People Living and Working
   Abroad', *International Financial Centres Yearbook 2004/05*, p. 11.
[26] *Investment International*, June 1996, p. 61.

3.13.6

Non-residents use 'Offshore Finance Centres' because they offer certain advantages not available in their own (home) jurisdiction. These include:

- no withholding tax;
- no personal income tax (for non-residents) or capital taxes;
- no exchange controls; and
- confidentiality.

3.13.7

The jurisdiction is likely to have a tailored regulatory environment. As stated above, the words 'tailored regulatory environment' should not be interpreted to mean the complete absence of regulation. Similarly, they do not mean no licensing is required or that scant attention will be paid to rules. Although this is not the norm, those words might bear such an interpretation in some jurisdictions. However, it is more likely to mean that, although similar standards are applied in the jurisdiction as are applied 'Onshore', the application of the regulations is focused on the particular type of business undertaken.

In the past, in some jurisdictions, 'banks' could be acquired in much the same way as any business can be acquired – and this had huge potential for abuse. The preference by far is that, normally, banks should only be owned by banks. In any event, regulators need to pay careful attention to those who fall into the category of 'qualifying shareholders' (i.e. those who are the largest shareholders). Further, material changes in shareholdings should be subject to regulatory approval.

3.13.8

'Offshore Finance' services companies in general and 'Offshore' banks in particular should – in principle – be subject to the same standards of control that financial services companies 'Onshore' must satisfy. The controls themselves need not be identical but they should be designed to satisfy the same objectives, for example adequacy of liquidity and capital, spread of assets, customer identity and so on. Where robust controls are not in place, problems are likely to ensue.

3.13.9

There is likely to be a cadre of professional advisors.

3.13.10

Economic and political stability are likely.

3.13.11

Good communication networks are likely to exist.

3.13.12

The jurisdiction is likely to have a benign fiscal environment (that is, no or low levels of tax on income and capital and no withholding tax or capital gains tax). Probably, interest will be paid gross and so the opportunity arises to defer the payment of tax – which represents a saving. Note that the payment is deferred, not eradicated. It is assumed that an OFC will be used for efficient tax planning because of the lower effective tax rates in that centre – avoidance and not evasion.

3.13.13

The IMF considers that the following characteristics are shared by many 'Offshore Centres' (see also section 3.4 above):

- Jurisdictions that have financial institutions engaged primarily in business with non residents;
- Financial systems with external assets and liabilities out of proportion to domestic financial intermediation designed to finance domestic economies; and
- More popularly, centres which provide some or all of the following opportunities: low or zero taxation; moderate or light financial regulation; banking secrecy and anonymity.[27]

Naturally, not every 'Offshore' jurisdiction is identical, but most jurisdictions will exhibit most of the characteristics described above – to

[27] 'Offshore Financial Centres – The Role of the IMF', 23 June 2000, p. 2.

some degree. This homogeneity will make it easier for a consumer to compare each jurisdiction and to assess the extent to which each one satisfies the criteria that the consumer considers are most important for him or her.

3.14 'Offshore' versus Onshore

The difficulties surrounding adequate definitions of 'Offshore' have been described in section 2.4 above, but it is just as difficult to define 'Onshore' as it is to define 'Offshore'. For example, while there might be general agreement that France, Germany and Italy are all 'Onshore' environments, it is not so easy to say why. Rather than try too hard, it might be agreed (somewhat unsatisfactorily) to regard an 'Onshore Finance Centre' as every type of finance centre that is not an 'Offshore Finance Centre'. Since this is not very helpful, there may be value in focusing on the characteristics of 'Onshore' rather than becoming entangled in an effort to establish a meaningful definition. See below for some further comments.

Speaking generally, six major sectors of finance have been identified as follows: 'commercial banking, investment banking, securities trading and broking, insurance and fund management'.[28] All these services are offered 'Onshore' and 'Offshore': in fact, 'Offshore' products used to be little more than 'Onshore' products repackaged. OFCs are not used because of exclusivity of their products and services – although some products and services available 'Offshore' are not available to residents of some 'Onshore' jurisdictions. (For example, companies registered 'Offshore' may invest in global assets through collective investment schemes that are also registered 'Offshore'. US citizens are denied access to these products from their 'Onshore' base.) A crucial difference in respect of 'Offshore' is that the services are 'packaged' differently. In fact, this is one of the reasons why there is a blurring of the distinctions between 'Onshore' and 'Offshore'. Some specific examples indicate that the figures involved are material. For example: 'Some 200 trust offices in the Netherlands . . . make a living from the creation and operation of (such) shell companies. These shells are also known as conduit companies, typically manufacture nothing, sell nothing, employ no-one and have no physical existence beyond a mailbox and a file drawer. But they

---

[28] David T. Llewellyn, *Global Pressures on the Banking Industry*, European Banking Report Seminar, Rome, 30 November 1994, p. 5.

take part in an estimated $1 trillion in transactions each year.'[29] (One estimate suggests that, in 2002, the conduit companies paid US$2.2 billion in tax.)

3.15 Some characteristics of 'Onshore' finance centres

The general characteristics of 'Onshore' financial services centres include:

- the jurisdiction will probably be a large, mainland jurisdiction;
- the finance industry will merely be one of several industries that contribute to Gross Domestic Product;
- the volume of business transacted is large in absolute terms;
- the number of service providers will not exceed the demand by much;
- most users of the services will probably be within the jurisdiction;
- the jurisdiction is likely to have a robust fiscal environment and requirements;
- the jurisdiction is likely to have a robust regulatory environment.

The Edwards report[30] cites three main criticisms of OFCs and seven points in their favour. The criticisms are as follows:

- their tax regimes induce particular industries to choose unsuitable locations offshore that deprive onshore jurisdictions of tax revenue to which they are due;
- secrecy and poor cooperation attracts and facilitates disreputable business and money laundering; and
- poor regulation: financial institutions can use low standards to build up a business that represents risk for its clients.

The favourable points cited in the Edwards report are as follows:

- the right to supply services;
- stability;
- risk spreading;
- convenience and simplicity;
- innovation and flexibility;

---

[29] 'Dutch Consider Regulation of an Ancient Financial Entity in Post Parmalat Backlash', March 2004, *Offshore Red*, p. 14.
[30] Michael Edwards, *Review of Financial Regulation in the Crown Dependencies*, Part 1, para. 2.14, 1998.

- regulation; and
- fiscal elements.

Where residents of a home jurisdiction consider that the tax rules are overly burdensome, they have few easy options. Possible alternatives (however unpalatable) include emigration, voting differently, reducing their standard of living or adopting alternative (legal) courses of action. Breaking the law (e.g. by evading tax) is not an option. In the final analysis, all such action is not only anti-social, but in the option. Inshore' centres have few feasible, acceptable alternatives other than to pay whatever rate of tax is demanded of them.

Regulation 'Onshore' is usually robust. The finance industry is built upon order and discipline. To limit the potential of would-be abusers of the financial system and to protect savers, investors and the payments system (on which the economy depends), detailed and prescriptive rules are established. Perversely, the majority of new rules are (frequently) developed directly after a catastrophe (which subject is taken up in a subsequent chapter). As an aside, a satisfactory regulatory system is a prerequisite for membership of the international economic and financial groupings with which 'Onshore' jurisdictions (for one reason or another) find themselves involved. Information on at least some of these groups is provided in Chapter 9.

Ironically, in some respects (e.g. some aspects of anti-money laundering procedures and the licensing and regulation of corporate and trust practitioners), the rules 'Offshore' are more developed than those 'Onshore' (including in FATF member countries).

It so happens that both London and the USA have certain characteristics (not least the number of accounts that belong to non-residents) that bring them near – if not within – the definition of an 'Offshore Finance Centre' – but this matter will be taken up in Chapters 17 and 18. This suggestion supports the argument that the classification of a financial environment is not quite as straightforward as one might suppose at first.

3.16 Capital flight

It has been said that: 'When capital is mobile it will seek its absolute advantage by migrating to countries where the environmental and social costs of enterprise are lowest and profits are highest. Both in theory and in practice the effect of global capital mobility is to nullify the Ricardian doctrine of comparative advantage.'[31] Further: 'The importance of flight capital as a potential source of deposits became increasingly evident to the large American financial institutions during the 1960s.'[32] The fact that this money is highly mobile means that the financial centres where it is located cannot know for how long they will enjoy its benefit. Accordingly, its mobility renders vulnerable any jurisdiction that depends on it. Information published by Russia's central bank suggests that, in 2004, the net outflow of private sector capital had increased from US$1.9 billion in 2003 to US$7.8 billion in 2004: 'spooked by the government's tax and legal proceedings against Yukos, investors moved their cash to offshore accounts according to analysts'.[33]

---

[31] John Christensen and Mark P. Hampton, *A Legislature for Hire: The Capture of the State in Jersey's Offshore Finance Centre*, as quoted in *Offshore Finance Centres and Tax Havens – The Rise of Global Capital*, ed. Mark P. Hampton and Jason P. Abbott, Macmillan Press Ltd, 1999, Chapter 7, p. 175.

[32] Ronen Palan, 'Offshore and the Structural Enablement of Sovereignty', in *Offshore Finance Centres and Tax Havens – The Rise of Global Capital*, ed. Mark P. Hampton and Jason P. Abbott, Macmillan Press Ltd, 1999, Chapter 2, p. 34.

[33] 'Global News, Russia', *Offshore Red*, February 2005, p. 2.

The service providers and the consumer (2)

The only certain means of success is to render more and better service than is expected of you, no matter what your task may be.[1]

4.1 Introduction

The previous chapter introduced three interest groups – the 'Offshore Centre' itself, the service providers and the consumers.

The focus of the last chapter was on the 'marketplace', while this chapter considers the service providers and the consumers.

It might be useful to distinguish between 'Offshore Services' – meaning the services provided to non-residents of the 'Offshore Centre' – and the 'Offshore Centre' itself – that is, a jurisdiction characterised by (inter alia) a predominance of business that is non-resident. Financial centres like London and New York provide a vast range of services to non-residents – and therefore might be described as 'Offshore' finance centres. It is unlikely that either London or New York would refer to itself or regard itself as an 'Offshore Centre' – although it has been acknowledged in London that the City transacts substantial amounts of non-resident business (see section 17.1 below). This distinction impinges upon other parts of the text, in particular in sections 17.2 and 18.2 with respect to the UK and the USA.

4.2 The service providers

'Offshore Centres' need to attract service providers to establish a real presence in the jurisdiction and to process as much business as possible through that location. According to Mr Jack Blum, former staff member of the US Senate Foreign Relations Committee, 'ultimately it is the banks and the financial institutions of the major countries that are the big

---

[1] Og Mandino, 1923–96.

players in this offshore world. Without them, without the access to the international payment system that these people provide, and without access to markets, you can close this whole thing down in a minute.'[2]

There is probably much truth in what Mr Blum says – although service providers other than banks contribute materially, for example insurance companies, captive insurance companies, stockbrokers, collective investment schemes, fund managers, custodians, corporate service providers, to name but a few. The third party in the transaction ('the final consumer') is the buyer of the services providers' products.

4.3 The consumers

The profile of 'Offshore' consumers is probably completely summed up thus: '[E]very Fortune 500 company and most of the Fortune 1000 companies and thousands of other enterprises and associations of individuals, or simply wealthy private persons, take advantage of the facilities offered by small islands and purpose-made international financial centres around the world.'[3]

4.4 Examples of services available 'Offshore'

In the previous chapter, the point was made that many services offered 'Offshore' are not peculiar to that environment as the list in Table 2 in Appendix 1 indicates. Meanwhile, the IMF has summarised the services that are provided from 'Offshore' jurisdictions as follows: banking (mainly inter-bank), private banking, collective investment schemes (including hedge funds and publicly marketed funds), asset management, incorporation of special purpose vehicles, establishment of trusts, structured financing, securitisation, estate management insurance (mainly for corporations), reinsurance and captive insurance.[4] Table 2 gives an indication of the range of services available.

One observer has said that international financial centres 'play a substantial commercial role facilitating tax-neutral transactions (often conceived in London or New York) as follows:

---

[2] Jeffrey Robinson, *The Laundrymen*, Simon & Schuster UK Ltd, 1998, p. 395.
[3] Dianna P. Kempe and Graham Wood, *The Bermuda International Business Guide 2003*, ISI Publications Ltd, p. 5.
[4] 'Offshore Financial Centres – The Assessment Program – A Progress Report and the Future of the Program', International Monetary Fund, 31 July 2003, p. 6.

- establishment and administration of mutual fund companies;
- structured debt and special purpose vehicles for bond markets, and other capital markets applications;
- insurance and reinsurance products;
- special purpose vehicles for securitisations;
- international tax and estate planning;
- international employee stock option plans; and
- shipping and aircraft financing structures.'[5]

4.5 'Offshore' banking

'Onshore' banks frequently establish subsidiaries and branches 'Offshore'. Their function may be the collection of deposits (used to fund lending by other parts of the group working 'Onshore') or maybe something more specialised like fund management or a subsidiary that provides trust services. The office 'Offshore' might be used to offer similar banking products as are available in mainland offices of the bank – but in an environment that may not be subject to any tax or to little tax on capital or revenue. There may be no withholding tax on dividends or interest, no capital gains tax, no corporation tax, no exchange controls – and there may be less onerous regulatory or reporting requirements. So there are advantages to customers and to the bank itself – which explains why there are substantial administration and management services provided to collective investment schemes by banks and other institutions from 'Offshore' bases.

The 'Offshore Environment' also accommodates what might be described as 'managed' enterprises, for example captive (see below) managers. In the case of banks, the 'managed bank' does not have a physical presence because it is managed by another 'legal person'. Thus, a properly licensed bank may actually manage the affairs of another bank which is also licensed – but licensed differently. The first bank (the manager) has a physical presence and staff, but the second bank only exists as a customer of the first. The second bank has its own customers, but the first bank manages those clients on behalf of the second bank. Managed banks should be distinguished from shell banks and from parallel branches and

---

[5] Richard Hay, 'International Financial Centres: Back on the Front Foot', *The 2005 Guide to International Financial Centres*, Euromoney Institutional Investor plc, February 2005, p. 1.

'brass plate' operations. It has been said that: 'Banking is the name of the game in the Cayman Islands, where there are more than 580 banks. Of these, 114 have a physical presence in the island; the rest have a brass plate operation.'[6] This type of operation has to be regulated very tightly to avoid abuse. For the sake of completeness, it should be stated that, in the short time that has elapsed since this quote was published, the figures have reduced (see section 16.4.7 below).

4.6 Insurance

There are a number of permutations on the general insurance theme; for example, protected cell captives, captives and reinsurance. These have been defined as follows: 'A captive insurance company is a separate legal entity which provides insurance for a non-insurer parent company's, and other corporate group members' risks. Protected cell captives, or rent-a-captives, enable several insured to share captive facilities with the business segregated from each other into cells. Reinsurance provides insurance for insurance companies' risks and producer-owned reinsurance companies are a specialised form of reinsurance captive.'[7] A 'captive' is the means by which an insurance company self-insures. It is owned by a company that is not an insurance company. This minimises the capital and reserves required. A subsidiary in an OFC may be established by an 'Onshore' insurer to reinsure certain risks underwritten by the 'Onshore' company. The advantages described above make this type of business attractive – and it becomes even more so if the capital and reserve requirements are low. It is estimated that there are around 4,000 captives globally. An increasing number of 'Offshore' centres have specific protected cell company legislation to accommodate this type of activity (e.g. Guernsey and Mauritius).

4.7 International Business Companies (IBCs)

International Business Companies (IBCs) are sometimes referred to as 'Offshore' companies, exempt companies or international companies.

---

[6] *International Wealth Management*, Supplement, 'International Financial Centres', Financial Times, September 2000, p. 49.
[7] 'Offshore Financial Centres – The Assessment Program – A Progress Report and the Future of the Program', IMF, 31 July 2003, p. 13.

One estimate suggests that 'there are some 680,000 companies incorporated in offshore jurisdictions'.[8] (It seems that many of the companies
referred to are IBCs.) Probably, the incorporation of companies is one of
the most popular services offered by OFCs. IBCs can be created very
quickly – and in some jurisdictions (e.g. Anguilla and Delaware) they can
be created online.

IBCs are limited liability companies. The shareholders are probably
individuals – whose identity will be a closely guarded 'secret'. For tax
purposes, the companies will not be resident in the jurisdiction where
the company was incorporated – although there must be a registered
office and an agent in that jurisdiction. These companies usually pay
no tax provided that the income generated by the company does not
originate within the OFC. Ordinarily, financial statements need not be
prepared, filed or audited. Such companies may be investment holding
companies, or used to raise capital (e.g. by way of issue of bonds) or to
hold assets ranging from ships to jewellery. IBCs are very flexible and (in
general) may conduct any activity that a corporate vehicle 'Onshore'
can conduct – without the consequent tax 'Onshore'. Thus, they are an
attractive method to accumulate revenue – on a gross basis.

A corporate constitution is required (or memorandum and articles
of association). Frequently, only one director is required, and that
director may be a corporate entity. Further, in some jurisdictions, bearer
shares are acceptable (although this is now less prevalent), and there may
or may not be a public register of shareholders. Therefore, the identity of
the true owners may not be (immediately) apparent. Establishment costs
are very low, and the speed of establishment means that there is little or
no regulatory control pre-incorporation (and sometimes not afterwards
either). Licensing may or may not be required, depending first on the
existence of a licensing regime and, secondly, on whether the licensing
regime considers the company's proposed activity to be licensable.

This type of company can be used as a 'Special Purpose Vehicle' (SPV) –
a particularly popular means of issuing asset-backed securities. (In summary, this allows the 'Onshore' company to transfer ownership of a
portfolio of assets to the SPV, which then offers securities to investors
elsewhere based on these assets). The tax benefits are considerable.

---

[8] Dianna P. Kempe and Graham Wood, *The Bermuda International Business Guide 2003*, ISI
Publications Ltd, p. 5.

SPVs can also be used to raise tier one capital and to exploit more liberal regulatory regimes 'Offshore'.

While most OFCs offer the incorporation of companies, the British Virgin Islands (BVI) probably has more companies incorporated than anywhere else. In some jurisdictions (e.g. Guernsey, Jersey, the Isle of Man, Malta and Mauritius), incorporating and managing companies on behalf of others is regarded as a licensable activity (see section 6.17 below). Different rules apply in different jurisdictions – and this is a good example of my earlier comments on 'packaging'.

> The complicating aspect of the IBCs and non resident trusts is that by design they have been created to provide an important degree of confidentiality to the beneficial owners. While IBCs and trusts may serve legitimate purposes . . . they can also be used for improper ends, including (i) their use to engage in illegal activities directly or (ii) holding the proceeds of illegal activities. Apart from the work done by the Offshore Group of Banking Supervisors [see sections 6.17 and 9.21 below], there are no international standards for regulating directly IBCs and non resident trusts, which now number in the hundreds of thousands, nor is there a consensus developing as to how individual IBCs and non-resident trusts could be regulated in 'Offshore' or Onshore centres. That said, some OFCs in the Caribbean and the UK Crown dependencies have begun what should prove to be a useful process of registering and regulating providers of services to those establishing trusts and companies.[9]

In fact, this is not new. Mauritius has been licensing what are known as 'Management Companies' since 1992. These Management Companies are basically providers of corporate and trust services – which include the establishment of corporate vehicles and trusts for clients. These companies are (now) regulated under the Financial Services Development Act 2001. Jersey and Guernsey have recently introduced legislation to which 'Corporate Service Providers' must conform (see section 6.17 below).

Formerly known as 'Incorporation Agents', Corporate Service Providers are the intermediaries that offer fiduciary services to clients. These services include the establishment of IBCs, providing registered office facilities and directors or acting as company secretary.

---

[9] 'Offshore Financial Centres, The Role of the IMF', 23 June 2000, p. 8.

4.8 Asset management

OFCs are frequently used by 'high net worth individuals' (HNWIs) to manage their assets. This keeps the assets outside their home jurisdiction and may protect those assets where the home jurisdiction has a fragile economy or uncertain financial environment. High net worth individuals use OFCs (particularly those with extensive tax treaties) as part of their tax mitigation strategies. Typically, they will use 'Offshore' companies, trusts and other 'Offshore' facilities to accommodate this strategy. Sometimes HNWIs use OFCs because they fear that their assets might be seized in their home environment (see section 4.10 below).

4.9 Collective Investment Schemes (CISs)

For the purposes of this text, the term 'collective investment scheme' (CIS) is used to describe an arrangement that enables investors (whether individuals or corporate entities) to pool money and to invest it in aggregate. The investors' interest is evidenced by shares or units which may be sold at any time. A CIS can be constituted as a trust, or as a company (or limited partnership) or by way of contract. Each is described below.

CISs come in many different shapes and sizes, but the term 'Collective Investment Scheme' has been used to describe them all since that is the term which the International Organization of Securities Commissions (IOSCO) has adopted. (Frequently, CISs are also referred to as schemes or funds.) The amount of money invested globally in CISs has fallen from a peak of US$12.25 trillion in 2000 to US$11.217 trillion in December 2002.[10] CISs offer a convenient means of saving because they:

- are flexible;
- reduce risk through diversification;
- limit costs through economies of scale; and
- are more likely to achieve finer prices because of the volume of their transactions.

---

[10] *Worldwide Mutual Funds Assets and Flows, Fourth Quarter 2002*, Investment Company Institute, Washington, as cited in *Managing Collective Investment Funds*, 2nd edn, Mark St Giles, Ekaterina Alexeeva and Sally Buxton, John Wiley & Sons Ltd, 2003, p. 13.

4.9.1 UCITS

An Undertaking for Collective Investment in Transferable Securities (UCITS) fund is an open-ended CIS (see below) which adheres to the EU's UCITS Directive. Satisfaction of the Directive's criteria means that the UCITS may be sold in any country within the European Economic Area.

4.9.2 Unit trusts

A unit trust is a CIS constituted as a trust and is formed under a trust deed under which a trustee is appointed to hold assets – which are pooled in trust – for the investors (who are referred to as 'unit holders'). The aggregate value of the units represents the worth of the trust. Although the units have no nominal value, they are all identical in value – which is the worth of the company divided by the number of shares in issue. The pooled money is invested in the name of the trustee (although the money and the assets acquired are owned by the unit holders). The whole process is administered by a manager. CISs in the form of a trust are prevalent in common law jurisdictions (see sections 4.10 and 18.3 below).

4.9.3 Companies

Although there is more than one permutation, companies are most frequently formed with limited liability. (Permutations include liability limited by guarantee or unlimited liability.) Limited liability companies are the most common type of vehicle used for CISs.

CISs may be open-ended (called mutual funds in the USA in which shares may be bought back from members and where new shares may be issued) or closed-ended (where the share capital issued is fixed and which requires a seller to obtain the approval of other shareholders before disposal). Closed-ended funds frequently have a finite life.

The partnership form is particularly useful for small numbers of institutional or professional investors – who become limited partners (while the management company becomes the general partner). The fund is not subject to tax, but the investors are personally liable. In this form, the life of the partnership is usually finite, which allows investors to liquidate their assets. This type of fund is particularly prevalent in 'Offshore' jurisdictions for hedge funds.

4.9.4 Hedge funds and 'Offshore'

Simply stated, hedge funds are collective investment schemes that are entitled to invest in almost anything, for example secondhand life policies, insurance covers or bets for hurricane loss, and commodity and equity derivatives. Hedge funds are entitled to invest in assets and to use techniques that are not permissible for collective investment schemes in general. Hedge funds can run short positions and leverage their portfolio by borrowing. The degree of risk and the fact that they are unregulated (which inter alia means that they are not obliged to disclose to the public what their asset portfolios comprise) combine to make them entirely unsuitable for most people. The fact that they may invest in complex and even custom designed derivatives means that the value of those assets may not be easily or accurately ascertained (since these instruments are unlikely to be listed on any exchange). Hedge funds were originally conceived as investment vehicles that were of specific interest to high net worth individuals but not the general public (in the USA the threshold for investment is US$1million). Accordingly, in the first instance, they were not given a high priority. However, this is now changing as more and more (ordinary) investors are lured by potential gains that have disappeared from many other types of investment. The Securities and Exchange Commission (SEC) in the USA is presently considering whether to regulate hedge funds fully. Some regulations came into effect in February 2005 (these require some funds to register with the SEC by January 2006). One operational consequence is the extent to which the rules apply, for example in respect of advisors who are overseas and who advise funds other than US funds (such as funds domiciled in the Cayman Islands and those which do not permit investment from US residents). Managers often earn an incentive fee which is paid by the fund itself out of its profits, which is in addition to the annual fee they earn. One problem that arises in comparing performance is that managers simply close funds that do not perform well, and this may affect the performance index of the funds that remain. (It is anticipated that, for 2005, in the US, hedge funds will have US$1 trillion under management, shared amongst 7,000 hedge funds. This should be compared with 2,500 hedge funds with US$400 billion a decade ago.[11])

---

[11] Anthony Slingsby, 'Hedging and Ditching – Not Yet!', *Offshore Investment.com*, April 2005, Issue 155, p. 21.

Amongst the factors that brought hedge funds to public attention was the near collapse of Long Term Capital Management (LTCM) – a hedge fund based in Greenwich, Connecticut. LTCM was founded in 1994 by John Meriwether, a former bond trader with Salomon Brothers. LTCM comprised a strong combination of traders and academics, whose market judgments and quantitative models were intended to combine to produce profits not otherwise available. The fund started with US$1.3 billion but within four years found itself on the verge of collapse. This was avoided by the involvement of a US$3.5 billion rescue package put together by the US Federal Reserve in which participants received 90 per cent of LTCM's equity. The people involved in LTCM included economists who were Nobel Prize winners and a vice-chairman of the Federal Reserve Board. LTCM's strategy was to identify securities that were mispriced in relation to each other – taking long positions in those that were priced cheaply and short positions in those priced expensively. Where differences existed, they were very small, which meant that LTCM was obliged to adopt large, highly leveraged positions to make profits. Despite this high leverage, LTCM relied on its complex models to correlate long and short positions to minimise net risk.

> [T]he ultimate cause of the LTCM debacle was the 'flight to quality' across the global fixed income markets . . . What LTCM had failed to account for is that a substantial portion of its balance sheet was exposed to a general change in the 'price' of liquidity. If liquidity became more valuable (as it did following the crises) its short positions would increase in price relative to its long positions. This was essentially a massive, unhedged exposure to a single risk factor.[12]

LTCM represented a fundamental problem that required attention to prevent systemic implications for the world's financial system, not least because it involved 20,000 derivatives contracts with seventy-five counterparties outstanding.

There may be some correlation between hedge funds and 'Offshore'. Both are said to be unregulated, which means that the principle of caveat emptor prevails. Secondly, because of certain exemptions that are provided in the US, hedge funds are not permitted to advertise and placements are private. '[I]nformation about the nature and performance of

[12] 'Case Study – Long Term Capital Management', www.erisk.com/Learning/CaseStudies/ref_case_ltcm.asp.

hedge funds has always tended to be masked in the protection of the professional secrecy of those running them.'[13] The common feature appears to be 'secrecy'.

4.9.5 Contractual

Funds in a contractual form are found in countries whose legal system is based on a civil code (e.g. France). The contract includes the rights of investors. This type of fund is formed under a contract made between the investor and the fund management company. The latter manages the assets, and appoints a depository to take responsibility for custody of the assets. Investors acquire units. This type of fund has no legal personality, which means that it is not taxable.

4.10 Trusts

As well as the incorporation of companies, the creation of trusts gives rise to substantial levels of business 'Offshore'. The 'trust concept' is said to date back to the Crusades and twelfth-century property rights. 'A departing Crusader would entrust his property to a trusted friend, to ensure his property passed to his lineal descendants in the event of his death and his widow's remarriage.'[14] Therefore, the ability of the Crusader to influence how his property would be dealt with continued after his death. 'They were subsequently used to reduce feudal dues: there is nothing new in the idea that trusts can be used to mitigate tax or protect assets.'[15]

Trusts are frequently private in nature, being a contract between (usually) two private persons. In explaining trusts, 'legal ownership' is distinguished from 'beneficial ownership'. Article 2 of the Hague Convention (see below) provides a description of the most fundamental characteristics of a trust (in order to enable the legal profession to determine whether a particular set of circumstances constitutes a trust for the purposes of the convention; accordingly, this is not a definition per se). Article 2 states:

---

[13] Anthony Slingsby, 'Hedging and Ditching – Not Yet!', *Offshore Investment.com*, April 2005, Issue 155, p. 20.

[14] 'Will the Government's Proposals Kill Off Trusts?', *Offshore Red*, March 2004, p. 13.

[15] Philip J. Hobson, 'The Statute of Elizabeth', www.trusts-and-trustees.com/library/statute_elizabeth.htm.

For the purposes of this Convention, the term 'trust' refers to the legal relationships created – inter vivos or on death – by a person, the settlor, when assets have been placed under the control of a trustee for the benefit of a beneficiary or for a specified purpose. A trust has the following characteristics:

a. the assets constitute a separate fund and are not part of the trustee's own estate

b. title to the trust assets stands in the name of the trustee or in the name of another person on behalf of the trustee

c. the trustee has the power and the duty, in respect of which he is accountable, to manage, employ or dispose of the assets in accordance with the terms of the trust and the special duties imposed upon him by law.

The reservation by the settlor of certain rights and powers, and the fact that the trustee may himself have rights as a beneficiary, are not necessarily inconsistent with the existence of a trust.

Often, it is not even necessary to identify the settlor (the person who creates the trust). Trusts are particularly useful vehicles and provide substantial anonymity. Trusts are used (inter alia) as a means of mitigating future tax liability by surrendering ownership of assets to a trustee, who assumes responsibility for administering the assets in accordance with the settlor's instructions for the benefit of specified beneficiaries. However, the validity of a trust may be subject to challenge and so, generally, the less control the settlor retains over the trust and its trustees, the less vulnerable the trust will be to challenge in this respect.

The main reasons for creating a trust include:

- to enable an individual during his lifetime to make provisions for others;
- to enable the distribution of assets in a way that is outside the laws of succession (which apply under the terms of a will);
- to enable the processing of transactions anonymously and confidentially;
- to avoid death or estate duties or inheritance tax liabilities;
- to shelter assets from litigation; and
- to minimise the effects of tax during a settlor's lifetime.[16]

---

[16] Alan Molloy, *The Offshore Investment Market*, Oak Tree Press, 1999, p. 36.

It is very rare for trusts to be regulated. There are a number of types of trusts, which include:

- The Foreign Grantor Trust, also known as the Asset Protection Trust (APT), is often used by professional people whose circumstances (principally arising from their occupation) expose them to risk of suit and unlimited liability. Consequently, they enter into an arrangement to transfer the ownership of their assets, thereby protecting those assets from litigation onshore. In this respect, APTs provide legal protection against improper claims. APTs should not be used to avoid liability for contractual debts that a person has incurred. If a professional person attempts to frustrate a potential attempt by any future creditor of the settlor of the trust while retaining access to the assets of the trust, the morality of the structure is called into question. For example, if a dentist in the USA injures a patient negligently, that patient will not be able to sue the dentist for assets that are owned by the APT located in an 'Offshore' jurisdiction. Although the dentist has protected his assets, the patient has been denied the proceeds of a (presumably) legitimate claim. This example presupposes legitimacy, but in fact some professionals would argue that they need an APT to protect themselves against illegitimate claims. Fraudulent conveyance is a particularly important criterion in demonstrating that an APT is valid (see the Statute of Elizabeth below). In some centres (e.g. Gibraltar in 1990), the legislation has been amended to accommodate enhanced creditor protection.
- A 'Life Interest Trust' arises where the assets of the trust pass to a beneficiary after the death of the life tenant. During his or her lifetime, the latter retains the right to trust property (including income).
- 'Accumulation and Maintenance Trusts' are frequently used to pay for education expenses or the living costs of children until the child reaches a predetermined age or until the child becomes an adult. They may give rise to inheritance tax onshore.
- Discretionary trusts are often treated with scepticism by regulators because of the potential for misuse. These trusts allow the trustees to decide when distributions of trust assets will be made and to whom. Such trusts are often used by families to hold assets such as property.
- Purpose trusts, where the benefit is for a purpose, not for a person or an entity. Normally (although not exclusively), purpose trusts are used in charitable scenarios.

In respect of trusts, different rules apply in different jurisdictions. For example, the Virgin Islands Special Trusts Act (VISTA Trust). This accommodates a BVI trust regime 'which allows trust assets to remain in trust for the life of the trust, rather than being sold simply to comply with outdated legal requirements, and which enables companies to be effectively managed by their directors without counter-productive interference by trustees. The new VISTA regime therefore enables settlors of trusts to retain effective control of trust assets at the company level (if this is required).'[17] Consider also the Special Trust Alternative Regime (STAR Trust), a regime for non-charitable purpose trusts.

Trusts are valuable instruments for a range of legal persons – their value is not restricted to individuals and families. Their uses include

> charitable and family purposes, the creation of a business entity (the so-called 'Massachussets' trust in the United States, developed in the nineteenth century), the formation of holding companies to concentrate the control of the stock of several corporations (the source of the so-called 'antitrust' laws in the United States, beginning in the late nineteenth century), and real estate investment trusts (to avoid limitations on ownership of land by incorporated companies). We now see on the one hand, massive pension funds and investment trusts and those savings schemes known in Britain as 'unit trusts', many of which are structured using the traditional trust mechanism, whilst, on the other hand, we see large amounts of debt structured and collateralised by 'trust indentures'.[18]

Thus, trusts may be used not only to protect the wealth of individuals and families but also for off balance sheet transactions and to acquire and dispose of a business. ('Unit Trusts' – a special type of Collective Investment Scheme (as described in section 4.9 above).)

4.10.1 The Hague Convention

The Hague Convention on the Law Applicable to Trusts and on Their Recognition is the foundation document in respect of their international development. Volume II of the Proceedings of the Fifteenth Session (8/20 October 1984) edited by the Permanent Bureau of the Conference and

---

[17] Humphry Leue, 'The British Virgin Islands', in *The 2005 Guide to International Financial Centre*, Euromoney Institutional Investor plc, February 2005, p. 6.

[18] Adair Dyer, 'International Recognition of the Trust Concept', www.trusts-and-trustees.com/library/trust_concept.htm.

issued by the Government Printing Office at The Hague in 1985, provides a complete history of the Hague Convention.

> The Hague Convention . . . was first conceived as an instrument which
> would build a bridge between the common law and the civil law countries
> providing uniform rules as to the law which applied to a trust and
> providing, for the civil law countries in particular, rules for recognition
> of this unknown form of property holding and for giving effect to the intent
> of the settlor of the trust in so far as was possible given the conceptual
> and technical differences between the property systems of the different
> countries.[19]

In the article just quoted, the author explained that, towards the end of
the 1970s, with the development of what was known as the common
market, civil law practitioners in Europe found themselves dealing increasingly with English and US trust matters as English and US citizens
moved to Europe to live. In so doing, they acquired property in civil law
countries. When they died, the property could conceivably form part of a
trust created by the expatriate. A problem arose because the systems for
registering land and categories of ownership of such civil law countries
did not cater for this type of property holding.

Similarly, as people from civil law countries moved to England or the
USA (common law countries) and acquired property, circumstances
arose where a will might be created that contained trust provisions
concerning their property. The complicating factor was that such trusts
might apply to an inheritance received by someone in a civil law country
of origin.

In principle, the rules of the Convention are universal and by definition therefore cover all trusts that are governed under the Convention's
rules, whether or not the country involved is a contracting state under
the Convention. There are two exceptions. Article 21 provides that 'a
contracting state may reserve the right to apply the provisions of the
Convention on recognition only to trusts, the validity of which is
governed by the law of a contracting state'.[20] Secondly, Article 13 states
that 'No state shall be bound to recognise a trust, the significant elements
of which, except for the choice of the applicable law, the place of

---

[19] Adair Dyer, 'International Recognition of the Trust Concept', www.trusts-and-trustees.
com/library/trust_concept.htm.
[20] Adair Dyer, 'International Recognition of the Trust Concept', www.trusts-and-trustees.
com/library/trust_concept.htm.

administration and the habitual residence of the trustee are most closely connected with states which do not have the institution of the trust or the category of trust involved'.

In making the previous points, Mr Dyer concludes that:

> The influence of the Hague Trusts Convention is not limited to its concrete application in the countries which are parties to it. Indeed, very little court practice seems to have been developed in those countries which have ratified. Yet for countries that have no private international law rules for trusts, the Hague Convention offers the only analysis and set of rules which have been negotiated in an international forum. Even in the common law countries the precedents for determining the applicable law for a trust are generally few and inconclusive.

4.10.2 Forced heirship

In a 1989 amendment to the Trusts (Jersey) Law 1984, forced heirship is said 'to relate to a legal rule restricting the right of a person to dispose of property during his lifetime so as to preserve such property for distribution at his death or having similar effect'. Thus, forced heirship requires that, on the death of an individual, his or her assets must be dealt with in a way that ensures the deceased person's heirs receive what is due to them.

So far as trusts are concerned, the implication is that a person must not dispose of property during his lifetime to trustees in circumstances that would deprive that person's heirs partially or completely of their rights to the property. To make sure this does not happen, some jurisdictions invoke forced heirship rules that restrict proposed transfers. If the transfer to a trust is not valid, the trust may not be valid and the trustees may have no title to the assets, so the implications are fundamental.

Forced heirship rules are most common in civil law countries (such as Europe). This compares with countries where English common law influence prevails, where generally no such restrictions apply. 'Under the European civil law jurisdictions there is an absolute indefeasible right to a share in the estate. There is no defence and the merits are not relevant.'[21]

---

[21] Anthony Dessain, 'The Forced Heirship Issue and Jersey Trust Law', www.trusts-and-trustees.com/library/v5no1.htm.

4.10.3 The Statutes Of Elizabeth

Although trusts are not peculiar to English common law jurisdictions, they predominate in common law environments. The Statutes of Elizabeth are part of English common law, dating back to the sixteenth century. (The UK Statute of Elizabeth was passed in 1571 but more recent provisions can be found in section 423 and 425 of the UK's Insolvency Act 1986.) The Statute is frequently cited in discussions concerning trusts in the UK's Crown dependencies. The cause of concern is that 13 Eliz. c. 5 sets aside 'fraudulent conveyances'.[22] The Statutes (there are more than one, dealing with both fraudulent conveyances and bankruptcy) are significant in determining whether the intention is to place property beyond the grasp of creditors of the settlor, and, if so, the conveyance may be 'set aside', that is to say, considered to be an invalid disposition of property.

> Only those jurisdictions that are independent from the UK Parliament and the Crown of the UK have constitutions permitting the repeal of English Common Law, such as this statute [the Statute of Elizabeth] or will permit argument supporting repeal . . . Otherwise Crown Dependent Territories may modify English Common Law, but not repeal it.[23]

4.11 Nominees

As the name suggests, a 'nominee' is appointed to represent someone else. For example, 'Nominee shareholders' means that the identity of the ultimate beneficial owner of a corporate entity will not be apparent immediately. 'Nominee directors' are said to represent the real directors, but this term is a misnomer since company law does not recognise the concept of nominee directors.

4.12 Shipping

The Geneva Convention on the High Seas 1958 states that: 'Ships shall have the nationality of the state whose flag they are entitled to fly.' The word 'registration' implies 'attributing a national character to a ship and

[22] Philip J. Hobson, 'The Statute of Elizabeth', www.trusts-and-trustees.com/library/statute_elizabeth.htm.
[23] 'Offshore Trusts and American and English Common Law Trusts are Creatures of Contract Law', World Newsstand, www.wealth4freedom.com/truth/banks8.htm.

a link from the ship to an ownership and control structure in that nation state (the Flag State) which is then duly recorded in the register of ships'.[24] The registration of ships goes back many years (to Imperial Roman days) and the Convention's words refer to closed registers, as opposed to the open registers which are sometimes referred to as flags of convenience. '[F]rom the 17th century onwards there is clear evidence of vessel owners living in one country, registering their ships in that of another to obtain protection during conflict, freedom from fishing restrictions and other reasons to gain usually a commercial advantage.'[25] The latter are criticised in that they are regarded as means for owners to adopt a veil of secrecy in that there is no economic link to the state whose flag they are flying. In the event of a hazard or a problem with environmental protection, the identity of owners may remain secret.

OFCs accommodate the ownership of ships, their registration and their management. An important study was published by the Seafarers International Research Centre in February 2003. The study (inter alia) analysed thirty-seven 'flag states' according to their regulatory approach. The 'Offshore' jurisdictions that were rated highly include Bermuda, the Cayman Islands, Cyprus, Hong Kong, the Isle of Man, Madeira, the Netherlands Antilles, the Philippines and Singapore. (As an aside, not all these jurisdictions regard themselves as being 'Offshore' in the first place.) By way of example, there are 300 ships on the Isle of Man's register and 466 on Bermuda's register. 'Shipping is continuing to experience strong growth of around ten per cent per annum, with over 400 merchant vessels and 22 super-yachts currently sailing under the Manx flag', according to the Isle of Man's figures.[26]

Some concern has been raised by the OECD (30 April 2003) that the secrecy surrounding the identity of the owners of ships could give rise to a 'maritime September 11 attack'. This could lead to new requirements that will provide disclosure of owners and more robust controls on shipping registers.

A flag state – which by definition has established a ship registry – has substantial obligations to the international community.

---

[24] 'St Kitts and Nevis as an International Ship Registry', *Offshore Red*, May 2005, p. 84.
[25] 'St Kitts and Nevis as an International Ship Registry', *Offshore Red*, May 2005, p. 84.
[26] 'Ships Register One of Two Best in the World', *Isle of Man Financial Review*, July 2005, p. 1.

4.13 Limited liability entities

Limited liability entities provide an alternative to the standard type of corporate entity. There are a number of permutations:

- Limited Partnerships (LPs). LPs provide limited liability. There are at least two partners, one of whom is a limited partner and one of whom is a general partner. The general partner has unlimited personal liability. The same person may be the general and the limited partner (although there must be two partners at all times).
- The Limited Liability Company (LLC). As the name suggests, the LLC has some characteristics of a corporation and some of a partnership: it is a hybrid. As for a corporation, the liability is limited to the amount paid on the shares held. As for a partnership, there is no tax at the level of the entity. LLCs appeared in 1990s. As a single member entity, an LLC may choose to be disregarded for US federal income tax purposes, and instead be treated as an extension of its owner. This provides certain tax planning opportunities, but the LLC needs to avoid creating a taxable presence in the USA (e.g. the member must not be a resident of the USA and must not trade in the USA or even have an office there).[27]
- The Limited Liability Partnership (LLP). There are two main categories, one of which protects the partners from any claim arising from the negligence of any other partner, but offers no protection in the event of a claim made against the partnership as a whole. The second category offers protection from all liabilities. This style has been adopted by some accounting firms.
- The Limited Liability Limited Partnership (LLLP). This type offers double protection – as a limited liability partnership with limited liability. This approach enables limited partners to control the partnership while having only limited liability. That said, a limited partner may be personally liable in a situation where he or she has been involved in a wrongful action.[28]

4.14 Foundations

Foundations are far from new, dating back to the Middle Ages. Historically, they have been used for charitable purposes, and, while they may

---

[27] Martin Berger, 'The US LLC – The Best of All Worlds', www.offshoreinvestment.com, November 2004, p. 8.
[28] Denis Kleinfeld, 'Limiting Liability with an LLE', *The OFC Report*, 2003, p. 21.

still be used for such purposes, they are now commonly used for estate planning purposes, particularly in civil law jurisdictions. (Not everyone is used to or comfortable with the concept of the trust. Importantly, a trust is not a legal entity in law per se. However, it is based on legal relationships. Foundations are legal entities – which are used in 'non-trust jurisdictions' to serve the purposes served by a trust in a 'trust jurisdiction'.)

Although a foundation is a distinct legal entity, it has no shareholders and it is administered in accordance with contractual principles – not fiduciary principles. The foundation is created when its charter is registered with the public registry by its founder. A founder may be a real person or a corporation or a trust. The founder then endows the foundation with assets, and this is called the 'patrimony'. This may be done while the founder is alive or after his or her demise by way of a will. Foundations may hold assets in their own name, for the purposes described in the constitutive documents. The founder is not the legal owner of the assets, and it is this separation which protects assets from potential creditors. That said, and depending on how the charter and constitutive documents have been structured, a foundation may allow a founder to retain more authority in dealing with assets than settlors may exercise under a discretionary trust.

Invariably, the charter includes the following: the foundation's name (which should include the word 'Foundation'), its purpose, duration and capital, how it may be liquidated, how beneficiaries are appointed, the members of the foundation's council, its domicile and the name and domicile of its registered agent and, importantly, the right to modify the charter. 'Under the Panamanian Private Foundation law, the Foundation is tax free on all income from sources generated outside Panama.'[29] In Europe, the Liechtenstein Family Foundation is very well known. The Panamanian Family Foundation is a newer rival.

4.15 Other services

The list of services offered 'Offshore' is virtually endless. One area of growing interest is what is sometimes referred to as 'business process outsourcing' (BPO) or 'back office' operations, which are basically administrative in nature. The focus is two-fold. First, in some jurisdictions

---

[29] 'Panama, A Rising Star in Offshore Asset Protection', *Offshore Red*, April 2005, pp. 68–9.

where space is at a premium (e.g. Jersey and Guernsey), there is increasing pressure to 'outsource' those services that use more manpower because such services are expensive where the labour supply is limited and adds least value. Secondly, some growing jurisdictions (especially where there is adequate space and lower labour costs, e.g. Mauritius) are willing to accommodate such business. There are some regulatory issues arising, but these are manageable. There are permutations that extend beyond financial services per se, and a whole new industry is gaining momentum, referred to as 'Offshoring'. Some additional comments will be offered in section 4.19 below.

One commentator has said: '[T]ax havens provide an essential escape route that enables capital to be preserved for productive purposes. In addition, it buttresses what is a core value of the West, namely freedom.'[30]

4.16 The consumer

In the same way that the OFC needs to attract service providers, the service providers need to attract clients. Thus, to a certain extent, the OFC needs to satisfy the consumer that the jurisdiction is appropriate for the sort of business that he wants to transact. Unless the environment is conducive, the OFC will not be able to attract clients and therefore will lose business. Thus, in promoting his own services, the service provider must convince the consumer that the 'Offshore Environment' from which those services will be offered is conducive. This demonstrates clearly the need for practitioners and the authorities (not regulators exclusively) in a jurisdiction to work in tandem to optimise results. In a sense, the regulator's role can be described as doing what is necessary to make a financial services environment conducive to good business.

4.17 What does the consumer expect from the market?

The consumer who uses an 'Offshore Finance Centre' will, generally speaking, have certain expectations that might include the following:

---

[30] Bob Stewart, 'The Moral Case for Tax Havens', www.lewrockwell.com, 30 October 2002.

- the environment must be able to retain his or her assets safely;
- the consumer will expect to be able to give effect to a tax optimisation strategy in the jurisdiction, that is to say, a strategy which allows him to pay no more tax on worldwide income than is absolutely necessary;
- there must be privacy (see section 3.9 above);
- there might be better returns on investment; and
- costs must be lower than in the consumer's home 'Onshore' environment.

In its 2000 report entitled 'Report of the Working Group on "Offshore Centres"', the Working Group of the Financial Stability Forum said that OFCs are used by the following:

- international companies, to maximise profit and to issue securitised products through special purpose vehicles;
- investors (including individuals and companies), to protect assets (from claimants and from those wanting to know investment positions) and to minimise income and withholding tax;
- financial institutions, to minimise tax and operate under a light regulatory regime and to assist customers to minimise tax;
- insurance companies, to accumulate reserves in a benign tax environment; and
- abusers, to launder the proceeds of crime using secrecy legislation as protection to defeat enquiries from law enforcement agencies.

The last bullet point sticks out – not because it is untrue but regrettably because criminals will always exploit every opportunity to their own advantage. Secrecy should be distinguished from confidentiality.

The quotations below indicate how some corporations have used 'Offshore' for tax purposes.

Enron operated 872 'Offshore' subsidiaries (692 of which were in the Cayman Islands), and managed to avoid US$409 million of tax between 1996 and 2000.

> Enron used a common technique among Onshore companies, i.e. directing profits to an Offshore partner which, after levying a fee, returns the profit Onshore in a format that is not taxable according to Onshore tax laws. An additional reason for Enron's extensive use of tax havens was that it allowed the company to make deductions for share options. By placing the cost of these options offshore, Enron's balance sheet was not affected.[31]

---

[31] Mattias Levin, 'The Prospects for "Offshore Financial Centres" in Europe', Box 1, CEPS Research Report, August 2002, p. 9.

Notice the use of terms in this quotation – as if 'Offshore' and 'tax havens' are synonymous.

Ingersoll Rand anticipated that, by moving to Bermuda, it will decrease its US tax bill by US$40 million. By reincorporating in Bermuda, Tyco International reduced its taxes by US$400 million in 2001[32] (see section 18.14 below). News Corporation's effective rate of tax is 6 per cent, achieved by using around 800 subsidiaries, including 'Offshore'. [33]

4.18 Contrary arguments

There are many who believe that OFCs want business at any price and that they will therefore do whatever is necessary to attract the business. If this means not asking too many questions, then OFCs will accommodate the needs of the customer.

The human weakness involved manifests itself not only in respect of 'Offshore' activity but in virtually every walk of life. Subsequent chapters explore some of the weaknesses to which the 'Offshore' environment is exposed, and the reader is left to judge for him or herself (see Chapter 13 below). However, in order to present a balanced argument, some of the weaknesses of the 'Onshore' environment are also described (see Chapter 14 below). Once again, the reader will be left to make a personal assessment. In doing so, it is important to compare like with like.

4.19 'Offshoring'

'Offshoring' refers to the practice of moving business activity to a lower cost location, which Deloittes (see below) says arises because of increasing pressures for cost reductions and because of competitive and business continuity issues arising after the terrorist attacks on 11 September 2001. Offshoring is not the same as 'Business Process Outsourcing' (BPO, i.e. the use of a third party to carry out certain processes). While BPO may be carried out anywhere, it is currently a popular activity in many 'Offshore Centres'.

---

[32] Jackie Johnson, '11th September and Revelations from the Enron Collapse Add to the Mounting Pressure on "Offshore Financial Centres"', Journal Of Financial Regulation and Compliance, November 2002, p. 346.
[33] *Ibid.*

A paper,[34] published by Deloitte Research in November 2003, described the potential that 'Offshoring' has for 'transforming the structure of the financial services industry'. Deloittes 'estimate that $356 billion of cost for the global financial services industry will be relocated offshore within the next five years . . . [N]early three of four major financial institutions will be offshore within two years.' The cost saving is estimated at US$138 billion.

If this paper is accurate, it seems like good news for 'Offshore' centres. However, the paper goes on to say that 'India is likely to continue as the key offshore destination.' This goes back to the problem of definition referred to at the outset. Is India an 'Offshore Centre' as defined in the opening chapters of this book? The key question is whether the centres described earlier as 'Offshore' are likely to benefit? Further, what effect might 'Offshoring' have on the long-standing efforts by the 'Offshore Finance Centres' to enhance their brand image as high quality jurisdictions (as opposed to low cost alternatives)? Meanwhile, overheads in general and salaries in particular are already lower in Malta and Mauritius than in most jurisdictions – excluding India.[35]

---

[34] Chris Gentle, 'The Cusp of a Revolution', Deloitte Research, November 2003.
[35] 'The Tide is Turning for Offshore', *Portfolio International*, November 2003.

5

The significance of taxation

> Picking important problems and fixing them is such a beguilingly simple
> idea, and appealingly non-partisan. Yet it turns out to be such a bugaboo
> to implement.[1]

5.1 Introduction

In the previous chapter, tax and regulation were identified as the two
factors that give rise to most debate and criticism about the 'Offshore'
environment. In fact, they are also amongst the most fundamental
factors that give value to operating 'Offshore' in the first place. This
chapter focuses on tax, and the next chapter discusses regulation.

There is at least one other reason why 'Offshore' plays such a significant role in world commerce – and that is in respect of asset protection.
In the widest sense, asset protection reduces to keeping what one owns.
In respect of some countries, the only way to protect assets is to remove
them from the jurisdiction – whether to prevent them from being seized
or consumed by punitive tax rates. Where seizure or sequestration is
possible or probable, the owner will take steps to move those assets
elsewhere. Further, in some jurisdictions, wealthy individuals are well
known and may be subject to kidnapping. This includes family members.
In such circumstances, the owner of the assets might consider that the
only way to protect the assets is to make them less open to public
scrutiny.

Professional people often use 'foreign grantor trusts' – also known as
the 'asset protection trust' (APT) – to transfer ownership of assets
elsewhere (frequently 'Offshore'), thereby protecting those assets from
litigation 'Onshore'. The APT is discussed fully in section 4.10 above.

---

[1] Malcolm K. Sparrow, *The Regulatory Craft*, Brookings Institution Press, 1998, p. 64.

Perhaps the most obvious way that the value of assets is depleted is through taxation. Tax is a key component in understanding the rationale for the existence of 'Offshore'. It is also an emotive subject, because, although its range is potentially endless, not all jurisdictions apply direct tax. In some, zero direct tax applies. In those jurisdictions where tax applies, the tax rates are not necessarily common. This gives rise to attempts by jurisdictions to compete on the basis of tax, and it has been said (by the OECD) that tax competition is wrong. The OECD's view is that there should be a level playing field, and it has sought certain commitments from some jurisdictions to eradicate wrongful competition in this respect. Accordingly, differentials arise in tax rates – which in turn make it possible for people to take action to avoid paying more than necessary. Tax harmonisation attempts to eradicate these differentials – but, while they remain, 'Offshore' jurisdictions are frequently used to mitigate tax. As the G7 countries reduce their corporate tax rates, the tax differential between 'Offshore' and 'Onshore' has narrowed.

While it is legitimate to avoid paying more than is due, it is not legitimate to evade a legal obligation to pay. The extent to which evasion has pervaded society is so vast that governments are losing vast sums of money that they need. From time to time, governments create tax amnesties to encourage errant tax evaders to repatriate capital and to assume their rightful tax responsibilities (see section 5.24 below). On the whole, these are very successful. Meanwhile, in the EU, very determined efforts have been made to ensure that Member States do not suffer because residents of one State are able to benefit because they do not declare revenue arising in another Member State. The rules and procedures are set out in the EU's Code of Conduct and in the Savings Directive.

Cross-border transactions give rise to tax complications between the home jurisdiction (of residence) and the host jurisdiction (the source of the revenue). Double Taxation Avoidance Agreements are used to deal with this problem. Further, in order to exploit differences between the tax treatment applied to ordinary residents and non-resident companies, ordinary persons sometimes incorporate companies abroad and process income through the incorporated entity. Controlled Foreign Company Rules (see section 5.25 below) have been designed to prevent the avoidance or deferral of tax by those persons who establish a company in an 'Offshore' jurisdiction.

This Introduction suggests that tax is multi-faceted. All these matters are explored in the next chapter.

5.2 In general

In the first place, tax is only necessary to fund spending. Consequently, nations that spend more have to raise revenue – and tax is a (convenient) way to generate that revenue. Some forms of tax are easier to collect than others. Goods passing from one country to another via a border check-point present a straightforward example of an easy way to apply tax. However, the imposition of tax is not so straightforward in all circumstances, for example the Internet. The Internet is transnational – which complicates tax gathering. The flexibility and freedom of choice provided to the consumer makes life difficult for the revenue authorities. One statistic that indicates the increasing significance of tax comes from the European Court of Justice, where it is reported that nearly half of the 'decisions on income and corporation tax since 1958 have been made in the past three years'.[2]

The Introduction to this chapter indicates the extent to which tax affects commercial and personal life. Complications arise because of the myriad permutations that arise both in how tax is applied and also in how it is collected. One helpful summary has been provided by Johns, who identified the following four basic approaches:

> A income is taxed only in the country where the owner resides;
> B income is taxed only in the country where it is earned;
> C income is taxed both in the country where the owner resides and where it is earned; and
> D the domicile principle – that is the country to which the individual will ultimately return is the key factor (UK).[3]

For the purposes of this part of the discussion, the focus will be on corporate taxpayers. In respect of a company engaged in international business, it is important to determine the basis on which the company is transacting business. If the basis is 'in a country', the company will be subject to tax in its home country, because it is linked in terms of residency. Alternatively, a company may transact business 'with a country', in which case the country is a source of revenue. Thus, a company may suffer tax at home on the basis of residency and abroad on the basis

---

[2] Peter Cussons, 'Anarchy in Europe's Tax Systems?', *The OFC Report 2004*, Campden Publishers, p. 30.
[3] Richard Anthony Johns, *Tax Havens and Offshore Finance – A Study of Transnational Economic Development*, Frances Pinter (Publishers) Ltd, 1983, p. 45.

of source. Accordingly, residency and source are described as 'the con-
necting factors', which are relevant in determining the jurisdiction of the
company for tax purposes.

Economic double taxation (see section 5.26 below) describes those
situations where the same income suffers tax twice. For example, all
other things being equal, the profit of a company is subject to tax.
Dividends are paid from profit that has suffered tax already, but, when
the dividend is paid to the shareholder, it is subject to tax again.

In mid-2002, there was substantial debate in the USA concerning a
proposal to change the basis of tax collection applied in that country,
from 'worldwide' to 'territorial'. The basis of the two approaches is
described below.

5.2.1 Worldwide tax system

As the name implies, a worldwide basis of taxation means that, no matter
where their citizens' income and capital arises, the home country makes
it subject to tax. Uruguay, Hungary and the USA are among the countries
that apply tax on the basis of worldwide income and capital. Where
countries levy tax on the worldwide basis, double taxation may arise
(and this might apply even though the person concerned lives in a
country other than the home country). This happens when a single
taxpayer's income suffers tax in two different countries.

5.2.2 Territorial tax system

The alternative approach is a territorial tax system, under which only
income earned within the borders of a country is subject to tax. Taxation
is based on the source of the income. The theory is that income that is
saved and invested should be taxed only once. This system prevents the
need for 'Offshore Centres' to be used as a means of avoiding tax. (See
sections 5.3 and 18.2 below.)

5.3 Tax avoidance

The Introduction to this chapter referred both to tax avoidance and to
tax evasion. No discussion about tax would be complete without reference to these emotive phenomena – because tax is so fundamentally
significant in all matters relating to the provision of financial services.

Tax avoidance should be distinguished from tax evasion. First, evasion of tax is a crime in most countries because it amounts to defrauding the exchequer of money that is rightly due to it.

Avoiding tax means using whatever strategies are available to ensure that one pays no more tax than the law requires. Avoiding tax is not a criminal act. For the purposes of this text, tax avoidance should be interpreted to mean legitimate actions designed to limit the amount of tax paid to an amount that represents only what is due. In his locus classicus Lord Tomlin said 'Every man is entitled, if he can, to order his affairs so that the tax attaching under the appropriate Acts is less than it otherwise would be.' Further, Lord Clyde has said in respect of the UK 'No man in this country is under the smallest obligation, moral or other, so to arrange his legal relations to his business or his property as to enable the Revenue to put the largest possible shovel into his stores. The Revenue is not slow – and quite rightly – to take every advantage that is open to it under the taxing structure for the purpose of depleting the taxpayer's pocket. And, the taxpayer is, in like manner, entitled to be astute to prevent, so far as he honestly can, the depletion of his means by the revenue.'[4] The emphasis expressed by Lord Clyde is different from that prevailing currently – which is perhaps demonstrated in the words of Lord Simon in *Latilla* v. *IRC* as follows: 'There is of course no doubt that they (tax avoiders) are within their legal rights, but there is no reason why their efforts . . . should be regarded as a commendable exercise of ingenuity or as a discharge of the duties of good citizenship.' Meanwhile, in 1981, the House of Lords decided that 'if the purpose of a step in some scheme was solely to avoid tax, the taxmen could ignore it, as if it had never happened'.[5]

Financial services activities are mobile by definition. It is axiomatic that active global companies and other legal persons will do all they can to minimise their tax bills. Is this any less than one might expect from globalisation and mobile capital?

Bringing this right down to the personal taxpayer, there can be little doubt that, by the very nature of things, most people would prefer to pay no tax at all but most people are willing to pay some – although we baulk

[4] G. C. Powell, 'Tax Havens and Measures Against Tax Evasion and Avoidance in the EEC' in J. F. Avery Jones, *Tax Havens and Offshore Finance – A Study of Transnational Economic Development*, Associated Business Programmes, 1974, p. 106.
[5] 'No Avoiding Mr Brown', *The Economist*, 20 March 2004, p. 35.

at the thought that there is any likelihood that we are paying more than we must.

This is where the problems begin, because, in order to assess what is due, all income (earned and unearned) must be taken into account. Simultaneously, every human being has a right to a degree of financial freedom and to confidentiality in respect of financial matters. In turn, this means that a tax collecting government must rely on the honesty and integrity of its taxpayers to disclose all that has to be revealed to enable the tax which they are due to pay to be calculated accurately. Alternatively, governments might only rely on this partially and simultaneously introduce certain checks to ensure that the taxpayer does not forget to include some items of income. The biggest 'gap' or potential weakness in the system is where taxpayers create income generating assets abroad which they do not disclose to the tax collector at home. One alternative for the tax collecting government is to capture adequate information to enable tax to be applied on a worldwide basis or to forget about income generated outside the home country. If the taxpayer fails to disclose, the tax collector might consider relying on the foreign country to tell the home country (see the comment on 'home' and 'host' in section 5.4 below) about income paid to one of its residents. To be effective, this strategy requires extremely tight legislation, which by definition will require the exchange of information which in turn will impinge upon personal privacy (which is protected by the 1948 Universal Declaration of Human Rights). This approach is replete with difficulties – as the debate concerning the EU Savings Tax Directive (see section 5.15 below) aptly demonstrates. Alternatively, the tax collecting government might acknowledge that this scenario will always give rise to tax seepage and might accept that the cost of taking no action is the amount of tax evaded.

The debate in the USA was fuelled by an increasing number of US corporate entities that were re-domiciling to Bermuda (which at the time was regarded by some as an 'Offshore' jurisdiction) or to other jurisdictions where the tax burden was less onerous than that which applied in the USA ('corporate inversion' – see section 18.14 below). This type of move means that the corporation ceases to pay US tax on overseas income. If the company maintains its main operations in USA, it will pay tax to the US Government on all income earned in the USA. Such companies are mitigating their tax liabilities in a totally legal fashion – much to the chagrin of some US politicians who regard such actions as 'unpatriotic'.

The US Senate twice passed legislation to prevent the new Homeland Security Department from doing business with companies that moved overseas; the Republican Leaders in the House of Representatives removed the provision in the final bill . . . California has been one of the more active US states seeking to ban firms who have switched their headquarters offshore from doing business with the government. Last September [2003], state law makers approved a bill, which will prohibit the state authorities from contracting with companies that have performed corporate inversions. The state of Connecticut also passed a similar bill last year [2003].[6]

This strategy enables a US corporation to compete on the same sort of terms as any other corporation based in a country where territorial tax applies (e.g. the Netherlands) (see section 5.15 below).

In order to avoid taxing income earned abroad twice, taxpayers in many countries may claim foreign tax credit for any tax paid to a tax authority abroad (e.g. if the tax rate abroad is 35 per cent and a corporation earns £100 in a foreign country that applies a 10 per cent rate of tax, the corporation will have paid tax of £10 abroad leaving £25 to be paid to the home tax authority).

At the level of individuals – where investors invest 'Offshore' – the norm has been that the fiscal authorities 'Offshore' will not provide details of income earned or generated outside the home country to the fiscal authority in the home country. OFCs describe this as their reluctance to enforce the fiscal legislation of governments abroad. OFCs are attractive to many consumers because of the strict confidentiality policies and unwillingness to exchange information. Despite this, it has been said that 'since the 1980s it has become increasingly difficult for UK residents or companies to use OFCs for tax planning [avoidance]'.[7] This is one way not to create tax harmonisation.

In early 2004, the UK's Chancellor introduced a new rule in his budget, based on the prevailing procedures in the USA. The Joint International Tax Shelter Information Centre is a task force established in the USA in 2004 to monitor aggressive corporate tax avoidance – mainly business structuring transactions, tax arbitrage by multinationals and transfer pricing (see section 5.27 below). The task force comprises

[6] Marion Williams, 'Offshore/Onshore and the Trusted Advisor', *International Financial Centres Yearbook 2004/05*, p. 23.
[7] Mark Hampton, *The Offshore Interface*, Macmillan Press Ltd, 1996, p. 115.

tax specialists from the USA, the UK, Australia and Canada. The rationale for the new rules in the UK is to invert the prevailing procedure of overturning a tax avoidance scheme. In the UK, it is necessary for the Revenue to know about a scheme to enable them to challenge it, possibly through the tax environment through the courts. However, some slip through the net. The new plan is to require both tax advisers and their clients to disclose their scheme from the start – on pain of penalty if they do not. Thus, the net is closing.

5.4 Home and host

The discussion concerning avoidance and evasion has to be interrupted to explain the reference to 'home' and 'host' in the previous section. There is a perception that 'Offshore Finance Centres' only exist because they enable wealthy people to evade tax. Before describing how this might happen, it may be useful to revisit the description of the terms 'home' and 'host' as applied to financial jurisdictions. For the purposes of the example that follows, the 'home' jurisdiction is the country where a depositor/investor is ordinarily resident and where he or she pays taxes. The location where a financial institution (e.g. a bank) has its head office will be the home jurisdiction of that bank. A 'host' jurisdiction is the country where a depositor/investor conducts his financial affairs. The depositor will earn interest gross of tax in the host jurisdiction. The location abroad where a bank establishes a subsidiary company will be the host jurisdiction (see section 2.4 above).

5.5 Tax evasion

Tax evasion is a generic term because there are more ways to evade tax than can be classified easily. Some methods to evade tax are very complicated while others are very basic – because taxpayers are not homogeneous.

The following illustration exemplifies evasion at its most basic. A depositor/investor removes capital from his or her home jurisdiction (i.e. the country where tax is due) and places that capital on deposit or uses it to invest in a savings plan (e.g. an insurance product, a pension plan, a collective investment scheme etc.) in an 'Offshore' jurisdiction. Traditionally, the French use Switzerland, Germans use Luxembourg and many of the rest use London and the USA. (More sophisticated techniques involve the establishment of a trust and/or an 'Offshore' company to absorb income and to benefit from double tax treaties.) In due course – and this means anything from days to years – the gain arising has to be taken into account – somewhere. On the maturity of the deposit (or on the redemption of the asset), the capital is repaid – together with any 'gain' arising – to its owner. The owner is (probably) obliged under the tax rules of the home country in which he or she lives to declare this gain, but, because the tax authorities of the host jurisdiction (the 'Offshore Centre') do not report the gain arising to the tax authorities of the home jurisdiction, the latter authorities may never know about this gain unless the resident of the home jurisdiction declares it. It is more than likely that the law in the home jurisdiction requires him or her to disclose this income. Many taxpayers will not consider themselves morally obliged to make such a report – even though they are legally obliged to do so. On this basis, the only loser is the home government, and such governments unsurprisingly object most strongly to this 'tax seepage'. The contrary argument is that lower tax rates would reduce any incentive to evade tax. All this precedes the EU's Tax Directive (which is described in section 5.15 below).

5.6 Two examples

5.6.1 Example 1

Mr A lives in Germany (home jurisdiction) and has accumulated the Deutschmark equivalent of £10,000. If he leaves this money in his bank account in Germany, where interest rates are (say) 10 per cent, he will earn interest of £1,000 gross in a year. If the tax rate in Germany is 25 per cent, then he will have to pay over £250 to the exchequer in Germany. If instead, he places his deposit with a bank in Luxembourg (the host jurisdiction where interest rates are also 10 per cent), he will still earn £1,000. However, Mr A and the bank in Luxembourg are the only people who know about this transaction and neither the bank nor the exchequer in Luxembourg will disclose this information to the exchequer in Germany (because of client confidentiality). Accordingly, unless Mr A discloses the interest he has been paid, the exchequer in Germany will (probably) not realise that he owes £250. If Mr A does not disclose, he is evading tax. All this precedes the EU Tax Directive (discussed in section 5.15 below).

5.6.2 Example 2

'[A]ssume you are a citizen of France. You save $1000 and receive an interest payment of $60 (6 per cent). Inflation is 3 per cent, so your real interest earnings are only $30. However you must pay a 59.7 per cent tax, or $35.82, on the $60 of interest, plus the $30 inflation tax ... This leaves you a net loss of almost $6 on each $1000 saved.'[8] On this basis, it is not hard to see why people look for more benign tax environments.

5.7 Tax competition

Generally speaking, competition leads to positive outcomes for consumers in that it helps to keep costs at acceptable levels and it promotes efficiency. By extension, tax competition is a good thing because it may encourage innovation and produce variety. This implies that consumers will make every effort to reduce their tax bills by seeking out ways to minimise their tax costs. Regrettably, the OECD's 'Harmful Tax Competition' report (see Chapter 12 below) described tax competition as harmful – which did not augur well for what the OECD was trying to achieve. Competition will not stifle economic development but inappropriate taxation might! In fact, when describing tax competition as 'harmful', it has to be remembered that it is only harmful because the high tax rate countries do not receive enough of it. Tax competition is not harmful to the individual taxpayer. It has been said that 'More objective and competent economists have clearly demonstrated that the concept of "harmful tax competition" is without intellectual merit, particularly given that most countries have taxes far above the revenue and growth maximising rates, so tax competition can only be beneficial.'[9]

'Governments of offshore financial centres serve their own and the world's interests by providing zero or low tax environments for global business and investment.'[10] When the OECD first published the list of criteria it used to determine whether or not a financial jurisdiction was a

---

[8] Robert W. Rahn, 'Economic Murder-Suicide', The Washington Times: Commentary, www.washtimes.com/commentary/20030611-093247-438lr.htm.
[9] Robert W. Rahn, 'Economic Murder-Suicide', The Washington Times: Commentary, www.washtimes.com/commentary/20030611-093247-438lr.htm.
[10] Terry Dwyer, '"Harmful" Tax Competition and the Future of "Offshore Financial Centres"', Journal of Money Laundering Control, Vol. 5, No. 4, p. 302.

tax haven, one criterion was whether the level of tax was low or nil. This was changed subsequently.

5.8 Tax harmonisation

Tax harmonisation means that taxpayers will pay the same amount of tax on their income and capital irrespective of its source or where they live or invest their money. Harmonisation can be achieved either directly or indirectly. The direct route is where jurisdictions combine to agree to levy tax at a uniform rate – for example VAT in the EU is charged at 15 per cent. The indirect route is where a country's residents are taxed on their worldwide income. As discussed above, this means that the taxpayer cannot mitigate that tax by moving to a lower tax regime. This route requires the tax assessor to know the quantum that represents the taxpayer's worldwide income – which requires the exchange of information.[11]

The rationale for tax harmonisation is entirely logical. The theory provides that the amount of tax payable on capital income is a core issue for entrepreneurs deciding where to locate. In the context of the EU, variable tax rates across the Member States cause distortion in the selection process (of where to locate) and encourages countries to reduce the costs in competing for capital. In turn, the theory suggests that tax rates will be set too low to meet social requirements. If the rates were standardised, the entrepreneur's decision would be based on criteria that are relevant to the corporation and to its business.

Governments are now seeking ways to harmonise taxes. Whether or not this is a legitimate goal remains to be seen, but the way that the OECD, the EU and the UN are trying to achieve it (by the exchange of information) has given rise to considerable controversy. Information exchange infers that countries with lower rates of tax would impose the rules of higher tax rate countries.

Currently, smaller countries offer tax incentives to global corporate entities to encourage investment. Tax harmonisation would prevent this. In turn, smaller countries would require some form of aid to compensate for lost income but, if the OECD were to be allocated control of that assistance, it would acquire considerable influence over how such countries would be allowed to finance their deficits.

---

[11] Andrew Quinlan, Special Alert, Center for Freedom and Prosperity, 18 July 2002.

In a report to the US Congress,[12] attention was drawn to the fact that 'a discussion of perceived UN imposed global taxation has received attention in the United States' three times. The most recent was at the International Conference on Financing for Development, held in March 2002 in Monterrey. The High-Level Panel on Financing for Development, a UN group chaired by Mr Zedillo, former President of Mexico, suggested several initiatives, including the creation of an international tax unit, the adoption of a global tax strategy and information exchange (which is not dissimilar to the OECD's proposal and which some equate with tax harmonisation). The theory is that global taxation might be the most appropriate way to address some of the global problems that the UN faces. It remains to be seen what the effects will be on national sovereignty because, currently, nations have exclusive authority to impose tax on their citizens. The proposal suggested runs contrary to how things stand presently and was not supported by the USA.

Not everyone agrees that tax harmonisation is a good thing (see Chapter 9). For example, Nobel Laureate Milton Friedman believes that 'The principle of "subsidiarity" – that government services be provided, and paid for, so far as is possible, at the level of government closest to the citizen – would be violated by any attempt to impose from the centre a uniform tax regime.'[13] Further, not everyone agrees that tax harmonisation (which has been and continues to be a contentious issue in Europe) is either necessary or positive. For example, 'Defeating tax harmonisation policies such as information exchange is critical if we want a world with freedom and sovereignty.'[14]

However, the detail of the debate and of that concerning the other arguments surrounding the effect on the UN itself is outside the scope of this book. Meanwhile, readers may care to refer to the OECD's report, 'Improving Access to Bank Information', for further information.

5.9 Tax and 'Offshore'

It is probably fair to describe 'Offshore Finance Centres' as low tax regimes. Their tax status gives rise to (at least) two important functions.

---

[12] Marjorie Ann Brown, 'Global Taxation and the United Nations: A Review of Proposals', Report for Congress, Congressional Research Service, 3 May 2002.
[13] Milton Friedman, 'Letter to the Center for Freedom and Prosperity', *CFP Weekly Update*, 15 May, 2001.
[14] 'US Institute Advises Bahamas to Resist EU/OECD Pressure', Tax-News.com, February 2003.

First, they promote competition. In this respect, the OECD's Business and Industry Advisory Committee has said that: 'Tax competition tends to keep tax burdens lower, which creates pressure for less wasteful, and, therefore, more efficient use of public funds. Secondly, tax competition is said to help retain more resources in the economy's productive sector. High rates of tax reduce capital formation. . .'.[15]

'But the offshore industry . . . makes its money out of providing facilities not for evasion of tax, but for its postponement and thereby leveraging wealth accumulation by reference to gross returns.'[16]

According to a UK Treasury discussion paper issued in February 2000, the UK's intention was to persuade Europe to replicate the USA's procedure to tax income irrespective of where it arises. The implication is that income accruing 'Offshore' would be liable to tax – even if not repatriated – provided that it is declared.

Is it possible that – as part of negotiations about other matters – the EU will force the UK to exchange information with Guernsey, Jersey and the Isle of Man? Yes, it is possible (see section 5.21 below). In this respect, it should be noted that Bermuda, the Cayman Islands (and others) have committed to exchanging information with members of the OECD by the end of 2005. This might mean that, in future, part of the capital held 'Offshore' will currently be subject to disclosure. By way of an example of how things are changing, it was reported recently that 'Ireland's Revenue Commissioners intend to use new powers to demand that tax avoiders hand over details of offshore bank accounts held with Irish financial institutions. The new powers will come into force in May [2004].'[17] (See also section 20.3 below.)

5.10 Tax and 'Offshore' and the OECD

The OECD's work and the commitments it has required 'Offshore Centres' to provide are dealt with in Chapter 12. But, fundamentally, 'the OECD does not seek to dictate to any country what its tax rate should be, or how its tax system should be structured'.[18] However, in

---

[15] Daniel Mitchell, a Senior Fellow at the Washington-based Heritage Foundation, as reported in an article published by the Wall Street Journal *Europe*, 29 June 2000.
[16] Nigel Morris-Cotterill, 'Secrecy Laws Under Assault', *The Banker*, August 2000, p. 62.
[17] 'Special Powers for Revenue Will Deepen Offshore Tax Inquiries', *Offshore Red*, March 2004, p. 5.
[18] 'The OECD's Project on Harmful Tax Practices: The 2004 Progress Report', OECD, 4 February 2000, p. 4.

respect of tax, the OECD wants OFCs and others to commit to exchange information with any OECD member state on request. In this respect, the OECD published a pro-forma agreement (the Model Agreement on Exchange of Information in Tax Matters) on 18 April 2002. The Agreement was formulated by a working group comprising OECD member states and the following OFCs: Aruba, Bermuda, Bahrain, the Cayman Islands, Cyprus, the Isle of Man, Malta, Mauritius, the Netherlands Antilles, Seychelles and San Marino. (Once again, not all of these jurisdictions regard themselves as 'Offshore Centres' : the use of the term 'OFC' is a convenient means of categorisation.)

The Agreement contains two important parts. The first part is a model treaty that could be used as a bilateral standard in formulating arrangements between OFCs and the more industrialised countries. The second part is a model treaty for multilateral arrangements (which might include a number of bilateral agreements) between OFCs and OECD member states.

Article 1 of the Agreement provides that the signatories will offer 'assistance, through [the] exchange of information that is foreseeably relevant to the administration and enforcement of the domestic laws of the Contracting Parties concerning taxes covered by this Agreement'. Further, 'information' means that which is 'relevant to the determination, assessment and collection of such taxes, the recovery and enforcement of tax claims or the investigation or the prosecution of tax matters'.

The pro-forma bilateral agreement excludes reference to the type of taxes that it will cover but the multilateral model refers to taxes on income or profits, capital, net wealth and estate, inheritance or gift taxes. Importantly, the model anticipates that the information 'shall be exchanged without regard to whether the conduct being investigated would constitute a crime under the laws of the country being asked for information if that is where the conduct occurred'.

As might be expected, the document provides: conditions for requests, a description of cooperation expected to be given to visiting tax authorities from abroad, clarification as to when a request can be declined – and the requirement to use all possible measures to accede to the request.

Requests for information should be made to the competent authorities within a jurisdiction. Those authorities must be able to provide: information concerning the person under scrutiny; what information is necessary and why; who might have the information; why it is thought that it is available in the jurisdiction that is being asked to provide it and confirmation that all measures possible have been taken in the home jurisdiction to obtain it.

The country asked to provide the information is not obliged to disclose anything that they would be unable to obtain in enforcing their own tax law or to provide 'information which would disclose any trade, business, industrial, commercial or professional secret or trade process'.

The effective date was 1 January 2004 in respect of criminal tax matters and 1 January 2006 for civil tax matters.

Meanwhile, the Committee on Fiscal Affairs has made the first substantive revisions (since 1977) to the OECD's Model Tax Convention in respect of its exchange of information provisions (Article 26). The changes include provisions to stop what are described as 'domestic tax interest' requirements from preventing the exchange of information. This Article now allows the disclosure of information to agencies that oversee tax administration and enforcement. Another new provision (Article 26 (5)) is designed to ensure that exchange of information is not hindered by bank secrecy rules.

5.11 Specific committments

As part of its commitment to the OECD, the Isle of Man reached an agreement on 4 October 2002 with the USA concerning the exchange of information on tax matters. The agreement requires a formal request to be made for assistance on an individual case-by-case basis – which must be under investigation in the home jurisdiction. Not all practitioners were happy about this arrangement but the island's Assessor of Income Tax said that: 'The benefits of having such an agreement in terms of international reputation and the business opportunities they open up far outweigh any business concerns.'[19]

The USA has signed similar agreements with other jurisdictions, including Antigua and Barbuda, the Bahamas, Bermuda, the British Virgin Islands, the Cayman Islands and the Netherlands Antilles. The Isle of Man's agreement followed on from a similar arrangement established by Guernsey on 19 September 2002. On 5 November 2002, Jersey signed a similar agreement, followed by Switzerland in 2003. The Bahamas was added to the list in December 2003 with the announcement that a Tax Information Exchange Agreement with the USA was to take effect from January 2004.

---

[19] Bob Campion, 'IoM Signs US Tax Agreement', *Portfolio International*, November 2002, p. 8.

5.12 The European Union and tax

The EU has been working on harmful tax competition since 1997. At that time, a package of matters was identified by the Monti Group (so named after its Chairman) and agreed by the EU Council, concerning which further action was needed to combat harmful tax competition in the EU. The package comprised three main elements: (1) a Code of Conduct on Business Tax; (2) a tax on savings; and (3) issues concerning withholding tax on cross-border interest and royalty payments between countries. With respect to the proposal for a Council Directive concerning the eradication of withholding tax on interest and royalties between associated companies based in different Member States, the relevant measures were agreed in November 2002.

Some comment on the significance for OFCs in respect of corporate taxation and in respect of taxation of income from savings is provided below.

The EU's approach differs to that of the OECD. The EU focused on all business taxation whereas the OECD was more interested in mobile financial services. Further, the EU favoured a withholding tax whereas the OECD favoured information exchange. Lastly, the OECD wants to enable all jurisdictions to tax its residents.

5.13 The Code of Conduct

It has been suggested that: 'Whilst there has been considerable media debate on the implications of the Savings Directive, it is the other element of the EU Tax Package, the Code of Conduct which has the most far reaching implications for both onshore and offshore centres.'[20] The purpose of the Code was to identify any tax measures in Member States and in their dependencies which were 'harmful'. Having identified such measures, the Code had two objectives. The first objective was to bring all variances into line with the principles of the Code ('rollback') and the second objective was to ensure that no new harmful tax measures were introduced ('standstill').

The Primarolo Report (Council of the EU, November 1999) identified sixty-six measures that existed in EU Member States and which were considered to be 'harmful'. These measures were prevalent in forty

---

[20] Letters, *Portfolio International*, April 2003, p. 15.

EU Member States, three in Gibraltar and twenty-three in Dependent Territories – were described as 'tax measures which provide for a significantly lower effective level of taxation, including zero taxation, than those levels which generally apply in the member State in question'. The Ecofin Council decided on 27 November 2000 that these measures should not be available after 1 January 2003 and that they should be eradicated completely by 2005. However, some extensions were agreed. For example, Jersey requested an extension to allow it to replace its tax exempt company with a zero rate tax environment. Jersey argued that it was necessary for the island to have a tax neutral environment to accommodate mobile cross-border business.

In 2002, Jersey was criticised by the UK Treasury for dragging its heels in respect of the Code of Conduct and on the automatic exchange of tax information. In July 2002, Gibraltar and the Isle of Man announced new tax measures that satisfied the Code. This involved the termination of practices whereby the tax treatment of local companies was different to that applied to 'Offshore' companies. Before the end of 2002, both Guernsey and Jersey announced measures to satisfy the Code. Information exchange on tax matters was no longer an issue. Had this agreement not been reached, it would have meant that the proposed withholding tax would have gained substantial momentum which was contrary to what the UK wanted.

5.14 The EU Savings Tax Directive: background

In respect of tax on savings, some Member States of the European Union – principally Germany – complained about the ease with which citizens of one Member State (e.g. Germany) could deposit money in another Member State (e.g. Luxembourg) and avoid reporting the interest arising to the tax authorities in the depositor's country of domicile. The problem is tax evasion.

The European Union spent a substantial amount of time debating the taxation of savings of non-residents. Subsequent to the EU summit meeting in December 1999 (Helsinki), there seemed to be little agreement between Member States on how to prevent EU citizens from evading tax on their savings income. Germany suggested there should be a EU-wide savings tax (the 'Draft European Union Directive on Savings Tax'). At their summit in Feira, Portugal, in July 2000, leaders of EU Member States undertook to agree the 'substantial content' of the

Directive before the end of 2000 and that, by the end of 2002, agreement should be reached with key non-EU countries.

5.15 The EU Savings Tax Directive summarised

Mr Frits Bolkestein, European Commissioner for Taxation and the Internal Market, has said that 'the principle of the directive is simple: to ensure that investors resident in the EU pay tax to the country where they live on interest income from their savings in other countries'. From another perspective, 'the Directive is designed to stop the flow of capital from high-tax nations to low-tax nations'.[21] In fact, the purpose of the Directive was to curb tax evasion. In practice, interest earned abroad by savers would be taxed at the same rate that applies in their home jurisdiction, but this requires the host jurisdiction to collate information about investors and pass it on to tax authorities elsewhere. The regime applies to individuals – and the principal impact will be on retail financial services. The idea was that there would be a seven-year period of transition – during which EU countries could impose a withholding tax on the savings of non-residents. The income arising was to have been shared. To make it work, all member states would have to automatically exchange information (with the tax authorities in the home country) relating to interest. Simultaneously, to minimise opportunities for tax evasion (by simply moving money outside the EU), Member States' dependent territories such as the Channel Islands would be required to adopt similar provisions. For the same reason, it was anticipated that Andorra, Liechtenstein, Monaco, San Marino, Switzerland and the USA would adopt similar provisions. The EU Savings Directive for 'Offshore' jurisdictions is significant.

5.16 Developments

Some Member States (excluding the UK, on the basis of the potential for harm (see below) that a withholding tax might have on the Eurobond market) had agreed to a 'co-existence' arrangement – but that was as far as agreement went.

The matter was problematic for more reasons than one. For example, the UK believed that the imposition of a withholding tax would drive

---

[21] Dan Mitchell, 'Davis Kills Goliath', *The OFC Report 2003*, p. 29.

away from the UK the 300 billion bond market based there. Instead, the UK proposed an agreement to exchange relevant information (on the savings income of non-residents) with other EU Member States. In practice, this would have meant that deposit takers in 'Offshore' juris-dictions would have been obliged to inform tax authorities in all EU countries about interest paid to their customers who were residents of those countries. The reaction of the Channel Islands was to describe the proposal as 'highly impractical and unrealistic',[22] and they declared that 'this position will not change should the EU adopt a common withholding tax'.[23]

Provisional agreement was reached on 27 November 2000. The meas-ures agreed included the 'elimination of 66 company tax measures identified as unfair in a "Code of Conduct" report by a working group . . . Luxembourg and Austria yesterday wrote into the council minutes that they would only agree the directive on savings taxes after a "binding decision" on the roll back of the 66 measures'.[24] (See above.) Further, it was agreed that three-quarters of the savings tax collected would be paid over to the country of residence of the depositor. The measures were 'unfair' because they created a competitive advantage vis-à-vis other Member States. It had been thought that both the tax on the Savings Directive and the Code of Conduct had to be agreed before the tax package became active. Belgium and the Netherlands refuted this. It was established that each measure would be addressed separately – which extended the timeframe.

Two problems arose in March 2001. First, Luxembourg objected to the way bonds were to be treated. In turn, Belgium (whose citizens frequently save by investing in tax-free bonds through banks (with secrecy laws) in Luxembourg) said it would not accept the Directive if Luxembourg's interpretation was accepted. This gave rise to potential for a veto. Secondly, on 4 March 2001, voters in Switzerland rejected any preparatory discussions regarding EU membership. Rejection was put down to EU demands for Switzerland to end its banking secrecy laws.

On 18 July 2001, the European Commission issued an amended Directive which required each Member State to exchange information

---

[22] Astrid Wendlandt, '"Offshore Centres" Reject EU Plan to Share Information', *Financial Times*, 25 July 2000.

[23] Tim Jones, 'The Making of a Classic Fudge', *European Voice*, 29 June/5 July 2000.

[24] Peter Norman, 'A Classic Compromise Between Two Extremes', *Financial Times*, 28 November 2000.

with other Member States concerning interest payments to people in one Member State but resident in another Member State. The Commission's proposal relied upon paying agents finding out the identity of the beneficial owner.

Since the Directive was contingent upon the agreement of all fifteen Member States and six non-EU countries (the USA; Liechtenstein; Switzerland; San Marino; Monaco and Andorra) and the dependent territories of Member States (e.g. Jersey), EU Finance Ministers agreed in October 2001 to enter into a dialogue with these non-member countries in an attempt to deal with this matter. In short, their mandate was to encourage these countries to adopt the same measures as members adopted whereby information would be exchanged on interest paid to non-residents.

For those countries (e.g. Luxembourg, Austria and Belgium and possibly Portugal and Greece) that were unwilling to make appropriate changes (to exchange information between tax authorities) too quickly, an interim arrangement (for seven years from 2003) was agreed. This involved a 15 per cent withholding tax on non-resident savings for the first three years of the transitional period rising to 20 per cent for the last four years.

Austria and Luxembourg (where banking secrecy is fundamentally important) said that their agreement was dependent upon a similar arrangement being concluded with financial centres that are not part of the EU (the USA, Switzerland, Liechtenstein, Andorra, San Marino, Monaco and the dependent territories of Member States, including Guernsey, the Isle of Man and Jersey). Luxembourg feared that, if it implemented a tax on savings leading to the mandatory exchange of information and the end of banking secrecy laws, money would move elsewhere, for example to Switzerland. The USA remained unconvinced.

The provisional agreement described above was due to take effect in 2003, subject to a unanimous vote scheduled for not later than 31 December 2002 when a broad range of tax measures, which included the Savings Tax Directive, were to have been decided. Even if all had gone according to plan, the Directive would not have required new legislation (where necessary) to apply before 2011.

On 13 December 2001, the EU's Council approved a draft, based on the EU Commission's draft dated July 2001. The Council increased the paying agent's role – which originally was restricted to finding out the identity of the beneficial owner. This meant that more information about the beneficial owner will be necessary (name, address and tax ID).

The operative date proposed was 1 January 2004, after which there would be regular exchanges of information.

A further problem developed in December 2001 when Luxembourg and Austria demanded a formal agreement to approve the (seven-year) transitional period from applying tax to exchanging information. This means that the six non-members of the EU will become subject to the same rules on exchanging information as EU members. This was agreed, and the EU has made it clear that these arrangements will come into operation after non-EU countries agree to do likewise.

Some of the UK's dependent territories remained unconvinced that the Directive was in their best economic interests. For example, McKeeva Bush, leader of the Cayman Islands Government, declared that the Cayman Islands 'will not commit to the Directive as it stands . . . [I]t is a very one-sided agreement'.[25] Meanwhile, the UK Government was equally determined to obtain adherence by all its dependent territories, which had already been achieved by 2002 in respect of Guernsey, the Isle of Man and Jersey.

A compromise was reached in January 2003, although the outcome included interest payments but not dividends received by natural persons (but not companies). Daniel Mitchell of the Heritage Foundation said that 'the new proposal is based on the same flawed principles of taxing economic activity in other nations and double-taxing income that is saved and invested'.[26]

5.17 The USA and the EU Savings Tax Directive

Some observers in the USA (and it is to be noted that US support was necessary to make the Directive work) considered the proposal to be an attack on sovereignty. One commentator said '[the] US Congress repeatedly decided, with few exceptions, not to tax the investment income of foreigners and not to report this income to foreign governments. The EU initiative seeks to protect uncompetitive European nations from the discipline of market forces. In particular it is an effort to preserve bad tax policy because it assumes there should be multiple taxation of income

---

[25] 'Cayman Islands Refuse to Commit to EU Directive', Bob Campion, *Portfolio International*, December 2002, p. 1.

[26] 'Free Market Leaders Denounce New Savings Tax Directive: US Will Not Support EU Tax Harmonisation Scheme, OECD Commitment Letters No Longer Binding', Center for Freedom and Prosperity, 27 January 2003.

that is saved and invested.'[27] Andrew Quinlan, of the Center for Freedom and Prosperity, was of the view that '[t]he European Union is pressuring the Bush Administration to support a cartel to prop up welfare states like France and Germany . . . The United States is [amongst] the world's biggest beneficiaries of jurisdictional tax competition . . . [I]nternational bureaucracies want to give high tax governments the power to tax income earned in low tax jurisdictions. This is a direct threat to America's economic interests.'[28] Daniel Mitchell, Senior Fellow at the Heritage Foundation, said that 'The EU information sharing proposal would have enabled foreign governments to tax US source income. And because the United States has attracted about $5 trillion of passive investment from overseas, the EU cartel would have harmed America's competitive advantage in the world economy.'[29] In July 2002, the USA hinted that it would not sign the EU's Savings Tax Directive, and the pace gathered against signing. In an address to conservative political groups in September 2002, the Chairman of the White House Council of Economic Advisers, Mr Glenn Hubbard, said that the US would not agree to the proposal to exchange information about the savings of foreigners deposited in the USA. In October 2002, Mr Larry Lindsey, the US President's senior economic adviser and Director of the National Economic Council, said: 'The Administration does not support the EU Savings Directive.'[30]

The view of the Centre for Freedom and Prosperity was that, because the EU failed to achieve support from the US, the Directive would fail. 'The EU Directive has numerous loopholes, the biggest of which is the United States . . . [T]he EU has decided to pretend that the United States is in compliance.'[31]

In fact, the USA opposes tax harmonisation (and the Directive was seen as an indirect means of tax harmonisation) and favours protection of confidentiality for taxpayers. The general consensus was that, without US involvement, the efforts (which until that stage had taken four years)

[27] Veronique de Rugy, 'Repel the Cartel', National Review Online, 7 June 2002, www. nationalreview.com/nrof_comment/comment-derugy060702.asp.
[28] Andrew Quinlan, Special Alert, Center for Freedom and Prosperity, 18 July 2002.
[29] 'US Administration Reiterates Opposition to EU Information Sharing Plans', Tax-News. com, Washington, 30 October 2002.
[30] 'US Administration Reiterates Opposition to EU Information Sharing Plans', Tax-News. com, Washington, 30 October 2002.
[31] 'The Level Playing Field: Misguided and Non-Existent', CF&P Foundation Prosperitas, October 2003.

to agree on how non-residents' savings should be taxed would come to an end. There was also an implication for the successful creation of a single financial market because the exchange of information on savings was a key part of this strategy. In short, the USA would be prepared to exchange information on request through bilateral tax agreements. Instead of relying on the automatic exchange of information in line with the EU model, the USA preferred to establish agreements with jurisdictions on a one-to-one basis (see section 5.11 above).

5.18 Switzerland and the EU Directive

By way of background, Switzerland has been described as 'politically and economically stable, its currency is rock solid, it has not imposed any capital controls in living memory and it has a well functioning legal system and regulatory framework . . . and . . . probably the most important competitive advantage Swiss financial institutions have to offer is banking secrecy.'[32]

As stated above, for the agreement to be effective, material changes to banking secrecy laws would have been necessary. This involved Switzerland (which controls 33.33 per cent of the world 'Offshore banking' market) and 'Offshore Centres'.[33] One of Switzerland's most senior bankers, Mr Lukas Muhlemann, Chairman of Credit Suisse, has said that Swiss banks would not 'systematically and routinely' submit the accounts of their 'Offshore' customers to tax authorities abroad.[34] 'As far as tax rates are concerned, we are not prepared to make our clients worse off than they would be in an EU country', according to Urs Roth, CEO of the Swiss Bankers Association.[35] In an effort to retain their banking secrecy, the Swiss had suggested a 'paying agent tax' proposal which was a permutation based on the model originally discussed in 2000 by the EU. The original model anticipated the application of a withholding tax throughout Europe, meaning that a resident of one European state would suffer the tax on money placed elsewhere. The Swiss suggestion

[32] 'A Survey of Switzerland', *The Economist*, 14 February 2004, p. 14.
[33] Robert Bell, 'European Union Financial Services Update', Compliance Monitor, July/August 2000, p. 244.
[34] William Hall, 'Swiss on Collision Course with EU Tax Policy', *Financial Times*, January 2001.
[35] 'Bankers Association Warns EU Over Banking Secrecy', www.swissinfo.org, 13 March 2003.

required the cooperation of all parties involved (an inherent weakness) so that paying agents outside the EU could not avoid paying tax. (The proposal extended the current Swiss withholding tax regime, which imposes a 35 per cent withholding tax on interest and dividend payments of domestic investors.) In practice, banks would deduct tax from the interest earned by investors from abroad and pay the amount deducted to the tax authority where the investor was resident.

Mr Bolkestein was disappointed that the EU had made little progress in dealing with Switzerland. He said: 'Many within the EU and elsewhere have grown rich by attracting the custom of tax evaders and are not in a hurry to lose that custom. Indeed, some of those calling for the strongest possible measures to fight the evasion of savings tax are doing so in the hope that by setting the standards unrealistically high, they will wreck the whole enterprise.'[36]

A list of sanctions (e.g. restricting investments by Swiss citizens) was prepared in case Switzerland failed to comply. Luxembourg opposed the imposition of sanctions on Switzerland and Mr Bolkestein conceded that, if sanctions were applied, they would only be effective from 2010.

All that proved unnecessary. On 13 May 2004, EU members agreed to sign nine bilateral treaties with Switzerland. The EU gave Switzerland membership in the Schengen Agreement (allowing free movement of people across borders in Europe) and in return Switzerland agreed to apply a withholding tax (progressively increasing from 15 per cent to 35 per cent) on the interest earned by EU residents on their savings. Thus, depositors will not be identified and the income arising will be paid to the relevant EU country. Simultaneously, Luxembourg was assured that its secrecy rules would not be subject to any changes that did not apply to Switzerland. As part of the deal, Switzerland agreed to contribute €650 million over a five-year period to the enlarged EU.

The EU's ECOFIN Council (the Council for Economic and Financial Affairs) considered proposing a fiscal amnesty for all of the EU, but the US stance strengthened the Swiss stance.

Although tax evasion (e.g. failing to disclose income to the tax authorities) is not a crime in Switzerland, tax fraud that involves making false statements and forging documents is a criminal offence. The Swiss will respond to enquiries from abroad about such matters. Banking

[36] Frits Bolkestein, 'I Cannot Stand Switzerland Cheating on Tax', *Financial Times*, 7 October 2002.

secrecy does not prevail in all circumstances, for example it does not protect money launderers or terrorists. Banks in Switzerland must know the beneficial owner of all assets. There is no great enthusiasm to join the EU, although, in 2002, the Swiss approved membership of the UN (by way of a referendum).

5.19 Agreement in the EU

Agreement was reached on 21 January 2003. The agreement provided that, with effect from 1 January 2004, twelve countries in the European Union will be obliged either to impose a withholding tax (the style to be adopted by Luxembourg, Austria and Belgium – all EU members) or to automatically exchange information on savings accounts maintained by non-residents. The next stage was to reach agreement with non-EU countries, principally Switzerland and the USA – but also Monaco, Andorra, San Marino and Liechtenstein. The tax rates will be: 1 January 2004 to 31 December 2006, 15 per cent; 1 January 2007 to 31 December 2009, 20 per cent and from 1 January 2010, 35 per cent. Luxembourg, Austria and Belgium agreed to exchange information if Switzerland agreed to relinquish bank secrecy. Although the Swiss did not agree to go so far as this, they agreed to impose a withholding tax (at rates described above) on EU residents' savings, the proceeds of which will be shared with the EU. 'According to Article 17.3 of the directive, EU members must unanimously agree before July 1, 2004 that the conditions of the directive have been met in order for it to be implemented.'[37]

One commentator said that: 'The agreement is fuller of holes than a colander, and depositors won't take long to make sure that their money is safe from information exchange (in the 12 EU states which will impose it) or from a withholding tax.'[38] That is to say, there is a distinct possibility that those depositors (and others) who do not want details of their affairs to be exchanged, will simply move their money to Austria, Belgium or Luxembourg, or perhaps even further afield, for example to Panama or Singapore. This represented a testing moment. The Society of Estate and Tax Practitioners said: 'Switzerland and the US are excused

---

[37] Center for Freedom and Prosperity, Strategic Memorandum concerning the London meeting of the OECD Sub-Group, 2 February 2004, p. 2.
[38] Jason Gorringe, 'Low-Tax Jurisdictions Puzzle Over Response to EU Savings Tax Deal', Tax-News.com, 24 January 2003.

from effective exchange of information on EU resident tax matters. This is despite the fact that OECD continues to insist that their competitors, smaller jurisdictions excluded from OECD membership, should still do so.'[39] Dr Mitchell, of the Center for Freedom and Prosperity, said: '[T]he EU's new proposal (an impractical co-existence model based on either withholding taxes or information exchange) clearly does not satisfy the "level playing field" requirement. This assumes of course, that it is even possible to implement and enforce the new EU Directive. This is highly unlikely.'[40]

The agreement could not have pleased the UK's Chancellor of the Exchequer, Gordon Brown, who proposed the automatic exchange of information in the first place. In January 2003, he committed the UK's dependent territories to the automatic exchange of information, but many OFCs did not feel obliged to honour such commitments unless and until the Swiss adhere. That said, this commitment does not affect those that have already signed information sharing agreements. The compromise solution adopted does not lend much support to aspirations for greater transparency. Fears were expressed within the 'Offshore Environment'. For example in a report published by Datamonitor, Oliver Guirdham said that 'UK Offshore territories are likely to be among the worst affected by the Directive . . . Datamonitor forecasts that fully compliant, information swapping territories are likely to lose 58 per cent of offshore funds and deposits invested by EU citizens by 2013. This will have a dramatic effect on financial services industries in the Offshore territories, such as those in the Channel Islands and the Caribbean.'[41] One other commentator suggested that 'Fully compliant territories are forecast to lose more than half of the offshore funds and deposits invested by EU citizens . . . This will effectively end the tax advantage of saving and investing in these territories for UK citizens.'[42]

Once the problems with Switzerland were ironed out in May 2004 (see section 5.18 above) talks began with the other 'outliers': Andorra, Liechtenstein, Monaco and San Marino.

[39] Ulrika Lomas, 'ECOFIN Met on Friday to Finalise the EU Tax Package', Tax-News.com, 10 March 2003.
[40] 'US Institute Advises Bahamas to Resist EU/OECD Pressure', Tax-News.com, February 2003.
[41] Amanda Banks, 'Report Warns Over Impact of Savings Tax Directive on "Offshore Centres"', Tax-News.com, 5 March 2003.
[42] 'EU Policy Will Hit UK "Offshore" Investment', *Offshore'Red*, April 2003, p. 28.

5.20 Other problems

The agenda of the ECOFIN meeting scheduled for 7 March 2003 included adoption of the agreement reached in January 2003 on the Directive after ten years of negotiations. The Italian Minister of the Economy prevented that by introducing new elements (including proposed changes in respect of cross-border taxes, milk quotas and other unrelated issues) which in turn required further discussions on 19 March 2003. Other issues concerning a desire by some EU members to revisit the Stability Pact's fiscal rules, may have prompted this. The Directive was due to be signed on 20 March 2003, but in the event it was actually signed on 3 June 2003 and was scheduled to come into effect on 1 January 2005.

5.21 The response Offshore

At the end of March 2003, Mr Laurie Morgan, President of Guernsey's Advisory and Finance Committee, announced that, if and when the EU tax package is adopted, Guernsey's Parliament would be asked to introduce a retention tax to be applied to the interest earned by EU depositors. This means that, from 1 January 2005, where a depositor is unwilling to authorise disclosure of relevant information to the depositor's home tax authority, Guernsey will deduct the relevant amount of tax and retain 25 per cent and pay the balance to the EU home country of the depositor. (Note, only individuals (from Europe) are affected, not companies and not most trusts. Guernsey has already ascertained that around 90 per cent of deposits placed in Guernsey would be unaffected.) Guernsey's announcement took the Isle of Man and Jersey by surprise in that Guernsey appears to have reached a decision and announced it without consulting the other two islands. This was abnormal.

Guernsey's announcement was followed by that of the Isle of Man and Jersey on 10 June 2003. Like Guernsey, the Isle of Man and Jersey announced that, when the Savings Directive takes effect, they will impose a withholding tax on interest paid to EU resident individuals rather than exchange information. If the investor agrees, information will be exchanged instead with the EU country in which the investor resides.

Interestingly, the EU Directive does not seem to apply to Bermuda, because its name was excluded from the list of jurisdictions drawn up at the Feira Summit in 2000 – unlike the Channel Islands and the Caribbean islands. (This appears to have been an error because those involved in drafting the rules were under the impression that Bermuda was not in the Caribbean. If Bermuda is to be involved, it looks like it will have to be on a voluntary basis.)

At that point in time, Austria, Belgium, Luxembourg, Switzerland, Guernsey, Jersey and the Isle of Man had all decided upon the withholding tax route. Meanwhile, '[b]anks in Singapore are already positioning themselves to capture a share of the $1 trillion that is expected to leave Europe if the Directive is implemented'.[43]

At the OECD's Global Forum in Ottawa in October 2003, the Chief Foreign Affairs Representative of Antigua and Barbuda said that 'the EU Council of Ministers has caused us to have to suspend our conditional commitment given to the OECD last year. And, I now formally advise this Forum of this decision by my Government to suspend our commitment until the OECD is able to convince its member states to become cooperative jurisdictions.'[44] This decision came about because of the decision of the EU Council of Economic and Finance Ministers on 21 January 2003 not to require EU members – Austria, Belgium and Luxembourg – to exchange information but to apply a withholding tax instead. (In due course, this was extended to Switzerland, Liechtenstein, Monaco, Andorra and San Marino.) The Representative said that this demonstrated the absence of an agreement within the OECD on the exchange of information on civil tax matters that OECD was trying to impose upon Antigua and Barbuda. The contradiction is that some EU members are exempted while non-EU countries are forced to comply with the same requirements.[45] (See Chapter 12.)

5.22 'Offshore' and the zero tax option

A significant development came at the end of June 2002 when the Isle of Man and Gibraltar announced their intention to create, from 1 January 2006, a corporation tax regime that applies to the majority of companies and which is simultaneously zero rated and which complies with the European Union's Savings Tax Directive and Code of Conduct on

---

[43] 'Singapore Set to Welcome Europe's Wealth', *Gulf Daily News*, Vol. 26, No. 156, Bahrain, 23 August 2003, as reported in 'The Level Playing Field: Misguided and Non-Existent', *CF&P Foundation Prosperitas*, October 2003.

[44] 'Antigua and Barbuda – Investing in Paradise', www.antigua-barbuda.com/busnss_politics/body_oecdglobalforum_ottawa.html.

[45] 'Antigua and Barbuda – Investing in Paradise', www.antigua-barbuda.com/busnss_politics/body_oecdglobalforum_ottawa.html.

Business Taxation. It is also transparent. At one stage, low or no tax was regarded as one of the badges that the OECD used to identify jurisdictions as 'Offshore Finance Centres' – although low or no income tax was not enough in itself to constitute harmful tax competition – it had to be combined with other factors (see section 12.3 below).

The characteristics of this strategy include: the registration of all companies for tax purposes; the availability of records for inspection; the recording of beneficial ownership; and the exchange of information is provided for. There is goal congruence here: legitimate business is encouraged and there are appropriate filters to discourage unwanted business. Companies engaged in financial services will be required to pay tax at a higher rate. In this respect, the Isle of Man is at an advantage over Gibraltar, Guernsey and Jersey because the income not generated by tax (estimated at £23 million) may be replaced by VAT, whereas in the latter centres there is no VAT. In the Isle of Man, income tax represents only 7 per cent of government revenue (£500 million for 2005–6), whereas VAT represents 56 per cent.[46] The standard zero rate will not apply to banks, which pay more tax on corporate profit than any other type of commercial enterprise. The standard rate of income tax in the Isle of Man is 10 per cent – and this is what the banks will continue to pay.

Soon afterwards, Jersey (19 November 2002) and Guernsey (22 November 2002) announced similar intentions.

> By 2006, Jersey must eliminate tax exemption to overseas companies that is not available to local business (that have to pay 20 per cent corporation tax). However, this tax contributes 202 million pounds to the annual budget of 365 million so another means must be found to generate this amount. This has given rise to some serious questions being posed by Jersey residents in respect of the prominence given to the Financial Services Industry in Jersey . . . [L]ike other tax havens, Jersey stands accused of kneeling at the alter of Transnational Capital where the high priests are local lawyers, transfer price specialists and tax planners performing feats of fiscal escapology that would have made Houdini proud. . ..[47]

---

[46] 'Editor's Note', *Offshore Red*, April 2005, p. 57.
[47] Marc Lopatin, 'Jersey Plans Corporation Tax Cut To Retain Its Haven Status', *The Times*, 2 January 2003.

5.23 Not everyone is happy

Meanwhile, the Cayman Islands took their concerns about being sub-
jected to the automatic application of the Directive to the European
Court of Justice, and, in March 2003, the Court of First Instance ruled
that neither the EU nor the UK could impose the Directive upon the
UK's dependent territories. Despite this, by March 2004, the Cayman
Island's Legislative Assembly succumbed and accepted the terms of the
Savings Tax Directive.

In the words of the Center for Freedom and Prosperity:

> Acting at the behest of Europe's welfare states, the Organization for
> Economic Cooperation and Development (OECD) has been fighting to
> undermine fiscal competition. Concerned that jobs and capital are leaving
> high-tax nations, the Paris-based bureaucracy wants low tax jurisdictions
> to help enforce the bad tax laws of OECD member nations by collecting
> private financial information about non-resident investors and sharing
> that information with the tax authorities from high tax nations.[48]

5.24 Tax amnesties

Tax amnesties are the flavour of the day. An amnesty was declared in
Cyprus for income and profit not previously declared till 31 December
2002.

An amnesty was announced by the Isle of Man to run from 9 April
until 31 October 2003. The scheme (the 'Penalty and Interest Remission
Scheme') was wide-ranging, covering failure to complete a tax return on
time to failure to notify the authorities about liability to VAT or tax.

However, it seems that tax amnesties may be even more popular
'Onshore' than 'Offshore', as the following examples suggest.

The Exchange Control Amnesty Bill represents an attempt by the
Government of South Africa to encourage taxpayers to repatriate money
from 'Offshore'. (One estimate puts the amount invested by South
Africans outside South Africa as US$50 billion.) The Bill exempted
investors from civil or criminal prosecution, but money repatriated
was subject to a 5 per cent tax. The amnesty was effective from 1 June
until 30 November 2003 and, as a result, offshore assets worth R65

---

[48] 'The Level Playing Field: Misguided and Non-Existent', *CF&P Foundation Prosperitas*,
October 2003.

billion were declared.[49] A subsequent report in March 2005 said that 'South Africa will receive an estimated R2.4bn ($414m) from levies raised from an amnesty for people who illegally took money offshore years ago, the Treasury said.'[50]

Naturally, there are consequences. For example, 'A recent Tax Amnesty in Italy caused Euro 300 billion to flow out of [Switzerland's] banks. The consequences of a similar amnesty currently under consideration in Germany would be even more severe given the higher level of German money in Swiss banks.'[51]

The trend is ongoing. For example, in December 2003, the French Budget Minister announced that France was considering the introduction of an amnesty for assets repatriated. (According to a report written by a member of the French National Assembly, over the last five years, €11 billion of assets left France because of high inheritance tax and wealth tax.)[52] France tried this before in 1986.

In 2003, a Bill was agreed in Belgium to encourage those with funds invested abroad to repatriate the money (at a cost somewhere between 6 per cent and 9 per cent). Belgians favour Luxembourg and Germans favour Switzerland to deposit their money. One estimate is that Belgians have deposited around US$190 million in foreign banks.[53]

Further, the IRS in the USA announced a three-month amnesty in 2003. As a result, the IRS collected US$170 million from tax and penalties in respect of money secreted 'Offshore'. The amnesty ended in March 2004, by which time around 10,000 people had made disclosures.[54] Meanwhile, in February 2005, 'Belgium's finance minister Didier Reynders said the country's tax amnesty scheme . . . had yielded around €496 million in additional tax revenue'.[55] In March 2005, Mexico offered a tax amnesty to individuals who have money 'Offshore'.

Not all amnesties are successful, for example the tax amnesty offered by Germany at the start of 2004.

[49] 'Global News – South Africa', *Offshore Red*, February 2005, p. 2.
[50] 'S. African Amnesty Worth $414m', *Offshore Red*, April 2005, p. 50.
[51] 'Editorial', *Offshore Red*, June 2003, p. 81.
[52] Ulrika Lomas, 'France Considers Tax Amnesty to Halt Capital Flight', Tax-News.com, 4 December 2003.
[53] 'Tax Amnesty Gathers Pace in Line with EU Savings Directive', *Offshore Red*, February 2004, p. 222.
[54] 'News Digest – Ireland', *Offshore Red*, April 2004, p. 30.
[55] 'Global News – Belgium', *Offshore Red*, March 2005, p. 26.

5.25 Controlled foreign companies

For tax purposes, most countries distinguish ordinary residents from non-resident companies. The latter usually receive more benign treatment than the former (e.g. residents are usually taxed on their worldwide income). In order to exploit these differences, ordinary persons sometimes incorporate companies abroad and process income through the incorporated entity. The idea is that the company will be tax exempt 'Onshore'. Taking the UK as an example, the 'controlled foreign company' (CFC) will not be resident in the UK, and it will be controlled to a large extent by individuals or companies who are resident there. The CFC must suffer tax at a rate that is less than 75 per cent of the rate that would have been payable if the company had been resident in the UK. Leaving aside the exemptions that may be claimed, the amount of the difference between the UK tax that would have been payable and the tax actually paid 'Offshore' is chargeable on UK companies which have at least a 25 per cent interest in the CFC. (One such exemption is called the acceptable distribution policy. Where the CFC pays to the UK residents a dividend that represents most of the CFC's profits (90 per cent), there will be no need to apply the normal CFC rules; since the dividend is taxable onshore, there will be no material amount of tax avoided.)

In order to prevent wrongful exploitation of CFCs, certain rules have been put in place to prevent the avoidance or deferral of tax in the home country by those persons who establish a subsidiary company in a lower tax 'Offshore' jurisdiction to which income will be diverted. (This can be used by some countries to discriminate against OFCs.) The home country of the parent corporation acquires some rights over subsidiaries (of the parent) that pay tax abroad at a low rate.

The sort of rules that countries apply to CFCs to allow the deferral of income include the following:

- Residents must not control or even have a substantial interest in the foreign company.
- The income placed in the foreign company must be 'passive' in nature, that is, not arising from an active commercial activity.
- The income suffers either no tax abroad or only a minimal amount.

Rules concerning CFCs were first applied by the USA in 1962. Incorporating companies for this type of purpose is particularly prevalent in 'Offshore Centres', and is a cause for concern in some 'Onshore' centres.

5.26 Double tax avoidance agreements

Clearly, double taxation is a commercial disadvantage that impinges upon economic development, and one of the means used to eradicate these effects is to use a double tax avoidance agreement (DTAs). This is a bilateral arrangement between two sovereign states that provides how the residents of each country will be taxed in respect of cross-border transactions. DTAs enable taxpayers to avoid paying tax twice on the same income.

At the outset, the International Chamber of Commerce identified the need to eliminate or at least reduce double taxation in order not to discourage international trade. The League of Nations was asked to assist, and as a result a Model Convention was drafted. In 1946, the UN Social and Economic Council's Fiscal Committee published a document. In due course, the OECD assumed responsibility and in 1977 published a Model Convention. This was followed by a new model in 1992 and revisions in 1995, 1997 and 2000. The commentary published at the same time is of great practical significance in interpreting the DTA. However, the OECD model is suitable for developed nations where the flow is two ways and revenue is shared on the residence principle. In order to assist developing nations – where the flow is more likely to be from the developed nation to the developing nation – the latter will suffer if the residence principle is applied. Accordingly, the UN drafted a Model Convention that is a compromise between the source and residence principles (but weighted towards the source principle), which was completed in 1980. This means that the UN model encourages investment flows from developed to developing countries while simultaneously accommodating sharing tax revenues with the capital-providing country. The relevant countries negotiate the withholding tax rate to be applied to dividend, interest and royalty payments.[56]

Some jurisdictions (e.g. Mauritius) have been able to channel substantial amounts of foreign investments through corporate vehicles incorporated in the jurisdiction, as a result of an extensive network of double taxation treaties. An increasing treaty network and growing regional investment prospects complement each other in that investors are given expanding opportunities for tax planning through the treaties.

---

[56] Noshir M. Lam, Mayur Nayak and Mitil Chokshi, *International Business and Tax Strategies*, Ketan Thakkar, 2002, pp. 270–4.

In this respect, substantial investment has flowed into India, China and South Africa through Mauritius, which currently has around thirty treaties. However, only legal persons and corporations that are resident in Mauritius (and liable to tax in Mauritius) may avail of benefits arising under DTAs. ('Offshore' jurisdictions do not normally enter into DTAs. Not surprisingly, Mauritius does not regard itself as an 'Offshore' jurisdiction.)

5.27 Transfer pricing

Ordinarily, legal persons buy and sell services at prices dictated by markets. The transactions are said to be made 'at arm's length'. Where related parties transfer services between themselves, they do so at what is referred to as the 'transfer price'. The tax implication is that, where the transaction is carried out at arm's length, the tax authorities are likely to accept that the buyer has not overpaid and that the supplier has not accepted less than it might have obtained elsewhere. Where the parties are related, and the transaction is not at arm's length, the tax authorities are less confident, especially if the parties to the transaction have different effective tax rates. In this scenario, there is a risk, arising from their relationship, that the price at which the services are transferred has been manipulated in such a way as to move the profit to whomever has the lower tax rate, thereby reducing the amount of tax that they jointly pay.

The global implication is that onshore tax authorities will want to make sure that transfer prices equate with arm's length prices – otherwise the taxable profit of the onshore taxpayer will be understated. In some circumstances, subsidiaries 'Offshore' (where the tax rate is likely to be lower) are used in this process.

Further information may be obtained from the OECD's 'Transfer Pricing Guidelines for Multinational Enterprises and Tax Administrations'.

5.28 Global forum on taxation

See section 12.15 below.

A description of regulatory and supervisory processes

Financial regulation is all about politics.[1]

6.1 Introduction

It has been said of regulatory agencies that 'Their missions are amorphous and multifaceted, their statutory obligations miscellaneous and poorly integrated. Each of their activities contributes towards some aspect of mission accomplishment, even if the tangled web of causes and effects makes linking specific actions to specific outcomes difficult or impossible'.[2] This chapter tries to identify some of the reasons why this may or may not be true. Regulation is inexact, it is not a science and there will be failures. Using the UK's FSA's terminology, a 'non-zero failure regime' does not apply.

In a previous chapter, tax and regulation were identified as the two factors that give rise to most criticism about the 'Offshore' environment. Chapter 5 focused on tax, and this chapter considers regulation.

According to the President of the FATF, 'effective regulation should not be seen as an option, it is a necessary cost which must be met if a jurisdiction wants to reap the benefits which flow from a financial services industry'.[3] In this respect, service providers in 'Offshore Centres' want to be able to demonstrate to prospective customers that they are regulated to a high standard. It seems that this reassures clients, although most accept this at face value without question and without any real understanding of what it means. For example, licensing in one jurisdiction may be little more than a formality while elsewhere it might be

---

[1] Philip Thorpe, 'Time to Wield the Big Stick', *Securities and Investment Review*, January–February 2004, p. 26.
[2] Malcolm K. Sparrow, *The Regulatory Craft*, Brookings Institution Press, 1998, p. 9.
[3] Interview: Jose Roldan, *The Financial Regulator*, Vol. 5, No. 2, p. 21.

a more meaningful process. So, it is not being licensed per se that matters. What really matters is the extent to which licensed institutions are regulated in their respective jurisdiction – and the quality of that regulation. For some, the licence is a 'must have' because it is a potent document. For example, an unscrupulous licensee (a licence-holding company) can use a licence to demonstrate that it has satisfied the regulator that it is credible, respectable and worthy of a consumer's trust.

On the other hand, some applicants (for licences to conduct licensable activity) want as little difficulty as possible when they apply for a licence. For such people, substance is much less important than form. This point is aptly demonstrated by the following quote:

> Regulators, under unprecedented pressure, face a range of demands, often contradictory in nature: be less intrusive – but more effective; be kinder and gentler – but don't let the bastards get away with anything; focus your efforts – but be consistent; process things quicker – and be more careful next time; deal with important issues – but do not stray outside your Regulatory authority; be more responsive to the regulated community – but do not get captured by industry.[4]

This chapter provides some comment on the meaning of regulation in general and in respect of regulation 'Offshore' in particular. This chapter presents a central theme of the book, because, as one commentator has said '[g]overnmental and regulatory environments profoundly influence the structure and scale of financial sector activities'.[5]

6.2 The rationale for regulation

Llewellyn cites what he calls the four key objectives of regulation as: '(1) systemic stability, (2) the safety and soundness of financial institutions, (3) consumer protection against hazardous behaviour of individual financial institutions, and (4) the maintenance of consumer confidence in the financial system and the integrity of financial institutions'.[6]

---

[4] Malcolm K. Sparrow, *The Regulatory Craft*, Brookings Institution Press, 2000, p. 17.

[5] Jeffrey Carmichael, 'Australia's Approach to Regulation', in *Aligning Financial Supervisory Structures with Country Needs*, ed. Jeffrey Carmichael, Alexander Fleming and David Llewellyn, World Bank Institute, September 2004, p. 99.

[6] David Llewellyn, 'Institutional Structure of Financial Regulation and Supervision', in *Aligning Financial Supervisory Structures with Country Needs*, ed. Jeffrey Carmichael, Alexander Fleming and David Llewellyn, World Bank Institute, September 2004, p. 23.

Meanwhile, Dale and Wolfe have said that there are three broad reasons for regulating financial institutions: (1) for consumer protection purposes; (2) because of moral hazard; and (3) to ensure the integrity of markets.[7] Moral hazard includes situations where depositors feel they can take more risks because, if anything happens to the institution to which they have entrusted their money, the government will compensate them. For example, in the USA, the Federal Deposit Insurance Corporation guarantees the first US$100,000 to depositors with insurance companies in respect of any amount they lose. In the absence of such a guarantee, the depositor may be more careful. The latter writers go on to say that consumer protection is afforded by (1) compensation schemes, (2) capital adequacy requirements to prevent insolvency and (3) by way of rules of business conduct. It is probably fair to summarise that academia suggests that the main reason for regulation is to prevent market failure.

It has been suggested that '[r]egulation comprises all the rules (both explicit and implicit) which significantly affect the way in which (financial) markets and firms operate, irrespective of who lays them down, so long as they have at least the implicit imprimatur of a government or international organisation'.[8]

The constituent parts of regulation (in the widest sense of that word) are described below, but, for the time being, regulation can be considered as a means to maintain order in a dynamic financial environment by the application of rules that aim to create economic efficiency (by avoiding market failure and by eradicating behaviour that prejudices the consumer).

In theory at least, the financial system should be able to operate efficiently without regulatory intervention. The Chief Executive of the International Securities Market Association, John Langton, believes that '[t]here is a role for statutory regulation where there is a demonstrable failure that the market is either unable, or unwilling to correct but too much statutory regulation is based on what "might" happen'.[9] Further, 'whenever there is imperfect information or markets (that is, always),

[7] R. Dale and S. Wolfe, 'The UK Financial Services Authority, Unified Regulation in the New Market Environment', *Journal of Banking Regulation*, Vol. 4, No. 3, 2003, p. 200.
[8] D. Gowland, *The Regulation of the Financial Markets in the 1990s*, Edward Elgar Publishing Ltd, 1990, p. 8.
[9] Edward Russell-Walling, 'A Necessary Autonomy', *International Securities 2004/05*, p. 131.

there are, in principle, interventions by the government'.[10] Why should this be so?

> In broad terms, financial markets fail to produce efficient, competitive outcomes for one or more of the following reasons:
>
> - anti-competitive behaviour;
> - market misconduct;
> - information asymmetry;
> - systemic instability.[11]

A brief comment on each is set out below:

6.2.1 Anti-competitive behaviour

Simply stated, competition is good and benefits an economy, so market forces should be allowed to apply. Whatever stifles that competition or dilutes it is problematic at best and bad at worst. No rules would be necessary if all the players adopted principles that were true and fair, because, in those circumstances, service providers would not be at any advantage over consumers.

6.2.2 Market misconduct

Misconduct impairs efficiency and prejudices the interests of bona fide participants. Therefore, it is in the interests of all participants to eliminate misconduct of all types. Carmichael has identified five areas on which he says market conduct regulation focuses, as follows: disclosure of information, conduct of business rules, entry restrictions through licensing, governance and fiduciary responsibilities and specified minimum financial strength criteria.[12] In practice, a number of 'techniques' are used. First, licensing may help to filter out undesirable people and their business. Secondly, in order to ensure proper conduct, a series of rules are frequently applied. Thirdly, organisations that are licensed must supply 'control information' to the regulator.

---

[10] Joseph Stiglitz, *Globalisation and its Discontents*, Penguin Books, 2002, p. 219.
[11] Jeffrey Carmichael and Michael Pomerleano, *The Principles of Regulation*, World Bank, 2002, p. 25.
[12] Jeffrey Carmichael, 'Australia's Approach to Regulation', in *Aligning Financial Supervisory Structures with Country Needs*, ed. Jeffrey Carmichael, Alexander Fleming and David Llewellyn, World Bank Institute, September 2004, p. 106.

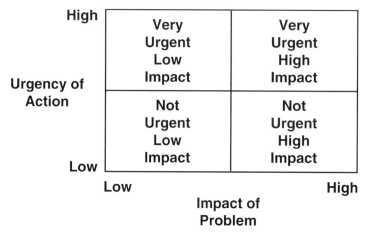

Figure 6.1. Regulation: problem/impact analysis

6.2.3 Conduct of business

This is a regulatory approach that is likely to be both intrusive and intensive – because its aim is to prevent problems. This idea is encapsulated in Figure 1 which tries to demonstrate that attention needs to be focused first on those situations where the perceived impact is high and action is deemed urgent. Attention can wait in situations where the impact is low and which are deemed non-urgent.

Action invariably costs money, and this is shown in the cost/ benefit analysis set out in Figure 2 (see section 6.3 below). The point is to use this approach to determine where regulatory resources should be focused. One of the fundamental purposes of regulation is to offer some degree of protection to those who need it. 'Regulators have learned the value of adopting customer service ideas for certain aspects of their business, but most are aware that they need a broader portfolio of ideas as they scratch for strategies that are at once economical with respect to the use of authority and genuinely effective in procuring compliance and mitigating risks.'[13] The allocation of resources is much more difficult in practice than the theory above suggests.

---

[13] Malcolm K. Sparrow, *The Regulatory Craft*, Brookings Institution Press, 2000, p. 3.

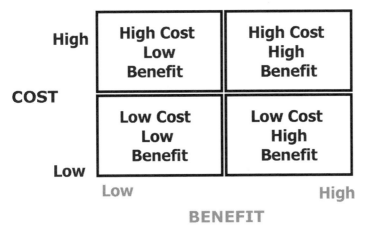

Figure 6.2. Regulation: cost/benefit analysis

6.2.4 Information asymmetry

People in general need protection for a number of reasons. One such circumstance is where a (financial) transaction involves a number of parties who do not all have the same amount of information. Obviously, the people with more information are better placed in taking action than those persons who are less well informed. Consumers must have adequate information to enable them to make informed decisions about their finances, but sometimes other people have more information than them. In such circumstances, there may be a need for some type of intervention to protect the less well-informed party. This scenario was expertly described in Akerlof's Lemon Theory,[14] which 'illustrates that a market with rampant informational asymmetries will under-perform compared to a market without or with less informational asymmetries, either by being illiquid or by ceasing to function altogether'.[15]

Many aspects of life are subject to some form or other of control, which fact is recognised by governments which provide for the public's well being in certain circumstances. These include areas where public

---

[14] G. A. Akerlof, 'The Market for Lemons: Quality Uncertainty and the Market Mechanism', *Quarterly Journal of Economics*, Vol. 84, No. 488, 1970.
[15] Jesper Lau Hansen, 'The Trinity of Market Regulation: Disclosure, Insider Trading and Market Manipulation', *International Journal of Disclosure and Governance*, Vol. 1, No. 1.

safety (e.g. air travel), public policy (e.g. the law), public health (medical care) or consumer protection is concerned. In respect of the regulation of financial markets, 'disclosure obligations and bans on insider trading and misinformation'[16] are the means used to avoid asymmetric information. However, in some scenarios, the amount of information per se is not the only criterion. As Carmichael and Pomerleano point out,[17] 'information asymmetry arises where products or services are sufficiently complex that disclosure by itself is insufficient to enable consumers to make informed choices . . . The issue involves the complexity of the product and the institution offering it. This problem is common in areas such as drugs and aviation and is particularly relevant in the area of financial services.'

Prudential regulatory techniques are used to deal with this phenomenon. The style is persuasive. The regulator is likely to have access to information about which the public is unaware. Carmichael and Pomerleano state therefore that the regulator's actions are designed to ensure that the investor is treated fairly. To achieve this, the regulator endeavours to make sure that the consumer is aware of whatever the regulator believes is reasonable for the consumer to know to help him make reasonable financial decisions. Prudential regulation involves capital and liquidity minima, licensing criteria and criteria concerning how licensees manage their licence holding activities. Not unsurprisingly, the consumer will have confidence in the system so long as he perceives it to be effective – and this is affected (inter alia) by the regulator's response when the consumer has been disadvantaged. Prudential actions include solvency and liquidity requirements, balance sheet controls and scrutiny of interrelationships with other financial institutions, etc.

6.2.5 Systemic instability

Where the failure of one institution creates a contagion effect, the whole financial system's stability may be impaired. And the most vulnerable part is the payments system. Positive protection depends on sound macroeconomic policies, and is supported by prudential mechanisms. Monetary policy is the core method employed to ensure stability.

---

[16] Jesper Lau Hansen, 'The Trinity of Market Regulation: Disclosure, Insider Trading and Market Manipulation', *International Journal of Disclosure and Governance*, Vol. 1, No. 1.
[17] Jeffrey Carmichael and Michael Pomerleano, *The Principles of Regulation*, World Bank, 2002, p. 26.

With respect to regulation, there is one insidious characteristic that must never be overlooked. It so happens that disasters may be latent for extended periods. In some respects, it is possible that the harmful effects of a bad decision will not be felt for years to come. (Licensing is a particular example.)

6.3 The cost/benefit analysis

Whatever regulatory structure is adopted, and the text shows that there are several options, 'the ideal regulatory structure at any point in time is that which provides the best cost/benefit ratio for providing systemic stability, safety and soundness of financial institutions and market efficiency and fairness'.[18] Like any other service, regulation costs money. The greater the degree and depth of the regulatory process, the greater the cost will be. As the services and the sophistication of the financial markets have increased, so also the scope and depth of regulation must expand to keep up. Probably, the cost of creating a system that was sufficiently sophisticated to eradicate all possibility of failure would exceed the benefit arising. In summary, 'a judgment has to be made as to how far the objectives of regulation (e.g. the protection of the consumer from all possible abuse) can reasonably be pursued and what cost it is reasonable to bear'.[19]

The regulatory system must be adequate for the task. It should be effective and cost-efficient. The intensity of regulation reflects the degree of risk identified. The problem is in knowing where to draw the line: how much is enough? Information concerning the costs of regulation 'Offshore' is not available. However, this point endorses the fact that 'Offshore Centres' need a certain critical mass – without which the appropriate legal and regulatory infrastructure will not exist. Cost is not the only factor that is relevant in considering the scope and depth of regulation, for example Regulators are expensive and to do the job properly requires appropriate people. Smaller 'Offshore Centres' must – despite their smallness – have an appropriate cadre of regulatory professionals if they are to have any chance of doing credible work. Despite the

---

[18] Jeffrey Carmichael, 'Summary of the Discussion', in *Aligning Financial Supervisory Structures with Country Needs*, ed. Jeffrey Carmichael, Alexander Fleming and David Llewellyn, World Bank Institute, September 2004, p. 13.

[19] Hans Falkena, Roy Bamber, David Llewellyn and Tim Store, *Financial Regulation in South Africa*, Financial Sector Forum, 2001, p. 9.

costs and despite the difficulties inherent in knowing how much is
enough, an acceptable standard must be maintained if an 'Offshore
Centre' is to be 'successful'. Like confidence in banking, credibility in
'Offshore Finance' is critical.

Since we live in a competitive and turbulent environment where there
is competition for scarce resources, and where profit is the reward for
enterprise, rules are necessary to ensure – to the extent that it is possible
to ensure anything – that all stakeholders have similarly equitable opportunities in all circumstances. For this reason, 'regulation should be a
dynamic process which changes to reflect the competitive climate and
market environment'.[20]

The extent to which the system operates inefficiently raises a question
about the value of regulatory intervention because the perceived advantages must be assessed in terms of perceived benefits. For example,
intervention might cost a lot more than the value of the benefit produced, but low cost might generate substantial benefits. The OECD
considers that 'the volume and complexity of laws, rules, paperwork,
and administrative formalities now reach an all-time high in OECD
countries, overwhelming the ability of regulators in implementing the
total load, the private sector in complying, and elected officials in
monitoring action. Too often, legislators issue laws as symbolic public
action, rather than as practical solutions to real problems.'[21]

As usual, the actual is never so simple as the theory, and to that extent
Table 2 indicates only some of the permutations that are possible.

Once again, the value lies in deciding where resources should be
allocated to derive the greatest benefit.

6.4 Core values

Simply stated, the regulatory process comes down to three decisions:
what, when, and how? That is to say, what is the regulator trying to
achieve? When is completion? How will the regulatory objectives be
achieved? The answers to these questions give rise to certain prompts
which in turn form the basis of the 'core values' for the regulator. For
example:

[20] Hans Falkena, Roy Bamber, David Llewellyn and Tim Store, *Financial Regulation in South
Africa*, Financial Sector Forum, 2001, p. 9.
[21] 'OECD Report on Regulatory Reform: Synthesis', 1997, p. 14, as reported in *The Regulatory Craft*, Malcolm K. Sparrow, Brookings Institution Press, 2000, p. 19.

- clarity of purpose;
- meaningful timeframe;
- strict adherence to commitments made;
- provision of adequate resources;
- integrity;
- efficiency; and
- quality of service.

6.5 A medical analogy

Perhaps the dual role of regulation can best be described with respect to a clinical analogy. No two 'Offshore Finance Centres' are identical – although, as previously discussed, many share common characteristics and traits. However described, there are certain factors or traits that are common to all 'Offshore' jurisdictions. Table 3 in Appendix 1 provides one way of characterising those factors. The table also makes a comparison between the application of these factors in 'Offshore' jurisdictions and the corresponding health factors in society as a whole.

First, in any social environment, the health of the population is a fundamental concern. While healthcare has many different aspects, perhaps the most fundamental is to make sure that the environment in which the population lives is conducive to life and well-being. The intention is not to create a sterile environment – because it will never be possible to eliminate completely what causes ill health. Rather the intention is to create a structure that will provide the highest quality of life as is possible (all other things being equal) and minimise the risk of anything that is life-threatening causing a harmful effect. A tolerable health environment will have to provide (inter alia) for sanitation, drinking water and waste disposal. There are different levels of response – not all societies deal with these factors in the same way. The needs of isolated communities will differ from those of large conurbations. This simple statement is an over-simplification, but may perhaps suffice for the sake of the analogy.

In respect of 'Offshore Finance Centres', 'conducive' implies stability and credibility, which in practical terms means the absence of bad news in general and no financial disasters in particular. External (potential) users of a jurisdiction will consider these factors closely in assessing whether a jurisdiction is conducive to their needs. The extent to which a financial centre is conducive is measured by its reputation – which acts like a thermometer, indicating a jurisdiction's relative well-being. Reputation reflects many variables, but, perhaps most importantly, reputation is an indication of how well the environment is considered to be protected against all the forces that might otherwise have a negative impact upon it. Note the word 'considered' – that is a perception, because sometimes there are weaknesses that are innate. (The significance of 'protection' is discussed elsewhere.) So how can jurisdictions obtain this protection? The answer is by adopting prudential supervision techniques and procedures.

Secondly, rendering the environment conducive for life and habitation is not a one-off exercise – it is an ongoing requirement, constantly evolving and changing in light of events and social demands. That being so, it is not only public health that is relevant, but also private health. This involves the provision of medical assistance – which in turn may be preventive, or reactive (and which provides assistance when people fall ill). Preventive medicine includes medical advice (e.g. on diet), the provision of inoculations, the availability of screening and X-ray procedures, check-ups etc. If human beings live in a healthy way, that is, by imposing certain disciplines upon themselves such as exercise, diet etc., they are likely (barring accidents) to have a better life and a tardier demise. Regulation is a preventive measure, because, in matters of regulation, prevention is always better than cure, which is why the licensing process is so important (primary prevention: see below). That being so, preventive measures may discourage infection and disease, but they cannot of themselves create health or even guarantee a germ-free environment. Dangers and risks remain. The objective of regulation is to manage risk, it does not attempt to eliminate it. Some risks or diseases have to be eradicated totally, while others must be managed. If something permeates the preventive net or filter, then a strategy to deal with that situation will be needed. Note the reactive element. Enhanced regulation always follows a disaster. This might be in the shape of direct medical assistance provided by medical practitioners in special facilities created for the purpose, i.e. hospitals or clinics.

The application for 'Offshore Centres' is that, if they conduct their affairs prudently, they are likely (barring accidents) to make a positive contribution to the world's economy and to the well-being and quality of life for their own licensees – and for a longer time than might otherwise have been the case. 'Offshore Centres' that do not conduct their affairs prudently will survive in the short term – but, without fundamental, self-imposed disciplines, they are unlikely to have a sustainable, long-term existence. The point is that, like humans who do not exercise discipline in how they live their lives, problems of one sort or another are likely to ensue – not necessarily immediately, but over time – for OFCs who do not control themselves. The preventive measures adopted in 'Offshore Finance Centres' and also reactive procedures when things go wrong are regulatory in nature.

For example, carriers of germs have the potential to pollute the whole environment. So financial institutions which want to establish in a jurisdiction must be screened in the first instance and at regular intervals thereafter. In the same way that humans have inoculations and medical check-ups, finance centres have their own type of diagnostic screening – referred to as the licence application process. Despite this precaution, some undesirable elements slip through the net, and so finance centres undertake continuous compliance checks to ensure that all is in order (secondary prevention). This compares to regular check-ups for human beings. Accordingly, regulation must be sufficiently effective to identify any potential licensee that is liable to damage the financial fabric of the jurisdiction and must also deal with potentially dangerous situations discovered thereafter. The regulator's role is to identify situations where risk is not being managed effectively (because, in such circumstances, there is potential for danger for the individual institution and also perhaps for the whole financial system) and then to indicate appropriate action to render the situation harmless before the potential becomes actual. In terms of finance, this is known as the contagion effect and supervisors must be alert to its potential in the same way as an epidemi-ologist must understand what is necessary to contain an infectious disease.

Failure to identify or to deal effectively with potential problems may precipitate some form of distress in the system – which may become public. Potential newcomers may be put off because of a perceived risk of infection.

In respect of health matters, there is substantial importance placed on the knowledge, skills and experience of practitioners – because they bear heavy responsibilities – and because failure may have disastrous consequences. In terms of financial services, substantial importance is placed on the quality of the regulators – who also have significant responsibilities.

Unless newcomers (licensees or people coming to live in the area) are willing to agree to adopt the preventive measures and ongoing medical check-ups (monitoring), they should not be allowed to join the commu-nity. However, there are costs as well as benefits involved in preventive action – and side-effects should not be overlooked. Jurisdictions might find it more economical to increase the intrusiveness of the licensing and regulatory processes than to completely discontinue operating as a finance centre. The idea is to achieve optimum balance between prevention and cure.

Thirdly, sometimes, special circumstances arise, despite having taken all the precautions that were reasonable. 'Reasonableness' suggests that the outcome represents a balance between all the relevant variables. For example, substantial sums of money might be expended on preventive care that produces only marginal benefits. Superficially, it might be argued that any benefits are worth it – and, in absolute terms, this is true – but, in relative terms, the healthcare budget is limited and, if the money is spent on this, there will be none left for that. Some hard decisions might have to be made. Special circumstances might include an epidemic of contagious diseases or illnesses that are 'new' (such as the SARS epidemic in Canada, China, Hong Kong and Singapore in 2003) or which have become virulent for some unknown reason.

In respect of 'Offshore Finance', special circumstances might include a situation where a licence-holding company is about to go under – or has just done so. If money has already been spent on contingency arrange-ments, these arrangements will come into play. If not, depending on the circumstances, a substantial amount of work may have to be undertaken very quickly. For example, the failure of a bank has many implications. This type of news is very sensitive, and, in order to limit damage, the fewer people who know the better. Depositors will be worried when the news breaks, and this might cause a 'run' on other banks. This might be prevented if action can be taken to prevent the failure. There are a number of permutations – but one is to sell the bank. In turn, the buyer will want to carry out some 'due diligence' – and this will take time. Every hour that passes might introduce new variables that could compli-cate the situation even further. A compensation scheme might already be in place and this might be triggered in the event of the default.

Fourthly, every society has what might be described as 'vulnerable groups'. They include the very old and the very young. They also include those with certain weaknesses who need additional support and assist-ance – which may be of short duration or may lead to a terminal situation.

'Offshore Finance Centres' also have vulnerable groups – and often the vulnerability is due to the institution itself. Such groups are likely to have raised prudential and regulatory concerns and their vulnerability is likely to have arisen from their own incompetence, for example through a failure to provide adequate solvency and liquidity – or by taking too many risks or too much risk. These groups require specific handling, and the order of priorities is to nurse the sick patient back to health or to prepare for closure in an ordered way – which leads on to the final area of similarity.

Lastly, the end situation for humans is death – which is part of life and therefore natural (all other things being equal). Death must be taken into account within the healthcare system. Although death is inevitable, it should not arise from negligence or from any deliberate action. Provision has to be made to ensure that there has been no 'foul play'. When people die of natural causes, there must be provisions for burial.

In respect of finance, there are occasions when, for acceptable reasons, a financial services provider considers it appropriate to terminate its activities. This is perfectly acceptable provided that its cessation comes about in an orderly and managed way – and without loss to any client. Difficulties are likely to arise in other circumstances – and not unlike the unexpected demise of someone who had appeared to be a healthy citizen, when a financial services company wants to 'close up shop' in what otherwise appear to be normal circumstances, some questions have to be asked.

Perhaps the importance of this analogy lies in the opportunity to compare one scenario with another to find out whether there are any additional lessons to be learned or predictors to be considered. There are a number of common denominators, but one important factor is that the diversity of human behaviour and circumstances leads to untold permutations that prevent perfection ever being possible. Healthcare does not promise perfect health or even escape from ill-health – it attempts to manage a number of potentially harmful factors and conflicting objectives in a positive, proactive manner to limit the dangers to well-being. Similarly, prudential supervision and regulation do not promise the eradication of financial crime or the enhancement of a jurisdiction's reputation through improved credibility and stability. These techniques are at best an effort to create and to maintain an environment in which financial services can develop and grow. Health practitioners and regulators have some techniques that they can apply usefully to this scenario – but the personal discipline that individuals can choose to apply to themselves is a very potent force in both community healthcare and in the provision of financial services. Interestingly, it should be noted that, in this respect, it is irrelevant whether the financial services are provided 'Onshore' or 'Offshore'.

6.6 Some structural theory

The structure adopted by regulatory and supervisory agencies is important – not least because it impinges upon the effectiveness of the agency itself. On that basis, there seems to be great value in considering the structure prior to introducing it. The Wallis Enquiry undertaken by Australia in 1996 is a case in point.

The traditional approach is to allocate separate disciplines to respective regulators – banks to one regulator, insurance companies to another etc.

6.6.1 Functional regulation

As the name suggests, the functional route means that regulation is applied on the basis of the functions of the licensee. This style focuses on how a company conducts its business and how it treats customers. As financial services companies diversify and as the distinctions between products becomes increasingly blurred, the applicability of the functional style reduces.

6.6.2 Institutional supervision

Institutional regulation means that the focus is on the institution and on its well-being irrespective of the functions involved. Llewellyn considers that, within an institutional structure, there are four main areas that warrant attention: systemic regulation and supervision; prudential regulation; consumer protection; and the need to ensure that competition exists within the financial system.[22] In practice, there is the hybrid style as well, which, as the name suggests, combines parts of both the functional and the institutional styles. Institutional supervision is particularly suited to the case of financial conglomerates.

---

[22] David Llewellyn, 'Institutional Structure of Financial Regulation and Supervision', in *Aligning Financial Supervisory Structures with Country Needs*, ed. Jeffrey Carmichael, Alexander Fleming and David Llewellyn, World Bank Institute, September 2004, p. 36. Further information is available in 'The Supervision of Financial Conglomerates (A Report by the Tripartite Group of Bank, Securities and Insurance Regulators)', July 1995.

6.6.3 Financial conglomerates

A financial conglomerate is generally understood to mean a group of companies that is involved in any two of banking, insurance and securities.

In 1993, a Tripartite Group of Bank, Securities and Insurance Regulators was formed on the initiative of the Basel Committee. The Group's remit was to consider a number of issues concerning the supervision of financial conglomerates because it was considered that the supervision of financial groups could not be effective if the individual components of the group were dealt with on an individual basis. Consolidated supervision or solo plus supervision were considered to be appropriate approaches in such circumstances. Acting in a personal capacity, they compiled a report entitled 'The Supervision of Financial Conglomerates', published in 1995. The report deals with three main issues: capital adequacy, supervisory cooperation; and group structures. A number of subsidiary matters are also dealt with, including contagion, large exposures, suitability/fit and proper, access and supervisory arbitrage.

The Group's work continued under the auspices of the Joint Forum on Financial Conglomerates (see section 9.19 below).

6.6.4 Prudential regulation and supervision

With respect to the development of regulation outside the central bank and the enhanced role of prudential supervision, it has been said that:

> Historically, central banks were charged with prudential supervision of banks because it complemented their functions in the areas of monetary policy operations, oversight of payments systems, and lender of last resort role. Over time, however, a number of developments altered the role of the central banks in the area of prudential supervision. Mainly as a result of the emergence of complex groups, the scope of prudential supervision broadened to include insurance undertakings, securities and investment business and funds management. The traditional role of the central bank did not easily extend to the prudential regulation of these financial sectors and, as a consequence, other regulatory bodies were established outside the central bank.[23]

---

[23] Liam O'Reilly, 'The New Structure of Financial Regulation in Ireland', in *Aligning Financial Supervisory Structures with Country Needs*, ed. Jeffrey Carmichael, Alexander Fleming and David Llewellyn, World Bank Institute, September 2004, p. 130.

> Prudential regulation – ensuring a firm's financial soundness and the
> adequacy of its control systems – is primarily conducted on an insti-
> tutional basis, while conduct of business regulation runs largely along
> functional lines.[24]

Prudential regulation and the assessment of conduct of business are different disciplines with different approaches. It was noted above that regulation and supervision are complementary processes. The focus of prudential supervision is on the protection of the financial system. Accordingly, it takes the solvency, safety and soundness of financial institutions into consideration. The object is to avoid systemic consequences arising through the failure of one or more institutions (the 'domino effect'). Operationally, this is achieved through the application of rules concerning capital adequacy and solvency. Since the role of banks is intrinsically linked to the efficacy of the payments system itself, supervisors will focus much of their attention on banks (and deposit takers) – but insurance companies also have very long-term contracts and short-term funding so solvency and liquidity are critically important for them also. Clearly, solvency and liquidity are important for every company – but they are more important for financial services companies than for others and, within this cadre, banks and insurance companies have the greatest potential for systemic harm if problems develop. An investment advisor may go into liquidation, but, if that company has no money belonging to clients, any damage arising will be more easily controlled than if clients' money was involved. (This is one reason why regulators insist that clients' money is always kept separate from that of the business itself.)

It is sometimes argued that the aims of prudential regulation and conduct of business regulation are different, but, according to Howard Davies, former Chairman of the FSA in the UK, these are two approaches to the same common objective – the protection of individuals' savings. '[T]he reason we want financial stability is so that individuals' money will hold its value and be reasonably secure and so that rational economic decisions can be made, which will promote investment and growth in the long run. Financial stability itself is a route to consumer protection.'[25]

---

[24] Michael Taylor, *Regulatory Leviathan: Will Super-SIB Work?*, CTA Publishing, 1997, p. 55.
[25] Howard Davies, 'Integrated Regulation in the United Kingdom', in *Aligning Financial Supervisory Structures with Country Needs*, ed. by Jeffrey Carmichael, Alexander Fleming and David Llewellyn, World Bank Institute, September 2004, p. 247.

6.6.5 Regulation

The focus of regulation is on how licensed financial services companies conduct their business not only with their customers but also with their peers and also how they behave towards the 'authorities' in the jurisdiction (which might include the regulator, the Financial Intelligence Unit etc.). Governments frequently establish rules requiring individuals and/ or organisations that accept money from an individual for investment purposes, to be subject to controls. (In this context, 'investment' should be interpreted widely to include bank deposits, securities and long-term insurance contracts.) This control process is frequently referred to as 'the regulation of financial services', but, however it is described, its function is more important than its name. Regulation comprises three core disciplines: licensing, regulation per se and compliance. The criteria arising from these three disciplines are inextricably linked; they are complementary and must be satisfied simultaneously, but finding the right balance is a hazardous process and one which the regulator faces daily. All centres want to grow – but not at any price.

6.7 Licensing

'Licensing' includes authorisation, permission, certification, approval or whatever process has been put in place by which a finance centre controls the population of those who may conduct (financial) 'licensable activity'. It should be noted that what constitutes 'licensable activity' in one jurisdiction need not constitute 'licensable activity' in another jurisdiction. For example, giving investment advice is a licensable activity in some jurisdictions – but not in all. At its most basic, a decision to license an applicant means that the regulatory authority is satisfied about the proposal and about the people behind it.

By definition, where jurisdictions license service providers, there has to be an 'application process'. The application process acts as a filter. The application process leads not only to the first decision within the regulatory process but arguably the most important. A good licensing decision can save much subsequent trauma. For the purposes of this discussion, it is assumed that the power to grant or to withhold a licence is vested in the regulator; but it sometimes happens that the authority to grant a licence vests in a government body ('the issuer') that is separate from the regulator. Unless the issuer and the regulator work closely and in tandem, the split function can lead to serious complications, arising not only through a lack of consistency but also because of the opportunity this type of situation affords to an applicant to play off the issuer and the regulator against each other.

The application process provides the means for the regulator to conduct adequate research and to make three critical assessments. The first assessment is whether or not the project constitutes licensable activity within the jurisdiction. At first sight, the question arises as to why an applicant would submit to the application process unnecessarily. The answer is that the applicant may (wrongly) believe that he needs a licence or he may just want the comfort of a document that he can use to demonstrate to others that he is 'bona fide' in the eyes of a regulator somewhere else in the world. The first question is whether the law of the jurisdiction provides that the activity for which a licence is being sought, requires a licence. The answer is not always clear cut. Another permutation is that an applicant may apply for one type of licence, but the regulator may believe that he requires a different type of licence.

Another scenario is that it is not always the case that licensable activity is easily or precisely defined, and, in such circumstances, the regulator must consider the activity very precisely before reaching a decision. For example, banking is a financial service that is very difficult to define, and this explains why banking legislation in many jurisdictions excludes a precise definition. In trying to determine whether a proposed activity constitutes banking, relevant questions might include whether money is accepted on deposit and whether interest is paid. Is the money used to finance lending? If the activity is licensable, is the jurisdiction prepared to consider licensing it? Even though it is licensable, the jurisdiction has a right to decline issuing a licence. This might arise for a number of reasons, such as the regulator being dissatisfied about some aspect of the application or about those behind it.

The application process is designed to clarify precisely what services the applicant proposes to provide and to identify the relevant risks and how the applicant proposes to manage those risks. The process includes finding out all relevant information about the people involved, including their skills, experience and qualifications. This is a derivation of the 'Know Your Customer' procedure (see section 6.9 below) that should be adopted by all financial services practitioners globally as part of their anti-money laundering procedures. 'Know Your Customer' is not only part of the anti-money laundering process, it is also part of the procedure that licensees should adopt to ensure that their prospective clients are 'fit and proper' (see section 6.8 below). The application process involves (inter alia) understanding not only who is behind the project (the beneficial owners), but also why they want a licence, whether they are regulated elsewhere, and, if so, where and to do what, their 'track record', the source of their funding, an assessment of their capital adequacy and solvency, a three- or five-year- business plan, and so on.

Problems can arise. First, those who want licences invariably want them the day before they applied, and the regulator is likely always to have more applications than resources to deal with them. Processing licence applications takes time, and the applicant or the representative of the applicant (e.g. a lawyer of a corporate service provider or agent) presses for quick answers because the client wants a quick response. If he does not get what he wants, the client will threaten to go elsewhere. Once the regulator begins to look at the application, questions arise. They may arise because the documentation has been completed without proper care or because questions on the application form have not been answered at all or, if addressed, not answered properly, or because the information provided has prompted further enquiry. Meanwhile, the applicant (or his agent) is pressing for a decision and affirms that the application form and all the documentation have been submitted correctly and in full. The regulator is charged with being too demanding, too slow, too literal in its interpretation of the rules and not sufficiently mindful of its customers' needs. The most usual criticism is that the regulator is venturing into matters of a commercial nature that have no regulatory significance – which is interpreted as confirmation that the regulator is not 'pro-business'. Regrettably, when a problem arises subsequently, it is very easy to charge the regulator with not having taken sufficient care at the licensing stage. This is a real dilemma. On the one hand, the regulator must exercise great care to avoid licensing someone or something that could adversely affect the reputation of the jurisdiction. On the other hand, the regulator is forced to respond more and more quickly – which by definition means more superficial analysis. This is where the applicant and/or his agent's ability to commit regulatory arbitrage (see section 6.25 below) is virtually unlimited. The regulator in this scenario may be used as a scapegoat by an unscrupulous applicant who tries to 'force' the regulator to approve the application (despite being defective) and, if he does not approve, the applicant will complain to everyone about how unprofessional the regulator is being.

6.8 The 'fit and proper' criterion

The 'fit and proper' criterion requires licensees to 'Know Their Customer' (see below). This is not a new concept. In fact, it can be traced
through existing legislation in the United Kingdom from section 41 of
the Insurance Companies Act 1982 to section 22 of the Building Societies
Act 1986 to the Banking Act 1987 and finally to the Financial Services
and Market Act 2001. 'Fit and proper' is a licensing criterion while
'Know Your Customer' is an anti-money laundering/terrorist financing
criterion. Thus, a licensee that does not have an adequate 'Know Your
Customer' procedure is unlikely to be fit and proper. Although 'Know
Your Customer' is most closely associated with the fight against money-
laundering '. . . [t]he Basel Committee's approach to KYC is from a
wider, prudential, not just anti-money laundering perspective. Sound
KYC procedures must be seen as a critical element in the effective
management of banking risks.'[26] By extension, the KYC criteria extend
beyond banking to other disciplines (see below).

The 'fit and proper' concept is subjective and nebulous – and therefore
difficult to define. Nevertheless, being 'fit and proper' suggests that a
person (and, in this case, the person may be either an individual or a
corporate entity) is likely to conduct business in an acceptable manner.
That is to say, the people behind the business will act with integrity and
conduct the affairs of the business in an honest and competent manner.

It is usual that the regulator will apply the test to beneficial owners
and to those who want to be shareholders, directors or senior managers
of companies engaged in 'financial services'.

The 'fit and proper' concept serves a number of important functions.
For example, being 'fit and proper' is a statutory pre-requisite in some
jurisdictions (e.g. Mauritius) to obtaining a licence – so it is a licensing
criterion. That is to say, even though all the technical tests concerning the
issue of a licence have been satisfied, the licence will not be issued unless
the regulator believes that the applicant is 'fit and proper'. That being so,
adoption of this criterion by a jurisdiction will show investors that
dishonest or incompetent licensees are unacceptable and that a code of

---

[26] 'Customer Due Diligence for Banks', Basel Committee on Banking Supervision, October
2001, pp. 3 and 4.

conduct must be satisfied by practitioners. This helps to provide comfort to investors and to stimulate confidence in the jurisdiction.

The 'fit and proper' test will be undertaken when an applicant applies for a licence, and on an ongoing basis thereafter. A licensee is expected to demonstrate fitness and propriety at all times.

The approach is normally cumulative, that is to say, the regulator may consider that, in a number of breach situations, the circumstances are not so serious as to suggest that the licensee has failed the test. However, considered on a cumulative basis, the regulator may conclude that there has been a lack of fitness and propriety.

Normally, the onus is on the applicant or licensee (as the case may be) to show that he or she is 'fit and proper', and not on the regulator to demonstrate the contrary.

There are three elements to the 'fit and proper' criterion: integrity, solvency and competence.

Integrity is difficult to define, but it embraces honesty and correct conduct whether in respect of clients, other licensees, the market or the regulator. Integrity demands an ongoing, disciplined approach to high standards of behaviour and honesty. Integrity manifests itself in many ways, such as in the creation of meaningful controls and procedures. Similarly, attitudes towards customers and the care of their assets reflect integrity. The process of time shows the degree to which integrity forms part of a licensee's attitude. Clearly, at the application stage, the regulator will have to assess the likelihood of the applicant acting with integrity once (and if) licensed.

Solvency means financial soundness. It includes being able to meet liabilities as they become due and, like integrity, it involves many factors, including whether the person has been the subject of any judgment or debt that remains outstanding or whether the person has made any arrangements with his creditors, filed for bankruptcy, had assets sequestrated, or been involved in these types of proceedings. It also includes whether the person has been adjudged civilly liable by a court for any fraud, misfeasance or other misconduct. Solvency applies both to the corporate licensee and to the principals behind the licensee.

Competence is not simply the avoidance of incompetence and negligence and mismanagement. It includes reliability and compliance with statutory rules, regulations and also codes of practice and guidance notes.

There are three parts to this third element of the 'fit and proper' test: qualifications, experience and performance. To demonstrate competence, people involved in the business of a licensee must be knowledgeable and efficient and comply with the rules. Employees must understand the business and the instruments and markets in which they operate. So a regulator will take into account the qualifications and experience of those involved (including controllers and directors), and the way in which business is transacted.

More generally, a licence holding company should be prudently and profitably managed and be capable of providing an efficient and reliable service to clients. The business should have adequate controls, and it should maintain sufficient records. A detailed business plan covering at least the first three years of operation is normally necessary.

Instructions and procedures must be in place to enable the licence-holding company to provide a high quality service to clients. This includes anti-money laundering procedures/anti-terrorist financing in general and verification of identity and suspicious transaction reporting (see section 8.9 below) in particular.

On the basis that most businesses rely on computer-based systems, competence includes information technology support that is adequate to maintain the integrity of the licensee's operating systems and security.

Competence emanates from an attitude of mind and is thus linked closely with integrity.

Examples of what might lead to the conclusion that a person is not 'fit and proper' might stem from discovering that the person has acted fraudulently or dishonestly or was convicted of a criminal offence and has not disclosed this fact to the regulator. The person may have been censured or criticised by a court or disqualified and/or prohibited by a court from being a director of a company. The person may have given the regulator false, inaccurate, misleading or incomplete information, or may have omitted to declare material information despite not being asked for it directly.

Jurisdictions adopt their own rules, but this description provides an indication of the type of principles that are likely to be included.

6.9 The 'Know Your Customer' criterion

Knowing one's customer is a part of the 'fit and proper' concept. A licensed service provider cannot claim to be acting competently or with integrity if it is not operating an effective 'Know Your Customer' (KYC) policy. KYC includes 'verification of identity', which is based on the premise that, if a service provider undertakes appropriate research on a prospective client before entering into a financial relationship with that person, there is a lesser probability that accounts will be opened (in ignorance) for undesirable people. The concept has a wide range of applications but is particularly apposite in respect of financial services. Accordingly, what constitutes 'undesirable' depends to an extent on the circumstances. For example, it might mean a money launderer in respect of a new banking customer but it could mean also a person who has falsified information on an application for a licence. KYC is part of the Customer Due Diligence Process (see sections 13 and 21 below).

Reverting to the axiom described above that, in regulation, prevention is always better than cure, it follows that it is much easier not to open a bad account in the first place than to open it and then to have to deal with the ensuing difficulties.

6.10 Capital adequacy in the EU

There are two important European Union Directives that concern capital adequacy. These are the revised Investment Services Directive (ISD) and the Risk Based Capital Directive (CAD3).

6.10.1 Investment Services Directive

Certain changes in the EU financial markets prompted new legislation on investment services. Even though the 1993 Investment Services Directive (ISD) was considered to be '"pivotal" to the integration of the investment services market'[27], its rules became outdated as the principles of the basis on which it was structured were in fact aimed at addressing the reality and situations of the industry in the late 1980s. Accordingly, as part of its Financial Services Action Plan, the EU recognised that, if the ISD were to remain the cornerstone of an integrated securities market, the ISD needed to be revised. A proposal for a new Directive for Investment Services and regulated markets was made to replace the 1993 Directive. The EU said that the new Directive – to be known as the Markets in Financial Instruments Directive (MiFID) – would 'increase harmonisation of national rules and meet two key prerequisites for the completion of the Internal Market in financial services. First it would give investment firms an

---

[27] Financial Services Policy Group, 'Action plan and Investment Services Reform', *Single Market News*, 2000, p. 3.

effective "single passport" . . . Second, it would make sure investors enjoyed a high level of protection.'[28] Following the Commission's proposal in November 2002 for an upgrading of the ISD, the new Directive was adopted in April 2004.

The MiFID provides (inter alia) for more efficient mutual recognition procedures between Member States. 'It is designed to adapt to changes in markets and trading technology, accommodate new instruments and facilitate, for example, competition between exchanges or between exchanges and newer alternative trading systems (ATS). It will also harmonise the operation of regulated markets, removing all concentration rules under which some Member States have required trades to be routed through national exchanges.'[29] Issues that arose included the provisions concerning transparency and conflicts of interest.

The MiFID is a 'framework directive' under the so-called Lamfalussy law-making model (see section 5 below), that distinguishes the 'framework principles' from the 'implementing technical' details. As a result, the MiFID, which aims at achieving more comprehensive harmonisation in the area of securities regulation, will be complemented by a number of implementing measures which, following consultation with the Committee of European Securities Regulators (CESR), will be issued by the European Commission in the form of Regulations and/or Directives.[30] (The CESR is made up of representatives from the Regulatory Authorities of Member States. The role of CESR is to advise the Commission in the field of securities. It may be consulted by the Commission on issues relating to securities, in particular for the preparation of draft implementing measures. See section 5 below.)

With effect from October 2006, Member States are required to adopt laws, regulations and administrative provisions to transpose the MiFID and the implementing measures which will be issued by the EC Commission. Firms and markets have another six months (until 30 April 2007) to adapt their structures and procedures to these new requirements.[31]

---

[28] Press Release, European Commission, Reference IP/02/1706, 19 November 2002, http://europa.eu.int/rapid/pressReleasesAction.do?reference=IP/02/1706&format=html.

[29] Alistair Milne, 'Capital Adequacy', *Securities Review,* July–August 2003, p. 26.

[30] C. P. Buttigieg, *Implementing the Markets in Financial Instruments Directive, Topic: Regulated Markets, MTFs and Systematic Internalisers – Transparency, Transaction Reporting and Freedom of Movement,* Malta Financial Services Authority Conference, June 2005, p. 2.

[31] Directive on Markets in Financial Instruments ('MiFID'): Commission Extends Transposition Deadline and Continues Consultation on Implementing Measures, European Commission, IP/05/759, June 2005, p. 1.

6.10.2 Capital Requirements Directive

The EU rules on capital adequacy date back to 1988 and are contained in the Capital Adequacy Directive 1993 and in the Consolidated Banking Directive 2000. Work on a new capital directive began in 1999. In July 2003, the European Commission issued its third consultative document on the proposed EU framework for regulatory capital. The Capital Requirements Directive will be an update of the 1993 Directive. After the Basel II rules (see section 6.10.4 below) were agreed in 2004, the European Commission made proposals for a new Capital Requirements Directive that would embrace banks and investment firms in the EU. There will be three levels:

- Pillar 1, simple/intermediate (due to become operational by the end of 2006, which corresponds to the Basel II timetable (see section 6.10.4 below)) and the advanced approach (from the end of 2007).
- Pillar 2, the supervisory review process; and
- Pillar 3, public disclosure.

The Directive is designed to ensure that banks and investment companies authorised under the ISD hold adequate capital. The rules are based on Basel II (see section 6.10.4 below) and are expected to apply to around 35,000 credit institutions in Europe and all financial firms operating in Europe including asset managers etc. One of the questions which non-banks were most interested in was not whether, but the extent to which the application of capital rules designed for banks will disadvantage them. Attempts have been made to exempt those investment firms whose range of services is very narrow from having to apply the operational risk charge.

Out of the five areas on which it was proposed to levy a capital charge, operational risk was the area about which there were greatest concerns. It represents the risk of loss arising as a result of a firm operating with weak procedures, systems, staff or even from external events. The application of a capital charge is as novel for banks as for other financial services. (The other four areas are: credit risk, position risk, settlement/counter-party risk and foreign exchange/commodity risk.) It is envisaged that investment firms will set aside capital based on the greatest of these areas (which is likely to be operational risk for non-banks). Currently, the amount of capital required is calculated by reference to an 'expenditure based requirement'. In future, the method to be adopted is that which requires the greater amount of capital.[32]

> The directive seeks to bring supervisory practices among the member states broadly into line and to enhance cooperation between supervisors. Specifically, it proposes a 'consolidated supervisor' for banking groups which operate across-border.[33]

The EU presented its proposals for a new Capital Adequacy Directive on 14 July 2004. A press release dated 14 July 2004 said that '[t]he proposal sets out new rules on capital requirements . . . [and] . . . reflects the flexible structure and the major components of the Basel II Accord, but has been tailored to the specific features of the EU market'.[34] The European Parliament plenary vote is expected to take place in September 2005.

6.10.3 Basel Capital Accord

In July 1988, the Basel Committee on Banking Supervision (BCBS) published the Basel Capital Accord, which established minimum capital standards and a common framework for measuring capital adequacy. These minimum standards and the measurement framework have been followed not only in member countries, but also in virtually all other countries having internationally active banks. The 1988 capital framework was not intended to be static but was intended to evolve over time. Perhaps, one of the most important attributes of the Accord was its simplicity. The core of the original calculation on the adequacy of bank capital was a calculation based on risk weightings applied to the assets which a bank carried on its balance sheet – and gave rise to what was known as Tier 1 and Tier 2 capital. The level at which banks were required to maintain capital was set at 8 per cent of risk weighted assets. Assets were allocated risk weightings, ranging from 0 per cent (for government debt) to 100 per cent (for unsecured lending to consumers). In due course, banks reduced their holdings of assets that required more capital (e.g. mortgages) and increased assets that carried low risk

---

[32] 'Regulatory Capital', *Securities and Investment Review*, November–December 2003, p. 16.
[33] 'Basel II and the Capital Requirements Directive', EurActiv.com, 23 June 2005.
[34] 'Commission Proposes New Capital Requirements for Banks and Investment Firms', Press Release, European Commission, IP/04/899, 14 July 2004.

weightings, so they were able to support more assets with the same amount of capital.

In the 1990s, banks became increasingly sensitive about how much capital they were required to maintain in their business, and developed sophisticated models for calculating that amount. A November 1991 amendment to the Accord provided more precision regarding the inclusion of general provisions or general loan-loss reserves as part of bank capital. In April 1995, the Committee issued revised proposals to incorporate within the Capital Accord the market risks arising from banks' open positions in foreign exchange, traded debt securities, equities, commodities and options. The main change from an initial proposal in April 1993 was that banks should be permitted, subject to strict qualitative and quantitative standards, to use their own internal models to measure market risk. An amendment at the end of 1995 had the effect of bilateral netting of banks' credit exposures in derivative products and expanded the matrix of add-on factors. Further work followed to expand the 1988 capital framework to make the capital of banks more sensitive to risks other than credit risk – its original focus. The risks incorporated include operational risk. The outcome was the Basel Committee's Capital Accord (referred to as Basel II).

6.10.4 Basel II

In 1999, the Committee proposed a new approach to capital adequacy. The revised framework was issued in June 2004. The Capital Accord recognised market risk and credit risk, but all other risks are regarded as being covered implicitly. The new approach – Basel II – leaves market risk unchanged but makes alterations to credit risk assessment, and introduces operational risk. It is an enhancement of the provisions of credit risk exposure in the current Accord but it differs from the latter because it requires capital to cover operational risk also. (This includes internal controls, people, procedures and external events.) Basel II aims to make the capital of banks more sensitive to risk.

Basel II is based on three pillars. Pillar 1 is quantitative: it specifies how much capital banks must provide against various types of risk – minimum capital requirements – by assigning risk weightings to different types of assets depending on their maturity date and on the credit rating of the counterparty. Pillar 1 has three dimensions: credit risk, market risk and operational risk. The definition of regulatory capital has not been changed by Basel II – and neither has the minimum capital

ratio (8 per cent) – the market risk part is not new. Under the operational risk part of Pillar 1, significant responsibilities are imposed upon
a bank's board, committees and senior management to approve and to
understand systems and operation of the credit rating system and the
variances it produces between theory and practice. Banks have some
options in measuring credit risk. The definition of risk weighted assets
has changed and more detailed weights are introduced, as compared to
Basel I. The most straightforward approach employs external data (supplied by credit rating agencies etc.). Alternatively, banks may use their
own internal ratings – the internal ratings based approach (IRB) – which
requires a substantial amount of data to be collated in-house. This allows
banks to use their own information to estimate the probability of a
default, and this will be adopted as part of the measurement of credit
risk. Banks are entitled to use their own Value at Risk ('VaR') models –
although it is likely that only the largest international banks will have the
resources to accommodate this concession. The probabilities will be
incorporated within a formula (the 'risk curve') devised by the Basel
Committee on Banking Supervision. This curve will be used to determine the level of capital that is appropriate for respective categories of
exposure.

This follows through to Pillar 2, which includes oversight responsibilities (which boils down to corporate governance and internal controls). Pillar 2 requires the regulator to assess the bank's management
and performance. Banks will have to increase their capital if a regulator
tells them they must.

Pillar 3 focuses on market discipline and disclosure. It requires banks
to make substantially increased disclosures about risks to capital and
profit. Pillar 3 complements the work of regulators and supervisors.
This will require 'business leaders to embed a risk culture that drives
employees to target appropriate customers, to abide by a formal code of
ethics, and to ensure that business processes are reliable and risk related
information is gathered and disclosed appropriately'.[35]

The Committee's intention was to incorporate Basel II within the
third Capital Adequacy Directive (CAD3; see section 6.10.4 above),
and thereby make it become part of the law prevailing within the
European Union. In the EU, Basel II and CAD3 apply not only to
'internationally active banks' but also to investment businesses and asset

---

[35] 'Basel II: Making the Smart Move: Frontiers in Finance', KPMG, November 2003, p. 26.

managers. (Compare this to the USA where it is anticipated that Basel II will apply to only the largest banks (see below).) The potential complexities of the new approach – not only for the institutions involved but also for the regulators involved – are not to be underestimated. For example, in its more sophisticated forms, the efficacy of the system depends on the VaR modelling that will produce the figures in the first place. This will be a crucial part of the process that will have to be controlled objectively because, once the model is adopted, assessment is based on the quantitative results of the model, not on objective human assessment of the circumstances that give rise to the exposure. Despite the technicalities involved, the calculation of how much capital is appropriate in a given set of circumstances cannot be absolutely accurate. Accordingly, other (simpler) methods may have some value still.

Some problems remain. One commentator said that:

> Basel II is highly discouraging to cross-border competition . . . [W]e must not copy Basel II into CAD and set it in stone for the next decade . . . A working document of November 2002 acknowledges this . . . But this flexibility does not go anything like far enough . . . Otherwise, political pressures are all too likely to create instead a framework that mistakenly applies sophisticated risk measurement to a mass of smaller financial institutions, places huge compliance costs on the industry, blocks competition, and encourages widely varying national differences in capital regulation and supervision.[36]

The new capital adequacy framework was due to be finalised by November 2003 and was due to come into force in 2006. In fact, it was not until 26 June 2004 that the central bank governors and the heads of bank supervisory authorities in the G10 endorsed the publication of the 'International Convergence of Capital Measurement and Capital Standards: A Revised Framework' (Basel II). The Basel Committee (see section 9.3 above) anticipates effective implementation by end 2006. However, Basel anticipated that the Advanced Internal Ratings Based approach for credit risk (IRB) and the Advance Measurement Approaches for operational risk would be available from end of 2007. Meanwhile, Wim Duisenberg, President of the European Central Bank, announced in September 2003 that, in Europe, a twelve-month delay in implementation (until the end of 2007) was likely in light of the complexity,

---

[36] Alistair Milne, 'Capital Adequacy', *Securities Review*, July–August 2003, p. 27.

prescriptive nature and cost to implement. Both China and India have rejected the adoption of Basel II. In the USA, only the ten largest banks will be obliged to adhere to the new rules (although around twelve more are likely to do so voluntarily).[37]

It has been suggested that 'capital requirements should not change significantly as a result of Basel . . . [C]apital requirements should drop substantially at a bank with a prime business portfolio that is well collateralised. On the other hand, a bank with a high risk portfolio will face higher capital requirements, and consequently limits on its business potential'.[38]

Although all issues had not been resolved at the time, Basel II was approved by the world's central bankers on 26 June 2004. It will come into force in stages as from the end of 2006.

6.11 The single passport

The free movement of capital and services within Europe was envisaged as far back as 1957 in the Treaty of Rome. Within the European Union, a licence issued by one Member State is valid in every other Member State – which means that a licensee in one EU country may establish a presence in another Member State and conduct licensable activity there without the need to obtain a licence in that location. The particular rules of the home state will prevail in most circumstances. In practice, the system could work better, but this might improve over time. That said, on 30 May 2005, UniCredit, Italy's largest bank, and HVB Group, Germany's second largest bank, confirmed that they were negotiating a merger. On 12 June 2005, the takeover was announced. Thirteen years after the creation of the single market, Europe's first significant banking merger happened. (Santander Central Hispano (Spain) acquired Abbey (UK) in 2004.)

While the theory of the Single Passport is entirely clear in theory, the committee of 'Wise Men' (see section 5 below) believed that the ambiguity in many of the EU's texts allowed different interpretations of the same rules affecting the same types of business. One text suggests that this 'violated the requirement of the so-called "competitive neutrality" of supervision – meaning that different supervisors in the EU should

---

[37] 'Bank Reform Faces Delay Says ECB', *Financial Times*, 11 September 2003, p. 1.
[38] 'Basel II: Making the Smart Move: Frontiers in Finance', KPMG, November 2003, p. 27.

implement the law in the same manner'.[39] Clearly, there is still some way to go before the Treaty of Rome's aspirations are fulfilled in respect of a pan-EU securities market.

6.12 Conduct of business

Conduct of business is nothing more than the application of good corporate governance procedures. 'The key to financial stability lies ultimately with the institutions themselves and in particular on their risk analysis, management and control systems.'[40] The significance should not be under-estimated, since '[t]he most fundamental change that is required to make globalisation work in the way that it should is a change in governance.'[41] Regulation is the discipline employed to help to ensure that legal persons adopt appropriate standards of activity and behaviour. Regulation also serves to ensure that the degree of risk undertaken is acceptable – relative to the resources of the licence-holding company – and that costs are not saved by cutting corners.

However, 'conduct of business rules' represent an additional cost to doing business. So, there has to be an appropriate balance to ensure that, where a situation demands it, adequate resources are allocated – and that there is demonstrable benefit arising from the cost. Some investors need more protection than others. For example, 'widows and orphans' (a term adopted to describe those who are most vulnerable whether actually widows or orphans or anyone else) deserve greater protection than high net worth investors (HNWIs) or professional investors (PIs) respectively. HNWIs can afford advisors and PIs are able to look after themselves. However, all investors are affected by what is referred to as 'asymmetry of information'. Frequently, 'investors' do not have all the information about financial organisations (e.g. banks) that they might need in order to assess the soundness of the institution to which they have entrusted their money – and, even where they have that information, they may not be able to interpret it correctly (see section 6.2 above). Accordingly, investors can rightly claim to need a measure of protection but

---

[39] Gerard Hertig and Ruben Lee, *Four Predicitions about the Future of EU Securities Regulation*, January 2003, p. 5.

[40] Hans Falkena, Roy Bamber, David Llewellyn and Tim Store, *Financial Regulation in South Africa*, Financial Sector Forum, 2001, p. 53.

[41] Joseph Stiglitz, *Globalisation and its Discontents*, Penguin Books, 2000, p. 226.

it is important to make absolutely clear to investors that the objective of
the legal and regulatory system is not to prevent or to minimise losses to
investors where such losses occur through developments in capital
markets . . . The principle that the investors must bear all the inherent
risks in their investment decision . . . characterises all capital market
investments . . . The objectives of the investor protection regime are to
protect investors against fraud, negligence and conflict of interests . . . fair
and transparent operation and that investors are adequately informed of
the risks involved in their investment.[42]

6.13 Regulation and crises

One feature of financial services regulation is that it is usually negative,
that is to say, it is designed to stop a practice that is considered undesirable. Further, financial services regulation is frequently reactive – which
is why much regulation currently in force in respect of financial services
has been introduced directly after a financial disaster. Walker puts it
this way: '[T]he historical development of financial markets has always
been accompanied by crisis and collapse.'[43] The Scandanavian countries
were a case in point in the 1980s. The Banking Act 1987 was enacted in
the UK after the collapse and rescue of Johnson Matthey. 'Similarly, in
the late 1990s, the governments of Indonesia, Republic of Korea, and
Japan announced wide ranging reforms almost as a way of penalising
agencies that were seen as having failed in their regulatory responsibilities . . . [L]ight regulation in Asia turned out to be under-regula-
tion.'[44] Examples of change include the collapse of single global
institutions like BCCI, financial crises such as the Asia crisis and
macro-economic changes. For example: 'The recent dismantling of
Japan's statutory separation of banks, securities firms and trust banks,
and the 1999 US legislation removing Glass Steagall restrictions on
banks' securities activities.'[45]

---

[42] White Paper on the Governance of CISs, Financial Market Trends, OECD, No. 88, March
2005, p. 142.
[43] George Alexander Walker, *International Banking Regulation Law, Policy and Practice*,
Kluwer Law International, 2001, p. 275.
[44] Jeffrey Carmichael, 'Australia's Approach to Regulation', in *Aligning Financial Supervisory
Structures with Country Needs*, ed. Jeffrey Carmichael, Alexander Fleming and David
Llewellyn, World Bank Institute, September 2004, pp. 95 and 103.
[45] R. Dale and S. Wolfe, 'The UK Financial Services Authority: Unified Regulation in the
New Market Environment', *Journal of Banking Regulation*, Vol. 4, No. 3, 2003, p. 206.

However, it has been rightly said that 'crisis provides an opportunity for supervisors to obtain from lawmakers the teeth they need, since legislative support is often easier to obtain during crisis. Nevertheless, care should be taken to dispel any unrealistic expectations that crisis can be prevented in the future solely by passing new laws or reorganising the agencies.'[46]

6.14 Regulation in practice

While the purposes of regulating financial services are fairly clear cut, regulatory methods adopted to achieve those purposes are not identical. The methods depend on the target of regulation. Dale and Wolfe have identified five main classifications of targets: banks, investment firms, insurance companies, fund managers and securities exchanges. These authors suggest that different regulatory methods are used because the characteristics of the target are different. For example, the relationship of a bank to its customer is that of debtor/creditor. The bank uses the customer's money in the way the bank thinks best – without reference to the customer. The balance sheet of a bank comprises liquid liabilities that are often short term in nature and long dated illiquid assets whose value (e.g. in a liquidation scenario) is uncertain. Depositors face the asymmetry of information (see section 6.2 above) problem, because the information at their disposal will not be adequate to enable them to assess the riskiness of the assets that their deposit liabilities are funding. Banks are vulnerable to systemic risk.

An insurance company is quite different. In this case, the balance sheet will have long dated liabilities and liquid assets. The liquidity transformation between banks and insurance companies is glaring.

In between, there are other categories. For example, '[t]he important principles in OFC securities business are those addressing information sharing and cooperation, market intermediation, and collective investment schemes'.[47] The assets of an investment firm should retain their value whether the firm remains viable or becomes insolvent because the

---

[46] Stefan Ingves, 'Issues in the Unification of Supervision: Lessons from the Swedish Experience', in *Aligning Financial Supervisory Structures with Country Needs*, ed. Jeffrey Carmichael, Alexander Fleming and David Llewellyn, World Bank Institute, September 2004, p. 160.

[47] 'Offshore Financial Centres – The Assessment Program – A Progress Report and the Future of the Program', IMF, 31 July 2003, p. 14.

assets should be liquid and the liabilities should be short and frequently secured. Fund managers are different again because the customer's money is invested on the customer's behalf – and remains intact despite what happens to the firm. Securities exchanges should not pose systemic risk. Accordingly, the regulatory tools used reflect the innate characteristic of the type of financial service provided. Table 4 in Appendix 1 provides a summary.

Regulating a bank means making sure that it does not fail. If it fails, there may or may not be 'lender of last resort' facilities available from the central bank. There might be contagion because there is systemic risk. Bank regulators will pay close attention to how risk is measured, the quality of the loan book, the appropriateness of provisions and the adequacy of capital. Regulating an investment firm means making sure that assets of the firm are clearly separated from those of the clients. The firm's assets must be liquid and easily redeemable at market prices. Valuations should be precise because prices are current and ascertainable. Insurance regulators will want to be sure of long-term viability. Solvency considerations and actuarial valuations are critical measures. Fund managers will have to demonstrate appropriate conduct of business procedures. Exchanges are often self-regulated.

It has been said that 'concerns about customer satisfaction – important though they are – cannot provide a foundation upon which to build effective regulatory strategy. Client satisfaction always has to be integrated with, and in some instances weighed against, mission accomplishment.'[48]

In this respect, '[e]vidence is mounting to justify questioning whether global financial institutions, operating transnationally to move money instantaneously across national borders, can be readily regulated or supervised by any one country . . . [E]ven the most sophisticated and best regulated financial centres have proved incapable of adequately overseeing the global enterprises they license.'[49] Further, 'the challenge for the regulator is to balance the public interest in controlling systemic and market risks without stamping out the new product developments'.[50] Where rules proliferate, there is always the risk that innovation will be stifled. This in itself is self-defeating. That said, it must be

---

[48] Malcolm K. Sparrow, *The Regulatory Craft*, Brookings Institution Press, 1998, p. 312.
[49] Jonathan M. Winer, 'How to Clean Up Dirty Money', *Financial Times*, 23–24 April 2002.
[50] T. Walmsley, 'Financial Regulation Report', *Financial Times*, May 1993, p. 17.

recognised that the tendency will be for rules to increase rather than to decrease. 'We live in a time of increasing demand for more effective regulation of financial reporting by companies.'[51] 'And we need to continue our work to promote a stable and predictable supervisory environment for banks world-wide.'[52]

We should not continuously and blindly increase the rules if there is a better way to attain the same objective. 'They [regulators] can ensure that standards of investor protection are met by mechanisms other than prescriptive rules, by better training, by professionalism or examinations.'[53]

It has been suggested of regulation that more formal and explicit 'business conduct' rules in the context of distinctions between types of financial institutions are being eroded and that:

> Regulation has become more interventionist and detailed, with regulatory authorities developing comprehensive rulebooks governing the way financial services are supplied. It seems that regulation and supervision are increasingly based on *functional* rather than *institutional* criteria (e.g. the consolidation requirements for banks and securities business) and that there is greater emphasis on capital requirements – rules on the allowable definitions of capital structure and capital adequacy. Lastly in this respect, information and disclosure requirements continue to be extended.[54]

6.15 Self-regulation

Arguably, the concept has proved to be more satisfactory in some parts of the global financial services industry than in others. For example, in the UK, the Banking Code and the Business Banking Code (which deal with conduct of business issues in respect of services like current accounts, personal loans and credit cards) represent types of self-regulation.

However, in the UK, self-regulation is more likely to be linked to the name of Professor L. C. B. Gower. In 1981, Professor Gower was commissioned by the UK Government to advise it on what needed to be done

---

[51] D. McBarnet, *Financial Markets: Regulation, Risk and a Global Economy*, Oxford University, Department of Socio-Legal Studies, 1992, p. 1.

[52] Robin Leigh-Pemberton, 'Recent Banking Difficulties', *Bank of England Quarterly Bulletin*, February 1993.

[53] T. Walmsley, 'Financial Regulation Report', *Financial Times*, May 1993, p. 17.

[54] Hans Falkena, Roy Bamber, David Llewellyn and Tim Store, *Financial Regulation in South Africa*, Financial Sector Forum, 2001, p. 81.

to protect investors in securities, including statutory changes and control of those involved in the industry. Professor Gower recommended a system that incorporated self-regulation within a statutory framework. It was envisaged that it would involve four self-regulatory organisations (SROs) which would operate under statute. The Council for the Securities Industry would coordinate the SROs and the Government was to supervise them. As it turned out, the Securities and Investments Board (SIB) became the key player. The SIB was a private sector organisation with which practitioners were deeply involved; its function was to oversee the regulators, i.e. the SROs. The Financial Services Act 1986 created the SIB with three SROs initially. In practice, the SIB was able to exercise only limited powers, for example it was not involved directly with the SROs.

It has been said that 'a lack of clear objectives, a lack of powers for [the] SIB, and the inappropriate extension of the concept of self-regulation crippled the Financial Services Act at birth'.[55] The system came under strain caused not only by a scandal in relation to the way that pensions were being sold at the time but also because of the profound changes that were happening in financial services globally. These changes blurred what were once distinct lines of demarcation between the products of different service providers. Banks were competing for business that was formerly considered as the business of insurance companies – and vice versa. New products were straddling what had been two disciplines so that it was unclear whether some products were investments or deposits.

The Labour Party (in opposition at the time) indicated that, if they assumed power, there would be a fundamental reform of the regulatory system. When they assumed power, they stuck to their electoral pledge in this respect with a vengeance. The reform turned out to be more fundamental than most people could have envisaged. On 20 May 1997, the UK's Chancellor of the Exchequer, Mr Gordon Brown, announced that the SIB would assume responsibility for a statutory securities commission and banking supervision, instead of the Bank of England (see section 6.20 below). Subsequently, these responsibilities were increased further to include building societies and insurance companies. Mr Brown said:

---

[55] Michael Taylor, *Regulatory Leviathan: Will Super-SIB Work?*, CTA Publishing, 1997, p. 11.

> It has long been apparent that the regulatory structure introduced by the
> Financial Services Act 1986 (FSA) is not delivering the standard of super-
> vision and investor protection that the industry and the public have a
> right to expect. The current two-tier system splits responsibility between
> the Securities and Investments Board (SIB) and the Self-Regulatory Or-
> ganizations (SROs) together with the Recognised Professional Bodies. This
> division is inefficient, confusing for investors and lacks accountability and
> a clear allocation of responsibilities. Reform is long overdue . . . [I]t is clear
> that the distinctions between different types of financial institution –
> banks, securities firms and insurance companies – are becoming increas-
> ingly blurred. Many of today's financial institutions are regulated by a
> plethora of different supervisors. This increases the cost and reduces the
> effectiveness of supervision.[56]

The SIB was dabbed as 'Super-SIB', at least until the name and style of
the new integrated regulatory authority had been approved. This turned
out to be the Financial Services Authority (FSA), which, although not the
world's first 'single regulator' (Sweden adopted this style much earlier)
still managed to set a certain style which others were to follow.

6.16 The Twin Peaks model

The Twin Peaks model was proposed by Michael Taylor, Director of
Regulation and Compliance Programmes at the ISMA Centre for Education and Research in Securities Markets at Reading University, UK, as an
alternative to Super-SIB. Mr Taylor suggested that:

> neither institutional nor functional regulation is now an appropriate way
> to regulate a market in which it is becoming increasingly difficult to
> distinguish a bank from a securities firm, or a credit derivative from an
> insurance contract or a deposit from an investment . . . [O]nly a regulatory
> approach based on objectives rather than institutions or products is a
> satisfactory solution to the problem of structuring a regulatory system.[57]

The objects of regulation have already been considered. To achieve what
Mr Taylor described as the three 'primary regulatory objectives',
he proposed allocating responsibility for the stability of the financial
system to one agency and allocating responsibility for the protection of

---

[56] Speech by UK Chancellor of the Exchequer to the House of Commons, 20 May 1997.
[57] Michael Taylor, *Regulatory Leviathan: Will Super-SIB Work?*, CTA Publishing, 1997,
p. 55.

individuals and the preservation of the integrity of the markets to a second agency. In practice, retail conduct of business could be separated from market integrity functions. This would have meant a prudential regulator (Financial Stability Commission), a consumer protection regulator (Consumer Protection Commission) and a transparency and integrity of markets regulator (Market Integrity Commission).

The Twin Peaks model was not adopted in the UK but the style adopted in Australia goes along Twin Peaks lines (see section 7.3 below). Safeguarding the payments system and maintaining systemic stability remain as functions of The Reserve Bank of Australia. Similarly, in the UK (as described elsewhere), the Bank of England shed regulatory responsibility but retained responsibility for systemic stability. This is feasible provided that those persons responsible for systemic stability have a positive and transparent working relationship with those persons entrusted with prudential responsibility.

6.17 Regulation Offshore

'More and greater regulation for offshore centres imposed from above has led to some underlying gloom around the world.'[58]

While the 'Onshore' and 'Offshore' environments have certain common features (see section 3.13 above), they are not identical. Accordingly, and speaking generally, the style of regulation applied 'Offshore' may well be different to that applied 'Onshore'. This does not mean that regulation 'Offshore' is inferior to regulation 'Onshore', it simply means that the styles are not identical – for reasons explained in earlier chapters.

Neither does this mean that a lower standard of customer care prevails or that the application of anti-money laundering rules is less intrusive or that the regulators are less diligent. It simply means that the 'rules' are tailored to the demands of the environment. Thus, where the same products and services are offered both 'Onshore' and 'Offshore', then ordinarily it would be reasonable to expect similar rules and standards. In theory at least, there should be no difference in the degree of risk between trading 'Offshore' and trading 'Onshore'. Frequently, this is not how it seems as discussed in section 3.15 above.

---

[58] Bob Reynolds, 'From the Editor', *Offshore Red*, July/August 2002, p. 117.

A significant matter in respect of 'Offshore' is the standard and extent to which regulation is applied there. As described earlier, there is a suggestion abroad that the rules are so benign that they impose little or no onus on those financial organisations that are subject to them.

In this respect, it has been said of financial services providers establishing 'Offshore' that '[t]ax neutrality has been the main driver . . . but some firms have also sought less onerous regulatory interference'.[59] The question is whether or not this is true. The answer will be left to the reader to determine – in due course.

6.17.1 Trust and company services providers

Meanwhile, Transparency International, an international non-governmental organisation whose object is to combat corruption, has said in a report entitled 'Corruption and Money Laundering in the UK',

> money laundering can take place using 'front companies' where a real business is conducted and illegal profits are mixed with legitimate revenues, as well as 'shell companies' that have no trading substance but conceal the identity of the ultimate owner of the assets controlled by the company. Service providers can set up the shell entities in a range of jurisdictions, provide registered offices, organise directors or company secretaries and arrange for people to act as trustees or nominee shareholders.[60]

Generally speaking, there are no rules concerning the provision of trust and corporate services, because, in most jurisdictions, this is not regarded as a licensable activity. In this respect, Transparency International has said that: 'It seems to us unconscionable that the UK Crown Dependencies and overseas territories have been pushed to introduce legislation, yet the UK itself lacks definitive plans to do so.'[61] A small number of jurisdictions (see section 7 above) represent the exception to this general rule. For example, Mauritius issued 'Guidelines for Management Companies (Corporate Service Providers)' in 1992. The Isle of

---

[59] 'What Future for "Offshore Financial Centres"?', *Compliance Monitor*, July/August 2000, p. 246.
[60] 'Lack of Regulation "Turning London into a Haven for Money Launderers"', *Financial Times*, 29 October 2004.
[61] 'Lack of Regulation "Turning London into a Haven for Money Launderers"', *Financial Times*, 29 October 2004.

Man enacted the Corporate Services Providers Act in 2000 (and updated it in 2002 – and is currently in consultation concerning rules for the provision of trust services). Guernsey issued the Regulation of Fiduciaries, Administration Business and Company Directors in 2000, and Jersey published the Financial Services (Extension) (Jersey) Law in 2000. (See section 7 above.)

In September 2002, a Working Group (comprising representatives of the Offshore Group of Banking Supervisors (OGBS) and representatives of four G7 countries (France, Italy, the Netherlands and the UK) and of the FATF, the IMF and the OECD) published the Trust and Company Services Providers Draft Statement of Best Practice (see section 7 above and section 9.21 below). The Statement of Practice provides for the following:

- a standard of integrity for all involved;
- statement of requirements in respect of proper business conduct;
- the latter might include corporate governance, customer due diligence and conduct of client business; and
- arrangements permitting regulators for AML/CFT purposes to obtain information on beneficiaries and owners of companies and those connected with trusts.

In February 2004, the OGBS Statement of Best Practice was supplemented by a paper entitled 'Securing Effective Exchange of Information and Supervision in Respect of Trust and Company Services Providers'.

The OGBS's work is timely and should help all jurisdictions involved in providing these services. This is a significant demonstration of how, in some respects, regulators 'Offshore' exercise greater controls than apply 'Onshore'. Despite that, as at the end of 2003, the Directors of the IMF 'noted that supervision and regulation of the non-banking sector, in particular needed to be strengthened in many OFCs'[62] ('non-bank financial institutions' includes corporate service providers).

Table 5 in Appendix 1 indicates the number of companies registered in some jurisdictions.

---

[62] 'IMF Executive Board Reviews the Assessment Program on Offshore Financial Centres', IMF, 24 November 2003.

It is estimated that 15,000 companies a year are incorporated in Hong Kong for offshore purposes and another 50,000 or so in the other offshore jurisdictions. This means that the total number of companies formed for offshore purposes exceeds 140,000 per annum. Estimates indicate that, by the turn of the century, a minimum of another half a million offshore companies will have been incorporated worldwide.[63]

6.18 Auditors and accountants

The auditor must undertake his work 'critically' and with 'professional scepticism'.[64] If it is accepted that the directors of a company are obliged to prepare the company's accounts and to ensure that the company satisfies its corporate responsibilities and that the auditor's job is to provide independent confirmation that the company has done so, the auditor will perform work that a regulator will find invaluable. 'An independent audit fulfils an essential role not only for the shareholders/regulators but also for the wider market participants in providing accurate information about a company.'[65]

Why should this be so? First, the annual accounts of a licence-holding company represent an important part of the information that Regulators use as part of their 'off-site supervision' (see section 6.19 below). The annual accounts differ from other types of information submitted in that the accounts are verified by an independent external professional person – the auditor. Accordingly, the annual audited financial statements of licensees are very significant for their regulators. In the UK, the Bingham report recommended that auditors should have the duty – not just the right – to report to the appropriate authority any adverse facts they came upon during their work. This is all good news for the regulator – who wants to be able to depend on an auditor's work.

---

[63] www.offshoresimple.com/tax_havens_history.htm.

[64] 'Objectives and General Principles Governing an Audit of Financial Statements: Auditing Practice Board', para. 11, p. 15, as quoted in D. Singh, 'The Role of Third Parties in Banking Regulation and Supervision', *Journal of International Banking Regulation*, Vol. 4, No. 3, 2003, p. 278.

[65] D. Singh, 'The Role of Third Parties in Banking Regulation and Supervision', *Journal of International Banking Regulation*, Vol. 4, No. 3, 2003, p. 281.

It is clearly important that the infrastructure of a financial services centre includes competent auditing firms. The practice of auditors (and accountants) has been called into question in many instances:

- (Enron is perhaps the most blatant example since it led to the demise of Andersen). During 2000, Enron 'paid Andersens about $52 million or $1 million per week for its work. Andersens' consulting fees at Enron exceeded its auditing fees for the first time in 1999, and, in 2000, totalled about $27 million compared to auditing fees of about $25 million'.[66] Further, a failure by Andersens to object does not preclude a finding that the Enron board, with Andersens' concurrence, knowingly allowed Enron to use high risk accounting and failed in its fiduciary duty to ensure the company engaged in responsible financial reporting.[67] Lastly, the US Subcommittee report cited above found that '[t]he independence of the Enron Board of Directors was compromised by financial ties between the company and certain Board members. The Board also failed to ensure the independence of the company's auditor, allowing Andersen to provide internal audit and consulting services while serving as Enron's outside auditor'.[68]
- 'The firm then known as Coopers & Lybrand, and individual partners were fined for their failures to report to IMRO (a UK regulatory agency) various regulatory breaches by the Maxwell Group.'[69]
- Barings Bank collapsed as a result of losses of $827 million, which emanated from losses incurred by Nick Leeson. These losses went undetected because of weak internal controls. 'Coopers & Lybrand audited Barings, including its worldwide subsidiaries . . . The case fundamentally calls into question the reliance placed on the internal

---

[66] Hearing Record 7b, Summary of Fees – Activity Overview (Audit Committee Presentation, 5/1/00), as quoted in 'The Role of the Board of Directors in Enron's Collapse', Report 107–70, Prepared by the Permanent Sub-Committee on Investigations of the Committee on Governmental Affairs, United States Senate, 8 July 2002, p. 58.

[67] 'The Role of the Board of Directors in Enron's Collapse', Report 107–70, Prepared by the Permanent Sub-Committee on Investigations of the Committee on Governmental Affairs, United States Senate, 8 July 2002, p. 24.

[68] 'The Role of the Board of Directors in Enron's Collapse', Report 107–70, Prepared by the Permanent Sub-Committee on Investigations of the Committee on Governmental Affairs, Finding 6, United States Senate, 8 July 2002, p. 54.

[69] D. Singh, 'The Role of Third Parties in Banking Regulation and Supervision', *Journal of International Banking Regulation*, Vol. 4, No. 3, 2003, p. 279.

controls at Barings, and a lack of the observance of the audit guidelines to determine whether the accounts give a "true and fair view".[70]

- 'Price Waterhouse paid BCCI liquidators $95m (£60m) and Ernst & Young paid $30m for their part in the closure of BCCI.'[71]

- As a result of conducting what was considered to be an improper business relationship with a software provider, Ernst & Young LLP was forbidden (16 April 2004) from accepting new SEC audit clients for six months and ordered to pay over US $1,686,500. 'EY partners acted recklessly and negligently in committing wilful and deliberate violations of well established rules that govern auditor independence standards in connection with business relationships with an audit client.'[72]

- In June 2005, it was reported that KPMG, 'one of the "Big Four" accounting firms that dominate auditing worldwide, said that it was negotiating with America's Department of Justice. It hopes to avoid a criminal indictment over its marketing of "abusive" tax shelters between 1996 and 2002.'[73] KPMG was charged with arranging 'dubious tax shelters that allowed rich individuals to claim over $11 billion in phoney losses and avoid $2.5 billion in taxes'.[74] The case was settled on 29 August 2005, with KPMG agreeing to pay fines of US $456 million, and agreeing to a number of conditions, including the cessation of its tax advisory business to private clients.

In October 2002, IOSCO published three papers that represent 'statements of principles to guide securities regulators in dealing with three critical areas necessary for investor confidence in securities markets. The principles describe essential features of regulatory systems requiring transparency and disclosure by listed entities; the independence of external auditors; and the need for public oversight of the audit function.'[75] The papers are:

---

[70] D. Singh, 'The Role of Third Parties in Banking Regulation and Supervision', *Journal of International Banking Regulation*, Vol. 4, No. 3, 2003, p. 280.

[71] 'Record BCCI Payout', *The Times*, 18 November 1999, p. 34, as quoted in D. Singh, 'The Role of Third Parties in Banking Regulation and Supervision', *Journal of International Banking Regulation*, Vol. 4, No. 3, 2003, p. 286.

[72] Initial Decision Release No. 249 Administrative Proceeding File No. 3-10933, In the Matter of Ernst & Young LLP Before the Securities and Exchange Commission, 16 April 2004.

[73] 'Crime and Punishment', *The Economist*, 25 June 2005, p. 96.

[74] 'Taxed', *The Economist*, 3 September 2005, p. 66.

[75] Press Release, IOSCO, 18 October 2002.

- Principles for Auditor Oversight;
- Principles of Auditor Independence and the Role of Corporate Governance in Monitoring an Auditor's Independence (October 2002); and
- Principles for Ongoing Disclosure and Material Development Reporting by Listed Entities.

On 16 March 2004, the European Commission proposed new rules that would apply to the audit of companies in Europe. The proposals include termination of the tradition for auditors to be self-regulating, replacing this practice with formal bodies (to be established by individual EC countries) that would be responsible for their regulatory oversight. The proposals also included:

- the establishment of independent committees by public companies, to engage and dismiss auditors;
- the requirement for auditors not from the EU to register with authorities locally; and
- the option to require the rotation of auditors.

Meanwhile, in the USA, the Public Company Accounting Oversight Board, whose job it is to regulate auditors in the USA said that initial inspections of the Big Four accounting firms had identified 'significant audit and accounting issues'. Despite the quality control system problems the Board had identified, its confidence in all was maintained. (The Board was formed in 2002 post-Enron and WorldCom, and the collapse of Arthur Andersen.)[76]

The KPMG tax shelter case referred to above is significant – not least because of the criminal prosecution of eight former employees, including seven former partners, for fraud.

6.18.1 Reporting accountants

The concept of the external auditor was first introduced in the UK's Banking Act 1987 (see below). The concept has been retained in sections 340–346 of the UK's Financial Services and Markets Act 2000, although the professional engaged in this capacity is now known as a 'skilled person'. A 'skilled person' may be engaged (under a contractual

---

[76] Floyd Norris, 'US Regulator Faults Big Four Accounting Firms – But Gently', *International Herald Tribune*, 27 August 2004.

arrangement) to provide 'a report on any matter' – from which the term 'reporting accountant' derives. Any report so prepared is addressed to the directors of the regulated firm. 'Skilled persons' must be approved by the UK's FSA but in practice they are frequently the auditor of the regulated firm. The concept has many advantages, but there has been an ongoing question about the independence of 'skilled persons'. A Treasury Select Committee that looked into this question after the collapse of Barings recommended that a firm other than the auditing firm should be used.

Some regulatory authorities 'Offshore' also use reporting accountants. This is particularly beneficial where the relevant authority does not have the skills in-house to do what has to be done – or does not have the manpower which a particular task may require. This type of engagement gives the reporting accountant a quasi regulatory function.

6.19 Supervision

With respect to financial services, the words 'regulation' and 'supervision' are used frequently as if they were synonyms. While there are no hard and fast rules in this respect, there might be value in considering one or two features that distinguish these disciplines. In one sense, supervision has a macro application whereas regulation has a micro application. 'But the main difference is that the protection of depositors is best pursued by setting requirements that apply bank by bank {supervision} rather than product by product or transaction by transaction {regulation}, such that the institution remains able to meet the demands of depositors as their claims fall due.'[77] It has been said elsewhere by the OECD that '[o]fficial financial supervision is concerned mainly with assessing the adequacy of governance systems and taking remedial actions when shortcomings are found'.[78] Walker refers to regulation as 'the body of legal rules, regulations or administrative requirements established by financial authorities or by market participants (generally referred to as self-regulatory systems) to limit or control the risks assumed by banks or other financial institutions and to the imposition of such provisions either generally or on the activities of a particular

---

[77] B. Quinn, 'The Bank of England's Role in Prudential Supervision', *Bank of England Quarterly Bulletin*, May 1993, p. 261.

[78] White Paper on the Governance of CISs, Financial Market Trends, OECD, No. 88, March 2005, p. 140.

bank or other institution'. He goes on to suggest that supervision refers to 'the associated or complementary process of monitoring or reviewing compliance by financial institutions with any specific sets of regulatory provisions imposed or with more general standards of prudent or proper behaviour in any particular market'.[79]

Stated simply within one sentence, 'prudential supervision' might be considered as the protection of the financial system within a jurisdiction, while 'regulation' might be considered as the protection of the consumer. 'Prudential supervision of banks makes the object of the exercise clear: it is concerned with the safety and soundness of the institution.'[80]

If this approach is adopted, supervision and regulation might be considered as complementary disciplines, designed to protect the jurisdiction that applies them. Thus, in a manner of speaking, supervisors and regulators are in the business of protection. This duty is not open-ended. There is only an extent to which regulators and supervisors can be expected to protect – but this matter is taken up elsewhere (see sections 6.2 and 6.12 above). The point should be made that the function of supervisors and regulators is not to serve licensees (see section 6.26 below). They serve taxpayers by ensuring that the jurisdiction and the licensees entitled to operate in that jurisdiction do so in accordance with the law and with the prevailing legislation and rules.

What may be said of one discipline within supervision (e.g. in respect of banking), may also apply to other disciplines such as investments and insurance. 'They [banking supervisors] seek to ensure that institutions have adequate capital and liquidity, "Fit and Proper" directors, managers and controllers and that there are systems and controls to monitor and contain the risk assumed . . . Supervisors, of course, cannot and should not second-guess the management of individual institutions.'[81]

Sambrook believes that 'supervision should be performed in a manner which will interfere as little as possible with legitimate business'.[82] While this is sound advice, it is not easily achieved, since rules have to be universally applied if they are to be fair – the concept that McBarnet

[79] George Alexander Walker, *International Banking Regulation Law, Policy and Practice*, Kluwer Law International, 2001, p. 1.

[80] B. Quinn, 'The Bank of England's Role in Prudential Supervision', *Bank of England Quarterly Bulletin*, May 1993.

[81] Robin Leigh-Pemberton, 'Recent Banking Difficulties', *Bank of England Quarterly Bulletin*, February 1993.

[82] D. Sambrook, 'Fundamentals for Offshore Success', *International Money Market*, 11 December 1992.

describes as rule-based competitive advantage.[83] McBarnet highlights three difficulties. First, there is the need to get the rules right in the first place; secondly, there is the need to adequately enforce the rules; and, lastly, there is the need to dissuade compliance in form although not in substance ('creative compliance'). 'New rules tend to simply mean new creative adaptations.'[84] From another point of view, there is always a temptation to resort to the lowest common denominator, that is, to deal with a new problem by formulating a new rule. 'Regulation in effect becomes a further stimulus for innovative use of law, both to defeat unwelcome regulation and to secure advantage over our competitors.'[85]

This compares with those specialist tax practitioners who are in business to devise clever schemes to avoid tax. As the rules become tighter, the innovations to defeat them become more elaborate and the system is perpetuated if yet more rules are introduced to defeat the innovations.

6.20 The UK model

Regulation and supervision are necessary in many systems – not least financial systems. The systems of regulation adopted in some 'Offshore Centres' are based on those that apply in the UK – so the UK is a model. It is therefore relevant to examine how these systems developed.

The supervision of banks in the UK was conducted on a non-statutory basis prior to the enactment of the Banking Act 1979. In fact, the only statute that related to supervision said of the regulator (the Bank of England – and referred to as 'the Bank') that:

> The Bank, if they think it necessary in the public interest, may request information from and make recommendations to bankers, and may, if so authorised by the Treasury, issue directions to any banker for the purpose of securing that effect is given to any such request or recommendation.[86]

---

[83] D. McBarnet, *Financial Markets: Regulation, Risk and a Global Economy*, Oxford University, Department of Socio-Legal Studies, 1992, p. 2.

[84] D. McBarnet, *Financial Markets: Regulation, Risk and a Global Economy*, Oxford University, Department of Socio-Legal Studies, 1992, p. 12.

[85] D. McBarnet, *Financial Markets: Regulation, Risk and a Global Economy*, Oxford University, Department of Socio-Legal Studies, 1992, p. 14.

[86] Bank of England Act 1946.

It is important to note that 'the Act imposes no specific requirement
on banks to comply with any directives that might be issued and lays
down no penalties for non-compliance'.[87] However, the Bank of England
had never used its powers under this Act. The Bank of England's own
description of the supervisory arrangements that existed prior to 1973/4
is as follows:

> [T]here was no overall supervision of deposit-taking institutions as such.
> On the other hand, it had long been accepted that the Bank had a
> supervisory role in relation to the fully recognised banks.

This approach to supervision first came under strain in the 1960s and
into the 1970s, with the growth in the number of banks operating in
London, and the consequent growth in competition. However, the cata-
lyst in the enactment of regulations was the 1973/4 banking crisis. ('The
Bank of England has estimated that a full-blown banking crisis costs the
country concerned an average of 16 per cent of GDP.'[88])

According to Penn,[89] the banking crisis was precipitated by 'fringe
banks' which did not pay sufficient attention to the management of their
liquidity and funded long loans with short-dated deposits. Further
problems resulted in an over-commitment to the property market. The
liquidity crisis that followed threatened to engulf even those who had
been managing their business prudently but who could not escape the
effects of a loss of confidence in the system. A rescue operation – known
as the 'lifeboat' – was mounted.

Penn points out that, in the aftermath of this crisis, it was clear that
one of the main reasons for the problems that arose was the lack of a
formal system of supervising the increasing number of deposit-takers
that had been joining the fringe of the banking system, but which were
outside the supervisory net.

At the end of 1977 and, apart from the secondary banking crisis, the
adoption of the first EC directive on the coordination of banking law (to
have been implemented by 15 December 1979) required legislation to be
put in place.

Accordingly, on 1 October 1979, the UK introduced a system requiring (by statute) that all deposit-takers should be authorised. Thus, the

---

[87] Morison, Tillet and Welch, *Banking Act 1979*, Butterworths, 1979, p. 16.

[88] David Shirreff, 'Open Wider, A Survey of International Banking', *The Economist*, 21 May
2005, p. 4.

[89] G. Penn, *Supervision Under the Banking Act 1979*, Butterworths, 1989, p. 11.

Banking Act 1979 represented the first attempt to put bank regulation on a statutory footing in the UK, although, to some extent, it seems merely to have formalised what was already understood.

The Banking Act 1987 came about because of difficulties in the UK. Penn suggested that the collapse and subsequent rescue of Johnson Matthey showed that the Banking Act 1979 was only the first move in UK regulation. The 1987 Act dispensed with the two-tier type of recognition that the 1979 Act had introduced.

On 20 May 1997, the UK's Chancellor of the Exchequer announced the intention to create the Financial Services Authority (FSA), whose responsibility would be to regulate all financial services in the UK in place of the Bank of England and a number of other agencies. The FSA was launched in October 1997 and assumed responsibility for banking and wholesale market supervision in June 1998. The FSA assumed full statutory powers in December 2001 – after the enactment of the Financial Services and Markets Act in June 2000. The FSA is privately incorporated. It is responsible to the UK Treasury (and indirectly to Parliament). The functions and responsibilities of the Treasury, the Bank of England and of the FSA are set out in an MOU dated 1997. On 31 October 2004, responsibility for the regulation of mortgages and long-term care insurance was allocated to the FSA and, on 14 January 2005, the FSA's responsibilities were widened and included the regulation of general insurance. This brought the number of firms regulated by the FSA to almost 25,800 as at 31 March 2005.

6.21 Consolidated supervision

Financial services companies used to be arranged along functional lines. That is to say, banks offered banking services exclusively and insurance companies offered insurance services exclusively. More recently, there has been a growing trend for the demarcation between what used to be discrete services to become less and less rigid, allowing one financial services group to offer a very wide range of financial services products. The traditional way to deal with the former functional style was to have a banking regulator, a securities regulator, an insurance regulator and so on. As demarcation has developed, so has the regulatory approach to it, principally in the form of consolidated supervision.

Regulators have had to adapt existing skills and to adopt new procedures to capture risks that appear in a consolidated scenario but which do not exist in a solo situation. Consolidated supervision applies to groups of companies. The procedure combines the risk profile of members to enable a composite assessment to be made of the group's risk – and how that risk is being managed. (Risk assessment is increasingly central-ised within organisational structures.) This goes hand in hand with an assessment of the adequacy of the group's capital.

The 1992 amendment to the Basel Concordat, 'Minimum Standards for the Supervision of International Banking Groups and their Cross-Border Establishments', introduced the post-BCCI requirement that international banks and banking groups should be supervised by a home country authority that capably performs 'consolidated supervision'. The present-day effect of this is that, before a bank can open a branch or a subsidiary company in an OFC, the regulator will probably require the bank to show that the home supervisor will be able to conduct consoli-dated supervision. This (inter alia) prevents establishment where the home country's bank conducts little business. 'Consolidated supervision matters because it enables the supervisor responsible to form a judgment about the totality of a group's activities, especially those that have the potential to damage confidence in the bank (the phenomenon known as "contagion"). It also helps ensure that no banking operation can escape supervision, no matter where it is located, and can prevent the double-gearing of capital. A lack of consolidated supervision of the whole BCCI group, and especially a failure to monitor the activities of the associated Cayman Islands-based holding company, ICCH, were contributory factors in its collapse.'[90]

In referring to recent financial crises in Latin America and Asia, the IMF has said that '[t]he absence of effective consolidated supervision by onshore supervisors proved to be the most important factor in permit-ting the exploitation of regulatory arbitrage offered in some OFCs through the transfer of assets and liabilities between "Offshore" estab-lishments and parent banks onshore'.[91] During the 1990s, there have been extensive global crises. Walker points out that:

> [t]he first major financial crisis of the 1990s began in Mexico in December 1994 . . . Before the financial crises in Asia during 1997 and 1998, most of the major Asian economies had experienced strong and sustainable growth . . . Underlying this economic performance however, a number

[90] 'Basle Concordat: Leading by Example Is No Longer Enough', Vol. 1, No. 3, *The Financial Regulator*, December 1996, p. 66.
[91] 'Offshore Financial Centres – The Role of the IMF', 23 June 2000, p. 5.

of potential sources of instability had already arisen. These included high relative levels of bank credit and short term debt, poor loan practices and fundamentally weak systems of bank supervision . . . The crisis in Asia began with the devaluation of the Thai baht on 2 July 1997 . . . [T]here was an almost immediate effect in other countries such as Malaysia, Indonesia and the Philippines . . . with the contagion then spreading into South Korea.[92]

6.22 Compliance

There appear to be at least three distinct elements within regulation and supervision: (1) licensing; (2) regulation; and (3) compliance. Subsequent to being licensed, the licensee is subject to ongoing regulation. Element (3) is testing to ensure compliance with the rules and conditions under which the licence has been issued. Compliance testing merely means that the business and its practices are checked against certain norms on an ongoing basis.

The interconnections – stated briefly – are as follows. Licensing includes the application process, i.e. the work carried out in order to determine whether a licence should be issued. Regulation begins once a licence is issued. A separate chapter (Chapter 7) has been devoted to this discipline, so suffice it to say here that regulation includes the work that arises in the ordinary course of the regulator's relationship with the licensee.

Once he or she issues a licence, the regulator assumes a degree of responsibility for the behaviour of its licensee, relative to the market of which it forms a part and relative to the consumers it serves. How can the regulator know what the licensee is doing? The answer is that it is not possible to know what every licensee is doing all the time – but the regulator has a responsibility to ensure that the licensee is operating in accordance with the prevailing legislation and in adherence to the terms of its licence on an ongoing basis. 'Compliance' is one name given to the discipline used to achieve that purpose.

There are two types of compliance: 'Offsite' and 'Onsite'. These two approaches are complementary. 'Offsite compliance' comprises the work undertaken to analyse and verify the information that licensees submit – whether in the form of specific regulatory returns (submitted on an

---

[92] George Alexander Walker, *International Banking Regulation Law, Policy and Practice*, Kluwer Law International, 2001, pp. 277–9.

ongoing monthly, quarterly or semi-annual basis), management accounts and/or annual audited financial statements. The data submitted
are analysed and cross-checked to identify precisely what is happening in
the licensee's business and whether there are any indications of adverse
or unusual trends. Regulators look for figures that appear to be inconsistent with past returns and the development of new trends. They look
for abnormalities and exceptions.

Other information may be required on a sporadic basis ('ad hoc'
reporting). An ad hoc report may be required to check something
specific that applies to the whole licence-holding population or it might
apply only to one licensee in isolation. The other source of information
is the grapevine. It is frequently the case that regulators receive anonymous information about a licensee – which may or may not be true – so it
has to be checked. Lastly in this respect, licensees often complain about
other licensees, but in doing so they invariably insist that the regulator
does not disclose the source of the information. All this information
represents the raw material used for offsite compliance testing.

'Onsite compliance' refers to the process of checking what takes place
in the business premises of the licensee, by way of 'compliance visits'
(sometimes called 'inspections'). In practice, a 'team' (maybe two or
three people) from the regulator will make a pre-planned (i.e. non-
surprise) visit and will carry out a series of checks. Ongoing, pre-
planned visits should be distinguished from surprise visits (i.e. those
carried out without warning) and from 'investigations', which usually
arise because of particular concerns that the regulator has. While the
terminology differs from jurisdiction to jurisdiction, the principles
remain the same.

Compliance visits serve a number of useful functions and should not
be regarded merely as an attempt to catch out the licensee. While these
visits provide an opportunity for regulators to identify weaknesses and
problems and to agree upon courses of action designed to remedy those
defects, the visits can be used to achieve more than this.

The visits also enable the regulator to offer feedback, comment and
opinion on the procedures and controls that the compliance team
observes during its visit. Lastly, the visits enable the licensee and the
regulator to build up rapport and to exchange views and to clarify any
areas of uncertainty or doubt.

Supranational 'regulators', including the Basel Committee, IOSCO,
the IAIS, the FSF and the OGBS, encourage regulators to undertake
compliance testing.

6.22.1 Risk-based supervision

The frequency of the visits and the style of the visit is likely to depend on the degree to which the regulator believes a licensee is exposed to risk – a 'risk-based' approach. Stated simply, risk-based supervision means that resources are allocated to wherever the regulator believes the risk is greatest. For example, 'the FSA [the UK regulator] takes a risk based approach to regulation'.[93] The FSA has developed a risk-based operating framework to identify the main risks to its statutory objectives and to assist in addressing those risks.[94]

It is the extent of the exposure that is important, so the regulator will want to assess how the perceived risks are managed and in so doing may consider:

- the relative competence, experience and qualifications of the people involved;
- the scope of the business and the 'riskiness' of the services provided;
- the regulatory track record of the licensee;
- the adequacy of controls in light of the risks; and
- the appropriateness of 'customer due diligence' and anti-money laundering systems etc.

With respect to the FSA, one observer has pointed out that:

> over 90 per cent of regulated firms are now small, that is they are without a dedicated supervisor, noted Callum McCarthy in the latest FSA Annual Report, published last month. How to address the potential threat from systemic failures by a major institution, while keeping in view the risk of cumulated weaknesses building at the smaller end of the market, represents an ongoing regulatory challenge.[95]

On average, every licensee might expect to be visited once every twelve months. This is merely a guide, as jurisdictions differ in their approach and in fact, until fairly recently, some did not conduct compliance visits at all.

Generally speaking, a licensee might be given around two weeks' notice of an inspection visit and a date will be arranged that is mutually

---

[93] Chief Executive's Report, Financial Services Authority (UK), *Annual Report 2004/05*, p. 11.
[94] 'A New Regulator for the New Millennium', Financial Services Authority, January 2000.
[95] 'Changing Shape', Vol. 17, No. 10, July/August 2005, *Compliance Monitor*, p. 1.

convenient. Visits might last between one day and ten days and are likely
to involve between two members of staff and a whole team – depending
on what type of entity is being tested (a small broker will not need the
same resources as a large bank). Once testing is complete, the staff
involved ('examiners') will compile a report – a summary of which will
(probably) be provided to the licensee.

The testing carried out onsite will follow a standard pattern (probably
using checklists) but will be tailored to take account of any exceptional
circumstances. 'Compliance testing checklists' are useful – not only as
prompts, but also as a means of ensuring consistency – but they must not
be used overly rigidly. Means and ends should not be confused.

In this respect, it has been said that '[f]inancial regulators that lack the
clear and unequivocal authority to enforce the provisions of the
governing legislation are unlikely to be taken seriously by the financial
community. The absence of effective powers of enforcement not only
undermines the authority of the regulator but, potentially, puts the
stability of the financial sector at risk'.[96]

6.23 Memoranda of Understanding

In May 2001, the Basel Committee published a statement prepared by
the Working Group on Cross Border Banking that includes a framework
for establishing bilateral arrangements (e.g. Memoranda of Understanding) between regulators in different countries. Notably, the Working
Group included members of the Offshore Group of Banking Supervisors.
This statement endorses the principle established in the 1975 Basel
Concordat concerning the need for regulators to be able to share information in certain circumstances. In light of the global nature of financial
services business, it is important for regulators and law enforcement
agencies to be able to build up intelligence and to share that intelligence
with others involved in similar activities elsewhere. This is frequently
achieved through the adoption of Memoranda of Understanding, which
are 'legal' documents that set out the manner in which one institution
will deal with another concerning the exchange of information. To be
effective, Memoranda of Understanding between regulators in different

---

[96] Peter R. Kyle, 'Establishing Legal Consistency for Integrated Regulation', in *Aligning Financial Supervisory Structures with Country Needs*, ed. Jeffrey Carmichael, Alexander Fleming and David Llewellyn, World Bank Institute, September 2004, p. 213.

countries should not be overly prescriptive. National legislation (such as rules protecting the confidentiality of bank customers' affairs) cannot be overridden. Cross-border establishments should be able to report to their head office to enable proper oversight.

6.24 A critical success factor

According to Johns,

> failure to appreciate the needs of multinational business to impress on onshore tax regimes and others the 'legitimacy' of their activities by the provision of local supervision of their activities led in many cases to very short run gains followed by a low reputation that circumscribed development or postponed substantial financial sector growth until a due period of time had elapsed and local supervisory powers had been instituted.[97]

This may be described as the classic failure of 'Offshore'.

All countries (including finance centres) have economies to support. Business generated contributes to gross national product and so such centres must make themselves attractive to those people around the world whose job it is to decide where to locate business.

From earlier research undertaken by the author,[98] it appears that the style, extent and pervasiveness of the prevailing regulatory system is of fundamental significance to such decision-makers in the overall decision to establish a presence in an 'Offshore Finance Centre'. The extent of the regulations, the level of intrusiveness and the effectiveness of the regulations are all considered to be very important.

There needs to be congruence between the regulatory standards of the organisation and the 'Offshore Centre'. It is considered that the centre's standards and business ethics should be discussed at an early stage in the application process. Also, the potential newcomer will hope that the regulations will not be more complex than what he is used to in his home jurisdiction.

No amount of regulation will prevent wrongdoing but rules will make such wrongdoing harder to accomplish. However, the regulations should be balanced so that they achieve all that is reasonable. Grey areas are

---

[97] Richard Anthony Johns, *Tax Havens and Offshore Finance – A Study of Transnational Economic Development*, Frances Pinter (Publishers) Ltd, 1983, p. 190.

[98] H. McCann, 'An Examination of What May Be Said to Constitute Success for an Offshore Finance Centre', unpublished thesis, August 1994.

disliked and should be clarified. There should be no doubt as to what is acceptable and what is not acceptable. The effort required in complying should not be under-estimated – especially for the smaller financial services companies and the smaller 'Offshore Finance Centres'.

Regulatory practice need not be visible. The absence of crises indicates effective regulation. Coordinated governmental support is a real advantage.

A further problem arises. It would be surprising if any finance centre – whether 'Onshore' or 'Offshore' – would describe itself as less than well regulated. Accordingly, the question is not simply whether a centre subscribes to all the appropriate principles promulgated by all the relevant organisations. Rather, the important question is the extent to which these worthy principles actually affect the practice of regulators and those whom they regulate. This is borne out by the efforts made by the Bank for International Settlements to assist regulators worldwide to test the extent to which licensees really adhere to the twenty five Core Principles described in section 9.3 below. Chapter 21 provides some tests that a consumer might use to assess the credibility of an OFC.

In describing why the City of London has been a successful financial services centre, a recent article suggests that 'its regulatory environment has been crucial . . . because of its favourable regulatory environment, the City dominates foreign exchange, international bonds and equities, and derivatives'.[99]

6.25 The European Central Bank

In January 2002, the European Central Bank (ECB) indicated its aspirations to be involved in banking supervision. The argument is that, in an integrated European market, the national central banks and the ECB should play a central role in banking supervision. The ECB believes that its right to be involved stems from the fact that, in the event of a disaster, it would be asked to assist in bailing out problem banks.

Opponents suggest that, because they have lost control of monetary policy, central banks in Europe consider that supervision is merely being used to fill a gap. Further, the ECB's remit under the Maastricht Treaty extends only to monetary policy, and to allow this proposal to happen will only lead to conflicts of interest.

---

[99] 'Tiner's Tightrope', *The Economist*, 20 September 2003, p. 39.

6.26 Regulatory arbitrage

Ordinarily, competition is a good thing – and cross-border competition amongst regulators is no exception, provided that it does not lead in practice to a reduction in standards in a race to attract new business. On the basis that this does not happen, regulators must work hard to maintain equilibrium in their regulatory system. Too much regulation is harmful – because it stifles innovation and creativity – and it is for these very reasons that the 'Offshore' environment has an undeniable raison d'être. There is correlation between too much homogeneity and too much regulation. An 'Offshore Finance Centre' should not promote itself either on the basis of its tax treaties – because this will encourage treaty shopping (see section 5.26 above) – or on the basis of its regulation – because this will encourage regulatory arbitrage.

However, regulatory arbitrage is not peculiar to OFCs. In 2004, German banks in Passau (a small town near the border with Austria) complained that 'Austrian bankers were stealing their business because of lighter Austrian regulation . . . The Austrians were attracting clients by advertising their lax rules.'[100] (The issue concerned the threshold at which banks are required to produce more information to demonstrate the financial status of a potential borrower – €250,000 in Germany and €750,000 in Austria.) Clearly, playing fields are far from level!

6.27 Regulatory independence

In practice, regulatory authorities will require a degree of independence from the government of the respective country they serve – if they are to carry out their work effectively. In this respect, '[c]onsultation with the regulated community should not offer them a vote in, or veto over, any action plan, for such plans may involve action against them. Regulators should be genuinely concerned to understand the perspectives of those they regulate, without giving up the prerogative to make (potentially unpopular) regulatory decisions.'[101] Perversely, consultation can be taken too far: the FSA in the UK has been taken to task for this very thing.

---

[100] David Shirreff, 'Open Wider, A Survey of International Banking', *The Economist*, 21 May 2005, p. 3.
[101] Malcolm K. Sparrow, *The Regulatory Craft*, Brookings Institution Press, 1998, p. 146.

'Regulatory capture' is at the other end of the spectrum. This refers to a situation in which licensees have more than an acceptable amount of influence over regulators – which means that licensees may materially affect formulation of the rules in their own favour. This sometimes happens when licensees have greater expertise than the regulator. How this is arranged will be peculiar to the jurisdiction concerned – but the principle is significant. However, regulators frequently wield substantial power and therefore they are accountable. Independence is not absolute and there must be proper controls and mechanisms in place to ensure that the regulatory organisation does not abuse the independence that it enjoys. The 'badges' include whether:

- the regulatory authority is accountable to Parliament through a minister;
- the minister responsible for the regulatory authority is empowered to change regulatory decisions in specific cases;
- the chairman is separate from the chief executive;
- the chief executive is appointed by the board;
- legislation provides the causes that give rise to dismissal of the chief executive;
- the regulatory authority is self-funding;
- the degree to which the regulatory authority is transparent (e.g. in respect of its policies and decisions);
- there is an appeals procedure, e.g. in respect of licence applications rejected or licences revoked; and
- the composition of the board conforms to good corporate governance principles.

In the Edwards Report (see section 3 below), Mr Edwards said that '[t]he task of regulation is better performed by suitably qualified independent professional people than by politicians or by government officials with other axes to grind'.[102] Mr Edwards went on to say that:

> There are also, however, some clear advantages in confining Regulatory Boards to non-political professional people . . . [T]he business of regulation is a professional task, requiring professional direction and impartial implementation. Regulators, like judges, need to be independent, impartial and professional, both in the reality and in the perception. It is

---

[102] Michael Edwards, *Review of Financial Regulation in the Crown Dependencies*, Part 1, para. 6.2.6, 1998.

difficult, however, for politicians, even if they have the necessary professional backgrounds, to be visibly impartial in this way when their daily tasks include public arguments about political strategies and public responses to political pressures and critics. It is also difficult for public figures to refuse to be drawn into discussion and controversy over particular regulatory decisions. For their own protection, therefore, it seems better that they should not serve on Regulatory Boards.

6.28 Promotion

Chapter 3 referred to the 'Offshore Finance Centre' as the market place where the 'sellers' and 'buyers' trade. In this respect, the jurisdiction must promote itself to encourage use of its services. The question arises as to who should be responsible for this type of marketing. It is suggested that it is inappropriate for the regulator to promote the jurisdiction in this way. The Edwards Report (see section 3 below) suggests that this type of role is incompatible with the impartiality expected of regulators in their licensing and regulatory duties.[103]

That said, irrespective of who is responsible, business development depends (inter alia) on the creation of an appropriate business environment – which might be described as a regulatory objective – even though the promotion itself is carried out by a non-regulator.

6.29 Summary

It seems that 'regulation (although central) is not the only key factor affecting the development of offshore finance'.[104] The objectives of regulation include the application of prudential norms and appropriate market conduct. There are three prudential norms: safety, soundness and stability. Market conduct includes integrity, transparency and consumer protection.

The principles of regulation include flexibility and responsiveness, competitiveness, good governance and relationships amongst regulators. The tools to make all this work include prudential standards, market conduct rules, enforcement regime, disclosure and a licensing regime. It has been suggested that:

---

[103] Michael Edwards, *Review of Financial Regulation in the Crown Dependencies*, Part 1, para. 6.9.10, 1998.
[104] Mark Hampton, *The Offshore Interface*, Macmillan Press Ltd, 1996, p. 67.

> The infrastructure of markets and institutions is usually improved by: (i) harmonising domestic regulatory standards with minimum international standards (including capital-adequacy standards); (ii) emphasising the importance of corporate governance rules; and (iii) ensuring that institutions and markets are subjected to appropriate compliance procedures.[105]

There is one crucial human dimension that must not be overlooked – or underestimated. There is an undeniable need for regulators and others to talk to each other. Failure to seek advice from or share information with each other (all other things being equal) can have far-reaching consequences. This is especially so in smaller 'Offshore' jurisdictions where there might be more than one authority responsible for licensing, regulation and compliance. In such cases, the greater the degree of coordination, the greater the probability of effective regulation.

---

[105] Hans Falkena, Roy Bamber, David Llewellyn and Tim Store, *Financial Regulation in South Africa*, Financial Sector Forum, 2001, p. 88.

7

The regulator and the regulatory authority

Mere looking, unguided by theoretical consideration of any sort, is from most scientific points of view wholly insignificant and without consequence.[1]

7.1 Introduction

The previous chapter considered the regulatory and supervisory processes. This chapter will focus on the people who are responsible for implementing those processes, how they carry out their function and the structures within which they operate.

Essentially, regulation is about changing the behaviour of regulated institutions.[2]

The following quote sums it up for some regulators. You don't need to be a masochist to work in financial markets regulation but it helps. You can never be right, you always cost too much and you can never know as much about the people you regulate as they do. Act too quickly on something and you are guilty of a knee-jerk reaction. Take your time and you are dragging your feet. Ask the institutions you regulate too many questions about possible changes and you are swamping them with consultation papers. Ask too few and you are high handed. Too many rules, you are suffocating the market; too few and you are asking for trouble.[3]

---

[1] N. R. Hanson, *Perception and Discovery*, Cambridge University Press, 1961.
[2] Hans Falkena, Roy Bamber, David Llewellyn and Tim Store, *Financial Regulation in South Africa*, Financial Sector Forum, 2001, p. 26.
[3] William Wright, 'Masochistic Tendencies of Regulators', Financial News Online, www.efinancialnews.com, 6 September 2004.

7.2 Evolving financial services

The role of the regulator must be considered within the context of the regulatory environment. Although this is a truism, a moment should be taken to remember some of the changes that have taken place within that environment – which itself reflects the evolving financial services markets.

It has to be said that standards 'Offshore' are changing. Originally, there were few rules so the first development was the introduction of general rules. This was followed by specific rules. The next development was the introduction of compliance controls and then demands for greater transparency. The latest development has been enhanced disclosure requirements and exchange of information.

Other 'structural' changes have taken place within the global financial services' environment. For example, some of the larger corporate entities have their own banks. The General Electric Company and the Ford Motor Company have been large corporate lenders in the USA for many years. A number of financial services (including loans) are provided by way of in house captive banks, such as Marks & Spencer and Tesco in the UK. 'Each week Wal-Mart processes more than a million transactions.'[4] These include money orders, pay-cheque cashing, a credit card with a 1 per cent cashback for in-store purchases, and express bill payments. 'Wal-Mart's British arm, ASDA, even offers insurance. . .'.[5] Some corporate entities are now more credible than their bankers. In the USA, industrial loan companies have existed for around 100 years: 'they are a favoured route for non-banks to get into banking while side-stepping federal restrictions on the separation of banking and commerce'.[6] Consider also that this is an era when negative interest rates are not unknown. 'After years of near zero interest rates, Japanese overnight call rates turned negative on January 24th [2003] for the first time in history: one European bank lent two others ¥15 billion ($127 million) and paid (rather than charged) them 0.01 per cent.'[7] (This arose because of costs that Japanese banks were having to absorb to borrow dollars – so they

---

[4] 'Supercentre Banking', *The Economist*, 3 September 2005, p. 65.
[5] 'Supercentre Banking', *The Economist*, 3 September 2005, p. 65.
[6] 'Supercentre Banking', *The Economist*, 3 September 2005, p. 65.
[7] 'Giveaway', *The Economist*, 8 February 2003, p. 74.

exchanged yen for dollars through swaps from foreign banks – and still made a profit.)

So, as financial services have developed and as the lines between those services became blurred, new scenarios have arisen for regulators and supervisors. As the number of financial services operators has diminished with mergers and acquisitions, the scope of the services of those who remain has become very much wider. Another factor that impinges is the scope of the distribution channels because they are likely to be global. Enter financial conglomerates and multidimensional financial services.

Naturally, this has brought new challenges for regulators – who need to be able to regulate on the basis of risk rather than on the basis of functional lines (see section 6.16 above).

7.3 Regulatory structures in practice

As regulators learn from their past experience and as economic circumstances change, there are inevitably consequences for regulatory structures. Traditionally, the functional style prevailed – banking business was regulated by banking regulators and insurance was regulated by insurance regulators (as stated in section 6.16 above). The main alternative to functional regulation was institutional regulation. Under this scenario, all the activities of one institution would be regulated by one regulator (see section 6.14 above).

Research undertaken by the World Bank at the end of 2002 identified six main regulatory structures that currently exist globally. (The fact that a number of models exist suggests that there is no single correct answer.) Broadly speaking, the models can be described as follows.

Of all these structures, the one that has probably given rise to most debate is what has been described above as the UK Model – that is, the single regulatory authority combining responsibility for all financial services – outside the central bank. In this respect, Llewellyn refers to 'the almost universal conclusion that, when financial supervision is concentrated (that is, a single agency is responsible for a wide area of supervision), the institution tends not to be the central bank'.[8]

---

[8] David Llewellyn, 'Institutional Structure of Financial Regulation and Supervision', in *Aligning Financial Supervisory Structures with Country Needs*, ed. Jeffrey Carmichael, Alexander Fleming and David Llewellyn, World Bank Institute, September 2004, p. 76.

Lastly, in this respect, it is important that, whatever style is adopted, the legislative infrastructure is sufficiently robust and replete to support any subsequent challenges made against the regulator. This is more than a mere truism, as practical experience often demonstrates. The infrastructure usually blends legislation and regulations – often referred to as secondary legislation. In summary, the choices are to create legislation that embraces all that is necessary – leaving little need for regulations – or to include only the framework in the legislation and use the regulations to supplement the law by providing the details. The latter style is much more flexible because it is much easier to change regulations than to change primary legislation. The skill is in obtaining an appropriate mix – because other factors impinge.

The following two examples show in a little more detail the extent to which approaches differ in practice. In Australia, as a result of the Wallis Inquiry in 1996, there are now four regulators:

- the Reserve Bank of Australia, responsible for monetary policy and systemic stability;
- the Australian Prudential Regulation Authority, responsible for the prudential regulation of insurance, deposit-taking and pensions;
- the Australian Competition and Consumer Commission, whose focus is competition; and
- the Australian Securities and Investment Commission, responsible for market conduct.

By contrast, on 1 May 2003, Ireland established the Irish Financial Services Regulatory Authority (IFSRA) as the financial services regulator under the Central Bank and Financial Services Authority of Ireland Act 2002. The IFSRA combines prudential and market regulation within the restructured Central Bank of Ireland – which was renamed the Central Bank and Financial Services Authority of Ireland (CBFSAI). Two Boards operate simultaneously within the CBFSAI – the Board of CBFSAI itself and the Board of the IFSRA – which is an autonomous, independent authority that is accountable for its own actions.

7.4 The single regulator

[T]here are important potential economies of scope to be gained from combining the prudential regulatory function under one regulatory agency. Furthermore, a single prudential regulator embracing all financial business is consistent with centralised risk management practised by diversified firms and the matching principle of consolidated supervision.[9]

The UK was not the first country to adopt a single regulatory authority – and it has certainly not been the last. As the previous section indicates, Ireland is amongst recent examples. The IFSRA combines prudential and market regulation within the restructured Central Bank of Ireland. Other jurisdictions have followed a similar course.

The style adopted by the UK since 1997 (see section 6.15 above) has given rise to a great deal of discussion about the most advantageous supervisory structure. The debate continues – not least because the answer is far from clear-cut. The only thing that may be said with any degree of certainty is that there is no single best answer. Much is still to be learned about whether and in what circumstances one structure is optimal.

For example, where a jurisdiction is about to establish as a financial services centre, or where the jurisdiction has only begun to operate as such, a single composite regulatory authority offers more advantages than the conventional style. Where responsibility for regulatory disciplines is spread amongst a number of 'authorities' in one jurisdiction, a great deal of care is necessary to ensure adequate coordination. The likelihood is that each unit will develop independently of its sister authorities – with its own culture, fee structure, hierarchy, conditions of employment, attitude to risk and other fundamental principles. 'Turf wars' can develop easily, and, if they exist, there may be a reluctance to share the very information that is key to enabling the regulatory framework to optimise its effectiveness. It would be difficult to create a single unit in such adverse circumstances – as the UK's story testifies (see below) – but to do so would be very advantageous.

The Edwards Report (see section 17.3 below) cites the following advantages for a single regulatory authority, 'especially in small jurisdictions':

- economies including accommodation, overheads, board servicing and support staff;
- flexibility and cross-fertilisation of professional staff;

---

[9] R. Dale and S. Wolfe, 'The UK Financial Services Authority: Unified Regulation in the New Market Environment', 2003, Vol. 4, No. 3, *Journal of Banking Regulation*, p. 210.

- contribution to supervision of conglomerates and investment businesses; and
- facilitation of corporate sectors.[10]

The case of the UK is instructive. The details are set out in section 6.15 above, but, for the purposes of this chapter, the difficulty in merging nine self-regulatory organizations (SROs) into one – some years after they had first begun to operate – was not easily achieved. The respective cultures of each SRO were disparate – as was the style and the response to regulatory breaches. The fines they imposed were different, and fundamentally these SROs were less cohesive than they might have been.

It must be stressed that the single regulatory authority does not fit all circumstances, but there are certainly some positive aspects to it.

However, discussion on a single regulatory authority is not restricted to individual jurisdictions; it has, for example, a certain application to the entire European Union. This refers to the debate whether there should be one central authority responsible for supervision of securities, insurance and banking. 'The EU Committee of Banking Supervisors (CEBS) has a key role in ensuring consistency among national supervisors, although it does not have an overall regulatory role. There is still debate as to the optimum level of harmonisation and some commentators have suggested there should be a single EU supervisor.'[11] The need to ensure cooperation and cohesive operational collaboration between the EU's member nations takes the debate to a different plane. Although the system of national regulation has a number of defenders, it may not always persist. That said, the difficulties involved in establishing the type of 'cross-border' rules necessary to make a pan-European regulator work effectively, should not be underestimated.

A group called Eurofi2000 published a report in November 2002 which it said demonstrated a positive approach towards centralised supervision in Europe for securities, insurance and banking (European Central Bank). This was not part of the strategy proposed by Mr Alexandre Lamfalussy and his 'wise men' – who developed some ideas about the development of securities markets and the enforcement of legislation in Europe. The Lamfalussy proposals were founded on committees (e.g. the Committee of European Securities Regulators: see

[10] Michael Edwards, *Review of Financial Regulation in the Crown Dependencies*, Part 1, para. 6.3.4, 1998.
[11] 'Basel II and the Capital Requirements Directive', EurActiv.com, 23 June 2005.

section 9.5 below) and the group's work on legislation to curb market abuse was scheduled for introduction in September 2003. Additional legislation, for investment services and prospectuses, is in the course of preparation.[12]

7.5 The implications Offshore

Clearly, many of the 'Offshore' jurisdictions are less mature in terms of experience than their 'Onshore' counterparts. In such circumstances, the 'Offshore' environment has an opportunity to learn from those that have trod a similar path before them. It is not surprising then that people 'Offshore' keep a close eye on developments 'Onshore'. The adoption of a single regulatory concept is a case in point.

Malta and Mauritius (which although once described as OFCs are no longer involved in 'Offshore' activity) are amongst those jurisdictions that have adopted the integrated regulatory route. It might be that regulation 'Offshore' is one scenario for which integrated regulation is particularly well suited.

However, there are usually fewer people working in regulatory authorities 'Offshore' than in 'Onshore' authorities. In fact, this is one of the criticisms levelled at 'Offshore' jurisdictions, that is to say, there are too few people employed to do what the job demands. The implication is that the job is not being done properly – which in turn gives rise to the criticism that there is either no regulation or ineffective regulation. What is the proper way to do the job?

7.6 Training and experience

Reference to the 'Offshore Centres' around the world indicates that many of the OFCs that exist currently are, or were, under British control. That being so, there is, or rather there was, a number of centres where the chief executive (whether so called or not) was a former employee of the Bank of England. Accordingly, Bahrain, Jersey, Guernsey, Hong Kong, the Isle of Man, Gibraltar and Bermuda, to mention a few, have all engaged former Bank of England trained officials. These people have obviously applied their earlier training and expertise in building up the regulatory muscle of the jurisdictions in which they work.

---

[12] 'Trojan Horses', *The Economist*, 15 February 2003, p. 69.

However, the Bank of England is no longer responsible for regulation and supervision which means (inter alia) that the Bank of England will not be providing such training in future. Further, senior staff in many of these jurisdictions have retired already or are due to retire in the near future, and so the next generation may be of a somewhat different breed. The point is that good training remains a significant factor in producing good regulators and we should not lose sight of the fact that the regulator's role is becoming more diverse and more significant.

One of the biggest problems for those centres that want to prepare adequately for the future is to train staff effectively. The main alternative – sending staff from the home jurisdiction to another country for extended training – is prohibitively expensive and it means that only one person benefits and also that person is away from the home jurisdiction for a long period. These two factors combine to produce a dilemma for the near future – the availability of appropriately trained staff for senior regulatory positions 'Offshore'. The quality of regulation depends on the quality of the training given to regulators.

It is critical to have appropriate people with relevant skills in regulatory organizations. 'Appropriate' should be interpreted to mean mature, competent, sensitive to the wider issues and capable of decision-making. These characteristics and traits must be combined with education and experience. On the face of it, many roles have similar requirements, but, as in so many other cases, the devil is in the detail.

In practice, the regulations produced by regulatory authorities are an attempt to assist licensees to know what is required of them – but in light of the pace of change in financial markets, the regulations cannot be exhaustive. As might be expected, the members of staff – at the 'coal-face' – are frequently required to make decisions that are fundamental and which may have far-reaching consequences because they may create precedents. Often, these decisions must be made quickly and in circumstances when all the facts are not available and where there is no precedent on which to rely. This means that, unless the right people are in the right roles, sound and prompt responses will not be forthcoming and progress is impaired. All sorts of factors come into play because the regulator frequently finds him or herself between a rock and a hard place. A decision is still required and, although there may be some who will query the decision after the event, they are frequently not around when the decision has to be made. Accordingly, a degree of maturity and presence of mind are called for.

'Offshore' regulatory authorities need to have people of the right calibre if that environment is ever to have any hope of shedding the adverse reputation that it has attracted from many quarters.

Training facilities that exist 'Onshore' are not restricted to persons who work 'Onshore'. The organizations listed below include 'Onshore' and 'Offshore' locations. The list is not exhaustive – it is merely provided to demonstrate that such facilities exist:

7.6.1 'Onshore'

The Bank of England's Centre for Central Banking Studies has been offering courses on central banking matters since 1990. In the UK, the Financial Services Skills Council (FSSC) was established in 2003 and licensed by the UK Government 'to work in partnership with employers to provide strategic and responsible leadership for training, education and development for the industry in the UK'.[13] The FSSC was asked by the UK's FSA to complete its examination review, and to determine which examinations were appropriate for particular regulated activities.

Many central banks (e.g. in India) establish their own training establishments. Some regulatory authorities (e.g. the FSA in the UK) offer secondments, but the number of places is limited and the demand is very high. The FSA also hosts an annual seminar for international regulators, and, while this is very useful, it is not training per se. In any event, authorities are accountable for their budgets, which ordinarily exclude the provision of training for regulators from every country around the world.

Canada's Office of the Superintendent of Financial Institutions (OFSI) provides a technical assistance forum for foreign regulators.

The Financial Stability Institute (BIS) provides very technical training on specific issues for regulators (e.g. Basel II). The Toronto International Leadership Centre for Financial Sector Supervision was established in 1988 with support from the Canadian Government, the Schulich School of Business at York University (Toronto), the Canadian International Development Agency and the World Bank. The IMF and the Financial Stability Institute have since added their weight to the project. Case

---

[13] Dr Chris Nakajima, 'Ensuring Competence in Money Laundering Prevention', Vol. 8, No. 3, *Journal of Money Laundering Control*, p. 198.

studies (e.g. in respect of systemic scenarios and failures of licence-holding companies) are used to prepare regulators from insurance, capital markets and banking environments. The case study approach is used because it enables students to learn from people who have actually been involved in real life scenarios that the study exemplifies.

7.6.2 'Offshore'

The Guernsey Training Agency Limited is owned by a charitable trust. The Agency's objective is to 'engender a training and development culture within all organizations throughout [Guernsey], and procure and facilitate high quality training and development programmes in all business sectors'.[14] Courses offered include (UK) Securities Institute courses, STEP courses, MScs in e-commerce and corporate governance, an MBA, and a diploma in personnel management.

The Isle of Man has its International Business School, which focuses on what they describe as the 'international finance industry'. It offers degree courses and research opportunities.

Jersey has established a Business School that offers a range of relevant courses including MBA and BSc degree courses.

Malta hosts the Malta International Training Centre. 'The Centre today is the recognised training body and examination centre of the CII (Chartered Insurance Institute), the Securities Institute, the Chartered Institute of Secretaries and Administrators and the Institute of Risk Management . . . [and] . . . has recently introduced courses leading to the examinations of the Institute of Sales, Marketing and Management.'[15]

> One recent hopeful development is the FIRST initiative – a $45 million fund to provide technical assistance and training for developing countries wanting to upgrade their supervisory systems.[16]

In considering training, the need for criminal prosecutors and judges to be helped in becoming aware of the legal perspectives of the issues with which they might be involved in respect of financial services should not be overlooked.

---

[14] Guernsey FSC, *Annual Report*, 2003, p. 53.
[15] 'Malta International Training Centre', www.middlesea.com/press/malta_international_training_cen.htm.
[16] Neil Courtis, 'Training Tomorrow's Supervisors', December 2002, Vol. 7, No. 3, *The Financial Regulator*, p. 72.

7.7 Operational implications

Regulators are often not popular people – in fact it has been said that, if a regulator is well liked by the people he or she regulates, then the regulator is probably not doing his or her job effectively. Naturally, a person does not have to be liked to be respected, but regulators must have the respect of their licensees. After all, in some senses the objects of the regulator and of the licensee are congruent.

This poses many problems in a small community – which OFCs often are. The regulator may find him or herself berating a licensee in a tense meeting in the afternoon and in the evening may be in a social setting with the same person (neither knowing in advance that the other would be there). Smallness and proximity enhance the potential value of the grapevine, but there are other effects also.

Regulators are often castigated. One frequent criticism is that they are not 'pro business'. One recent example of this arose in the UK when Prime Minister Tony Blair said in a speech to the Institute for Public Policy Research (June 2005) that the FSA's actions were detrimental to businesses that were well run. Mr Blair said that the UK's regulatory authority was 'seen as hugely inhibiting of efficient business by perfectly respectable companies that have never defrauded anyone'.[17] This type of comment is potentially very harmful to the credibility of the UK's regulatory authority. Regulators are also accused of insensitivity or lack of professional experience. The charge is made that regulators are ruining a centre's business. However, the most frequently repeated claim is that of 'over-regulation', concerning what are described as 'commercial decisions'. These are not the type of comments that encourage government ministers – so they should not be made lightly – and it is the responsibility of those who believe these things to be able to demonstrate why. Unfortunately, this is the type of criticism that anyone can make at any time without being expected to justify it, and this is particularly damaging to what the regulatory authority is trying to achieve.

Trade groups (i.e. associations of professional people within a jurisdiction representing all or a part of the population of practitioners) have a particularly significant role to play. These people are a sample of the population of those who generate revenue – for the economy, for their

---

[17] Gavin Stamp, 'FSA under Fire after Blair Speech', BBC News, http://newsvote.bbc.co.uk;, 10 June 2005.

company and for themselves. Their focus is on profit generation and
their role increases their sensitivity towards commercial issues. Regulators need such groupings to help them understand what is happening
commercially in the jurisdiction and in the world at large. Thus, it is
advantageous for regulators and trade groups to establish a rapport and
to develop the sort of synergies that will enhance the revenue generating
capabilities of the jurisdiction. Frequently, in practice, this rapport takes
a great deal of effort and time – not only to cultivate but also to
maintain. Here are the opposite points of view – expressed in extreme
terms to demonstrate the point.

It is feasible that within a trade group there are people whose job and
salary and maybe bonus or commission is based on the profitability of
their organization (whether they own it themselves or it is owned by
others). In carrying out their role, these people will prefer as much
latitude and as little interference as possible. Ordinarily, they do not
want this latitude to enable them to operate wrongfully – but in their
view to operate efficiently – that is without too much attention to fine
detail and tight procedures. This keeps costs under control and enhances
the bottom line. Licensed institutions have obligations that sometimes
conflict with the profit generation motivation. Time spent on regulatory
matters means less time spent on profit generating activity – which
means that it should be kept to a minimum.

Licensees must never be allowed to forget their fiduciary responsibilities – and this is probably the area in which most tensions exist
between the regulator and the licensee. The regulator believes that proper
controls are necessary to manage the risks to which the regulator feels the
business is exposed. Practitioners often believe this emphasis on controls
simply adds additional costs to the operation – which in turn reduces
profitability. Their focus is frequently on the near term.

It is feasible that within a trade group there are people who believe
that the regulatory authority comprises people whose job depends on the
success of members of the trade group – although they suppose that the
regulators do not realise that. They may consider that regulators are not
risk-takers – and, more frequently than not, they have never even worked
in the industry that they regulate. They see regulators baulk at decisions
and take overly long to make up their mind. They look upon regulators
as insensitive to the commercial aspects of transactions they are asked to
approve and unwilling to allow any meaningful risk – thereby restricting
business. Regulators are said to be rule-based and meet every situation

with a new rule because they lack the imagination and creativity to deal with a problem in any other way.

It is conceded that the two approaches described are at either end of the spectrum, but they have been described in this way to show a fundamental dichotomy. The objective is to bring the extreme views to the table for discussion and to create a third alternative approach that balances the concerns and aspirations of the two interest groups. It has been said that '[o]ver emphasising customer service can lead those on the receiving end of Regulatory encounters to feel entitled to be pleased; and they will use every avenue open to them to retaliate'.[18]

In a telling comment from *The Banker*, a recent article said that:

> Banks persistently complain about regulation. A survey of bankers' regulators and analysts by City of London Think Tank, the Centre for the Study of Financial Innovation, underlined fears that the burden of regulation will continue to rise due to growing pressure on governments to crack down on financial crime and mismanagement. This is probably true. But who can blame government and the regulators when banks are showing themselves to be irresponsible in some of their basic duties? Pointing the finger at a few bad apples is no longer credible; too many banks have been caught out. Financial institutions have no one to blame but themselves.[19]

It has been said of the UK's FSA that:

> A very large amount of FSA energy went into dealing with accountability and the need for consultation. While the objective is worthy, it has produced a snowstorm of consultation papers, which as the FSA now acknowledges, has led to regulatory overload for small and medium sized regulated entities. The approach to consultation also provides an insight into FSA 'design philosophy': the processes adopted by the FSA are intended to be robust and 'review proof' but usually at the cost of efficient and expeditious action. And overall, the tendency for the policy process and policy output to be seen as ends in themselves has produced a mini industry within the FSA, with too many hands being applied.[20]

This quotation clearly demonstrates that, for regulators, it is very hard to please any of the people any of the time – although it has to be said

---

[18] Malcolm K. Sparrow, *The Regulatory Craft*, Brookings Institution Press, 2000, p. 64.

[19] 'Taking Care of Business Ethically Must Be Priority for New Year', *The Banker*, 1 January 2004, as reported in *GPML Global Press Review*, United Nations Office on Drugs and Crime, Vol. 2, No. 1, 5 January 2004.

[20] Philip Thorpe, 'Time to Wield the Big Stick', Securities and Investment Review, January–Febuary 2004, p. 26.

that the FSA issued around 235 consultation papers in its first three
years.

7.8 Is there an answer?

In fact, there is an answer but it is not an easy answer – and the burden
falls on the regulator.

There is a line that delineates acceptability from non-acceptability in
all regulatory matters – whether it is a licensing decision or a decision
whether to allow a transaction or a decision to implement a certain
procedure in certain circumstances. Wherever that line is, the regulator
must find it and operate within its boundaries – every day. The trouble
is finding that line. There is no formula for this line. It cannot be
plotted. It is invisible – but it exists and, when it is crossed, it is clear
because crossing it usually creates strong reactions. Finding it requires
knowledge, sensitivity and maturity. It also involves much practice and
patience.

Good regulators learn to accept criticism objectively – learning from
what is valid and avoiding reacting to what is vindictive and puerile.
In light of the asymmetry of information, regulators often have more
information than other people – and some of this information cannot be
revealed publicly. This sometimes leads to situations where regulators
have to accept invalid public criticism without retort. Part of the secret is
to be able to separate the issue from the person raising it – and ignoring
any aggression or insults in the manner in which issues are raised.

Being a good regulator requires a number of personal attributes which
include: strong discipline, complete integrity, ability to communicate
effectively and a sense of humour. However, while these aspirations
and sentiments are true, the essence of the problem is much deeper. In
his book, *The Regulatory Craft*, the author says that its central concentration '. . .is that while apparently simple ideas about risk control and
problem solving remain for the most part very poorly understood, they
represent the opportunity for profound changes in regulatory practice
and should be adopted as foundations for reform'.[21] The point is made
later that 'if risk control counts, then we must learn how to count it. But
for now, we have to put off the counting long enough to tease out
the underlying nature of the performance we seek to measure.'[22]

---

[21] Malcolm K. Sparrow, *The Regulatory Craft*, Brookings Institution Press, 2000, p. 10.
[22] Malcolm K. Sparrow, *The Regulatory Craft*, Brookings Institution Press, 2000, p. 122.

Further, 'teams face a powerful and natural temptation to monitor implementation of their plan, rather than abatement of the problem. Requiring attention to measurement issues before action planning obliges a project team to work out what success would look like (that is what indicators would move in what directions, or what intelligence reports they might expect to receive), before they craft solutions.'[23]

There are probably many factors that affect the amount of trust that practitioners have in their regulators – some of which are listed below. The level of trust is neither fixed nor absolute. It is rather dynamic and subject to change. The regulatory factors are under the direct influence of the regulator while the external factors include both matters that are outside the control of practitioners (such as the global economy) and factors over which the practitioner has complete control.

One approach is rule-driven. Another is to let the industry try to sort itself out, but, if it fails to do so, the regulator takes control.

7.9 Boards

It has been said that 'no matter which model is chosen, arrangements for strong internal governance are needed if the system is to operate effectively. These arrangements should cover at least the agency's independence, accountability and transparency.'[24] This probably summarises the board's responsibilities. In an 'Onshore' centre, the board of a regulatory Authority is likely to comprise experts in financial services and related disciplines. The mix of skills increases the probability of good decisions being made. The same range and depth of skills and experience may or may not be available 'Offshore'.

Those with less regulatory experience 'Offshore' will instead have other experience that can be brought to bear on the situation in hand – and will increase their experience in the meantime. The point is to develop the synergies that exist. The value of a small number of board members from outside the jurisdiction should not be under-estimated. This style has been adopted by the regulatory authority in Jersey.

The board must acknowledge its own limitations. The board cannot and should not make every decision. Some matters are best left to the

---

[23] Malcolm K. Sparrow, *The Regulatory Craft*, Brookings Institution Press, 2000, p. 143.

[24] Jeffrey Carmichael, 'Summary of the Discussion', in *Aligning Financial Supervisory Structures with Country Needs*, ed. Jeffrey Carmichael, Alexander Fleming and David Llewellyn, World Bank Institute, September 2004, p. 13.

management. Failure to delegate will prevent the board from focusing on its area of expertise – strategic planning and decision-making. It will also prevent management from maturing. One approach is for the board – so far as is possible – to exclude itself from making management decisions about specific regulatory issues. (At some point in some scenarios, it may be necessary for the board to become involved, so the previous suggestion is not intended to be a rigid rule.) Since the board will not be deciding upon every issue, members must let management know in advance which matters should be brought to the board's attention – by way of exception reporting or a simple update or for whatever reason. Similarly, boards must avoid the creation of too many committees and hierarchies of decision-making – otherwise the speed and efficiency – for which most markets are looking – will be harder to achieve.

One important task for the board is in respect of communication. Regulators are sometimes regarded as too powerful – so the board must manage the relationship with government and with stakeholders to prevent tensions in this respect.

7.10 Enforcement

In financial services centres, there must not only be sound regulatory processes but also the culture to enforce those processes. This means that, when wrongdoers are identified, there has to be an apparatus in place to deal with them – fairly but also forcibly.

This is another area where the peculiar circumstances that prevail 'Offshore' have to be considered. By definition, 'Offshore Centres' are small and generally people know each other. That being so, there might be a tendency to 'overlook' certain situations because of the potential implications on the local practitioner involved. Similarly, in smaller, less mature centres, there is a risk that aggrieved parties will expect the appropriate minister (or whoever may be in a position of authority) to intervene. Those in such positions are best placed to stop this. Obviously, the regulatory response to any situation must be dispassionate and objective – but this might be more easily achieved if the regulator and the practitioner have not known each other all their lives. This is more likely to be the case in larger 'Onshore' centres.

In any event, the legislation should provide a hierarchy of punitive measures. This might begin with a (mild) warning, followed perhaps by a more severe warning or warnings. The next level is the issue of a 'Direction', which, as the name suggests, is a direct requirement made of the licensee by the regulator to take a particular course of action or to desist from adopting or continuing to adopt a course of action. There are a number of additional permutations which may be applied simultaneously. These include whether the public should be informed by way of a press notice, and, if so, at what stage. The licensee's licence may be restricted or additional restrictions may be added (e.g. on what new business may be added or the imposition of more onerous capital or liquidity requirements).

Frequently, this is where most regulatory action ends. It is suggested that, where there is capacity to impose monetary penalties or fines, the regulator will be much better placed to attain the cooperation of licensees. The establishment of a punitive regime that involves monetary penalties is not simple. The jurisdiction's law might not allow this, so specific legislation may have to be enacted. The level of the fine is problematic. For example, how does one quantify the gravity of the wrongdoing? Will the same penalty apply for a smaller licensee as for a larger licensee? Is the penalty affected by how long the licensee has been licensed? Should the fine be weighted according to whether it has recurred, or to the profitability of the offending licensee or according to the regulatory record of the licensee, and so on? Many issues arise. There is general agreement that, when a licensee has to pay up – and especially if the public is made aware that the licensee has been censured – the licensee's compliance is assured. Interestingly, licensees are often more influenced by the fact that the public will be made aware than by the amount of the penalty. If licensees do not respect the regulator voluntarily, their respect must be attained in some other way.

The last resort is what is referred to as the 'nuclear option' in regulation: the revocation of a licence. No regulator relishes having to withdraw a licence – but that has to be the ultimate deterrent. Naturally, it will only be interpreted as such if it is actually applied – fairly but forcibly.

Table 8 in Appendix 1 indicates the types of punitive action that regulators apply (although not all regulators have identical powers). The jurisdiction's legislation is the source of the regulator's authority. Without appropriate legislation, the regulator's hands are tied behind his back.

In one sense, suspension is a regulatory tool and not a punitive measure per se. A licence may be suspended as a preliminary step to revocation – and may be applied, for example, to protect the public. In this sense, it is a regulatory tool. In light of the fact that a suspended licence means that a licensee may no longer accept new business, it is punitive.

7.11 The regulatory cycle

'Offshore' jurisdictions evolve. Table 9 in Appendix 1 describes how this evolution happens and some of the implications arising.

This analysis represents one permutation. The four phases described are not discrete. One phase merges into another almost imperceptibly at first but the transition is definite nevertheless. The timeframes quoted are no more than best estimates. Some jurisdictions become stuck and do not develop much, if at all. Other jurisdictions may benefit from some circumstances quite out of their control but which, nevertheless, allow them to find a niche which they can exploit (Bermuda and insurance is a case in point). The global economic cycle also affects how long jurisdictions linger in one phase or another. It must be remembered that the 'Offshore' concept is relatively new. The most mature 'Offshore Finance Centres' such as Jersey (if Jersey can be described as an OFC) are only some forty years old.

7.12 Evolution of 'Offshore Finance Centres'

Table 9 in Appendix 1 includes one perspective on how financial services centres develop. The progressions described are not discrete – one phase merges into another. Further the time frames suggested are very difficult to determine because no two financial services centres are identical.

7.12.1 Phase 1: new

In a 'new' centre (i.e. one that has only recently become an OFC), it is likely that, if there is any regulation, it will be superficial and the financial services infrastructure in which it exists will be substantially undeveloped. If asked, practitioners in such a jurisdiction might say that, although there are no detailed regulatory rules in place at that time, they adhere to international best practice. They might support this approach with a description of specific activities in which they engage in order to try to demonstrate to anyone who might ask the efficacy of the regulatory process. However, a question arises concerning what 'international best practice' means. If it means the standards described elsewhere (e.g. those published by the Basel Committee, IOSCO, the IAIS etc.), then the jurisdiction – although new – will have achieved a great deal in a short space of time. Ordinarily, it is very unlikely that a new centre will have had the opportunity to introduce such detailed and sophisticated rules at the beginning of or even early in its life. Even if this was possible, the newly regulated practitioners in that jurisdiction are unlikely to have the systems or experience to cope with these sophisticated rules at that very early stage. Further, any other activities in which the new jurisdiction says it engages should be probed – just to make sure that there is substance as well as form. For example, it is easy to state that a regulatory authority conducts compliance testing, but the real question is the extent and the quality of the work. In short, wrong impressions can be given easily – albeit unintentionally.

At this early stage, and if it is to survive, the jurisdiction needs to create critical mass quickly and the more rules that exist and the more intrusive the rules are, the longer that growth will take. The jurisdiction will expect fast growth and may be willing to sacrifice some quality to achieve it – but this will be far from obvious to most people. (A typical example of the asymmetry of information potential that was described earlier.) Further, in that new centre, no one will know how much regulation is appropriate because there are no precedents on which the authorities may rely for guidance. The only sensor is what the practitioners find acceptable.

The practitioners will not want any hurdles to business. They will stress the need for the jurisdiction to make the environment 'consumer-friendly' in order to attract new business. Practitioners will expect the regulator to provide rapid processing of licence applications, to ask as few questions as possible, to require as little documentation to be submitted as possible, to levy as low fees as possible and to give only positive responses to applications. These features, it will be argued, are necessary to avoid 'over-regulation'.

Unfortunately, the term 'over-regulation' can mean almost anything! For their part, the regulators will (probably) agree that there should be no more regulation than necessary and that their intention is to achieve an appropriate balance. Regulators will be aware of the need for the jurisdiction to be competitive – but they are unable to do their job properly and at the same time meet the aspirations described above. Accordingly, there must be some degree of trade-off. The kernel of this very fundamental dilemma is knowing where the point of equilibrium lies.

In effect, attaining that level is a very complex and sensitive process which requires skill and experience. Some of the factors that impinge upon it include: the influence of the supranational authorities; the maturity of the jurisdiction; the exposure to risk; the real experience of the practitioners; the comparative rules applied in competing jurisdictions; the quality of the business to which the jurisdiction aspires; the degree to which consumers need to be protected; the objective assessment of how much is enough and so on.

In a new centre, there will be many simultaneous developments and the pace of change will be rapid, as long as new business keeps coming in. There will be more focus on development than on regulation. In these circumstances, it is probable that there will be a satisfactory relationship with the regulator, because the regulator only says 'no' infrequently. In fact, licensees may have helped to establish the regulatory authority in the first place and may be part of its board or may be closely involved with government in some other way that impinges upon the regulatory authority. At this stage in the evolutionary process of the 'Offshore' jurisdiction, the regulator will probably not influence the business environment to any marked degree because of the 'novelty' element in this new scenario.

7.12.2 Phase 2: young

The transition from Phase 1 to Phase 2 may take between three and five years. As the new centre develops and business increases, the pace of change is likely to increase. This is when the practitioners are likely to submit myriad forms of new applications for consideration by the regulator. This is because the jurisdiction is at a stage when it will consider almost anything – but perversely when it has rules for nothing (or very little).

This vacuum creates the potential for problems and exploitation. The establishment of trade associations may happen at this stage. They are likely to become strong in a short space of time. They have substantial positive potential. Recourse by such associations (when they fail to achieve their objective) to the highest authority in the jurisdiction will by this stage have become commonplace. These factors combine to create some strains in the relationship of practitioners with the regulator – who will now consult practitioners about all proposed changes. One of the hallmarks of a 'young' jurisdiction is that the players have not yet learned to sort out their differences (typical in any period of change) privately and quietly. Any flexing of muscles in the public arena (of which there is likely to be more than a little) has a perverse effect. It wastes opportunity for synergy, it dissipates resources that could have been used for a more positive purpose and it demonstrates clearly to the outside world that this jurisdiction is not yet mature. Although this seems perverse, operators have influence. All it takes is for a group of practitioners to convince the relevant government minister that the rules are too tough. The minister is in a difficult position because he must demonstrate to the electorate that his policies are working – and he may not have as much time as the regulatory rules need to be accepted. He or she can intervene (directly or indirectly) by 'encouraging' the regulator to be less demanding. This means a reduction in standards in order to build up the business. Regrettably, 'quick fixes' do not work. The outcome is problems in the medium (not short) term.

The regulators will make a decision at this stage – consciously or not. This decision concerns the extent to which they will act as regulators or as administrative processors. Does regulation exist merely in form or in substance? Are applications rubber-stamped, or analysed objectively and approved only if they meet pre-determined and objective criteria?

If the Regulator is worth his salt, he will test each application objectively and, as a result, he is unlikely to agree everything. If he agrees everything (or virtually everything), he demeans the regulatory process by reducing it to rubber-stamping. This will affect the entire regulatory process. The standard of completed applications will fall, the business for which a licence is requested will be of lower quality, more compliance problems will arise, and, eventually, the jurisdiction's international reputation will suffer. Decisions may take a little time, and both these factors will have a slightly adverse effect on the relationship of the practitioner with the regulator. So long as business is booming, that relationship will suffer no material or lasting ill effects.

Meanwhile, the financial services infrastructure will be developing simultaneously. This phase will highlight (inter alia) the quality of auditors and accountants and also whether the legal profession can cope with the legislative implications of transactions that are global in perspective. If they cannot, they must learn quickly or stay out of that business. (Regrettably, many do not recognise that the decision is that stark and will try to bluff their way. Their lack of experience and shallow knowledge will be very apparent to any potential client (and this applies especially to the higher value corporate client) from abroad and will make promotion of the jurisdiction even more difficult.) The most prudent jurisdictions will be preparing students for a larger and deeper role in the future and will facilitate new educational programmes and courses of study within the jurisdiction.

In this important phase, standards will be established. This is a critical time in creating positive bonds between practitioner and regulator. It is at this stage that clear and decisive leadership will assist most practitioners.

7.12.3 Phase 3: developed

A jurisdiction is not likely to become 'developed' within ten years of establishment. By this time, a new sense of purpose has percolated through and everyone in the financial services sector (and beyond) begins to realise that they are in this business together and that the success of the jurisdiction will depend (inter alia) on how effectively the practitioners and the regulator and other relevant authorities interact.

The pace of change has slowed – but not materially – although the growth in business has fallen noticeably. By this stage, there will have been adequate opportunity for the regulator to have employed an appropriate number of staff and to have introduced relevant legislation and regulations. Whether such people have been hired remains to be seen. The supranational authorities are adamant that OFCs need to have appropriate staff in place if they want to be taken seriously. The 'rules' are now more extensive and the approach has become more intrusive. The decrease in business compared to the heady days is a source of concern – because practitioners are sensitive to the bottom line.

It is probable that the influence of the trade associations will have grown but so also will the level of maturity of the players, who will begin to realise that two heads are always better than one.

The financial services infrastructure is now in a position to complement the future growth of the jurisdiction and the jurisdiction's university, or educational system will focus more and more on appropriately qualified professional people who will contribute to the jurisdiction's aspirations for success.

7.12.4 Phase 4: mature

A financial services sector that is more than twenty years old is likely to be regarded as mature. Mature jurisdictions need not be progressive jurisdictions. By this stage, it will be very clear which are which. For those that are progressive, there is likely to be a wide range of regulation that covers all aspects of financial services because the jurisdiction now has substantial experience over a range of economic cycles. The growth in the level of business is likely to have slowed materially and the need for extensive change has fallen away. Now the practitioners – through their trade associations – will have a great deal of influence with the regulator. The most mature jurisdictions will demonstrate a collaborative relationship between practitioners and the regulator, and this will create opportunities to exploit whatever synergies that exist. There will always be differences of opinion between the latter two groups, but there will be no overt hostility which means the external world will be substantially unaware of such differences.

The question is whether senility follows maturity and, if so, what dilemmas that is likely to bring with it. Maybe, like the very young, the very old will need to be prompted and assisted by considering the example of those who are somewhat younger but with more energy and capacity for change. Time will tell. 'Eventually, and some say inevitably, the rule based system becomes top heavy and turns into an economic liability; sympathy for the plight of the regulated industries begins to grow, regulators lose respect as their authoritarian stance alienates the public, and reformist pressures begin to push the other way.'[25]

7.13 Regulatory immunity

Regulators are not immune from suit. However, in order to prevent this fact of life from stopping regulators doing their duty, most legal systems provide the regulator with statutory protection or immunity – in certain circumstances.

Generally speaking, a regulator might find himself liable to a depositor or to an investor who had suffered loss as a result of handing over his money to an entity licensed by that regulator if the aggrieved party can establish that:

- the regulator owed a duty of care to the claimant; and
- the regulator breached that duty; and
- the claimant suffered loss.[26]

Relevant case law demonstrates that depositors/investors cannot sue a regulator for losses resulting from a breach of statutory duty[27] or for losses flowing from the negligent licensing or supervision of a regulated

---

[25] Malcolm K. Sparrow, *The Regulatory Craft*, Brookings Institution Press, 2000, p. 34.
[26] Charles Proctor, 'Regulatory Immunity and Legal Risk', December 2002, Vol. 7, No. 3. *The Financial Regulator*, p. 28.
[27] *Davis* v. *Radcliffe* [1990] 1 WLR 821 (PC).

entity, or the failure to withdraw a licence at an appropriate time.[28] In the latter case, it was found that having a licence was not tantamount to some sort of official approval. (See section 13.6.1 below.)

Statutory immunity does not apply where a regulator has acted in bad faith. (Public officers such as regulators must act for the public good. In so doing, they need to be confident that their immunity is appropriate. This will enable them to take decisions based on regulatory rationale – and free from political influence. The public should be made aware, for example, that rescues are not automatic – each case must be considered on its own merits – and that the government is not the lender of last resort.)

7.14 Conclusion

Regulatory processes are subject to all sorts of influences – but perhaps the human dimension is the most volatile and unpredictable. When business levels drop and some licensees move abroad, citing 'over-regulation' as the cause, the powers that be may be forced to reconsider their regulatory approach. If this happens at the wrong time or for the wrong reasons, there is regression that undermines the rationale for the implementation of those rules in the first place. The power of the practitioner should never be under-estimated – but that power can be a force for good and the authorities have an obligation to try to assist the practitioners to use their influence positively and in the best interests of the future success of the centre.

One fundamental question is the extent to which the level of regulation that prevails in a particular jurisdiction is a reflection of what licensees are expected to be willing to tolerate – as opposed to the level and style of regulation that the circumstances seem to demand. Further, good ideas matter, but the influence of politics must not be under-estimated. In his book concerning the operations of the World Bank and the IMF, Joseph Stiglitz said that 'I saw that decisions were often made because of ideology and politics. As a result, many wrong-headed decisions were taken, ones that did not solve the problem in hand but that fit with the interests or beliefs of the people in power.'[29]

---

[28] Charles Proctor, 'Regulatory Immunity and Legal Risk', December 2002, Vol. 7, No. 3, *The Financial Regulator*, p. 28. *Yuen Kun-Yeu* v. *Attorney General of Hong Kong* [1988] AC 175 (PC).

[29] Joseph Stiglitz, *Globalisation and its Discontents*, Penguin Books, 2002, p. x.

There is no single prescription – which means that alternative opinions are important – so open and frank discussions should be encouraged. The more objective the discussion, the more valuable the output is likely to be. The more hypocrisy involved, the less valuable the output is likely to be.

Money laundering

> Where there is laxity, or even more importantly the perception that there
> is laxity in controls, in banking and investment supervision and regula-
> tion, money launderers will be attracted.[1]

8.1 Introduction

Money laundering is probably one of the more prevalent crimes in
modern society, and one that is – in the view of some – inextricably linked
to the 'Offshore' environment. Whether this is fair or not remains to be
seen, but clearly, because it is trans-national in character, it requires a
global response. 'The overall concept and fundamental principle of international cooperation is based on the functional theory of collective security. The assumption that nations could deal with common problems
through collective and concerted efforts is better than acting in isolation.'[2]

In respect of the tragic events which took place on 11 September 2001,
one commentator[3] has drawn attention to the following general weaknesses in the financial system:

- While the Al-Qaeda terrorists were able to send US$500,000 from
  Dubai for use at ATMs in Florida, it has not been possible to trace the
  remitter of the funds.
- Massive outflows of money preceded the collapse of the peso in
  Mexico in 1994.
- Vast sums of money vanished as governments collapsed in Ecuador,
  Peru and Argentina.

---

[1] Rosalind Wright, 'The Hiding of Wealth: The Implications for the Prevention and Control
of Crime and the Protection of Economic Stability', Vol. 9, No. 3, February 2002, *Journal
of Financial Crime*, p. 239.

[2] Abdullahi Y. Shehu, 'International Initiatives Against Corruption and Money Laundering:
An Overview', Vol. 12, No. 3, *Journal of Financial Crime*, p. 221.

[3] Jonathan M. Winer, 'How to Clean Up Dirty Money', *Financial Times*, 23 April 2002.

- Pyramid schemes caused major upheaval in Albania, Bulgaria and Latvia.
- Theft of money from the governments of the Democratic Republic of the Congo/Zaire, Indonesia, Nigeria and Russia.
- Financial losses in Japan, South Korea and Taiwan, which were hidden offshore.
- Enron was a large user of 'Offshore Centres'.[4]

Note the spread of these weaknesses across the 'Offshore'/'Onshore' divide. 'The International Monetary Fund (IMF) estimates that between US$500 bn and $1.5 trn is laundered every year through the global financial system.'[5] The website of the International Money Laundering Information Network, http://www.imolin.org, is a useful reference.

In a paper entitled 'Money Laundering: The Role of Legislation in Developing Economies', D. C. Jayasuriya referred to a description of the law enforcers problems, as cited by a prosecutor from the UK's Serious Fraud Office, as follows:

> The modern criminal exploits territorial and jurisdictional boundaries; he may commit crimes and cause loss simultaneously in different jurisdictions and launder his profits through many more. He may then escape justice altogether by fleeing to another which permits no extradition, keeping his funds hidden from his victims. Even within the Commonwealth we are finding that arrangements made 20 years ago are becoming out of date. They were not designed for a world where money can pass untraceable through ten banks in as many minutes and where 200 limited companies are formed in a day, and sold the next, by one agent on one island.[6]

8.2 Which jurisdictions are most at risk?

There is no question over which jurisdictions are at risk: *all* jurisdictions are at risk. Money laundering is transnational. However, the question

---

[4] Enron was an energy trader, and was was the seventh largest company in the USA, until its collapse in 2001. It had more than 440 companies registered in the Cayman Islands.
[5] Justin Madubuko, 'Lobbyists Slam the UK Over Dirty Laundry Loopholes', *Portfolio International*, July 2003, p. 2.
[6] Paper provided to attendees at the Sixteenth International Symposium on Economic Crime, Jesus College, Cambridge, September 1998, quoting T. Howse, 'Investigation and Prosecution of Fraud in the European Communities', Vol. 18, No. 4, 1992, *Commonwealth Law Bulletin*, p. 1412.

posed by the title suggests that some jurisdictions might be more exposed than others.

> From experience of money laundering cases at the SFO [Serious Fraud Office in the UK], it is possible to draw some general points:
>
> - Money laundering is prevalent where there are corrupt, negligent or unaccountable governments;
> - The way money is laundered is the same whether the proceeds of the crime arise from fraud, political corruption, drug dealing or terrorism;
> - Countries with favourable tax regimes will attract dirty money;
> - Money laundering will take place where financial institutions which receive dirty money pay only lip service to the law, regulations or good practice;
> - Money laundering can only take place where there are sophisticated professionals, such as lawyers, accountants and bankers, who are willing to be actively engaged in criminal acts or simply shut their eyes to the truth.[7]

One commentator has suggested that:

> [T]here are literally dozens of nations in this world where the government's revenue is less than the profits made by the drug cartels. Wherever this occurs, the danger is that those nations are ripe for picking. The traffickers move in and the country becomes a laundryman's playground.[8]

8.3 United Nations initiatives

The UN's work in respect of corruption and anti-money laundering is encapsulated in a number of conventions. For example, the Single Convention on Narcotic Drugs of 1961 and the Convention on Psychotropic Substances of 1971 – which preceded the United Nations Convention Against Illicit Traffic in Narcotic Drugs and Psychotropic Substances of 1988, known as the Vienna Convention. The latter was the first important international initiative against drug trafficking. The Convention made drug trafficking a criminal offence and also limited banking secrecy and financial privacy in certain circumstances. In fact, the

---

[7] Rosalind Wright, 'The Hiding of Wealth: The Implications for the Prevention and Control of Crime and the Protection of Economic Stability', February 2002, Vol. 9, No 3, *Journal of Financial Crime*, p. 240.

[8] Jeffrey Robinson, *The Laundrymen,* Simon & Schuster UK Ltd, 1998, p. 397.

Convention represented the first attempts to take action against money laundering. The UN has also published its Convention on Transnational Organized Crime. This Convention – which was adopted in Vienna on 19 December 1988 – created certain offences and relevant sanctions. Article 3(1)(b) contains a definition of money laundering. Article 5 encourages member states to adopt appropriate procedures (such as identification, tracing, freezing and seizing of assets) to be used to confiscate the proceeds derived from the offences created in Article 3.

The draft UN Convention Against Transnational Organized Crime was adopted in Palermo in December 2000 and came into force in September 2003. The Convention attempts to encourage cooperation amongst members both to prevent and to combat crime. Members are required to legislate against and to confirm adherence to a checklist of certain criteria which includes the criminalisation of the laundering of the proceeds of crime (Article 6). Article 6(1–2) expanded predicate offences to include 'serious offences' both within and outside the jurisdiction. In respect of the latter, Article 6(2)(b) provides that, to be a predicate offence, the offence must be a criminal offence under the domestic law that applies in the state that is trying to apply the Article. Shehu points out that 'this is one of the controversial issues involved in the recovery of funds stolen by political leaders and kept in foreign bank accounts'.[9] Article 7 refers to measures used to prevent the financial system from being used to launder the proceeds of crime and to assist in tracing funds suspected to be of criminal origin (e.g. reporting requirements for cross-border movements of cash or negotiable instruments). Article 27(1–3) concerns cooperation amongst law enforcement agencies in combating money laundering including the need for exchange of information and bilateral/multilateral agreements to achieve this.

8.3.1 Money laundering defined

The definition of money laundering that is used most frequently comes from the United Nations Convention Against Illicit Traffic in Narcotic Drugs and Psychotropic Substances (1988) (the Vienna Convention)[10] and the United Nations Convention Against Transnational Organized

---

[9] Abdullahi Y. Shehu, 'International Initiatives Against Corruption and Money Laundering: An Overview', Vol. 12, No. 3, *Journal of Financial Crime*, p. 223.

[10] See http://www.incb.org/e/conv/1988/.

Crime (2000) (the Palermo Convention).[11] These have been summarised (see Vienna Convention, Articles 3(b) and (c)(i), and Palermo Convention, Article 6(i)) as follows:[12]

> The conversion of property, knowing that such property is derived from any [drug trafficking] offence or offences or from an act of participation in such offence or offences, for the purpose of concealing or disguising the illicit origin of the property or of assisting any person who is involved in the commission of such an offence or offences to evade the legal consequences of his actions.

> The concealment or disguise of the true nature, source, location, disposition, movement, rights with respect to, or ownership of property, knowing that such property is derived from an offence or offences or from an act of participation in such an offence or offences.

> The acquisition, possession or use of property, knowing at the time of receipt that such property was derived from an offence or offences or from an act of participation in such offence or offences.

Money laundering may be considered as a process by which the proceeds of criminal activity are made to appear as if they are and always have been legitimate tender. Section 302(3) of the US Patriot Act says 'money launderers subvert legitimate financial mechanisms and banking relationships by using them as protective covering for the movement of criminal proceeds and the financing of crime and terrorism, and, by so doing, can . . . undermine the integrity of United States financial institutions and of the global financial and trading systems upon which prosperity and growth depend'. Money laundering attempts to make money from illegal sources appear as if it is legitimate while terrorists use money whose source is often legitimate to acquire materials that are used to perpetrate illegal acts of violence for political purposes.

8.4 The criminalisation of money laundering

There are now few countries that do not have legislation in place to make money laundering a criminal offence and to facilitate the tracing and seizure of the proceeds of drug-related crime. The pace of developments

---

[11] See http://www.undcp.org/ adhoc/palermo/convmain.html.
[12] Paul Allan Schott, *Reference Guide to Anti-Money Laundering and Combating the Financing of Terrorism*, 2nd edn, World Bank, 2004, pp. 1–2.

in this respect has increased markedly in the (relatively) recent past. For example, it was only in 1986 that money laundering was 'criminalised' in the USA.

8.5 A summary of some problems arising

One of the difficulties in dealing with this crime is that there are so many possible ways in which it may be carried out. One feature of financial activity is that it is evolving as new innovations are introduced. The FATF recognises that the methods adopted by launderers change as countermeasures are developed. For example, 'increasingly sophisticated combinations of techniques, such as the increased use of legal persons to disguise the true ownership and control of illegal proceeds and an increased use of professionals to provide advice and assistance in laundering criminal funds'.[13] This poses a fundamental problem for regulation in general, and for anti-money laundering techniques in particular, because in these two areas it is often the case that procedures are designed as a reaction to problems. Major difficulties arise where the regulatory responses lag too far behind the criminal activity.

The FATF considers that 'existing anti-money laundering laws are undermined by the lack of regulation and essentially the numerous obstacles on customer identification, in certain countries and territories, notably Offshore Financial Centres'.[14] On this basis, there is some value in considering at least some aspects of money laundering. One interesting statistic is that money laundering is said to churn 2–5 per cent of gross world product every year.[15]

The World Drug Report estimates that the annual turnover from drug trafficking globally is around US$400 billion, while the proceeds of all forms of organised crime are estimated to be as high as US$1 billion. [16] The same report suggests that the proceeds of financial fraud probably exceed the total from drug trafficking. 'According to the US Treasury, in

---

[13] FATF, *Annual Report*, 20 June 2003, para. 16, p. 4.
[14] 'Report on Non Cooperative Countries and Territories', FATF, 14 February 2000, p. 1.
[15] 'All Havens in a Storm', *The Economist*, 1 July 2000, p. 86.
[16] United Nations International Drug Control Program, *World Drug Report*, Oxford University Press, 1997, as quoted in 'Financial Havens, Banking Secrecy and Money Laundering', United Nations Office for Drug Control and Crime Prevention, Issue 8 of the UNDCP Technical Series, Double Issue 34 and 35 of the *Crime Prevention and Criminal Justice Newsletter*, 1998, p. 34.

1998 alone, some $70bn left Russia for "Offshore" accounts in Nauru which has 10,000 people, one main road and 400 banks ... A UN official estimates that as much as $100bn is being laundered in the country. President Vladimir Putin has also complained of $20bn leaving the country each year in capital flight, in which illegal funds are often said to be included.'[17] In section 302 of the US Patriot Act, which President Bush signed on 26 October 2001, there is an informative statistic. It says that: 'The Congress finds that: money laundering, estimated by the International Monetary Fund to amount to between 2 per cent and 5 per cent of global gross domestic product, which is at least $600,000,000,000 annually, provides the financial fuel that permits transnational criminal enterprises to conduct and expand their operations.'

The difficulty is that it is impossible to quantify, with any degree of accuracy, the extent of the problem, because there is no way of knowing which frauds have been perpetrated successfully. All that is known is that the figures are huge. Some unquantifiable proportion finds its way 'Offshore'. A recent book suggests that 'such figures are useful to confirm that the phenomenon of money laundering is of sufficient scale to warrant public policy attention, but their quality is not good enough to provide guidance for policy . . . Confronting this reality is critical because ignorance about the volume of money laundering is an important conditioning reality for policymakers as well as for any assessment of the [anti-money laundering] regime's effectiveness.'[18] (It is interesting to note that precisely the same sentiments might be said of the 'Offshore' environment itself.)

By way of a practical example, if a financial institution is asked to open an account but declines to do so because it is not happy about some aspect of the account opening process and the prospective client walks away without opening the account, should the financial institution submit a Suspicious Transaction Report (see section 8.9 below)? Many financial institutions would like to think that they have no obligation because the account was not opened. However, the 2003 edition of the UK's Joint Money Laundering Steering Group's guidance notes, published in January 2004 (published after the Money Laundering Regulations 2003 which were published in December 2003), makes it clear that

---

[17] 'Editorial', 2001, Vol. 5, No. 1, *Journal of Money Laundering Control*, p. 5.
[18] Peter Reuter and Edwin M. Truman, *Chasing Dirty Money – The Fight Against Money Laundering*, Institute for International Economics, 2004, p. 10.

this is not acceptable in the UK. A report must be made if money laundering is suspected. This is also part of the FATF's revised (June 2003) recommendations.

It has been suggested that anti-money laundering 'has become a key issue for senior management because the possibility of an anti-money laundering related failure now poses significant potential reputational risk, both domestically and for banks' international operations. . ..'[19]

8.6 Money laundering and Offshore

The advantage that the 'Offshore' environment offers the launderer is that, having moved dirty money out of the jurisdiction where it became tainted, an investigator will have to overcome certain practical and time-consuming difficulties (not least obtaining evidence) before the launderer is endangered. By this time, the money will probably have been success-fully merged with all the rest of the money in circulation, after which it will become more deeply camouflaged by a series of complex transactions. That said, there is an innate risk for a launderer to involve an 'Offshore' jurisdiction in the process because it poses an extra dimension of risk. Laundering does not depend on bank secrecy per se. Perversely, Jose Roldan, a former President of the FATF, believes that 'the use of remote jurisdictions by money launderers is another indirect indicator that we are being effective in the fight against money laundering'.[20]

Professor Rider points out that:

> The transactions which are used to obscure the source of the relevant funds will be structured in such a manner as to render it almost impossible for admissible evidence to be obtained, which would allow a court to establish the derivation of the money. Law enforcement agencies often refer to this process as layering, but this rather implies that with diligence the true facts may be uncovered through a progressive investigation. While there have been cases where dedicated, extremely lucky, well resourced investigators have been able to peel-off a series of layers to reveal what in fact took place, in the case of the more sophisticated structures, the concept of layering is too simplistic. Certain operations are structured in a manner which resembles a mosaic or kaleidoscope rather than a layer-cake. Transactions will not be progressive, but parallel, establishing mutual

---

[19] *Global Anti-Money Laundering Survey 2004*, KPMG, October 2004, p .4.
[20] Jose Roldan, Interview, Vol. 5, No. 2, The Financial Regulator.

obligations which can be married or crossed, often on a contingent basis, and which would not be substantiated to the satisfaction of a court applying conventional legal rules.[21]

Thus, it seems that the launderer has (almost) perfected a method of perverting the system to achieve his own criminal ends. The main method of monitoring transactions adopted by 94 per cent of respondents to a survey carried out by KPMG is staff vigilance.[22]

8.7 Action taken by OFCs to prevent money laundering

The most influential grouping of 'Offshore' entities is the Offshore Group of Banking Supervisors (OGBS) (see section 9.21 below). The OGBS is committed to the FATF's 40+9 Recommendations. Commitment to the 40+9 is a criterion for membership of the OGBS. Apart from this funda-mental adherence to international standards in this respect, members of the OGBS have demonstrated their commitment by their willingness to publish their respective Mutual Evaluation Reports (see section 8.21 below). Table 1 in Appendix 1 shows that, as at March 2004, there are no members of the OGBS that have failed to publish their IMF FSAP/ Module 2 reports. (By way of contrast, reluctance has been expressed by certain members of the FATF in publishing their reports.)

More generally, reputation – on which credibility is founded and of which regulation is a platform – is probably a financial centre's most valuable asset. Credible centres will want to protect their reputation by employing robust anti-money laundering procedures in general and intrusive Customer Due Diligence procedures in particular.

This being so, money launderers – being as astute and as adaptable as they are – must weigh up the cost (including the opportunity cost of the time and effort that it takes) of defeating the protective systems that individual jurisdictions have established or whether it is easier to try a different method. 'The UK Treasury recently estimated that the cost of laundering money has risen to 25 per cent of the money laundered from about 5 per cent in the 1980s.'[23]

---

[21] Barry A. K. Rider, 'The Control of Money Laundering – A Bridge Too Far?', paper submitted to the Sixteenth International Symposium on Economic Crime, Jesus College, Cambridge, September 1998.

[22] *Global Anti-Money Laundering Survey 2004*, KPMG, October 2004, p. 22.

[23] A. Courtenay, 'Washed and Brushed Up', *The Banker*, October 1996, p. 72.

In fact, the general response of OFCs to the types of dilemmas described above is little different to the responses of the 'Onshore' finance centres. The main weapon relied upon by OFCs is legislation. It should be said that the degree to which the rules apply is sometimes greater 'Offshore' than 'Onshore'. It is frequently stated – and this will be anathema to some – that it is more difficult to open an account 'Offshore' than it is 'Onshore'.

Despite all the measures taken by so many jurisdictions, money laundering prevails globally, and so the question must be asked – why? Some think this is the fault of the 'Offshore' jurisdictions. In the Edwards Report (see section 17.3 below), Mr Edwards said that: 'Some of the overseas prosecutors and regulators I met, perhaps influenced by re- sponses received in other Offshore Centres, assumed that there was no point in asking the Islands for assistance in the investigation of crimes or regulatory offences, since no assistance would be forthcoming.'[24] (The specific islands referred to were Guernsey, the Isle of Man and Jersey – but some might say that this comment could be applied to all 'Offshore Centres'.)

On the other hand, it has been suggested that 'the OECD has been successful in demonising the so-called tax havens by raising the false spectre of money laundering while marginalizing its political leaders through diplomatic double-speak'.[25]

8.8 The fight against money laundering

Action taken to prevent money laundering is very costly, but whether the action being taken is appropriate or not remains to be seen. This matter is pursued in section 8.17 below.

However, the problem is not simply that the cost/benefit ratio is skewed unfavourably. There are other factors to be considered, such as those relating to the rights of citizens. Some measures adopted in the fight against money laundering have resulted in infringements of civil rights, including the right to privacy. Even unwitting accomplices can be called to account – despite not knowing that 'dirty' money was being laundered with their assistance.

---

[24] Michael Edwards, *Review of Financial Regulation in the Crown Dependencies*, Part 1, para. 15.4.11, 1998.
[25] 'The Case for International Tax Competition: A Caribbean Perspective', *CFP Foundation Prosperitas*, Vol. 2, No. 2, April 2002.

It is a fact of life that some 'operators' both Onshore and 'Offshore' pay less than full attention to the Customer Due Diligence procedures. Failure to do so may breach the law and will in any event almost certainly lead to problems – in the medium to long term. On the basis that prevention is better than cure, it seems likely that, in future, more and more attention must be paid to the placement stage – since the problem of discovery is aggravated once placement has taken place.

In the meantime, regulators both 'Onshore' and 'Offshore' will continue to focus their efforts in sensitising over and over again senior management of banking and financial services companies to know their customer and to refuse to accept any business about which they are suspect. This type of paradigm will only be effective if licensees comply because they know it to be in their own best interest to do so and not because a regulator tells them they must. In this respect, 84 per cent of respondents to a survey undertaken by KPMG in 2004 believed that the burden of anti-money laundering requirements placed upon them are acceptable.[26]

A recent article in *Compliance Monitor* may be relevant, even though it was not focused on money laundering. The article said that 'The recent trend in regulatory philosophy is to place greater reliance on general management responsibility rather than the enforcement of rigid rules . . . In particular, UK regulators are currently involved in various plans to make directors and senior managers more clearly responsible for their firm's compliance with regulatory standards.'[27] Sometimes these officials are referred to as 'Principal Officers'. Whether this stretches to anti-money laundering procedures remains to be seen, but the FATF's Recommendations clearly require key individuals to be fit and proper.

To do so will focus the attention of senior management on their precise responsibilities for ensuring that appropriate standards prevail. After all, the culture of the organisation is largely a reflection of the style and attitude of the most powerful and influential people within it. '[W]hile everyone must act with integrity, due care, skill and diligence while carrying out their controlled functions, senior managers are additionally responsible for the management, organisation and control of

---

[26] *Global Anti-Money Laundering Survey 2004*, KPMG, October 2004, p. 6.
[27] D. Stephens and J. Neill, 'Managers and the Regulators', PriceWaterhouseCoopers, *Compliance Monitor*, August 1998, p. 45.

the business.'[28] This means that senior managers are well placed to introduce or to enhance – as the case may be – levels of accountability (see section 18.16 below). In this respect, there is less value in apportioning blame – which is reactive – than with ensuring that appropriate levels of control exist at all levels within the organisational hierarchy – which is a proactive element in strategic planning. If this requires a paradigm shift, so be it.

In line with the FATF's recommendation, more jurisdictions are widening the range of predicate offences. Originally, only drug trafficking was a predicate offence.

Meanwhile, in October 2000, EU countries agreed to increase the penalties for money laundering. Perhaps more importantly, the EU agreed to do more to overcome whatever impedes criminal investigations in respect of banking secrecy laws and confidentiality in respect of tax matters. The maximum sentence for money laundering will be at least four years. (By comparison, this exceeds the level in some countries (e.g. Austria) but is less than elsewhere (e.g. the UK where it is fourteen years).)

It is not only so-called 'Offshore Finance Centres' that are at risk. For example, a member of Canada's Financial Transactions and Reports Analysis Centre ('Fintrac') suspects that C$22 million was processed through Canadian financial institutions in the year to March 2003. A conference at which Fintrac was represented was told that 'Canada is a haven for money launderers and there are more active terrorist groups operating in the country than anywhere else in the world.'[29] It was reported in March 2005 that 'Canadian direct investment in offshore financial centres has risen eight fold since 1990 to C$88bn in 2003 according to Statistics Canada.'[30] (In Canada, thirteen provincial and territorial agencies regulate the securities business. If a firm wants to sell securities, provide investment advice or sell mutual funds, it must register with the securities commission in ten provinces and three territories. This requires form filling, fees and slightly different regulatory requirements. The Governor of the Bank of Canada, Mr David Dodge, is on record as saying that 'foreigners considered the country a regulatory wild west'.[31] Only two members of IOSCO (see section 9.16 below) do

---

[28] Jonathan Edwards and Simon Wolfe, 'Compliance: A Review', Vol. 13, No. 1, *Journal of Financial Regulation and Compliance*, p. 54.

[29] Karen Howlett, 'Canada Is a Haven for Dirty Money, Conference Told', GlobeandMail.com, 11 May 2004.

[30] 'Canadian Investment in OFCs up Eightfold Since 1990', April 2005, *Offshore Red*, p. 51.

[31] 'An End to the Wild West?', *The Economist*, 18 June 2005, pp. 68–9.

not have a national or supranational regulator, Bosnia-Herzegovina and Canada.)

A more recent factor in the fight against money laundering is the Financial Intelligence Unit.

8.9 Financial Intelligence Units

Financial Intelligence Units (FIUs) have been in operation since the early 1990s. They are specialist, centralised, governmental agencies that act as central intelligence gathering units. They process the information fed to them and pass on to appropriate governmental agencies whatever intelligence they are able to collate. The rapid exchange of information (between financial institutions, law enforcement agencies and the jurisdictions themselves) is a core objective and, when accomplished at the pre-investigative or intelligence stage, increases the potential for successful action.

FIUs provide an opportunity for effective coordination between multiple law enforcement agencies that might be involved in particular investigations. This is advantageous at all times, but especially when those agencies have parallel or even competing jurisdictional authority. FIUs also enable coordination of Suspicious Transaction Reports (STRs) (see below) so that their analysis and the intelligence that results can be exploited optimally.

It is not possible for a provider of financial services to know that a client has criminal intentions. However, suspicions may arise as a result of enquiries, observations and trends. Such suspicions must be reported by way of STRs to FIUs – for whom this is the main source of intelligence. This is a passive means of detecting money laundering, and, as such, it is open to criticism because money launderers circumvent the system and the process is subject to overload as large numbers of STRs are submitted. (This is entirely to be expected since failure to submit an STR renders an individual person guilty of an offence. Accordingly, to be on the safe side, people are likely to report and avoid personal culpability rather than not report and risk the consequences.) In such circumstances, there is always a risk that the system will be saturated by reports and thereby become dysfunctional. Meanwhile, honest citizens are affected. It is becoming more difficult to open a bank account; transactions are scrutinised more closely; and the administration surrounding even simple transactions is growing. FIUs also obtain spontaneous submissions of information from other FIUs.

The system is founded on the premise that one piece of information in the hands of one agency might mean very little, but, if all the single pieces of information about the same person or transaction in the hands of a number of agencies is collated, a more meaningful and comprehensive picture may be apparent. FIUs act as coordinators, and, by collating a number of pieces of intelligence, they might be in a better position to spot something that would not be possible to spot in other circumstances.

For this exchange of information to work properly, there has to be complete confidence by those who are disclosing information that it will remain secure in the hands of the FIU. Previous comments on the importance of confidentiality 'Offshore' will indicate the sensitivity of this type of disclosure. In order to make the disclosure possible in the first place, a jurisdiction's legislation will have to authorise the disclosure. The majority of 'Offshore Centres' have FIUs (as can be seen by Table 24 in Appendix 1).

8.10 The Egmont Group

The Egmont Group's first meeting – attended by fifteen countries – was at the Egmont-Arenberg Palace in Brussels in 1995. As of June 2004, the Egmont Group – which began as an informal forum for FIUs – had grown to include ninety-four members (see Table 24 in Appendix 1). The Group's goal is to 'seek ways to develop among participants more effective[32] and practical cooperation, especially in the areas of information exchange and [the] sharing of expertise'.[33] The Group defines an FIU as follows: 'a central, national agency responsible for receiving (and, as permitted, requesting), analysing and disseminating to the competent authorities, disclosures of financial information: (i) concerning suspected proceeds of crime, or (ii) required by national legislation or regulation, in order to counter money laundering'.[34] FIUs often act as

---

[32] 'Statement of Purpose of the Egmont Group of Financial Intelligence Units', 24 June, 1997.

[33] The Egmont Group of Financial Intelligence Units, 'Information Paper on Financial Intelligence Units and the Egmont Group', www.oecd.org/fatf/Ctry-orgpages/org-egmont_en. htm. p. 3.

[34] The Egmont Group of Financial Intelligence Units, 'Information Paper on Financial Intelligence Units and the Egmont Group', www.oecd.org/fatf/Ctry-orgpages/org-egmont_en. htm. p. 4.

a focus for their respective countries' anti-money laundering programmes. FIUs provide an effective means for exchanging information
rapidly – between jurisdictions, between financial institutions and
between law enforcement authorities and prosecutors.

The Group's 'Principles for Information Exchange' provide that:

> FIUs should be able to exchange information freely with other FIUs on
> the basis of reciprocity or mutual agreement and consistent with proced-
> ures understood by the requested and the requesting party. Furthermore,
> the Egmont members have agreed that information exchanged between
> FIUs may be used only for the specific purposes for which the information
> was sought or provided. The requesting FIU may not transfer the infor-
> mation shared by a disclosing FIU to a third party, nor make use of the
> information in an administrative, investigative, prosecutorial, or judicial
> purpose without the prior consent of the FIU that disclosed the infor-
> mation.[35]

The Group acts as a forum in which each member undertakes to share
information with every other member in accordance with prescribed
procedures. The Group continues to grow in terms of members and in
stature. In fact, the establishment of the Egmont Committee in 2002
reflects the pace of growth. The Committee coordinates the Heads of the
FIUs, and Egmont has five working groups. The Committee comprises
the Chairs of each working group (described below) and representatives
from Asia, Africa, Europe, the Americas and Oceania. The working
groups are (1) Legal; (2) Operational; (3) Training/Communications;
(4) Outreach; and (5) Information Technology. The Outreach Working
Group identifies potential new members, while the Legal Working Group
reviews applications for membership, handles legal matters and coordinates the work of the other working groups. The Operational Working
Group brings together FIUs on strategic projects, while the Training
Working Group is responsible for identifying training opportunities.
Lastly, the Information Technology Working Group addresses IT issues.
The Committee and the working groups meet three times each year.

The Egmont Group celebrated its tenth anniversary at its thirteenth
plenary meeting in the United States held from 27 June to 1 July 2005,
with the addition of seven new members, bringing total membership to

---

[35] 'The Egmont Group of Financial Intelligence Units Exceeeds the 100 Member Mark
During Its Annual Meeting Hosted by the Financial Crimes Enforcement Network',
Egmont Group, 29 June 2005, p. 4.

101. The new members are: the FIUs from Bosnia and Herzegovina, Honduras, Peru, the Philippines, Montenegro, Qatar and San Marino.

8.11 Alternative remittance systems

In some countries, 'underground banking systems' have been in operation so long (pre-dating banking) that they are regarded as traditions. Frequently, such systems have ethnic or cultural roots. They include *hawala* (associated with India and Pakistan), *fei chien* (associated with Chinese communities), *padala* in the Philippines, *hundi* in India, *phoei kwan* in Thailand and the black-market peso exchange in Latin America. By definition, they create what the FATF refers to as 'alternative remittance systems'. 'According to the United Nations, some $100bn flows through the informal banking sector. It is estimated for example, that remittances to Pakistan through hawalas are in the range of $3–$5bn annually, larger than the remittances received through the formal banking sector.'[36]

In common with banking, these systems allow value to be transferred but without any physical movement of currency, and, most importantly, they rely on trust – a characteristic innate to all financial transactions. Minimal information is required from users, and even less is recorded. Usually, they operate outside the national financial and regulatory systems. This means that they pose fundamental problems for law enforcement agencies engaged in detecting money under suspicion. Identification procedures are replaced by a code word. They transmit value by some form of 'netting' or 'book transfer system'. They are secure and cheap and allow circumvention of the standard currency exchange rules. Although physical cash may be exchanged, it is frequently the case that a token is used. Fundamentally, they provide anonymity to the user – they are opaque. This means that the absence of statistical information is an acute problem. The prevalence of such systems and their increasing usage make them of particular interest to criminals and of particular concern to law enforcement agencies.

The US Department of the Treasury Financial Crimes Enforcement Network ('FinCEN', the FIU in the USA) has described the black-market

[36] James Fisher, James Gilsinan, Ellen Harshman, Muhammed Islam and Fred Yeager, 'Assessing the Impact of the USA PATRIOT Act on the Financial Services Industry', Vol. 8, No. 3, *James Journal of Money Laundering Control*, p. 245.

peso exchange mechanism as 'the single most efficient and extensive money laundering "system" in the Western Hemisphere'.[37,38]

8.12 The Wolfsberg Anti-Money Laundering Principles

The Wolfsberg Principles – made public on 30 October 2000 – represent an initiative of the private sector and are named after the United Bank of Switzerland's training centre where they were agreed. It took two years to compile the Principles. Eleven banks subscribed to the process, namely ABN Amro Bank NV, Banco Santander Central Hispano SA, Barclays Bank, the Chase Manhattan Private Bank, Citibank NA, the Credit Suisse Group, Deutsche Bank AG, the Hong Kong and Shanghai Banking Corporation, JP Morgan, Société Générale and UBS AG.

The eleven Principles represent a set of guidelines that reflect the responsibilities of the management of banks in the fight against money laundering in private banks. Bank regulators have a part to play, but the voluntary creation and adherence to these types of 'guidelines by bankers for bankers' represents a new approach. The new approach is based on the tenet that it is the reputation of the banks that is at stake and so it is in their best interests to curb the abuse of their organisations – and money laundering represents such an abuse.

8.13 'Customer Due Diligence for Banks': a Basel Committee paper

The concept of 'customer due diligence' goes beyond the identification and verification of the client. It includes the identification of the potential risks of a business relationship. According to the Review of the FATF Forty Recommendations Consultation Paper, the overall objective of the customer due diligence process is for financial institutions to know their customers so that institutions can recognise when financial activity is unusual and therefore potentially suspicious and/or derived from or intended for use in criminal/terrorist activity; and to have sufficiently accurate records available to assist with investigations.

---

[37] 'Colombian Black Market Peso Exchange', FinCEN Advisory Issue, No. 9, as quoted in George Gilligan, 'Going Underground – The Not So New Way to Bank', Vol. 9, No. 2, *Journal of Financial Crime*, p. 2.
[38] Further information may be obtained from the FATF's website (see Appendix 2 below).

International best practice recommends that financial institutions should undertake customer due diligence checks. Customer due diligence checks include:

- identifying the direct customer;
- verifying the customer's identity;
- identifying the person who exercises beneficial ownership and control;
- verifying the identity of the beneficial owner and/or the person on whose behalf a transaction is being conducted; and
- conducting ongoing due diligence and scrutiny.

The 'CDD Paper', as it is called, is based on the Basel Committee's view that, in the absence of due diligence, banks (although the same comment applies to all financial services practitioners) may be exposed to reputational, operational, legal and concentration risks. The focus is on how banks can ensure that they have adequate procedures to ensure that they actually know the identity of persons with whom they are dealing.

The CDD Paper arose from deficiencies that the Basel Committee identified as part of its review of 'an internal survey of cross-border banking in 1999'. The deficiencies ranged from material gaps to non-existent procedures. The Committee resolved to research further what 'know your customer' procedures were already in place and to prepare standards for all banks in all countries to consider adopting. This work was delegated to the Working Group on Cross-Border Banking, and a consultative document was prepared, refined and then issued, '. . . in the expectation that the KYC [know your customer] framework presented here will become the benchmark for supervisors to establish national practices and for banks to design their own programmes'. (The Group comprised members of the Basel Committee and of the Offshore Group of Banking Supervisors.)

A paper was prepared and, in January 2001, was issued as a consultative document. The paper was revised to take account of the comments received and was reissued in October 2001 under the title 'Customer Due Diligence for Banks'. The intention was that the framework presented in the CDD Paper would become 'the benchmark for supervisors to establish national practices'.[39] The CDD Paper made it clear that the

---

[39] 'Customer Due Diligence for Banks', Basel Committee on Banking Supervision, October 2001, p. 2.

standards presented in the paper were intended to be consistent with those promulgated by the FATF. On the basis that rigorous due diligence standards are necessary for organisations other than banks, the anti-money laundering perspective adopted in the paper is based on the belief that 'similar guidance needs to be developed for all non-bank financial institutions and professional intermediaries'.[40]

The CDD Paper provides more precise guidance than was set out in earlier papers published by the Committee on what are referred to as 'the essential elements of [know your customer] standards and their implementation'.[41]

The paper forms part of the assessment criteria used by the IMF/World Bank in their Financial Sector Assessment Programs (see section 10.09 below).

8.14 Terrorist financing

'The problem with terrorist financing is that the funds are often not the proceeds of crime.'[42] This poses great problems in detection.

In response to the terrorist attacks in the USA on 11 September 2001, action was taken by the FATF at an extraordinary plenary meeting on 31 October 2001 when the organisation's role was expanded to include combating terrorist financing. Eight Special Recommendations were issued and jurisdictions were asked to ratify a 1999 UN resolution on terrorist financing. Jurisdictions were asked to make terrorist financing a criminal activity. Jurisdictions were also asked to ensure that their legislation enabled them to freeze assets and to cooperate in investigations – not least by reporting suspicious transactions. All jurisdictions were given until 30 September 2002 to adhere to these Recommendations. (See also Chapter 11.) Surprisingly, some jurisdictions did not meet this deadline. 'The least comprehensive legal frameworks were to be found in Austria, Australia (which had yet to comply in any sense with three of the recommendations), Greece, Mexico and Hong Kong.'[43]

The results[44] of the action taken since 11 September 2001 include:

---

[40] 'Customer Due Diligence for Banks', Basel Committee on Banking Supervision, October 2001, p. 3.
[41] The quotations in this sub-paragraph are taken from the CDD Paper (p. 2).
[42] Bob Campion, 'In the Shadow of September 11', October 2002, *Portfolio International*, p. 10.
[43] Bob Campion, 'In the Shadow of September 11', October 2002, *Portfolio International*, p. 10.
[44] Bob Campion, 'In the Shadow of September 11', October 2002, *Portfolio International*, p. 10.

- in the year since September 2001, US$112 million of terrorists' assets were frozen;
- 165 countries ordered terrorists' funds to be blocked;
- 288 legal persons were subject to blocking;
- more than 80 countries have enacted or will enact legislation dealing with the financing of terrorists;
- US$34 million was frozen within the USA;
- US$78 million was found outside the USA, and of this US$39 million was frozen in Switzerland.

Another update – this time from the US Department of the Treasury, and dated 16 January 2004 – stated that, since September 2001:

- 1447 accounts, containing more than US$139.1 million in assets, have been frozen worldwide, including US$36.7 million in the USA;
- US$64 million in additional terrorist-related assets have been seized by authorities globally;
- 345 individuals and organisations have been listed as 'Specially Designated Global Terrorists' (SDGTs) under Executive Order 13224;
- countless millions in additional funds have been prevented from flowing to terrorists by the disruption of terrorist financing networks, by the deterrence of donors, and by international efforts to secure the world financial system from the financing of terror.[45]

Suicide bombers set off explosions in London on 7 July 2005, – killing fifty-seven people and injuring many others. Further (failed) attempts took place on 21 July 2005. In response, the UK Government convened a special meeting of EU Interior Ministers on 13 July to endeavour to speed up the adoption of EU anti-terror measures – which have been in the pipeline since the train bombings in Madrid (11 March 2004). The EU Commission proposed transposing into EU law, an existing FATF recommendation that requires money transfers into or out of Europe to include the name, address and the account number of the person transmitting the money (with a simplified procedure for transfers within and between Member States). The objective is to allow money transferred to be traced. Records must be kept for five years, and a failure to provide this information will allow the bank to refuse to transfer and possibly submit a Suspicious Transaction Report. Meanwhile, on 13 July 2005, EU

---

[45] State Department Press Releases, 16 January 2004, as reported in *GPML Global Press Review*, United Nations Office on Drugs and Crime, Vol. 2, No. 3, 19 January 2004.

Ministers convened a special meeting of the Justice and Home Affairs
Council and resolved to bring forward completion dates on measures
(already in the pipeline) to counter terrorism.

8.15 The EU and anti-money laundering

The EU's First Directive on Money Laundering was dated 1991. The
Directive focused on laundering the proceeds of the sale of drugs
through the financial sector in general. Its object was to 'harmonise'
the national legislation enacted in Member States, thereby eliminating
opportunities for arbitrage between Member States. The Directive gave
rise to the initial efforts to identify customers, to report suspicious
transactions and to keep appropriate records.

An agreement was approved by the EU's Parliament on 13 November
2001 which extended the EU Directive to include a wide range of criminal
activities (the 'all crimes' approach) and extended the reporting population to include certain non-financial professions (see below). The cadre
of professionals included notaries and independent legal professionals,
when their work involved them in 'financial or corporate transactions,
including providing tax advice'. Lawyers and other legal advisers were
exempted from reporting when the relevant information was 'obtained
either before, during or after judicial proceedings, or in the course of
ascertaining the legal position for a client'.[46]

On 4 December 2001, the EU adopted the Second Directive on Anti-
Money Laundering. The Directive amended the European Council
Directive on Prevention of the Use of the Financial System for the
Purpose of Money Laundering (91/308/EEC) and dated 1991. The new
Directive widened the range of predicate offences and extended the
obligations of the 1991 Directive. The new Directive included certain
non-financial professions and activities within the definition of 'relevant
financial business'. This included professional intermediaries such as
estate agents, lawyers and accountants, and people who deal in goods
of high value including jewellers, auctioneers and casino operators.
The obligations regarding customer identification and the obligation to
file Suspicious Transaction Reports were widened. Member States were
obliged to incorporate the provisions of the Directive into domestic

---

[46] Joint Text Approved by the Conciliation Committee Provided for in Article 251(4) of the
EC Treaty.

legislation by 15 June 2003, 'but only around half the member states have done so'.[47] Therefore, France, Greece, Italy, Luxembourg, Portugal and Sweden are to be sent formal requests by the European Commission to implement the Directive.

The EU formulated the Paris Declaration on 8 February 2002. This represents an action plan to combat money laundering. The Declaration prevents EU companies from establishing subsidiary companies or branches or even representative offices in any jurisdiction that has been blacklisted by the OECD or by the FATF. Similarly, entities in such countries will not be able to open offices in an EU country.

The Third Directive on Anti-Money Laundering was published in June 2004. The European Parliament approved the Bill in May 2005 and the Ecofin Council adopted the Directive on 7 June 2005. It is expected to take effect from the end of 2007. Its purpose is to consolidate the previous directives and to incorporate the provisions of the FATF's recent (June 2003) revisions of its Forty Recommendations. (The intention was to repeal the 1991 Directive (as amended in 2001) and to replace it with a new consolidated text.) The Directive provides for the seizure of assets by means of civil law (as opposed to criminal law) procedures. The Third Directive enhances the definition of money laundering to include, for example, scenarios where legitimate money is used to finance terrorism, and it will also make provision for the protection of employees who report transactions that they consider to be suspicious.[48] The definition has been extended to include concealing or disguising the proceeds of a wider range of serious crimes and the funding of terrorism. The Directive embraces life insurance intermediaries and company services providers (including trusts). It requires financial advisors to identify the beneficiaries of trusts (who will receive more than 10 per cent of the trust's assets) and has caused some ripples in both 'Onshore' and 'Offshore' because of the implications for confidentiality. Further, the Directive will also cover anyone providing a service that involves cash of €15,000 or more.

[47] 'Money Laundering', EurActiv.com, 27 May 2005.
[48] 'Justice and Home Affairs: Commission Unveils Plans to Tackle Organized Financial Crime', *Europe Information*, 28 April 2004, as cited in *GMPL Global Press Review*, 10 May 2004, Vol. 2, No. 12, United Nations Office on Drugs and Crime, p. 20.

8.16 The Basel Committee and anti-money laundering

Although the Basel Committee focuses its attention on banks, the application of the principles described in at least two of the Committee's publications is not restricted exclusively to banks. Certain aspects also apply to non-bank financial services companies.

8.16.1 Statement of Principles on Prevention of Criminal Use of Banking System

In 1988, the Basel Committee published a paper entitled 'Prevention of Criminal Use of Banking System'. The Committee recognised that banking supervisors had 'a general role to encourage ethical standards of professional conduct among banks and other financial institutions'. That being so, the Committee published this paper as a 'Statement of Principles' to which (it was hoped) there would be international agreement. The Committee pointed out that the Statement was not a legal document and that implementation depended on national practice and law. Rather, the Statement was described as 'a general statement of ethical principles which encourages banks' management to put in place effective procedures to ensure that all persons conducting business with their institutions are properly identified; that transactions that do not appear legitimate are discouraged; and that cooperation with law enforcement agencies is achieved'.

Interestingly, the paper/Statement recognised that 'the first and most important safeguard against money-laundering is the integrity of banks' own management and their vigilant determination to prevent their institutions becoming associated with criminals or being used as a channel for money-laundering'.[49]

8.16.2 Customer due diligence for banks

The Basel Committee published its paper entitled 'Customer Due Diligence for Banks' ('CDD Paper') in October 2001 (as described in section 8.13 above).

---

[49] The quotations in this subsection are taken from paragraph 6 of the paper.

8.17 Future action

The fight against money laundering is a costly business. One estimate of the 'direct up-front' cost of compliance with anti-money laundering laws in the UK is approaching £1 billion. The comparable figure for the USA is around US$3000 million.[50] The Governor of New Mexico was quoted in the *New York Times* (30 December 2000) as saying: 'The federal anti drug budget in 1980 was roughly $1 billion. By 2000, that number had climbed to nearly $20 billion, with the states spending at least that much. Yet according to the federal government's own research, drugs are cheaper, purer and more readily available than ever before.'[51] According to an analyst at Celent Communications, 'US banking, securities and insurance industries will spend a total of $10.9 billion on anti-money laundering prevention from now until the end of 2005 . . . Celent estimates that $856.6 billion will be laundered worldwide in 2002 . . . to reach $926.6 billion by the end of 2005.'[52] Further, 'Celent estimates that financial firms in Europe and America spent over $5 billion on tackling money laundering last year [2003]. American firms accounted for $3.6 billion of this, up from $700m in 2000 . . . in part because more were required to install AML [anti-money laundering] systems under the Patriot Act.'[53] Clearly, '[t]he cost of AML compliance has risen significantly over the past three years, with the average reported increase being 61 per cent . . . Transaction monitoring activity has been the main cause of increased AML spending.'[54] It is likely that costs will continue to rise.

So far as the results are concerned, 'the UK recovery rate is just 0.02 per cent . . . According to new research by money laundering expert Mike Adlem, out of an estimated £250 billion that is currently laundered through the UK each year, just £46 billion has ever been recovered at a cost of £400 million.'[55] Mr Adlem has said that Britain's attempts to combat money laundering are 'pathetic' and that 'we need to stop and

[50] Barry Rider, 'Minding Other People's Wealth – Editorial', Vol. 12, No 3, *Journal of Financial Crime*, p. 198.
[51] 'Taxation, Money Laundering and Liberty', Vol. 9, No. 4, *Journal of Financial Crime*, April 2002, p. 342.
[52] 'Money Laundering Is a Growth Industry', OffshoreOn.com, 29 October 2002.
[53] 'Coming Clean', *The Economist*, 16 October 2004, p. 73.
[54] *Global Anti-Money Laundering Survey 2004*, KPMG, October 2004, p. 6.
[55] 'Failing to Combat Money Laundering', *Investment International News*, 12 April 2005.

completely rethink things'.[56] Some of the procedures adopted thus far and an indication of the resources allocated to dealing with money laundering have been described above. Despite all this, the problem is far from solved. 'The [US] Justice Department's most recent data states that fewer than 1/1000th of one per cent of currency transaction reports are used in a criminal conviction',[57] and 'fewer than 1000 people per year have been convicted of money laundering in the USA since it became illegal'.[58] Further, 'as at 31 December 2004, over 2.1 million Suspicious Activity Report Forms had been filed with FinCEN' in the USA (see section 9.9 below).[59]

Clearly, the measures adopted so far have not been successful, so it is likely that, in the future, there will be an increasing need to justify this sort of spending by demonstrating tangible results. It has been suggested that 'the best way to combat drug trafficking must be to include methods which deprive criminals of their profits . . . [T]he day the drug problem is defeated, the money laundering problem will also be defeated.'[60]

The fight continues as more novel methods to launder money are continuing to be developed. For example, in this respect, the 'SAR Activity Review – Trends, Tips and Issues' is a useful source document. The seventh issue (published on 16 August 2004) analyses 'the suspected use of United States-based shell corporations and foreign shell banks by some Eastern European criminals to move money through correspondent bank accounts'.[61] The Review says that 397 SARs that involved shell corporations, Eastern European countries and correspondent bank accounts were filed between April 1996 and January 2004. The quantum of money involved was almost US$4 billion. (see section 13.5 below for comment on shell banks). 'The use of shell corporations and shell banks to launder money and possibly finance terrorist activities is a concern shared by government Financial Intelligence Units worldwide.'[62]

---

[56] Tom Bawden, 'UK's Bid to Trace Dirty Money Is "Pathetic"', 15 March 2005, www. timesonline.co.uk/newspaper/0,171-1525951,00.html.

[57] A. Quinlan, 'Center for Freedom and Prosperity Statement on State Hearing', 18 July 2001.

[58] 'Taxation, Money Laundering and Liberty', April 2002, Vol. 9, No. 4, *Journal of Financial Crime*, p. 342.

[59] *The SAR Activity Review – By the Numbers*, Issue 4, May 2005, p. 1.

[60] Jeffrey Robinson, *The Laundrymen*, Simon & Schuster UK Ltd, 1998, p. 396.

[61] *FinCENnews*, US Department of the Treasury Financial Crimes Enforcement Network, 16 August 2004.

[62] *The SAR Activity Review – Trends, Tips & Issues*, Issue 7, August 2004, p. 4.

Further, the Review also describes 'food stamp trafficking', in which people who receive aid for food from the government sell their 'Electronic Benefit Transfer' cards for less than their value. 'An estimated $395 million of food benefits are diverted each year from their intended purpose through food stamp trafficking and associated money laundering activities.'[63]

8.18 FATF and IMF/World Bank

The IMF's work in respect of anti-money laundering is managed by the Financial Markets Integrity Division, part of the Monetary and Financial Systems Department.

At the end of a twelve-month pilot programme – that focused on how anti-money laundering and anti-terrorist financing standards could be applied consistently all over the globe, and in which the FATF's Recommendations have been used as test criteria – the FATF encouraged the IMF and the World Bank to make their assessments a permanent part of the Financial Sector Assessment Program. At a seminar that preceded the FATF's plenary meeting in February 2004, attendees concluded that more must be done in collecting and sharing information. The intentions are good – but the results (in terms of solving the problems) are discouraging. The questions that must be asked include whether we are doing the right thing and whether we are doing the thing right. 'Perhaps a new approach to anti-money laundering needs to be developed . . . [B]usiness and jurisdictions risk sinking under a sea of the misguided application of compliance . . . [T]here has to be a more focused solution.'[64] The FATF issued their new methodology in 2004 and, in March 2004, the IMF and World Bank agreed to use this methodology in their Financial Sector Assessment Program (see sections 10.14 and 11.12 below). In this respect, it has been said that

> [a]ssessments of compliance with AMLCFT standards include judgments about how well the system is implemented. This goes beyond just evaluating supervisory practices. It includes evaluations of the functioning of the

---

[63] Theodore Macaluso and V. A. Alexandria, 'The Extent of Trafficking in the Food Stamp Program', Food and Nutrition Service, 2003, as cited in *The SAR Activity Review – Trends, Tips & Issues*, Issue 7, August 2004, p. 10.

[64] Alan Morgan-Moodie, 'Knowing Me, Knowing You', *Portfolio International*, March 2004.

criminal justice system, including the courts, in enforcing AMLCFT laws
and regulations . . . The firms themselves are supposed to be governed by
ethical parties. These entities are expected to have systems and procedures
in place that deter them from being misused by their customers for
laundering the proceeds of any serious crime. Assessing compliance with
these standards is a natural consequence of the Fund's work on oversight
of the financial sector.[65]

The emphasis seems to be changing continuously. Originally, it was
said that OFCs were fundamentally to blame because of lax procedures
and ineffective regulations. Then new rules were introduced, then FIUs
were in focus, then more rules, and now the FATF believes that charities
and unregulated money transfer systems require more attention than
mainstream financial institutions. Even as other activities come under
the spotlight, and despite all the efforts to remedy this problem, it
continues to worsen. The answer seems to be that we do not know what
the answer is – but, before we choke business further, there may be
value in considering whether there may be a different paradigm. 'In
North America, 70 per cent of all respondents [to a KPMG survey]
believe the [anti-money laundering] requirements are acceptable but
need improvement, against only 18 per cent who feel that they are
acceptable and effective.'[66]

8.19 Assets recovery

In some countries, there are agencies whose role it is to recover assets
from those with no legitimate right of ownership and which have been
obtained unlawfully. One such agency, the Assets Recovery Agency
(ARA), was established in the UK under the Proceeds of Crime Act
2002. The philosophy is that criminals damage society in general when
they are allowed to retain assets that have been obtained unlawfully.
Damage derives from the potential that these assets may be used to
perpetrate further crimes and also because it is unjust that criminals
may enjoy their ill-gotten gains after their prison sentence. More fundamentally, if crime is to be controlled, society must be able to see that it
does not pay.

---

[65] R. Barry Johnston and John Abbott, 'Placing Bankers in the Front Line', Vol. 8, No 3,
Journal of Money Laundering Control, p. 215.
[66] *Global Anti-Money Laundering Survey 2004*, KPMG, October 2004, p. 30.

In the UK, the ARA is an independent government agency that became operational in February 2003. Cases are referred to the ARA by police, customs and law enforcement agencies according to certain criteria. The ARA provides training for other agencies such as the police and customs, and investigates cases with the intention of obtaining a post-conviction confiscation order. The ARA uses its civil recovery powers to sue for the recovery of the proceeds of unlawful conduct. Interestingly, the Director of the ARA may operate under the tax rules that the Inland Revenue would apply. This power is invoked where there are reasonable grounds to suspect that income, gains or profits deriving from crime exist and which are chargeable to tax. All the defendant's property is subject to tax. The ARA is empowered to request international assistance in obtaining restraint and confiscation orders.

It has been reported[67] that, as at 31 March 2004, twelve months after it began to operate, the ARA had sixty-two cases under investigation and had frozen assets to the value of £14.8 million. As at 15 November 2004, the ARA had £20 million worth of property under restraint and was dealing with 160 referrals from law enforcement agencies and had instituted litigation in forty cases. At that stage, five cases had been processed through the courts, and orders had been made for £5.5 million.

[67] 'Freezing, Leasing and Timing', *Money Laundering Bulletin*, December 2004/January 2005, Issue 119, p. 3.

9

Some international organisations and groupings

Like water finding its own level, entrepreneurial business, when constrained in one place, will emerge in another. When restrictions in one place become too burdensome, too discouraging and perhaps too punitive, the businessman will look elsewhere.[1]

9.1 Introduction

This chapter focuses on some of international organisations whose role impinges upon the 'Offshore' environment.

9.2 Bank for International Settlements

Founded in 1930, the Bank for International Settements (BIS) operates as a bank in that it processes transactions between the national central banks that comprise its membership. In fact, it is the 'central bankers' bank'. In addition, the BIS operates as a research centre and a discussion forum for members – of whom there were thirty-two until 1997 when nine new members were invited to join by subscribing for shares. As at July 2005, the number of members had increased to fifty-six.[2] The Board of Directors comprises representatives of the G10.

---

[1] D. G. Hanson, *Service Banking*, Institute of Bankers, London, 1979, p. 272.
[2] Algeria, Argentina, Australia, Austria, Belgium, Bosnia and Herzegovina, Brazil, Bulgaria, Canada, Chile, China, Croatia, Czech Republic, Denmark, Estonia, the European Central Bank, Finland, France, Germany, Greece, Hong Kong, Hungary, Iceland, India, Indonesia, Ireland, Israel, Italy, Japan, Latvia, Lithuania, Macedonia, Malaysia, Mexico, the Netherlands, New Zealand, Norway, the Philippines, Poland, Portugal, Romania, Russia, Saudi Arabia, Serbia and Montenegro, Singapore, Slovakia, Slovenia, South Africa, South Korea, Spain, Sweden, Switzerland, Thailand, Turkey, the UK and the US.

9.3 Basel Committee on Banking Supervision

'The Basel Committee was established after the closure of Franklin National in the United States and the collapse of the Bankhaus Herstatt in Germany, in particular, as a result of heavy foreign currency losses suffered by each.'[3] In fact, '[n]ational bank supervision had until then [the early 1970s] been largely ignored at the Governors' meetings while national supervisory and regulatory authorities considered developments unfolding in international financial markets to be irrelevant. It was only in 1974 with the establishment of the Basel Committee that banks' supervisory issues would be elevated to being an issue of international as well as national concern.'[4]

Originally known as the Committee on Banking Regulations and Supervisory Practices, the Basel Committee is an advisory body that was established in 1974 by the G10 central banks in the aftermath of serious disturbances in international currency and banking markets after the collapse of Bankhaus Herstatt. The Basel Committee operates under the auspices of the Bank for International Settlements, which provides the Committee's Secretariat in Basel. Although the Basel Committee exerts substantial influence, it has no legal force or formal supervisory authority per se.

The Basel Committee sets the standards for world banking regulation and supervision. It meets three or four times each year to formulate broad supervisory standards and statements of best practice in the banking sector. (The Committee's approximately twenty-five task forces and working groups also meet regularly.) Its main objectives are 'to strengthen international cooperation, improve the overall quality of banking supervision worldwide, and to ensure that no foreign banking establishment escapes supervision'.[5]

The Basel Committee provides a forum for ongoing cooperation between member countries on banking supervisory matters. Its conclusions do not have, and were never intended to have, legal force. Rather,

---

[3] George Alexander Walker, *International Banking Regulation Law, Policy and Practice*, Kluwer Law International, 2001, p. 155.

[4] George Alexander Walker, *International Banking Regulation Law, Policy and Practice*, Kluwer Law International, 2001, p. 39.

[5] 'Response of the Basle Committee on Banking Supervision and of the International Organization of Securities Commissions to the Request of the G-7 Heads of Government at the June 1995, Halifax Summit', Montreal, May 1996.

its broad supervisory standards, practices and guidelines are used by individual authorities to implement detailed arrangements – statutory or otherwise – which are best suited to their own national systems. In this way, the Basel Committee encourages convergence towards common approaches and standards without attempting detailed interventions in member countries' supervisory techniques.

9.3.1 The Concordat

The BIS established the Committee on Banking Regulations and Supervisory Practices (the Cooke Committee). Originally, the Committee formulated outline principles concerning the supervision of the activities of international banks overseas. In particular, the Committee emphasised some rules in respect of allocating responsibility amongst the regulators involved. In September 1975, the Committee established five general guidelines in their Concordat in a paper entitled 'Report on the Supervision of Banks' Foreign Establishments'. The Concordat established clearly two core rules for supervision: the need for global inclusion (that is to say, all internationally active bank operations must be subject to some type of regulation) and the adequacy of regulatory techniques.

9.3.2 The revised Concordat

The Concordat was revised and expanded in May 1983 with the publication of 'Principles for the Supervision of Banks' Foreign Establishments'. The collapse of Banco Ambrosiano Holdings (based in Luxembourg) in 1982 led to this revision. (This failure drew attention to the importance of including intermediate companies – and, in this case, bank holding companies and joint ventures – in formal regulatory reviews.[6]) The Concordat described certain principles for sharing supervisory responsibility between host and home supervisors in respect of the foreign branches of banks, for their subsidiaries and for joint ventures. The revision in 1983 aimed at encompassing the increasing need for consolidated supervision of internationally active banking groups' constituent entities – wherever their activities were conducted. Further, the revision included authorisation procedures for banks' foreign entities. In

---

[6] For further information, see Charles Raw, *The Moneychangers – How the Vatican Bank Enabled Roberto Calvi to Steal $250 Million for the heads of the P2 Masonic Lodge*, 1992.

particular, '[h]ost authorities are specifically required to ensure that parent authorities are informed immediately of any serious problems that arise in a parent bank's foreign establishment while parent authorities are to inform host authorities of any difficulties that may affect the parent bank's foreign establishment'.[7]

The purpose of the supplement to the Concordat in April 1990 was to improve the flow of prudential information between parent and host supervisors.

9.3.3 The Basel Capital Accord

See section 6.10.3 above.

9.3.4 The Minimum Standards[8]

The collapse of BCCI in 1991 led to the publication of the Basel Committee's Minimum Standards in 1992. The Minimum Standards are:

- all international banks should be supervised by a home country authority that capably performs consolidated supervision;
- the creation of cross-border banking establishments should receive the prior consent of both the host country and the home country authority;
- home country authorities should possess the right to gather information from their cross-border banking establishments;
- if the host country determines that any of these three standards is not being met, it could impose restrictive measures or prohibit the establishment of banking offices.

More generally, the Committee addresses a wide range of supervisory issues. Papers published include topics such as the supervision of banks' foreign exchange positions, the management of banks' international lending (i.e. country risk), the management of banks' off-balance sheet exposures, the prevention of the criminal use of the banking system, the supervision of large exposures and managing derivative risks. The Committee actively encourages cooperation between its members and

---

[7] George Alexander Walker, *International Banking Regulation Law, Policy and Practice*, Kluwer Law International, 2001, pp. 102–3.
[8] Edited Version of the Response of BCBS and of IOSCO to the Request of the G7 Heads of Government at the June 1995 Halifax Summit, Basle, September 1995.

other banking supervisory authorities around the world and maintains close relations with regional banking supervisory associations. Contacts are further strengthened by biennial international conferences of banking supervisors, held since 1979. The Committee believes that the development of close personal contacts between supervisors in different countries has greatly helped in handling and resolving problems affecting individual banks as they have arisen.

In response to the blurring of distinctions between banking and securities, the Committee works closely with the International Organization of Securities Commissions (IOSCO). One outcome of this cooperation was a joint report, in May 1995, setting out a framework for supervisory information about the derivative activities of banks and securities firms. Members of the Basel Committee also work with securities and insurance regulators on the supervision of financial conglomerates. A discussion paper on this matter was issued in July 1995.

In addition, the Committee has worked with other international bodies such as accountancy experts in the publication of occasional papers. The Committee's Secretariat is provided by the Bank for International Settlements in Basel, where the Committee's meetings normally take place every three months. The Secretariat is mainly staffed by professional supervisors on temporary secondment from member institutions. In addition to undertaking the secretarial work for the Basel Committee and its subcommittees, it stands ready to give advice to supervisory authorities in all countries and conducts several annual training programmes for bank supervisors.

The Committee's members comprise G10 member countries, together with Luxembourg and Sweden. The institutions represented on the Basel Committee are set out in Table 1 in Appendix 1. Representatives are heads of supervision or senior executives of the central bank (or other authority responsible for banking supervision). Most countries have two representatives, except Luxembourg (with one member) and the USA (with four members).

9.4 Overview of the work of the Basel Committee[9]

Over twenty years, the Basel Committee has developed a box of supervisory tools, the rationale for which is based on a rather limited number

[9] 'Opening Remarks by the Chairman of the Basle Committee on Banking Supervision', International Conference on Banking Supervisors, Stockholm, 12 June 1996.

of precepts: coverage should be comprehensive; capital should be adequate; good qualitative standards should be in place; and controls within the firm and the market itself should impose discipline on banks.

9.4.1 Comprehensive coverage

Comprehensive coverage means that no bank should escape effective supervision. The 1975 Concordat and its subsequent refinements, and the Committee's 1992 minimum standards, simply impose minimum conditions for the supervisory system to be consistent across countries.

Consolidated supervision, whereby a banking group is treated as a single entity, is a further condition for comprehensiveness. In practice, many, if not all, regulatory requirements would prove ineffective if market participants were allowed to circumvent them through subsidiaries or complex group structures.

9.4.2 The Core Principles for Effective Banking Supervision

The Core Principles were published by the Basel Committee in September 1997. The Principles include a requirement for bank supervisors, whether 'Onshore' or 'Offshore', to ensure that 'banks have adequate policies, practices and procedures in place, including strict "know your customer" rules, that promote high ethical and professional standards in the financial sector and prevent the bank being used intentionally or unintentionally by criminal elements.' The Core Principles include a framework for the conduct of consolidated supervision. This is very difficult to implement. At one stage, it was said that 'out of those countries for which consolidated supervision was relevant, only 28 per cent were rated fully or largely compliant, with 72 per cent found seriously wanting'.[10]

9.4.3 Capital adequacy

See also section 6.10 above.

Capital is not only a cushion against losses. First and foremost, it is the stock of wealth shareholders invest in a bank to earn a return. A capital requirement thus represents a way to stimulate owners and managers to

---

[10] 'Offshore Finance Centres', IMF Background Paper, 23 June 2000.

ensure the 'safe and sound conduct' of their business. 'Safe and sound' means handling risks that can be borne.

9.4.4 Internal controls

As the risks banks incur grow more complex, their measurement becomes more difficult. Moreover, the increased marketability of financial instruments has greatly increased banks' ability to make rapid changes in the composition of their portfolios and their exposure to risk. For these two reasons, it is virtually impossible for any single person within a bank, let alone anyone outside, to value its asset portfolio accurately. Monitoring by management, owners and the market is becoming increasingly dependent on banks' own internal control systems.

9.4.5 Disclosure

In the past, bank supervisors did not place a great deal of emphasis on the issue of transparency and disclosure. This attitude has changed. 'The ultimate aim is to stimulate the market's own defences.'

9.5 Committee of European Securities Regulators

The European Union's Economic and Finance Ministers asked the 'Committee of Wise Men' (see section 7.4 above) to:

- assess the current conditions for implementation of the regulation of securities markets in the EU;
- assess how the mechanism for regulating securities markets in the EU can best respond to developments in these markets;
- propose scenarios for adapting current practices to ensure greater convergence and cooperation in day-to-day implementation.[11]

In responding, the Wise Men drew attention to a number of key problems, including the slowness of the legislative process and the lack of consultation and transparency. The absence of a mechanism for adopting and updating Directives arising from market developments was a particular concern. Attention was also drawn to the fact that there

---

[11] Gerard Hertig and Ruben Lee, 'Four Predictions about the Future of EU Securities Regulation', January 2003, p. 3.

were too many (in excess of forty) regulatory authorities responsible for EU securities markets. 'A critical concern of the Wise Men was that many of the Directives in the financial services field failed to distinguish between core principles and the detailed provisions necessary to implement these principles, and were indeed excessively detailed.'[12]

The Wise Men proposed a four-level approach (referred to as the Lamfalussy Process) to cater for passing both primary and secondary legislation. A split was created between 'framework principles' (Level 1) and 'implementing measures' (Level 2). Level 1 comprises directives and regulations which had to be adopted by the Council of Ministers and by the European Parliament, whereas Level 2 comprises technical measures adopted by the European Commission under powers arising from Level 1 legislation. Level 2 amendments would be based on a procedure first developed in 1987 called Comitology. The European Securities Committee was established to assist the EU in advisory matters arising under Level 1 and in regulatory matters arising under Level 2. A second committee, the Committee of European Securities Regulators (CESR), was also established to provide advice especially in relation to technical implementation measures arising under Level 2. Level 3 functions concerned smooth and timely implementation of action necessary in member states from Level 1 and Level 2 work. Lastly, in this respect, the object of Level 4 is to facilitate integration in the single market for financial services. It focuses on strengthening and enforcing EU legislation amongst member states. This is needed. Consider (for example) the following – '. . .The European Union for its part is aiming for financial market integration, but is being held back by its own diversity and by political disagreements about the purpose of national banking systems. For the past couple of years Italy has been the pariah, seemingly resisting one of the EU's fundamental principles: the free flow of capital among member countries. . .'[13]

The Forum of European Securities Commissions (established in 1997) provided the means that allowed Europe's national securities regulators to work together voluntarily to create common approaches to the implementation of EU legislation. This work was taken over by the Committee of European Securities Regulators (Level 3). The CESR is an independent

---

[12] Gerard Hertig and Ruben Lee, 'Four Predcitions about the Future of EU Securities Regulation', January 2003, p. 3.
[13] David Shirreff, '"Open Wider": A Survey of International Banking' *The Economist*, 21 May 2005, p. 4.

network of national securities regulators, created in June 2001, comprising regulators responsible for drafting standards in a timely manner. It is one of two important committees – the other being the EU Securities Committee (EUSC) – comprising senior treasury officials who will approve new legislation. The CESR's role is to advise the EU Commission on how to achieve consistency throughout the EU. The CESR drafts text based on Commission mandates. 'At present, [the] CESR produces at level 3 administrative guidelines, interpretative guidelines, interpretative recommendations, common standards, peer reviews and comparisons of regulatory practices to improve [the] consistent application and enforcement of EU legislation.'[14] The CESR's members are the national securities regulators of EU member countries plus Norway and Iceland.

The following example describes how it is intended that the CESR will function. Within the drafting of the Investment Services Directive and Basel II within the Third Capital Adequacy Directive (CAD3), substantial detail concerning CAD3 was placed in appendices. This enabled the EUSC and the CESR to consider the provisions that remain unresolved under the Comitology procedures. (The Comitology procedures were recommended in a report produced in 2001 by the Committee of Wise Men, whose Chairman was Baron Alexandre Lamfalussy. The procedures provide for amendment (by a committee) of rules that are shown not to be working. The intention is to enhance progress.) 'There is however concern that the Lamfalussy process will ultimately result in proscriptive rules across the EU.'[15]

Meanwhile, it should be noted that regulation sometimes stretches beyond borders. For example, the EU Financial Conglomerates Directive of 2002 means that regulators in the USA must supervise groups on a consolidated basis.

9.6 The Enlarged Contact Group on the Supervision of Collective Investment Funds

This informal group of regulators of collective investment schemes was established in 1970. Membership was at one time restricted to regulators

---

[14] Arthur Docters van Leeuwen and Fabrice Demarigny, 'Europe's Securities Regulators Working Together under the New EU Regulatory Framework', 28 May 2004, Vol. 12, No. 3, *Journal of Financial Regulation and Compliance*, p. 206.
[15] Jonathan Edwards and Simon Wolfe, 'Compliance: A Review', Vol. 13, No. 1, *Journal of Financial Regulation and Compliance*, p. 48.

in EU Member States. Membership now extends to Brazil, Canada, Hong Kong, Japan, Mexico, Norway, Switzerland, South Africa and the UK Crown dependencies. The group meets annually.

9.7 The European Union

The aspiration for a European Union can be traced back to the 1950s. The purpose was to combine countries in Europe with common purposes. On the one hand, this included no more wars and, on the other hand, it meant a single economic area without borders or barriers. The European Coal and Steel Community of 1951 eventually became the European Economic Community (1973), which subsequent to the Maastricht Treaty of 1991, became the European Union, with twenty-five Member States and around 455 million citizens. (See Table 25 in Appendix 1.) On 29 May 2005 and by way of a referendum, voters in France rejected the EU Constitution by a 55 per cent majority. Within three days, voters in the Netherlands followed suit (62 per cent).

Although the single market for financial services has still not been achieved, more progress has been made on the wholesale side than on the retail side (e.g. banking, personal investments and payments). The factors that have retarded progress arise, for example, from failures to harmonise tax and conduct of business rules.

The EU's Second Banking Directive provides for branches to be opened under the 'European Passport', but, 'despite the principle of mutual recognition, which is supposed to allow retail banks to operate branches in other EU countries under the supervision of their home regulator, simply opening branches in other countries does not win many retail customers'.[16] Further, despite the Investment Services Directive providing for the sale of collective investment schemes across Europe, it turns out that selling financial services across national borders requires substantial rules to work. There are similar problems with cross-selling insurance, arising from consumer protection issues and tax, to name only two difficulties.

However, on a more positive note, the single currency (the euro) has been in operation since 2002.

---

[16] David Shirreff, 'A Blurred Euro-Vision: A Survey of International Banking', *The Economist*, 21 May 2005, p. 14.

9.8 The Financial Action Task Force[17]

The Financial Action Task Force (FATF) was established by the G7 Economic Summit in Paris in 1989 as an independent international body whose purpose is 'to examine measures to combat money laundering'.[18] The FATF is located in the premises of the OECD in Paris, and is funded 'by its members on an annual basis – in accordance with the scale of contribution to the OECD. This scale is based on a formula related to the size of the jurisdiction's economy'.[19] The FATF describes itself as a 'policy making body . . . [whose] . . . primary goal is to generate the political will necessary for bringing about national legislative and regulatory reforms . . . [to combat money laundering]'.[20] It also describes itself as 'an inter-governmental body whose purpose is the development and promotion of policies, both at national and international levels, to combat money laundering and terrorist financing'.[21]

The FATF relies on a Secretariat (which comprises ten staff members), a Steering Group (for advising the FATF's President) and on working groups to pursue its mandate. The Steering Group comprises the President, the immediate Past-President and the President-Designate. The FATF operates under a temporary lifespan, and requires a specific decision to continue to exist.

One year after its establishment, the FATF issued its Forty Recommendations to combat money laundering. While it is important for countries to implement the FATF's Recommendations, doing so has many operational implications – not least because member countries have disparate legal systems. This renders the application of standardised applications a sensitively balanced job.

The FATF's remit was extended in 1996 to include the laundering of the proceeds of 'serious crimes' (which term each member country must define as it sees fit), but which an interpretative note refers to as those crimes from which the proceeds are large. Another interpretative note stipulates that tax confidentiality ('the fiscal excuse') should not be used as a means to avoid cooperation. Many money laundering investigations

---

[17] See also sections 11.2 et seq. below.
[18] FATF, *Annual Report*, 1997–8, para. 8.
[19] FATF, *Annual Report*, 2004–5, p. 10.
[20] See www.fatf-gafi.org.
[21] 'FATF Targets Cross-Border Cash Movements by Terrorists and Criminals', FATF, 22 October 2004, p. 2.

involve tax, so the aim is to prevent the fiscal excuse from being used to avoid reporting suspicious transactions.

At an extraordinary plenary meeting held in Washington on 29–30 October 2001, the FATF extended its remit to include combating the financing of terrorism. The FATF issued eight new 'Special Recommendations' in this respect, which, together with the existing conditions, became known as the 40+8 Recommendations.

The FATF issued revised Recommendations in 2003 and a ninth Special Recommendation was added in 2004.

On 14 May 2004, members resolved to renew the FATF's mandate for another eight years, to 2012. The extended mandate agreed in 2004 included considering the integration of the two sets into a single unit.

9.9 Financial Intelligence Units

The role of FIUs is described in section 8.9 above. As Table 24 in Appendix 1 suggests, they exist virtually everywhere, and include:

- FinCen, the US Department of the Treasury's Financial Crime Enforcement Network;
- NCIS, the UK National Criminal Intelligence Service;
- TRACFIN, 'Treatment of Information and Action Against Clandestine Financial Circuits', founded in 1990 as part of France's Ministry of Finance (Tracfin centralises intelligence and investigates activities brought to its attention; it does not prosecute).

9.10 The Financial Stability Forum[22]

The Finance Ministers and Central Bank Governors of the G7 countries met in Washington on 3 October 1998. It was decided at this meeting to invite Mr Hans Tietmeyer, President of the German Bundesbank, to consider how the stability of the international financial system might be enhanced.

In his report, 'International Cooperation and Coordination in the Area of Financial Market Supervision and Surveillance', which was submitted on 20 February 1999, Mr Tietmeyer recommended the establishment of the Financial Stability Forum. The Finance Ministers and Central

---

[22] See section 10.2 below.

Bank Governors of the G7 countries approved the recommendation and the composition of the new entity.

The FSF, which is supported by a Secretariat, is located at the BIS in Basel. The FSF was established on 14 April 1999 and meets twice yearly. The FSF 'promotes international financial stability through information exchange and international cooperation in financial supervision and surveillance . . . [it] . . . seeks to coordinate the efforts of these various bodies in order to promote international financial stability, improve the functioning of markets and reduce systemic risk'.[23] Membership includes authorities from the largest financial jurisdictions that are responsible for financial stability, the IMF, the World Bank, the OECD, the Basel Committee, IOSCO and the International Association of Insurance Supervisors. There are currently forty members.

The work in which the FSF is engaged currently includes:

- raising corporate governance standards;
- establishing effective auditor oversight;
- strengthening international accounting standards;
- reviewing the operations of credit rating agencies; and
- considering potential conflicts of interest in financial institutions.

> The [FSF] remains engaged with a number of other concerns, including efforts to strengthen supervisory, regulatory and information exchange practices in Offshore financial centres.[24]

The FSF attaches 'particular importance to all OFCs improving cross-border cooperation and information exchange practices . . . [T]he IMF should evaluate both the ability of OFC authorities through their existing procedures to obtain relevant information on financial activities originating in their own jurisdictions, as well as the willingness to share this information with foreign authorities in a cooperative, non-discriminatory, timely and effective manner.'[25]

9.11 G7/G8/G10

When it was first established in Rambouillet (France) in 1975, the G7 – as it came to be known – comprised France, Germany, the UK, Italy,

---

[23] Financial Stability Forum, www.fsforum.org.
[24] 'Current Focus of the Financial Stability Forum', *FSI World*, Issue 10, January 2004.
[25] Press Release, Financial Stability Forum, 5 April 2004.

Japan and the USA. Canada joined the Group in 1976 and the European Community joined in 1977. Membership was fixed at that stage. The world's seven major industrial democracies are represented by their respective heads of state. Russia has been involved in a 'post-summit dialogue' with the Group since 1991. Russia participated fully in 1998 (which prompted the establishment of the G8).

The Group meets annually. Their remit includes domestic and international economic and political issues and includes:

> macroeconomic management, international management, international trade and relations with developing countries. Questions of East–West economic relations, energy and terrorism have also been of recurrent concern. From this initial foundation, the summit agenda has broadened considerably to include microeconomic issues such as employment and the information highway, transnational issues such as the environment, crime and drugs and a host of political-security issues ranging from human rights through regional security to arms control.[26]

The G10 currently comprises Belgium, Canada, France, Germany, Italy, Japan, the Netherlands, Sweden, the UK and the USA. The G10 arose from 'negotiations surrounding the establishment of the General Agreement to Borrow ("GAB") in 1961 and 1962 . . . The GAB was set up as a device for providing additional liquidity to the IMF by a decision of the executive board of the IMF. . . . The function of the G10 was to provide for intergovernmental consultation in connection with the implementation of calls on the lines of credit extended to the IMF under GAB although this has subsequently been extended.'[27]

9.12 G20

This group of finance ministers and central bank governors was established in September 1999 at a meeting of the G7. The meeting of the G7 in June of that year had made a 'commitment to work together to establish an informal mechanism for dialogue among systemically important countries, within the framework of the Bretton Woods institutional system'. The Group's mandate is to 'promote discussion and study and review policy issues among industrialized countries and emerging markets with a

---

[26] 'What Is the G8?', G8 Research Group at the University of Toronto, 30 June 2003.
[27] George Alexander Walker, *International Banking Regulation Law, Policy and Practice*, Kluwer Law International, 2001, p. 30.

view to promoting international financial stability'. Initially, its members
included the G7 members plus Argentina, Australia, Brazil, China, India,
Mexico, Russia, Saudi Arabia, South Africa, South Korea and Turkey.[28]

9.13 The International Accounting Standards Committee

The IASC emanates from the private sector. It was formed in 1973 by
the accounting profession with the object of harmonising accounting
principles globally.

9.14 The International Association of Insurance Supervisors

The IAIS, whose headquarters is in Basel, was formed in 1994 and
comprises members that are insurance regulators and supervisors from
more than 160 jurisdictions. Their function is to:

- cooperate to ensure improved supervision of the insurance industry on
  a domestic as well as on an international level in order to maintain
  efficient, fair, safe and stable insurance markets for the benefit and
  protection of policyholders; and
- unite in their efforts to develop practical standards that members may
  choose to apply.[29]

The IAIS is guided by an Executive Committee and three main
committees, Technical, Emerging Markets and Budget.

The IAIS has compiled six Principles and eight Standards. The IAIS
says that the Principles 'identify areas in which the insurance supervisor
should have authority or control', as follows:

1. insurance core principles and methodology;
2. principles applicable to the supervision of international insurers and
   insurance groups and their cross-border business operations;
3. principles for the conduct of insurance business;
4. principles on the supervision of insurance activities on the internet;
5. principles on capital adequacy and solvency; and
6. principles on minimum requirements for supervision of re-insurers.

The Insurance Core Principles were first issued in 1997 and were
revised in 2000 and most recently in 2003. 'The 28 Principles cover all

[28] 'What Is the G20?', G8 Research Group at the University of Toronto, 30 June 2003.
[29] IAIS, 'Insurance Principles, Standards and Guidance Papers', Foreword, October 2003.

aspects of insurance industry regulation and supervision – from licensing a company to winding it up. Principles addressing such issues as transparency of the supervisory process, assessment and management of risk, consumer protection, and anti-money laundering have been added . . . [They] provide a globally accepted framework for the regulation and supervision of the insurance sector.'[30]

The IAIS expects insurance supervisors to make self-assessments of the extent to which the Principles are being observed in their respective jurisdiction. The IAIS has developed a programme to assist supervisors to review their systems 'objectively and comprehensively in order to improve them'.[31]

'Standards focus on particular issues and describe best or most prudent practices.'[32] The IAIS has published Supervisory Standards on:

1. licensing;
2. on-site inspections;
3. derivatives;
4. asset management by insurance companies;
5. group coordination;
6. exchange of information;
7. evaluation of the re-insurance cover; and
8. supervision of re-insurers.

The IAIS has also published eight Guidance Papers and, in 2002, Principles for the supervision of reinsurance and captive reinsurance.

9.15 International Monetary Fund

9.15.1 The context

The Second World War reduced international trade to a very low ebb. Even before that war ended, some work had begun on how to encourage world trade. The point was to promote multilateral trade and (relatively) stable exchange rates were considered a key component. The ideal criteria included:

- changes in exchange rates to be agreed;
- multiple exchange rates;

---

[30] IAIS, 'Insurance Core Principles Self Assessment Programme', July 2004, p. 2.
[31] IAIS, 'Insurance Core Principles Self Assessment Programme', July 2004, p. 2.
[32] IAIS, 'Insurance Principles, Standards and Guidance Papers', Foreword, October 2003.

- abolition of restrictions on acquiring foreign currency; and
- all currencies to be freely convertible.

The Gold Standard offered certain advantages but its disadvantages included its rigidity (gold had to be exported whenever balance of payments was adverse) and loss of independent decision-making authority over monetary policy. By comparison, free exchange rates meant fluctuating rates and freedom to determine domestic policy. Ideally, the best solution was to create a way forward that created both sets of advantages.

9.15.2 The Bretton Woods Agreement

A conference was arranged in New Hampshire, USA, in July 1944. Forty-four countries convened to establish a system for managing exchange rates which system was to replace the foreign exchange market that had prevailed under the Gold Standard. The Americans (Harry Dexter White) and the British (John Maynard Keynes) suggested different approaches, but both agreed on the desirability of:

- promoting multilateral trade through stable exchange rates and unrestricted convertibility of currencies;
- creation of an international organisation to administer the scheme;
- an international currency;
- gold as part of international settlements.

The conference adopted the Bretton Woods System – which meant fixing the values of all foreign currencies against the US dollar (subject to a certain adjustment mechanism) – and the value of the dollar to gold. The system lasted until the early 1970s.

9.15.3 The Creation of the IMF

The conference also resolved to establish the International Monetary Fund (IMF) and the International Bank for Reconstruction and Development (World Bank). The World Bank started operations on 25 June 1946 and the IMF commenced business on 1 March 1947.

Article 1 of the IMF's Articles of Agreement sets out the Fund's six objectives (and three functions) summarised as follows:[33]

---

[33] George Alexander Walker, *International Banking Regulation Law, Policy and Practice*, Kluwer Law International, 2001, p. 24.

1. to promote international monetary cooperation;
2. to facilitate expansion and balanced growth in international trade;
3. to promote exchange rate stability;
4. to assist in the establishment of a multilateral payment system;
5. to make its general resources temporarily available to members experiencing balance of payments difficulties (subject to certain conditions); and
6. to seek reductions in the duration and magnitude of payments imbalances.

The IMF's functions were stated as follows:

1. to administer a code of conduct with regards to exchange rate policies, current account payments and convertibility;
2. to provide members with financial resources to enable them to observe the code of conduct while correcting or avoiding payments imbalances; and
3. to provide a forum in which members could consult and collaborate on international monetary matters.

In summary, the IMF became the administrator of the new arrangements and assumed responsibility for maintaining surveillance over the international monetary system.

9.16 International Organization of Securities Commissions

The International Organization of Securities Commissions (IOSCO) was formed in 1983. Its members' objectives are:

- To cooperate together to promote high standards of regulation in order to maintain just, efficient and sound markets;
- To exchange information on their respective experiences in order to promote the development of domestic markets;
- To unite their efforts to establish standards and effective surveillance of international securities transactions;
- To provide mutual assistance to promote the integrity of their markets by a rigorous application of the standards and by effective enforcement against offences.[34]

---

[34] IOSCO, *Annual Report*, 2002, Appendix 2, p. 22.

Table 9.28 in Appendix 1 provides an analysis of membership, which, as at May 2005, comprised 108 Ordinary Members, nine Associate Members and sixty-five Affiliate Members. IOSCO works through Standing Committees and through Regional Committees. The Standing Committees comprise the President's Committee (107 Ordinary Members and seven Associate Members), the Executive Committee (twenty-one Ordinary Members), the Technical Committee (seventeen Ordinary Members), the Emerging Markets Committee (eighty Ordinary Members), together with the Emerging Markets Committee Advisory Board (twelve Ordinary Members) and the SRO Consultative Committee (fifty-two Ordinary Members). The Regional Committees cover the following areas: Africa/Middle East (twenty Ordinary Members), Asia-Pacific (twenty-two Ordinary Members and four Associate Members), Europe (forty-four Ordinary Members) and Inter-America (twenty-four Ordinary Members and four Associate Members).

The President's Committee comprises those persons who are presidents of member organisations. The purpose of the President's Committee is to assist IOSCO to achieve its purposes. The Executive Committee comprises nineteen members and meets as circumstances require. The Executive Committee's remit includes strategic planning and management issues. There are two specialised working committees (the Emerging Markets and the Technical Committee) and four Regional Standing Committees (Africa/Middle East, Asia-Pacific, Europe and Inter-America).

The Emerging Markets Committee 'endeavours to promote the development and improvement of [the] efficiency of emerging securities and futures markets by establishing principles and minimum standards, preparing training programs for the staff of members and facilitating exchange of information and transfer of technology and expertise'.[35] This Committee was established in 1994 (replacing the former Development Committee) and has the following Working Groups: Disclosure; Institutional Investors; Derivatives; Clearing and Settlements; and Market Incentives.

The Technical Committee has sixteen members, each of whom represents the largest and most highly developed and international markets. This Committee focuses on major regulatory issues that impinge upon international securities transactions and coordinates appropriate

---

[35] IOSCO, *Annual Report*, 2002, Appendix 2, p. 23.

practical responses to those issues. The remit also includes the promotion and adoption of common rules globally. Since 1990, the Technical Committee has concentrated on five functional areas as follows, each under a Working Group (WG): Multinational Disclosure and Accounting (WG1); Regulation of Secondary Markets (WG2); Regulation of Market Intermediaries (WG3); Enforcement and the Exchange of Information (WG4); and Investment Management (WG5). In turn, the Technical Committee has established Standing Committees and Project Teams to assist it. Each Working Group works according to a mandate from the Technical Committee that relates to a particular issue.

The SRO Consultative Committee is made up of fifty-two affiliate members of IOSCO, all of whom represent SROs and securities and derivatives markets in both developed and emerging markets. According to IOSCO's website,[36] the SROCC 'is committed to assisting persons in understanding the regulatory requirements of its member self-regulatory organisations . . . to assist persons contemplating foreign business operations . . . It also contains information that may assist investors in verifying the registration status of brokers or investment advisors, information on customer dispute resolution procedures and other investor protection information.'

In October 2003, IOSCO announced the adoption of its Methodology for Assessing Implementation of the IOSCO Objectives and Principles of Securities Regulation. The document is designed to assist in identifying where a jurisdiction's securities regulations fall short of the international standards described in the IOSCO Principles. IOSCO has compiled thirty Principles about which the Methodology says that they 'set out a broad general framework for the regulation of securities, including the regulation of (i) securities markets, (ii) the intermediaries that operate in those markets, (iii) the issuers of securities, and (iv) the sale of interests in, and the management and operation of, collective investment schemes'. The Principles were updated in June 2003.

At its Annual Conference in October 2003, IOSCO adopted its Methodology for Assessing Implementation of the IOSCO Objectives and Principles of Securities Regulation. The purpose of the Methodology is to assist regulators in conducting assessments of the extent to which IOSCO's Principles have been implemented.

---

[36] www.iosco.org/committees/srocc

The Principles (which were first adopted in 1998 and last updated in June 2003) represent a general framework for the regulation not only of securities markets but also for market intermediaries, issuers of securities and also for the 'sale of interests in, and the management and operation of collective investment schemes'.[37] The Principles are not intended to be a checklist. From time to time, IOSCO issues resolutions to provide 'content to the more broadly stated IOSCO Principles'.[38] Meanwhile, the framework aims to protect investors, to reduce systemic risk and to ensure fair, efficient and transparent markets.

IOSCO has adopted a Multilateral Memorandum of Understanding (MMOU) as a means of raising standards in respect of regulatory cooperation and exchange of information. In April 2005, IOSCO resolved to require all its members to become signatories by 1 January 2010. IOSCO is presently (July 2005) engaging in an exercise to identify non-cooperative jurisdictions with a view to engaging with them in discussions concerning change.

9.17 The International Securities Market Association

Based in Switzerland, the ISMA is both a (UK) trade association and a self-regulatory organisation at the same time. Under the UK's Financial Services and Markets Act 2000, the ISMA is classified as an International Securities Self-Regulating Organization (the only one of its kind).

9.18 The International Trade and Investment Organization

The ITIO describes itself as a grouping of small and developing economies (SDEs) set up in March 2001 to help the latter to respond to global tax and investment challenges. It explicitly considers the development implications of these challenges. Members comprise: Anguilla, Antigua and Barbuda, the Bahamas, Barbados, Belize, the British Virgin Islands, the Cayman Islands, the Cook Islands, Malaysia, St Kitts and Nevis, St Lucia, Turks and Caicos and Vanuatu. The Commonwealth Secretariat, the Pacific Islands Forum Secretariat and the Caricom

---

[37] 'Methodology for Assessing Implementation of the IOSCO Objectives and Principles of Securities Regulation', IOSCO, 16 October 2003, p. 1.
[38] 'Methodology for Assessing Implementation of the IOSCO Objectives and Principles of Securities Regulation', IOSCO, 16 October 2003, p. 2.

Secretariat have 'Observer' status. The objective of the ITIO is to assist small developing countries to deal with international initiatives that impinge upon them.

9.19 The Joint Forum

The Joint Forum was established in 1996 under the aegis of the Basel Committee on Banking Supervision, the International Organization of Securities Commissions and the International Association of Insurance Supervisors to deal with issues that are common to the banking, securities and insurance sector respectively. On 2 August 2004, the Joint Forum published a report for consultation entitled 'Outsourcing in Financial Services', which service is of growing importance for some OFCs.

The document includes nine guiding, high level principles 'designed to assist regulated entities in determining the minimum steps they should take when considering outsourcing activities. These include establishing a coherent policy and specific risk management programmes as well as determining the types of issues that should be considered in contracts.'[39]

9.20 Moneyval[40]

Moneyval is the new name of the PC-R-EV Committee, which was established in 1997 by the Commission of Ministers of the Council of Europe.

9.21 The Offshore Group of Banking Supervisors

Following the First International Conference of Banking Supervisors held in London in 1979, the Basel Committee on Banking Supervision decided that there would be virtue in initiating a meeting of banking supervisors representing 'Offshore Centres'. The end of the 1970s had seen considerable expansion of international loan activity with many loans being booked through 'Offshore Centres' for tax reasons. The Basel Committee member countries were concerned that the banks for which they were

---

[39] The Joint Forum, Press Release, 'Joint Forum Provides Outsourcing Guidance to the Financial Sector', 2 August 2004.
[40] See PC-R-EV Committee, sections 9.25 and 11.11.3 below.

responsible were at risk because their subsidiaries or branches in 'Offshore Centres', through which loans were booked, were not subject to a sufficient standard of supervision.

The first meeting of the OGBS was held in 1980 in Basel. The OGBS enabled 'Offshore Centres' to define their common ground more clearly, to identify the extent to which the exchange of information with other supervisory authorities could be compatible with their general function as 'Offshore' refuges from the fiscal and monetary policies of other countries, and to establish a positive, constructive and coordinated response to the approaches made by other supervisory authorities for assistance in the effective supervision of international banks.[41]

The twelve initial members had expanded to nineteen by 2000 – around which level the number has more or less settled. These included Aruba, the Bahamas, Bahrain, Barbados, Bermuda, the Cayman Islands, Cyprus, Gibraltar, Guernsey, Hong Kong, the Isle of Man, Jersey, Labuan, Macao, Mauritius, the Netherlands Antilles, Panama, Singapore and Vanuatu. Admission to membership depends upon the satisfaction of certain admission criteria.

The FATF's report for 1999 confirmed that the following members of the OGBS had formally committed themselves to the Forty Recommendations by way of ministerial letters sent to the FATF: Bahrain, Cyprus, Gibraltar, Guernsey, the Isle of Man, Jersey, Malta, Mauritius and Vanuatu. (Malta is no longer a member of the OGBS.) (See section 8.7 above.) The OGBS is represented at all FATF meetings. Further, the FATF recognises the OGBS as a competent authority in the conduct of mutual evaluations, which places the OGBS on a par with the FATF-style regional bodies.

In 1997, the FATF established a strategy in respect of its relationship with non-members which the report (described above) says is 'directed towards supporting the various activities of other regional and international bodies involved in the fight against money laundering'. As part of this strategy, a Select Committee of the Council of Europe and the OGBS initiated a programme of mutual evaluations, designed to assess the measures taken by respective members to protect their jurisdiction against money laundering.

The OGBS, together with the Basel Committee on Banking Supervision, formed a working group in 1996 to prepare a report on the

---

[41] Colin Powell, 'A Briefing Note', Offshore Group of Banking Supervisors, February 2002.

supervision of cross-border banking, which was subsequently endorsed by the International Conference of Banking Supervisors. The report dealt with issues arising in the supervision of cross-border operations of international banks. The report made certain recommendations concerning the exchange of information between supervisors. Further collaborative work between the OGBS and the Basel Committee resulted in the publication in 2001 of 'Customer Due Diligence'. This report provides detailed guidance on the 'know your customer' principle (see section 8.13 above).

Most recently, and in conjunction with representatives of G10 countries, the OECD, the IMF and the FATF, the OGBS undertook some work in producing a 'Best Practice' paper for the regulation of trust and company service providers (see section 6.17 above) and a further report by a working group on the exchange of information.

Two other specialised fora (the Offshore Group of Insurance Supervisors and the Offshore Group of Collective Investment Scheme Supervisors) also exist to serve practitioners in their respective area of expertise. A few words about each:

9.22 The Offshore Group of Insurance Supervisors

The Constitution of the Offshore Group of Insurance Supervisors (OGIS) describes its objectives as follows:

> To provide mechanisms and forums whereby insurance supervisors from jurisdictions concerned with cross border insurance business may discuss areas of mutual interest and concern and formulate appropriate policies;
>
> To provide assistance and encouragement to appropriate non member jurisdictions to establish regimes for the supervision of cross border insurance business at least to standards equivalent of those of the Group;
>
> To represent the interests of the Group at international insurance forums;
>
> Generally, to promote the proper supervision of cross border business.[42]

The OGIS was formed on 14 October 1996.

---

[42] Offshore Group of Insurance Supervisors, Constitution, October 1998.

9.23 The Offshore Group of Collective Investment Scheme Supervisors

This Group held its inaugural meeting, attended by representatives from six jurisdictions, on 1 December 1997. The Group's objectives are stated as:

> To encourage the application of high standards of supervision and regulation based on international principles with the aim of maintaining adequate protection of markets and market users;

> To facilitate the cooperation and sharing of knowledge, experience and training among Offshore Regulators and Supervisors of Collective Investment Schemes;

> To provide a forum for discussion of international issues of relevance to the Collective Investment Scheme industry.[43]

9.24 The Organization for Economic Cooperation and Development

The OECD, based in Paris, was created in 1961, during the early years of the 'Cold War', by twenty-four of the leading industrialised nations. The purpose was to act as a consultative body, research centre and forum on high level economic issues.[44] The intention was to distribute US money and economic expertise to Europe. As Europe developed, the OECD became a focal point for those rich nations that symbolised it. That is not to say that today the OECD comprises only rich nations as the list that follows will demonstrate.

The OECD comprises thirty of the richest countries in the world. These countries are: Australia, Austria, Belgium, Canada, Czech Republic, Denmark, Finland, France, Germany, Greece, Hungary, Iceland, Ireland, Italy, Japan, Luxembourg, Mexico, the Netherlands, New Zealand, Norway, Poland, Portugal, Slovak Republic, South Korea, Spain, Sweden, Switzerland, Turkey, the UK and the USA. (Russia has submitted an application for membership.) The OECD is responsible for the promotion of policies that will lead to economic growth amongst its members. In a

---

[43] Offshore Group of Collective Investment Scheme Supervisors, Press Release, 1 May 1998.
[44] George Alexander Walker, *International Banking Regulation Law, Policy and Practice*, Kluwer Law International, 2001, p. 30.

booklet distributed at OECD meetings in Paris in April 2003, the OECD's Secretary General described the essence of the organisation as being 'a steering group for the world's economy'.

9.25 The PC-R-EV Committee

See section 9.20 ('Moneyval') above and section 11.11.3 below.

9.26 The UN Offshore Forum

This was an initiative of the UN's Office for Drug Control and Crime Prevention launched at a plenary meeting in March 2000. The aim was to prevent criminals from using OFCs for laundering money. OFCs were expected to make a political commitment to minimum performance standards.

9.27 The World Bank

Section 9.15 above contains relevant background concerning both the IMF and the World Bank. The World Bank comprises the International Bank for Reconstruction and Development (IBRD), the International Development Association (IDA), the International Finance Corporation (IFC), the Multilateral Investment Guarantee Agency (MIGA) and the International Centre for Settlement of Investment Disputes (ICSID). The brief description below[45] of each of the five organisations that make up the World Bank Group shows that they are closely associated.

It is interesting to note the connection between loans from the World Bank and regulation. 'Since 1990, 71 per cent of financial sector adjustment loans have included conditions related to prudential regulation. Conditions related to bank supervision were attached to 88 per cent of loans after 1990 . . . Regulators know that their choice of policies influences the availability of finance.'[46]

---

[45] See web.worldbank.org.
[46] Jonathan Ward, 'Is Basel II Voluntary for Developing Countries?', Vol. 7, No. 3, *The Financial Regulator*, December 2002, p. 53.

9.27.1 The International Bank for Reconstruction and Development

Established in 1945, the IBRD 'aims to reduce poverty in middle-income and creditworthy poorer countries by promoting sustainable development through loans, guarantees, and non-lending – including analytical and advisory services . . . Owned by member countries, IBRD links voting power to members' capital subscriptions – in turn based on a country's relative economic strength.' There are 184 members and cumulative lending is US$360 billion.

9.27.2 The International Development Association

The IDA was established in 1960 and has cumulative lending of US$135 billion. 'Contributions to IDA enable the World Bank to provide $6–7 billion per year in interest free credits to the world's 78 poorest countries, home to 2.4 billion people . . . IDA helps provide access to better basic services (such as education, health care, and clean water and sanitation) and supports reforms and investments aimed at productivity growth and employment creation'.

9.27.3 The International Finance Corporation

Established in 1956, the 'IFC's mandate is to further economic development through the private sector. Working with business partners, it invests in sustainable private enterprises in developing countries and provides long-term loans guarantees and risk management and advisory services to its clients. IFC invests in projects in regions and sectors underserved by private investment and finds new ways to develop promising opportunities in markets deemed too risky by commercial investors in the absence of IFC participation.' There are 175 members and the committed portfolio is US$21.6 billion.

9.27.4 The Multilateral Investment Guarantee Agency

'MIGA helps encourage foreign investment in developing countries by providing guarantees to foreign investors against losses caused by non-commercial risks . . . MIGA provides technical assistance to help countries disseminate information on investment opportunities.' MIGA was established in 1988 and has 157 members.

9.27.5 The International Centre for Settlement of Investment Disputes

ICSID was established in 1966. It has 134 members and 'helps to encourage foreign investment by providing international facilities for conciliation and arbitration of investment disputes . . . Many international agreements concerning investment refer to ICSID's arbitration facilities.'

PART II

The present

The middle third of the book (Chapters 10 to 12) focuses on 'the present', which covers the period from the late 1990s (approximately 1998) to 2005. This section examines the extent to which 'Offshore' has been criticised, and explores whether it is fair to blame 'Offshore Centres' for not doing more to disenable criminals from laundering the proceeds of crime 'Offshore'. Some of the problems that affect the global financial services network are considered. The extent to which the 'Offshore' environment has become the focus of global attention is perhaps best understood by reference to work undertaken at the end of the 1990s by the Financial Stability Forum, the Financial Action Task Force and the Organization for Economic Cooperation and Development. An analysis of the work of these three organisations is spread over three chapters. Whether there is any correlation between 'Offshore Finance' and small island jurisdictions is considered briefly.

Supranational focus (1): the Financial Stability Forum and the International Monetary Fund

> Outcomes matter, but no more than the fairness of the processes that produce them.[1]

10.1 Introduction

> For the past ten years, the 'Offshore' industry has been constantly under fire with claims that it was facilitating the laundering the proceeds of drugs trafficking and other offences.[2]

This chapter and the next two describe work carried out in respect of the 'Offshore' environment by some supranational organisations: the Financial Stability Forum (FSF), the International Monetary Fund (IMF), the World Bank, the Financial Action Task Force (FATF) and the Organization for Economic Cooperation and Development (OECD).

This particular chapter focuses on the work of the Financial Stability Forum (FSF), and on the International Monetary Fund (IMF) and the World Bank, beginning with the FSF. The FSF itself has been described in Chapter 9, so the outline that follows merely serves to place the work of the FSF in respect of 'Offshore' in context.

10.2 The work of the Financial Stability Forum

With reference to its work on 'Offshore' in particular, 'the objective of the FSF's OFC initiative is to strengthen the supervisory, regulatory information sharing and international cooperation practices of OFCs on a lasting basis'.[3] At its inaugural meeting on 14 April 1999, the FSF

---

[1] W. Chan Kim and Renee Mauborgne, January 2003, 'Fair Process: Managing in the Knowledge Economy', *Harvard Business Review*, January – February 1997, pp. 65–75.
[2] Nigel Morris-Cotterill, 'Secrecy Laws under Assault', *The Banker*, August 2000, p. 62.
[3] Tenth Meeting of the FSF, Paris, 10 September 2003, FSF Press Release, www.fsforum.org/press/press_releases_60.html.

created a Working Group on 'Offshore Finance Centres'. The Working Group was asked to:

- consider the uses of OFCs and the possible role they have had or could play in posing threats to the stability of the financial system;
- evaluate the adherence of OFCs with internationally accepted standards and good practices; and
- make recommendations, to enhance problematic OFCs' observance of international standards.[4]

A survey (of both 'Onshore' and 'Offshore Finance Centres') to obtain appropriate information was approved in September 1999 and sent to jurisdictions at the end of November 1999. An interim communiqué dated September 1999 stated that 'governments must maintain strong internal financial controls and tighten supervision and regulation of domestic financial institutions and Offshore banking centres, including measures to deter money laundering'.

The survey took the form of a questionnaire (no meetings or face-to-face communication between the FSF and those surveyed took place). Thirty major financial centres and thirty-seven other centres with what were described as 'significant offshore finance activities',[5] were surveyed.

By way of example, the questionnaire included the following:

- Who licenses banks, insurance companies and securities companies?
- How many are there of each, and what volumes of business do they transact?
- What checks are made on licence applicants from abroad?
- Precisely what work is carried out as 'host supervisor', both onsite and offsite, and by how many people?
- Information on access to a licensee's records and approach to cross-border supervision, including onsite access and contacts with home country supervisors.
- Measures to combat money laundering and whether particular countries have been reviewed.
- Whether local entities are supervised in the same way as entities from abroad.

---

[4] 'Report of the Working Group on Offshore Financial Centres', April 2000, p. 6.
[5] Financial Stability Forum, Press Release, 26 May 2000.

- Able to share information with home country supervisors and foreign law enforcement agencies.
- Whether the responding jurisdiction has concerns with particular home supervisors.

The results of the survey were used to classify jurisdictions that were considered to have significant 'Offshore' activities, of which there turned out to be forty-two. The survey distinguished jurisdictions according to their perceived quality of supervisory standards and degree of cooperation into three categories. The FSF pointed out that 'the categorisation of OFCs into these three groupings is based on responses of OFC supervisors and the impressions of a wide range of Onshore supervisors at a particular point in time. The categorisation does not constitute judgements about any jurisdiction's adherence to international standards . . . It should not be used as an assessment.'[6] The categorisations were based on whether the jurisdictions are 'generally perceived as having legal infrastructures and supervisory practices, and/or a level of resources devoted to supervision and cooperation relative to the size of their financial activities and/or a level of cooperation that are largely of good quality and better than in other OFCs'.[7] (Note the word 'impressions' and the term 'generally perceived'.)

The jurisdictions that satisfied these criteria were classified as Group 1. A Group 2 classification was better than a Group 3 classification but not so good as a Group 1. Group 3 jurisdictions were considered to be inferior to Group 2; it was said that their 'scale of financial activity has the greatest potential impact on global financial stability'.[8] The categorisation allocated to each of the forty-two countries that the FSF assessed is shown in Table 17 in Appendix 1. The table shows that eight jurisdictions were classified as Group 1, nine as Group 2 and twenty-five as Group 3. If the FSF's classifications were accurate, this does not say a great deal that is positive about most of the 'Offshore' jurisdictions.

The table excludes some places like Delaware (USA) that might have been mentioned. Comparison with the list of 'tax havens' which the OECD identified (see Chapter 12 and Table 20 in Appendix 1) gives rise to some fundamental questions.

---

[6] Financial Stability Forum, Press Release, 26 May 2000.
[7] Financial Stability Forum, Press Release, 26 May 2000.
[8] Financial Stability Forum, Press Release, 26 May 2000.

The Group's work was completed in March 2000 and its conclusions were published in the Report of the Working Group on Offshore Financial Centres in April 2000 (the 'FSF Report'). The conclusions were endorsed by the FSF on 26 March 2000 and made public on 5 April 2000.

The 'key' recommendations made by the FSF were:

1. That an assessment process for assessing OFCs' implementation of relevant international standards be put in place;
2. That the IMF take responsibility for developing, organising and carrying out an assessment process for OFCs; and
3. That priority for assessment be placed on those OFCs whose procedures for supervision and cooperation are in place, but where there is substantial room for improvement; and on OFCs with the most significant financial activity.[9]

The FSF Report concluded, inter alia, that 'OFCs, to date, do not appear to have been a major causal factor in the creation of systemic financial problems.'[10] Despite the significance of this conclusion, it seems to have been forgotten in the aftermath of the publication of the Report. In fact, instead of the matter ending there, additional work ensued. The Report continued that 'OFCs that are unable or unwilling to adhere to internationally accepted standards for supervision, cooperation and information sharing create a potential systemic threat to global financial stability'.[11]

Consequently, the FSF Report recommended the establishment of a framework 'to encourage such jurisdictions to adhere to relevant international standards'.[12]

The FSF Report took account of the volume of business being processed through OFCs and, in light of that, the Report identified the need for appropriate disclosure mechanisms and also for supervisory standards in OFCs to be compatible with international standards. That is, the Report identified certain prudential standards and concerns about market integrity. In the absence of appropriate standards, OFCs were exposed to abuse – which could lead to international financial instability – and this was compounded by an inability to share information which in turn might hamper international efforts to combat what was

---

[9] 'Offshore Financial Centres, The Role of the IMF', 23 June 2000, p. 3.
[10] 'Report of the Working Group on Offshore Financial Centres', April 2000, p. 1.
[11] Financial Stability Forum, Press Release, 26 May 2000.
[12] Financial Stability Forum, Press Release, 26 May 2000.

unacceptable regulatory structures – or even crime. The bottom line is that weak standards in OFCs might lead to abuses that have international implications.

Although the Working Group's general conclusions were made public on 5 April 2000, the classification of OFCs did not form part of the published text. It was not until 26 May 2000 that jurisdictions were made aware[13] of the group in which FSF intended to classify them. In a letter to each jurisdiction, the FSF's Chairman said that '[t]he Forum concluded that it would be in the public interest to release a grouping of OFCs based on the results of the survey . . . The attached embargoed text will be publicly released on 26 May [2000], identifying the placement of jurisdictions.'[14]

Recommendation 5 of the Report identified certain incentives to encourage changes. Five types of incentive were presented for consideration ('Disclosure-type incentives . . . Membership-type . . . Provision of assistance . . . Supervisory incentives and Other official incentives'). The incentives included positive action such as provision for training and secondments and financial assistance, and also negative action such as increased reporting requirements.

It was stated that all members of the G20 had undertaken to carry out similar reviews within their respective financial sectors. The report was forwarded to G7 and G20 ministers and governors, and to the respective heads of the World Bank and the IMF.

Although the FSF started this work, they did not finish it because subsequently (May 2000), to help achieve its objective, 'the FSF asked the International Monetary Fund (IMF) to develop and carry out a process for assessing OFCs' adherence to relevant international standards and codes'.[15] Further, '[t]he FSF has also asked the [IMF] to take on the main responsibility for conducting these assessments'.[16] Perhaps some discussions took place behind the scenes because, subsequently, it was reported that '[t]he FSF considers that the key to addressing most of the problems with these OFCs is through the adoption and implementation of international standards, particularly in cross-border cooperation'.[17]

---

[13] Grouping of Offshore Financial Centres, Press Release, www.fsforum.org.
[14] Letter from FSF (Mr Crockett) dated 22 May 2000.
[15] Tenth Meeting of the FSF, Paris, 10 September 2003, FSF Press Release, www.fsforum.org/press/press_releases_60.html.
[16] 'Offshore Finance Centres', IMF Background Paper, 23 June 2000.
[17] 'Offshore Finance Centres', IMF Background Paper, 23 June 2000.

The IMF agreed to accept this responsibility.[18] In fact, 'the FSF attaches particular importance to the publication of the IMF assessments as a means of enhancing transparency and enabling the position of individual OFCs to be evaluated by all concerned parties'.[19]

The manner in which this matter was managed gave rise to considerable disquiet 'Offshore' – and to considerable confusion. Consider the following comment: 'Neither the FATF nor the IMF has the capacity to play a police or enforcement role regarding compliance and each seems to be casting about for answers regarding an enforcement formula . . . The OECD, FATF and IMF are searching for models to manage compliance and supervision, and as yet have no real idea of how to proceed. For example, the Financial Stability Forum (FSF) has a mandate, through supervision and assessment reports, to ensure the structural stability of the international financial system. That would imply that it is the FSF, rather than the IMF, that should conduct national institutional assessments. However, it has disappeared from the scene.'[20]

10.3 Some reactions to the FSF Report

Perhaps the most significant factor concerning this Report (apart from the results) was the methodology adopted by the FSF. Although the FSF itself was not named, the 'Directors [of IMF] expressed concern that some recent public announcements of lists by other bodies were not based on well developed criteria nor took into account all of the relevant facts.'[21] Did the IMF mean the FSF? One journal's headline was 'Offshore Centres up in Arms over Judgemental "Hit List"'.[22] Gibraltar's reaction was one of extreme disappointment to the FSF's categorisation.[23] Malta was said to have reacted 'angrily'[24] but the Cayman Islands agreed 'to

---

[18] 'Actions Against Abuse of the Global Financial System', Report of the G7 Finance Ministers to the Heads of State and Government, Okinawa, July 2000, and 'IMF Board Reviews Issues Surrounding Work on Offshore Financial Centres', IMF News Brief, No. 00/62.

[19] Tenth Meeting of the FSF, Paris, 10 September 2003, FSF Press Release, www.fsforum.org/press/press_releases_60.html.

[20] Gilbert N. M. O. Morris and Padideh Tosti, 'The Coming Anti-Climax: Review of the OECD/FATF Initiatives', *Tax Notes International*, 25 June 2001 p. 3283.

[21] 'An IMF Review of Experience and Next Steps: Assessing the Implementation of Standards', IMF, Public Information Notice 01/17, 5 March 2001.

[22] *International Money Marketing*, June 2000, p. 1.

[23] 'Offshore Centres up in Arms over Judgmental Hit List', June 2000, *International Money Marketing*, p. 1.

[24] 'Offshore Centres up in Arms over Judgmental Hit List', June 2000, *International Money Marketing*, p. 1.

begin cooperating with US tax authorities in criminal and civil cases . . .
The United States had already begun an information exchange with
Bermuda.'[25]

Almost immediately, regulators 'Onshore' (and 'Offshore') began to
advise their licensees to exercise greater care in dealing with particular
entities 'Offshore' that were identified. It was supposed that those jurisdictions in Group III would lose business and that costs would increase as
business migrated elsewhere – presumably to Group I centres. Some of the
Group 1 jurisdictions were already at saturation point. Group II centres
were 'forced' to try to upgrade to Group I.

Bearing in mind Luxembourg's reluctance to exchange information,
some find it difficult to reconcile the FSF's categorisation of Luxembourg
as a Group I jurisdiction.

Further, the G7 – the organisation sponsoring the FSF Report –
includes the USA and the UK amongst its members despite the fact that
both these countries have a substantial amount to gain from reducing the
amount of tax they lose as a result of their residents depositing money
'Offshore'. (Chapter 17 focuses on the UK, and Chapter 18 focuses on the
USA.)

The FSF reviewed its initiative and issued a communiqué in that
respect after its meeting in Rome at the end of March 2004. The FSF
said that, at that stage, nearly all the forty-two jurisdictions that it had
identified as having 'offshore financial activities' had been assessed by the
IMF – and that as a result of the initiative, 'significant reforms' had been
established. The FSF believed that 'shortcomings in the independence of
the regulator, the level and quality of technical supervisory skills and
onsite and offsite inspections are recurrent concerns. In addition, resources of regulators and supervisors are insufficient if compared with
the workload required by effective prudential activity and cooperation.'[26]

In a press release dated 11 March 2005, the FSF announced 'a new
process to promote further improvements in offshore financial centres . . .
[t]he 2000 list has served its purpose and is no longer operative'. This
was very welcome news to practitioners 'Offshore' since many of them
believed that the list had not been scientifically compiled in the first place
and therefore presented results that were unsatisfactory. This weakness

[25] 'Tax Schemes Cost Put in Trillions of Dollars', 20 June 2000, *Washington Post*, p. A19.
[26] 'FSF Reviews its Offshore Financial Centres (OFCs) Initiative', Press Release, Financial
Stability Forum, 5 April 2004, p. 1.

had been compounded by the introduction of the Financial Sector Assessment Program – which made the FSF listing redundant. The FSF said that:

- Thirty-nine of the forty-two jurisdictions identified as having offshore financial activities had undergone an initial assessment by the IMF;
- thirty-four of the thirty-nine have published their initial assessment reports[27];
- an additional two have confirmed their intention to publish;
- the FSF believes that 'significant reforms were initiated by many OFC jurisdictions in response to the FSF initiative and the IMF assessment program';
- 'there is a continuing need to ensure that OFCs meet international standards'.

The FSF announced a process 'based on objective criteria and due process . . . that will include a set of initiatives by its members . . . and appropriate steps by the FSF itself' to promote further improvements. The process referred to action by standard setting bodies, assessments by the IMF, initiatives by national authorities, provision of technical assistance and the FSF's own role. In respect of the latter, the FSF stressed the need for further progress by some OFCs and announced the establishment of a group to review reports by IOSCO, the IMF and others. The FSF will consider what, if any, follow-up action is necessary and 'will retain the option to engage directly with respect to a problematic OFC'. The FSF will review these initiatives in March 2008.

10.4 A comment

The FSF seems to have been pleased with the outcome of its work. Whether it has sufficient cause to be so remains to be seen. The method adopted by the FSF to collect its data does not bear scrutiny. The FSF stated that the categorisation of OFCs was based on responses of OFC supervisors and the 'impressions' of 'Onshore' supervisors. This filled no one with any confidence. Further, the 'survey' was conducted at a particular point in time – but did not accommodate ongoing assessment. Even though the FSF said that their categorisation did not constitute judgements about any jurisdiction, it was inevitable that it would be

---

[27] See www.imf.org/external/np/pp/eng/2005/022505.htm.

treated as such. The FSF said their categorisation should not be regarded as an assessment – but this is exactly what happened and the reputation of many legitimate 'Offshore' jurisdictions was affected as a result.

It was perhaps just as well then that the FSF stopped because, although this did not remedy the harm done, it limited the damage at least. Perversely, though, the FSF's interest in OFCs did not stop there, even though (as has been stated above) the FSF concluded that OFCs had not caused systemic financial problems, they took another track.

Since the FSF Report was published, the IMF has taken over. They have introduced a battery of more meaningful checks (see section 10.9 below) which are factually based and do not rely on 'impressions'. Many OFCs have undergone IMF/World Bank assessments and have demonstrated that their status *now* is better than what the FSF categorisation *estimated* it was at the time of the report. Despite that, the FSF refused to amend its categorisations. Naturally, the OFCs that have made material and fundamental changes felt tarnished by the FSF's categorisations. Although it took until 2005 for the FSF to move forward from this unfortunate attempt to categorise some jurisdictions, the matter was resolved. The FSF never withdrew or amended its categorisations – it merely announced that they had become obsolete.

10.5 The International Monetary Fund

As a consequence of the Financial Stability Forum's report (described above), a system was developed for assessing OFCs. The system included self-assessments at one end of the spectrum and Financial Sector Assessment Programmes (FSAPs) at the other.

A communiqué issued by the IMF's Interim Committee in 1999 said that 'governments must maintain strong internal financial controls and tighten supervision and regulation of domestic financial institutions and offshore banking centres including measures to deter money laundering'. On 22 January 2000, a communiqué issued by the G7 finance ministers and governors stated that 'We remain concerned about Offshore havens which undermine international standards of financial regulation and which are shelters to avoid or evade payment of tax.'

The IMF had two overriding concerns: the adequacy of the supervision and the availability of data.[28] The implication of inadequate

---

[28] 'Offshore Financial Centres: The Assessment Program', International Monetary Fund, 31 July 2003, p. 5.

supervision was said to be facilitation of fraud (including money laundering) and the encouragement of regulatory arbitrage. Weak supervision could impair the quality of consolidated supervision for those entities with subsidiaries etc. in 'Offshore Finance Centres'. Lastly, cross-border risks could not be assessed accurately without adequate information. The materiality was reflected by the volume of transactions that were being processed through these centres (see section 2.8 above).

10.6 The International Monetary Fund and OFCs

In the IMF's view,

> [t]he major risks that OFCs could pose for the international financial system are associated with prudential and financial integrity concerns . . . The institutions most likely to generate stability concerns are banks that have a large presence in offshore markets . . . OFCs are a potential conduit for the proceeds of crime to gain access to, and to be laundered through, global financial markets . . . Concerns about possible risks posed by OFCs are exacerbated by the lack of information about their operations.[29]

The International Monetary and Financial Committee issued a communiqué on 16 April 2000, which requested 'the Executive Board to undertake an assessment of the recommendations relevant to the Fund'.[30] The IMF's recommendations were formalised in July 2000 when the IMF included 'Offshore Financial Centres' in a voluntary assessment programme. The IMF 'noted that only limited evidence is available thus far on the direct risks posed by Offshore Financial Centres and Offshore Finance vehicles for the global financial system'.[31] The stated intention was 'to help members identify gaps and reduce potential vulnerabilities in their financial systems and improve the coverage of statistics on activities of OFCs in financial markets'.[32]

---

[29] 'Offshore Financial Centres: The Assessment Program', International Monetary Fund, 31 July 2003, p. 7.

[30] Communiqué of the IMF's International Monetary and Fiscal Committee, para. 22, 16 April 2000.

[31] 'Assessing the Implementation of Standards: An IMF Review of Experience and Next Steps', IMF, March 2001, p. 5.

[32] 'Offshore Financial Centres: The Assessment Program: An Information Note Prepared by the Monetary and Exchange Affairs Department', 29 August 2002.

10.7 The IMF's OFC Assessment Program

On 23 June 2000, the IMF published a paper entitled 'Offshore Financial Centres – The Role of the IMF'. This paper contains the 'OFC Assessment Program', which has two platforms: Assessment and Technical Assistance. The IMF's paper recommended a modular approach, as described below.

The IMF contacted forty-four jurisdictions with significant levels of cross-border business or with 'Offshore' legislation to invite their participation in a cycle of IMF-promoted assessments of the prevailing supervisory and regulatory systems. There was an initial meeting with representatives of all centres in September 2000 to explain the way forward. The Assessment Program dated July 2003 states that supervisory deficiencies identified in OFCs are similar to those identified in other countries. The weaknesses identified included 'shortcomings in the independence of the regulator and constraints on both the level and the quantity of technical supervisory skills'.[33] The report analyses the weaknesses identified in banking supervision, insurance supervision and securities regulation and supervision.

Phase 2 started in November 2003, at which stage the Assessment Program became a standard part of the IMF's work. Phase 2 had

the following four elements:

- Regular monitoring of OFCs' activities and compliance with supervisory standards;
- Improved transparency of OFC supervisory systems and activities;
- Technical assistance in collaboration with bilateral and multilateral donors;
- Collaboration with standards-setters and the onshore and offshore supervisors to strengthen standards and exchange of information.[34]

By the time the IMF had published its update in March 2004, forty-one out of forty-four jurisdictions involved at the start of the programme had been assessed already – or were in the process of being assessed (under a Module 2 or Financial Sector Assessment Program (FSAP)

---

[33] 'Offshore Financial Centres: The Assessment Program: A Progress Report and the Future of the Program', IMF, 31 July 2003, p. 12.
[34] 'Offshore Financial Centres: The Assessment Program: An Update', IMF, 12 March 2004, p. 4.

(see section 10.9 below)). This marked the end of the first part of the programme. The assessments indicated that the absence of adequate resources in OFCs causes a shortage of appropriate numbers of people with adequate skills – which in turn leads to what were referred to as 'shortcomings in the supervisory systems'. Compliance with assessed standards were found to be higher in jurisdictions that had higher levels of income.

The standards by which jurisdictions are assessed are described below.

10.7.1 Module 1 assessments

The idea is that jurisdictions can start off with a self-assessment of compliance with certain standards, called a Module 1 assessment. Technical assistance is offered where required. These self-assessments are intended to lead to an assessment led by a member of the IMF's staff. This could take the form of a Module 2 assessment or else could be a FSAP review (described as a Module 3 in the case of non-members).

10.7.2 Module 2 assessments

Module 2 assessments are independent assessments of supervisory standards carried out by specialised regulators from the IMF. The compliance of supervisory and regulatory systems with international standards are tested in respect of banking (and insurance and securities where appropriate). The effectiveness of both anti-money laundering procedures and also procedures to combat the financing of terrorism are tested. Each assessment will be based on standard principles adopted for the relevant discipline. For example, the banking assessments are based on the Basel Core Principles and the insurance assessment will be based on the core principles of the IAIS. The standards provided by IOSCO and by the FATF are also used. 'The average cost per Module 2 assessment is estimated at about $150,000.'[35] Instead of the Module 2 assessment, members may request an FSAP assessment (which includes a review of domestic financial vulnerabilities also).

---

[35] 'Offshore Financial Centres: The Assessment Program: A Progress Report and the Future of the Program', IMF, 31 July 2003, para. 45, p. 21.

10.7.3 Module 3 assessments

The third type of assessment is Module 3, for non-OECD members. The comprehensive Module 3 or Financial Sector Assessment Program assessments are aimed at identifying significant risks and vulnerabilities (see section 10.9 below). They include not only reviews of the observance of regulatory and supervisory standards and codes (as for Module 2) but also an assessment of the vulnerabilities of a jurisdiction and domestic and potential cross-border risks. Module 3 OFC assessments comprise 'assessments of financial risks, relevant financial sector standards and codes, and cross-border effects of the relevant OFC'.[36]

10.8 Financial System Stability Assessments

'The Financial System Stability Assessment (FSSA) assessments derived from FSAP findings and Article IV consultations, is the main tool for identifying financial system vulnerabilities, contributing to the bilateral Article IV surveillance of member countries.'[37] (Under Article IV of the IMF's Articles of Agreement, the IMF holds bilateral discussions on macroeconomic policies with its members on an annual basis.) The FSSAs include assessment of risks to macroeconomic stability arising from the finance sector and whether that sector could absorb such shocks.[38] This module links into the first two modules and to the IMF's Article IV surveillance. In this respect, 'the FSSAs focus on strengths, risks and vulnerabilities in the financial system'.[39] The result enables an overall assessment of stability to be compiled. The IMF's 'Directors agreed that the FSSAs are the preferred tool for strengthening the monitoring of financial systems under the IMF's bilateral surveillance.'[40]

---

[36] 'IMF Reviews Experience with the Financial Sector Assessment Program and Reaches Conclusions on Issues Going Forward', IMF, Public Information Notice 01/11, 5 February 2001.

[37] 'Offshore Financial Centres: The Assessment Program', International Monetary Fund, 31 July 2003, p. 9.

[38] FSSA Country Reports are available at www.imf.org/external/np/fsap/fsap.asp.

[39] Paul Hilbers, 'The IMF/World Bank Financial Sector Assessment Program', IMF, February 2001.

[40] 'IMF Reviews Experience with the Financial Sector Assessment program and Reaches Conclusions on Issues Going Forward', IMF, Public Information Notice 01/11, 5 February 2001.

10.9 Financial Sector Assessment Programs

The FSAP, which was launched in May 1999, derived from the financial crises of the late 1990s. It is voluntary, and the FSAP reports are treated as confidential documents for the relevant national authority. Publication is voluntary. For example, Cyprus, Gibraltar and Panama publicly disclosed their IMF assessments, and were applauded by the Financial Stability Forum for doing so.[41] Other jurisdictions also published their respective reports. Media reports have indicated that other centres (e.g. Liechtenstein (OFC assessment by the IMF in November 2002) and the Bahamas (Article IV consultation) as reported in the September 2003 edition of *Offshore Red*) have fared well in their respective assessments. Not all centres have fared so positively. In the same edition of *Offshore Red*, reference was made to a critical report by IMF on Vanuatu. 'This report will add further to the troubles experienced by Vanuatu. Its reputation as a non-cooperative jurisdiction has led to public skirmishes with the Organization for Economic Cooperation and Development and the Financial Action Task Force. In addition, the Australian National Tax Office has named Vanuatu as its number one target.'[42] (It should be noted that many OFCs do not undergo Article IV consultations.)

Like other aspects of financial regulation, the assessment programs are based on the premise that prevention is better than cure. The FSAP program focuses on the financial sectors of the countries under review. The rationale is that, in assessing strengths and vulnerabilities in 'financial systems', potential problems will become apparent. This will allow remedial action to be taken and will help to prevent a problem and, in turn, this will contribute to financial stability. 'Financial systems' include not only different types of service providers (e.g. insurance companies, banks or mutual funds) but also different types of financial markets (e.g. money markets or securities markets). The focus extends to payments systems and to the legal and regulatory framework. What is the role of the World Bank? The intention was that the IMF would be responsible for assessing data dissemination and fiscal transparency and that the World Bank would

---

[41] 'Financial Stability Forum Holds its Seventh Meeting', Bank for International Settlements, 5 April 2002.
[42] 'IMF Savages Vanuatu in Recent Report', September 2003, *Offshore Red*.

take the lead in three areas covered by Reports on Observance of Standards and Codes: (i) corporate governance, (ii) accounting and auditing, and (iii) insolvency regimes and creditor rights.[43]

The IMF has traditionally focused on the two-way linkages between financial sector soundness and macroeconomic performance on the one hand, and support policies that reduce the likelihood of financial crises and lessen the severity of those that do occur on the other . . . [whereas] . . . the Bank has focused on the importance of the financial sector development and poverty reduction. A well functioning financial system has been shown to be important for economic growth, which is a key element for poverty reduction. In this connection, the Bank has traditionally supported the development and strengthening of countries' financial sectors.[44]

The IMF's focus is on systemic stability while the World Bank's focus is on development.

Assessments under the FSAP, in addition to evaluating observance of relevant financial sector standards and codes, consider risks to macroeconomic stability stemming from the financial sector and the capacity of the sector to absorb macroeconomic shocks.[45]

The IMF has said that

[t]he FSAP, a joint IMF and World Bank effort introduced in May 1999, aims to increase the effectiveness of efforts to promote the soundness of financial systems in member countries . . . work under the program seeks to identify the strengths and vulnerabilities of a country's financial system; to determine how key sources of risk are being managed; to ascertain the sector's developmental and technical assistance needs; and to help prioritise policy responses.[46]

The FSAP program creates reports on FSSAs and Reports on the Observance of Standards and Codes (ROSC's) – as described in section 10.8 and 10.10 below, respectively.

[43] 'Reports on the Observance of Standards and Codes', World Bank Group (undated).
[44] Paul Hilbers, 'The IMF/World Bank Financial Sector Assessment Program', IMF, February 2001.
[45] 'Offshore Financial Centres: The Assessment Program: A Progress Report', IMF, 25 February 2005, p. 4.
[46] Financial Sector Assessment Program, IMF, www.imf.org/external/np/fsap/fsap.asp.

The assessments are carried out by IMF/World Bank staff, together with external experts from IOSCO, the Basel Committee and the IAIS. The three components that comprise the assessment of the financial system are as follows:

> (1) an assessment of stability of the financial system, including macroeconomic factors that could affect the performance of the system and conditions in the system that could affect the macro-economy; (2) an assessment of the extent to which relevant financial sector standards, codes and good practices are observed: and (3) an assessment of the financial sector's reform and development needs. The team identifies actions that would strengthen the financial system, together with any needed contingency plans, and provides a detailed evaluation of the monetary and fiscal implications of these actions.[47]

The assessment also considers the adequacy of the regulatory environment in terms of both capacity and practice. The Basel Core Principles for Effective Banking Supervision are used as a benchmark. Further, there is also an assessment of the potential for system development (e.g. in respect of pension funds and capital markets). 'Practice has shown that financial crises usually occur when both types of indicators [macro-prudential analysis such as large short term borrowing in a foreign currency in excess of a country's foreign exchange reserves and micro-prudential indicators] point to vulnerabilities, that is, when financial institutions are weak and face macroeconomic shocks'[48] Stress tests and scenario analysis are used for this purpose as are standards assessments (i.e. tests that are designed to measure the extent to which relevant financial sector standards and codes are both implemented and observed). However, the assessment is not an end in itself and, that being so, the results are fed into other work.

In respect of the IMF, the results of the FSAP become part of a Financial System Stability Assessment (FSSA). With respect to the World Bank, the FSAP leads into the preparation of a Financial Sector Assessment (FSA). The FSAP forms the basis of the Bank's determination whether and what assistance (including technical assistance) will be provided to the country concerned.

---

[47] Paul Hilbers, 'The IMF/World Bank Financial Sector Assessment Program', IMF, February 2001.

[48] Paul Hilbers, 'The IMF/World Bank Financial Sector Assessment Program', IMF, February 2001.

FSAP missions usually last around two weeks. The assessors leave a draft report with the jurisdiction for comment. Meanwhile, the draft is reviewed by specialists within the IMF and by external reviewers as appropriate.

10.10 Standards

Fundamentally, the core value of international standards includes consistent definitions which apply geographically. It has been said that:

> international standards enhance transparency as well as multilateral surveillance. They help to better identify weaknesses that may contribute to economic and financial vulnerability, foster market efficiency and discipline, and ultimately contribute to a global economy which is more robust and less prone to crisis. At the national level, international standards provide a benchmark that can help identify vulnerabilities as well as guide policy reform.[49]

The relevant standards (which date from the second half of the 1990s) include:[50]

- International Accounting Standards;
- International Standards on Auditing;
- Core Systems for Systemically Important Payment Systems;
- Core Principles for Effective Banking Supervision;
- Objectives and Principles of Securities Regulation;
- Insurance Supervisory Principles;
- Supervision of Financial Conglomerates;
- ten key principles of information sharing;
- the Forty Recommendations of the Financial Action Task Force;
- principles of corporate governance;
- the Specific and General Data Dissemination Standards;
- the Model Law on Cross Border Insolvency; and
- Orderly and Effective Insolvency Procedures.

The IMF pointed out that, since 1995, there has been general consensus on the need to strengthen the global financial system. The focus has been on both increased transparency and on the implementation of

---

[49] 'Reports on the Observance of Standards and Codes', World Bank Group (undated).

[50] Hans Falkena, Roy Bamber, David Llewellyn and Tim Store, *Financial Regulation in South Africa*, Financial Sector Forum, 2001, p. 90.

relevant standards and codes. It was said that 'standards are designed to promote sustained growth and greater stability in international financial markets'.[51]

The IMF identified eleven standards that are relevant to their assessment work as follows:

1. the IMF's Special Data Dissemination Standard/General Data Dissemination System;
2. the IMF's Code of Good Practices on Fiscal Transparency;
3. the IMF's Code of Good Practices on Transparency in Monetary and Financial Policies;
4. the Basel Committee's Core Principles for Effective Banking Supervision;
5. IOSCO's Objectives and Principles for Securities Regulation;
6. the International Association of Insurance Supervisory Principles;
7. the Committee on Payments and Settlements' Core Principles for Systemically Important Payments Systems;
8. the OECD's Principles of Corporate Governance;
9. the International Accounting Standards Committee's International Accounting Standards;
10. the International Federation of Accountants' International Standards on Auditing; and
11. paragraph 3 of the Staff Paper on Insolvency and Creditor Rights.

10.10.1 Reports on the Observance of Standards and Codes (ROSCs)

In January 1999, the IMF started a pilot programme based on assessments of members' adherence to certain relevant standards – referred to as Reports on the Observance of Standards and Codes (ROSCs). These have since been adopted as part of the joint IMF/World Bank's FSAP work. The ROSCs 'provide a systematic and structured way of organising and presenting information on standards assessments to help guide and inform the surveillance process'.[52]

---

[51] 'Assessing the Implementation of Standards: An IMF Review of Experience and Next Steps', IMF, 5 March 2001.
[52] 'Assessing the Implementation of Standards: An IMF Review of Experience and Next Steps', IMF, 5 March 2001.

10.11 Anti-money laundering and combating the financing of terrorism

In April 2001, the IMF agreed upon the value of developing a methodology to assess standards to counter money laundering.

The methodology was pilot-tested for twelve months as part of the standards used in FSAP work and also as part of the IMF's OFC programme. This programme was expanded in November 2001 to include procedures to combat the financing of terrorism and legal and institutional structures. The final methodology has been in use since October 2002 and reflects the FATF's Recommendations. As part of the pilot, forty-one countries were assessed for compliance – thirty-three of which assessments were conducted by staff from the World Bank and the IMF. The pilot was considered to be successful, and the FATF encouraged the World Bank/IMF to use it in future on a permanent basis.

The review of the results of the pilot programme indicated that:

> [m]ost higher-income countries have in place well developed rules and safeguards, but often exhibited gaps related to measures to combat terrorist financing. In middle-income countries, frameworks are often in place but much more needs to be done to put them into practice. Low-income countries need assistance in strengthening many aspects of their financial sectors and have been slower in focusing on money laundering and terrorist financing concerns.[53]

Meanwhile, the World Bank stated that it had been increasing its efforts to combat financial abuse by focusing on '(i) strengthening government and institutional capacity to fight corruption, promote good governance and public financial management; (ii) strengthening financial systems primarily through the joint Bank/Fund FSAP follow-up assistance and (iii) helping countries develop sound market infrastructure through legal and judicial reform, corporate governance, accounting and auditing and market transparency'.[54]

In pursuit of the strategy described, the Bank and the IMF developed a draft anti-money laundering methodology as part of the FSAP assessment programme. Their methodology was based on the prudential

---

[53] 'World Bank Enhance Efforts at Combating Money Laundering, Terrorist Financing', Press Release No. 04/70/, IMF, 2 April 2004.

[54] 'Proposed Action Plan for Enhancing the Bank's Ability to Respond to Clients in Combating Money Laundering and the Financing of Terrorism', World Bank (undated).

supervision principles compiled by the Basel Committee, by the International Association of Insurance Supervisors and by IOSCO – and with reference to the FATF's Forty Recommendations. The World Bank and the IMF agreed to '[g]ive attention to anti-money laundering issues in the Bank's diagnostic work, especially the voluntary Financial Sector Assessment Program (FSAP) and Report on Observance of Standards and Codes (ROSC) exercises'.[55] As a result, the World Bank and the IMF have set themselves a target of ten visits per year. These will be conducted under the FSAP regime (joint IMF/World Bank) or the OFC regime (IMF).

Distinction was drawn between the FSAP and the ROSC work and the anti-money laundering work. The former will be used to assess adherence to the FATF's Forty Recommendations – including criminal and civil law enforcement measures while the latter excludes law enforcement measures. The methodology was expanded in 2002 to include measures to combat the financing of terrorism – and the legal framework employed in dealing with financial abuse. The revised methodology took account of the additional eight special recommendations adopted by the FATF in respect of terrorism and which have been described elsewhere. (A subsequent methodology was introduced in 2004 to incorporate changes arising from the revisions to the Forty Recommendations made by the FATF.) Where technical assistance was to be offered in future, it might include the adequacy of supervisory regimes and the legal framework to combat financial abuse. Specific training materials were to be produced for this new area of focus. Since assessments carried out after September 2004 were to be carried out according to the new style, there was a flurry of international activity to train new trainers in the new methodology.

10.12 A summary of the results between 2001 and 2004

10.12.1 2001

Based on assessments conducted up to the end of 2001, an Information Note ('IN') published said that 'weaknesses in banking supervision stemmed from inadequate anti-money laundering measures, insufficient independence of the regulator and poor onsite and offsite surveillance. Insurance supervision was weaker in general, with market conduct, onsite inspections and information sharing and cooperation requiring

---

[55] 'Proposed Action Plan for Enhancing the Bank's Ability to Respond to Clients in Combating Money Laundering and the Financing of Terrorism', World Bank (undated).

particular attention . . . The assessments had also identified issues common to all sectors, including a need for improved legal frameworks for anti-money laundering and combating the financing of terrorism (AML/CFT) and found that supervisory capabilities were constrained by high costs and skill shortages. Cross sectorial information sharing also required enhancement.'

10.12.2 2002

It was anticipated that four FSAPs and thirteen other assessments would be accomplished during 2002. Five Module 2 reports and one FSAP report have been published.

The work carried out in 2002 included a review of AML/CFT proced- ures and comparisons with the Basel Committee's Core Principles for Effective Banking Supervision. There was limited assessment of the insurance and securities sectors because of their limited significance in the small jurisdictions. The IN identified some patterns as follows:

1. Observance of principles of effective banking supervision was de- scribed as 'quite modest'. This was apparent in 'small low income jurisdictions where outdated legislative provisions, inadequate budget- ary resources and limited supervisory skills are, as would be expected, the main constraining factors'.
2. Although the limitations apply to both the domestic and the 'Offshore' sectors, they are more pronounced in the latter when the supervisory authorities are not the same.
3. Regulators have too little knowledge of corporate entities registered in the jurisdiction.
4. The supply of supervisory skills is too little.
5. Enhancement of legislation and/or supervisory practices concerning AML/CFT was encouraged.

The IMF said that 'most of the major centres have strengthened their laws, regulations and supervisory arrangements to meet international standards either ahead of or as a result of the assessments. Some smaller jurisdictions with weak supervisory capacity have reduced their offshore activity, and requested technical assistance to improve their regulatory and supervisory arrangements.'[56]

[56] 'IMF Executive Board Reviews the Assessment Program on Offshore Financial Centres', IMF, 24 November 2003.

10.12.3 2003[57]

Table 11 in Appendix 1 sets out the Summary Status of OFC assessments at the end of 2003. On 5 November 2003, the Executive Board of the IMF carried out a review of the OFC assessment program that began in 2000. They decided that 'the regular monitoring of OFCs should become a standard component of the work of the Fund'.[58] As a result, IMF staff recommended in their July 2003 progress report that the OFC pro- gramme would become an integral part of the IMF's work which should encompass the following:

- regular monitoring of OFCs through offsite analysis, and risk focused and periodic assessment missions;
- improving the transparency of OFC supervisory systems and activities;
- providing technical assistance in collaboration with bilateral and multi- lateral donors to strengthen supervisory and regulatory systems; and
- collaborating with the standard setters and the onshore and offshore supervisors to strengthen standards and exchanges of information.[59]

The same report described the major elements of the monitoring programme, as follows:

- Development and maintenance of information on the main activities in OFCs;
- Immediate priority would be given to completing the current round of assessments and to updating AML/CFT assessments;
- Risk focused assessments of jurisdictions tied to issues of specific concern;
- Periodic Module 2 assessments of all OFCs not subject to FSAPs;
- Close coordination with the FSAP program to identify weaknesses in consolidated supervision;
- Assessments of OFCs would continue to be voluntary, with the support of members to ensure the success of the program;
- The OFC initiative would continue for the time being as a separate program from the FSAP.[60]

---

[57] 'Offshore Financial Centres: The Assessment Program: A Progress Report and the Future of the Program, Supplementary Information', IMF, 3 November 2003.

[58] 'IMF Executive Board Reviews the Assessment Program on Offshore Financial Centres', IMF, 24 November 2003.

[59] 'Offshore Financial Centres: The Assessment Program: A Progress Report and the Future of the Program', IMF, 31 July 2003, p. 16.

[60] 'Offshore Financial Centres: The Assessment Program: A Progress Report and the Future of the Program', IMF, 31 July 2003, p. 16.

It was further proposed that transparency would be enhanced by reclassifying Module 2 reports as staff reports. Originally, under the technical assistance modus operandi, Module 2 reports contained two volumes. The first comprised a summary assessment of compliance with codes and standards and a description of the jurisdiction's activities, the supervisory system, ROSCs (including recommendations for correcting deficiencies identified in ROSCs). Volume 2 was a detailed assessment of the standards. Volume 1 and summary assessments of compliance with standards were available to Board members – with the jurisdiction's approval. The new arrangement provides that Volume 1 – and ROSCs – would be circulated to Board members.

10.12.4 2004

In March 2004, the IMF published an update on its assessment programme for OFCs. The update includes the following findings:

- Compliance levels for OFCs are, on average, more favourable than those for other jurisdictions assessed by the Fund in its financial sector work;
- Nevertheless shortcomings remain in the supervisory systems of many of the OFCs;
- Compliance with the standards tends to increase with the income of the jurisdiction assessed;
- While compliance rates were generally high in the areas relevant for their business, the assessments identified the following main areas of weakness . . .[61]

In respect of banking, the update said that 40 per cent of jurisdictions needed to strengthen the independence of their supervisors and improve their resources. Oversight of banks' credit and market risks also needed improvement. Onsite inspection at insurance companies needed improvement and in respect of securities, it was said that supervisors needed more powers and resources. Further, contingency plans were needed to deal with the failure of firms that give advice on securities. In respect of anti-money laundering and the combating of the financing of terrorism, there were deficiencies in rules applicable to branches and subsidiaries abroad. Transactions with higher risk countries needed more

---

[61] 'Offshore Financial Centres: The Assessment Program: An Update', IMF, 12 March 2004, p. 8.

monitoring, and focus was required on ensuring that adequate AML/CFT programmes were properly applied by all licensees. Strengthened measures were necessary in imposing anti-money laundering requirements in respect of alternative remittance systems and in assisting in investigations by other countries with respect to the financing of terrorism.

An analysis of the publication status of reports under the Module 2 and FSAP programmes was included in a further update, entitled 'Offshore Financial Centres – The Assessment Program – An Update'[62] (See Tables 11 and 12 in Appendix 1 below.) In summary, as at 12 March 2004, of the forty-four jurisdictions that had been contacted about these programmes, twenty-eight assessments had been completed. Of the sixteen that were incomplete, thirteen were in train and three had not been started. At that stage (March 2004), the IMF had already begun to implement the actions described above as part of the November 2003 review.

It so happens that, after a FSAP assessment, every jurisdiction's public relations machinery finds much about the outcome to demonstrate that the centre has passed with flying colours. It seems that, in such circumstances, human nature dictates that we maximise our strengths but minimise our weaknesses. For example, after the assessments carried out in Guernsey, the Isle of Man and Jersey, all three centres were described as 'basking in the praise they received from the International Monetary Fund . . . jostling to release statements welcoming the IMF reviews, which highlighted their comprehensive regulatory frameworks and overall high standards'. However, less publicity was given to action that the IMF required to be undertaken. '[T]he Isle of Man and Jersey were told to update their on-site supervisory process. Jersey was told to adopt an anti-terrorism Act. Guernsey was told to enhance the powers of its regulator and to address a resource deficit in its banking division. And all three were told to make their regulators more independent.'[63]

Nevertheless – and in their favour – the following comments were taken from one issue of one journal concerning the assessments:

> Gibraltar is generally effective and ranks as a well-developed supervisor, according to an IMF assessment of the jurisdiction . . . An IMF assessment of the offshore banking sector in Cyprus said supervision was 'generally

---

[62] IMF, 12 March 2004.
[63] Jacqui Canham, 'Crown Dependencies Revel in IMF Praise', January 2004, *Portfolio International.*

effective and thorough'. . . Jersey's financial regulatory and supervisory
system complies well with international standards according to an IMF
report on the offshore financial centre . . . Hong Kong's financial sector
regulatory system is well developed by international standards an IMF
report on *offshore financial centres* has concluded . . . [A]n IMF assessment
of standards and codes found that authorities in Mauritius have made
'substantial progress' and are upgrading key financial sector legislation
and regulations . . . [T]he IMF said in its latest assessment of *international
financial centres* that Switzerland's supervisory system was effective.[64]

Besides the positive reports, notice the adoption of dual terminology –
'offshore financial centres' and 'international financial centres'. Confusion prevails.

10.12.5 2005

The IMF published a progress report on 25 February 2005, in which it
stated that the first phase of the OFC assessment programme was
virtually complete.[65] (See Table 12 in Appendix 1.) The following comments are taken from that report:

- 'Compliance levels for OFCs are, on average better than in other
  jurisdictions assessed under the FSAP . . . Jurisdictions with low levels
  of income have a much lower rate of compliance with all the assessed
  standards than wealthier jurisdictions. Such jurisdictions often have
  low volumes of financial activity and many of the poorer jurisdictions
  have eliminated or are phasing out their OFC activities' (para. 5);
  Table 4 of the report (see Table 12 in Appendix 1 below) contains a
  very enlightening summary on the numbers of jurisdictions that
  comply with the Principles and Recommendations related to cooperation and to information sharing.
- 'On average, OFCs meet supervisory standards superior to those of
  other jurisdictions though with deficiencies in lower income jurisdictions' (para. 6). '50% of offshore jurisdictions comply with every
  principle and recommendation directly concerned with cooperation
  and information exchange as opposed to 47% of other assessed
  jurisdictions' (footnote 5).

[64] 'European News', June 2004, *Offshore Red*, pp. 77–8.
[65] 'Offshore Financial Centres: The Assessment Program: A Progress Report', IMF, 25
February 2005, p. 3.

Appendix 1 to the report contains a very detailed summary of assessments so far undertaken on forty-six jurisdictions – and includes relevant updates. This information is summarised in Table 30 in Appendix 1 below.

The IMF said that their Information Framework (see section 2.10 above) would allow 'more intensive offsite monitoring of activities' (para. 9) in financial centres and reminded readers that the Framework provides a template that jurisdictions can use in disseminating their figures.

Tables 2 and 3 of the IMF's report provide summary analyses arising from assessments undertaken on those international and offshore financial centres contacted so far. Table 2 deals with Module 2 Assessments and Table 3 deals with FSAP Assessments. These tables are most instructive.

10.13 The OFC programme: phase 2

Presumably, focus will now turn to the second phase, which the IMF's Directors agreed (November 2003) should incorporate the following elements:

- regular monitoring of OFCs' activities and compliance with supervisory standards;
- improved transparency of OFCs' supervisory systems and activities;
- technical assistance in collaboration with bilateral and multilateral donors;
- collaboration with standard-setters and the onshore and offshore supervisors to strengthen standards and exchanges of information.[66]

---

[66] 'Offshore Financial Centres: The Assessment Program: A Progress Report', IMF, 25 February 2005, p. 7.

Supranational focus (2): the Financial Action Task Force

OFCs have more recently become a major target of the FATF and OECD because some of them are increasingly viewed as offering opportunities for money laundering and tax evasion as well as raising obstacles to anti corruption investigations.[1]

11.1 Introduction

This is the second of three chapters devoted to the work in respect of the 'Offshore' environment that has been carried out by certain supranational organisations. The work of the Financial Stability Forum (FSF), the International Monetary Fund (IMF) together with that of the World Bank was considered in the previous chapter. This chapter focuses on the work of the Financial Action Task Force (FATF).

An outline of the FATF has been provided in section 9.8 above, so the introduction that follows merely serves to place the work of the FATF in context.

11.2 The work of the Financial Action Task Force

The Annual Report for 2004–5 states that the FATF carries out the following tasks:

- it sets international AML/CFT standards;
- it monitors compliance with AML/CFT standards;
- it promotes worldwide application of the FATF's standards;
- it encourages compliance of non-FATF members with FATF standards; and
- it studies the methods and trends of money laundering and terrorist financing.

---

[1] 'Offshore Financial Centres', IMF Background Paper, 23 June 2000.

The FATF works closely with international financial institutions in compiling, applying and promoting international standards, principal among which are the Forty Recommendations and the Nine Special Recommendations. 'It is estimated that about 130 jurisdictions representing 85 per cent of the total world population, and about 90–95 per cent of global economic output have made at least a political commitment to implement the 40 Recommendations.'[2]

The IMF and the World Bank recognise both the latter as international standards for combating money laundering. In 2002, both sets of Recommendations were added to the list of standards on which Reports on the Observance of Standards and Codes (ROSCs, dealt with in more detail in section 10.10 above) are compiled. The IMF, the World Bank and the FATF have now agreed upon a common methodology to assess adherence.

As part of an initiative to identify anti-money laundering weaknesses in both member and non-member countries, the FATF published a document entitled 'Report on Non-Cooperative Countries and Territories' (the 'FATF Report') on 14 February 2000. The FATF Report focused on (unnamed) countries and territories that were described as 'uncooperative' in the war against money laundering.

The FATF Report described twenty-five criteria[3] that the FATF had used to identify 'detrimental rules and practices which impeded international cooperation in the fight against money laundering.'[4] The criteria were classified under four areas: (1) loopholes in financial regulations; (2) impediments arising through other regulatory rules; (3) obstacles to cooperation; and (4) inadequate resources to detect, prevent and repress money laundering. The FATF Report described the means that would be used to encourage uncooperative jurisdictions to implement appropriate international standards – and identified some countermeasures that member countries might use to protect themselves against possible abuse.

Interestingly, the FATF Report said '[t]he legitimate use by private citizens and institutional investors of certain facilities offered by many financial centres, including Offshore centres, is not put in question. An

---

[2] Abdullahi Y. Shehu, 'International Initiatives Against Corruption and Money Laundering: An Overview', Vol. 12, No. 3, *Journal of Financial Crime*, p. 233.

[3] See Appendix 3, 'Criteria for Defining Non-Cooperative Countries'.

[4] 'Review to Identify Non-Cooperative Countries: Increasing the Worldwide Effectiveness of Anti-Money Laundering Measures', FATF, 22 June 2000, para. 5, p. 2.

essential aspect of this issue is to make sure that such centres are not used by transnational criminal organisations to launder criminal proceeds in the international system. It is also important that they are not used by criminal organisations to escape investigation in other jurisdictions.'[5]

The FATF Report set the scene for the action that the FATF was to adopt thereafter. This began with the establishment of four regional review groups, whose job it was to review the prevailing anti-money laundering regimes in a number of jurisdictions – against the twenty-five criteria. Each jurisdiction was asked to provide relevant information both in writing and orally. The FATF then analysed the information it had collated, and, on 22 June 2000, it published another report entitled 'Review to Identify Non-Cooperative Countries: Increasing the World-wide Effectiveness of Anti-Money Laundering Measures' (the 'FATF Report 2').

Page 2 of the FATF Report 2 starts a summary of a review of what were described (page 3) as 'a first set of jurisdictions . . . Jurisdictions marked with an asterisk are regarded as being non-cooperative by the FATF.' The review included a comment on each of twenty-nine jurisdictions (see Table 22 in Appendix 1 below) that had been considered, and specified areas for attention where necessary. The FATF Report 2 said 'there is a wide variance in both the character of the money laundering threat posed by different jurisdictions and in the status of efforts to implement anti-money laundering controls'.[6]

11.3 Non-cooperative countries and territories

The FATF reviewed a total of 47 jurisdictions and listed 23 jurisdictions as ['non-cooperative countries and territories' (NCCTs)] based on their overall regulatory framework, customer identification, suspicious transaction reporting, criminalisation of money laundering and international cooperation. All jurisdictions unwilling to respond to requests or having laws or regulations prohibiting international exchange of information between judicial authorities were placed on the NCCT list.[7]

---

[5] 'Report on Non-Cooperative Countries and Territories', FATF, 14 February 2000, p. 9.
[6] 'Review to Identify Non-Cooperative Countries: Increasing the Worldwide Effectiveness of Anti-Money Laundering Measures', FATF, 22 June 2000, para. 62, p. 12.
[7] FATF, *Annual Report* 2004–5, p. 12, 10 June 2005.

The FATF Report 2 identified fifteen jurisdictions that the FATF considered to be NCCTs. These countries were the Bahamas, the Cayman
Islands, the Cook Islands, Dominica, Israel, Lebanon, Liechtenstein, the
Marshall Islands, Nauru, Niue, Panama, the Philippines, Russia, St Kitts
and Nevis and St Vincent and the Grenadines.[8] The FATF Report 2 said
(para. 64) that these jurisdictions had 'serious systemic problems' and
encouraged immediate remedial steps.

Table 23 in Appendix 1 below analyses the conclusions of the FATF
Report 2 and traces subsequent changes to the list of NCCTs. As at 30
July 2005, Myanmar, Nauru and Nigeria comprise those jurisdictions
that remain on the NCCT list (last changed on 11 February 2005).

Recommendation 21 provides for special measures against jurisdictions that do not adhere to the 'rules'. The Recommendation States that
'financial institutions should give special attention to business relations
and transactions with persons, including companies and financial institutions, from the [NCCTs] mentioned in paragraph 64'.[9]

Additional special measures were developed[10] that should be 'gradual,
proportionate and flexible'. These included:

- Stringent requirements for identifying clients and enhancement of
  advisories (see below), including jurisdiction-specific financial advisories, to financial institutions for identification of the beneficial
  owners before business relationships are established with individuals
  or companies from these countries;
- Enhanced relevant reporting mechanisms or systematic reporting of
  financial transactions on the basis that financial transactions with such
  countries are more likely to be suspicious;
- In considering requests for approving the establishment in FATF
  member countries of subsidiaries or branches or representative offices
  of banks taking into account the fact that the relevant bank is from a
  NCCT;
- Warning non-financial sector businesses that transactions with entities
  within the NCCTs might run the risk of money laundering.

[8] 'Review to Identify Non-Cooperative Countries: Increasing the Worldwide Effectiveness
of Anti-Money Laundering Measures', FATF, 22 June 2000, para. 64, p. 13.
[9] 'Review to Identify Non-Cooperative Countries: Increasing the Worldwide Effectiveness
of Anti-Money Laundering Measures', FATF, 22 June 2000, para. 65, p. 13.
[10] See 'Criteria for Defining Non-Cooperative Countries and Territories', 14 February 2000,
www.fatf-gafi.org.

In the absence of appropriate action by NCCTs, 'FATF members would then need to consider the adoption of counter measures'.[11] In fact, the FATF members issued 'advisories' to all licensees within their jurisdiction – advising them of the extra care required in analysing transactions passing through the named territories. ('Advisories' are tantamount to warning notices.) Naturally, there is a 'reputational' issue arising for those jurisdictions so listed and against which other jurisdictions have taken this sort of action. This is a serious development for those involved since, in the final analysis, it could lead to a loss of business.

The FATF plenary decides upon changes to the list of NCCTs. The criteria adopted by the plenary include whether a jurisdiction has properly dealt with the deficiencies already brought to its attention – and the first critical step in this respect is whether the necessary legislation and rules have been put in place. 'The FATF attaches particular importance to reforms in the area of criminal law, financial supervision, customer identification, suspicious activity reporting and international cooperation.'[12]

The outcome of a subsequent review of the list of NCCTs was published in the FATF's twelfth Annual Report (published on 22 June 2001). The Bahamas, the Cayman Islands, Liechtenstein and Panama were removed from the list of NCCTs. The initiative achieved some success – not least because many of the jurisdictions listed as non-cooperative made significant progress in achieving the changes demanded of them. However, the following six jurisdictions were added to the list: Egypt, Guatemala, Hungary, Indonesia, Myanmar and Nigeria. A detailed description of the precise developments is available from the FATF's publication (dated 22 June 2001) entitled 'Review to Identify Non-Cooperative Countries or Territories: Increasing the Worldwide Effectiveness of Anti-Money Laundering Measures'. This was the FATF's second review.

As at June 2001, the list of NCCTs comprised seventeen jurisdictions: the Cook Islands, Dominica, Egypt, Guatemala, Hungary, Indonesia, Israel, Lebanon, the Marshall Islands, Myanmar, Nauru, Nigeria, Niue, the Philippines, Russia, St Kitts and Nevis and St Vincent and the

---

[11] 'Review to Identify Non-Cooperative Countries: Increasing the Worldwide Effectiveness of Anti-Money Laundering Measures', FATF, 22 June 2000, para. 67, p. 13.
[12] 'Annual Review of Non-Cooperative Countries or Territories', FATF, July 2004, para. 13, p. 4.

Grenadines. In a press release dated 22 June 2001, '[t]he FATF calls on its members to request their financial institutions to give special attention to businesses and transactions with persons, including companies and financial institutions, in these countries or territories'.

Further, in the same press release, the FATF recommended 'additional countermeasures (including the possibility of enhanced surveillance and reporting of financial transactions and other relevant actions) as of 30 September with respect to Nauru, the Philippines and Russia unless their governments enact significant legislation which addresses identified money laundering concerns'.

After their plenary meeting, the FATF announced in their press release dated 7 September 2001 that additional countermeasures would not be required against Russia because significant legislation had been enacted. Nevertheless, Russia remained on the NCCT list (but, within a short time, became a member of the FATF). Anti-money laundering legislation enacted by Nauru was considered to be unsatisfactory. If amendments were made by 30 November 2001, countermeasures would not be applied. The Philippines had not enacted legislation – and, unless this was done by 30 September 2001, the FATF recommended to members that additional countermeasures should be adopted. Two additional countries were added to the NCCT list: Grenada and the Ukraine. Accordingly, the NCCT list comprised nineteen countries as at September 2001. The NCCTs were the Cook Islands, Dominica, Egypt, Grenada, Guatemala, Hungary, Indonesia, Israel, Lebanon, the Marshall Islands, Myanmar, Nauru, Nigeria, Niue, the Philippines, Russia, St Kitts and Nevis, St Vincent and the Grenadines and the Ukraine.

The FATF called on members to request their financial institutions to give special attention to businesses and transactions with persons, including companies and financial institutions, in these countries or territories.

The list was further amended in June 2002 when Hungary, Israel, Lebanon and St Kitts and Nevis were removed. As at June 2002, the list of fifteen NCCTs comprised the Cook Islands, Dominica, Egypt, Grenada, Guatemala, Indonesia, the Marshall Islands, Myanmar, Nauru, Nigeria, Niue, the Philippines, Russia, St Vincent and the Grenadines and the Ukraine. The FATF members were advised to alert their financial institutions to pay special attention to businesses and transactions with financial institutions in countries on the list.

The next revision was in October 2002, when Russia, Dominica, Niue and the Marshall Islands were removed from the list of NCCTs which at that stage therefore comprised the Cook Islands, Egypt, Grenada, Guatemala, Indonesia, Myanmar, Nauru, Nigeria, the Philippines, St Vincent and the Grenadines and the Ukraine. Of the eleven NCCTs remaining, there were only four OFCs listed. Further, the FATF recommended that countermeasures should be adopted against Nigeria and Ukraine.

The list was again reviewed in February 2003. At that time, Grenada was removed from the list of NCCTs and the additional countermeasures imposed against Ukraine were withdrawn but Ukraine remained on the list for the time being. Meanwhile, the FATF recommended that its members impose additional countermeasures (from 15 March 2003) against the Philippines – because of its failure to enact relevant legislation. At that stage, the list of NCCTs comprised the following ten jurisdictions: the Cook Islands, Egypt, Guatemala, Indonesia, Myanmar, Nauru, Nigeria, the Philippines, St Vincent and the Grenadines and Ukraine. The next review was scheduled for 18–20 June 2003 (the FATF's next plenary meeting) – by which time a review of the Forty Recommendations was due to have been completed.

At its plenary meeting on 20 June 2003, the FATF removed St Vincent and the Grenadines from the list of NCCTs. Countries listed at that stage therefore were the Cook Islands, Egypt, Guatemala, Indonesia, Myanmar, Nauru, Nigeria, the Philippines and Ukraine. 'Three years after the release of the first review of NCCTs, it remains clear that this initiative has triggered significant improvements in anti-money laundering systems throughout the world. Of the twenty-three jurisdictions placed on the NCCT list in 2000 and 2001, only nine remain there.'[13]

At its plenary meeting in February 2004, the FATF removed Ukraine and Egypt from its list of NCCTs – leaving only seven jurisdictions – as follows: the Cook Islands, Guatemala, Indonesia, Myanmar, Nauru, Nigeria and the Philippines. On 2 July 2004, Guatemala was delisted, leaving only six jurisdictions. Although countermeasures against Myanmar and Nauru were withdrawn in October 2004, both countries remained on the NCCT list.

In February 2005, the Cook Islands, Indonesia and the Philippines were removed from the list of NCCTs. After that, the list comprised three countries: Myanmar, Nauru and Nigeria.

Classification as a NCCT has many implications. For example, in the UK, the Money Laundering Regulations 2003 (published in December

---

[13] FATF, *Annual Report* 2002– 3, 20 June 2003, para. 118, p. 26.

2003) empower the UK Treasury to prevent a financial entity from starting business or from continuing business with a person based in a country that is subject to the FATF's countermeasures.

> Leaders of the G7 group of the world's most industrialised countries meeting in Okinawa, Japan, have asked their domestic financial institutions to pay special attention to transactions with countries on the Financial Action Task Force (FATF) blacklist published in June . . . The G7 said it would block loans from agencies such as the IMF if listed countries do not cooperate.[14]

In July 2004, the FATF's President said that '[t]he NCCT process has been very successful in encouraging countries to take necessary action to clean up their financial systems'.[15]

11.4 Some negative comment

Monaco was not blacklisted by the FATF, but a French parliamentary report had (the same week) accused the jurisdiction of being an 'Offshore Finance Centre' that facilitated money laundering.[16]

Liechtenstein said that the FATF's process lacked transparency and that the country's blacklisting had been inappropriate.[17]

The Cayman Islands expressed astonishment at the country's blacklisting, pointing out that the extent of its efforts to deal with money laundering had not been recognised.[18] 'The Cayman Islands has passed four anti-money laundering bills in the wake of its FATF listing.'[19]

A senator in Jersey (which has been a UK Crown dependency for nearly 800 years) submitted a formal request to the island's leading civil officer for a referendum on independence from the UK.[20]

---

[14] 'G7 Checks FATF List', *International Wealth Management*, Financial Times, August 2000, p. 8.

[15] 'FATF Tackles Terrorism Financing, Delists Guatemala', FATF, 2 July 2004.

[16] Guy de Jonquieres, 'Taskforce Cracks Down on Money Laundering', *Financial Times*, 25 June 2000.

[17] Guy de Jonquieres, 'Taskforce Cracks Down on Money Laundering', *Financial Times*, 25 June 2000.

[18] Guy de Jonquieres, 'Taskforce Cracks Down on Money Laundering', *Financial Times*, 25 June 2000..

[19] 'Centres Respond to FATF', September 2000, *International Wealth Management*, p. 11.

[20] Astrid Wendlandt, 'Island Tax Haven Moves to Vote on Autonomy', *Financial Times*, 29 August 2000.

In an article published in the *Journal of Money Laundering*,[21] reference was made to the FATF's strategy to 'name and shame'. Consideration of the FATF's previous experiences with two countries (as follows) is an interesting comparison.

Although Austria joined the FATF in 1990, no action was taken to prevent the use of anonymous accounts until February 1999 (although since February 1996 it had not been possible to open new accounts). Austria responded only when the FATF warned its members to pay special attention to cheques issued by Austrian banks in Austrian schillings.[22] The FATF threatened to suspend Austria's membership of the FATF if it did not take action to prevent the use of anonymous accounts.[23] 'It has taken ten years to get Austria, a FATF member, to change its laws.'

In September 1996, the FATF expressed concern that Turkey did not have anti-money laundering legislation. As a result, the FATF applied Recommendation 21, which alerted financial institutions to the need to treat as special, business relations and transactions with Turkish persons.[24] Turkey responded by November of the same year. 'It took six years for Turkey to comply, and a further four years to achieve more effective regulation.'

This is not to infer that the FATF has not done a good job – it merely demonstrates the need for the 'level playing fields' philosophy to have a wider application than merely OFCs.

11.5 Some positive comment

Many OFCS have taken decisive action. Consider a few examples as follows:[25]

- The Bahamas said that it intended to correct deficiencies in its anti-money laundering measures.
- St Vincent and the Grenadines revoked the licences of six 'Offshore' banks for failure to comply with regulations.

---

[21] Jackie Johnson, 'Blacklisting: Initial Reactions, Responses and Repercussions', June 2001, Vol. 4, No. 3, *Journal of Money Laundering Control*, p. 211.
[22] OECD News Release, 11 February 1999.
[23] FATF press release, 3 February 2000.
[24] FATF press release, 19 September 1996.
[25] James Canute, 'Caribbean Tax Havens Seek Refuge With the WTO', *Financial Times*, 3 October 2000.

- The British Virgin Islands expressed its intention to strengthen legislation to reduce opportunities for money launderers.

> Concern about being included on the [FATF] blacklist had already prompted Israel and Liechtenstein to speed up plans to fight money laundering.[26]

Larry Summers, US Treasury Secretary, said that the FATF Report was a 'landmark step to limit the capacity of drug dealers, terrorists, organised criminals and corrupt foreign officials to launder their ill-gotten gains through safe havens'.[27]

Mr Stuart Eizenstat, US Deputy Treasury Secretary, said of the success of the FATF initiative that it has 'been wildly beyond anything we would ever have anticipated . . . [and] . . . [T]he countries on the first list were not necessarily the worst offenders'.[28]

11.6 Some 'neutral' comments

A certain amount of the bluster that followed the publication of the FATF's Report and subsequent lists was to be expected. The fact of the matter is that, post-publication, many OFCs took definitive and precise action. It is a great shame that this action was merely a reaction to the FATF's work and that it did not happen as part of a general OFC initiative which jurisdictions took of their own volition.

It might be argued that no one OFC would have been willing to take unilateral action because to have done so would have placed it at a competitive disadvantage. The extent to which such an argument is valid remains to be seen but this type of tardy reaction is the very stuff that those who are sceptical about the 'Offshore' environment use to demonstrate the unacceptability of 'Offshore'.

11.7 11 September 2001

At around 12:45hrs GMT on 11 September 2001, one of four hijacked aircraft (all of which had been on internal flights in the USA) crashed

---

[26] Guy de Jonquieres, '15 Blacklisted in Global Fight on Money Laundering', *Financial Times*, 22 June 2000.

[27] Guy de Jonquieres, 'Taskforce Cracks Down on Money Laundering', *Financial Times*, 25 June 2000.

[28] Edward Alden, 'Blacklist Leaves a Mark on Money Laundering', *Financial Times*, 5 December 2000.

into the North Tower of the World Trade Center in New York. Some eighteen minutes later, the second of the four hijacked planes crashed into the South Tower. Within two hours, both towers collapsed, causing thousands of deaths. The third hijacked aircraft crashed into the side of the Pentagon in Washington. The fourth hijacked plane crashed in Pennsylvania. Subsequent investigation showed that Osama Bin Laden and his Al-Qaeda network (based in Afghanistan) were responsible. This was described as the largest terrorist attack that the world had ever experienced.

The USA responded by declaring war against terrorism in general and in particular by bombing the Taliban for refusing to hand over the perpetrator. The USA took wide-ranging diplomatic, political and economic action in response.

Economic action was focused on identifying the global assets of Osama bin Laden and those of his accomplices. The President of the USA issued an Executive Order on 24 September 2001 blocking the transactions and freezing the assets of twenty-seven named individuals. The list included the names of eleven terrorist organisations and as many terrorist leaders, three charitable organisations and one corporate body. The President warned the global financial community that any person who transacted business with anyone named would not be allowed to transact business with the USA. The Order widened the powers of the Treasury and established the Foreign Terrorist Asset Tracking Centre which was made responsible for the identification of foreign terrorist groups and for assessing how and by whom they were funded – which information would be passed on to law enforcement agencies to enable pre-emptive action to freeze assets before they can be used for wrongful purposes.

On 28 September 2001, the UN's response to the 11 September atrocities was (inter alia) the unanimous adoption of a wide-ranging resolution to combat terrorism. The resolution required the UN's 189 members to take action against networks of terrorists in their territory and to prosecute them or hand them over to the USA. Bank accounts were to be frozen and no funding was to be allowed. Governments were required to report their progress in addressing these requirements within three months (31 December 2001).

On 26 October 2001, new legislation was introduced in the US, the Patriot Act, designed (inter alia) to combat money laundering. (See section 18.12 below.)

Action was taken by the FATF at an extraordinary plenary meeting on 31 October 2001 when the organisation's role was expanded to include combating terrorist financing. In pursuit of this objective, the FATF is engaged in a process to identify weaknesses in the procedures that are currently adopted globally. Special Recommendations (of which there were eight at the time, but the number increased by one in October 2004) and 'guidance' were issued on how the Special Recommendations should be implemented. This work is driven by a working group established for that purpose. The Special Recommendations included (inter alia) the requirement for members to implement and to ratify the 1999 United Nations Convention for the Suppression of the Financing of Terrorism and other related resolutions but in particular United Nations Security Resolution 1373.

On 30 October 2001, the FATF adopted the following Special Recommendations on terrorist financing:[29]

1. ratify and implement the 1999 UN Convention for the Suppression of the Financing of Terrorism;
2. include terrorism in predicate offences under money laundering rules;
3. freeze and confiscate terrorist assets;
4. impose reporting requirements on suspicious transactions related to terrorism;
5. formalise the greatest possible measure of mutual legal assistance and information exchange in connection with terrorism;
6. set up licensing and registration systems for money/value transmission services;
7. force financial institutions to include originator information on funds transfers and related messages that are sent through the payment chain;
8. review laws relating to entities that can be abused for the financing of terrorism (e.g. NGOs).

Other requirements included making the financing of terrorism a criminal offence. Terrorist organisations were to be criminalised, as were their acts. It was recommended that these offences should become money laundering predicate offences in future.

Countries were asked to make sure that their legislation allowed the freezing and confiscation of assets of terrorists and all such assets were to be so treated with immediate effect. Suspicious transaction reporting on terrorism (similar to that already in force regarding money laundering)

---

[29] 'Special Recommendations on Terrorist Financing', FATF, 30 October 2001, www.fatf-gafi.org/TerFinance_en.htm.

was required by member countries. The importance was stressed of cross-border mutual assistance (by way of treaty or other agreements) to other countries in relevant investigations. Improved and precise information was to be disclosed on all money transfers – which should be a licensable activity. Lastly, there was a requirement to focus on the potential for non-profit organisations to be abused in financing terrorism.

Members of the FATF were required to undertake a self-assessment by 31 December 2001. It was intended that additional guidance would be issued by the FATF in February 2002 and that the Forty Recommendations would be revised to incorporate the Special Recommendations described above. By June 2002, work was to start on identifying jurisdictions that had not made appropriate arrangements to meet these new needs. It was decided by a plenary session in February 2002 that the FATF would publish a list of all jurisdictions that did not have adequate measures to deal with the financing of terrorism. The FATF agreed to produce a self-assessment questionnaire to this end in February 2002.

It was decided, in June 2002, that the FATF would consider what measures to adopt in response to the countries that had been listed in June 2001 and which had failed to make adequate progress.

11.8 The Forty Recommendations

The Forty Recommendations were first issued in 1990, and were revised in 1996. The FATF issued eight Special Recommendations in October 2001 and at the FATF meeting held in Paris on 20–22 October 2004, the FATF added Special Recommendation (IX). The focus of the new measure is cross-border movements of currency and monetary instruments related to terrorist financing and money laundering. Through this new measure, the FATF is encouraging countries to stop such movements and to confiscate the money involved. Enhanced sharing of information concerning movements of illicit cash related to terrorist financing and money laundering is also encouraged.

- In May 2002, a public consultation paper was issued which described current issues and presented proposals for action and invited all countries, relevant organisations and the financial sector for comments. There were more than 150 responses. A working group was formed in October 2002 to discuss issues that arose and to expand the existing Recommendations to take account of these matters. A forum was convened in October 2002. The group included representatives from the private sector. Further consultation took place in April 2003 and the results were discussed at a special FATF plenary meeting in Paris at the beginning of May 2003. At the end of its plenary meeting in Berlin in June 2003, the FATF issued a revised version of its Forty Recommendations – which had been agreed on 18 June 2003. No fixed date for implementation was specified, but member countries were encouraged to start immediately to make preparation for implementation. Compliance was to be tested through a new round of mutual evaluations, but the commencement date depended upon when the new methodology to test compliance will be completed. This was expected to be in the first half of 2004. The most important changes include:[30]

- specifying a minimum list of designated categories of predicate crimes for money laundering (that is, crimes that underpin the money laundering offence);
- expanded due diligence for financial institutions by extending some anti-money laundering requirements to deal with the financing of terrorism, including reporting of suspicious transactions;
- refined measures to apply to higher risk customers and transactions by introducing risk-based application of customer due diligence; this means allowing simplified customer due diligence in certain circumstances and introducing enhanced measures for higher risk customers and transactions, correspondent banking, non-face-to-face customers and politically exposed persons;
- imposing specific conditions and customer due diligence for business and transactions for which reliance is placed on third parties for undertaking customer due diligence;
- extending anti-money laundering and combating financing of terrorism measures (including customer due diligence, record-keeping and suspicious transaction reporting) to certain businesses and professions that are not financial; these include casinos, real estate agents, dealers in precious metals and stones, lawyers, notaries, other legal professionals and accountants and trust and company service providers;
- including additional key institutional measures, notably regarding Financial Intelligence Units, and strengthening international cooperation;
- prohibiting shell banks; and

---

[30] 'Status Report of the Work of the IMF and the World Bank on the Twelve Month Pilot Program of AMLCFT Assessments and Delivery of AMLCFT Technical Assistance', IMF, 5 September 2003, p. 9, and 'New Anti-Money Laundering Standards Released', 20 June 2003, www.oecd.org.

- improving the transparency of legal persons and beneficial owners, including trusts and companies issuing bearer shares.

Note that the revised 40+8 Recommendations include explicit provisions for trust and company service providers, and for the identification of customers by third parties (which is a feature of this latter type of business – see section 10.10 below). This is of particular interest 'Offshore', where a substantial amount of such business is sourced.

11.9 Joint working of the World Bank, the IMF and the FATF

Combating money laundering was once the preserve of the FATF, but, on 11 October 2002, the FATF announced:

> that it will collaborate with the IMF and the World Bank on an important initiative in the international fight against money laundering and the financing of terrorism . . . [T]he IMF, World Bank and the FATF have developed in recent months a common methodology to assess the countries in the world in compliance with the FATF recommendations. To this end, this methodology will be used by the FATF, the IMF and the World Bank.[31]

The methodology referred to is a common method of assessing compliance and will be used in drafting the FSAP and ROSC reports in future.

> On 24 March 2004, the Executive Board of the International Monetary Fund (IMF) reviewed the Twelve-Month Pilot Program of Anti-Money Laundering and Combating the Financing of Terrorism (AML/CFT) Assessments jointly undertaken by the IMF and World Bank, and adopted proposals to make such assessments a regular part of Fund work. As part of the review, the Executive Board endorsed the revised 40 Recommendations of the Financial Action Task Force (FATF) as the new standard for AML/CFT Reports on the Observance of Standards and Codes (ROSCs) that will be prepared, as well as the revised methodology to assess that standard. Drawing on the positive experience under the 12 month program (see Press Release No. 02/52), the Executive Board decided to expand the Fund's AML/CFT assessment and technical assistance work to cover the full scope of the expanded FATF recommendations.[32]

---

[31] 'Russia, Dominica, Niue and Marshall Islands Removed from FATF's List of Non-Cooperative Countries and Territories', FATF, 11 October, 2002.

[32] 'IMF Executive Board Reviews and Enhances Efforts for Anti-Money Laundering and Combating the Financing of Terrorism', IMF, Public Information Notice No. 04/33, 2 April 2004.

One of the implications is that assessors (including those from the FATF and all FATF-style regional bodies; see section 11.11 below) need to be trained to use the new methodology.

11.10 Membership

When the FATF started in September 1998, seven countries were identified as target members (Argentina, Brazil, China, India, Mexico, South Africa and the Russian Federation). Of these, all but two (China and India) have become members. That said, on 21 January 2005, China was admitted as an Observer – but the intention is to transfer to full membership in due course (although the FATF is unable to specify when). Meanwhile, the FATF has entered into a dialogue with India regarding possible membership. (India enacted its anti-money laundering legislation, the Prevention of Money Laundering Act, on 1 July 2005.) Membership comprises thirty-one governments and two regional organisations (see Table 18 in Appendix 1). The latest members to be admitted (June 2003) were the Russian Federation and South Africa (which countries had been 'Observers' since October 2002 and February 2003 respectively). 'However, the FATF has perhaps approached the limit of members if it is to continue to retain its current structure and character.'[33]

The criteria for membership are:[34]

- to be fully committed at the political level: (i) to implement the 1996 Recommendations within a reasonable time frame (three years), and (ii) to undergo annual self-assessment exercises and two rounds of mutual evaluations;
- to be a full and active member of the relevant FATF-style regional body (where one exists), or be prepared to work with the FATF or even to take the lead, to establish such a body (where none exists);
- to be a strategically important country;
- to have already made the laundering of the proceeds of drug trafficking and other serious crimes a criminal offence; and
- to have already made it mandatory for financial institutions to identify their customers and to report unusual or suspicious transactions.

---

[33] 'FATF Mandate Renewed for Eight Years', FATF, 14 May 2004, para. 6, p. 2.
[34] FATF, *Annual Report* 2002–3, 20 June 2003, para. 38, p. 10.

The list of members was last updated on 27 July 2004 and remains unchanged as at 30 July 2005.

As well as fully fledged members as described above, the FATF has seven FATF-Style Regional Bodies (FSRBs – see Para 11.11 below) and 20 other international organisations as Observers. See Table 18 in Appendix 1.

11.11 FATF-style regional bodies

There are five FATF-style regional bodies (FSRBs) – as described below. See Appendix 2 for their web addresses. It should be noted that the Offshore Group of Banking Supervisors is deemed to be an FSRB (see section 9.21 above).

11.11.1 Asia-Pacific Group on Money Laundering

The purpose of the APG 'is to ensure the adoption, implementation and enforcement of internationally accepted anti-money laundering and counter terrorist financing standards as set out in the FATF's Forty Recommendations and the FATF's Eight Special Recommendations. . .'.[35] The APG members include Australia, Bangladesh, Brunei Darussalam, Cambodia, Chinese Taipei, the Cook Islands, Fiji, Hong Kong, India, Indonesia, Japan, Macau, Malaysia, the Marshall Islands, Mongolia, Nepal, New Zealand, Niue, Pakistan, Palau, the Philippines, Samoa, Singapore, South Korea, Sri Lanka, Thailand, Tonga, the USA and Vanuatu. There are twelve Observers to the Group. The Group arranges workshops and, since 2000, has been conducting mutual evaluations, summaries of which are available to the public.

11.11.2 Caribbean Financial Action Task Force

The CFATF comprises states and territories in the Caribbean basin that in common have implemented measures to defeat money laundering. Twenty-one of the FATF's members entered into a Memorandum of Understanding in 1996, which represents the basis on which the CFATF operates. The CFATF conducts self-assessment exercises, undertakes mutual evaluations (summaries of which are available to the public)

---

[35] www.fatf-gafi.org/Ctry-orgpages/org-apg_en.htm.

and offers/coordinates training and technical assistance. The following (twenty-six) countries are members of the CFATF: Anguilla, Antigua and Barbuda, Aruba, the Bahamas, Barbados, Belize, Bermuda, the British Virgin Islands, the Cayman Islands, Costa Rica, Dominica, the Dominican Republic, Grenada, Haiti, Jamaica, Montserrat, the Netherlands Antilles, Nicaragua, Panama, St Kitts and Nevis, St Lucia, St Vincent and the Grenadines, Suriname, Trinidad and Tobago, the Turks and Caicos Islands and Venezuela.

11.11.3 *Council of Europe Select Committee of Experts on the Evaluation of Anti-Money Laundering Measures ('Moneyval')*

Moneyval is the new name of the PC-R-EV Committee, established in 1997 by the Commission of Ministers of the Council of Europe. The Committee was charged with carrying out self and mutual assessment exercises on the anti-money laundering measures which the twenty-six countries that comprise the Council of Europe and which were not members of the FATF, had implemented. Moneyval's mandate includes combating terrorist financing. It is a sub-committee of the European Committee on Crime Problems of the Council of Europe (CDPC).[36] The Committee comprises the following Council of Europe Member States – which are not members of the FATF: Albania, Andorra, Armenia, Azerbaijan, Bosnia and Herzegovina, Bulgaria, Croatia, Cyprus, the Czech Republic, Estonia, Georgia, Hungary, Latvia, Liechtenstein, Lithuania, Macedonia, Malta, Moldova, Poland, Romania, the Russian Federation, San Marino, Serbia and Montenegro, Slovakia, Slovenia and the Ukraine.

Moneyval has five 'Observer Jurisdictions' (Canada, the Holy See, Japan, Mexico and the USA) and twelve 'Observers'. Moneyval's role includes conducting self-assessment and mutual assessments of members, summaries of which are available to the public. Each of the twenty-five member countries may appoint three experts to serve on Moneyval. Plenary meetings are held twice a year.

11.11.4 *Eastern and Southern Africa Anti-Money Laundering Group (ESAAMLG)*

The Group comprises eleven members that have signed the Group's MOU (Botswana, Kenya, Malawi, Mauritius, Mozambique, Namibia,

---

[36] FATF, *Annual Report* 2002–3, 20 June 2003, para. 90, p. 20.

Seychelles, South Africa, Swaziland, Tanzania and Uganda) and three members that have yet to sign (Lesotho, Zambia and Zimbabwe). There are in addition two 'Observer Jurisdictions' (the UK and the USA) and three 'Observer Organizations'. The Group describes its purpose as 'combat[ing] money laundering by implementing the FATF Forty Recommendations', and this was expanded later to include countering terrorist financing.[37] In practice this involves mutual evaluations (open for inspection as they become available), self-assessments, consideration of typologies, development of appropriate manpower resources and coordinating technical assistance. The Group was formed in 1999.

11.11.5 Financial Action Task Force on Money Laundering in South America ('GAFISUD').

GAFISUD, which was established in 2000, describes its purpose as working 'toward developing and implementing a comprehensive global strategy to combat money laundering and terrorist financing as set out in the FATF Forty Recommendations and FATF Eight Special Recommendations'.[38] The Group's activities include carrying out mutual evaluations (reports of which are available for inspection) and coordination of training. The Group's nine members are Argentina, Bolivia, Brazil, Chile, Colombia, Ecuador, Paraguay, Peru, and Uruguay. There are five 'Observer Jurisdictions' (France, Mexico, Portugal, Spain and the USA) and three 'Observer Organizations' (the Caribbean Financial Action Task Force, the Financial Action Task Force and the Inter-American Development Bank).

11.11.6 Eurasian Group (EAG)

The EAG was formed in Moscow in October 2002, and was admitted as an Observer to the FATF. As well as the Russian Federation, the EAG comprises Belarus, China, Kazakhstan, Kyrgyzstan and Tajikistan.

11.11.7 Middle East and North Africa Financial Action Task Force (MENAFATF)

At the FATF meeting in October 2004, it was anticipated that a new regional body would be formed, comprising fourteen countries from the

---

[37] www.fatf-gafi.org/Ctry-orgpages/org-esaamlg_en.htm.
[38] www.fatf-gafi.org/Ctry-orgpages/org-gafisud_en.htm.

Middle East and North Africa, as follows: Algeria, Bahrain, Egypt, Jordan, Kuwait, Lebanon, Morocco, Oman, Qatar, Saudi Arabia, Syria, Tunisia, the United Arab Emirates and Yemen. The Group, whose head-quarters will be in Bahrain, began operations in November 2004.

11.12 Update

The year 2003 was significant for the FATF for at least two reasons which have ongoing implications. First, the IMF and the World Bank officially recognised the FATF's 40+8 Recommendations on anti-money launder-ing and terrorist financing ('AML/CFT') as appropriate standards for combating money laundering and terrorist financing. This led to the development of a common methodology to assess compliance. The FATF issued this methodology in 2004, and, in March 2004, the IMF and the World Bank agreed to use this methodology in their Financial Sector Assessment Program. Thus, the FATF's 40+8 Recommendations will be the standard against which the prevailing AML/CFT processes in all jurisdictions will be tested using the methodology described above.

Secondly, probably the most important development for the FATF was that its thirty-three members renewed the organisation's mandate for a further eight years, until 2012. Previous mandates have been for periods of five years, so the extended renewal period indicates that members believe that much remains to be accomplished. The new mandate in-cludes the following tasks:

- to continue establishing the international standards for combating money laundering and terrorist financing;
- to ensure global action in combating money laundering and terrorist financing, including building stronger cooperation with the IMF and the World Bank;
- to ensure that members implement the revised 40+9 Recommenda-tions in their entirety and in an effective manner;
- to increase its membership appropriately; and
- to enhance relationships between the FATF and the FATF-style re-gional bodies.[39]

Mr Kader Asmal from South Africa was installed as President with effect from 1 July 2005.

---

[39] The Mandate for the Future of FATF (September 2004–December 2012).

12

Supranational focus (3): the Organization for Economic Cooperation and Development

> Good government, sophisticated financial firms and regulators who are honest and competent cannot eliminate the risk of financial calamity altogether, but they can reduce it to bearable proportions.[1]

12.1 Introduction

This is the third of three chapters devoted to the work of supranational organisations in respect of the 'Offshore' environment. The work of the Financial Stability Forum (FSF) was considered first, and then the work of the IMF and the World Bank. The work of the Financial Action Task Force (FATF) was considered in the previous chapter and, in this chapter, the focus is on the Organization for Economic Cooperation and Development (OECD).

Relevant background information has been provided already (see section 9.24 above) on the OECD so the introduction that follows merely serves to place the OECD's work in context.

At the outset, it is useful to remember that '80 per cent of the total offshore finance services industry is located in the OECD countries, excluding their colonies. The remaining 20 per cent is in the non-OECD countries, with even this segment dominated by a few large centres such as Hong Kong and Singapore which, conveniently, the OECD has not named as tax havens. This means that approximately less than 10 per cent of offshore business in the world is done in the targeted jurisdictions.'[2] Further, the OECD is on record as saying that OFCs 'have been mentioned as cases where harmful and unfair tax competition takes place because they are simply used as institutions to avoid or evade tax'.[3]

---

[1] 'A Place For Capital Controls', *The Economist*, 3 May 2003, p. 15.
[2] 'The View from the Smaller Offshore Financial Centres, Extracted from the OECD and Small Jurisdictions', December 2002, and published in *Offshore Red*, February 2003, p. 255.
[3] 'Harmful Tax Competition: A Conceptual and Empirical Analysis', OECD Working Party No. 2 on Tax Policy Analysis and Tax Statistics, 14 November 1996.

12.2 OECD Report on Harmful Tax Competition

The focus of the OECD was turned to the 'Offshore' environment some time ago. The tax reforms that have taken place over a number of years – designed to make countries more attractive to investors – have led to a situation where 'virtually every high tax country has adopted some type of preferential tax regime'.[4] OECD was concerned about the introduction of 'harmful tax practices' that led to the tax laws of other countries being abused. This led to defensive measures being taken to prevent tax evasion – but this inevitably made the tax system more complicated and therefore more expensive to administer and led to concerns amongst taxpayers about the fairness of the system. There was also concern that the globalisation process made it easier for taxpayers to evade their fiscal responsibilities to their own countries. The OECD believed that 'Globalisation of the economy has had the side effect of opening up new ways in which companies and individuals can avoid taxes that are legally due. As the level of taxpayers' activities outside national borders expands, governments cannot always rely on domestic sources of information to enforce their tax laws.'[5] This is where 'Offshore' enters the fray because it has been asserted that '[a] key element in this process of the growing international mobility of capital has been the growth of offshore finance'.[6] The implication was that honest taxpayers were likely to have to pay even more tax than previously to make up for what was being lost through evasion. To place this matter in context, it may be useful to bear in mind that the OECD has said that '[t]he OECD project does not seek to dictate to any country what its tax rate should be, or how its tax system should be structured. It seeks to encourage an environment in which free and fair tax competition can take place.'[7] The progression of events is described below.

---

[4] *International Tax Havens Guide 2002.*
[5] The OECD's Project on Harmful Tax Practices, 'The 2001 Progress Report', OECD, 14 November 2001, p. 5.
[6] Mark P. Hampton, *The Offshore Interface*, Macmillan Press Ltd, 1996, p. 1.
[7] The OECD's Project on Harmful Tax Practices, 'The 2001 Progress Report', OECD, 14 November 2001, p. 4.

12.3 The sequence of events

12.3.1 May 1996

In May 1996, the OECD's Committee on Fiscal Affairs was asked by the OECD Council to 'develop measures to counter the distorting effects of harmful tax competition on investment and financing decisions and the consequences for national tax bases, and report back in 1998'.[8] Most of the ensuing work was carried out by the Committee's subsidiary, the Forum on Harmful Tax Practices.

12.3.2 April 1998

Certain research was undertaken prior to the publication of a report in 1998. The Forum requested each member to carry out a self-assessment of its preferential tax regimes in light of the criteria. The self-assessment was followed by a peer review on each preferential regime that was identified. This research involved a review of jurisdictions that seemed to satisfy the criteria.

The results of the OECD's Committee on Fiscal Affairs' work on harmful tax competition were published in a report entitled 'Harmful Tax Competition – An Emerging Global Issue' (the '1998 Report'). The report embraced harmful preferential tax regimes and harmful tax practices, and the role of tax havens therein. The focus was on geographically mobile activity. Two OECD member countries – Luxembourg and Switzerland – abstained from the 1998 Report.

At the time, the OECD said that 'the project is not primarily about collecting taxes and is not intended to promote the harmonisation of income taxes or tax structures . . . nor is it about dictating to any country what should be the appropriate level of tax rates. Rather, the project is about ensuring that the burden of taxation is fairly shared and that tax should not be the dominant factor in making capital allocation decisions. The project is focused on the concerns of OECD and non-OECD countries, which are exposed to significant revenue losses as a result of harmful tax competition.'[9]

---

[8] Foreword, 'Harmful Tax Competition, An Emerging Global Issue', OECD, 1998.
[9] 'Towards Global Tax Cooperation, Report to the 2000 Ministerial Council Meeting and Recommendations by the Committee on Fiscal Affairs, Progress in Identifying and Eliminating Harmful Tax Practices', Executive Summary, OECD, 2000, p. 5.

The OECD established four criteria to define a tax haven. In itself, this was a significant development because – as previously mentioned – while terms like 'tax haven' and 'Offshore' had been in common usage for a long time, there was substantial variation of opinion about what they meant. The most significant criterion concerned tax. 'No or only nominal taxation is a necessary condition for the identification of a tax haven.'[10] The other three criteria were: absence of substantial activities, lack of transparency and lack of effective exchange of information. The 1998 Report made nineteen recommendations to deal with what were described as harmful tax practices.[11]

The 1998 Report distinguished tax havens as 'countries that are able to finance their public services with no or nominal income taxes and that offer themselves as places to be used by non-residents to escape tax in their country of residence' from countries which have potentially harmful preferential tax regimes 'which raise significant revenues from their income tax but whose tax system has features constituting harmful tax competition'.[12] 'A preferential tax regime was considered to be potentially harmful if it had features that suggested that the regime had the potential to constitute a harmful tax practice even though there had not been an overall assessment of all the relevant factors to determine whether the regime was actually harmful.'[13] Preferential tax regimes are identified by: low or zero effective tax; 'ring fencing'; non-transparency regime; and absence of effective exchange of information.

Characteristics of a tax haven are considered harmful if they facilitate illegal activity (such as tax evasion or money laundering). Low or no income tax is not enough in itself to constitute harmful tax competition – but when either is combined with other factors (such as unwillingness to exchange information) a problem is likely to arise. Interestingly, the OECD Report draws attention to the style of advertising and promotion used by some tax regimes – which it says is an indication of the extent to which a jurisdiction is used primarily to avoid and to evade tax. This seems to endorse a point made in an earlier report published by OECD,[14]

---

[10] 'Harmful Tax Competition, An Emerging Global Issue', OECD, Box 1, 1998, p. 23.
[11] 'Harmful Tax Competition, An Emerging Global Issue', OECD, April 1998, p. 3.
[12] 'Harmful Tax Competition, An Emerging Global Issue', OECD, 1998, para. 42, p. 20.
[13] The OECD's Project on Harmful Tax Practices, 'The 2004 Progress Report', OECD, 4 February 2004, p. 5.
[14] 'Harmful Tax Competition, An Emerging Global Issue', OECD, 1998, para. 51, referring to 'International Tax Avoidance and Evasion: Four Related Studies', OECD, 1987, p. 22.

which stated that 'a good indicator that a country is playing the role of a tax haven is where the country or territory offers itself or is generally recognised as a "tax haven"'. (An advertisement that appeared at the time is a very clear example of what the OECD meant. The advert described the services of a practitioner in Andorra, which in turn was described as 'the last 100 per cent tax haven in Europe'.[15]) The OECD's point was that, if you as a jurisdiction – or the people who promote the jurisdiction's financial services – refer to the jurisdiction as a 'tax haven', do not be surprised if that is how people in general – including the OECD – refer to you. The point that the OECD was making could not have been described more accurately than by reference to this advert.

The 1998 Report contained a number of recommendations. Recommendation 16 was to produce a list of tax havens within twelve months of the date of the report. Subsequent to publishing their report, the OECD appointed a contact country to liaise and coordinate information being exchanged and to conduct bilateral discussions with jurisdictions being reviewed.

The 1998 Report (inter alia) conceded that even some of the OECD's own members manifested certain attributes that were characteristic of tax havens – but these were due to cease by 2005. In this respect, one observer said that 'most OECD countries are themselves tax havens'.[16] The report suggested that Canada, Germany, Greece, Italy, the Netherlands, Norway and Portugal had preferential tax regimes.

12.3.3 1999

Based on the information obtained from the research, a technical evaluation was made (in 1999) concerning which jurisdictions met the criteria. The evaluation produced a list of preferential tax regimes that were potentially harmful. Each jurisdiction listed had until 31 July 2001 to commit to eliminating harmful tax practices. These practices had to be removed by April 2003 (unless the harmful regime was in place before 31 December 2000, in which case the remedial deadline was 31 December 2005). Failure to take corrective action within the timeframe allocated

---

[15] International Wealth Management, August 2000, *Financial Times*, p. 36.
[16] Marshall J. Langer, 'Harmful Tax Competition: Who Are the Real Tax Havens?', International Tax Planning Conference, International Tax Planning Association, New Orleans, 20 November 2000.

would mean that the jurisdiction would be listed automatically (on 31 July 2001) as an '*uncooperative* tax haven'. A range of 'possible defensive measures . . . identified to date as a framework for a common approach'[17] against uncooperative tax havens had already been prepared. (A report was due to be made to the OECD Council by June 2003 describing which of these regimes were actually harmful.)

12.3.4 2000

In 2000, forty-seven jurisdictions were identified as having potentially harmful tax regimes, and each was invited to comment on the application of the tax haven criteria relevant to their jurisdiction. In January of the same year, the Committee considered the evaluations that had been made. The Committee confirmed the list in May 2000 and the Council confirmed it on 16 June 2000. The Committee was asked to initiate a dialogue with the jurisdictions listed to encourage them to commit to eliminating their harmful tax practices.

12.4 Advance commitments

12.4.1 June 2000

On 19 June 2000, the OECD announced that six jurisdictions (Bermuda, the Cayman Islands, Cyprus, Malta, Mauritius and San Marino) had provided an advance commitment to eliminate harmful tax practices by 2005, thereby avoiding classification as a 'tax haven'. More advance commitments were made thereafter (see below).

One week later (26 June 2000), the OECD published another report,[18] 'Towards Global Tax Cooperation: Progress in Identifying and Eliminating Harmful Tax Practices' (the '2000 Report'). This report was published by the Forum on Harmful Tax Practices, whose remit is to monitor the implementation of the Guidelines and Recommendations described in the Report on Harmful Taxation. The Forum reports to the

[17] 'Towards Global Tax Cooperation', Report to the 2000 Ministerial Council Meeting and Recommendations by the Committee on Fiscal Affairs, Progress in Identifying and Eliminating Harmful Tax Practices, OECD, 26 June 2000, p. 25.
[18] 'Towards Global Tax Cooperation', Report to the 2000 Ministerial Council Meeting and recommendations by the Committee on Fiscal Affairs, Progress in Identifying and Eliminating Harmful Tax Practices, OECD, 26 June 2000, p. 17.

Committee of Fiscal Affairs (originally established in 1971). The June 2000 report identified thirty-five jurisdictions out of the original population of forty-seven jurisdictions whose tax regimes had been regarded as potentially harmful. The thirty-five jurisdictions were categorised as 'tax havens'. (See Table 20 in Appendix 1 below.) The 2000 Report also identified potentially harmful tax regimes in countries that were members of the OECD and introduced the framework of 'coordinated defensive measures' that might be used to deal with the effects of the harmful tax practices. The report also described a process to enable jurisdictions to commit to eliminate harmful tax practices.

The OECD said that the 'harmful' tax practices carried on by member and non-member countries (and their dependencies) arise from the development of tax systems encouraged by the globalisation of business and enable 'tax havens' to develop. Where tax regimes have been established to attract mobile business, they are considered to be harmful because (inter alia) they 'erode the tax bases of other countries . . . and . . . undermine the fairness and neutrality of tax systems'.[19] A further backdrop was provided by Jeffrey Owens, Head of the OECD's Fiscal Affairs Division who said that 'the economic crisis in Asia had shown the need to establish a set of rules for globalisation', and by Nicholas Bray, an OECD spokesman, who referred to the OECD's recognition that 'some territories had become dependent on financial services designed to attract investment from those seeking to escape taxes'.[20] Interestingly, the 1998 Report focused on shell companies initially. The emphasis changed to ring fencing, and then again to the 'tax haven' element at the end. The report envisaged the use of coercion (e.g. through possible cancellation of treaties and other measures that are not tax related) to force 'tax havens' to cooperate.

In respect of 'Offshore', a joint working group of the OECD and OFCs was established. The absence of agreed definitions concerning transparency, non-discrimination and sharing of information were the three areas of concern. Meanwhile, on 24 November 2000, the OECD published a document entitled 'Framework for a Collective Memorandum of Understanding on Eliminating Harmful Tax Practices'. The idea was to offer a template for a Memorandum of Understanding to jurisdictions,

---

[19] Jeffrey Owens, Tax in 2010, *OECD Observer*, 27 June 2000.
[20] Barry James, 'Tax Havens Face OECD Threat of Sanctions', International Herald Tribune, 14 June 2000.

adoption of which would be taken to show alignment with the OECD's programme. The commitment was to last from July 2001 until December 2005. It was intended that punitive measures would be adopted against the thirty-five tax havens (by July 2001) if the terms of the three criteria set out in the MOU were not agreed in principle.

There were three milestones as follows:

1. By 31 December 2001, a plan to achieve transparency and exchange of information was to be formulated. Regimes that attracted business without substantial activity were to be eliminated.
2. By 31 December 2002, access to details of beneficial owners to be achieved. Adherence to accepted accounting standards was required.
3. By 31 December 2003, procedures to exchange information on criminal tax matters are to be in place. There should be access to necessary bank information, and there should be transparency of tax systems.

If the OECD enforced its threat, it would mean that, unless they complied, the OFCs might be denied access to international banking networks or securities markets. OFCs risked being disbarred from accepting clients from other jurisdictions and also risked access being denied to favourable tax treaties with OECD member countries.

The approach adopted by the OECD gave rise to a degree of sensitivity. It is unjust to attribute wrong intentions to the whole population because a sample gives rise to doubt and the stigma attached to a pejorative categorisation makes the struggle for credibility harder for those centres that do not deserve to be castigated. The degree of sensitivity is perhaps best described by reference to some reactions to the OECD's 'naming and shaming' exercise. Examples are provided in section 12.10 below.

Meanwhile, in September 2000, the committed jurisdictions formed a working group with OECD 'to establish a programme of effective exchange of information . . . The group has focused on . . . developing an instrument . . . for effective exchange of information and . . . adequately protect the confidentiality of taxpayer information'.[21]

---

[21] The OECD's Project on Harmful Tax Practices, Centre for Tax Policy and Administration, 'The 2001 Progress Report', OECD, declassified on 14 November 2001, p. 12.

12.5 More advance commitments

The OECD announced on 13 December 2000 that the Netherlands Antilles and the Isle of Man had also made commitments. Interestingly, the Isle of Man's Commitment Letter specified that the island would not honour its commitment unless and until all OECD members agreed to conform to the same rules. This became known as 'the Isle of Man Clause' and appeared in a number of Commitments provided subsequently.

The OECD convened a joint OECD/Commonwealth meeting in Barbados on 8–9 January 2001. The meeting included representatives of OECD, Caribbean jurisdictions, the IMF, the World Bank, the UN, the WTO and others. It was agreed to establish a Joint Working Group co-chaired by Australia and Barbados. The Group's remit was to identify an acceptable process to enable jurisdictions to commit to the three criteria (described above) other than by adopting them within a Memorandum of Understanding. The deadlines described above became blurred – although the MOU was not removed – and neither were the deadlines.

The Task Force met in London on 26–28 January 2001. The result was inconclusive. The OECD and the Commonwealth Secretariat disagreed vehemently. European and Middle East jurisdictions met in Paris in February, and the OECD convened a conference for the Pacific region in Japan in February 2001. The conclusions of the January meeting were submitted. Further proposals were considered at an OECD/Commonwealth Task Force meeting in Paris (1–2 March 2001). Once again, the meeting ended inconclusively.

12.6 Two approaches

The OFCs affected by the OECD Report fell into at least two camps. The first camp comprised those six countries that gave advance commitments and those amongst the thirty-five nations listed as tax havens that were taking action aimed at encouraging the OECD to remove them from the list. (In the course of time, the number categorised by camp one increased – with a corresponding reduction amongst those with different views.)

The second camp included 'the Opposition', and comprised: Antigua and Barbuda, Barbados, the British Virgin Islands, the Cook Islands, Dominica, Malaysia and Vanuatu. The Opposition comprised those 'small and developing jurisdictions of the Joint Working Group' that opposed the changes that the OECD required. The Opposition was represented by the Centre for Freedom and Prosperity and by Prime Minister Owen Arthur from Barbados.

Representatives of the Opposition and representatives from the OECD formed the OECD–Commonwealth Joint Working Group, which comprised: Antigua and Barbuda, Barbados, the British Virgin Islands, the Cook Islands, Malaysia, Malta and Vanuatu. Its purpose was to make joint representations to the OECD in respect of the OECD's tax initiative.

In May 2001, the US Treasury Secretary, Mr Paul O'Neill, made an announcement that showed (inter alia) that the new US administration (under President Bush) did not support the OECD's initiative in the same way as the previous administration (under President Clinton). Mr O'Neill made it clear that the USA did not share the view that low rates of tax are suspicious per se. Further, the suggestion that one country had a right to interfere with the tax system of another country was fundamentally unacceptable. Some Americans were not convinced. They believed that the initiative could force taxes upwards in the USA. (Throughout, Delaware and others were registering companies with no substantial activities so the stance of the USA was understandable, but the US also had reservations concerning the effects on some small 'Offshore' jurisdictions.) The stance taken by the USA forced the OECD to amend its original initiative. The change meant that offering preferential tax benefits to foreign investors was no longer considered to be a factor that would trigger sanctions (see below). Further OECD countries were required to deal with their own preferential tax regimes by 2003.

OECD representatives met tax officials from the USA and elsewhere (June 2001). The OECD made some changes to its original strategy as a consequence of this meeting. For example, the 'ring fencing' criterion was dropped. That is, the OECD conceded that it would not impose sanctions on a jurisdiction that offered tax concessions to companies and investors from abroad, that had no 'substantial activities' in the country. This was known as the ring fencing criterion, because the tax benefits arising were only available to non-resident investors or where the transactions involved were all international. The USA was opposed to the ring fencing criterion (see above). The changes were described in 'The OECD's Project on Harmful Tax Practices: The 2001 Progress Report'.

Defensive measures had been scheduled to take effect from 31 July 2001. On 3 July 2001, the OECD said that no measures would be taken against non-OECD members until at least 2003 – which is the same deadline imposed on OECD members. In the 2001 progress report (declassified in November 2001), the deadline for making commitments – and thereby avoiding being categorised as 'uncooperative' – was extended from 31 July 2001 to 28 February 2002. Committed jurisdictions had until 2005 to implement their plan to eliminate harmful tax practices.

Meanwhile, the critical factors which would be used to assess whether a jurisdiction was an uncooperative tax haven had reduced to transparency and a willingness to share information (undefined). 'A committing jurisdiction also agrees that its governmental authorities should have access to beneficial ownership information regarding the ownership of all types of entities and to bank information that may be relevant to criminal and civil tax matters . . . In the case of information requested for the investigation and prosecution of a criminal tax matter, the information should be provided without a requirement that the conduct being investigated would constitute a crime under the laws of the requested jurisdiction if it occurred in that jurisdiction.'[22]

12.7 More commitments

Aruba, Bahrain, Seychelles and Tonga submitted their respective commitment on 23 August 2001.

12.8 Exchange of information

The focus then shifted to the exchange of information. The OECD agreed to seek commitments in respect of transparency and the exchange of information.

One criterion that the OECD had adopted in assessing whether or not a jurisdiction was uncooperative was whether there was evidence of 'substantial activities'. The suggestion was that, in the absence of 'substantial activities', the jurisdiction might be trying to attract inward investment that was purely tax driven. The OECD subsequently concluded that the method adopted to determine the absence of substantial activity, 'whether there were factors that discouraged substantial

---

[22] The OECD's Project on Harmful Tax Practices, Centre for Tax Policy and Administration, 'The 2001 Progress Report', OECD, declassified on 14 November 2001, p. 11.

domestic activities', was inappropriate.[23] Instead, 'uncooperativeness' was to be determined by reference to the transparency and exchange of information criteria only. 'In applying the transparency and exchange of information criteria many factors are relevant, including a relaxed regulatory framework, which reduces transparency and makes it less likely that the information needed for effective exchange of information will be available.'[24]

The most important issues concerning sharing information between regulators and others about the beneficial ownership are found in the G7's Ten Key Principles on Information Sharing produced in 1998 and in the G7's Ten Key Principles for the Improvement of International Co-operation Regarding Financial Crime and Regulatory Abuse produced in 1999.

The OECD's priority is the exchange of specific information, whereas the EU requires an automatic exchange of information.

12.9 Even more commitments

The jurisdictions that have committed are regarded as 'cooperative jurisdictions'. As described above, the original deadline had been set for November 2001, by which time those countries that had not already made their commitment were required to do so. This deadline was extended to 28 February 2002. Just before the latter deadline, Antigua and Barbuda, Jersey, Guernsey, Gibraltar, Grenada and St Vincent and the Grenadines also made commitments (to improve the transparency of their tax systems and to establish appropriate systems for the exchange of tax information with OECD countries before 2005). St Vincent and the Grenadines was in the news again in 2004. At the OECD's Global Forum in Berlin, the OECD accepted two proposals by the jurisdiction. The first concerned the postponement of discussions on the imposition of sanctions on countries that failed to meet the OECD's requirements and the second was that the OECD should not dictate that jurisdictions should comply by 2006.

Once the deadline had passed, those jurisdictions that had not committed were regarded as 'uncooperative'.

---

[23] The OECD's Project on Harmful Tax Practices, Centre for Tax Policy and Administration, 'The 2001 Progress Report', OECD, declassified on 14 November 2001, p. 10.

[24] The OECD's Project on Harmful Tax Practices, 'The 2001 Progress Report', OECD, 14 November 2001, p. 10.

12.10 Uncooperative tax havens

On 18 April 2002, the OECD named seven jurisdictions that had not committed to their initiative on transparency and the effective exchange of information. These were Andorra, Liberia, Liechtenstein, the Marshall Islands, Monaco, Nauru and Vanuatu. Table 21 in Appendix 1 below traces the changes to the list. The jurisdictions originally listed (which were thereby blacklisted as 'uncooperative tax havens') were Andorra, Liberia, Liechtenstein, the Marshall Islands, Monaco, Nauru and Vanuatu. The 'coordinated defensive measures' that OECD members could take against such centres were due to commence in April 2003.

Vanuatu expressed its defiance, thereby risking being blacklisted and simultaneously increasing the potential that investors from abroad may think twice about transacting business in that centre – with a consequent effect on Vanuatu's economy. However, in May 2003, Vanuatu finally capitulated to the OECD's demands after some two years of resistance.[25] At this stage, the list of 'uncooperative tax havens' comprised six jurisdictions, as follows: Andorra, Liberia, Liechtenstein, the Marshall Islands, Monaco and Nauru.

However, all the commitments were predicated on the understanding that OECD countries would commit similarly. In light of the stance taken by Luxembourg and Switzerland (neither of which have supported any of the reports) to protect their banking systems, it was difficult at that stage to imagine how this could happen.

The next update on those jurisdictions that were classified by the OECD as 'uncooperative tax havens' was published in December 2003. With the removal of Nauru, the list then comprised five jurisdictions as follows: Andorra, Liberia, Liechtenstein, the Marshall Islands and Monaco. As at 30 July 2005, this list remains unchanged.[26]

12.11 Some reactions to the OECD's 1998 Report

Regrettably, the report published in 1998 did not distinguish between individuals focused on evading tax and the entirely legitimate tax optimisation strategies of multinational corporations. It is also difficult to

[25] Vanuatu's Letter of Commitment can be accessed at www.oecd.org./pdf/M00041000/M00041258.pdf).
[26] See www.oecd.org/document/57/0,2340,en_2649_33745_30578809_1_1_1_1,00.html.

say why 'Offshore Centres' have been criticised while OECD member countries doing the same thing escaped censure. It has been said that the '1998 study implicitly levelled charges of fiscal piracy against the international financial centres, with suggestions that IFCs used secrecy to assist clients with evasion of taxes imposed by the larger countries. The OECD prescribed the antidote of transparency, and demanded that the IFCs enter into agreements for exchange (i.e. provision) of information in order to facilitate better enforcement of taxes by its member states. IFCs rightly recognised the OECD demands as unprecedented, particularly in view of a long-standing rule in international law that no country is obliged to lend unilateral assistance to another in the enforcement of its taxes.'[27]

This 'un-level playing field' has since been the source of lengthy debate. Many, many comments were expressed at the time, including the following.

- The authorities in Jersey considered that the OECD Report was 'seriously flawed' and could wreck Jersey's economy.[28]
- Laurent Fabius, France's Finance Minister, was prepared to 'cease all financial relations of whatever type' with countries classified unfavourably.[29]
- Caricom, (representing fourteen members of the Caribbean community) described the OECD's methodology as 'amateurish'.[30]
- 'These disturbing developments, such as the OECD's initiative on Harmful Tax Competition, the main aim of which is to prohibit capital flow from high tax nations to low tax or no tax countries, abrogate the rule of law, disregard national sovereignty and put in place procedures to remove the right to privacy. Such movements are being brought forward with threats to use their economic might to bring to heel all those who do not agree. This behaviour endangers the very foundation of the force which we all seek to harness.'[31]

---

[27] Richard Hay, 'International Financial Centres: Back on the Front Foot, The 2005 Guide to International Financial Centres', February 2005, Euromoney Institutional Investor plc, p. 1.
[28] Carl Mortished, 'Jersey Attacks OECD Tax Haven Report', *The Times*, 27 June 2000.
[29] 'All Havens in a Storm', *The Economist*, 1 July 2000, p. 86.
[30] 'All Havens in a Storm', *The Economist*, 1 July 2000, p. 86.
[31] Michael Alberga, Presentation, *Center for Freedom and Prosperity's Update*, 31 January 2001.

- 'The OECD attack has nothing to do with economic principle and everything to do with political expediency.'[32]
- It is by no means generally accepted that tax competition is 'harmful' and, even if every nation was involved, it does not mean that the OECD policies would be effective. 'This is manifestly untrue. The OECD vision is completely contrary to good tax policy. The academic literature clearly shows that low rate, consumption based territorial tax systems maximise economic growth.'[33]

Further, many of the adverse effects attributed to tax competition, similarly apply to tax per se (see para. 30 of the 1998 Report).

Thirdly, since the so-called 'tax havens' are not members of the OECD, a question arises as to what remit the OECD has to deal with them.

Fourthly, one of the tenets of banking is the confidentiality of customers' affairs. However, the right of individuals to privacy is now less certain than it used to be. 'Easier access to banking information is an acceleration of a process that has been going on for some time . . . [N]ow access . . . is driven not by those trying to control drugs trafficking, terrorism, child prostitution, corruption and the like but by the demands of tax collectors.'[34] International cooperation to deal with wrongdoing should not necessarily mean the eradication of financial privacy.

In an article published by the *Wall Street Journal* on 29 June 2000, Daniel Mitchell, a Senior Fellow at the Washington-based Heritage Foundation, argued that the EU's failure to impose a tax on savings throughout the EU has led to efforts to curb financial privacy. Mr Mitchell also said that the OECD's work involves dangers because cartels are only successful if consumers have no alternatives. Thus, the EU may find that, in an attempt to protect those nations that impose high rates of tax (which it seems they would like low tax nations to collect), the result will be a migration of jobs and capital – reducing international investment and world growth. Mr Mitchell thinks the cartel will not work and that non-OECD jurisdictions will attract the business that will surely migrate if a tax oligopoly is created. Mr Mitchell thinks that not all tax havens will

---

[32] Paul Baxendale-Walker, 'OECD Demands and International Law, The OFC Report 2004', p. 21.

[33] 'The Level Playing Field: Misguided and Non-Existent', *Center for Freedom and Prosperity Foundation Prosperitas*, October 2003.

[34] Nigel Morris-Cotterill, 'Secrecy Laws under Assault', The Banker, August 2000, p. 62.

cooperate with the OECD's wishes and so some are likely to profit from migrating business as a result.

'In essence the OECD is arguing that the rest of the world should be forced to design their legal and administrative systems to facilitate the application of residence-based income taxation by OECD countries.'[35] Further, 'by targeting certain countries while exempting the United States and others, the OECD initiative is inconsistent with national treatment and most favoured nation treaty commitments as a member of the WTO'.[36]

Some believe that the true objectives of the FSF report were more to do with information for tax purposes – in support of the OECD report – rather than increased anti-money laundering efforts and better regulation.

Although the OECD originally decried the plight of locals who are not allowed the same tax concessions as non-residents, this is not abnormal. In fact according to a recent article in *The Economist*, 'such incentives are a normal tool of economic policy . . . witness the special economic zones of China, or the incentives available to multinationals that set up in Singapore'.[37] In fact, the OECD's free market ideology seems to be at odds with the criticism levelled at the jurisdictions criticised: it is not the competition that is harmful, it is the practices.[38] Is it not a legitimate aspiration for taxpayers to want lower tax rates and should the OECD be setting tax strategies for member countries?

Some questions have arisen as to why Switzerland and Luxembourg (both of which are members of the OECD) have been excluded from the OECD's Report.[39] It seems that these member countries are unwilling to commit to the standards required of OFCs. Further, the USA, Hong Kong, Singapore and the UK are all excluded from the list.

It is surprising that Delaware, the Dakotas and Florida all escaped mention despite the fact that their rules do not dissuade money laundering and that they seem to satisfy the 'harmful tax' criteria.[40]

Panama's Minister of Foreign Relations complained that, because the OECD had labelled Panama as a tax haven, other countries had applied

[35] Terry Dwyer, 'Harmful Tax Competition and the Future of Offshore Financial Centres', Vol. 5, No. 4, *Journal of Money Laundering Control*, p. 308.
[36] David R. Burton, 'Towards a Global Tax Cartel', *Policy*, Summer (December–February) 2002–3.
[37] 'Havens and Haven'ts', The Economist, 24 June 2000, p. 107.
[38] Christopher Adams and Astrid Wendtlandt, 'Offshore Centres Fight Sea Change in Their Ways', *Financial Times*, 24 July 2000.
[39] Patience Wheatcroft, 'Paradigm Lost for the Dot-Coms', *The Times*, 27 June 2000.
[40] Nigel Morris-Cotterill, 'Secrecy Laws under Assault', *The Banker*, August 2000, p. 62.

sanctions against his country. He said that, in the legislation of Mexico, Argentina, Venezuela, Brazil, Spain and Italy, Panama was regarded as a tax haven.[41]

It has been argued that the OECD is attempting to create tax harmonisation by way of encouraging the adoption of a taxation policy based on worldwide income, thereby eradicating any incentive to migrate capital to a lower tax area. This strategy requires exchange of information which in turn dilutes an individual's rights to privacy.

Actions are said to speak louder than words. It remains to be seen therefore what will be the implications of the words of the Ambassador of Antigua and Barbuda. On 15 October 2003, Mr Ronald Sanders announced that his jurisdiction, was no longer willing to work with the OECD. Instead, his jurisdiction, together with one other (unidentified at the time), determined to form a group to consider the level playing field concept (until 2004). Mr Sanders' rationale was that, since the EU allowed three of their members – together with five others – to apply a withholding tax (see section 5.14 above) instead of undertaking to supply information, they increased the unevenness of the playing field to the extent that it became unsustainable. The original commitment of many jurisdictions (including that of Antigua and Barbuda) was predicated on the understanding that, if all OECD countries failed to comply with the standards by 31 December 2005, those jurisdictions would no longer consider themselves bound to their commitment. On this basis, two jurisdictions withdrew from the fray.

> For developing countries, there is obligation without representation – a governance gap.[42]

12.12 The Center for Freedom and Prosperity

The Center for Freedom and Prosperity (CFP) was 'formed to protect tax competition, financial privacy and fiscal sovereignty . . . [its] . . . immediate priority is to lead the fight against the so-called "harmful tax competition" initiative'.[43]

---

[41] 'Panama Attacks OECD over Sanctions', *Offshore Red*, November 2002, p. 187.
[42] Jonathan Ward, 'Is Basel II Voluntary for Developing Countries?', Vol. 7, No. 3, The Financial Regulator, December 2002, p. 57.
[43] 'News Release on OECD and Tax Competition', *Center for Freedom and Prosperity*, 22 November 2000.

The CFP has been in the middle of the ensuing exchanges. The CFP argued that governments were under pressure to reduce taxes in order to retain investment – and this acts as a check on the amount of power they have. Those nations that impose high taxes do not want to have to compete with lower tax nations and so they resort to dictating to these nations how to manage their fiscal affairs. The CFP considers that the OECD approach represents an attack on four fronts: on taxpayers themselves, on free trade and global commerce, on sovereignty and on privacy.[44]

The Center has suggested that:

> In a globally liberalised world where trade barriers are falling, tax competition is a legitimate strategy for economic development. Not only do sovereign states have a right to use their tax systems to lure foreign investment; they owe a duty to their citizens to use all and every legitimate means to generate economic activity and growth . . . If trade liberalisation and globalisation are designed to integrate economies and peoples, tax competition is the best way for many developing countries to participate in the world economy.[45]

The Center concludes that:

> It is self-evident that the proposals of the OECD are morally suspect, legally dubious, smack of imperialism more reminiscent of the 19th century rather than the 21st century, and at a rudimentary level are an affront to the dignity and self respect of Caribbean people.[46]

12.13 Some clarifications by the OECD

The OECD said that a number of misunderstandings had arisen about 'the scope, objectives and implications' of their work. These were summarised in an article in the *Financial Regulator* in which Dr William Witherell, Director of Financial, Fiscal and Enterprise Affairs at the OECD, attempted to provide some clarification. The points he made included:[47]

[44] 'The Case for International Tax Competition: A Caribbean Perspective', *Center for Freedom and Prosperity Foundation Prosperitas*, Vol. 2, No. 2, April 2002.
[45] Based on a document produced by the Coalition for Tax Competition, created by the Center for Freedom and Prosperity and dated 21 November 2000.
[46] 'The Case for International Tax Competition: A Caribbean Perspective', *Center for Freedom and Prosperity Foundation Prosperitas*, Vol. 2, No. 2, April 2002.
[47] 'FATF Told: "Physician, Heal Thyself"', Tax-News.com, 31 October 2002.

- The focus is to establish the effective exchange of information and transparency for tax purposes.
- The aim is to prevent wealthy people from escaping from their share of tax.
- The object is to provide equal treatment of resident and non-resident investors.
- The purpose was to detect and to prevent violations of civil and criminal tax law.
- 'Ring fencing' must stop.
- The objects were not: harmonisation of taxes at high rates, forcing countries to alter their tax structures, or attacking legitimate tax planning.
- It is a misconception to believe that the OECD is threatening the fiscal sovereignty of small states.
- No distinction was made between small and large countries or between member and non-member countries.
- The OECD welcomed competition that is fair.

12.14 Behind the corporate veil: using corporate entities for illicit purposes

In May 2000, and arising out of the general concern about the potential for corporate entities such as corporations, trusts, foundations and partnerships to be used for wrongful purposes including money laundering, corruption and financing of terrorist activity, the FSF's Working Group on Offshore Financial Centres invited the OECD to carry out some research. The OECD was asked to consider whether any mechanisms could be developed to prevent this type of misuse by providing supervisors and law enforcement agencies with the capability of obtaining appropriate information on beneficial owners and the authority to share that information with authorities elsewhere. The OECD believed that this approach would minimise the potential for misuse of such vehicles. In response, the OECD Steering Group on Corporate Governance produced their report 'Behind the Corporate Veil: Using Corporate Entities for Illicit Purposes'.

The report excluded the examination of listed corporations and financial services companies, but included trusts, corporations, foundations and partnerships with limited liability. Most concerns arose over international business companies, trusts, exempt companies and foundations in jurisdictions that provide a substantial degree of secrecy and which do not have the means to enable the authorities to identify the true owner.

Regrettably, only OECD countries were involved in preparation of the report, although its focus was on such vehicles in non-OECD countries. The report did not deal with corporate vehicles in OECD countries, although 'OECD member countries control approximately 80 per cent of the global trade in financial services provided to non-residents'.[48] Instead, the report focused on 'Offshore', when it said that:

- The potential for misuse was greater in some OFCs because, in those centres, corporate vehicles were allowed to be excessively secret.
- Shell companies offer substantial potential for misuse and this type of company constitutes a large proportion of corporate vehicles established offshore.
- Some OFCs tolerate facilities that obscure beneficial ownership (e.g. bearer shares, nominee shareholders, nominee and corporate directors, flee clauses and letters of wishes).
- There are insufficient mechanisms to enable the identification of true owners; in fact some jurisdictions protect anonymity through secrecy laws that prevent disclosure of beneficial ownership.

The report recommended the establishment of adequate measures to enable the relevant authorities to obtain details on ownership and control quickly, to enable investigation and information sharing in the event of need.

Concerning detailed information on ownership and control, the report said that:

- this information should be available or else obtainable;
- adequate systems to oversee and to control this information should be in place; and
- it should be possible to share this information with investigators from abroad who are carrying out supervisory functions.

Three main scenarios were identified by the OECD, as follows.

12.14.1 Disclosure to the authorities ab initio

Might be appropriate where:

---

[48] 2000, Vol. 5, No. 3, *Financial Regulator.*

- the investigatory system is weak;
- there is substantial ownership of corporate vehicles by non-residents;
- there are many shell companies;
- there are options to enhance anonymity.

12.14.2 Intermediaries

Where there are intermediaries involved in forming and managing corporations, they might be able to maintain the information. This might be appropriate where:

- there are adequate mechanisms to monitor compliance by the intermediaries, who will be responsible for obtaining and maintaining the relevant information;
- there is an adequate number of intermediaries

12.14.3 Reliance on an investigative system

This might be appropriate where:

- the authorities are adequately empowered to obtain the information;
- the track record on enforcement is positive;
- the judicial system is effective; and
- the information is available in the jurisdiction.

The report anticipated that some jurisdictions might rely on one option or adopt more than one to fit prevailing circumstances.

In May 2001, the OECD published a report entitled 'Report on the Misuse of Corporate Vehicles for Illicit Purposes'. 'The report utilized a largely anecdotal, non-introspective and non-benchmarked approach rather than any form of scholarly research methodology.'[49]

The report encouraged regulatory authorities to ensure that they could obtain information on the beneficial owners of corporate vehicles, as a means of preventing their misuse for wrongful purposes. The Finance Ministers of the G7 endorsed the report in July 2001 and it was released on 27 November 2002 as 'Behind the Corporate Veil: Using Corporate Entities for Illicit Purposes'.

---

[49] 'Towards a Level Playing Field', International Tax and Investment Organization and the Society of Trust and Estate Practitioners, September 2002.

12.15 Model Agreement on Exchange of Information on Tax Matters

The Agreement[50] aims 'to promote international cooperation in tax matters through exchange of information.'[51] It was developed by the Global Forum Working Group on Effective Exchange of Information. The Group's members include Aruba, Australia, Bahrain, Bermuda, Canada, the Cayman Islands, Cyprus, France, Ireland, the Isle of Man, Italy, Japan, Malta, Mauritius, the Netherlands, the Netherlands Antilles, Norway, San Marino, Seychelles, Slovak Republic, the UK and the USA. The Agreement embraces information exchange in respect of civil and criminal tax matters – and applies even where the requested country does not need the information for itself. The relevant authorities must be able to obtain and hand over information held by financial institutions (including banks) and fiduciaries – and it extends to beneficial owners. It offers protection for bona fide taxpayers – for example, by excluding fishing expeditions and by requiring the requesting authority not to pass on the information without permission from the requested authority.

12.16 OECD Global Forum on Taxation

A meeting was convened in Ottawa in October 2003 and attended by forty governments (OECD and non-OECD) that were committed to the principles of transparency and effective exchange of information for tax purposes. 'In pursuit of these principles, the participants agreed to establish a small group to develop proposals for consideration by the Global Forum for achieving a global playing field and a process by which this work could be taken forward.'[52] The Group established a sub-group to consider how the level playing field issue could be progressed. Terms of reference were agreed. 'In developing proposals, the members of the Sub-Group were guided by the objective of the global level playing field: to achieve high standards of transparency and information exchange in a way that is fair, equitable and permits fair competition between all

[50] See www.oecd.org/ctp/.
[51] The OECD's Project on Harmful Tax Practices, 'The 2004 Progress Report', OECD, 4 February 2004, p. 13.
[52] OECD Global Forum on Taxation, 'A Process for Achieving a Global Level Playing Field', Annex 1, OECD, 4 June 2004.

countries large and small, OECD and non-OECD.'[53] The aspiration is that every country should meet these standards so that lack of transparency and lack of effective exchange of information do not hinder appropriate competition. The intention is to prevent business migrating to jurisdictions where transparency is lacking and where there is no effective exchange of information for tax purposes. The Forum met next in Berlin on 4 June 2004 and defined a 'global level playing field' as being 'fundamentally about fairness to which all parties in the global forum are committed. In the context of exchange of information, achieving a level playing field means the convergence of existing practices to the same high standards for effective exchange of information on both criminal and civil taxation matters within an acceptable timeline for implementation with the aim of achieving equity and fair competition.'[54] The OECD was given a mandate to review the information exchange practices of OECD and non-OECD countries and to report at the next meeting in November 2005. This will be a significant test as to whether its own members are willing to meet standards that the OECD has tried to enforce on non-members.

12.17 Behind the corporate veil

As discussed above, the OECD produced a report entitled 'Behind the Corporate Veil'. It began by stating that its intention was to treat 'Offshore' and 'Onshore' centres similarly – and, in the view of one commentator, '[t]here then follows a wholesale demolition of Offshore Centres'.[55] The 'Offshore Centres' had insisted that they and 'Onshore' centres should be treated the same way – but this was not to be.

The International Tax and Investment Organization (ITIO) and the Society of Trust and Estate Practitioners (STEP) commissioned a review of the report 'in an attempt to provide a broader and more objective basis for policy formulation'. The review, dated September 2002, was called 'Towards a Level Playing Field' and was prepared by Stikeman Elliott, a Canadian law firm, on behalf of the ITIO and STEP.

[53] OECD Global Forum on Taxation, 'A Process for Achieving a Global Level Playing Field', OECD, 4 June 2004, p. 2.
[54] 'A Process for Achieving a Global Level Playing Field', OECD Global Forum on Taxation, 4 June 2004, p. 2.
[55] Bob Reynolds, 'Editorial', *Offshore Red*, October 2002, p. 169.

The ITIO and the STEP believed that the report was influential to the extent that it was being used by the FATF, the FSF and the European Union despite being flawed – in their opinion – for two reasons. First, only OECD countries had been involved in its preparation; and, secondly, its focus was on non-OECD countries. The logic applied was that, if the preparation was flawed, the conclusions were unlikely to be reliable. The review made the point that 'OECD countries control approximately 80 per cent of the global trade in financial services provided to non-residents . . . [so] . . . the OECD is unlikely to be an impartial referee in regulating a market where its member countries have a significant commercial interest'.

The review expressed concern that rules for the cross-border exchange of financial information were 'being developed with a mixed agenda, which includes combating transnational crime'. To be fair and effective they must be applied evenly and the information gatherers must take account of financial privacy and human rights. The point is that international financial centres, small and developing countries and professionals involved in trusts and estates want to be able to contribute to the discussion. Further, the review says that 'Delaware limited liability companies and trusts administered in Switzerland' (which vehicles are used in OECD countries) are not considered.

The review made it clear that those who had been excluded from the debate believed that corporate vehicles should not be misused. The review proposed a consensual process – including all jurisdictions that may be affected – which promoted the application of the same rules for all countries involved in similar activities – and which agreed not to direct the trade in services away from small, developing countries and which took account of personal privacy rights.

The review was a timely reminder of the potential for redirecting business to jurisdictions that are not embraced by the new rules. This is a serious problem now but may be even more serious if the trade in services continues to grow relative to the level of world trade. Further, as information accumulates, the potential for unauthorised access increases. As information is exchanged across borders, the potential for misuse becomes greater. The review is an important document because it says that its conclusions are based on a 'comprehensive benchmarking review of the regulation of corporations, trusts and limited partnerships in fifteen OECD and non-OECD countries'.

PART III

The future

The last third of the book (Chapters 13 to 22) begins with a synopsis of how things stand and covers some of the factors that may be relevant to 'Offshore' in the years to come.

A comparison of two of the world's largest – and most respected – financial services centres – the USA and the UK – is provided – and this leads into consideration of whether 'Offshore' is really the cause of so many global woes – or whether it is being used as a scapegoat. This section attempts to summarise the problems and to identify some options for the future – post FSF, FATF, OECD and the catastrophic events of 11 September 2001 in the USA. Finally, this part provides a checklist that consumers might use in deciding where to transact 'Offshore'.

13

Some problems 'Offshore'

> Regulatory functions represent an anomaly in the context of customer-driven government.[1]

13.1 Introduction

Reference was made in the opening chapter to the pejorative sense in which the word 'Offshore' is often used. This chapter explores some of the reasons why this might be the case.

13.2 Background

At the outset, it is perhaps pertinent to emphasise that, on the face of it, there is no reason why the 'Offshore' environment should be any more exposed to any form of wrongful activity than the 'Onshore' environment. Analysis of the products offered in both environments indicates that by and large the same types of products and services are offered in both places. Further, a comparison of the regulatory procedures applied 'Offshore' and 'Onshore' indicates that, while not identical in practice, they are similar in principle. The previous chapters refer. All other things being equal, there is no reason on the face of it why there should be more problems 'Offshore' than 'Onshore' – unless other variables apply.

Despite all this, practitioners 'Offshore' frequently say that, when problems arise 'Offshore', they seem to attract substantial attention – perhaps even more attention than they would have received if the problems had occurred 'Onshore'. While this attention (and by extension the criticism that goes with it) has been justified some of the time, practitioners affirm that it has not been appropriate in all circumstances.

---

[1] Malcolm K. Sparrow, *The Regulatory Craft*, Brookings Institution Press, 2000, p. 2.

A small example of the adverse opinions that have been expressed about 'Offshore' include the following: '"Offshore Finance Centres" are unlikely ever to be able to shed their slightly unsavoury air.'[2] '[OFCs'] activities arouse deep suspicion among tax authorities and police forces.'[3] And 'Offshore . . . is regarded with the deepest suspicion.'[4]

Regrettably, the time that has lapsed between when these opinions were first expressed and the present time has not diluted that suspicion by one iota. In fact, since these opinions go back some years, the inference is that none of this is new. What gives rise to this type of opinion requires some further comment.

Part of the stigma may stem from the derivation of the term 'Offshore Finance Centre'. An earlier chapter drew attention to the 'tax haven' label. To place these comments in some historical context, a 1997 press report suggested that 'international organised crime . . . launders an estimated $1 trillion a year in illegal money through offshore tax havens'.[5] On the basis of this type of statement, it is little wonder that credible 'Offshore Finance Centres' do not want to be referred to as 'tax havens'. That being so, this term was gradually replaced by the term 'Offshore Finance Centre' – not least when jurisdictions were referring to themselves. However, even this change of style was not enough to make the public in general and financial cognoscenti in particular forget the 'unsavoury' attitude described above. In fact, any small degree of authenticity that may have distinguished an 'Offshore Finance Centre' from a 'tax haven' has now vanished. Importantly, the term 'tax haven' has been given a degree of legitimacy – because it has been adopted by the OECD in its Harmful Tax Competition Report (see Chapter 12 above).

13.3 The extent of the problem

'Research by the US Federal Reserve indicated that of the funds held by OFCs a sizeable minority – perhaps in excess of $500 billion – was believed to represent the proceeds of criminal activities, such as drugs,

[2] 'Survey of European Finance and Investment Offshore Centres', *Financial Times*, 18 April 1991.
[3] P. Gartland, No Crime Please, We're OFCs', *Accountancy*, December 1992.
[4] J. Authers, 'Building Societies, Investing Offshore', *FT Quarterly Review of Personal Finance*, January 1994, p. 8.
[5] 'Criminal Paradise Lost as Cayman Islands Come Clean', *Sunday Times*, 22 June 1997, p. 19.

money laundering, insider trading or tax evasion.'[6] While this quantifi-
cation is useful, it excludes the potential for harm that is created by
giving rise to a perception that 'Offshore' is negative because no controls
are exercised in that environment. It has to be said that, for some, the
perception is virtually a reality. Consider this quote:

> The existence of what could be called the offshore interface has under-
> ·mined national governments' abilities to impose higher taxes both on
> individuals and companies, has facilitated money laundering and other
> illegal activities, and has weakened the power of both national and inter-
> national supervisory bodies to regulate the financial system.[7]

Clearly, these are powerful indictments.

13.4 Some underlying principles

As stated earlier, probably the most important characteristic that an
'Offshore Finance Centre' must be able to offer is confidentiality. At the
same time, confidentiality is perhaps the one characteristic that renders
'Offshore Finance Centres' most vulnerable.

Then (with respect to 'Offshore') there are certain factors that, if they
exist, will facilitate, or at least do not militate against, wrongdoing. These
factors include: legislation that is itself inadequate or which is inadequately
enforced; absence of a (meaningful) licensing regime; weak regulation and/
or regulators; incompetent and/or inexperienced management in licence-
holding companies; unlicensed institutions carrying on licensable activity;
little or no compliance testing; failure to adhere to international accounting,
auditing and regulatory/supervisory standards, not least in respect of controls; non-adoption of corporate governance principles; inadequate 'know
your customer' and payments systems; and so on. (Naturally, these factors
would impinge upon any financial services environment, but this part of the
discussion focuses on 'Offshore' financial environments.)

Accordingly, the problem and the solution revolve around getting the
balance right. For example, client confidentiality is not a weakness, it is a
strength. However, where confidentiality becomes secrecy that is used to
mask dubious practice or criminal activity, this represents an abuse and
must not be tolerated. The answer is to offer an appropriate level of

---

[6] Paul Stribbard, 'International Reports, A Brief Review', *Private Wealth Investor*, June 2001,
p. 16.
[7] Mark P. Hampton, *The Offshore Interface*, Macmillan Press Ltd, 1996, p. 2.

confidentiality – but not enough to enable this fundamental right to be exploited adversely. It is in this respect that there may be some value in distinguishing confidentiality from secrecy.

13.5 Are there any common features in frauds Offshore?

Interestingly, frauds 'Offshore' differ little from frauds 'Onshore' – and in many respects the differences are more apparent than real – except in tax matters – which, to some extent, might explain why 'Offshore Centres' are considered as tax havens. However, there are perhaps some features that are often central to wrongdoing 'Offshore'. These include:

- prosecutions are not commonplace;
- knowing how the systems work will help resolve issues 'Offshore' more quickly;
- 'Offshore Centres' are used in a wide variety of ways, for example to establish companies, to deposit money, to launder money, and to avoid stricter regulation elsewhere;
- the collusion of bank employees makes a fraud much easier to accomplish;
- the use of a number of jurisdictions and (frequently) numerous shell companies to obscure the final destination of the funds;
- weak 'know your customer' procedures and less than robust procedures in banks;
- the exploitation by fraudsters of any situation where it is easy to make deposits and the difficulties for investigators in tracing the destination of the funds; and
- the fraud does not usually emanate from 'Offshore'; rather, 'Offshore' is used to accomplish it.

Both 'shell banks/branches' and 'parallel owned banks' offer potential for abuse. Shell banks are 'licensed in an OFC [and] are not affiliated with a supervised financial group and whose management resides elsewhere'.[8] By extension, shell branches have a limited physical presence. All the important decisions are taken elsewhere. Parallel owned banks are those which have a unit 'Offshore' and another 'Onshore' – and

[8] 'Filling a Gap in Global Surveillance Finance and Development', in Salim M. Darbar, R. Barry Johnston and Mary G. Zephirin, *Assessing Offshore Financial Centres*, September 2003, p. 35.

which are both owned by common shareholders but are not connected in a subsidiary/parent relationship. These organisations are frequently paper-based only.

13.6 A few examples of frauds

The range of wrongful activity perpetrated 'Offshore' includes: money laundering, tax evasion, 'Nigerian letters', advance fee frauds, credit card frauds, prime bank guarantees, wrongful use of 'Offshore' companies, and many more. (For the avoidance of doubt, Nigeria is not an 'Offshore Finance Centre'.) Here are examples of three types of fraud:

- Ponzi schemes are swindles in which abnormally high rates of return are paid to initial investors out of funds contributed by later investors, who end up losing all of their money when the house of cards falls down.
- Pyramid schemes involve the collection of money from individuals at the bottom (new investors) to pay the initial investors at the top, with all the emphasis on bringing in new members/investors and not on selling the product or service.
- Smurfing occurs where numerous deposits of small amounts are made – each being below a reporting threshold. Frequently, the money is transferred to another account which is often in another country.
- A phoenix firm is where the directors of one limited company move with the assets to a new company, leaving the liabilities behind and avoiding claims from customers.[9]

Here are two examples of major frauds in which the 'Offshore' environment was used predominantly:

13.6.1 BCCI

The fraud perpetrated at the Bank of Credit and Commerce International (BCCI) is one of the best-known cases of banking fraud and simultaneously one of the most blatant examples of the abuse of 'Offshore'. Eventually, after years of investigation into its affairs, BCCI collapsed.

---

[9] Financial Services Authority, *Annual Report* 2004/5, p. 35.

BCCI was backed by Abu Dhabi's ruling family and by the Bank of America (which in 1977 owned 45 per cent of BCCI). BCCI was founded in 1972 in Pakistan by Aga Hassan Abedi and was incorporated in Luxembourg. Mr Abedi's aspiration was to create a global retail bank whose market would be the developing world. BCCI grew very quickly. For example, by 1982, it had 280 branches in fifty-seven countries. It opened in the UK in 1972 (the operational headquarters) and had forty-five branches in the UK by 1979. By 1988, the bank had 1.3 million depositors and US$15.7 billion on deposit.[10] In 1988, seven of its bankers were arrested in Florida on charges of drug trafficking and money laundering. The BCCI banking network was shut down by banking regulators globally in 1991, at which time its debts exceeded US$16 billion.

'The Bank had claimed to make profits that seem to have been largely fictitious and had been wholly indiscriminate about its customers providing services for drug traffickers, dictators, terrorists, fraud merchants, intelligence agencies, arms dealers and the like.'[11] There was more than one post mortem on what came to be known in some quarters as the Bank of Crooks and Criminals International. But the report prepared by the Foreign Relations Committee of the United States Senate is probably one of the most comprehensive. The report says of the bank that:

> from its earliest days [it was] made up of multiple layers of entities, related to one another through an impenetrable series of holding companies, affiliates, subsidiaries, banks within banks, insider dealings and nominee relationships. By fracturing corporate structure, record keeping, regulatory review, and audits, the complex BCCI family of entities . . . was able to evade ordinary legal restrictions on the movement of capital and goods as a matter of daily practice and routine.[12]

---

[10] 'Old Wounds', *The Economist*, 10 January 2004, p. 58.
[11] 'Financial Havens, Banking Secrecy and Money Laundering', United Nations Office for Drug Control and Crime Prevention, Issue 8 of the UNDCP Technical Series, Double Issue 34 and 35 of the *Crime Prevention and Criminal Justice Newsletter*, 1998, p. 35.
[12] The Executive Summary of the BCCI affair, A Report to the Committee on Foreign Relations, United States Senator John Kerry and Senator Hank Brown, December 1992, 102nd Congress, 2nd Session, Senate Print, pp. 102–40, as reported in 'Financial Havens, Banking Secrecy and Money Laundering', United Nations Office for Drug Control and Crime Prevention, Issue 8 of the UNDCP Technical Series, Double Issue 34 and 35 of the *Crime Prevention and Criminal Justice Newsletter*, 1998, p. 35.

BCCI routinely used 'Offshore Finance Centres' and other centres where bank secrecy prevailed over bank confidentiality. The bank's structure added another layer of complication which tangled the web even further. Headquarters was in Luxembourg but offices were globally dispersed. Notably, the bank was not subject to regulatory oversight by any one regulator because, even though activities were separated globally, the two sets of auditors involved considered their own respective area of responsibility but neither considered the effect of the combined activities of the organisation. One commentator believes that 'BCCI is a perfect example of how the offshore system is a godsend to the laundrymen.'[13]

More than US$12 million of assets were seized by regulators. Amongst the many questions arising was how the bank had been allowed to do what it had been doing for so long (for example, the 'know your customer' rules were not enforced).

The BCCI case underlines the importance of consolidated supervision (see sections 6.19 and 6.21 above) which, in summary, requires that the totality of 'financial services' operations are taken into account as well as its individual parts in reaching conclusions about regulatory acceptability. In practice, there are many operational difficulties in compiling an accurate picture of a diversified financial services group whose operations are global in nature, and therefore fall under the purview of many regulators. A 'lead regulator' is normally appointed.

While BCCI's collapse was the most notable banking catastrophe 'Offshore', it was not the only one. (Although not dealt with here, the case of Meridian International Bank in 1995 is also relevant.)

If it is any comfort, 'it is now unlikely that a bank owned and incorporated in an OFC could establish operations in other major financial markets on anything like the scale achieved by BCCI or even Meridian Bank'.[14]

Many legal problems arose. For example, it was said that the Bank of England had acted unlawfully in issuing a licence to BCCI in the first place. (In 1980, the Bank of England regarded BCCI as a 'Licensed Deposit Taker'. However the Bank of England never licensed BCCI as a bank per se.) The Bank of England said it relied on the assessment by the regulator in Luxembourg (where BCCI was incorporated, although its

---

[13] Jeffrey Robinson, *The Laundrymen*, Simon & Schuster UK Ltd, 1998, p. 361.
[14] 'Offshore Financial Centres, The Role of the IMF', 23 June 2000, p. 5.

main place of business appears to have been in the UK). Whether the
Bank of England was entitled to rely on Luxembourg in these circumstances remains to be seen. Depositors also questioned why the Bank of
England did not revoke BCCI's licence in 1990 or 1991. They believe that
it was clear then that the bank was insolvent and that it was being
managed fraudulently. The Bank of England believed that a rescue was
still possible at that stage.

The problems caused by the collapse of BCCI were still being felt in
2004. On 12 January 2004, the Bank of England, BCCI's regulator, found
itself in court defending an action for misfeasance brought against it
by Deloitte & Touche, BCCI's liquidator. Deloittes 'claims that the
Bank "knowingly or recklessly" failed to supervise BCCI properly in
the 12 years before BCCI imploded, and is seeking GBP 850,000 ($1.5
million) in damages' for the 6,500 depositors in the UK whom it
represents.[15] Note that the Bank of England cannot be sued for negligence, so the charge is 'misfeasance in public office'. One suggestion in
mid-2004 was that it could cost the Bank of England up to £100 million
to defend the case, but the point made in the Bank's annual report for
2003/4 was that the Bank could not settle a case in which twenty-two
members (both present and former) of the UK's central bank had been
accused of dishonesty.

13.6.2 Enron

Until its failure in December 2001 (when it filed for bankruptcy protection), Enron was the world's largest energy trading company and the
seventh largest corporation in the USA. Its international operations
included involvement in about 25 per cent of global natural gas and
energy deals.

The company's modus operandi involved the sale of energy products
(e.g. natural gas and electricity) for delivery at a date in the future. This
led to the sale of financial instruments designed to protect customers
from adverse movements in the price of the products it sold. However,
these deals appear to have been less transparent than they might
have been.

Many employees lost not only their jobs but also their retirement
savings (with pension plans based on Enron's shares). The role of Arthur

---

[15] 'Old Wounds', *The Economist*, 10 January 2004, p. 58.

Andersen (Enron's auditor) was called into question amidst charges of shredding documents and destroying e-mails just before Enron went bankrupt. The auditing firm was convicted in May 2002 for obstructing justice during an investigation into the collapse of Enron. The Arthur Andersen partnership collapsed. On 31 May 2005, the Supreme Court in the USA overturned the conviction because the trial judge's instructions to the jury did not make it clear that it was necessary for the jurors to find that, in shredding documents relating to the audit, the auditor had knowingly subverted an investigation by illegal behaviour. (This decision does not, however, vindicate Andersen.) The role of the Chairman of Enron, Kenneth Lay, and other senior executives (former President, Jeffrey Skilling, and former Chief Financial Officer, Andrew Fastow) came under scrutiny. The problem came to a head when Sherron Watkins, a former vice president, 'blew the whistle'.

The group had around 2,000 subsidiaries in twenty-three states and sixty-two countries. Further, 881 of the subsidiaries were 'Offshore', 692 in the Cayman Islands, 119 in Turks and Caicos, 43 in Mauritius, 8 in Bermuda, 6 in Barbados, 4 in Puerto Rico, 2 in Hong Kong, 2 in Panama, and 1 in each of Aruba, the British Virgin Islands, Guam, Guernsey and Singapore. Delaware hosted 685 subsidiaries 'which the US General Accounting Office cites as a . . . haven for money launderers (see *Law Offshore*, December 2000)'.[16] The company went from what might have been described superficially as strength to strength, until October 2001 when a provision of £24 million ($35 million) had to be made to cover losses arising in two partnerships (LJM Cayman LP and LJM2 Co-Investment LP) that were established in the Cayman Islands in 1999 to absorb debt from Enron's balance sheet and to obscure losses.

The US Justice Department launched a criminal investigation; other investigations followed, including one by the Securities and Exchange Commission. Investigations focused (inter alia) on the use of 'Offshore' partnerships and the company's tax compliance (it seems that the company paid no tax in four out of the five years to 2000).

13.7 Some 'Offshore Centres' in particular

Earlier chapters described some characteristics of 'Offshore Centres' and then – using the criteria developed by the OECD – identified some

---

[16] 'Enronitis Spreads, Focus Shifts to Offshore Centres', Offshoreon.com, 7 February 2002.

centres that satisfied those criteria. The point has been made already that, while there is a degree of homogeneity, no two centres are identical. This is particularly well demonstrated by reference to the centres described below – all of which have particular traits and characteristics that require special attention. Subsequent chapters (chapters 17 and 18 respectively) will examine the UK and the USA in particular.

13.7.1 Switzerland

Switzerland is a member of the OECD but is not a member of the EU (although two-thirds of its exports go to European Union countries). Switzerland does not regard itself as an 'Offshore Finance Centre'. The FATF does not regard Switzerland as a 'Non-cooperative country or territory' and the OECD has not classified Switzerland as a tax haven.

It is axiomatic to link Switzerland with banking secrecy. 'It is estimated that Swiss banks look after about DM 2 trillion ($870 billion) for wealthy foreigners, most of which has been lured into the country by the assurance that information on this money will under no circumstances be provided to officials in the depositors' home countries.'[17]

One observer believes that '[i]n the particularly difficult area of tax evasion, the Swiss have probably got it right'.[18] In principle, tax evasion is a financial crime. However, in practice, the regulations only apply where financial companies there directly assist clients to evade tax overseas. Compare the situation in Switzerland with that prevailing in China: 'China, for example, recently sentenced an individual to death for tax evasion.'[19]

However, Switzerland has been pressured by the EU to harmonise the taxation of interest to prevent outflows of capital from elsewhere (principally Germany) to non-EU countries (such as Switzerland and Liechtenstein). It appears that, in future, Switzerland will prevent foreigners from using the country as a means to evade tax. In the article referred to above, Mr Kaspar Villiger, Federal Finance Minister, has said: 'We cannot regard tax evasion abroad any less seriously when at home we treat it with a withholding tax of 35 per cent.'

---

[17] Konrad Mrusek, 'Swiss Bankers Bob and Weave', *Frankfurter Allgemeine Zeitung*, 17 October 2000.
[18] Cameron Niles, 'Middle Ground', *Offshore Finance USA*, January/February 2001, p. 56.
[19] Richard Hay, 'International Financial Centrres and Information Exchange', June 2005, Issue 157, *Offshore Investment*, p. 2.

The Swiss will retain bank secrecy until the EU Directive on taxing interest payments is agreed (see section 5.15 above). A change in the law will be required to remove banking secrecy, and this will require a referendum.

Switzerland was criticised for having had (around) SFr1 billion of General Abacha's money in its banking system (see section 14.4 below). The banks involved were publicly rebuked by the Swiss Federal Banking Commission. Former Yugoslav President, Slobodan Milosevic, and others, had more than US$57 million in Swiss accounts. However, when it came down to it, the bill that would have controlled Swiss banks more tightly was defeated by thirty-four votes in October 2000 (eight-nine for and fifty-five against).

In a referendum on 3 March 2002, 54.1 per cent of the Swiss electorate voted in favour of Switzerland joining the United Nations. This was interpreted by some as a sign that Switzerland would be willing to bear its share of global responsibilities and was seen as a move to greater openness. This vote may pave the way for membership of the European Union at some future time.

13.7.2 Seychelles

The Republic of Seychelles (population 77,000), guaranteed for itself a place in the financial history books when it enacted the Economic Development Act on 27 November 1995. The object of this piece of legislation according to the authorities was to attract investment. Investors who invested at least US$10 million in an approved investment scheme were guaranteed immunity from prosecution in all criminal matters. They were also protected from seizure of assets provided no serious crimes were committed in Seychelles.

Investors became citizens with diplomatic status. Assets could not be compulsorily acquired (unless drug trafficking or violence had been committed in the Seychelles). The FATF and the international community reacted strongly and, on 2 April 1996, money laundering was rendered an extraditable offence in the Seychelles.

The FATF responded by warning financial institutions to examine carefully their links with Seychelles banks and corporations because they regarded this legislation as an open invitation to money launderers.

The Government of Seychelles repealed the legislation in July 2000. Seychelles has since adopted a different paradigm. For example, Seychelles has introduced legislation regulating international corporate and trustees service providers.

13.7.3 Grenada

Grenada's leading 'Offshore' bank, the First International Bank of Grenada, collapsed in August 2000. The bank's capital was said to be a gem worth US$25 million.

13.7.4 Antigua and Barbuda

In 1999, a large money laundering operation was discovered. Foreign politicians were said to be involved. In the aftermath, twenty-six 'Offshore' banks were closed down. As at 2003, there were twenty-one licensed 'Offshore' banks, of which eleven were shell banks not represented by any physical presence on the island.[20]

13.8 A balanced perspective

Every commercial enterprise involves risk, and the examples cited above show that financial services facilities 'Offshore' are subject to abuse. These examples indicate some of the risks involved, but should not be interpreted to mean that 'Offshore' equals risk and caveat emptor is the only rule that applies. Meanwhile, the 'Offshore' environment is too important to be marginalised because the potential cannot be controlled. The secret is in achieving an appropriate balance.

Whether 'Offshore' poses more risk than 'Onshore' remains to be seen. This is pursued in the next chapter.

---

[20] Mark Wilson, 'Islands in the Sun', *Money Laundering Bulletin*, June 2004, p. 9.

14

Some problems 'Onshore'

[L]aw typically specifies only a part of the role that society expects regulatory and enforcement agencies to play.[1]

14.1 Introduction

Reference was made in the opening chapter to the pejorative sense in which the word 'Offshore' is often used, and the previous chapter explored some of the reasons why this should be. This chapter focuses on some of the problems that have arisen 'Onshore'. To place this aspect in context, it is interesting to note that, in their recent review of work they carried out in assessing 'Offshore' centres, the Directors of the IMF noted that (as at end 2003) 'some onshore financial centres potentially pose greater risks to international financial stability [than offshore centres]'.[2]

14.2 Some quotable quotes

Some observations were included in the last chapter to show the disparity of views about the perceived quality of the environment under review. This chapter similarly presents some views for consideration. It has been said that:

> it is generally easier, cheaper, faster and more reliable for money launderers to use retail or merchant banks in so called 'onshore centres'.[3]

> In the UK the Treasury estimates that the black economy is about 8 per cent of GDP.[4]

---

[1] Malcolm Sparrow, *The Regulatory Craft*, Brookings Institution Press, 2000, p. 244.
[2] 'IMF Executive Board Reviews the Assessment Program on Offshore Financial Centres', IMF, 24 November 2003.
[3] Nigel Morris-Cotterill, 'The Colour of Money', *The Hindu*, 18 January 2001.
[4] 'Knowing How to Know Your Customer', *Private Wealth Investor*, July/August 2002, p. 14.

Between 1980 and 1996, almost two-thirds of all IMF member countries
had experienced significant banking sector problems.[5]

14.3 French parliamentary reports

The Peillon-Montebourg Commission, under the leadership of Socialist
Deputy Arnaud Montebourg, focused its attention on a number of
finance centres including Liechtenstein (March 2000), Monaco (June
2000), Switzerland (February 2001), the UK, Gibraltar, the Crown
Dependencies (October 2001) and Luxembourg (January 2002). The
team compiled a report on each jurisdiction.

In respect of Switzerland, the team was not impressed by the country's
banking secrecy rules, and concluded that legislation on money laundering was ineffective and improperly enforced. For its part, the Swiss
Bankers' Association described the report on Switzerland (which ran to
almost 400 pages) as 'a very sloppy analysis of selective source material'.[6]

The report (10 October 2001) on the City of London was not met with a
positive response either. The City was condemned and the UK's dependent territories were categorised as havens used by criminals for their funds.

In January 2002, Luxembourg was similarly castigated, this time for
using words not backed by appropriate action. In response, the Ministry
of Justice in Luxembourg issued a press release on 22 January 2002
rejecting 'as unfounded the accusations made against it . . . Luxembourg
cannot accept the accusation of being a State that deliberately refuses to
participate in the fight against financial crime . . . Luxembourg considers
that the Peillon-Montebourg report lacks objectivity.'

14.4 The Abacha affair

General Sani Abacha, who died in 1998 of a heart attack, was a former
dictator of Nigeria. The Nigerian Government has been trying to recover
around US $4 billion of missing assets from the deceased's estate since
his death; the action continues. The UK's *Financial Times* reported
(15 January 2001) on a review carried out by the UK's Financial Services
Authority into the Abacha affair. It said that, of US $514 million of

[5] George Alexander Walker, *International Banking Regulation Law, Policy and Practice*,
Kluwer Law International, 2001, p. 276.
[6] Annabel Newman, 'Swiss Bankers Slam French Report', *Portfolio International*, April 2001,
p. 11.

Nigerian money that was paid from Switzerland, US $126 million was processed by one Jersey-based bank. Of the US $514 million, US $123 million was transferred through the UK in the first place (US $83 million from UK banks and US $40 million from a number of financial institutions in Jersey).

The Nigerian authorities asked for the UK's assistance using the 'civil route' (which involves disclosing evidence) as opposed to pursuing the 'criminal route' (on the basis that the allegation was that public funds had been stolen for personal use). This created a problem because the legislation in the UK prevented the UK Government from freezing bank accounts in the UK until criminal proceedings had started in Nigeria. Individuals had not been charged in Nigeria before the UK's assistance was requested – which meant that the UK's assistance was delayed. (Compare France or Switzerland, where criminal proceedings begin when the magistrate starts his work, thereby allowing assets to be frozen more quickly.) Almost nine months after the request for legal assistance was filed, the UK Home Secretary consented to assist the authorities in Nigeria. The UK's FSA had indicated (8 March 2001) that US$1.3 billion had been processed through twenty-three UK banks. This type of delay causes great frustration to the country requesting assistance. This situation was the catalyst for a review in the UK. Compare the response of the UK to that of its near ('Offshore') counterpart, Jersey, where the authorities offered prompt assistance by freezing a number of accounts. In April 2002, the Abacha family agreed to return US $1billion, in return for charges being dropped against Abacha's son and another associate. (This brought the total identified for return to Nigeria to US $2 billion.)

In 1999, the authorities in Switzerland froze US $700 million. In August 2004, Switzerland undertook to return US $500 million to Nigeria (which is estimated by the Nigerian authorities as being around 25 per cent of the money Abacha stole between 1993 and 1998, when he was in office).

14.5 Corporate governance

Corporate Governance involves a set of relationships between a company's management, its board, its shareholders and other stakeholders. Corporate Governance also provides the structure through which the objectives of the company are set, and the means of attaining those objectives and monitoring performance are determined.[7]

---

[7] 'OECD Principles of Corporate Governance', OECD, 2004, p. 11.

More practically, corporate governance is about making sure that managers remain accountable to shareholders.

On the basis of this definition, it is not surprising that it has been said elsewhere in respect of financial services that '[u]ltimately, all aspects of the management of a financial institution are corporate governance issues . . . If a firm has a good corporate governance culture, a host of other regulatory requirements will automatically fall into place, such as a proper compliance culture and adequate risk-management systems.'[8] More particularly, with respect to regulators and supervisors, Das and Quintyn have identified four fundamental requirements for appropriate regulatory governance, as follows: independence, accountability, transparency and integrity.[9] Llewellyn believes that, in regulatory and supervisory authorities, corporate governance norms are important because 'they determine the effectiveness and efficiency of the agency's operations; they have a powerful impact on the agency's credibility, authority and public standing; and they have an important impact on the authority and credibility of an agency's attempt to encourage and require effective corporate governance arrangements with regulated firms'.[10]

In the UK, corporate governance principles revolve around the Cadbury, Greenbury and Hempel Reports. The Combined Code is a restatement of these reports. It applies in respect of all accounts from 1998 onwards. There are two sections entitled respectively 'Principles of Good Governance' and 'Code of Best Practice'. The Turnbull Guidance represented an attempt to describe how the Combined Code should be interpreted. There appears to be a degree of fragmentation in respect of corporate governance that impairs its effectiveness. For example, no one

[8] Hans Falkena, Roy Bamber, David Llewellyn and Tim Store, *Financial Regulation in South Africa*, Financial Sector Forum, 2001, pp. 36 and 61.

[9] Udaibir S. Das and Marc Quintyn, 'Crisis Prevention and Crisis Management: The Role of Regulatory Governance' in Robert Litan, Michale Pomerleano and V. Sundararajan, eds., *Financial Sector Governance: The Role of the Public and Private Sectors*, Brookings Institution Press, Washington DC, 2002, as quoted in Jeffrey Carmichael, Alexander Fleming and David Llewellyn, *Aligning Financial Supervisory Structures with Country Needs*, World Bank Institute, 2004, chapter 2, p. 82.

[10] Udaibir S. Das and Marc Quintyn, 'Crisis Prevention and Crisis Management: The Role of Regulatory Governance' in Robert Litan, Michale Pomerleano and V. Sundararajan, eds., *Financial Sector Governance: The Role of the Public and Private Sectors*, Brookings Institution Press, Washington DC, 2002, as quoted in Jeffrey Carmichael, Alexander Fleming and David Llewellyn, *Aligning Financial Supervisory Structures with Country Needs*, World Bank Institute, 2004, chapter 2, p. 83.

entity appears to be responsible for regulating adherence to corporate governance principles.

Ms Monica Ridruejo, a Spanish Member of the European Parliament, has drawn up a draft report for the European Parliament's Committee on Economic and Monetary Affairs. The draft report says (inter alia) that '[t]he [European Investment Bank] . . . fails to comply with good corporate governance rules, which it is required to observe in its capacity as a public bank and the largest supranational lending institution in the world'.[11] The EIB is jointly owned by EU countries. The problems concern disclosure of directorships, which disclosure is relevant (and necessary under the Bank's Code of Conduct) in respect of potential conflict of interest scenarios. The article quoted above goes on to say: 'Its board of directors includes people with directorships on at least 11 commercial banks or other companies but the EIB's annual report and website only refer to two of them.' The draft report suggests that senior management and directors should be required to produce an 'annual statement of income, assets and conflicts of interest'. The draft report was not received positively.

As stated above, an appropriate regulatory culture means little more than the adoption of good corporate governance principles. The weakness is that all practitioners will affirm their approval of and approbation for all that sound governance policies entail, but, in practice, this often proves not to be the case. These words are so easy to say, but, like most things to do with regulation, it is what happens in practice that counts.

The Financial Stability Forum regards the OECD's Principles of Corporate Governance as one of the Twelve Key Standards in assessing the soundness of financial systems. As such, 'they form the basis of the corporate governance component of the World Bank/IMF Reports on the Observance of Standards and Codes'.[12] The Chair of the OECD's Steering Group on Corporate Governance, Ms Veronique Ingram, said that 'The revised Principles emphasise the importance of a regulatory framework in corporate governance that clearly defines the responsibilities between different supervisory, regulatory and enforcement authorities.'[13] The Principles were issued in 1999 and cover six areas: the legal and regulatory framework; shareholders' rights; treatment of

[11] G. Tremlett, 'Conflicts at the Heart of the EIB', *Observer*, 7 March 2004, p. 4.
[12] 'OECD Principles of Corporate Governance', OECD, 22 April 2004, p. 9.
[13] 'OECD Issues New Principles', *Chartered Secretary*, June 2004, p. 7.

shareholders; stakeholders; transparency; and responsibilities concerning disclosure to the board.

Meanwhile, in the US, the Sarbanes–Oxley Act has caused substantial controversy (see section 18.16 below). In particular, section 406 of the Act says that issuers must (periodically) disclose whether their senior financial officers must adhere to a code of ethics, and, if not, explain why. The code must be publicly available. However it seems that the Act 'is not in fact proving to be the unalloyed blessing that its creators envisaged . . . [I]t was designed in a panic and rushed through in a blinding fervour of moral indignation.'[14]

Some of the 'corporate governance' type problems that have arisen include the following (see also sections 17.9 and 18.15 below).

14.5.1 France

> France, riven by money laundering and graft scandals reaching to the highest levels of government, is one of the most corrupt of all developed countries . . . according to a recent international study. The report, by Transparency International, shows that, among large developed nations, France is only outdone in the corruption stakes by Italy. Experts say graft affects every corner of life, from sport to politics. So endemic is it, they argue, that it simply represents the French way of doing business . . . Corruption runs from the top to the bottom of French society. A government report in 1996 estimated that the cost of tax evasion in France could be as high as £21 billion per year – equal to two-thirds of the revenue from income tax.[15]

14.5.2 USA

In 1989, the US Government – through the Federal Home Loan Bank Board – was forced to guarantee the assets of almost all savings and loan institutions. This turned out to be one of the most expensive banking failures ever – at a cost of US $124 billion. 'At the root of the problem had been moral hazard: recklessly managed financial institutions had enjoyed cheap funding because the lenders knew they would be bailed out by the deposit insurer, the Federal Savings and Loans Insurance Corporation.'[16]

---

[14] 'Damaged Goods', *The Economist*, 21 May 2005, p. 9.
[15] 'France Sells Its Soul for a Fistful of Francs', *Observer*, 1 July 2001.
[16] David Shirreff, 'Don't Start from Here: A Survey of International Banking', *The Economist*, 21 May 2005, p. 8.

14.5.3 Parmalat

Parmalat, Italy's largest food company, and owned by the Tanzi family, is even more up to date. The case of Parmalat is described more fully because of the direct implications for 'Offshore'. It has operations in 139 plants in thirty countries, employs more than 36,000 people, and generates annual sales of around US$9.2 billion through 214 subsidiaries.

Parmalat encountered liquidity problems towards the end of 2003. On the face of it, the company's large debts were offset by large cash and asset balances, but, on 8 December 2003, the company had difficulty in redeeming a bond of €150 million. Further difficulties ensued, this time in connection with accessing €500 million invested in a Cayman Island-based collective investment scheme. Enrico Bondi was engaged to re-structure the company's finances, but, before he had an opportunity to do much, the company announced that, to protect its creditors, while attempting to restructure its finances, it intended to go into adminis-tration. (The bankruptcy legislation enabling this was only enacted one month before the scandal became public.)

References were made to 'complex international financial arrange-ments and heavy use of off-balance sheet transactions in derivatives such as swaps and options'.[17] The company had more than 120 special pur-pose vehicles in the Netherlands which had issued US $6 billion in bonds.[18] One estimate suggested that there were more than 250 'Offshore' companies established globally (including in the Cayman Islands, Malta and Mauritius). Administration was precipitated by the discovery of a €4 billion hole in the company's accounts. A criminal investigation was launched. 'The probe focuses on Parmalat's Cayman Islands subsidiary, Bonlat, which was last week accused of providing documents falsely showing some Euro €4 billion in assets.'[19] Bonlat was owned by a Maltese company. It appears that the problem surrounds a letter, purportedly emanating from the Bank of America, confirming that the subsidiary had €4 billion on deposit with the bank. It was reported that '[o]n the face of it, a financial holding company seems to

---

[17] 'Parmalat to Seek Administration', BBC News, 23 December 2003.
[18] 'Dutch Consider Regulation of an Ancient Financial Entity in Post Parmalat Backlash', *Offshore Red*, March 2004, p. 14.
[19] 'Parmalat to Seek Administration', BBC News, 23 December 2003.

have been used to grab cash from the operating company, before losing the money through silly use of derivatives and other speculative financial dealings'.[20] The company had set off the large (non-existent) balances reported by the subsidiary against the large amounts of debt on its own balance sheet – but no one queried why such a (seemingly) cash-rich company needed so much debt.

Meanwhile, it was suggested that Mr Tanzi, the firm's founder and former chairman, had siphoned off €800 million. Mr Tanzi and five other executives of the firm were arrested.

Grant Thornton had been Parmalat's auditor from 1990, but, in accordance with Italy's rules regarding the rotation of auditors, Deloitte & Touche became the company's auditor in 1999. However, Grant Thornton did not resign as auditor of Bonlat, and, until December 2003, relied on the letter from the Bank of America as evidence that Bonlat had that amount of assets. At that time, the Bank of America said that the document was forged and Bonlat had no such assets. (It seems that the auditor sent the letter requesting confirmation of the subsidiary's balances through Parmalat's internal mail service.)

By the end of December 2003, Lorenzo Penca, Chairman of Grant Thornton in Italy, had resigned following his arrest in connection with the Parmalat fraud. Meanwhile, the estimate of the amount involved rose to €8 billion, and Dutch regulators announced that they were opening an investigation into shell companies established by Parmalat and which raised more than €5 billion worldwide.

Common features with other frauds include:

- weak auditing practices;
- non-executive directors were not independent (family members and friends);
- Mr Tanzi was both Chairman and Chief Executive; and
- people with knowledge did not make their suspicions known.

> Giulio Tremonti, Italy's finance minister, has suggested that more effective local regulation might have prevented the fraud. He has proposed a law that would change the regulatory responsibilities of the country's different agencies.[21]

[20] 'Milking Lessons', *The Economist*, 3 January 2004, p. 46.
[21] 'Parma Splat', *The Economist*, 17 January 2004, p. 51.

The implications included a reform of financial regulation, with the announcement on 3 February 2004 that the Italian Cabinet had approved proposed legislation to create a new regulator (the proposed name of which was the Authority for the Protection of Savings) to replace Consob (currently responsible for the regulation of the securities market).

Meanwhile, in March 2004, a judge rejected a fast-track procedure on the basis of 'market rigging' charges, indicating that it is not likely that a trial will begin for a very long time.

In the aftermath of the fraud, there were many repercussions. Frits Bolkestein, EU Commissioner for the Internal Market, said that '[t]he financial services industry had better get its act together, and do so fast. We need some real industry leadership to stand up and take charge: to clear out the crooks, expose their unscrupulous practices and curb excessive greed.'[22] The same article included a warning from Mr Bolkestein that 'the role and regulatory control of offshore centres also needed to be tightened'.[23] Further, 'Brussels will target offshore centres in a tightening of corporate governance after the Euro 4 bn ($5.2bn) Parmalat accounting scandal.'[24] Before leaving office, Mr Bolkestein proposed sweeping corporate governance reforms to force transparency in respect of intra-group relations and to make directors responsible for company reports. 'In a bid to prevent future scandals [like Enron and Parmalat] firms would have to disclose in their financial statements details of off-balance sheet items, including special purpose vehicles and activities in offshore centres where supervision is scarce . . . The proposed new rules will ask all companies to fully disclose their ownership structure and their relations with subsidiaries and units offshore to provide a clearer picture of their control structure for shareholders and creditors.'[25]

In respect of another issue in Italy (though this time domestic and not on anything like the same scale as Parmalat), *The Economist* reported in

---

[22] P. Blum, 'EU Warns of Tough Brussels Action over Financial Scandals', www.efinancial-news.com, 12 February 2004, as reported in *GPML Global Press Review*, 16 February 2004, Vol. 2, No. 7, p. 13.

[23] P. Blum, 'EU Warns of Tough Brussels Action over Financial Scandals', *Financial News*, 12 February 2004, as reported in *GPML Global Press Review*, 16 February 2004, Vol. 2, No. 7, p. 14.

[24] R. Hailey, 'Brussels to Target Offshore Sites in Financial Regulation Squeeze', *Lloyd's List*, 12 February 2004, as reported in *GPML Global Press Review*, 16 February 2004, Vol. 2, No. 7, p. 14.

[25] 'EU to Unveil Governance Shake-Up Soon', *Business Times*, Singapore, 17 September 2004.

January 2005[26] that, since 1991, anti-money laundering legislation capped cash transactions at 20 million lire (€10,000). However, no penalties were applied to accounts that were operated by means of a passbook whose balance exceeded that threshold. Reflecting the requirements of an EU Directive, the Italians issued a decree in early 2004 (which was to take effect from the end of January 2005) imposing heavy penalties on such accounts where the balance exceeded €12,500. On 21 January 2005, the effective date was deferred till 31 July 2005. Implementation may have been rendered difficult because of the number of such passbook accounts that are still operational (one estimate puts the figure at 10 million, so it is possible that the balance on a material number of these may breach the law). Elsewhere, passbook accounts are old-fashioned and are no longer common – except perhaps in respect of older people and children. However, because of the 'bearer' element, they are very useful for money laundering purposes. This is yet another example of how a simple and convenient financial instrument – mainly used by widows and orphans – can be abused by wrongdoers.

> But worse than Parmalat was the sale of many thousands of bonds issued by unrated Italian companies and offered to Italian mutual funds with minimal due diligence. Many of the bonds defaulted, damaging customers' confidence in Italian banks and bankers.[27]

It was reported in July 2005 that 'Calisto Tanzi, the founder and former Chairman of Parmalat was ordered by an Italian Judge to stand trial in September (along with 15 others) on fraud charges related to the bankruptcy in 2003 of the dairy company. The Judge sentenced 11 people in the same case this week under plea bargain deals.'[28]

> The saga cast regulators, bankers and auditors in a desperately unfavourable light for not spotting the fraud much more quickly than they did . . . Maybe Enrico Bondi, special administrator of Parmalat, has done too good a job of cleaning house. Rather than breaking up the firm, he decided to keep it alive and save thousands of jobs. In July Parmalat revealed healthy first half profits. It is planning to relist on the Milan stock exchange in October.[29]

---

[26] 'Pass', *The Economist*, 29 January 2005, p. 67.
[27] David Shirreff, 'Allegro ma non Troppo: A Survey of International Banking', *The Economist*, 21 May 2005, p. 15.
[28] 'Business', *The Economist*, 2 July 2005, p. 9.
[29] 'Another Year, Another Scandal', *The Economist*, 6 August 2005, p. 55.

14.5.4 National Australia Bank

In a report after a scandal involving NAB's currency options team, the Australian Prudential Regulation Authority said that 'NAB's internal control systems failed at every level to detect the irregular currency options trading . . . [A]s long as the business unit turned a profit, other shortcomings could be overlooked.'[30] NAB is Australia's largest bank.

14.5.5 Shell

Shell was accused of announcing falsified figures in respect of its oil reserves between 1998 and 2003. The UK's Financial Services Authority accused Shell of market abuse. The FSA imposed a fine of £17 million for misconduct amounting to market abuse. The US Securities and Exchange Commission meanwhile imposed their own fine of US $120 million.[31] One newspaper commented that '[t]he reserves fiasco revealed a serious lack of central audit reporting within the group'.[32]

14.5.6 Banca Antonveneta

Italy's governance problems did not end with Parmalat. There were contested bids for Banca Antonveneta by Banca Popolare Italiana (BPI) and ABN Amro.

> After ABN Amro announced in March that it would bid for Antonveneta, BPI raised its small stake in the bank to 29 per cent in several steps that involved allegedly illegal financial manoeuvres, now the subject of investigation. The central bank approved each step. Against this background, Italy's magistrates stepped in. Several weeks ago in Milan prosecutors launched a probe into allegations that BPI had violated securities laws. On July 25 they confiscated shares owned by BPI and ten investors amounting to 4 per cent of Antonveneta's stock. On July 27 Consob suspended, belatedly, its approval of BPI's bid. The Bank of Italy finally followed suit. On August 2 a Milan judge ordered Gianpiero Fiorani, BPI's boss, suspended from his job for 60 days, for fear that he might tamper

[30] 'Regulator Reins in NAB with New Measures', *Financial Times*, 25 March 2004, p. 19.
[31] 'FSA Exposes Long Running Deception by Shell Executives', http://businesstimesonline. co.uk, 25 August 2004.
[32] 'Shell Becomes a Normal Company', *Financial Times*, 29 October 2004.

with evidence . . . All this has left Italy's reputation as a sensible place in which to invest more than a little damaged.[33]

14.5.7 American Interntional Group

In its annual report for 2004, AIG, the world's largest insurer, reduced the net income figure reported by US $1.32 billion to US $9.73 billion compared to figures originally released in February. 'Over the past five years, the company said that the total amount overstated was $3.9 billion . . . In its new filing with the SEC, AIG acknowledged accounting improprieties, including "improper or inappropriate transactions" and transactions that may have involved misrepresentations to members of the management, regulators and AIG's independednt auditors.'[34]

14.6 A long list

The list of corporate scandals onshore is lengthy. Here are a few examples: ABB, Elan, EM.TV, Enron (USA), Kirsch (Germany), Lernout & Hauspie (Belgium), Royal Ahold (the Netherlands), Skandia (Sweden), WorldCom (USA) and so on. The following quote summarises some of the events of 2003:

> [A] raft of banking scandals hit the headlines. Money laundering con-
> tinued to be an issue, with Abbey National fined a record £2.3m for
> failings in its procedures and Citibank and Union Bancaire Privée in
> Switzerland named in investigations into the laundering of public money
> by General Sani Abacha, the former Nigerian dictator. Wall Street Banks
> came to a $1.4bn settlement with the regulator on conflicts of interest but
> the story did not die down as an analyst at Bank of America Securities (not
> involved in the settlement) was fined in December and Bank of America
> itself promised to cooperate with the authorities in the on-going investi-
> gation of the $7000bn mutual fund industry.[35]

A recent edition of *The Economist*[36] listed the following

---

[33] 'Another Year, Another Scandal', *The Economist*, 6 August 2005, p. 54.
[34] 'News', *Chartered Secretary*, July 2005, p. 8.
[35] 'Taking Care of Business Ethically Must Be Priority for New Year', *The Banker*, 1 January 2004, as reported in *GPML Global Press Review*, United Nations Office on Drugs and Crime, 5 January 2004, Vol. 2 No 1.
[36] 'The World This Week, Business', *The Economist*, 20 August 2005, p. 7.

Commerzbank confirmed that its Chief Executive, Klaus Peter Muller, is being investigated by German authorities as part of a money laundering inquiry involving a Russian telecoms firm . . . Germany's financial regulator BaFin has opened a formal inquiry into possible insider trading in shares of Daimler-Chrysler . . . J. P. Morgan, Chase and Toronto-Dominion Bank agreed to settle their part in a lawsuit brought by Enron against ten banks that it alleges 'aided and abetted' the accounting fraud which led to the energy trader's bankruptcy in 2001. J. P. Morgan will pay $350m and Toronto-Dominion at least $70m.

Auditors have been involved as follows. Enron's and WorldCom's problems were followed by the criminal conviction and bankruptcy of Andersen (but note that, on 31 May 2005, the Supreme Court in the USA overturned the conviction: see section 13.6.2 above), KPMG was embarrassed over Xerox, PriceWaterhouseCoopers over Tyco and Deloittes over Adelphia. On the basis of reliance upon auditors globally (but not least in respect of financial services centres), this is not encouraging reading. Since regulators depend a great deal on the work of the external auditor, this situation is parlous for the regulator.

'. . . The right response is to adopt the strongest, not the laxest, regimes possible. And that means enforcement of international accounting standards and tough regulation of auditors.'[37] (In this respect, from 1 January 2005, all groups listed in the European Union have been required to prepare their annual accounts in accordance with the International Financial Reporting Standards (IFRS). It has been estimated that this affects 7,000 companies.[38])

14.7 Bearer shares

Many 'Offshore Finance Centres' have been berated because of their tolerance of bearer shares. In response, most OFCs listened to the criticism voiced – concerning how easily bearer shares could be used for fraudulent business – and took action to prevent such abuses. In France, Germany, Italy, Spain and the UK, bearer shares are still acceptable.

[37] 'Ahold Out', *The Economist*, 1 March 2001, p. 12.
[38] 'So Far, So Good', *The Economist*, 18 June 2005, p. 69.

14.8 European Union

It was reported (October 2004), in a study by PricewaterhouseCoopers, that all twenty-five members of the recently enlarged European Union (see Table 9 in Appendix 1 below) has one or more tax rules that contravene European Community treaty law.[39]

The European Commission provides funds to the Centre for European Policy Studies (CEPS). Recently, the CEPS produced a paper that 're-inforces the impression that European financial regulation is a chaotic building site rather than the advertised level playing field. It argues that coordination between regulators is not developed enough to handle a Europe-wide financial crisis, and that consumers . . . do not have enough say in shaping financial sector reform.'[40]

14.9 A closing comment

'. . . Decades of international cooperation on regulatory standards through the Basel Committee didn't stop BCCI or Barings or Daiwa. Fraud is fraud, and there is only so much one can do to detect it and to prevent it from happening.'[41] This is probably a fair statement, but there is no inference that remedial action is restricted to either 'Onshore' or 'Offshore' centres exclusively.

---

[39] PriceWaterhouseCoopers study, as reported in www.offshoreinvestment.com, Issue 151, November 2004, p. 4.
[40] David Shirreff, 'A Blurred Euro-Vision: A Survey of International Banking', *The Economist*, 21 May 2005, p. 16.
[41] Wai Wong, 'Corporate Governance: The Debate Continues', *Chartered Secretary*, October 2000, p. 20.

15

Small islands and 'Offshore'

[T]he safest way for a developing country to demonstrate equivalent standards to the rich countries is to adopt (superficially) identical standards.[1]

15.1 Introduction

It is worth noting that, 'of the ten richest countries in the world in terms of GDP per head, only two have more than 5 million people: the United States with 260 million and Switzerland, with 7 million. A further two have populations over 1 million: Norway with 4 million and Singapore, with 3 million. The remaining half dozen have fewer than 1 million people.'[2] The point is that jurisdictions do not need to be large to be successful – but that does not mean that it is easier for small jurisdictions to be successful. Nevertheless, size may be a significant variable. Many of the jurisdictions which are regarded as 'Offshore Finance Centres' are small islands – and this chapter explores some of the implications.

15.2 Economic expedience

It has been said that '[s]mall jurisdictions must not lose heart at the global project taking place around them – it does not necessarily spell their doom and decline and may indeed provide them with new, niche opportunities'.[3]

---

[1] Jonathan Ward, 'Is Basel II Voluntary for Developing Countries?', *The Financial Regulator*, December 2002, Vol. 7, No. 3, p. 55.

[2] 'When Small is Beautiful', *The Economist*, 20 December 2003, p. 117.

[3] David Fabri and Godfrey Baldacchino, *The MFSC: A Study in Micro-State Dependency Management?*, p. 159, as quoted in *Offshore Finance Centres and Tax Havens: The Rise of Global Capital*, ed. Mark P. Hampton and Jason P. Abbott, 1999, Macmillan Press Ltd, Chapter 6.

Small islands have at least one thing in common with other jurisdictions – which is that all must pay their way. Some island centres have
found that the establishment of an 'Offshore' finance industry is one way
to achieve this. 'Most OFCs are located in small island economies and
offshore finance is often seen as a useful economic development strategy
for such places.'[4] It has to be said that the fundamental requisites for
entering this market were less demanding previously than currently, but,
as a subsequent chapter shows, there are still many centres that want to
establish themselves as financial services centres. Like everything else, the
higher the quality, the higher the cost.

A jurisdiction considering establishing an 'Offshore' financial services
activity (see also Chapter 21 below) should consider the following
requirements: political stability; credibility; positive international reputation; local consensus; and a sound financial infrastructure. Probably,
most jurisdictions believe that they satisfy all these criteria already:
'OFCs provide a useful and relatively inexpensive strategy of economic
development for a number of small states and islands.'[5] This statement
bears scrutiny. For example, the cost of establishing and maintaining an
effective regulatory authority is far from cheap – if substance is to prevail
over form. It has been said that, 'while a financial centre can be a useful
addition to their economy, significant infrastructural investment is
needed to provide an internationally accepted minimum supervisory
system.'[6] Internationally, inadequate funding is not an acceptable excuse
for failure to adopt appropriate regulatory practices or to adhere to
international standards. If this fundamental criterion cannot be overcome, then it would be better if the services that require the (additional)
regulatory resources were to stop (or not start as the case may be).
'Jurisdictions with low levels of income have a much lower rate of
compliance with all the assessed standards than wealthier jurisdictions.
Such jurisdictions often have low volumes of financial activity and many
of the poorer jurisdictions have eliminated or are phasing out their OFC

---

[4] *Offshore Finance Centres and Tax Havens: The Rise of Global Capital*, ed. Mark P. Hampton
and Jason P. Abbott, 1999, Macmillan Press Ltd, Chapter 1 ('The Risk (and Fall?) of
Offshore Finance in the Global Economy, Editors' Introduction'), p. 6.

[5] *Offshore Finance Centres' and Tax Havens: The Rise of Global Capital*, ed. Mark
P. Hampton and Jason P. Abbott, 1999, Macmillan Press Ltd, Chapter 1 ('The Risk (and
Fall?) of Offshore Finance in the Global Economy, Editors' Introduction'), p. 15.

[6] 'Filling a Gap in Global Surveillance, Finance and Development', in Salim M. Darbar,
R. Barry Johnston and Mary G. Zephirin, *Assessing Offshore Financial Centres*, September
2003, p. 35.

activities.[7] The other side of this coin is that the funding in many jurisdictions comes from licence fees, so the implications of (additional) resources must be taken into account in setting fees. Naturally, if the fees are too high, the jurisdiction risks lack of demand. The additional implications listed below imply that the practice is less straightforward than the theory.

Nevertheless, many small islands have created a successful 'Offshore' finance sector from fairly humble beginnings – and the strategy has paid off. To quote merely two examples: at one time, one person in four in Jersey worked in the finance sector and the Isle of Man derives nearly 40 per cent of its national income from its finance sector.

Subsequent to all the attention that has been given to 'Offshore' in the recent past, the controls that now need to be adopted to make an 'Offshore' centre credible demand a certain critical mass. Those jurisdictions that are unable to generate this critical mass still need the controls and should not delude themselves by believing that less rigorous or fewer controls will suffice. Trying to cut corners in this area is precisely the sort of approach that has created negative feelings and suspicions about the integrity of 'Offshore'. However, 'the impact of large neighbours on island OFCs can be serious, ranging from economic pressure or the threat of sanctions, judicial pressure to break local bank secrecy laws, direct action in covert operations such as Tradewinds, or unilateral treaty re-negotiations which reduce offshore advantages. Island and microstate economies, by virtue of their smallness and openness often have no alternatives to developing service industries such as OFCs.'[8] The problem of critical mass should not be underestimated. The IMF has said that: 'The lower income jurisdictions face the biggest challenge to build their supervisory capacity. Some of these jurisdictions with limited resources may first have to decide whether the benefits of developing a financial centre will outweigh the cost of achieving internationally acceptable minimum supervisory standards.'[9]

Mutual assistance requests (where a jurisdiction receives a request from prosecutors elsewhere for assistance in connection with a prosecution case: see section 3.10 above) are a case in point. In order for the

---

[7] Mark Hampton, *The Offshore Interface*, Macmillan Press Ltd, 1996, p. 117.
[8] 'Offshore Financial Centres, The Assessment Program, An Update', IMF, 12 March 2004, p. 9.
[9] IMF's Progress Report, para. 5, 25 February 2005, see section 10.12.5 above.

system to work effectively, an appropriately sophisticated prosecution system must be in place already – and the jurisdiction must be able
to bear whatever costs arise (which may include litigation). This is an
area of vulnerability – and this fact will not escape the attention of
criminals. On the assumption that the conduct which prompted the
request in the first place has taken place abroad, a letter of request must
be sent to the relevant country. It may take some time to collect the
relevant evidence – especially if extradition is involved. The attendant
costs for the 'Offshore' jurisdiction may be material.

On the other side of the coin, the developments in technology have
made a real impact in this respect. What would otherwise have been
insurmountable difficulties in respect of location and time differences are
no longer problematic criteria. For example, it is possible to incorporate
companies online in some jurisdictions.

15.3 The services of OFCs are in demand

Despite the fact that the 'Offshore' concept has existed for a relatively
short time, the volume of business transacted 'Offshore' is very large. The
data to support this have been provided already, but, to emphasise the
point being made here, some additional data are quoted below. For
example, it has been said that 'foreign direct investment by G7 countries
in a number of jurisdictions in the Caribbean and in the South Pacific
island states, which are generally considered to be low tax jurisdictions,
increased more than five fold over the period 1985–1994, to more than
\$200 billion'.[10] Further, 'over 1 trillion dollars (US) is invested in offshore
funds and . . . the number of funds has increased by more than 1400 per cent
over the last 15 years'.[11]

Growth continues, but at a slower pace than in the heyday of the 1970s
and early 1980s. Since then, the attractiveness and need for 'Offshore
Finance Centres' has declined because of global changes[12] including:

- the OPEC surpluses have not recurred;
- the reduction/elimination of reserve requirements;

---

[10] 'Harmful Tax Competition – An Emerging Global Issue', OECD, 1998, para. 35, p. 17.
[11] Jeffrey Owens, 'Tax in 2010', *OECD Observer*, 27 June 2000.
[12] 'Financial Havens, Banking Secrecy and Money Laundering', United Nations Office for
Drug Control and Crime Prevention, Issue 8 of the UNDCP Technical Series, Double
Issue 34 and 35 of the *Crime Prevention and Criminal Justice Newsletter*, 1998, p. 22.

- reduced levels of taxes; and
- liberalised regulations.

Apart from these factors, it has been said that 'tax havens and OFCs are central to the operation of the contemporary financial markets'.[13] This point is pursued later because it is a matter of some debate. Amidst all the changes described, there are some more fundamental 'drivers'. If there is to be a continuing role for OFCs, they must be able to demonstrate their legitimate status within the global financial environment. In fact, 'this process of attempted legitimisation of OFCs is commonly defined by pointing to the danger that, if the attractiveness of the more respectable centres was reduced, the same activities would move to more delinquent jurisdictions which would be harder to control. It is certainly true that there is no shortage of states attempting to break into the offshore market, and that the lack of other economic opportunities makes many of them vulnerable to corruption.'[14]

15.4 Small islands offer a conducive infrastructure

It might be reasonably asked what particular characteristics small island states manifest that make them particularly appropriate as financial services centres. 'Small states (often islands) which generally had been (and sometimes still remain) colonial dependencies, offered a number of advantages. Their colonial heritage generally gave them a modern style legal system, a currency tied to that of the mother country, and in many cases the benefit of tax treaties which had been extended to them. Their small populations could not easily generate revenues to finance the government.'[15]

The attractiveness of small islands is nothing new. 'Over the past thirty years, a large number of minor states and small island economies (SIEs) around the world have attracted "Offshore Finance" and tax haven activity. Their low levels of effective taxation, minimal regulatory

---

[13] *Offshore Finance Centres and Tax Havens: The Rise of Global Capital*, ed. Mark P. Hampton and Jason P. Abbott, 1999, Macmillan Press Ltd, Chapter 1 ('The Risk (and Fall?) of Offshore Finance in the Global Economy: Editors' Introduction'), p. 13.

[14] *Offshore Finance Centres and Tax Havens: The Rise of Global Capital*, ed. Mark P. Hampton and Jason P. Abbott, 1999, Macmillan Press Ltd, Chapter 3 ('Offshore: The State as Legal Fiction', by Sol Picciotto), p. 68.

[15] *Offshore Finance Centres and Tax Havens: The Rise of Global Capital*, ed. Mark P. Hampton and Jason P. Abbott, 1999, Macmillan Press Ltd, Chapter 3 ('Offshore: The State as Legal Fiction', by Sol Picciotto), p. 53.

regimes and bank secrecy made these offshore finance centres (OFCs) highly attractive to global financial capitalism.'[16] Further, 'SIEs offer geopolitical advantages that are particularly attractive to the interests of financial capitalism, namely, tax advantages, independence from onshore regulation, judicial independence, and secrecy in the political and banking spheres. Their relatively unsophisticated status – evidenced by the limited experience of both politicians and civil servants in matters relating to financial services regulations – create a political economy in which sophisticated legal and tax accounting professionals are able to persuade the key players within the state to introduce a variety of devices which serve their special interests.'[17]

The innate opportunity that OFCs offer for market research on new products and services is not to be underestimated: '[T]here are plenty of examples where the more flexible and innovative atmosphere of offshore has enabled offshore centres to invent or pioneer products and services which remain largely exclusive to the offshore world' (captives; cell companies; limited liability partnerships; managed banks; asset protection trusts).[18]

Two factors which contribute are the time zone and proximity to a larger trading country. An OFC, appropriately located, can provide an interface that enables trading to continue in an OFC that is just opening as the market elsewhere is closing. Proximity to 'Onshore' is implied by the word 'Offshore' and some centres use this to describe themselves, for example, as 'Offshore Europe'. However, for the reasons provided in the opening chapters, this type of description is now less popular than hitherto.

Small islands must be able to take measures to attract mobile business if they are to nurture the economy of their own domicile. The

[16] *Offshore Finance Centres and Tax Havens: The Rise of Global Capital*, ed. Mark P. Hampton and Jason P. Abbott, 1999, Macmillan Press Ltd, Chapter 7 ('A Legislature for Hire: The Capture of the State in Jersey's Offshore Finance Centre', by John Christensen and Mark P. Hampton), p. 166.

[17] *Offshore Finance Centres and Tax Havens: The Rise of Global Capital*, ed. Mark P. Hampton and Jason P. Abbott, 1999, Macmillan Press Ltd, Chapter 7 ('A Legislature for Hire: The Capture of the State in Jersey's Offshore Finance Centre', by John Christensen and Mark P. Hampton), p. 168.

[18] *Offshore Finance Centres and Tax Havens: The Rise of Global Capital*, ed, Mark P. Hampton and Jason P. Abbott, 1999, Macmillan Press Ltd, Chapter 9 ('Financial Regulation and Supervision Offshore: Guernsey: A Case Study', by Christopher M. Le Marchant), p. 215.

attractiveness of 'Offshore Finance' includes the potential to expand the infrastructure of small islands to include service providers of all types (for example, accountants and lawyers), who have benefited to no small degree from the opportunities that arise 'Offshore'. The opportunities spawned by this type of activity in a small island state may be significant because they are not restricted to the two professional activities described above. For example, new businesses need computer hardware and software, office premises, staff, furniture and other office equipment. They also need utilities and an ongoing supply of materials. In summary, there are many spin-offs.

15.5 There is a natural good fit

'Offshore financial centres and small island locations may appear to have been intended for each other.'[19] There may be no satisfactory alternative.

> From a strictly cultural, closed economy perspective, many small jurisdictions are simply non-viable. To make matters worse, long and deep colonial penetration has established a standard of living more akin to extant Western levels amid one which is simply impossible to maintain on the basis of natural resource endowment and productive capacity. They have thus placed themselves as strategically internationally attractive platforms . . . International Finance, and its diverse economic spin-offs, is a lucrative form of transfer one would rather not go without.[20]

This absence of satisfactory alternatives for many small island states has been recognised by the UN and by the OECD because these factors are inextricably linked to economic expediency and/or necessity. To operate properly as an OFC requires substantial resources and some jurisdictions do not have the critical mass to generate enough contribution to enable the appropriate infrastructures to be created and maintained (see above). The worst possible outcome is that lower standards are adopted. The other possibility is unwillingness to spend because until

---

[19] *Offshore Finance Centres and Tax Havens: The Rise of Global Capital*, ed. Mark P. Hampton and Jason P. Abbott, 1999, Macmillan Press Ltd, Chapter 6 ('The MFSC: A Study in Micro-State Dependency Management?', by David Fabri and Godfrey Baldacchino), p. 141.

[20] *Offshore Finance Centres and Tax Havens: The Rise of Global Capital*, ed. Mark P. Hampton and Jason P. Abbott, 1999, Macmillan Press Ltd, Chapter 6 ('The MFSC: A Study in Micro-State Dependency Management?', by David Fabri and Godfrey Baldacchino), p. 161.

recently it was considered unnecessary to raise standards too high since this would inhibit new business. These are critical factors because the room (globally) for jurisdictions without appropriate standards is reducing at a very rapid rate – and rightly so.

15.6 The involvement of outsiders

In all walks of life, including 'Offshore', those who are inexperienced learn most from those who already have an appropriate level of skill and/ or experience. Consequently, at the outset, and possibly for some years, new and fairly new OFCs will probably feel the need to engage expatriates, either as consultants or on the basis of a short, perhaps renewable contract. Sometimes this gives rise to difficulties. Expatriates are expensive because by definition they have very particular skills and experience which the engaging jurisdiction wants to hire (not to acquire) for a short time. Further, expatriates frequently derive from a country where the level of salaries is higher than in the island jurisdiction that wants to engage them. Salary levels and value for money may become contentious issues. On the other hand, expatriates will not know as much about the local environment as residents, and have less at stake since after their assignment ends their responsibilities terminate. Importantly, expatriates must be able to develop a rapport with those who engage them because (almost by definition) tensions will develop as changes are proposed and implemented.

Accordingly, the involvement of 'foreigners' should not be taken for granted, and neither should the effect of the local environment on the foreigners engaged. 'The latter [expatriates] must accept a condition of cultural alienation which, however, affords at least a comfortable degree of social distance. Keeping oneself at arm's length may not provide the best views and details of the case material, but it certainly provides a platform from which one can more comfortably expand one's views and criticism.'[21]

The expatriate regulator in an 'Offshore' jurisdiction is frequently in an invidious situation. He or she may be resented by both regulatory

---

[21] *Offshore Finance Centres and Tax Havens: The Rise of Global Capital*, ed. Mark P. Hampton and Jason P. Abbott, 1999, Macmillan Press Ltd, Chapter 6 ('The MFSC: A Study in Micro-State Dependency Management?', by David Fabri and Godfrey Baldacchino), p. 158.

colleagues and local practitioners. The first group may regard the new-comer as some sort of rival or unnecessary 'know all'. The second group may consider the newcomer as a meddler who knows little or nothing of any local matter of importance, including the local legislation and peculiarities of the local environment. The foreigner must learn to man-age these relationships quickly or he or she will not survive, irrespective of the potential to add value.

When changes are proposed by such expatriates, they may be un-acceptable because they will be regarded as disadvantageous to new business. The 'new boy on the block' will – for a time – find it difficult to persuade practitioners of the need to change. This may be because they resent the newcomer or because they are too short-sighted or prejudiced or perhaps because they are too comfortable to accommodate any change, but, importantly, it may be because they are right. Time usually tells who has got it right. (See section 7.12 above.)

'Creating this industry's equivalent, desirable legislation, competent practitioners and efficient courts is the work of seasoned professionals: lawyers, accountants, trust officers and marketing specialists. Govern-ments elected from tiny populations must face up to the fact that they have to turn to such professionals, both local and imported, to meet the evolving and ever more sophisticated needs of the international consumer – or else they will fail and the business will go elsewhere.'[22]

15.7 Apparent dominance of finance within the economy

At first sight, the dominance of finance within the economy of an island environment is unproblematic. However, if and when the development of products and services within the jurisdiction compete more than marginally for scarce resources, problems may ensue. Many factors impinge on decisions concerning the allocation of resources – and proper weight must be given to them all if the economy is to be in equilibrium – all other things being equal. Thus, divergent opinions may arise in respect of how much resource should be devoted to what.

---

[22] Susan Le Murra Kelly, 'Introduction', in *The OFC Report 2004*, p. 9. Some further insight in respect of integrating staff (albeit in a different context) is provided in a chapter. 'Creating an Effective Regulatory Culture in Estonia' by Andres Trink, in *Aligning Financial Supervisory Structures with Country Needs* (edited by Jeffrey Carmichael, Alexander Fleming and David Llewellyn), pp. 223 *et seq.* (World Bank Institute, September 2004).

Difficult decisions may have to be taken concerning immediate needs and medium- to long-term needs. To what extent should a sacrifice be made today to provide for tomorrow?

Depending on circumstances, other problems may be (unwittingly) created if sufficient numbers of 'outsiders' arrive in a small island. This might lead to increased demand and therefore higher prices for accommodation – making it more difficult for (local) young people to be able to afford their own homes. Further, foreigners will import their own preferences and values – which might distort local preferences and priorities. Islanders may – in due course – feel that their very culture is threatened to the extent that they would prefer to sacrifice the added value if only the foreigners would return to wherever they came from.

15.8 Lack of influence externally

It is a truism that, globally, larger nations exert more influence than smaller nations – whether in respect of 'Offshore Finance' or not. However, the irony is that smaller islands are probably substantially more adaptable and flexible than their larger 'Onshore' neighbours. Herein lies an opportunity to develop niche strategies. However, the secret is not to throw out the baby with the bath water. It is not possible to be all things to all people and small islands sometimes try – to discover in due course that it is to their cost. In respect of 'Offshore' activity, flexibility and adaptability should not be interpreted to mean that the island jurisdiction should try to be all things to all people or that the promoter of the business should expect to receive everything he requests.

Further, because of their limited influence, small islands sometimes join together in trade organisations (or similar) so that their cumulative influence exceeds the sum of their individual voices. This is the basis on which (for example) the Offshore Group of Banking Supervisors has earned the opportunity to influence the prestigious Basel Committee on Banking Supervision.

The Organization of Eastern Caribbean States (OECS) comprises eight small, independent island states which include Antigua and Barbuda, Dominica, Grenada, St Lucia, St Vincent and the Grenadines, Montserrat, St Kitts and Nevis and the British Virgin Islands. The OECS is in the process of creating an economic union and already has a common currency, aviation and telecommunications authority. The Eastern Caribbean Central Bank regulates domestic finance for the eight islands and administers the common currency. A regional stock exchange was launched in 2001, as was the Eastern Caribbean Securities Regulatory Commission. The concessions that once protected the sugar, rum and banana industries have diminished. Tourism remains important, but produces less revenue than is needed to compensate for depleted contributions to GDP from elsewhere – and 'Offshore Finance' services provide the answer.

Joining forces produces many synergies and creates potential that would otherwise be impossible to generate.

15.9 Currency of advantages

It has been said that a trader is only as good as his last deal. The same might be said of small islands. The turbulence of the economic environment and the pace of change within the financial environment – brought about at least in part by globalisation – requires continuous adaptation by small islands – if they are to retain their attractiveness. It is therefore of little value to stand still if the services being demanded by users of 'Offshore' islands are in a continuous change mode. Failure to keep up is to be left behind. The implications of this type of need should not be underestimated, since the cost of appropriate technology and manpower is not insignificant.

> Island governments must be forever alert to the possibility of institutional divestment and to the fact that their meso-economic actors are not obliged to have local national loyalties: their allegiance is to the wider global company advantage and not to any narrow specific national territorial advantage.[23]

The changing global environment is in some respects not conducive to financial services since investors do not like change – especially because longer term investments are based on criteria that the investor anticipates will not change before the investment matures. However, when change is the order of the day, it would be suicidal for 'Offshore Centres' not to keep up. Finance centres that fail to innovate and to exercise creativity on an ongoing basis will lose their way (see below).

---

[23] R. A. Johns and C. M. Le Marchant, 'Offshore Britain: The British Isles Finance Centre Since the Abolition of UK Exchange Controls', *National Westminster Bank Quarterly Review*, May 1993, p. 54.

15.10 Uniqueness

As the book of Ecclesiastes reminds us, there is nothing new under the sun. We should therefore remember that, in respect of 'Offshore Finance Centres', what seems like a unique idea today will be copied almost immediately by others serving similar markets. There is substantial homogeneity in the 'Offshore' arena and excess demand (by jurisdictions) over the supply of acceptable business. Small islands probably have to adopt some sort of niche service, skill or activity. Failure to do so will be a limiting factor on the extent to which the jurisdiction can be promoted abroad successfully. Without doubt, successful development has more to do with unique characteristics than with general characteristics. It has been said that '[t]he fundamental competitive advantage of a small economy is the ability to be hospitable to the world, [and] . . . nimble'.[24] The key question is what makes the jurisdiction different from every other jurisdiction – because it is these differences that demonstrate uniqueness. The only alternative is sameness – which, in this case, is not a clever marketing strategy.

15.11 Value of the business generated

The fact of the matter is that there are too many jurisdictions competing for the limited pool of (acceptable) business. One of two things happens. Either, the jurisdiction attempts to win the business – virtually at any price – and this reduces the value of attracting the business in the first place. 'Consequently, the logic that drives almost all small island economies towards "Offshore Finance" may signal their demise.'[25] Alternatively, the jurisdiction drops its standards and accepts inferior business (of which there is always a more than sufficient supply). The latter course is likely to be catastrophic in the medium to long term and the former course is not optimum either. The answer probably lies somewhere in between the two (the future for 'Offshore' is explored in Chapter 20 below).

---

[24] Alvin Wint, 'Trouble in Paradise', *The Economist*, 23 November 2002, p. 50.
[25] *Offshore Finance Centres and Tax Havens: The Rise of Global Capital*, ed. Mark P. Hampton and Jason P. Abbott, 1999, Macmillan Press Ltd, Chapter 8 ('Mahathir, Malaysia and the Labuan International Offshore Finance Centre: Treasure Island, Pet Project or Ghost Town?', by Jason P. Abbott), p. 207.

The OECD's work has added another dimension to the status of 'Offshore Centres'. If such jurisdictions impose the OECD's tax rates, it is likely to worsen the plight of the economy because no new business will come and what is already there may migrate. Unemployment will rise and GDP will decline.

15.12 Concentration of business

> Typically, island micro-states suffer from the 'concentration phenomenon'; those which have entered the international finance industry do so with a small number of 'flagship' institutions on which the destiny of a whole industry often depends. Much hope and therefore much responsibility is placed on what are often no more than a handful of institutions and typically one small regulatory body.[26]

Like all systems, the 'Offshore Finance' system will operate best when it is in equilibrium.

Regulatory resources are often minimal 'Offshore'. Without adequate regulation, a jurisdiction will never win the credibility needed for long-term success. In the meantime, the regulated population will exert too much influence, and will, given the slightest opportunity, dictate the terms. Their leverage boils down to giving them what they demand or else they will leave. This is a vicious circle which serves no useful purpose and will lead inevitably to stagnation and an introverted focus.

If a jurisdiction cannot attain the critical mass it needs to operate effectively, its attempts to move forward in an appropriate direction will take a very long time to achieve. This will lead to suggestions that regulatory requirements are too onerous and preventing new business being stimulated. If the response is to reduce standards, this will be the first step on a slippery slope that is destined to produce sub-optimal results.

15.13 Conclusion

This chapter can be concluded by the following quotation – which concerns developing countries, and by extension small island jurisdictions.

---

[26] P. Selwyn, 'Industrial Development in Peripheral Small Countries', in *Development Policy in Small Countries*, ed. P. Selwyn, Croom Helm, Beckenham, 1975, as cited in *Offshore Finance Centres and Tax Havens: The Rise of Global Capital*, ed. M. P. Hampton and J. P. Abbott, Macmillan Press, 1999.

Most important, developing countries need effective governments, with strong and independent judiciaries, democratic accountability, openness and transparency and freedom from the corruption that has stifled the effectiveness of the public sector and the growth of the private. What they should ask of the international community is only this: the acceptance of their need, and right, to make their own choices, in ways which reflect their own political judgments about who, for instance, should bear what risks. They should be encouraged to adopt bankruptcy laws and regulatory structures adapted to their own situation, not to accept templates designed by and for the more developed countries[27]

15.14 Population Density Comparatives

Table 15 in Appendix 1 provides some comparative figures for a number of international financial services centres.

---

[27] Joseph Stiglitz, *Globalisation and its Discontents*, Penguin Books, 2002, p. 251.

16

Some information on particular centres

A man who has lived in many places is not likely to be deceived by the local errors of his native village; the scholar has lived in many times and is therefore in some degree immune from the great cataract of nonsense that pours from the press and the microphone of his own age.[1]

16.1 Introduction

It has been estimated that 13 million people are employed in financial services jobs in mature industrial economies.[2] In the introduction to this book, mention was made of perceptions that members of the public have about 'Offshore'. Sadly, many of these perceptions derive (at least in part) from what appears to be relative ignorance about the 'Offshore' environment. This is perhaps most acute in respect of statistical information.

16.2 What is the problem?

In one sense, the absence of detailed information should not be much of a surprise since 'confidentiality' is one of the pillars on which 'Offshore' environments are constructed. In another sense, why should there be any gaps in aggregate figures? Is there something to hide?

Some figures are available through the Bank for International Settlements, but these are incomplete because, according to the IMF,[3]

- only major OFCs report and, as non-reporting OFCs grow, the absence of their figures is even more important;
- the data that are available do not fit the patterns of data already developed;

---

[1] C. S. Lewis, *The Weight of Glory: Learning in War-Time*, pp. 58–9.
[2] 'The Cusp of a Revolution', *Deloitte Research*, November 2003.
[3] 'Offshore Financial Centres', IMF Background Paper, IMF, 23 June 2000.

- off-balance sheet activity is not counted; and
- relevant data for non-bank financial institutions are excluded. This includes insurance companies, mutual funds, private trusts and international business companies.

Additional information is available through the IMF's Coordinated Portfolio Investment Survey (see section 2.09 above) and through the Information Framework (see section 2.10 above). Supplementary information is also available from the respective websites and annual reports of each jurisdiction.

16.3 What do we know?

'Statistics relating to "Offshore Centres" are currently often inadequate for monitoring and analysis.'[4] Nevertheless, information that is available includes the data, as it applied in 1998, set out in Table 16 in Appendix 1.

Note the value of 'Global Assets Under Management' relevant to the value of 'Global Foreign Direct Investment'.[5]

Leaving the debate about confidentiality to one side for the time being at least, sufficient is known to demonstrate that the quantum of business transacted 'Offshore' is a material amount. For example, '[a]ccording to figures published by the US Senate there are around US$15.5 trillion funds under management, $5 trillion in "Offshore Centres"'.[6] Further, '[t]here are up to 100 tax havens across the world today, depending on your definition of the term'.[7]

Other figures suggest that there are roughly seventy OFCs – the aggregate population of which is 1.2 per cent of the world's population and 3.1 per cent of the world's GDP. Between them, they manage 25 per cent of the world's assets.[8]

---

[4] News Brief No. 00/62, IMF, 26 July 2002.

[5] Mattias Levin, CEPS Research Report, August 2002, Table 1, 'Offshore Financial Centres in Perspective' (citing UNCTAD, 'World Investment Report 1999: Foreign Direct Investment and the Challenge of Development', New York, United Nations, 1999, and Ingo Walter, 'Globalisation of Markets and Financial-Centre Competition', paper presented at the Institut fur Welwirtschaft, Kiel, Germany, 1998).

[6] Paul Stribbard, 'International Reports – A Brief Review', *Private Wealth Investor*, June 2001, p. 16.

[7] 'Gangsters' Paradise Lost', *Observer*, 'Business' section, 24 February 2002.

[8] 'The Prospects for Offshore', *Offshore Red*, October 2002, p. 180.

Further, '[t]he "Offshore" fiduciary sector encompasses businesses in some 47 jurisdictions and territories, directly employing some 250,000 people, and holding assets in excess of [US$10 trillion] . . . the amount of money Offshore [is] estimated at 60 per cent of the world's money'.[9]

One estimate suggests that '$25 trillion is lodged in offshore accounts throughout the world'.[10]

> [S]ome of the largest US fortunes in the financial services industry these days are parked offshore. 'The money involved is clearly in the billions' says Offshore hedge fund expert Antoine Bernheim. There are individual [hedge fund] managers who have deferrals that exceed $100 million or $200 million.[11]

It has been said that 'foreign direct investment by G7 countries in a number of jurisdictions in the Caribbean and in the South Pacific island states, which are generally considered to be low tax jurisdictions, increased more than five fold over the period 1985–1994, to more than $200 billion'.[12] Further, 'over 1 trillion dollars (US) is invested in "Offshore" funds and . . . the number of funds has increased by more than 1400 per cent over the last 15 years'.[13]

The OECD's estimate of the amount held in 'Offshore' funds amounts to US$1,000 billion.[14]

> BIS data suggest that, for selected OFCs, on balance sheet cross border assets reached a level of $4.6 trillion at end of June 1999 (about 50 per cent of total cross border assets) of which $0.9 trillion was in the Caribbean, $1 trillion in Asia and most of the remaining $2.7 trillion was accounted for by the IFCs, namely London, the US, IBFs and the JOM.[15]

> Germans alone are thought to have more than Euros 300 billion ($320 billion) stashed in offshore accounts.[16]

---

[9] Tim Bennett, *International Initiatives Affecting Tax Havens*, Reed Elsevier (UK) Ltd, 2001, p. iii.

[10] 'Swiss Bank Laws Attacked', CNN.com/World/, 21 February 2001.

[11] Hal Lux, 'Rich, Offshore, Taxable?', *Institutional Investor*, September 2002, p. 13.

[12] 'Harmful Tax Competition – An Emerging Global Issue', OECD, 1998, para. 35, p. 17.

[13] Jeffrey Owens, Tax in 2010, *OECD* Observer, 27 June 2000.

[14] Astrid Wendtlandt, 'Guernsey Stands Alone in the Face of Economic Sanctions', *Financial Times*, 27 July 2000.

[15] 'Offshore Financial Centres', IMF Background Paper, 23 June 2000.

[16] 'The Taxman Cometh', *The Economist*, 25 January 2003, p. 70.

It is estimated that one third of the wealth of the world's 'high net worth individuals', or approaching $6 trillion out of some $17.5 trillion, may now be held offshore: that is, outside the jurisdictions where the individuals live (Merrill Lynch & Gemini Consulting, *World Wealth Report*, 1998). The Crown Dependencies probably have about 5 per cent of this market.[17]

These figures aptly demonstrate at least two points: (1) the absence of agreed definitions causes problems; and (2) although the 'Offshore' environment is material, no one knows how material. This point has not been lost on the supranational regulatory authorities.

16.4 General information

The text below indicates some general data about some OFCs. It is not intended to be exhaustive.

16.4.1 Antigua and Barbuda

Location	British West Indies, 270 miles southeast of Puerto Rico.
Geography	A twin-island state, 170 square miles.
Economy	Main industry, tourism,[18] generating more than 50 per cent of GDP.
Legal	Embodies principles of English common law.
WTO	Member.

16.4.2 Aruba

Location	33 miles off the coast of Venezuela (part of the Kingdom of the Netherlands).
Area	20 miles by 5 miles.
Population	96,000.
GDP	US$21,200 per capita (tourism generates 43 per cent of GDP).[19]
Languages	Dutch, English, Spanish and Papamiento.

[17] Michael Edwards, 'Review of Financial Regulation in the Crown Dependencies', Part 1, para. 2.2, 1998.
[18] Financial Services Regulatory Commission, www.fsrc.gov.ag/antigua_glance.asp.
[19] 'Aruba Wins Positive Vote from IMF Mission', Vol. 10, No. 6, *Offshore Red*, July/August 2005, p. 138.

16.4.3 Bahamas

Location	A chain of more than 700 islands in the north Atlantic Ocean, 60 miles southeast of Florida.
Area	14,000 square kms.
CISs	700 (US$125 billion under administration).[20]
Licensees	123 bank and trust licencees, 80 bank licencees and 107 trust licensees.[21]
Population	315,000.
Political status	Independent from UK since 1973.
Economy	Dependent on tourism (60 per cent of GDP and 40 per cent of labour force) and financial services (15 per cent of GDP and 14,000 employees). Manufacturing and agriculture contribute less than 10 per cent of GDP.
Language	English.
Ratings	Standard & Poors Sovereign Long Term Credit Rating 'A–' and Short Term 'A–2'.

16.4.4 Barbados

Location	300 miles off the northern coast of South America.
Area	21 miles by 14 miles.
Population	264,000.
Language	English.

16.4.5 Bermuda

Location	600 miles off the east coast of the USA.
Area	25 square miles.
Population	62,000.

---

[20] Wendy Warren, 'Strengthening the Bahamas' Position', *Offshore Investment*, September 2004, p. 21.

[21] 'IMF Review of Bahamas Sees Progress in Regulatory Regime', *Offshore Red*, November 2004, p. 180.

General	The first exempted company was incorporated in the 1930s. A British Dependent Territory, Bermuda has had its own elected Parliament since 1622. A common law jurisdiction. Major international re-insurance jurisdiction, with 1,400 insurance and re-insurance companies.
Banks	Four. Combined balance sheet of banks and deposit companies (Q4 – 2004) BD$20.5 million.[22]
CISs	Q4, 2004, 2,011; total net asset value US$158.2 billions (see previous reference).
International companies	13,509;[23] 12,309 registered companies.
GDP	US$3.9 million (see previous reference).
International business	15.8 per cent of Bermuda's output in 2002 (2003 Economic Review).
Offshore CISs	US$133 billion of assets.[24]
Captives	1,426 (estimated); total assets US$49 billion; net premiums US$9.8 billlion.

16.4.6 British Virgin Islands

Location	60 miles east of Puerto Rico, comprising 40 islands, of which 16 are inhabited.
Financial services	Generates 45 per cent of GDP.
Captives	350, with 20 managers.
CISs	2,500 (with nearly US$100 billion under management).
Population	22,000.
Language	English.
Registered companies	around 635,000.[25]

[22] Bermuda Monetary Authority, *Report and Accounts 2004*, p. 31.
[23] Government of Bermuda, Bermuda's Economic Review, 2003.
[24] 'Bermuda Follows Lead of SEC and Steps Up Fund Regulation', *Offshore Red*, December 2004/January 2005, p. 195.
[25] Humphry Leue, 'The British Virgin Islands, The 2005 Guide to International Financial Centres', Euromoney Institutional Investor plc, February 2005, p. 4.

16.4.7 Cayman Islands

Location	Three islands (Grand Cayman, Little Cayman and Cayman Brac) in the Caribbean Sea between Honduras and Cuba.
Area	259 square kms.
Population	41,000.
Banks	313.[26]
Funds	Approx 6,178.[27]
Trust companies	123.[28]
Company managers	68.[29]
Insurance	721 (Classes A and B).[30]
General	Colonised from Jamaica during the eighteenth and nineteenth centuries. Administered by Jamaica since 1863 but remained a British dependency after Jamaica became independent in 1962.
Economy	No direct tax; 40,000 registered companies. Total banking assets exceed US$500 billion. Stock exchange opened in1967. Tourism, mainly from the USA, 70 per cent of GDP (75 per cent of currency earnings). 90 per cent of food and consumer goods imported. Very high output per capita and very high standard of living. Cayman banks and trust companies, US$748 billion in assets; fifth largest banking centre in the world.[31]
Language	English.

16.4.8 Cook Islands[32]

Location	South Pacific, near New Zealand, comprising 16 islands.
Population	26,000.

[26] Cayman Islands Monetary Authority, *The Navigator*, Vol. 20, March 2005, p. 1.
[27] Cayman Islands Monetary Authority, *The Navigator*, Vol. 20, March 2005, p. 1.
[28] Cayman Islands Monetary Authority, *The Navigator*, Vol. 20, March 2005, p. 2.
[29] Cayman Islands Monetary Authority, *The Navigator*, Vol. 20, March 2005, p. 2.
[30] Cayman Islands Monetary Authority, *The Navigator*, Vol. 20, March 2005, p. 2.
[31] Spencer Privett, 'Hedge Funds in the Cayman Islands', *Offshore Red*, March 2004, p. 16.
[32] 'IMF Financial Sector Review', as cited in 'The Cook Islands – An IMF Financial Sector Review', *Offshore Red*, February 2005, p. 14.

Language	English.
Banks	3 domestic and 15 international banks.
Insurance	20 'Offshore' insurance companies.
Companies	800 international companies.
Trusts	2,100 (6 trustee companies).
Offshore	Contributes 8 per cent of GDP; 20 entities employ 80 people.

16.4.9 Delaware

| General | There are in excess of 300,000 companies created under the law of Delaware. |
| Population | 843,000. |

16.4.10 Gibraltar

Legal	A common law jurisdiction located in continental Europe. Currency – Sterling.
Population	30,000.
GDP	£333 million (1997).
Financial services	60 per cent of workforce.
Exempt companies	Approximately 8,500 offshore firms qualify for the Exempt Company Tax Scheme.[33]

16.4.11 Guernsey

Population	60,000.
Assets	£24.8 billion of assets under management.[34]
Funds	£73.6 billion as at 31 December 2004.[35] (As at the end of March 2005, the figures for open and closed ended funds respectively were £36.3 billion and £23.6 billion.)[36]

[33] 'EU Calls on UK to Phase Out Gibraltar Tax Breaks by 2010', *Offshore Red*, February 2005, p. 6.
[34] Astrid Wendtlandt, 'Guernsey Stands Alone in the Face of Economic Sanctions', *Financial Times*, 27 July 2000.
[35] 'Guernsey Financial Sector Posts 30 Per Cent Increase in 2004', *Offshore Red*, June 2005, p. 102.
[36] 'Guernsey Reports Bumper Investment Returns in Q1', *Offshore Red*, Vol. 10, No. 6, July/August 2005, p. 125.

Banks	54.[37]
GDP	£870 billion.
Companies	16,071 (as at 31 December 2003).
Bank deposits	£70.4 billion (as at 31 December 2004).[38]
Employment	2,652 people employed in finance sector as at June 2004.[39]

16.4.12 Hong Kong

| Population | 6.8 million. |
| Companies | Local, 65,558; Overseas, 7,279; Total, 518,980. |

16.4.13 Isle of Man

- Standard & Poors Long Term Credit Rating AAA.
- Unemployment 0.9 per cent.
- Total bank deposits €28.25 billion (March 2003).
- 145 captive insurance companies.
- 120 experienced investor funds (June 2003).

Population	76,000.
Contribution	37 per cent of national income derived from the financial sector.[40]
GDP	£1 billion.
Companies	36,126.[41]

---

[37] 'Guernsey Financial Sector Posts 30 Per Cent Increase in 2004', *Offshore Red*, June 2005, p. 102.

[38] 'Guernsey Financial Sector Posts 30 Per Cent Increase in 2004', *Offshore Red*, June 2005, p. 102.

[39] 'Guernsey Financial Sector Posts 30 Per Cent Increase in 2004', *Offshore Red*, June 2005, p. 102.

[40] Isle of Man, Financial Services Commission, *Annual Report*, 2004.

[41] Isle of Man, Financial Supervision Commission, *Annual Report*, 2003, (figures as at 31 March 2003).

16.4.14 Jersey

Population	87,400.
Assets	Total deposits (June 2005) were £173 billion.[42] One person in four works in the financial sector.[43]
Deposit-takers	50 (peak was 82 in 1997).[44]
Funds managed	£112.6 billion.[45]
Insurance companies	168.
Financial services	The financial industry accounts for '28 per cent of total employment, 70 per cent of GDP and 66 per cent of total tax receipts'.[46]
GDP	£1.5 billion

16.4.15 Labuan

Offshore banks	57.[47]
Offshore insurance	102.
General insurance	US$436.2 million gross premium (2004).[48]
Listings	26 (market capitalisation $10.1 billion).[49]
Trust companies	20.
Leasing companies	54.
Population	60,000.
Companies	2,700 (international).[50]

[42] 'Jersey Reports Bullish 2nd Quarter Results', Tax-News.com, 29 August 2005.
[43] Jon Ungoed-Thomas and Martin Jay, 'Channel Islands Face Tax Haven Threat', *Sunday Times*, 21 May 2000.
[44] 'Jersey Reports Bullish 2nd Quarter Results', Tax-News.com, 29 August 2005.
[45] 'Jersey Reports Bullish 2nd Quarter Results', Tax-News.com, 29 August 2005.
[46] 'Hong Kong and Jersey: A Comparison of Major Financial Jurisdictions', *Offshore Red*, February 2004, p. 230.
[47] 'Malaysia's PM Renews Push for Labuan as a Strategic OFC', *Offshore Red*, October 2004, p. 151.
[48] 'Labuan's Banks Post Increased Profits', *Offshore Red*, June 2005, p. 104.
[49] 'Labuan's Banks Post Increased Profits', *Offshore Red*, June 2005, p. 104.
[50] 'Asia/Pacific News – Malaysia', *Offshore Red*, March 2005, p. 32.

16.4.16 Liechtenstein

Location	Between Switzerland and Austria.
Area	61 square miles.
Population	34,000.
Status	A member of the European Economic Area.
Language	German.
Banks	16 (managing assets worth SFr104 billion).[51]
Trust companies	350.

16.4.17 Luxembourg

Location	Central Europe, bordered by France, Belgium and Germany.
Population	440,000.
Area	1,000 square miles.
Sector	177 banks (balance sheet footings as at end November 2002 was €667 billion), 100 insurance companies, approximately 250 reinsurance companies, and 1,955 collective investment schemes. Net assets as at end 2002 were €844.5 billion.
Contribution	Almost 40 per cent of GDP is linked to financial services.
EU	Member.
OECD	Member.
Language	French and German.
General	Not an official member of the G10 but the Central Bank of Luxembourg is a member of the Basel Committee with one member.

16.4.18 Malta[52]

Population	392,000.
Currency	Maltese lira.
Assets	Lm 1.9bn (US$4.4 billion) on deposit (31 July 2000).
EU	Member since 1 May 2004.

[51] Thomas Piske, 'Liechtenstein: The 2005 Guide to International Financial Centres', Euromoney Institutional Investor plc, February 2005, p. 12.
[52] David Marinelli, 'Malta', The OFC Report, 2005, p. 127.

GDP   12 per cent contributed by financial services sector.
Double taxation   41.
agreements

16.4.19 *Mauritius*[53]

Location   2,400 Km off the southeast coast of Africa.
Population   1,200,000.
Area   720 square miles.
Currency   Mauritian rupee.
Regulators   Bank of Mauritius (central bank) and the Financial
                    Services Commission (NBFIs).
Economy   Financial services generated 10 per cent of GDP in 2004.
Employment   Financial services sector employs 10,000 + people.
Banks   23 (June 2004).
Corporate   81 providers.
services
Insurance   20.
companies
Stockbrokers   11.
Corporate   23.
trustees
Portfolio   16.
managers
Leasing   12.
companies
Global   25,274 (7,590 GBC1 and 17,684 GBC2).
business
companies
CISs   327 global collective investment schemes and 27 local.
Listed   42.
companies
Market   MuR 70.4 billion.
capitalisation

[53] Ministry of Industry and Medium Enterprises, Financial Services and Corporate Affairs, 17 June 2005 (figures as at March/April 2005).

16.4.20 Montserrat

Location	Caribbean, 1,500 miles southeast of Miami.
Area	40 square miles.
Population	12,000.

16.4.21 Nauru

Location	Central Pacific Ocean.
Area	9 square miles.
Population	9,000.
Currency	Aus$.
Language	English.

16.4.22 Netherlands Antilles

Location	Caribbean, 40 miles off the coast of Venezuela, 100 miles east of Puerto Rico.
Geography	Two groups of islands (5 islands in total); main island – Curacao.
Population	140,000.
EC	Associate Member.
Government	Parliamentary democracy.
Economy	Oil refining, shipping and repairs, tourism and financial services.

16.4.23 Switzerland

Population	6,500,000.
Financial services	Employs 220,000 people and contributes 11 per cent of GDP; 356 banks.[54]

---

[54] 'A Survey of Switzerland', *The Economist*, 14 February 2004, p. 13.

| Other | The Swiss maintain that Switzerland is not a tax haven. It is not a member of the EU (in 2001, 77 per cent of the Swiss people rejected talks on EU membership). Tax evasion is not a criminal act. Described as the world's largest private banking centre with US$1.2 trillion in assets held by non-residents.[55] It is estimated that 39 per cent of all funds placed offshore by EU nationals are placed in Switzerland.[56] Not an official member of the G10, but the Swiss National Bank is a member of the Basel Committee. Member of the OECD. |

16.4.24 St Vincent and the Grenadines[57]

Banks	17 (7 domestic and 10 international).
Insurance	13 motor and general, 8 long-term and life, and 3 international insurance companies.
CIS	5 (and 6 managers).
Legal	Common law.
Economy	Tourism is the prime industry.
Trusts	413.
International business companies	6,342.
Independent	From 1979.
Total assets	US$109 million (aggregated from all offshore banks).[58]

16.4.25 Turks and Caicos

Population	17,500.
Assets	US$1 billion deposits in banks and trust funds.[59]

---

[55] 'Swiss Tax Decision Could See Singapore Shine as a Haven', *Offshore Red*, November 2003, p. 175.

[56] 'Editor's Note', *Offshore Red*, November 2003, p. 177.

[57] www.stvincentoffshore.com/offshore_indus.htm (figures as at May 2003).

[58] 'Regulation in St Vincent and the Grenadines', *Offshore Red*, October 2004, p. 160.

[59] Michael Peel, 'Haven Hopes Raising its Game Will Reap Rewards', *Financial Times*, 27 July 2000.

16.4.26 Vanuatu

Location   Comprises 100 islands in the South Pacific.
Business   Reduction in number of offshore banks from 130 to 34 in
              2003.
Banks   3 (local).
Population   170,000.

The UK and 'Offshore'

Change is not made without inconvenience, even from worse to better.[1]

17.1 Introduction

The typical perception of an 'Offshore Finance Centre' was described in the introduction to this book. However, not all OFCs conform to this perceived description, and perceptions concerning what distinguishes 'Offshore' from 'Onshore' can be misleading. This chapter describes some of the traits that make the UK not dissimilar to more familiar 'Offshore Finance Centres'. Meanwhile, it has been said that 'the UK has tolerated the creation of OFCs in its own dependent territories such as the [Channel Islands] [see section 17.4 below] and Gibraltar. In addition, it has encouraged some of its overseas dependent territories in the Caribbean to set up offshore centres.'[2] Accordingly, the UK is not unfamiliar with the 'Offshore' concept.

By way of a backdrop, the UK – like all other countries – has a number of ongoing problems, such as crime. One estimate of the total cost of crime to the UK puts it 'in the region of £50 million per annum . . . [and] . . . assets derived from organised crime represent around 2 per cent of the UK's Gross Domestic Product'.[3] Another estimate says that 'Assets derived from crime probably represent around 2 per cent of the United Kingdom's Gross Domestic Product (GDP) or GBP18 million, up to half of which is the value of illegal drug transactions in the UK.'[4]

In March 2000, the UK's Treasury Minister said, concerning 'Offshore', that:

---

[1] Richard Hooker, 1554–1600.
[2] Mark Hampton, *The Offshore Interface*, Macmillan Press Ltd, 1996, p. 69.
[3] Susan Singleton, 'Stand and Deliver', *Chartered Secretary*, June 2003, p. 18.
[4] Assets Recovery Agency, 'Making Sure Crime Doesn't Pay', www.assetsrecovery.gov.uk.

[t]he policy of the United Kingdom Government on offshore centres can be summed up as follows:

1. We have no problem, in principle, with centres who earn their living from providing financial services to non-residents. This activity is not confined to offshore centres. Many onshore centres, including London and New York, do substantial non-resident business.
2. It is important that all financial centres comply with world standards regardless of whether onshore or offshore.
3. We support the initiatives underway in various international bodies to encourage all jurisdictions to improve standards.
4. We consider that the true distinction is not between onshore and offshore centres, but between centres which comply with international standards and those which do not.[5]

17.2 Is London an 'Offshore Finance Centre'?

A short while ago, Mr Gavin Cassey, Chief Executive of the London Stock Exchange, was reported to have put 'the worth of financial services across the UK as a whole at some 20 per cent of GDP'.[6] According to one article, London has more foreign banks (570) than any other centre. They manage in excess of 50 per cent of UK banking sector assets (totalling €2.6 billion) and have a large proportion of the management of overseas clients' non-domestic portfolios. London's favourable tax system is cited as one of its two major advantages (the other being the competitive pricing structure).[7] According to *The Economist*, 'financial services are Britain's single biggest export earner, with exports worth £13 billion ($19 billion) in 2001'. Figures released in July 2005 show that 'British insurance companies, banks and other financial institutions achieved net exports of £19 bn ($31.92 bn) in 2004, almost three times higher than their contribution to the UK's balance of payments a decade ago.'[8] It has been estimated that 87 per cent of all 'Offshore' transactions take place in London, Tokyo and New York.[9]

---

[5] Colin Powell, 'Foreword' in *International Financial Centres Yearbook 2004/05*, p. 2.
[6] 'Three Wise Men', Vol. 13, No. 1, July/August 2000, *Compliance Monitor*.
[7] *International Wealth Management*, Supplement, 'International Financial Centres', September 2000, p. 7.
[8] Chris Giles, 'City of London Drives Surge in UK Financial Exports', *Financial Times*, 18 July 2005.
[9] 'Last Gasp for the Old Tax Haven', *Offshore Red*, February 2004, p. 229.

Although international clients using the financial services offered by the City of London might (informally) regard it as an 'Offshore Finance Centre' in the broadest sense, the City's private bankers might suggest that its robust reputation prevents the City being regarded as an 'Offshore Centre' in the narrowest sense. Leaving aside the semantics, by whatever name it is dubbed, the City is frequently used as a pure OFC. And, despite the fact that London might regard itself as well-regulated, a recent article has suggested that a French parliamentary mission investigating money laundering denounced London's lack of cooperation.[10] It has been said that 'the second most important tax haven in the world is located on an island. It is a city called London in the United Kingdom.'[11] Further, it has been suggested that 'London . . . is one of the largest offshore markets in the world. Financial services comprise a significant portion of the UK's invisible exports, as do non-resident clients of the UK's financial institutions. Dollar-wise, London does much more offshore business than smaller, more concentrated offshore centres could ever hope to undertake.'[12]

Even so, an 'EU-commissioned report . . . estimated that Britain alone is losing £85 billion a year through tax avoidance, much of it lured away by specially crafted "designer" tax regimes in places like Jersey.'[13]

The UK offers a range of facilities that practitioners 'Offshore' might use to the advantage of overseas clients because, so long as they do not conduct business in the UK, such people are broadly exempt from UK tax. One might be forgiven for wondering how this could be, especially since the UK's Chancellor of the Exchequer has treated Guernsey, the Isle of Man and Jersey in no light way for acting similarly.

17.3 The Edwards Report

Arising from criticism over what was considered to be loose financial regulation in some UK dependent territories, the UK Government, in 1998, commissioned Mr Michael Edwards, a former civil servant

[10] 'Havens and Haven'ts', *The Economist*, 24 June 2000, p. 107.
[11] Marshall J. Langer, 'Harmful Tax Competition: Who Are the Real Tax Havens?', International Tax Planning Conference, 20 November 2000.
[12] John R. Aspden, *International Wealth Management*, Supplement – 'International Financial Centres', September 2000, p. 21.
[13] 'Gangsters' Paradise Lost' *Observer*, 'Business' section, 24 February 2002.

employed by the UK's Treasury, to review the operation and practice of regulation in Guernsey, Jersey and the Isle of Man.

In essence, Mr Edwards' report, entitled 'Review of Financial Regulation in the Crown Dependencies', was positive about these three centres. Mr Edwards concluded that the reputation of the jurisdictions indicated 'stability, integrity, professionalism, competence and good regulation'. The report was published in four parts. Part 1 provided a general commentary and recommendations, while a separate part was devoted to each of the three respective jurisdictions. The changes agreed upon were identified in a White Paper entitled 'Partnership for Progress and Prosperity: Britain and the Overseas Territories' (see section 17.5 below).

Mr Edwards is attributed with the creation of the appellation 'International Finance Centre' instead of the already tarnished and bruised 'Offshore Finance Centre'.[14]

17.4 The Crown dependencies

Guernsey (which includes Sark) and Jersey comprise the Channel Islands. These, together with the Isle of Man, are part of Great Britain – but not part of the United Kingdom. These three islands host significant financial services business. The constitutional relationship of each island with the Crown – from 13 June 2001 – has been administered by the Lord Chancellor. (Previously, the responsibility lay with the UK's Home Office.) In response to OECD criticism, it has been said that: 'Every one of our Crown jewels is self-financing . . . By contrast, five member countries of the OECD receive aid totalling $7.305 billion. Then again, the OECD accusations against these island states are not that they are economically incompetent. It is that they are too competitive.'[15]

17.5 The UK's overseas territories

The White Paper described above ('Partnership for Progress and Prosperity: Britain and the Overseas Territories') was presented to the UK Government in 1999. The White Paper renamed that group of countries

---

[14] Michael Edwards, 'Review of Financial Regulation in the Crown Dependencies', Part 1, para. 3.2.3.

[15] Paul Baxendale-Walker, 'OECD Demands and International Law', The OFC Report 2004, p. 21.

known formerly as the 'UK's Dependent Territories' as the 'UK's Overseas Territories'. These Territories 'are scattered around the globe. All
except Gibraltar are islands or are parts of islands . . . The biggest
concentration is in the Caribbean.'[16]

There are thirteen Overseas Territories, namely, Gibraltar (also part of
the EU); Bermuda; the Pitcairn Islands; the British Virgin Islands;
Anguilla; the Turks and Caicos Islands; the British Antarctic Territory;
the Cayman Islands; Montserrat; Ascension Island, St Helena and Tristan
da Cunha (which together form one territorial unit); the Falkland
Islands, South Georgia, the South Sandwich Islands (which also together
form one territorial unit); the Chagos Archipelago; and the Sovereign
Base Areas in Cyprus.

An article published at the time said that, '[w]hilst recognising that
some of the UK Overseas Territories are world leaders in the Offshore
Finance Services Industry, Mr Cook [the UK's Foreign Secretary] called
for the highest international standards of financial regulation in all the
territories'.[17] Every overseas territory was expected to provide evidence
by the end of 1999 that it had implemented the following measures:

- measures covering standards of regulatory legislation;
- membership of bodies such as the FATF and the Basel Group of
Banking Supervisors;
- measures to combat money laundering, comprising all financial institutions;
- measures to facilitate checking companies based elsewhere but incorporated in the territory; and
- legislation permitting full cooperation with overseas investigations.

The Foreign Secretary's intention was that the UK's Overseas Territories would all apply the same rules in dealing with money laundering and
concealing profit derived from crime, to eradicate regulatory arbitrage
between the centres. However, it gave rise to an issue for the global
population of 'Offshore Finance Centres' concerning how fair competition could be achieved amongst 'Offshore Centres' that were not
amongst the UK's Overseas Territories.

[16] John White, 'The Overseas Territories: A Personal Reflection', *Duncan Lawrie Journal*,
Autumn, 2000, p. 17.
[17] 'Comment', *International Money Marketing*, 20 February 1998.

The UK's Chancellor of the Exchequer had nevertheless made known his desire to eradicate what has been referred to as 'designer taxation' and to ensure that the UK's Overseas Territories are in line.[18] (See section 17.2 above.) The Chancellor had promised his European counterparts that he would try to persuade the UK's Overseas Territories to cooperate. He could not directly compel them but he could take other indirect measures to coerce adherence (e.g. by forcing UK banks to close branches 'Offshore').

The Overseas Territories Bill received its second reading in the UK's House of Commons on 22 November 2001. It changed the name of the Dependent Territories to Overseas Territories – as described above. As a result, citizens of Overseas Territories will be able in future to renounce their British citizenship (which gives a right of abode in the UK, and free movement in the EU).

17.6 The KPMG Report

As well as renaming these territories, the White Paper recommended a review of the financial regulation pertaining in each Overseas Territory. The Overseas Territories Department of the UK's Foreign and Commonwealth Office, together with the governments of the Caribbean Overseas Territories and Bermuda, 'funded and organised a study, by . . . KPMG of financial regulation in the territories. The aim was to undertake a thorough, comprehensive objective review for each territory of existing legislation, regulatory policy and practice and to identify any measures needed to enable the territory to meet international regulatory standards.'[19] Representatives from the UK Treasury and from the UK Foreign and Commonwealth Office agreed the 'terms of reference' with the jurisdictions – and with KPMG as the auditor involved. KPMG recruited a group of former regulators to assist. A 100-page questionnaire was sent to each jurisdiction, and this was followed up by a visit. The remit was found to be less precise than was necessary. Judgments proved to be necessary in such areas as company formation (where rules regarding licensing and regulation had not yet been agreed).

---

[18] Patience Wheatcroft, 'Paradigm Lost for the Dot-Coms', *The Times*, 27 June 2000.

[19] John White, 'The Overseas Territories: A Personal Reflection', *Duncan Lawrie Journal*, Autumn, 2000, p. 21.

The review was completed in October 2000 and the jurisdictions agreed to publish an action plan by 15 January 2001 and had until 30 September 2001 to implement the recommendations – which included:

- the establishment of an independent body responsible for regulation;
- legislation and processes to enhance anti-money laundering procedures; and
- legislation to enable information gathering and sharing.

By February 2001, most of the six centres involved had responded positively to the recommendations made, as follows.[20] For their part, KPMG's review said of Anguilla that '[it] has many of the features necessary to be considered a well regulated jurisdiction'. Of the British Virgin Islands that '[t]he BVI has made demonstrable efforts to bring its financial regulatory system into line with international standards'. And, of the Turks and Caicos Islands it said that '[m]uch progress has been made in enhancing the regulatory framework, with a considerable volume of legislation passed'.

In response to the recommendations, the Government of Bermuda said '[t]he report clearly serves to validate the rigour and effectiveness of Bermuda's regulatory systems and practices.' The Government of the Cayman Islands said: 'In general, the review is welcomed as useful and will be accorded close consideration.' The Government of Montserrat said: 'If the government is unable for any reason to meet substantially the recommendations of the report, it will recognise that there will be no option but to review its involvement in offshore finance.'

A joint statement by the UK's Treasury and Foreign and Commonwealth Office on 23 May 2002 indicated that the UK Government was pleased with the progress that had been made in implementing the recommendations in the original report. For example, all six jurisdictions concerned had adopted anti-money laundering procedures and four of the six (the British Virgin Islands, Bermuda, Montserrat and the Turks and Caicos Islands) had established an independent regulatory authority.

By June 2002, only one jurisdiction (Montserrat) had satisfied the changes that had been asked of it. The original deadline for completion

---

[20] Ken Hunter, 'Spin Doctors', *Offshore Finance*, May/June 2001, p. 51.

was September 2001. Anguilla, the Cayman Islands and Bermuda had still some work to do at that stage.

17.7 A comment

It seems that the UK Government's actions reflected pressure from the rest of Europe on the UK to do something about its dependent/overseas territories. However, there is a limit to the action that is possible because the jurisdictions involved have the responsibility of looking after their own fiscal affairs. That said, great pressure was brought to bear in respect of the EU withholding tax on savings by non-residents (see Chapter 5 above). This resulted in an announcement (4 June 2002) that Guernsey and Jersey had agreed to introduce legislation to enable the exchange of information about the savings of citizens of the European Union. At that stage, the Isle of Man was thought likely to follow suit – and it eventually did so. The full background is described in Chapter 5.

17.8 Anti-money laundering

The UK's Home Office 'estimates that dirty money represents about two per cent of gross domestic product or approximately £18 billion'.[21] Another article stated that '[o]fficial estimates suggest GBP25bn ($46bn) is laundered through the UK every year'.[22] Note that the actual amount of money laundered is unknown. It has been reported that 'the UK law enforcement authorities removed some 3,400 kilos of heroin from the supply chain in 2001/2002. Confiscation orders and drug cash seizures in 2000/2001 resulted in GBP23.5 million being removed from circulation, with the potential of preventing the importation of up to a further 1,175 kilos of heroin.'[23]

Although the UK's Financial Intelligence Unit (the National Criminal Intelligence Service, NCIS) received 18,404 suspicious transactions reports in 2000,[24] '[t]he Head of the UK Home Office's judicial cooperation unit . . . admitted that the government had done little to prevent money launderers using British financial institutions to hide the

---

[21] 'London: The Anti-Money Laundering Capital', *Offshore Red*, September 2003, p. 136.
[22] 'Lack of Regulation "Turning London into a Haven for Money Launderers"', *Financial Times*, 29 October 2004.
[23] Assets Recovery Agency, 'Making Sure Crime Doesn't Pay', www.assetsrecovery.gov.uk.
[24] 'Knowing How to Know Your Customer', *Private Wealth Investor*, July/August 2002, p. 14.

proceeds of criminal activity'.[25] Ms Harris said that it was only possible
once or twice per annum to confiscate assets on behalf of other governments. Most applications did not satisfy the UK's rules (such as evidence
that a criminal prosecution was under way in the country making the
request). Prior to the establishment of the Financial Services Authority in
the UK, only the Bank of England (at the time) undertook any anti-
money laundering initiatives. None of the self-regulatory organisations
considered that this fell directly within their remit.

> That the industry needs to do more is undeniable . . . [F]ifteen of the
> banks investigated in connection with US$1.3 billion of funds associated
> with the former President of Nigeria, that passed through the UK, were
> deemed to have major deficiencies in their money laundering controls.[26]

More recently, the legislation has been updated. The Proceeds of
Crime Act 2002 – which replaced the money laundering provisions in
the Criminal Justice Acts of 1988 and 1993 – will be brought into effect in
stages which started in December 2002. The Act introduced new powers
to investigate money laundering and to trace the proceeds of crime.
These powers include requirements for financial institutions to identify
any account maintained by anyone connected to an investigation and to
provide information on transactions processed through such accounts.
In the first three months the legislation was operative, 'Customs & Excise
seized more than £4 billion'.[27] Further, the Money Laundering Regulations 1993 and 2001 have also been revised. The revisions include a
provision which makes any assistance provided by a banker in respect
of the transfer of criminal property a possible offence which carries a
sentence of up to fourteen years' imprisonment.

The following quote puts the current situation in perspective:

> The experts seem agreed that the sums of money laundered through
> London alone each year amount to many billions of pounds, possibly
> more than £100 billion.[28]

Further:

---

[25] 'Too Little, Too Late?', *Financial Regulator*, Vol. 5, No. 3, p. 12.
[26] Timon Molloy, 'Must Do Better', *Money Laundering Bulletin*, Issue 86, September 2001,
    p. 4.
[27] Susan Singleton, 'Stand and Deliver', *Chartered Secretary*, June 2003, p. 19.
[28] Michael Edwards, 'Review of Financial Regulation in the Crown Dependencies, Part 1,
    para. 14.8, 1998.

Transparency International (TI), a global organisation that seeks to free the financial markets of corruption, said in a report that London's financial centre has become a haven for money launderers washing dirty money through a cycle of UK-based financial institutions.[29]

The Financial Services and Markets Act 2000 delegated the fight against financial crime to the Financial Services Authority. The existing Regulations (which derive from the requirements imposed by the First EU Directive on Money Laundering) in the UK were replaced in 2003 by the Money Laundering Regulations 2003,[30] which came into force on 1 March 2004. The Regulations (which replace the Money Laundering Regulations 1993 and 2001) will implement the provisions of the EU's Second Directive on Money Laundering (considered in Chapter 8 above). Under the Regulations, any person that carries on a 'relevant business' must adopt certain anti-money laundering procedures and relevant training in the same field.

The biggest change brought about by the Regulations is the enlargement of those industries now caught by the rules – the scope of which is wider than required by the Directive. The Regulations embrace real-estate agents, auctioneers, auditors and accountants, dealers in items of high value and auctioneers, providers of trust and company services, insolvency practitioners, lawyers, casinos etc. All will be brought within the remit of the Regulations. There was some criticism about the late introduction (i.e. in December 2003, that is, after the period for public consultation had ended) of a requirement for businesses involved in the provision of services relating to the formation, operation or management of a company or trust to comply with the Regulations. The criticism is that this means that companies ranging from management consultants to advertising agencies may also have to comply. The term 'money laundering' now covers all crimes.

The number of Suspicious Activity Reports (SARs) anticipated by the National Criminal Intelligence Service (NCIS) was expected to reach 10,000 in 2003. The number of reports quadrupled between 2000 and 2002, with particular growth after the tragic events of 11 September 2001. 'An independent evaluation conducted by KPMG found the system for dealing with these reports "falling short of its aims" and in need of an

[29] Justin Madubuko, 'Lobbyists Slam the UK over Dirty Laundry Loopholes', *Portfolio International*, July 2003, p. 2.
[30] SI 2003/3075.

overhaul. KPMG's report, which was published earlier this year [2003], also found the NCIS overwhelmed by the number of SARs with a backlog of 58,000.[31] Under the Proceeds of Crime Act 2002, there is no minimum threshold for reporting a suspicious transaction.

17.9 Problems in the UK

Although the problems are not restricted to the UK (or to the USA, as the next chapter demonstrates), there have been an increasing number of fines imposed in the UK for unsatisfactory adherence to the rules. For example, in late 2002, the Royal Bank of Scotland was penalised and, in early 2003, the Northern Bank suffered a similar fate.

'Abbey was found not to have properly identified one in three banking customers and to have failed to ensure suspicious activity reports were promptly reported to the National Criminal Intelligence Service.'[32] On 15 January 2004, the Bank of Scotland was fined £1.25 million by the FSA because 'In over half of a sample of accounts tested the bank had failed to retain either a copy of the customer identification evidence or a record of where this evidence could be obtained.'[33]

Further, Equitable Life (said to be the world's oldest life insurer) almost collapsed in 2000. A report into the matter was published on 8 March 2004. The report's author, Lord Penrose, concluded that, for a prolonged period, Equitable Life's management suggested that there would be better bonuses than the underlying assets could provide. Lord Penrose said that the firm's solvency was bolstered by 'the consistent . . . adoption of the weakest valuation basis in addition to valuation practices of . . . "dubious actuarial merit".'[34] This, together with the fact that the board members were unaware of the situation because of a deficit in skills and information implies something less than acceptable. They relied on the data supplied by an actuary – who was also the firm's chief executive – and who later came in for serious criticism. Losses were estimated at £3 billion, a loss of

[31] 'Suspicious Activity Overwhelms Regulator', *Financial Times*, 20 September 2003, p. 11.
[32] Mark Williamson, 'Bank of Scotland Fined £1.25m for Breaching Money Laundering Rules', *The Herald*, 16 January 2004, as reported in *GPML Global Press Review*, United Nations Office on Drugs and Crime, Vol. 2, No. 3, 19 January 2004.
[33] Mark Williamson, 'Bank of Scotland Fined £1.25m for Breaching Money Laundering Rules', *The Herald*, 16 January 2004, as reported in *GPML Global Press Review*, United Nations Office on Drugs and Crime, Vol. 2. No. 3, 19 January 2004.
[34] 'Equitable Life – A Sorry and Convoluted Tale', *The Economist*, 13 March 2004, p. 40.

25 per cent on the savings of policyholders. This debacle led to some changes in insurance regulation in the UK.

In its annual report for 2004/5, the Financial Services Authority in the UK stated that:

> [I]n May 2004, we fined Carr Sheppards Crosthwaite £500,000 for systems and controls failings in its compliance function . . . In August [2004], we fined the Bank of Ireland £375,000 for failing to take reasonable care to establish and maintain effective systems and controls to counter the risk that its bank drafts might be used to further financial crime or to ensure its staff understood their anti-money laundering responsibilities. . . In August [2004], we fined the Shell Transport and Trading Company plc and the Royal Dutch Petroleum Company NV (Shell) £17 million for committing market abuse and breaching the listing rules. In November [2004], we fined Evolution Beeson Gregory Limited £500,000 and Christopher Potts £75,000 for market abuse as a result of short selling of the shares of Room Service Group plc . . . In December [2004], we fined Bradford & Bingley plc £650,000 for the widespread selling of precipice and with-profit bonds. The firm had not made suitable recommendations to customers, had not maintained adequate records of sales, did not have in place adequate systems and controls to prevent and ultimately address these failures.

In July 2005, it was reported that 'Citigroup was fined £14m ($25m) by Britain's Financial Services Authority for failing to conduct a controversial euro-zone bond deal last August with "due skill, care and diligence".'[35]

17.10 Companies and trust service providers

In Policy Research Paper 003, dated October 2004, Transparency International drew attention to the failure of the UK Government to enact legislation to regulate providers of trust services and services that include the formation and administration of companies. The paper compares the UK's approach with that of many 'Offshore' finance centres that have such legislation in place already. Although, in the UK, these activities fall within the scope of the EU's Second Money Laundering Directive, under the Money Laundering Regulations 2003 they remain unregulated.[36]

---

[35] 'Business', *The Economist*, 2 July 2005, p. 9.
[36] 'Corruption and Money Laundering in the UK – One Problem – Two Standards', Policy Research Paper 003, Transparency International (UK), October 2004, p. 5.

18

The USA and 'Offshore'

[O]ur strategy and our mission may change, but our values never do.[1]

18.1 Introduction

This chapter continues the 'Onshore/Offshore' comparison by examining the assertion that the USA – like the UK – manifests many of the traits of an 'Offshore Finance Centre'. It has been suggested that 'New York, London and Tokyo control between them nearly 60 per cent of the global market for offshore banking and capital markets'.[2] To put this chapter into context, 'industry accounts for only 16 per cent of jobs in America',[3] but there is in excess of US$1.7 trillion of foreign money on deposit in US banks.[4] On the other hand, 'J. P. Morgan Chase estimates that $650bn of profit earned abroad by US companies over decades has never been taxed by the US'.[5] Other figures indicate that, as at September 2003, there was in excess of US $2.3 trillion of foreign funds in US banks. The figures indicate that more than 50 per cent comes from the UK and the Caribbean.[6] Meanwhile, 2003 was a record year for US banks, generating US $120 billion in profit – US$17.9 billion of which was made by Citibank alone.

Reference has been made to 'the structural anarchy in America's supervision of its financial institutions'.[7] The supervisory structure is

---

[1] Mike Eskew, Chairman, United Parcel Service.
[2] Richard Hay, 'International Financial Centres and Information Exchange', *Offshore Investment*, Issue 157, June 2005, p. 3.
[3] 'What's in a Name?', *The Economist*, 17 January 2004.
[4] An excerpt from a letter from New York Governor George Pataki to Treasury Secretary Snow urging withdrawal of IRS interest program, as reported in the Center for Freedom and Prosperity's e-mail update of 10 April 2003.
[5] 'Big US Firms Prefer the Cayman Islands', *Offshore Red*, July/August 2004, p. 98.
[6] US Treasury International Capital Reporting System, Chart CM-A, US Liabilities to Foreigners Reported by US Banks, Brokers and Dealers with Respect to Selected Countries, January 2004.
[7] 'Hall of Fame', *The Economist*, 24 January 2004, p. 67.

not straightforward – not least because there are so many regulators involved – and, when this is the case, there is inevitably an overlap – as the article went on to explain. The Federal Reserve is in overall control of the financial system – including complex financial holding companies that own banks. The larger banks can choose to be regulated by state charter (i.e. by one of the fifty-four state banking departments) or by national charter under the oversight of the Comptroller of the Currency (itself a branch of the Treasury). 'The Comptroller's oversight of national banks, with "sole visitorial authority" – i.e. exclusive powers of inspection – was established by Abraham Lincoln in 1864.'[8] State regulators, together with local branches of the Federal Reserve, are responsible for bank holding companies and for some very large banks. The remainder come under the Comptroller of the Currency. 'Each State tends to have its own approach to bank regulation'[9] and anomalies abound concerning who is responsible for what. For example, the Comptroller of the Currency's responsibilities include Citigroup (perhaps the most global of all global banks) but the Comptroller only became responsible for J. P. Morgan Chase (the second largest bank in the USA) in November 2004, which previously fell under state regulators and the New York Federal Reserve.

Banks that are smaller do not fall under the remit of the Federal Reserve system but instead are chartered by state regulators. Institutions such as savings banks and industrial loan corporations (quasi-banks whose deposits are insured by the Federal Deposit Insurance Corporation (FDIC) and whose owners include Volkswagen and BMW) fall under the supervision of the FDIC. 'Thrifts' (a type of savings bank, some of which are owned by very large conglomerates such as General Electric and General Motors) fall under the Office of Thrift Supervision, while credit unions (of which there are more than 9,000 in the USA) fall under the National Credit Union Administration.

Although the legislation that had prevented banks from going beyond state boundaries changed in 1994 (Under the Riegle–Neal Act), the present situation has arisen because national banks were previously unknown.

---

[8] 'American Bank Regulation – Spitzer's Trials', *The Economist*, 25 June 2005, p. 98.
[9] David Shirreff, 'Don't Start from Here: A Survey of International Banking', *The Economist*, 21 May 2005, p. 7.

Meanwhile, the Securities Exchange Commission is responsible for complex financial holding companies that own broker-dealers. 'Insurance companies, some of which own or are part of banking groups, are supervised at the state level, and state supervision is coordinated to some extent by the National Association of Insurance Commissioners.'[10]

The Comptroller of the Currency has codified the law to assist the consolidation of the banking industry. One outcome is that it has been suggested that state regulators should no longer be involved in regulating national banks. A furore ensued, and Congress became involved.

Since 1999 (as a result of the Gramm–Leach–Bliley Act), financial groups may compete across divisions of insurance and commercial and investment banking.

This is the backdrop to the following additional information concerning the US approach to financial services in general and to 'Offshore' in particular.

18.2 Is the USA an 'Offshore Finance Centre'?

'It does not surprise anyone when I tell them that the most important tax haven in the world is an island. They are surprised, however, when I tell them that the name of the island is Manhattan.'[11] In this respect, '[t]he US is the world-leading beneficiary of tax competition. We have more than $8 trillion in foreign investment . . . The United States is the world's largest tax haven. Non-resident foreigners can invest in US stocks and bonds and pay little or no tax.'[12] If this income is not reported – which is normally the case – it will not be easy for the income to be taxed elsewhere. 'With few exceptions, the US Government does not tax the investment income of non-resident foreigners.'[13] (This income may be put at risk if the USA enters into agreements to exchange information.)

---

[10] David Shirreff, 'Don't Start from Here: A Survey of International Banking', *The Economist*, 21 May 2005, p. 7.

[11] Marshall J. Langer, 'Harmful Tax Competition: Who Are the Real Tax Havens?', International Tax Planning Conference, 20 November 2000.

[12] A. Quinlan, Statement on State Hearing, Center for Freedom and Prosperity, 18 July 2001.

[13] 'The Adverse Impact of Tax Harmonisation and Information Exchanges on the US Economy', *Prosperitas*, November 2001, www.freedomandprosperity.org/Papers/taxharm/taxharm.shtml.

[O]ur tax and privacy laws make the United States a tax haven for foreign
investors. This has resulted in $7 trillion to $10 trillion of capital from
overseas being invested in our economy.[14]

It has been said elsewhere that 'America is the best tax haven in the
world. Low taxes and a strong commitment to financial privacy combine
to attract more than $9 trillion in foreign capital to the US economy'.[15]
Further,

> the biggest tax haven of all, however, is the United States. America satisfies
> every single criterion. Most importantly, American lawmakers have quite
> deliberately chosen not to tax the bulk of the investment income earned by
> non-resident aliens. Combined with the fact that the US Government
> generally does not require the income to be reported – either to the
> Internal Revenue Service or to a foreign tax authority, this makes America
> a safe repository for international flight capital.[16]

The tax systems of some jurisdictions are based upon 'source of income
rules' where tax is only applied to income generated from within that
jurisdiction. 'Territorial taxation is a much better approach. This reform
would protect America's economic interest while also reducing opportunities for tax evasion. Territorial taxation would help make American
companies more competitive and it also facilitates tax competition.'[17]
So, if no income arises in that country, no tax is applied. Uruguay,
Hungary and the USA are examples of such countries. By extension, the
USA might be regarded as a tax haven for someone living in the USA who
is not an American but who has income from outside the USA.[18]

Thus, while the USA will go to some lengths to obtain 'tax information' on residents of the USA, non-residents who invest in the USA
are protected from similar scrutiny from foreign governments. This is

[14] Donald Manzullo, Member of the US Congress, as reported in 'Tax Talk in Tokyo',
Offshore Finance USA, May/June 2001, p. 47.
[15] Veronique de Rugy, 'Repel the Cartel', National Review Online, 7 June 2002, www.
nationalreview.com/nrof_comment/comment-derugy060702.asp.
[16] 'The Adverse Impact of Tax Harmonisation and Information Exchanges on the US
Economy', *Prosperitas*, November 2001, www.freedomandprosperity.org/Papers/tax-
harm/taxharm.shtml.
[17] 'The Adverse Impact of Tax Harmonisation and Information Exchanges on the US
Economy', *Prosperitas*, November 2001, www.freedomandprosperity.org/Papers/tax-
harm/taxharm.shtml.
[18] Howard Fisher, 'Is There a "Perfect Tax Haven"', *Offshore Investment*, Issue 117, June
2001, p. 39.

because it is unlawful to disclose information on an individual's business activities to a foreign government in the absence of a treaty between the two countries.

> The United States is a low tax jurisdiction, the United States is a tax haven and the United States is the world's biggest beneficiary of international tax competition. The overall tax burden in the US is 29 per cent of GDP, compared to 43 per cent of GDP in the European Union.[19]

18.3 The legal system encourages the use of OFCs

The USA has adopted the English common law system based on precedent and statutes (as opposed to the civil law system which derives from Roman law and is based on detailed written codes). One fundamental feature of the common law system was that it was based originally on relatively few rules – which made the whole thing more comprehensible. The law in the USA has developed in a way that differs from this basic principle.

In fact, the level of litigation in the USA is at a very high level. In the eyes of some, this is a vicious circle that feeds on itself, encouraging even more litigation and reducing the threshold at which litigation becomes a feasible course of action. It is unlikely that this trend produces any respect for the rule of law – because it gives rise to a situation where violations are punished not by civil fines but instead by treating them as felonies which carry prison sentences. In respect of protecting one's assets, the natural consequence (at least for professionals who risk being sued) is that more and more people consider preventive action – which includes moving assets 'Offshore'.

18.4 The link to 'Offshore'

'Offshore' banks are not permitted to advertise in the USA, unless they submit to similar regulation as banks operating in the USA. So, people using 'Offshore' jurisdictions cannot do so easily. However, the following figures suggest that this is not really a problem because it has been said that the US banking sector is the largest user of 'Offshore' centres – which position it has maintained since the fourth quarter of 2000 according to the Bank for International Settlements. 'US banks alone

---

[19] Dan Mitchell, 'OECD's Progress Report', CFP Strategic Memo, 19 November 2001.

accounted for $601 billion, or one third of all offshore claims, with most of the money going to Cayman Islands and Jersey.'[20]

18.5 Money laundering and the USA

A report entitled 'Private Banking and Money Laundering: A Case Study of Opportunities and Vulnerabilities', was published in November 1999 by the US Permanent Senate Sub-Committee. (The same Sub-Committee had made eight prior investigations into money laundering activities.) The report estimated that between US $500 billion and US $1 trillion was laundered through banks every year and, of this sum, around half was processed through US banks.

The report focused on four case histories covering the period from 1992 to 1999: Raul Salinas (brother of former Mexican President, Carlos Salinas), Asif Ali Zardari (husband of former Pakistan Prime Minister, Benazir Bhutto), El Hadj Omar Bongo (President of Gabon) and General Sani Abacha (late President of Nigeria).

The people involved were heads of state and their close relatives. Their banker was Citibank Private Bank – although the report clarifies that the problems identified involve the private banking industry generally. The topics covered included due diligence, secrecy and anti-money laundering controls. Analysis is beyond the focus of this book; nevertheless, the research is of particular relevance to international finance in general and to abuses in particular. On 30 October 2000, eleven global investment banks adopted guidelines on due diligence. These became part of the Wolfsberg Principles (see below and Chapter 8 above).

A report published by the Democratic staff of the Senate Investigations Sub-Committee in February 2001 charged a number of very important banking institutions in the USA with facilitating money laundering. These names included J. P. Morgan Chase, Citigroup and the Bank of America. The problem arose because of 'correspondent banking' relationships that the banks had with foreign banks. (The services offered by the US banks allowed the smaller foreign banks to process payments for immediate value. It is estimated that the Clearing House Interbank Payments System (CHIPS) in New York processes around US$1,000bn every day.) Some of these foreign banks had unsatisfactory control mechanisms in place, but, by virtue of their relationship, they had access to the US banking system.

---

[20] BIS, Quarterly Report, December 2003, Reuters News Service, as reported in 'US Banks Extend Lead as Biggest Offshore Users', Forbes.com, 7 December 2003.

There has been sensitivity in this area since it was discovered (in 1999) that the Bank of New York had processed around US $7 billion of suspicious Russian funds.

Meanwhile, 'the US Treasury Department estimates that 99.9 per cent of the criminal money in the USA is laundered successfully'.[21]

18.6 The Wolfsberg Principles

Eleven of the largest banks (including UBS, Credit Suisse, Citigroup, Barclays, HSBC, Deutsche, Société Générale, ABN Amro and Banco Santander Central Hispano) agreed some new rules, in the form of a voluntary code, the Wolfsberg Principles (which were agreed at Wolfsberg in October 2000). These guidelines are part of an initiative by Transparency International (a non-government group based in Berlin which focuses on curbing corruption globally; see also sections 6.17, 17.8 and 17.10 above).

18.7 The FATF and the USA

'According to self assessment exercises conducted on the implementation of the FATF's Forty Recommendations, the USA came third from the bottom, after Canada and Mexico, among the 29 industrialised nations surveyed.'[22] '[T]he FATF placed the US third from bottom in a survey of 29 industrialised nations. Only Canada and Mexico scored worse.'[23] It seems that, out of twenty-eight recommendations which required specific action, the USA complied with only seventeen (and in fact only ten members had implemented all twenty-eight recommendations). Further, '[i]n its assessment of how closely it follows the new recommendations, America admits that insurance companies, stockbrokers and bureaux de change do not have to report suspicious transactions'.[24]

18.8 'Know your customer'

The 'know your customer' rules that are part of the FATF's requirements, and which are at the centre of Wolfsberg's anti-money laundering

---

[21] Daniel J. Mitchell, 'US Government Agencies Confirm That Low-Tax Jurisdictions are Not Money Laundering Havens', *Journal of Financial Crime*, October 2003, Vol. 11, No. 2, p. 128.

[22] Editorial, Vol. 5, No. 1, 2001, *Journal of Money Laundering Control*, p. 5.

[23] 'From the Editor', *Offshore Red*, July/August 2001, p. 109.

[24] 'Follow the Money', Leader, *The Economist*, 1 June 2002, p. 73.

guidelines, represent one of the most important weapons against money launderers. Despite that, in 1999, the US Congress refused to tighten existing rules in face of criticism that to do so would threaten civil liberties. That said, all cash transactions whose value exceeds US $10,000, must be reported.

However, in light of the terrorist atrocities that took place in the USA on 11 September 2001, anti-money laundering legislation that had been waiting in the legislative queue for attention was given much higher priority. (See section 18.2 above.) 'Certainly the fact that there [has been] a Republican rather than a Democrat President in the USA since January 2001 seems to have had a slowing effect on the momentum and timetables of the OECD and FATF initiatives.'[25]

> The US has seized more than $100 million in assets linked to Al-Qaeda and Osama Bin Laden since first attempting to block his finances in 1998. In the three weeks since the latest attacks, US officials have seized $6 million in assets and blocked 30 accounts in the US and 20 overseas.[26]

18.9 Comparatives in the USA

Alaska, Delaware and Nevada actively promote asset protection rules through specific legislation. Thereby, a client's affairs are protected from disclosure (e.g. Alaska's 'Offshore' trust law). Nevada does not levy income tax, either personal or corporate, and the identity of beneficial owners is not part of public records, and bearer shares are allowed. Tax information is not disclosed to any other state or to the federal government. Montana and Colorado have 'Offshore' banking laws.

No mention is made of any of these things in the FATF or OECD reports.

18.9.1 Nevada

The following quotations from the promotional literature of a service provider in Nevada are significant:

---

[25] George Gilligan, 'Going Underground – The Not So New Way to Bank', Vol. 9, No. 2, *Journal of Financial Crime.*
[26] 'Bush Launches a War on Terrorist Financing', October 2001, Vol. 6, No 7, *Offshore Red*, p. 164.

For some, the most appealing aspect of incorporating in [this jurisdiction] is the respect for privacy. [This jurisdiction] does not keep the identity of shareholders in the public record. In other words, who owns a corporation is no-one's business but the owner. If someone is pursuing your assets and they suspect that you might own a related corporation in this jurisdiction, they're going to have more hurdles in discovery than in most [territories]. A record search, for example, generally ends up as a dead end . . .

A nominee officer is not required to know the shareholders or even their names. The nominee need only know from whom he or she is to take instructions, and where the list of shareholders is kept – not necessarily who is listed on the shareholder ledger. Not only can you save income tax levied from your home [territory], you can also build a firewall of privacy to protect assets . . .

With the help of a skilled professional, you so arrange your finances that the business in your home [territory] continually owes money to your Company [in this jurisdiction] – so much so that the business in your home [territory] shows little or no profit. The profits show up in your Corporation [in this jurisdiction] where there is no . . . income tax and where no one knows you own the company . . .

[This jurisdiction] does not require tax reports, and it does not share the information it does gather . . .

If a corporation is sued, the corporate shareholders are not personally responsible for the liability. It is a thing that is apart from you – it is not you – even though you may control it and enjoy great benefits from it. For example, the corporation could accumulate debts that benefit you, and then go bankrupt, leaving your estate out of the settlement.[27]

It is suggested that the sentiments expressed here would cause great trouble for any 'Offshore Finance Centre' that dared to publish them.

18.9.2 Delaware

Delaware is a sovereign state within the United States. It is not subject to scrutiny by the OECD or by the FATF. Delaware is said to be home to only one-third of 1 per cent of Americans.

---

[27] Peter Neville, 'Implications for Financial Intermediaries', *Journal of Financial Crime*, July 2002, p. 75.

America's corporate scandals have wreaked havoc with other institutions empowered to regulate the nation's errant businessmen. The Securities and Exchange Commission (SEC) lost a chairman, as did the New York Stock Exchange – and both have lost plenty of prestige. Yet Delaware has escaped, once again, untouched.[28]

Delaware became an 'Offshore' jurisdiction on 1 October 1992 when the Delaware Limited Liability Company Act became effective and tax-free status for non-resident companies became a reality in the US.[29]

The *New York Times* published an article on 29 November 2000 that referred to a Congressional inquiry that had established that it was relatively easy for foreigners in the USA to form shell companies using false identities to enable money laundering. More than US $1.4 billion was involved. Accounts had been opened by Irakly Kaveladze, a Russian immigrant. He established more than 2,000 companies in Delaware for Russian brokers, for whom he set up bank accounts. The report casti-gated the banks for failure to perform any due diligence checks. The inquiry was initiated by Senator Carl Levin, who said that:

We routinely and legitimately criticise foreign countries that allow the creation of corporations with secret ownership for the purpose of hiding money. Yet, some American states, including Delaware, let companies incorporate without disclosing owners and officers, and that allows the establishment of a private corporation that can be used for money laun-dering.[30]

A filing fee of US $100 is required to establish a company in Delaware that will have no tax liability to the federal government.

No information about the members or the beneficial owners is requested. No financial information about the company is required. No address information, identification of the location of the company's offices or operations is requested . . . Delaware registered agents are not required to maintain records on the beneficial owners of Delaware companies.[31]

The types of entity that are available in Delaware include the following:

---

[28] 'Triumph of the Pygmy State', *The Economist*, 25 October 2003, p. 23.
[29] Rick Bell, 'Offshore Financial Centres USA – Delaware', The OECD Report 2003, p. 181.
[30] Raymond Bonner, 'Inquiry Grows in Laundering of Money', *New York Times*, 29 Novem-ber 2000.
[31] Rick Bell, 'Offshore Financial Centres USA – Delaware', The OECD Report 2003, p. 181.

- tax-exempt limited liability companies;
- Delaware business trusts that allow the client to fix the relationship between the trustee and the beneficiary;
- Delaware holding companies;
- Delaware general corporations; and
- Delaware close corporations, which do not need a board of directors.

Remote access to the Division of Corporations means that all filings receive immediate attention.

> Three times in the past century Delaware faced explicit federal threats to its influence. Yet today, even as Americans choke with disgust at monstrous executive pay, corporate looting and spineless boards, no one in power suggests that supposedly business friendly Delaware should be stripped of its authority.[32]

18.10 Qualified intermediary status

Ordinarily, 30 per cent withholding tax is applied to dividends on US securities which are paid to intermediaries outside the USA and overseas intermediaries must disclose the identity of the beneficial owners of US stocks unless the intermediary becomes a 'Qualified intermediary' (QI). However, an intermediary may not apply to the Inland Revenue Service (IRS) for QI status unless the jurisdiction where the intermediary is based can demonstrate that its 'know your customer' rules are of an acceptable standard. In this respect, the IRS is responsible for deciding which jurisdictions will be regarded as 'qualified jurisdictions'.

It is clearly important for jurisdictions where there are intermediaries who have clients who want to deal in US stocks to apply for and to obtain recognition as a 'qualified jurisdiction'.

18.11 The US and the OECD's Harmful Tax Initiative

While President Clinton was in office, the USA had supported the OECD's initiative in respect of what the OECD referred to as 'tax havens'. It took a little while for the Bush administration to clarify its approach. The attitude of the USA to the OECD's Report on Harmful Tax Competition was summed up on 10 May 2001 by Mr Paul O'Neill, the Treasury Secretary:

---

[32] 'Triumph of the Pygmy State', *The Economist*, 25 October 2003, p. 23.

I share many of the serious concerns that have been expressed recently about the direction of the OECD initiative. I am troubled by the underlying premise that low tax rates are somehow suspect and by the notion that any country, or group of countries, should interfere in any other country's decision about how to structure its own tax system. I also am concerned about the potentially unfair treatment of some non-OECD countries. The United States does not support efforts to dictate to any country what its own tax rates or tax system should be, and will not participate in any initiative to harmonise world tax systems. The United States simply has no interest in stifling the competition that forces governments like businesses to create efficiencies . . . The work of this particular OECD initiative, however, must be refocused on the core element that is our common goal: the need for countries to be able to obtain specific information from other countries upon request in order to prevent the illegal evasion of their tax laws by the dishonest few. In its present form the project is too broad and it is not in line with this administration's tax and economic priorities.[33]

This view supports that advocated by the US's Heritage Foundation which believes that there should be consolidated action against crime but not the indiscriminate exchange of private financial information by governments to enforce tax laws. This statement marks the end of what the Foundation referred to as the first phase of the battle over tax competition. It was followed by debate about information exchange and the conditions and circumstances under which such exchange is acceptable. The argument is that the enforcement of tax laws on an extraterritorial basis, 'fishing expeditions' for information and ignoring a jurisdiction's right to determine what is a crime, are all unacceptable.

18.12 The USA Patriot Act

After the terrorist attacks in New York, Washington and Pennsylvania on 11 September 2001, the USA responded by declaring war against terrorism (see section 11.7 above). The USA took wide-ranging diplomatic, political and economic action in response. This included the International Money Laundering Abatement and Anti-Terrorism Financing Act which is Part III of the USA Patriot Act (which is an acronym for

---

[33] 'The US Announces its Stand on the OECD Harmful Tax Initiative', Vol. 3 No. 10, June 2001, *Private Wealth Investor.*

'Uniting and Strengthening America by Providing Appropriate Tools Required to Intercept and Obstruct Terrorism').

The USA Patriot Act is a robust piece of legislation that became law on 26 October 2001. It enables the USA to take action against anyone, anywhere who breaches the anti-money laundering rules that apply in the USA. For example, the USA claims jurisdiction over any part of any bank's global operation if that bank has money on deposit with a bank in the USA or processes any payments through the USA. Part III strengthens the provisions put in place by the Bank Secrecy Act and by the Money Laundering Control Act. Generally speaking, the relevant provisions deal with the prevention, detection and prosecution of money laundering and the financing of terrorism. In signing the Act on 26 October 2001, President Bush said that it would help to defeat terrorism and at the same time to protect the constitutional rights of US citizens. He said that this legislation would assist in identifying, dismantling, disrupting and punishing terrorists before they strike. The law regarding the sharing of information was changed but so also was the culture of the agencies engaged in the fight against terrorism. In summary, the Act requires financial institutions to:

- Establish a more formalised anti-money laundering (AML) program;
- Designate an AML compliance officer;
- Implement an ongoing training program;
- File Suspicious Activity Reports (SARs) on an ongoing basis;
- Verify identity of new account customers;
- Determine whether potential customers appear on any list of known or suspected terrorists provided to financial institutions by any government agencies;
- Continual reporting and information sharing.[34]

The USA finally adopted the 'know your customer' principles that legislators in the USA had rejected for so long (see section 18.8 above). That said, the legislation quoted above has much to say about the identification of those who try to open accounts from outside the USA and on correspondent banking requirements. Whether this means that the focus is external remains to be seen.

---

[34] James Fisher, James Gilsinan, Ellen Harshman, Muhammed Islam and Fred Yeager, 'Assessing the Impact of the USA PATRIOT Act on the Financial Services Industry', Vol. 8, No. 3, *Journal of Money Laundering Control*, p. 243.

> In private, however, bankers with long experience of financial crime say
> that many of the rules introduced since September 11 to keep terrorists
> out of the mainstream financial system will not achieve their aim . . .
> Before September 11, America lagged Europe in its rules against money
> laundering. With the Patriot Act passed in October last year, America has
> caught up and in some cases has gone beyond Europe.[35]

It should be noted that the terrorists needed no more than US $500,000
to finance the destruction they caused – and this money was processed
through the United Arab Emirates.

18.12.1 UN Convention for the Suppression of the financing of Terrorism

Members of the UN were able to sign and to ratify the International
Convention for the Suppression of the Financing of Terrorism (Convention 54/109, dated 19 December 1999) from 10 January 2000. Prior to 11
September 2001, only forty-two countries had signed and only four
(Botswana, Sri Lanka, the UK and Uzbekistan) had ratified it.[36] Between
11 September 2001 and 19 February 2002, ninety more countries signed
and thirteen more had ratified the Convention. However, at that stage,
the US had 'not yet ratified or fully implemented the 1999 United
Nations International Convention for the Suppression of the Financing
of Terrorism, which was the first proposal on the Task Force's October
list. Neither have Germany, Italy and Japan.'[37]

In response to the attacks of 11 September 2001, the UN Security
Council adopted Resolution 1373, which required members of the UN to
take certain measures to prevent and combat terrorism. These included
immediate action to freeze funds and any other financial asset or resource
of any person involved in terrorist acts, whether they have committed
these acts, attempted to commit them or facilitated their commission. In
this respect, a Counter Terrorism Committee was established to monitor
implementation of the steps required under Security Council Resolution
1373. As at the end of 2003, 'all the 191 member states [of the UN] had

---

[35] 'Anti-Money Laundering: "The Needle in the Haystack"', *The Economist*, 14 December
2002, p. 81.
[36] Jackie Johnson, '11 September 2001: Will It Make a Difference to the Global Anti-Money
Laundering Movement?', Vol. 6, No. 1, *Journal of Money Laundering Control*, p. 12.
[37] 'Don't Relax', Leader, *The Economist*, 1 June 2002, p. 12.

submitted reports detailing the steps and measures they had taken to implement the resolution'.[38]

18.13 Information exchange treaties

In July 2001, the US Treasury Secretary, Mr Paul O'Neill, said that, within twelve months, the USA intended to implement tax treaties with half of the thirty-five countries that the OECD had identified as tax havens. This would enable the USA to pursue suspected criminals through individually tailored treaties. This strategy seems to be much more effective than trying to compel such centres to amend their tax structures. The first such agreement was established (27 November 2001) with the UK Government on behalf of the Cayman Islands (a UK Overseas Territory). The Cayman Islands is one of the largest banking centres in the world (see section 16.4.7 above).

The agreement covers the exchange of information, upon request, in respect of tax evasion and civil and administrative tax matters that concern US federal tax. The question is what this will mean for the future of the 'Offshore' environment. Treaties have been signed since with many other jurisdictions, including Antigua and Barbuda, Bermuda, the Bahamas, Barbados, the Cayman Islands, Jamaica, the Netherlands (in respect of Aruba) and Trinidad and Tobago.

On the other hand, it has been suggested that '[t]ax harmonisation is a direct threat to America's economic interests . . . At a minimum, "information exchange" would drive several hundred billion dollars out of the US economy. The capital flight easily could exceed $1 trillion.'[39]

18.14 Corporate inversion

Corporate inversion (see section 18.3 above) refers to 'a legal transaction through which the corporate structure of a United States based multinational group is altered so that a foreign corporation replaces the existing US parent corporation as the head of the corporate group. By relocating their headquarters offshore, American businesses can avoid

---

[38] Abdullahi Y. Shehu, 'International Initiatives Against Corruption and Money Laundering: An Overview', Vol. 12, No. 3, *Journal of Financial Crime*, p. 227.
[39] 'The Adverse Impact of Tax Harmonisation and Information Exchanges on the US Economy' *Prosperitas*, November 2001, www.freedomandprosperity.org/Papers/tax-harm/taxharm.shtml.

the high and complex income taxes that their foreign competitors don't have to pay.'[40] The corporate objective is to mitigate tax, but critics of inversion label the procedure as an 'unpatriotic' means of evading tax. Between twenty and thirty corporations have inverted.

This is another example of the dangers of perceptions that are wrong. In fact, even though a US corporation 'inverts', its structure does not alter in any way other than as described above. Inversion is a legitimate procedure that attempts to place US companies on a par with foreign companies trading in world markets. Such US companies pay around 40 per cent tax in aggregate – compared to the average 30 per cent tax rate paid in most developed countries. In addition, and unlike companies incorporated abroad, companies incorporated in the USA must pay tax on any income they earn abroad. Consequently, US firms are at a disadvantage because they must either pay more tax than their competitors or refrain from transacting business in the USA.

18.15 Problems in the USA

Like every other jurisdiction, whether 'Onshore' or 'Offshore', commercial activity brings with it a series of problems. Here are some of the difficulties that have faced the USA in the recent past:

18.15.1 General

Individuals that have been punished by the courts for financial crime include John Rigas and his son Timothy (former Chief Executive and Chief Financial Officer respectively of Adelphia Communications). 'They stole $100 million and hid $2 billion in corporate debt, thus looting and defrauding shareholders.'[41] The article just cited refers to others that have been sentenced within the past twenty-four months. The list includes: Andrew Fastow (Enron), ten years; Martin Glass (Rite Aid), eight years; Jamie Olis (Dynegy), twenty-four years; and Sam Waksal (Im-Clone Systems), seven years. The former Chief Executive of WorldCom, Bernie Ebbers, was sentenced to twenty-five years in prison for his role in the bankruptcy of the company. One person who was tried but found not

---

[40] Grover Norquist and Damon Ansell, 'The Case for Inversion', *Offshore Red*, June 2003, p. 93.
[41] 'Off to Jail', *The Economist*, 25 June 2005, p. 81.

guilty was Richard Scrushy, founder and former Chief Executive of HealthSouth (provider of services to outpatients). The case of Mr Scrushy is interesting not least because he 'was the first Chief Executive to be charged with knowingly filing false statements under the Sarbanes–Oxley Act . . . [T]he firm's restated results released on June 27th [2005] put the total misstatement at $3.9 billion.'[42]

The problem is not restricted to individuals. Consider the case of Deloitte & Touche Wealth Management, which was fined US $750,000 for inadequate compliance arrangements between 1997 and 2001. These were described as 'systemic and continued for a prolonged period of time'.[43]

The problem is not restricted to one discipline. For example, in response to a scandal that arose in October 2004 involving insurance companies colluding with brokers and inflated prices, one commentator said: 'The inability of state regulators to oversee properly an insurance industry now dominated by big firms adds to the already strong case for Congress to create a federal regulator to monitor the industry nationwide.'[44] In May 2005, one observer said that 'In the past year, all the biggest American banks – Citigroup, J. P. Morgan Chase and Bank of America – have been in trouble of one kind or another.'[45] One of the latter cases, together with others, are described below.

18.15.2 Citigroup

In the USA, Congressional investigators found that Citigroup, for example, has held assets for the sons of Mr Abacha; Raul Salinas de Gortari, a brother of the former President of Mexico, who is in prison for masterminding a murder; Asif Ali Zardari, husband of a former Prime Minister of Pakistan, who is in jail for corruption; President Omar Bongo of Gabon, subject of a French corruption enquiry; and two daughters of former President Suharto of Indonesia. Citigroup says that it has overhauled its procedures to make sure it does not accept corruption linked deposits. A bank spokesman said Citigroup 'applauded the efforts of the Treasury department to combat money laundering. But

---

[42] 'Face Value – With God on His Side', *The Economist*, 2 July 2005, pp. 9 and 66.
[43] 'News', *Compliance Monitor*, February 2004, p. 6.
[44] 'Reprehensible', *The Economist*, 23 October 2004, p. 13.
[45] David Shirreff, 'Don't Start from Here: A Survey of International Banking', *The Economist*, 21 May 2005, p. 11.

Citigroup was among a consortium of leading New York banks that led an effort in late December to water down the new guidelines.'[46] Further, '[t]he General Accounting Office (GAO), the investigative arm of the US Congress, has rebuked Citigroup for not following government guidelines to prevent money laundering and for allowing up to $800 m in Russian "funny money" to pass through 136 of its accounts between 1991 and January 2000. The report is . . . especially embarrassing for Citigroup coming one year after an inquiry into the possible laundering of $100 m in Mexican drug money.'[47] That said, Citigroup's profit in 2003 was US $17.85 billion (said to be more than any other company – ever!). As the result of an investigation undertaken between November 2003 and April 2004, Citibank Japan was required by the Financial Services Authority to suspend new operations from 29 September 2004 and to close down four offices (with effect from September 2005). These measures represent the cumulative result of a number of breaches of legislation and regulations.[48] Citigroup has faced other problems as well. In June 2005, it was reported that Citigroup 'had lost information on 3.9 million current and former customers when some unencrypted computer tapes went astray while being handled by United Parcel Service'.[49] Stealing data – which frequently includes personal information – which in turn sometimes end up as stealing identities is a growing crime.

18.15.3 Xerox

In June 2003, the Securities and Exchange Commission imposed a five-year ban on Paul Allaire, the boss of Xerox in the late 1990s, preventing him from acting as a director or officer of a public company. There was also the possibility at the time of a criminal investigation by the Department of Justice. Mr Allaire was in charge of Xerox at the time it 'injected non-existent profits into its accounts to the tune of $1.4 billion'. In fact, the SEC fined Mr Allaire US $1 million and ordered him to pay US $7.6 million as 'disgorgement' of the fraud. However, the company's byelaws indemnified its executives from any such punitive measure – which

---

[46] Joseph Khan, 'Clinton Seeks to Keep Foreigners from Hiding Wealth in US', *New York Times*, 16 January 2001.

[47] 'Citigroup Rebuked over Laundering', *The Banker*, January 2001.

[48] Mayumi Negishi, 'Citibank Japan Ordered to Close Four Offices over Legal Breaches', *Japan Times*, 18 September 2004.

[49] 'Hot Data', *The Economist*, 25 June 2005, p. 18.

means that Xerox will pay the US $7.6 million on Mr Allaire's behalf, and another US $11.8 million which the SEC has levied on five other Xerox executives. Described by the SEC as 'a particularly egregious fraud', the net result is that Mr Allaire has a net gain of US $6.6 million. Xerox's byelaws are not uncommon in the USA. The moral hazard is compounded by Xerox's intention to claim the money from its insurers. In short, those involved have suffered little punishment for the fraud that was perpetrated while they were in charge. Directors' and officers' insurance has been used for a purpose for which it was never intended.[50]

18.15.4 Mutual funds

There are said to be more than 95 million investors with more than US $7 trillion invested in mutual funds in the USA. In April 2003, the Securities and Exchange Commission in the USA initiated an inquiry into sales of mutual funds and investigations concerning the trading procedures of some funds. (Unlawful trading includes late trading and market timing. Late trading is illegal. It allows special clients to buy shares – after the market has closed – at the closing price. This enables buyers to use information released late in the day to process trades – while other would-be buyers have to wait until the market reopens the next day. Market timing refers to the practice of using time differences between markets to transact rapid short-term trades at non-current prices. This reduces the value of the fund for standard investors and allows traders to make profits.)

In one case, a settlement was reached in September 2003 by Canary Capital Partners Hedge Fund. 'Canary, two related entities and their manager Edward Stern agreed, without admitting wrongdoing, to pay $40 million over allegations of unlawful trading . . . [In another case, the SEC found that] . . . Putnam had committed securities fraud by not disclosing self-dealing by several of its employees.'[51] Putnam agreed to make changes to its corporate governance, ethics and compliance standards and agreed to pay restitution and fines, the amount of which was to be agreed. The full results of the inquiry were released on 13 January 2004. The inquiry established that six brokers and thirteen

[50] 'Directors' Insurance – Double Indemnity', Leader, *The Economist*, 14 June 2003, p. 14.
[51] Ben Maiden, 'SEC Faces Critics over Mutual Funds Scandal', *International Financial Law Review*, December 2003, p. 21.

fund companies improperly promoted the sale of mutual funds in circumstances where the incentives were not disclosed transparently. The identity of those involved was not disclosed at that stage – although this information became public later – and included such names as FleetBoston. On 15 March 2004, it was announced that a settlement had been reached as follows: 'a $675 m agreement with Bank of America and FleetBoston Financial . . . [B]oth banks' mutual-fund subsidiaries were alleged to have allowed "market timers" to trade in and out of their funds, generating higher costs that ate into long-term investors' returns.'[52] Janus Capital paid a fine of US $50 million and paid another US $50 million to investors to settle allegations of improper trading and reduced fees by another US $125 million.[53] Strong Financial paid US $140 million in settlement of charges.[54] The story seemed never-ending: in June 2004, Bank One agreed to pay US $50 million in respect of a settlement concerning the improper trading of mutual funds.

18.15.5 Vivendi Universal

The Securities and Exchange Commission charged Vivendi Universal and two of its French executives with systematic fraud between 1999 and 2002. Vivendi almost collapsed in 2002. The case was settled in December 2003.

18.15.6 UBS AG

The Federal Reserve fined UBS AG US $100 million in May 2004. Switzerland's largest bank was accused of sending dollars to Cuba, Libya, Iran and Yugoslavia in violation of sanctions imposed against those countries.

18.15.7 Riggs National Bank

Riggs National Bank has been called the 'bank of presidents', having been bankers to more than twenty first families. In May 2004, it was announced that Riggs had been fined US $25 million. The charge was for alleged

---

[52] 'Unsettling', *The Economist*, 20 March 2004, p. 103.
[53] 'The World This Week', *The Economist*, 1 May 2004, p. 9.
[54] 'The World This Week', *The Economist*, 29 May 2004, p. 9.

violations of the Bank Secrecy Act. The Treasury's Financial Crimes
Enforcement Network said Riggs was being fined for 'wilful, systemic
violations of the anti-money laundering program and suspicious activity
and currency transaction reporting requirements'.[55] In January 2005, 'the
bank pleaded guilty to money laundering offences concerning the accounts of various foreigners, including Augusto Pinochet, the former
dictator of Chile'.[56] The bank was fined US $16 million. On 10 February
2005, the bank was sold to PNC Financial (a Pennsylvania bank) for US
$654 million (although the agreed price in July 2004 was US $779 million).

18.16 Sarbanes–Oxley Act

The Sarbanes–Oxley Act of 2002 was the USA's response to the corporate
scandals (including Enron) that rocked the country in 2001–2. The
purpose of the legislation is to 'protect investors by improving
the accuracy and reliability of corporate disclosures made pursuant to
the securities laws'.[57] In summary, the Act:

- created a new Public Company Accounting Oversight Board to oversee auditors;
- requires auditors to report to an independent audit committee;
- makes chief executives and chief financial officers responsible for the
  accuracy of financial statements;
- protects whistleblowers who report fraud;
- emphasises the importance of internal controls;
- imposes new requirements for internal controls over financial
  reporting and deterring and detecting fraud; and
- introduces substantial penalties and criminal sanctions.

It has been suggested that, while the Act contains important provisions arising from the need to deal with conflicts of interest amongst
auditors, and to prevent auditors from becoming too familiar with the
client company's managers, it went too far in some respects, for example
with respect to the severe criminal penalties that managers may face.
Further, the cost implications are substantial. 'A survey by the FEI, an

[55] Mark Felsenthal, 'Fed Orders Reviews for Diplomats' Bank', Reuters news service.
[56] 'Riggs National Bank and PNC – A Deal of Trouble', *The Economist*, 12 February 2005,
   p. 67.
[57] House of Representatives Conf Report, No. 107-610, 2002 p. 1.

association of top financial executives, found that companies paid an average of $2.4m more for their audits last year than they had anticipated (and far more than the statute's designers had envisaged).'[58] Perversely, this windfall has brought substantial benefits to the very profession whose work above all others was at the heart of the scandals that provoked the legislation in the first place – although it might be argued that the failures were more to do with corporate governance matters than with accounting per se. 'Many of the problems at Enron remained hidden because the relationships between its managers and its auditors, Arthur Andersen, were far too warm.'[59] In accordance with section 301 of the Act, the SEC (in 2003) created a rule requiring national securities exchanges to disallow listing where the issuer's audit committee had not established an appropriate complaints procedure for complaints concerning accounting, auditing, internal controls and whistleblowing. The audit committee must develop compliance procedures in respect of the types of misconduct described above.[60]

Euopean companies that are listed on the New York Stock Exchange – or that deal with other companies so listed – are also affected by this Act.

---

[58] 'Special Report: Sarbanes–Oxley', *The Economist*, 21 May 2005, p. 82.
[59] 'Special Report: Sarbanes–Oxley', *The Economist*, 21 May 2005, p. 83.
[60] Standards Relating to Listed Company Audit Committees, Exchange Act Release Nos. 33-820,34-47654, 17 CFR paras. 228, 229, 240, 249 and 274, 25 April 2003.

19

Can the problems be identified?

One of the most dangerous errors instilled into us by nineteenth century progressive optimism is the idea that civilization is automatically bound to increase and spread. The lesson of history is the opposite.[1]

19.1 Introduction

Previous chapters have shown the extent to which the global 'Offshore' environment has been the focus of substantial attention in the recent past. Why should there be so much interest all of a sudden? After all, 'Offshore' is nothing new, so why should it arouse so much attention and action just at the time it did? Were there new issues – or have the old issues assumed greater significance? Or is this bout of attention stirred up by paranoia – or what?

19.2 What are the issues?

It seems that, in respect of at least three areas of the global economy, 'Offshore Finance Centres' are considered to be material. The three areas are:

- global financial stability;
- money laundering; and
- tax evasion.

Some comments about each follow. But, before that, it has to be recognised that much of the blame attaching to 'Offshore Finance Centres' derives from the fact that, until quite recently (say, within the last twenty years), regulation was light, cross-border cooperation was not general and transparency was limited in these jurisdictions. (To place this

---

[1] C. S. Lewis, *Rehabilitations.*

into context, there was no banking legislation in the UK until 1979. Therefore, things may not be so extreme as they first appear.) That said, as this text has demonstrated, many things have changed in the intervening period. Most 'Offshore Finance Centres' have gone to great lengths to improve their status internationally – not least in respect of legislative developments. However, legitimacy does not depend merely on having appropriate legislation in place – it must be properly applied. Most 'Offshore Finance Centres' realise this and are in the process of showing by their deeds that this is the case. They must be given the chance to prove themselves if we are to move forward.

There are of course some additional charges – the 'fair play' arguments. These include claims that OFCs dilute the tax revenue of G7 countries and that they absorb money from emerging countries and thereby make it more difficult for such countries to develop. It is not possible to refute such arguments categorically – in the same way that it is not easy to say why some people go hungry even though there is enough food in the world to feed them. It might be argued that, if the tax rates in G7 countries were lower, there might be less incentive to avoid tax abroad. One argument is no fairer than the other. Similarly, it is not the responsibility of OFCs to provide for the development of under-developed countries.

19.3 Global financial stability

It has been said that '[s]ome of the characteristics of OFCs raise concerns about potential risks to international financial stability'.[2] No one would argue that global financial stability is unimportant, but the Financial Stability Forum (FSF) has concluded that OFCs are not a threat to global financial stability. Whether this is ever likely to change remains to be seen, but, for the time being at least, the threat has not crystallised and it is therefore inappropriate to behave as if it had. It might be preferable to focus more attention on how OFCs might complement efforts to maintain global financial stability. This is a very complex phenomenon – and any one factor, such as regulation, will be inadequate in isolation to deal with all the permutations and variables. In any event, excess

---

[2] Salim M. Darbar, R. Barry Johnston and Mary G. Zephirin, 'Assessing Offshore Financial Centres – Filling a Gap in Global Surveillance', *Finance and Development*, September 2003, p. 35.

regulation is a negative force because it stifles creativity. Further, it is liable to suffocate the business that promoted OFCs in the first place. Market forces will not prevent business relocating 'Offshore': the business will merely locate elsewhere or adopt a different form.

So what role might regulation satisfy? If financial services are to be developed and maintained in any centre (whether 'Offshore' or 'On-shore'), a satisfactory regulatory system is a prerequisite. Without regulation, there is unlikely to be stability. In the previous sentence, the word 'satisfactory' should be interpreted to mean that the regulatory system must be robust, independent and transparent although 'lack of transparency does not cause crises nor can transparency inoculate a country against crises'.[3] (Nevertheless, transparency is likely to increase. For example, when the UN Convention Against Corruption becomes effective globally, there is likely to be more banking transparency – which will affect international financial services centres. The Convention has already been signed by several governments as far back as 2003.) The word 'regulation' does not imply rigidity and inflexibility, which are likely to result from the improper application of regulations. Ideally, regulatory action should take the form of incremental corrections – not absolute control.

Much has already been written about what constitutes acceptability in respect of regulatory matters. The review of regulation in the UK's White Paper, 'Partnership for Progress and Prosperity: Britain and the Overseas Territories' (described in Chapter 14 above), cites four papers which address this particular issue. They are:

- 'Objectives and Principles of Securities Regulation' (IOSCO);
- 'Core Principles for Effective Banking Supervision' (Basel Committee);
- 'The Supervision of Cross Border Banking' (Basel Committee and the OGBS); and
- 'Insurance Principles, Standards and Guidance Papers' (IAIS).

These papers contain much useful comment – not least concerning the benefits of regulators cooperating across borders. It is entirely logical for countries to cooperate in the fight against international crime – and adherence to the provisions described in these documents is a very

---

[3] Joseph Stiglitz, *Globalisation and its Discontents*, Penguin Books, 2002, p. 211.

effective starting point. This type of adherence will help to eliminate 'regulatory arbitrage' as described in section 6.25 above.

Many 'Offshore' jurisdictions already have treaties that provide for mutual assistance between the jurisdiction and other countries. This type of mutual assistance indicates a responsible attitude and a willingness to deal with wrongdoing. However, mutual legal assistance treaties are agreed in order to combat international crime. They must not be used for purposes other than those for which they were originally intended – such as the collection of tax.

In respect of regulation, prevention is always better than cure. The first step on the road to probity is to ensure that appropriate legislation is in place. The second step is to enforce the legislation and the third step is to assist other countries to do the same. It is likely that, increasingly, pressure will be brought to bear on centres with inferior legislation or unacceptable operational standards or which are unwilling to extend assistance to curb wrongdoing. This pressure will emanate from at least two sources. The first is from consumers (as defined in Chapter 4). Companies will avoid using centres that have unacceptable moral and ethical standards and the effect will be a marked downturn in business. The second source is the global community of supranational regulators. If individual centres do not exert self-discipline, then discipline will be imposed. Regrettably, OFCs have not paid sufficient attention to this truism in the past.

In the midst of all this, there is a general approach which dictates that 'Offshore' jurisdictions – in common with larger 'Onshore' countries (such as the USA) – do not assist other countries to enforce their legislation (unless the alleged offence is an offence 'Offshore' as well). The application of this principle is perhaps most acutely felt in respect of tax. Whether nations with high tax rates can expect nations with lower tax rates (which are often 'Offshore' jurisdictions) to assist the home government to ensure that its citizens adhere to the home country's tax rules remains to be seen. A resolution of this dichotomy would enable great progress to be made.

In summary, while there is likely to be consensus that global financial stability is fundamentally significant, there is no consensus about whether OFCs are a threat (potential or actual) in this respect – even though the FSF has said that they are not. This incongruence detracts from the synergy that might otherwise be available as a result of greater cohesion between 'Offshore' (a material component of the global financial environment) and 'Onshore'. Further, while appropriate regulation

will contribute to attaining financial stability, it is only one of myriad
controls and checks that might be employed.

19.4 The money laundering threat

The argument has been made that the way to prevent major crime (e.g.
drugs trafficking, terrorism and tax evasion) is to prevent money laundering. In the absence of appropriate evidence, this argument is not
persuasive per se. Governments around the world have expended vast
resources to combat money laundering but there has been no concurrent
reduction in drugs trafficking, terrorism and tax evasion. For example,
the State Governor of New Mexico has been quoted as saying: 'The
federal anti-drug budget in 1980 was roughly $1 billion. By 2000, that
number had climbed to nearly $20 billion with the states spending at
least that much. Yet according to the federal government's own research,
drugs are cheaper, purer and more readily available than ever before.'[4] As
if the greater availability is not enough, 'fewer than 1,000 people per year
have been convicted of money laundering in the US since it became
illegal. The amount of money confiscated is a tiny fraction of 1 per cent
of the total amount of money the government says is laundered each
year.'[5] So there are now more drugs around than there used to be and yet
fewer people have been caught peddling them despite the fact that

> [b]etween 1987 and 1995, the government collected 77 million currency
> transaction reports, something of the order of 62 tons of paper. Out of
> that, it was able to prosecute 3,000 money laundering cases. That is
> roughly one case for every 25,000 forms filed. In other words, entire
> forests had to be felled in order to prosecute one case. But it gets worse:
> Of the 3,000 money laundering cases prosecuted, the government man-
> aged to produce only 580 guilty verdicts. In other words, in excess of
> 100,000 reports were filed by innocent citizens in order to get one convic-
> tion. That ratio of 99,999 to one is something we would not normally
> tolerate as a reasonable balance between privacy and the collection of
> guilty verdicts.[6]

---

[4] Gary Johnson, Governor of New Mexico, *New York Times*, 30 December 2000.
[5] 'Why the War on Money Laundering Is Counter Productive', a presentation by Richard
     W. Rahn, at the Conference on 'Anti-Money Laundering 2001', 30 January 2001.
[6] Former Federal Reserve Governor Lawrence Lindsey, as reported in 'Why the War on
     Money Laundering is Counter Productive', presentation by Richard W. Rahn at the
     Conference on 'Anti-Money Laundering 2001', 30 January 2001.

There appears to be no evidence to suggest that the experience of any other country is better than that of the USA – which is that, despite all the effort, action taken thus far has not been successful.

'A Commonwealth spokesman characterised the issue of money laundering as a red herring. This is not about money laundering he said. It's about the competition for global capital.'[7] Is it possible to deal with money laundering by focusing on the proceeds of the crime instead of the criminal offence per se? This is the basis of the philosophy of the thinking behind – for example – the Assets Recovery Agency in the UK (see section 8.19 above) and the Criminal Assets Bureau in Ireland.

In respect of terrorism, the evidence is no more compelling. There can be no doubt that the threat of terrorism is real and must be dealt with – but it is not clear that 'Offshore Finance Centres' are being used by terrorists to launder money to the extent being suggested. Not everyone agrees – and, in light of the horrific terrorist acts perpetrated by Osama bin Laden on the American people on 11 September 2001, Spain in 2004 and London in July 2005, it is easy to understand why people are anxious to take action to starve terrorists of access to the world's financial systems. This is entirely appropriate. Reactions expressed include:

> A genuine attack on banking secrecy. . .will involve shutting down the offshore finance industry. No other solution will do . . . The banking industry needs to freeze offshore centres and offshore banks out of the system. True, most 'Offshore' business is legitimate. It consists of companies who want to manipulate their tax accounts, and rich people who want to hide their money from divorce lawyers. But it has created a system in which tracking terrorists is virtually impossible.[8]

A senior US Government official is reported to have said that, '[i]f necessary, we will use the considerable persuasive powers of the US to close certain [offshore] centres down'.[9] Perhaps that official had evidence to support the sort of action that was being suggested – in which case, the evidence should be presented to allow the appropriate action to be taken. If that is not the case, we must be careful not to adopt extreme

---

[7] Patrick Tracey, 'Global Tax Forum Proposed by Offshore Tax Jurisdictions', Bureau of International Affairs, 30 January 2001.

[8] Matthew Lynn, 'Time to End Banking Secrecy', *Bloomberg.com*, 10 February 2001.

[9] Conal Walsh, 'America Wants to Scrap the World's Tax Havens', *Observer*, 23 September 2001.

positions that are not tenable. Using a sledgehammer to crack a nut is not a prudent way forward.

The attack on 'Offshore' goes on:

> Offshore banks that facilitate money laundering have been tolerated until now precisely because they have served the interests of many within the financial and business community . . . [G]lobalisation provides criminals with a complex and opaque international financial system, where few questions are asked about the origin of money.[10]

The extent to which this is true remains to be seen but – to add some balance – even the most sensitive information retained by banks can be obtained by a court order.

It should be borne in mind that the FATF said: 'The legitimate use by private citizens and institutional investors of certain facilities offered by many financial centres, including Offshore centres, is not put in question.'[11]

Meanwhile, we should not lose sight of the fact that the Universal Declaration on Human Rights guarantees fundamental rights to privacy – which includes financial privacy. The question is how this right can be preserved – because it is a legitimate right that should not be abused.

In summary, it seems that more money is laundered through OECD countries than through any other country grouping. It also seems that that USA and the UK are used more than any other country to launder money. On the basis of the information contained in the preceding chapters, it seems legitimate to question whether the 'Offshore' environment poses any greater opportunities to the global fight against money laundering than that posed by the 'Onshore' environment. However, none of this is really the kernel of the matter. The key question is whether there is any concerted action that can be taken to deal with these problems. Ongoing finger-pointing – and all that follows – merely absorbs limited resources and presumably amuses those who continue to benefit from the authorities not 'getting their act together'. In any event, it seems that it is time for a rethink of the strategy employed to defeat drug trafficking because, despite the resources allocated to this problem, the solution has not been found thus far. For example, it may

---

[10] Leif Pagrotsky (Minister of Trade for Sweden) and Joseph Stiglitz (Professior of Economics at Columbia University and Nobel Prize winner, 2001), 'Blocking the Terrorists' Funds', *Financial Times*, 7 December 2001.
[11] 'Report on Non-Cooperative Countries and Territories', FATF, 14 February 2000, p. 9.

be more productive to increase the resources devoted to determining how the demand for drugs can be reduced.

Some care has to be exercised to ensure that the amount of attention being devoted to anti-money laundering procedures – important though they are – does not reach a point where the amount of resource left to deal with (other) regulatory issues is too little. Getting the right balance is easier said than done.

19.5 Tax evasion

There is a great deal of confusion about the extent to which 'Offshore Finance Centres' are used to evade tax. The opening chapters described how confusion can easily lead to misperceptions which, when not refuted, can easily appear to be reality. The same applies to tax evasion. The first confusion arises because of the failure to distinguish between tax avoidance and tax evasion. The background has been described in some detail in Chapter 5. The second main confusion arises because inadequate care is taken to distinguish between the bona fides of the government imposing the tax in the first place. Some are corrupt – not all are honest and democratic.

Competition is good, not bad. If tax competition is 'harmful', that implies that other forms of competition may be harmful also – or at least suspect. This type of argument is difficult to defend. It has been said that tax competition is wrong because it will lead to a reduction in the revenue of the government imposing high rates of tax. While this is a distinct possibility, it does not follow in logic that thereby tax competition is wrong. Governments should be free to set their own tax rates, but, in so doing, they must accept responsibility for the implications of setting a tax rate that is so high that taxpayers will not accept it. Inevitably, this will lead such taxpayers to take alternative action. In the absence of a uniform global tax rate, there will always be an inclination to arbitrage. Meanwhile, capital flight must give a message to the government concerned.

There is a fine line here. On the one hand, consumers have a right to financial privacy. On the other hand, it is very easy to transfer money across borders and, in turn, this means that criminal activity in general and evading tax in particular becomes less difficult.

Questions have arisen about precisely what was reviewed in the FSF, the OECD and the FATF reports – and it seems that the distinction between tax avoidance and tax evasion is part of the dilemma. One

journalist has suggested that '[t]his is not about morals or even about
money laundering. It is about competition and an attempt to stem a
flight of funds from high tax countries to low tax countries.'[12] The
argument she made was that the direct measures necessary to stem the
flight of capital might lead to an exodus of people so the focus has
instead been turned on those jurisdictions where the cash can be deposited on a tax-free basis temporarily. This is likely to have an effect on
the economies of such jurisdictions.

The problem seems to be that 'Offshore Finance Centres' provide
the sort of opportunities that the higher rate tax jurisdictions cannot
provide for their citizens. Accordingly, since these jurisdictions cannot
control the actions of their citizens outside their own borders, they will
try to stop them some other way. The style chosen is to try to close down
the 'Offshore Finance Centres'. Is it not possible for the higher rate
centres to use their tax revenue more efficiently? If not, the advances in
technology that may occur over the next decade will make the control
process even more difficult than now – and what will happen to financial
privacy then?

The OECD has recognised that competitive forces 'have encouraged
countries to make their tax systems more attractive to investors. In
addition to lowering overall tax rates, a competitive environment can
promote greater efficiency in government programs.'[13]

In summary, 'Offshore Finance Centres' provide many opportunities
to people who want to minimise – by legitimate means – the amount of
tax they pay. Regrettably, the same services can be used in the same
jurisdictions by those who want to minimise – by illegitimate means –
the amount of tax they pay. That potential has been used to decry some
centres – but not all. For example, the UK and the USA do not suffer the
same criticism as do small 'Offshore Finance Centres' although they are
used similarly in many instances. Lastly in this respect, the example of
nuclear power was cited earlier to demonstrate how factors other than
'Offshore Finance Centres' can be used either for good or for evil. Even if
there were no 'Offshore Finance Centres', high tax nations would still not
receive all the tax they are due – so the problem does not arise merely
because of the existence of OFCs.

---

[12] Patience Wheatcroft, 'Paradigm Lost for the Dot-Coms', *The Times*, 27 June 2000.
[13] 'The OECD's Project on Harmful Tax Practices: The 2001 Progress Report', OECD,
    Centre for Tax Policy and Administration, declassified on 14 November 2001, p. 4.

Meanwhile, it has been suggested that 'many OECD governments appear to be exploiting the political climate post-September 11 to promote information exchange policies that have more to do with limiting tax competition than enhancing international efforts to apprehend terrorists and criminals'.[14]

19.6 What next?

It may be that part of the reason why OFCs are still referred to in pejorative terms is because of a lack of clear understanding about their role. It may be that greater efforts will be required by the OFCs themselves to adopt appropriate 'marketing' strategies to deal with this issue. According to Catherine Creech, a Washington-based attorney, 'anything that is "Offshore" has a negative implication to it these days'.[15] It has also been said that '[t]he billions of dollars in the Cayman Islands and other such centres are not there because those islands provide better banking services than Wall Street, London, or Frankfurt; they are there because the secrecy allows them to engage in tax evasion, money laundering, and other nefarious activities. Only after September 11 was it recognised that among those other nefarious activities was the financing of terrorism.'[16] This is a strong statement, which, in light of the preceding, seems more than a little unfair.

As for global financial stability, the answer does not lie in introducing greater regulatory controls, but perhaps in a different paradigm based on governance and refinement of the controls that exist already. To do otherwise will increase costs and bureaucracy even further – and, unless the outcome will be beneficial, greater inconvenience for consumers and lower dividends for shareholders will only increase frustrations further.

19.7 Summary

OFCs have got a bad name – and this is sometimes deserved, but not always. OFCs are a convenient whipping boy – and, as small jurisdictions, they often lack adequate critical mass and resources to defend

---

[14] David R. Burton, 'Towards a Global Tax Cartel', *Policy*, Summer (December–February) 2002–3.

[15] Hal Lux, 'Rich, Offshore, Taxable?', *Institutional Investor*, September 2002, p. 13.

[16] Joseph Stiglitz, *Globalisation and its Discontents*, Penguin Books, 2002, p. 228.

themselves effectively. In this respect, they have failed to optimise their potential for the synergy that would arise through combining their respective critical mass by joining forces and as a result have allowed a contrary public relations mechanism to decimate their image. OFCs are not as bad as they are sometimes made out to be – although they are often their own worst enemy.

Even if the concept of 'Offshore' did not exist, the threats to global financial stability, the seemingly uncontrollable growth of money laundering and the hardy perennial of tax evasion would not fall into line and everybody would not live happily ever after. So, what is the answer? The next chapter presents some ideas.

20

Offshore's future

> The most serious problems afflicting our society today are manifestly moral, behavioral and spiritual and therefore are remarkably resistant to government cures.[1]

20.1 Introduction

The global village is a reality. For the 'Offshore' environment, this means, on the one hand, that, if it is to optimise its value, 'Offshore' must be acknowledged as an integral part of the global economy, and, on the other hand, it must demonstrate that its standards are at least equal to those applied elsewhere in the global financial environment.

That said, nearly every attribute of an 'Offshore Finance Centre' exemplifies the fact that the same attributes that have contributed to making the 'Offshore' environment so conducive for international business, also represent its Achilles' heel in the here and now. Accordingly, the 'Offshore' environment must decide which course it is going to follow – continuous improvement or gradual decline. Expressed in this way, there is no real decision to be made – except that, if 'Offshore' is to continue to exist, ways and means must be found to accommodate all those who want to use its services legitimately. Logically, this means also that ways and means must be found to prevent those who want to use 'Offshore' for illegitimate purposes.

20.2 A glimpse of the future

By way of context, it has been estimated that the world's population is increasing by around 90 million persons per year – many of whom are

---

[1] William Bennett, *American Enterprise*, as quoted in R. Warren, *The Purpose Driven Church*, Zodervan, 1995, p. 20.

born in China. Further, 30 per cent of the current population is un-
employed – but all of us want a higher standard of living. The extent to
which these developments can be financed will cause many political and
economic debates – but inevitably taxes will increase. One commentator
believes that the following trends will influence the development of the
'Offshore' industry worldwide:

- The spectacular growth in South East Asia;
- The after-effects of the collapse of the Soviet Union;
- The emergence of South America, India and China as economic power-
  houses;
- Volatility in currency markets.[2]

While knowledge gained from past experience is a helpful lesson for
the future, it cannot be considered as more important than that. Any
anticipation of what the future may hold is conjecture at best – but, on
the basis that to be forewarned is to be forearmed, it makes sense to
consider whatever information is available. As with all disciplines, this is
quite a challenge because of the complexity of the environment and the
many conflicting signals. However, there is at least one thing in respect of
'Offshore' that is certain – and that is, in the future, the dichotomy
between 'Offshore' and 'Onshore' will not focus on geographical location or on perception but on precisely how well financial services centres
are regulated. That said, regulation is not important per se – it is only
important to the extent that its effectiveness (or otherwise) will be felt as
a major component of reputation – which, as a yardstick of safety, will be
a determining factor in how willing investors are in doing business with
particular centres.

The future will be shaped by some compromises. The growth in
financial crime internationally suggests that information about the ultimate ownership of assets must be made accessible – for the purposes of
bona fide criminal investigations. This means that those who are engaged
in the business of offering financial services will be required to maintain
full information on beneficial ownership. Access should be provided to
law enforcement agencies and to regulators – under appropriate authority and in specified circumstances. A balance between confidentiality and
transparency that takes reasonable account of the interest of all parties
must be achieved. In the future, it is likely that the veil of 'secrecy' that

---

[2] www.offshoresimple.com/tax_havens_history.htm.

has surrounded the 'Offshore' environment for many years will continue to be lifted, 'Offshore' will become more transparent than ever, and OFCs will no longer be used for transactions that have to be protected by opacity. Transparency will become the order of the day and will be supported by blacklists for those who cannot or will not operate at an acceptable level. That said, the point should be made that, in this respect, corporate business should be distinguished from personal business (private banking). Issues surrounding confidentiality and the exchange of information are much less sensitive in respect of corporate business than they are in respect of personal business.

There must be clarity in respect of legislation on tax evasion. It is unlikely that tax evasion will become acceptable – so practitioners and clients must be sure what the law demands to avoid tax mitigation schemes crossing the somewhat philosophic divide that separates such schemes from evasion. In fact, in 2004, a spokesperson has said on behalf of PriceWaterhouseCoopers in the UK that:

> The [Inland] Revenue is especially targeting individuals who hide their assets offshore. The Special Compliance Office, the tax department investigation unit, is clamping down on avoidance and evasion, and in the most serious cases individuals will be prosecuted. At the same time, the Revenue is pursuing people who have settled funds into offshore trusts and demanding inheritance tax from them. The move comes amid new wide-ranging legislation to tackle tax planning and the setting up of the new Avoidance Intelligence Unit.[3]

This is because those who assist others to evade tax are likely to be punished more severely in future than at present. Unless these simple parameters are satisfied, business will migrate to less well-developed and less controlled centres – which will exacerbate the current problems.

Generally speaking, there are many legitimate business opportunities – which in turn means that there is no need for 'Offshore Finance Centres' to involve themselves in tax evasion. That said, it is likely that businesses that do not need a physical presence 'Onshore' will make for the 'Offshore' environment. It seems that tax competition will continue (because competition, including tax competition, is generally a good thing). More countries will lower their tax rates and make changes to

[3] 'Revenue Casts Nets To Offshore Assets', *Offshore Red*, June 2004, p. 74.

the way tax liability is calculated – and these factors will prompt more changes.

It is also worth considering the source of competition in the future. Will the East replace the West as the direction from which 'Offshore' business will flow? For example, the rapid development of Shanghai in the past ten years is an indication of how quickly things can change. China is now a member of the World Trade Organization and an Observer at the FATF and has become more receptive to business from abroad. Asia is another area of potential interest to investors.

> The political and economic catalysts that influenced the growth of the offshore industry in the eighties and nineties will continue to influence growth in the next two decades. These catalysts are:
>
> - Political and economic instability;
> - Market globalisation and deregulation;
> - The internalisation of business;
> - The lifting of trade barriers;
> - A trend towards steady global economic growth;
> - A global relaxation of foreign exchange controls.
>
> In addition to political and economic catalysts there are also global tax related catalysts that continue to influence the growth of the offshore industry. These include:
>
> - High tax regimes;
> - More effective tax recovery;
> - The opportunities of utilising double taxation treaties.[4]

Further, it behoves 'Offshore' jurisdictions to make very clear what their requirements are in respect of mutual legal assistance. It is not as if these provisions do not exist – so there should not be any problem in publicising the information. The value in doing so includes avoidance of having to reject a request for assistance because it has not been served properly. Rejection is more than likely to give the impression that the 'Offshore' jurisdiction is unwilling to cooperate and is being obstructive instead of being helpful. This will not impress the jurisdiction abroad – or the FATF! Meanwhile, it has been suggested that '[t]ax free companies with anonymous ownership are no longer available in the international

---

[4] www.offshoresimple.com/tax_havens_history.htm.

financial centres; so tax free US limited liability companies (LLCs) are now common substitutes'.[5]

Some believe that we are moving towards international free trade where imports may be totally free from tariffs and where national governments may be funded by tax levied on worldwide income. This system will be supported by mechanisms to eradicate double taxation. This suggests that there is a need to develop synergies where possible but not at the cost of competition. Are these two factors mutually exclusive? The new environment is likely to change not only the payments system but also the role that banks play in it; for example, the need for cash will diminish as 'smart cards' become more prevalent. The traditional role of banks will continue to change. (In a report issued by IBM Consulting Services in May 2003, it was suggested that in Europe the prospects for 'Onshore' banking are better than those for 'Offshore'. The report added that revenue in the 'Offshore' banking market decreased by 5 per cent in 2002.)[6] The product/market life cycle will be much shorter than ever before as individuals accumulate wealth and their preferences become more demanding. 'In 2002, the global wealth of high net worth individuals (HNWI – an individual with financial assets of at least USD1 million, excluding home real estate) grew 3.6 per cent to USD27.2 trillion. 200,000 people around the world became millionaires – a 2.1 per cent increase to 7.3 million people. The number of ultra-HNWIs (individuals with financial assets of more than USD30 million) rose 2 per cent to 58,000 people, their combined wealth growing an estimated 3.6 per cent.'[7]

The point was made at the outset that statistical information about the 'Offshore' environment is sketchy at best. But, based on the estimates that are available, it seems that no more than US $500 million was invested in 'Offshore' funds in 1989. Within ten years, the figure is estimated to have grown to over US $5 trillion and some suggest that the figure will be around US $6 trillion by 2010. (All this excluding any damage caused to the potential for growth caused by the discovery of bad practice in the US mutual funds industry towards the end of 2003.)

[5] Richard Hay, 'International Financial Centres and Information Exchange', *Offshore Investment*, Issue 157, June 2005, p. 3.

[6] Justin Madubuko, 'Banks Dismiss Claim That Industry Is Dying', *Portfolio International*, June 2003.

[7] 'Low Growth in World Wealth', *Offshore Investment.com*, Issue 138, July/August 2003, p. 4.

According to Booz Allen Hamilton's report on wealth management,[8] OECD nations comprise more than 16 million individuals each of whom has over €500,000 to invest in a market that will be worth more than €35 trillion by 2004. The report points out that private banking has relied upon the 'Offshore' market to generate tax-efficient investment products and profit. The IBM Consulting Services report referred to above says that 'Offshore banks need to adapt the traditional model based on secrecy and move towards a more international approach to take advantage of the rapid growth of the cross-border segment.'[9]

All other things being equal, the effects of the three reports described in Chapters 10 to 12 are likely to be mitigated by fewer scandals, and this will improve the reputation of 'Offshore'. But it is not reputation per se that is significant: it is the degree to which investors are comforted by what that reputation means (see section 20.4 below). Reputation is a type of barometer or yardstick. In the meantime, the BIS has said that 'the trend to place deposits offshore was [and still is] increasing'.[10] Accordingly, OFCs might focus their attention (inter alia) on winning credibility and therefore equivalence in global finance by very close compliance with the FATF's Recommendations, the OECD's rules and positive FSAP reports from the IMF and the World Bank.

What does all this mean for tax havens, 'Offshore Finance Centres', international financial services centres – or whatever they are called? The extent to which such centres adopt a different paradigm will affect their success – or otherwise!

20.3 Do observers believe that 'Offshore' will continue to exist?

The jury is still out on whether 'Offshore' has a future or not. However, as the Offshore Group of Banking Supervisors has wisely pointed out, the dichotomy between 'Offshore' and 'Onshore' is less significant than the dichotomy between financial centres that comply and those that do not comply with agreed international standards.[11]

---

[8] 'Wealth Management: The Challenge', Vol. 3, No. 10, *Private Wealth Investor*, June 2001, p. 12.
[9] Justin Madubuko, 'Banks Dismiss Claim That Industry Is Dying', *Portfolio International*, June 2003.
[10] *BIS Quarterly Report*, December 2003, as quoted in 'BIS Says US Banks Are the Biggest Users of OFCs', *Offshore Red*, February 2002, p. 219.
[11] Colin Powell, 'Offshore Group of Banking Supervisors – A Briefing Note', February 2002.

Consider the following views.

Sir Howard Davies, former Chairman of the Financial Services Authority in the UK, has said that 'Offshore Finance Centres' face a 'bleak future' unless their anti-money laundering regulations are improved. 'Political leaders in the G7 economies in particular, are very concerned by what they see as dangerous gaps in the world's defences.'[12]

> Notwithstanding the current clouds over Offshore Financial Centres, it is hard to see anything but increased demand for their services so long as there is scorn elsewhere for the 'Obvious and simple system of natural liberty' which commended itself to the Physiocrats and Adam Smith.[13],[14]

> Can there be a more moral case for tax havens than tax efficiency, restraints on government power to grab the income of its citizens, the preservation of capital to increase prosperity and freedom to enjoy private property?[15]

> Globalisation and the growth of the knowledge economy are unstoppable now. Despite the OECD, the FATF and EU initiatives, offshore jurisdictions have a bright future as major e-business centres. And clean, well-run offshore centres stand to play a significant role in facilitating the growth of the global, knowledge economy.[16]

'The outlook for OFCs therefore looks rather bleak.'[17] The environment in which OFCs operate is considered to be getting more difficult as the advantages which OFCs could once offer are being eroded. The route forward is diversification within a very robust regulatory framework.

> My crystal ball shows the offshore jurisdictions flourishing but having to yield a great deal more information about what they are doing and to whom. At the same time, the offshore world needs to be on the lookout for competition from onshore jurisdictions.[18]

---

[12] Paul Lashmar and Heather Tomlinson, 'The Sun Goes Down in Tax Free Paradise', *Independent News*, 11 October 2001.
[13] Adam Smith, *An Inquiry into the Nature and Causes of the Wealth of Nations*, Oxford, 1776, p. 687.
[14] Terry Dwyer, 'Harmful Tax Competition and the Future of "Offshore Financial Centres"' Vol. 5, No. 4, *Journal of Money Laundering Control*, p. 312.
[15] Bob Stewart, 'The Moral Case for Tax Havens', lewrockwell.com, 30 October 2002.
[16] William A. Woods, 'Why Legitimate Companies Use Offshore Financial Centres', OffshoreOn.com, 18 October 2002.
[17] 'The Prospects for Offshore', *Offshore Red*, October 2002, p. 180.
[18] Milton Grundy, 'Offshore Legislation 2003: Introduction', The OFC Report 2003.

After ten years of haggling, EU members have struck a deal that will close
tax havens all across Europe.[19]

In the 21st century, offshore locations have a worthwhile and profitable
role to play but only as modern, efficient and transparent centres.[20]

IFCs which maintain tax neutrality and responsive regulatory environments will thrive in a connected world.[21]

In fact, not all jurisdictions will survive – as the following two
quotations aptly anticipate. First, 'Nauru has been in political and
economic crisis since early January [2003] . . . [I]t squandered its
resources and is now riven with major financial and structural problems . . . [I]ts offshore centre is reputed to have laundered money for the
Russian mafia.'[22] (In fact, President Dowiyogo had undertaken to stop
Nauru's involvement in 'Offshore' services, but the President died
abroad and so implementation of this decision was deferred until after
the election to appoint his successor.) Secondly, 'Grenada's offshore
sector has virtually disappeared. In 2000 when these agencies [OECD,
FATF and IMF] started their good works, the sector employed around
300 people. Now almost everyone has left.'[23]

While many jurisdictions will survive, their future status will be
different from their current status. For example, 'the number of companies registering in the Cayman Islands has steadily decreased over the
past three years'.[24] A further example of how fast things are changing is
reflected by the following incident. As a result of a crackdown by the
Irish authorities, the banks in Ireland that have operations 'Offshore'
were asked by the Revenue to contact customers to encourage them to
disclose undeclared assets before the end of March 2004 to avoid investigation. In April 2003, 'the Bank of Ireland wrote to around 400 customers with accounts at its Jersey branch warning that the Revenue
Commissioners will be looking into their accounts in June to ascertain

---

[19] 'The Taxman Cometh', *The Economist*, 25 January 2003, p. 70.
[20] 'From the Editor', *Offshore Red*, May 2003, p. 57.
[21] Richard Hay, 'International Financial Centres: Back on the Front Foot, The 2005 Guide
to International Financial Centres', Euromoney Institutional Investor plc, February 2005,
p. 3.
[22] 'Nauru', *Offshore Red*, March 2003, p. 7.
[23] 'From the Editor', *Offshore Red*, March 2003, p. 9.
[24] 'Cayman Islands', *Offshore Red*, April 2003, p. 27.

whether they have evaded Irish taxes'.[25] It was reported subsequently that the 'investigation into the tax affairs of customers of the Bank of Ireland Trust Company in Jersey netted more than €100 million in unpaid taxes from 254 people'.[26] In due course, the Chairman of the Irish Revenue Commissioners announced[27] that 250 of those customers had voluntarily disclosed information relating to trust accounts maintained in Jersey.[28] One journal reported as follows:

> Some €150 million rolled into the Revenue after it told Bank of Ireland to write to its customers who held trusts in its bank in Jersey advising them to settle their tax affairs. Another €46 million was netted after similar letters were sent to customers of Irish Life & Permanent's Isle of Man subsidiary. Since then Ireland's Revenue Chairman has met the Chief Executive of 10 Irish financial institutions which were asked to write to customers of their offshore companies to stress the benefits of disclosure. Some 15,000 people contacted the tax authorities about a possible tax liability and these paid a further €500 million before an early June [2004] deadline . . . [The Revenue Commissioner] has also subsequently been granted powers to demand that these institutions also hand over details of customers who have accounts at subsidiary companies in other jurisdictions.[29]

In April 2005, 'Ireland's Revenue Commission said it would seek court orders to compel all life assurance companies to surrender information on customers who may have used investment products to evade tax.'[30] The other side of the tax amnesty coin is the investigation. In this respect it was reported in early 2005 that '[f]ive major Irish Revenue investigations have taken €1.62bn in the past five years. A sixth inquiry is due to begin and will target funds hidden by way of single premium insurance policies according to Commissioners.'[31] The USA has taken

[25] Jason Gorringe, 'Jersey Business Braces Itself for Increasing Scrutiny from IR', Tax-News.com, 8 May 2003.

[26] 'Special Powers for Revenue Will Deepen Offshore Tax Inquiries', *Offshore Red*, March 2004, p. 5.

[27] Irish Revenue Commission, *Annual Report 2004*, Chairman,

[28] 'BOI Customers Disclose Jersey Accounts to Tax Commission', *AMS Group Offshore Update Newsletter*, 25 June 2003.

[29] 'Irish Revenue Pulls in Euro 650m from Offshore Accounts', *Offshore Red*, July/August 2004, p. 98.

[30] 'Revenue Commission to Seek Court Order in Insurance Enquiry', *Offshore Red*, May 2005, p. 78.

[31] 'European News – Ireland', *Offshore Red*, February 2005, p. 6.

certain steps in a not dissimilar direction by the proposed enactment of the Tax Shelter and Tax Haven Reform Act. Section 2210 of the Act:

- increases the penalties on persons who promote abusive tax shelters, knowingly aid or abet taxpayers who understate their tax liability, or fail to disclose abusive tax shelters or offshore bank accounts;
- prevents abusive tax shelters;
- requires economic substance for transactions to be eligible for tax benefits; and
- deters uncooperative tax havens.[32]

The message is that people using 'Offshore' must be able to demonstrate that they are doing so legitimately. In the UK, the Inland Revenue has issued 'production orders' that require companies operating credit cards to surrender details of those persons who hold 'Offshore' credit and debit cards.[33]

20.4 The influence of the work of the supranational autorities

The platform on which the OECD report (and in fact the FSF and the FATF reports) was built includes transparency and greater cooperation in general and the exchange of information in particular.

Unfortunately, the emphasis that the OECD placed on its work at the outset may not have been focused as precisely as it might have been. Even the title adopted ('Harmful Tax Competition') was less than appropriate because there is nothing wrong with tax competition per se. The problems arise with harmful tax practices – but that was not the original emphasis.

Further, there is probably a degree of agreement amongst most 'Offshore Finance Centres' that, when there is adequate reason to suspect wrongdoing, they will be willing to cooperate by sharing information in appropriate circumstances and subject to due legal process being served. However, there is objection to non-members of the OECD being required to adopt standards that are not met by the members themselves. There is also an objection to governments trying to enforce their law on an extraterritorial basis. 'Fishing expeditions' are not

---

[32] 'Tax Haven Reform Bill to Target Abusive Tax Shelters', *Offshore Red*, June 2005, p. 99.
[33] 'Offshore Credit Card Holders Facing Probe', Vol. 10, No. 6, *Offshore Red*, July/August 2005, p. 124.

welcome. (The term 'fishing expedition' refers to an inquiry which is general in nature and not part of an investigation into a specific event or person, in the hope that the trawl for information will reveal something that will incriminate someone.) The dual criminality principle must be respected because all jurisdictions have a right to determine what constitutes a crime.

20.5 Is the focus appropriate?

'Offshore Finance Centres' have been the subject of much criticism – not all of which is justified. If one wants to evade tax, one does not need to go 'Offshore' to do it. For example, if cash is used, the paper trail ends. Further, it is quite clear from previous chapters that the facilities made available by large OECD countries to non-residents are not totally different to what is made available by 'Offshore Finance Centres' to non-residents. It has been said that

> [t]o escape high taxation by Europe's welfare states or outright confiscation by Marxist and other dictatorships, foreigners have been putting their earnings into US bank accounts, where the currency is relatively stable and their privacy was protected. Congress has encouraged this practice since 1921 to attract capital to the US economy by exempting from US taxation the interest earned on deposits of non-resident foreigners ... [There is] ... an estimated $41.7 trillion in US bank assets from foreign depositors.[34]

Accordingly, the problem is not merely one of servicing non-residents. Honesty in respect of reporting income must be focused on the individual taxpayer – who after all is the person responsible. It cannot be logical to hold a service provider in the shape of an 'Offshore' jurisdiction responsible for the actions of people who use its facilities wrongly – provided that the centre does not condone or facilitate criminal activity.

What seems to have started as uncertainty whether 'Offshore Finance Centres' contribute to global financial instability – and which was proved to be incorrect – moved on to blaming 'Offshore' for encouraging money laundering and tax evasion. This latter was also disproved. The FSF report concluded, inter alia, that 'OFCs, to date, do not appear to have been a major causal factor in the creation of systemic financial

---

[34] John Berlau, 'Tax Collector for the World', InsightMag.com, 13 July 2001.

problems.'[35] In February 2005, the IMF has said in its latest progress
reports that

> Compliance levels for OFCs are, on average better than in other jurisdic-
> tions assessed under the FSAP [and that] . . . [o]n average, OFCs meet
> supervisory standards superior to those of other jurisdictions though with
> deficiencies in lower income jurisdictions . . . 50 per cent of offshore
> jurisdictions comply with every principle and recommendation directly
> concerned with cooperation and information exchange as opposed to 47
> per cent of other assessed jurisdictions.[36]

It has also been said that:

> Fighting against drug dealers and terrorists is a noble endeavour, so
> proponents of tax harmonisation are cleverly using the money laundering
> issue as a weapon to besmirch the reputation of the low-tax jurisdictions . . .
> [T]ax havens are neither the source nor the destination for a dispropor-
> tionate share of the world's criminal proceeds.[37]

Previous chapters have shown that money laundering is a global
phenomenon and that launderers do not limit their activity to 'Offshore
Finance Centres'. This text has already referred to the FATF's view that
'[t]he legitimate use by private citizens and institutional investors of
certain facilities offered by many financial centres, including Offshore
centres is not put in question'.[38] Despite the resources invested in trying
to deal with money laundering, the indications are that it is worsening
not improving – and there is no indication that it can be controlled
easily. The proceeds of the crimes that predicate money laundering have
pervaded the most prestigious institutions in the most respected and
well-regulated 'Onshore' centres. Meanwhile, '[o]pium cultivation is
surging across Afghanistan . . . Last year the country produced almost
4,000 tonnes, 75 per cent of the world's opium. The trade generated
US $1 billion for farmers and US$1.3 billion for traffickers, the United
Nations says. This is more than half of Afghanistan's national income.'[39]

---

[35] 'Report of the Working Group on Offshore Financial Centres', FSF, April 2000, p. 1.
[36] 'Offshore Financial Centres, The Assessment Program, A Progress Report', IMF,
25 February 2005, paras. 5 and 6, p. 5.
[37] Daniel J. Mitchell, 'US Government Agencies Confirm That Low-Tax Jurisdictions Are Not
Money Laundering Havens', October 2003, Vol. 11, No. 2, *Journal of Financial Crime*, p. 127.
[38] 'Report on Non-Cooperative Countries and Territories', FATF, 14 February 2000, p. 9.
[39] Amy Waldman, 'Afghan Economy Blooms as Opium Crop Hits Record', *Sun Herald*,
11 April 2004, as cited in *GMPL Global Press Review*, 13 April 2004, United Nations Office
on Drugs and Crime, p. 3.

The thorny question of tax evasion is a hardy perennial. 'Offshore Finance Centres' are said to turn a blind eye to the proceeds of tax evasion and accept the business, asking few questions in the process. Surely, this is another of those cases where prevention of the problem is preferable to trying to cure the way in which the problem manifests itself. Each country must police its own law. Naturally, where there has been wrongdoing, mutual assistance treaties can be used to pursue the wrong-doers – but according to the natural rules of justice. Not everyone with wealth 'Offshore' derived it by evading tax – and they do not retain their wealth 'Offshore' for tax reasons only. Not all centres agree on what constitutes tax evasion. The Swiss approach is a case in point.

It has been suggested that 'Offshore Finance Centres' encourage wrongdoers because their regulations are either lax or non-existent. These questions concerning the efficacy of regulation 'Offshore' prompted a massive worldwide exercise to establish new legislation where gaps were identified and to tighten up how existing regulations and legislation were enforced. The raft of legislation that ensued and the pace at which it was enacted contributed to massive uncertainties which in turn made those on the verge of a business activity stop and ponder what further changes might be made. Naturally, change causes apprehension and people entering into long-dated contracts tended to hold back – just in case. (Corrective action arising from the 11 September attacks also made people hesitate in entering into further contracts.) Even a quick analysis of what is on the statute books of many 'Offshore Finance Centres' will testify to the extent of the regulatory and legislative changes that have taken place in the recent past. So, it would be incorrect to suggest that in general there are material lacunae in legislation 'Offshore'.

> Unfortunately, money laundering laws often focus on process rather than results. Indeed, many of the blacklists are based on how many laws a nation has enacted and how many rules it has imposed on its financial services sectors – not on whether the jurisdiction is actually a place where dirty money is laundered. There is very little cost–benefit analysis and very little discussion of whether law enforcement resources are being effectively utilised.[40]

---

[40] Daniel J. Mitchell, 'US Government Agencies Confirm That Low-Tax Jurisdictions Are Not Money Laundering Havens', October 2003, Vol. 11, No. 2, *Journal of Financial Crime*, p. 130.

While there is some truth in this comment, it should be made clear that enacting relevant legislation is an attempt at making and keeping financial environments clean. There is probably general agreement that 'sifting through millions of financial transactions or placing onerous burdens on banks, accountants and lawyers to report "suspicious" activity is of questionable efficacy'.[41] The same point is made by Professor Barry Rider:

> I fully recognise the importance of attention being given to the funds and profits of organisations that seek to abuse or subvert our values. As in all things, however, there is a need for balance and caution in evaluating the efficacy of actions, which are far from cost and risk free . . . If we really do not think that all the laws, procedures and other constraints aimed against the improper laundering of wealth, achieve more than disruption, then surely this needs to be properly evaluated and the processes rendered accountable.[42]

The fact is that, despite the plethora of new rules, they are only a means to an end and not the end in itself. It is the culture that has to change – as the failure of anti-money laundering legislation, rules and actions testify. The focus – not the intention or the will – appears to be misplaced. If it was just a matter of creating legislation, regulations, codes, guidelines etc., or focusing effort, the problem would be resolved already. (Note that there is a hierarchy in this respect – as implied by the terms 'primary' legislation (the law) and 'secondary' legislation (the regulations made under primary legislation).) The tendency is for the legal draftsman to place all the principles in primary legislation and to expand those principles in the regulations. The importance of rules, codes, guidelines and practice notes depends on how they are provided for within primary legislation. For example, in Mauritius, rules carry weight because the legislation says that breach of a rule may give rise to criminal liability. While issued under the authority of primary legislation, codes, guidelines and practice notes are usually advisory in nature – that is, they are used to explain how things should be done or how a particular

---

[41] G. Mather, 'Money Laundering Fight Could Hit the Wrong Targets', *The Times* (UK), 2 October 2001, as cited in Daniel J. Mitchell, 'US Government Agencies Confirm That Low-Tax Jurisdictions Are Not Money Laundering Havens', October 2003, Vol. 11, No. 2, *Journal of Financial Crime*, p. 130.

[42] Barry Rider, 'More of the Same', 2004, Vol. 7, No. 4, *Journal of Money Laundering Control*, p. 294.

legal provision is interpreted. They do not usually have the force of law but breach of a direction (see section 7.10 above) to adhere to a code, guideline or practice note will (depending on the law) be treated as a failure to comply with the law – which would normally require compliance with a direction.

20.6 Regulation

Regulation is not a science. While many scientific methods can be incorporated in its execution, it is at best inexact and requires ongoing subjective assessments in 'what if' scenarios. It is like the pilot who must incrementally adjust his course from when he leaves one airport until he arrives at his destination. Fine-tuning is always required and sometimes more severe action is necessary. By definition, 'regulation' means order – the opposite of chaos – and regulators therefore like everything to be in order. In the turbulent and global economic environment in which we live, the pace of change constantly frustrates attempts to maintain order. This means that regulators are not always in complete control – which explains why major regulatory action always follows a disaster. In short, the proliferation of guidelines, rules, regulations and legislation is a best effort to exert control because it is an axiom of regulation that one should not try to regulate what cannot be controlled.

In fact, regulators and service providers (meaning those carrying out financial services activity that is licensable) enjoy a degree of goal congruence, and, if this could be developed, less prescriptive regulatory regimes might be possible. If it was possible for such service providers to adopt a reasonable course of action because it made sense as opposed to it being forced upon them, there may be better quality financial environments. 'Reasonableness' suggests that in the circumstances it may not be optimal but it is certainly not unacceptable.

Regulation involves protecting consumers by managing risk. The emphasis is likely to shift in future to greater education of the public about the risks to which the public is exposed – rather than increased rules to limit the potential for harm. So it is likely that the consumer will have to accept greater responsibility for (financial) decisions made. To assist, the regulator will probably have to focus more on preventative (pro-active) measures rather than a reactive picking up of pieces. That said, prevention is not easy, and, even if smaller, less acceptable centres close down, the problem will migrate elsewhere, possibly even to 'Onshore'.

The style, intrusiveness, quality and approach to regulation all have a direct bearing on decisions about where financial services businesses locate. Contrary to what might be imagined, financial services companies do not migrate to those jurisdictions where regulation is lax – otherwise the second-rate jurisdictions would have attracted the best names to their location, which they have singularly failed to do. The short-term advantage may be felt on the bottom line this year but the 'reputational' risk in so doing may be felt on the bottom line for years to come. Profit-maximisation exists in theory, but arguably not in practice. In financial services, longevity is a core attribute. Licensees consider that there is good marketing mileage in being able to say – and to demonstrate – that they are licensed in a robustly regulated financial services centre.

Regulators 'Offshore' – not unlike their 'Onshore' counterparts – have acquired certain skills pertaining to the environment in which they work. These skills are frequently common to both environments. Regulators 'Offshore' should welcome visits from the IMF, the FATF and the OECD – and from any other international agency that cares to call – because this is an opportunity to exchange skills. The outcome may be that the consumer and the jurisdictions involved will both be served simultaneously to their respective advantage. (That said, many 'Offshore' jurisdictions would attest to having been reviewed by Edwards, KPMG, the FATF, the IMF, the OECD etc., and could be forgiven for wondering how much is enough.)

20.7 Aspiring OFCs

Although the attractiveness in becoming an 'Offshore Finance Centre' may have waned (see section 20.9 below), it has not been lost completely for at least some aspirants – despite all the attention focused on such centres in the recent past. The effects are demonstrated in existing centres and in respect of others that aspire to be OFCs. In respect of the former, the Prime Minister of Malaysia is reported as saying that the prospects for the growth of offshore activities in the next few years are good. 'The Labuan IOFC has been established to offer a wide and integrated range of offshore financial services that include offshore banking, insurance, trusts fund management, leasing and Islamic finance.'[43]

---

[43] 'Malaysia's PM Renews Push for Labuan as a Strategic OFC', *Offshore Red*, October 2004, p. 151.

In respect of the latter, it has been said that:

> As new technologies reduce the importance of physical proximity to major onshore financial centres so a new generation of offshore financial centre (OFC) has emerged. Remote jurisdictions bereft of natural resources and too remote to benefit significantly from the global economy have established OFCs characterised by strict bank secrecy, criminal penalties for disclosure of client information and a policy or practice of non-cooperation with law enforcement agencies of other countries. This new generation of OFCs has succeeded in attracting brass plate banks, anonymous financial companies and asset protection trusts.[44]

Consider the following additional examples: 'In 2001, countries as diverse as New Zealand, Puerto Rico, Israel, Jordan, South Korea [Jeju], India [Mumbai], Anjouan and Iceland took various steps to establish themselves as "Offshore Centres".'[45] For example, it has been reported that 'India's Maharashtra State Government is continuing its push to develop Mumbai into an international financial centre'.[46] There are some advantages in doing so for an economy seeking new growth because, as Dan Mitchell of the Heritage Foundation explains in the article just quoted, '[t]he ability to attract international capital is the single best way for a jurisdiction to boost its economy'. Potential for added value exists for those jurisdictions that carry out the task properly.

By way of background, here are brief comments on some of the jurisdictions involved. Anjouan. The Anjouan 'Offshore Centre' was created by Law No. 1 in 1999. Companies that want to register or to become licensed must engage a registered agent – of which there is currently one. A summary of the Anjouan 'Offshore Centre'[47] says that, '[a]lthough Anjouan is clearly not an international financial centre, it maintains the advantage of being a relatively unknown offshore haven which has not attracted attention or bad publicity . . . [and offers] . . . a business-friendly, liberal and stress free regulatory environment'. Simultaneously, 'positive identification of company owners is required . . . [although] . . . Anjouan will absolutely not cooperate with foreign governments except in serious criminal cases,

---

[44] Jeffrey Owens, 'Global Financial Markets Need Global Rules', in *The 2005 Guide to International Financial Centres*, Euromoney Institutional Investor plc, February 2005, p. 8.

[45] Brendan Harrison, 'New Arrivals', *Offshore Finance USA*, January/February 2002, p. 8.

[46] 'Mumbai in IFC Talks with Reserve Bank', *Offshore Red*, February 2005, p. 8.

[47] www.anjouanoffshore.com.

which do not include tax-related matters. Anjouan is not a party to any
treaties regarding taxation or exchange of information or Mutual Legal
Assistance ... [In fact] ... few countries even maintain diplomatic relations
with Anjouan.' An 'Offshore' bank or captive insurance company can
be licensed within forty-eight hours. Comoros gained independence from
France in 1975, and has experienced nineteen coups or attempted
coups since.

The Seychelles' fledgling 'Offshore Finance Centre', established in
1995, is expanding its business with the intention of becoming a fully
fledged 'Offshore Finance Centre'. The International Corporate Service
Providers Act was enacted in December 2003, and the Prevention of
Terrorism Act was enacted in 2004. Other recent legislation includes
the Protected Cell Companies Act 2003 and the Limited Partnerships
Act 2003. The Central Bank of Seychelles Bill 2004 was approved by the
National Assembly in December 2004. This legislation provides a degree
of independence to the Central Bank.

In Slovakia, the government has imposed a flat-rate tax of 19 per cent.
It has been said that 'the government is transforming the country into a
tax haven for Central Europe'.[48]

'Aspiring' centres should not lose sight of the resources and effort
required to make 'Offshore' business successful. For example, consider
the investments made by Bahrain and the current programme in Dubai.
It has been estimated that the Bahamas spent US$35 million in develop-
ing its financial sector. The approach of other centres may also be of
assistance to the newer centres. For example, in Ireland, the authorities
have developed a very flexible structure that is sensitive to customer
demands – and which has proved to be very successful.

An 'Offshore' regime was introduced in Hungary in 1994, where there
are currently more than 1,000 'Offshore' companies, which paid US$84
million in corporate income tax in 2002.[49] The 'Offshore' regime is
unlikely to continue in Hungary in light of the country's accession to
the EU in 2004. By the end of 2003, the tax allowances and customs
facilities had already come under scrutiny as part of discussions about
accession. After 31 December 2002, it was no longer possible to obtain an
'Offshore' licence. Meanwhile, 'Offshore' companies are entitled to take

[48] 'Slovakia to Become European Tax Haven', DW-World, 6 January 2004.
[49] Gabor B. Szabo and Tunde Darvai, 'The Beginning of the End or the End of the
Beginning', Offshore Investment, September 2003, p. 3.

advantage of over sixty double taxation agreements and enjoy 3 per cent corporate income tax (until the end of 2005).

New legislation in Qatar provides for the establishment of an international financial centre there.[50] The plan is that the sector will be the responsibility of the Qatar Financial Regulatory Authority, which will be the licensing authority. Qatar confirmed its intentions in January 2005. The centre will not be regarded as an 'Offshore' centre, although tax will be relatively benign. The centre began operations in June 2005.

20.8 A step in the right direction

The fundamental solution is that 'Offshore Finance Centres' must not allow themselves to be used for wrongful purposes. The other side of this coin is that, even when 'Offshore Finance Centres' behave properly, they may still be perceived to be fundamentally flawed at best and evil at worst. How is it possible to change the public's attitude, and what do OFCs stand to gain?

Marshall Goldsmith, an 'executive coach', says, concerning change, that the secret is to measure the perception of change, i.e. the extent to which observers think one is changing. 'It's much harder to change people's perceptions of someone's behaviour than to actually change that person's behaviour.'[51] Accordingly, Mr Goldsmith advocates a process whereby a person will say how he intends to change his behaviour and then asks for feedback at intervals thereafter from those who know the person concerning the success of the change strategy. Mr Goldsmith says that this reduces scepticism and, the longer the period until a slip, the less sceptical observers become until a stage is reached where a slip is properly interpreted as a slip that deserves the benefit of the doubt – as long as it is not repeated.

We already know that there are strong perceptions about 'Offshore' in general – and therefore a degree of scepticism about anything remotely connected with that environment. If Mr Goldsmith is correct, there may be value for OFCs in trying to change the public perception of them by stating their strategies for change and then have repeated checks on progress. How could this be achieved?

---

[50] Lorys Charalambous, 'Qatar Establishes International Finance Centre', Tax-news.com, 13 January 2005.

[51] Gardiner Morse, 'Conversation – Behave Yourself: Excerpts from a Conversation with Marshall Goldsmith' *Harvard Business Review*, October 2002, p. 22.

Stephen Covey advocates the Greek philosophy he summarises as *ethos* (credibility), *pathos* (empathy) and *logos* (logic).[52] Dr Covey's approach – which involves all three of these factors in combination – may have some significance for 'Offshore' centres as they determine their strategic direction for the future.

An approach based on *ethos* (credibility) implies that OFCs must be pro-active exhibiting a degree of professionalism and positive attitude that manifests itself in cooperation and integrity – which in turn is likely to inspire trust and inspiration. This leads into *pathos* (empathy), which revolves around the emotional management of a situation. It requires effort in understanding the problems of others and engaging in creative communication. In summary, *ethos* points to an attempt to align with another person's point of view. In turn, this points to *logos*, which enables meaningful search for new alternatives based on *ethos* and *pathos*. This type of approach has much to commend it in determining an appropriate way forward.

Whatever mechanism is developed, it needs credibility to have any chance of success. One way forward might be for the World Bank to establish a Central Offshore Forum. There are many permutations that are possible, but one is that the Forum could become a self-regulatory organisation (SRO) for 'Offshore' activity. As such, the SRO might become responsible for standard tests, for example transparency, anti-money laundering, information sharing and so on. It might produce a ranking of 'Offshore Finance Centres' based on the World Bank/IMF's FSAP reports (which themselves incorporate consideration of the provisions arising from best practice documents published by the Basel Committee, IOSCO, the IAIS, the FATF and so on). The results of the FSAP reviews might be used to create a 'catalogue' of OFCs throughout the world. The 'catalogue' could be produced on all OFCs on a regular basis. This is a very simplistic suggestion – replete with problems and unanswered questions – but it is intended as no more than an example. In this respect, Walker has suggested that 'it is highly unlikely (if not wholly impossible) that a single international body or agency will be established to regulate financial markets'.[53]

---

[52] Stephen R. Covey, *The 8th Habit – From Effectiveness to Greatness*, Simon & Schuster, 2004, pp. 374–7.

[53] George Alexander Walker, *International Banking Regulation Law, Policy and Practice*, Kluwer Law International, 2001, p. 328.

This approach is very transparent and provides the public with an indication of how each centre fares when tested against best practice criteria. This might lead to decreased scepticism and a more realistic approach to how OFCs can be brought within the group of credible financial services centres. The term OFC might even become redundant in the course of time – but, more importantly, the pejorative sense in which this term is used might be proved to be inappropriate. Further, it might help consumers to decide where to locate their business because a large part of the analytical work involved in such a decision will have been done already (see Chapter 21 below). Finally, this type of approach might assist in limiting the potential for regulatory arbitrage.

Naturally, none of this will solve all the problems with 'Offshore' but it might be a step in the right direction.

20.9 The future summarised

The starting point may be in reflecting on the following statement made by the FATF: 'The legitimate use by private citizens and institutional investors of certain facilities offered by many financial centres, including offshore centres, is not put in question.'[54]

What sort of business should OFCs aim to attract? In this respect, Johns has identified two consequential effects that involve what he refers to as 'industrial slippage' and 'erosion of actual or potential tax bases'. The first is where there is a diversion of activity from a higher tax centre to a lower tax centre of trade or activity but using the offshore jurisdiction as part of a paper trail – where no real business is transacted. 'In this case, the haven merely seeks to attract income leakages from the economies whence its clients originate and little real financial centre development takes place.' The second is where the activity is an actual function carried out in the jurisdiction. 'Such activity may be of a positive sum variety, whereby the supply of international financing facilities is actually added to, or of a zero sum variety, whereby onshore activities are appropriated and replaced by offshore business.'[55] If 'Offshore Finance Centres' are to survive, they will need less of the former and much more of the latter. In 1983, Johns

[54] 'Report on Non-Cooperative Countries and Territories', FATF, 14 February 2000, p. 9.
[55] R. A. Johns, *Tax Havens and Offshore Finance: A Study of Transnational Economic Development*, Frances Pinter (Publishers) Ltd, 1983, p. 35.

was sufficiently far-sighted to note that '[c]oordinated onshore policy seems imminent in respect of international tax authority discussions, information exchanges, and the simultaneous audits of the same company at the same time by two or more national tax authorities'.[56] One observer has asked 'Will information exchange kill the offshore world? No. The main attraction of IFCs [International Financial Centres] is not secrecy. Their fundamental appeal is the provision of a tax neutral platform, in a manner similar to London's role as host of the Eurobond market.'[57]

As to the future, one commentator has suggested that '[o]ffshore financial centres now play an essential role in international commerce and trade. There will always be a need and a place for offshore financial centres . . . However, it will only be those jurisdictions which adopt a responsible attitude towards regulation and supervision of their industry that will be allowed to survive and prosper.'[58] In fact, this is borne out by recent history because the jurisdictions that have prospered most are those that have sought to improve regulation. The Edwards Report says that:

> [T]he authorities in any finance centre have clearly to accept that high standards of regulation will drive away some categories of business just as it will encourage others. They have also to accept that, when regulation is improved, some good business may be lost as well as bad . . . [T]he commitment to high standards is very much in the Islands' own interests as well as being an absolute obligation. In the longer term, good regulation is likely to attract more business than it drives away. The business it attracts will, moreover, be likely to be good business. The business it deters will in many cases be business that the Islands would rather not have.[59]

It could, therefore, be that business will leave less reputable jurisdictions as a result of the three reports described above – and migrate to jurisdictions with higher standards. The UK dependent territories worry that they are being forced to adopt procedures that will lead to a loss of

---

[56] R. A. Johns, *Tax Havens and Offshore Finance: A Study of Transnational Economic Development*, Frances Pinter (Publishers) Ltd, 1983, p. 228.

[57] Richard Hay, 'International Financial Centres and Information Exchange', *Offshore Investment*, June 2005, Issue 157, p. 2.

[58] N. Braham, 'The Offshore Evolution', *Finance International*, Spring 1996, p. 30.

[59] Michael Edwards, 'Review of Financial Regulation in the Crown Dependencies', Part 1, para. 17.2, 1998.

business that other, less well-regulated jurisdictions will attract. 'But, as legitimate rationales for offshore finance centre utilisation diminish . . . the ability of criminal transactions to hide in the intricacies of legitimacy ought logically to diminish also.'[60] In fact, 'the use of OFCs by UK residents and companies has arguably been undermined since the 1980s by the combination of increasing tax legislation and the lowering of direct tax rates in the UK'.[61] The suggestion is that, in the future, there will be fewer 'Offshore' centres. In this respect, the IMF has said that 'many of the poorer jurisdictions have eliminated or are phasing out their OFC activities'.[62] Those that remain will be more transparent and more 'professional' in their approach. Enhanced regulation will be the norm. It might be expected that zero tax will become less prevalent – unless the terms satisfy OECD norms – but, perversely, in the UK Dependent Territories, the EU Savings Directive has encouraged zero direct tax (see below). It is possible that 'Offshore' jurisdictions will be able to play a greater part in policy formulation as their credibility grows internationally. In turn, this will help to decrease the suspicion with which OFCs are still regarded. 'Offshore' will be different in many ways, not least because practitioners will be operating in a different financial environment.

Another commentator considers that '[w]ith the passage of time, the death of tax havens seems to be inevitable'.[63] (For example, Banco Bilbao Vizcaya, Argentina, 'closed nine of 36 offshore units it had in 2003 and four others were being liquidated'.[64]) Sombre words about the demise of tax havens (which may or may not include 'Offshore Finance Centres') have to be balanced with those of other commentators (for example, 'the future for no-tax centres is not nearly as terminal as it appeared a few weeks ago').[65] (The context of the comment was the announcement by the Isle of Man in June 2002 of the intention to introduce a zero-rate

---

[60] 'Financial Havens, Banking Secrecy and Money Laundering', United Nations Office for Drug Control and Crime Prevention, Issue 8 of the UNDCP Technical Series, Double Issue 34 and 35 of the *Crime Prevention and Criminal Justice Newsletter*, 1998, p. 49.

[61] Mark Hampton, *The Offshore Interface*, Macmillan Press Ltd, 1996, p. 116.

[62] 'Offshore Financial Centres, The Assessment Program, A Progress Report', IMF, 25 February 2005, para. 5, p. 5.

[63] Akiko Hishikawa, 'The Death of Tax Havens', 20 June2002, www.bc.edu/bc_org/avp/law/lwsch/journals/bciclr/25_2/10_TXT.htm.

[64] 'Leading Spanish Bank Closes Offshore Operations', *Offshore Red*, March 2005, p. 26, quoting from Banco Bilbao Vizcaya's Annual Audit Report in February 2005.

[65] Bob Reynolds, 'From the Editor', *Offshore Red*, July/August 2002, p. 117.

corporation tax regime that also satisfied EU requirements). Another
commentator has said that '[t]here will always be a need for offshore
financial centres and there will always be a way for those centres to
operate'.[66]

In any event, it may be that the requirement for greater transparency
and more robust regulation in the 'Offshore' community will produce
less wrongdoing. However, a fully open and transparent market means
perfect information which – as any economist will confirm – produces
lower returns on investment. The answer will be clearer in the process of
time. Meanwhile, OFCs must adapt to the changes in the environment in
which they operate and seek out other services that may not be tax-
related. Despite the FSF's affirmation that the results of its report should
not be used to assess 'Offshore Finance Centres', it is likely that this will
be the very purpose to which its report and the others will be used. Anti-
money laundering legislation is likely to become tougher (e.g. to include
the requirement to report suspicion of laundering the proceeds of tax
offences) and client confidentiality is likely to become less robust. 'Provided that the local court is satisfied, often on the basis of probabilities,
that an offence has been committed, it will generally order the release of
bank information.'[67] This is enhanced by the establishment of mutual
legal assistance agreements and by Memoranda of Understanding. In the
past, this has been sufficient to deal with fraud, drug trafficking etc., but
not tax evasion (which is now less easily distinguished from tax avoidance), which is now the focus of attention. Hence, the increased interest
in 'Offshore Finance Centres'.

Inevitably, as the culture of 'Offshore Finance Centres' changes, their
rationale will also change. As a consequence, they will be forced to adopt
a new paradigm. This is likely to involve higher standards and greater
transparency in an attempt to increase credibility and to improve reputation. In referring to his advice that the British 'Offshore' islands
should aspire to and deliver high standards, Mr Edwards, in his report,
said that:

> The continuing pursuit of such standards may sometimes discourage
> business, especially less reputable business. As many professionals have
> remarked however, the Islands' best interests must lie in continued devel-
> opment of good business and rejection of business which is questionable

---

[66] Terry L. Neal, The Offshore Solution, MasterMedia Publishing Corp, 2001, p. 294.
[67] Nigel Morris-Cotterill, 'Secrecy Laws under Assault', The Banker, August 2000, p. 62.

or worse . . . [M]oreover, high standards will encourage, not discourage, the growth of business.[68]

This may lead to a greater focus on corporate business. In any event, lax regulation and the lack of transparency are weaknesses that OFCs can afford no longer – if they want to remain in business. Repercussions are inevitable for those centres that fail to meet the new standards. Many OFCs are considering alternative products as a means of generating revenue – so the pressure to which OFCs have been subjected has prompted a more global perspective. Further, as more of the services that may have been peculiar to 'Offshore Finance Centres' at one time become equally available 'Onshore', the 'Offshore' environment will lose out. 'We will continue to see smaller OFCs – those less able to respond – fail to locate the stamina and imagination for the commercial challenges ahead.'[69] The OECD has pointed out that:

> The level playing field serves as a goal . . . [and] . . . the overall objective of the level playing field is to facilitate the creation of an environment in which all significant financial centres meet the high standards of transparency and effective exchange of information on both criminal and civil taxation matters.[70]

This maps out the road to the future.

Insofar as the prevention of money laundering and terrorist financing is concerned, even more vigilance will be required – despite the fact that it is already widely reported that it is currently much more difficult to open a new account 'Offshore' than 'Onshore'. More activities will be brought within the scope of the regulations that currently apply (mainly) to financial services companies in more places. These will include: casinos, investment advisors, lawyers, company services providers, accountants and dealers in property and items of high value. Abusers of financial systems will expand their creativity in searching for means to thwart the increasingly elaborate surveillance systems. In so doing, they will use all the types of professional advice described above – even more than currently – and they will blend legitimate with illegitimate business in ways so subtle that it will become increasingly difficult to separate the

---

[68] Michael Edwards, 'Review of Financial Regulation in the Crown Dependencies', Part 1, para. 4.1, 1998.

[69] Bob Reynolds, 'From the Editor', *Offshore Red*, December 2003/January 2004, p. 201.

[70] 'A Process for Achieving a Global Level Playing Field', OECD Global Forum on Taxation, 4 June 2004, pp. 2 and 8.

one from the other. For example, a business that operates mainly on cash can lower the price of the commodity it is selling which is likely to increase the amount of cash flowing through it, thereby making it easier to 'place' dirty money. Consequently, there will be an increase in the number of suspicious activity reports that will be submitted to the authorities. (This trend has already been evidenced. 'Two thirds of banks indicate that they have generated a greater number of suspicious activity reports (SARs) over the last three years.'[71]) This will have regulatory implications. The permutations are endless.

In earlier chapters, there was discussion on the fine line between perception and reality in financial services. This is really bad news for the 'Offshore' environment because the general perception of it is less than favourable – and the recent reports have contributed to this. But does this mean that the 'Onshore' environment – the main alternative to 'Offshore' – is sanitised, free from abuses, money laundering, fraud or tax evasion? Obviously, the answer is negative. The global financial services environment will continue to be abused so long as there are people around who think they can get away with it – and they are not very particular where they process their transactions, only that the environment chosen allows them to get away with it.

However, this is entirely the responsibility of the environment. All pollution is harmful and it is therefore not in the long-term best interests of any jurisdiction to allow behaviour that will ultimately adversely affect its economic prosperity. A medium-to-long-term perspective is required. Meanwhile, many OFCs are reviewing their legislation to keep pace with the changing circumstances of business worldwide and to satisfy the new demands arising from the reports described above. One important question is where will all this navel gazing end, because '[t]he lists have provoked a flurry of defensive moves.'[72] The 'Offshore' environment is dynamic and perhaps the pace of change in the future will be even faster than it has been in the past. The proof of the pudding is in the eating, however, because the question is whether there is capacity to enforce all the legislation that has been enacted. In some centres, this will be difficult to achieve and such centres will degrade their standards or opt out of the 'Offshore' business altogether.

---

[71] *Global Anti-Money Laundering Survey 2004*, KPMG, October 2004, p. 6.
[72] 'All Havens in a Storm', *The Economist*, 1 July 2000, p. 86.

Maybe the focus is misplaced, because, as Johns pointed out, 'competitiveness does not exist exclusively on the ability to serve given demand patterns at low prices, but to a large and growing extent in the creation of demand for "new" products through product innovation'.[73] Clearly, the IMF does not anticipate that all OFCs will survive. In their July 2003 progress report on OFCs, they said that: 'In cases where jurisdictions conclude that the costs of achieving the internationally required supervisory standards exceed the benefits, if requested, staff would provide technical assistance to advise on the process for winding up.'[74]

Presently, most 'Offshore' subsidiaries are exempt from the rules that apply to controlled foreign companies. UK companies use such subsidiaries 'Offshore' to avoid tax. However, in his 2002 Budget Speech on 17 April 2002, the UK's Chancellor of the Exchequer, Mr Gordon Brown, created reserve powers to enable his government to exclude UK companies from those exemptions in certain circumstances. In January 2005, it was reported that the UK's Inland Revenue had established a special unit to deal with entrepreneurs who use 'Offshore' bank accounts to avoid paying tax. 'Using new powers, the Inland Revenue is said to have applied pressure on banks and financial institutions with a UK presence to deliver a list of offshore accounts.'[75]

Many 'Offshore Financial Centres' have experienced reductions in the level of business (although most choose not to draw too much attention to it). For example, in Barbados, the figures indicate that, in 1996, 4,137 international business companies were active. This figure had dropped to 2,123 by 2004.[76] The number of people employed in the sector had fallen also.

The Netherlands Antilles' New Fiscal Framework abolished the distinction between 'Onshore' and 'Offshore' companies, and, in Mauritius, the distinctions between what was formerly known as the 'Offshore' regime and 'Onshore' is being phased out gradually. Aruba is another example. The announcement that all Aruban companies will be taxed at a uniform rate of 35 per cent has been heralded as the end of that jurisdiction's status

---

[73] R. A. Johns, *Tax Havens and Offshore Finance: A Study of Transnational Economic Development*, Frances Pinter (Publishers) Ltd, 1983, p. 246.

[74] 'Offshore Financial Centres, The Assessment Program, A Progress Report and the Future of the Program', IMF, 31 July 2003, p. 19.

[75] 'Inland Revenue to Target Offshore Entrepreneurs', *Offshore Red*, February 2005, p. 5.

[76] 'News Digest, Barbados', *Offshore Red*, April 2004, p. 27.

as a tax haven. On 6 November 2002, the Prime Minister of Barbados announced an initiative to harmonise the fiscal regime for 'Onshore' and 'Offshore'. Malta no longer distinguishes between the two.

Finally in this respect, many OFCs are too small to deal with all the regulatory responsibilities that arise in a complex global financial environment. It is likely therefore that greater collaboration will be needed in the future, and this has begun already, for example previous chapters showed that OFCs joined together to make representations to the OECD.

Caricom is a good example. Established in July 1973, Caricom is the name adopted by the Caribbean Community and Common Market. It comprises Antigua, the Bahamas, Barbados and St Kitts and Nevis, together with associates Anguilla, the British Virgin Islands and the Turks and Caicos Islands. These countries have created the Caribbean Single Market and Economy (CSME) and the Caribbean Court of Justice (CCJ). The CSME focuses on the free movement of goods and services in the area, and caters for the free movement of professional people. The legal systems of these countries are diverse. The idea of the CCJ is for it to be the first appellate court for the area, replacing the Privy Council in this respect. The proposals have not been agreed, but aptly show that jurisdictions are thinking about how and to what extent they can collaborate with each other.

A further example is the way in which a number of jurisdictions collaborated to create the Eastern Caribbean Securities Exchange (Anguilla, Antigua, Dominica, Grenada, Montserrat, St Kitts and Nevis, St Lucia and St Vincent and the Grenadines). The Exchange commenced trading on 19 October 2001.

The Caribbean Regional Technical Assistance Centre assists countries in the region. It serves to improve their economic and financial management services. These include 'Offshore Finance' sector supervision and regulation. (Management of public expenditure, tax policy and financial statistics are also included.) The Centre was inaugurated in Barbados on 5 November 2001.

In fact, 'Offshore Finance Centres' may be better placed if they were represented by a single representative body.

In an article[77] discussing a consultation paper published by the FATF containing new provisions in respect of corporate vehicles, a suggestion

---

[77] 'Shell Games', *The Economist*, 26 October 2002.

was made that the proposals were unlikely to win the favour of those who might be required to implement them. One proposal is for FATF members to amend their legislation to require companies other than those that are publicly traded to identify their beneficial owners – and to eliminate bearer shares. Further, banks should identify the owners of their corporate clients and the names of trustees, settlors, protectors and beneficiaries of trusts should be registered. The article anticipates that Austria, Belgium, Germany and Switzerland will not relinquish bearer shares easily, and that the UK and the USA will oppose the registration of trusts.

When rules are imposed on 'Offshore Finance Centres' but not on the larger FATF members, more anomalies are created. The rules – all other things being equal – must apply to all those involved in financial services. The consequence of not doing so is a form of regulatory discrimination.

A large number of important anomalies have been described in earlier chapters, but perhaps amongst the most glaring is the situation that obtains in Delaware and Nevada. *The Economist* referred to the conclusion of a study undertaken by the General Accounting Office in the USA (sponsored by Senator Carl Levin of Michigan) which said that 'it was easy for foreign entities to hide their identities in Delaware shell corporations and launder money'. Senator Levin acknowledged that USA was doing what they criticised other countries for doing, that is, to allow the identity of the true owners of corporations to remain hidden.

> The offshore world now has an increasingly sustainable and resilient model, which is more sensitive to the needs of the dominant countries. Well resourced IFCs which maintain tax neutrality and responsive regulatory environments will thrive in a connected world.[78]

Meanwhile, a speech by the UK's Prime Minister, Mr Tony Blair, on 26 May 2005 attacked the UK's regulatory authority, the FSA, for imposing rules unnecessarily. Mr Blair said that:

> in my view, we are in danger of having a wholly disproportionate attitude to the risks we should expect to run as a normal part of life. This is putting pressure on policy making, not just in government but in regulatory bodies, on local government, public services, in Europe and across parts of the private sector, to act to eliminate risk in a way that is out of all

[78] Richard Hay, 'International Financial Centres and Information Exchange', *Offshore Investment*, Issue 157, June 2005, p. 3.

proportion to the potential damage. The result is a plethora of rules, guidelines, responses to 'scandals' of one nature or another that ends up having utterly perverse consequences . . . But something is seriously awry when . . . the Financial Services Authority that was established to provide clear guidelines and rules for the financial services sector and to protect the consumer against the fraudulent, is seen as hugely inhibiting of efficient business by perfectly respectable companies that have never defrauded anyone . . . A civil servant or regulator who fails to regulate a risk that materialises will be castigated. How many are rewarded when they refuse to regulate and take the risk? Bodies set up to guard the public interest have one-way pressures. It is in their interest never to be accused of having missed a problem. So, it is a one-sided bet. They will always err on the side of caution . . . A natural but wrong response is to retreat in the face of this change. To regulate to eliminate risk. To restrict rather than to enable . . . So what to do? First, recognise the problem. Some public discussion of it helps engender a more sensible debate. Instead of the 'something must be done' cry that goes up every time there is a problem or a 'scandal', we make it clear we will reflect first and regulate only after reflection. Second, start to roll back the tide of regulation in specific areas: here, in Europe, in respect of the regulatory bodies themselves. Third, replace the compensation culture with a common sense culture.[79]

It remains to be seen what Mr Blair's words mean for the future of regulation 'Onshore' – never mind 'Offshore'. If we are talking about Europe and the large 'Onshore' centres where there has been much criticism about the increasing cost of regulation, that is one thing, but it would be difficult to reconcile Mr Blair's words with the type of ongoing criticism made about 'Offshore' centres for doing the opposite of what he is suggesting. It is true that 'rules that are neglected do no good at all. They do not change behaviour beneficially.'[80]

20.10 What about products for the future?

On the basis that communication, knowledge and information are playing a more significant role in the global economy than ever before, it seems prudent to inquire how these factors are likely to affect 'Offshore'.

---

[79] www.number-10.gov.uk/output/Page7562.asp.
[80] Adam Samuel, 'More Better Regulation: Perhaps Tony Blair Is Right', *Compliance Monitor*, July/August 2005, p. 9.

One writer has suggested that competitive advantage may be achieved 'Offshore' provided that there is neutral taxation on cross-border income flows, more flexible regulation for global activity and privacy of data and trade secrets. If these apply, he says that 'Offshore Finance Centres' are likely to be acceptable places for the following businesses:

- e-procurement operations;
- B2B exchanges;
- Data warehouses;
- Intangible asset holding companies; and
- digital distribution sales entities.[81]

Notably B2B operations are web-based and are therefore fully electronic and are not bound by the same restraints as other types of business in respect of physical location. Further, there are not the same restrictions as apply where a business is dealing with consumers – since, by definition, one business is dealing with another. '[A] B2B exchange operates a globally uniform, closed contractual system under which the rules regulate how contracts are formulated, how trades are settled and paid for, and how disputes are dealt with.'[82]

Data warehouses 'Offshore' means that digitally recorded data are stored in a neutral environment, which means in turn that the data is not subject to data protection rules that apply elsewhere.

Intangible asset-holding companies can be used to locate intellectual property assets.

Mr Woods goes on to describe certain tests, which, if satisfied, would mean that a motion picture is an intangible asset – owned outside the USA – which would mean that royalties arising from the distribution of the asset outside the USA are not taxed in the USA. Some 'Offshore Finance Centres' are already involved in offering this service. Bermuda, the Isle of Man and Malta are amongst the jurisdictions that have already been used for this purpose. It has been reported that '[t]he Isle of Man is fast becoming recognised as a centre of excellence for the provision of

---

[81] William A. Woods, 'Why Legitimate Companies Use Offshore Financial Centres', OffshoreOn.com, 18 October 2002.
[82] William A. Woods, 'Why Legitimate Companies Use Offshore Financial Centres', OffshoreOn.com, 18 October 2002.

specialised financial and regulatory services to the global space and satellite industry'.[83]

According to Datamonitor, 'expansion of Offshore outsourcing will grow at a compound annual rate of 18 per cent between now [2003] and 2005'.[84]

It is unarguable that trade in services has been growing rapidly – and that it is likely to continue to do so in the future. However, the future success of 'Offshore Finance Centres' is not guaranteed. 'The US Treasury has declared an amnesty for Americans who have hidden assets offshore . . . The Bahamas and Cayman Islands are keeping a close watch on the US Government.'[85]

Meanwhile, the trend for banks to unbundle their risks is likely to continue. ('Securitisation', as it is called, means that risk is passed on – elsewhere in the system but not that the risk disappears.) The process is managed by way of derivatives, interest rate swaps, futures and asset-backed securities. These types of assets frequently appear on the balance sheet of insurance companies, mutual funds and pension funds. Most importantly, the trend for banks to create risk transfer by way of credit derivatives is likely to gather pace not least for insurance companies. (Note that credit exposures have been at the core of many bank failures.) 'Banks have tended to pool the cheapest (that is, the most heavily discounted) risks into baskets of assets which they then securitise. Rating agencies have assisted with this process by assigning ratings to these asset pools, ignoring the variations in the quality of individual credits within each rating band.'[86] The question is, how far down the line can such risks be passed? To the policyholder?

Pension funds will continue to move towards defined contribution schemes and away from defined benefit schemes. Individuals will be called upon to take increasing responsibility for their own needs after retirement.

[83] Tom Maher, 'Joining the Space Race', www.offshoreinvestment.com, December 2004/ January 2005, p. 22.
[84] 'Outsourcing to Grow', *Portfolio International*, July 2003, p. 3.
[85] 'Carib Fears at US Savings Crackdown', *Portfolio International*, February 2003.
[86] David Shirreff, 'Crusader Castles: A Survey of International Banking', *The Economist*, 21 May 2005, p. 26.

21

How to assess an 'Offshore Finance Centre'

Morality in the marketplace depends on the decisions made by each individual economic agent . . . [E]conomic success depends upon morality.[1]

21.1 Introduction

This chapter highlights some information that might be relevant to anyone who might be anticipating using an 'Offshore Finance Centre' or who already uses an OFC but who wants some objective criteria by which to assess it. The criteria that follow are merely indications. It is most unlikely that anyone will go to the extent of collating all the information that follows. (Even financial services companies anticipating establishing a presence are unlikely to go to these lengths.) However, the extent of the criteria listed indicates that there may be a lot more information available than most people realise.

21.2 The significance of reputation

Generally speaking, two reasons are usually cited to explain why 'Offshore Finance Centres' attract so much business. First, it is said that there is likely to be no tax or, if there is tax, it will probably be at a nominal rate. Secondly, it is said that there will be no effective regulation. By extension, the latter are often offered as the reasons why the world's tax evaders and money launderers use such OFCs – because it is said that anything is possible in such places. The extent to which the public's perception has been influenced by fiction (like *The Firm*, by John Grisham) or by fact (like the arrest of the Chairman of Vanuatu's Financial Services Commission on charges of laundering US $14 million

---

[1] Charles Colson and Nancy Pearcey, *How Now Shall We Live*, Marshall Pickering, 1999, p. 390.

from the island's shipping registry)[2] remains to be seen. This chapter shows that there is more to success than one might at first imagine.

In the first place, like any other 'living' organism, an 'Offshore Finance Centre' assumes a distinct personality. One of the factors that contribute to the personality of an 'Offshore Finance Centre' is its reputation. Reputation is the core criterion around which the business ethic of the centre develops – because, like banking, 'Offshore Finance' is all about trust and confidence.

Reputation reflects public opinion and, by extension, anything that impinges upon reputation (even a name – see below) is significant because it has the potential to be a critical influence. 'From inside, the main risk is a loss of reputation. Offshore Centres, even more than the large onshore centres, live by their reputations. Their problems, real or perceived, tend to receive disproportionate coverage in the world's press.'[3]

Thus, for those 'Offshore Centres' whose reputation is less than wholesome, negative perceptions have only a marginal effect, but for those 'Offshore Centres' whose reputation is good, even a negative suggestion can be harmful. The fulcrum is very sensitive. Although it takes years to accumulate a positive reputation, it can be lost very quickly.

In all matters relating to finance, reputation is paramount. Reputation amounts to what is generally known about a centre or, more danger- ously, what is perceived about a centre. Investors/depositors/insureds ('consumers') are primarily concerned that, once their money has been handed over to a banker or investment house or insurer or any fiduciary ('financial services practitioners'), they will be able to get their money back when the transaction matures at some future time. As a result of the asymmetry of information (where consumers do not have all the infor- mation they need to make their own assessment of the 'fit and proper' status of the financial services practitioner (see section 6.2 above)), consumers must make a value judgment about that practitioner. This is a very important part of a financial transaction because, in some transactions (such as insurance), the lifespan of the transaction may stretch over forty years.

Thus, the status of the practitioner is very important for consumers not only at the outset of the transaction but also on an ongoing basis

---

[2] 'FSC Chairman Held by FBI over $14m', *Offshore Red*, February 2003, p. 238.
[3] Michael Edwards, 'Review of Financial Regulation in the Crown Dependencies', Part 1, para. 2.13, 1998.

until the transaction matures. Although consumers will also expect that the maturity value will represent an appropriate return on their original investment, their most fundamental requirement is the safety of the amount originally invested. Accordingly, the reputation of the practitioner is a critical factor affecting whether the transaction will or will not take place. The 'fit and proper' test applies to the people involved and to the firm itself (see section 6.8 above).

On a higher level, potential investors may well consider the reputation of the finance centre where the intermediary is located before considering the reputation of the intermediary him/herself. If the finance centre's reputation is poor, the investor may well decide that the reputation of the practitioner does not even have to be considered. Accordingly, the centre's reputation may be considered as a gateway.

Reputation is therefore important for the service provider, for the consumer and for the 'Offshore Finance Centre' from where the practitioner sells his services.

21.3 What's in a name?

The significance of a name is aptly demonstrated by an article that appeared in a supplement to the *International Wealth Management*[4] journal. Previously, that journal had published a guide to 'Offshore Finance Centres'. In the introduction, the journal referred to the blurring of the distinction between 'Offshore' and international finance, and went on to explain that '[i]t is for this reason that we have produced a guide to international finance centres this year rather than our usual "Offshore Centres"'. The publishers were sensitive to the fact that, even though the philosophy of their annual guide had not changed, they had to change the reference to 'Offshore' to avoid causing problems. Similarly, the OFC Report says that, for a long time, the journal 'stalwartly clung to the epithet offshore centre . . . [s]adly the term has become so tarnished by the breadth of watchdogs that the industry has been compelled to look around for another expression, far removed from the negative connotations associated with shady characters, disreputable banks and suitcases full of drug money.'[5] The term chosen instead was 'international financial services centres'.

---

[4] 'Introduction', *International Wealth Management*, Supplement, September 2000, p. 5.
[5] 'Introduction', *The OFC Report 2004*, p. 9.

The term 'Offshore Finance Centre' has been used frequently in a pejorative sense but never more so since the publication of the reports by the OECD, the FATF and the FSF (as described in Chapters 10, 11 and 12 above). So, 'Offshore Finance Centres' are no longer happy about being referred to as such. Interestingly, the IMF sent invitations to forty-six jurisdictions to participate in its Information Framework (see section 2.10 above). The IMF says that 'three of these questioned their classification as OFCs, or noted that their offshore activities had been, or were being, phased out'.[6]

A report by the Australian National University (June 2002)[7] has indicated that 'Pacific Island jurisdictions have suffered as a result of their policy of becoming Offshore Financial Centres.' Naturally, the researcher has to consider whether this type of assessment is accurate or not, and, if it was accurate when it was written, is it still true?

If the term 'Offshore Finance Centre' was/is problematic, the term 'tax haven' is even more so – for the reasons explored earlier. Consequently, jurisdictions no longer describe themselves in these terms. That said, there seems to be no question about the acceptability of the word 'Offshore' for some jurisdictions. For example, the Chief Minister of the British Virgin Islands, Dr Orlando Smith, is reported as saying recently that '[t]he new BVI Business Companies Act was designed to safeguard the attributes that have made the BVI the world's premier offshore company domicile'.[8]

In Chapter 5, reference was made to one method adopted by the US Treasury to thwart terrorist financing and crime – by entering into information-sharing agreements with the 'tax havens' identified by the OECD. This enables the USA to pursue suspected criminals through individually tailored treaties. This strategy is much more effective than trying to compel such centres to amend their tax structures en bloc. Will this be a new trend for the future of the 'Offshore' environment?

In any event, '[t]here is no empirical evidence supporting the claim that OFCs contribute to a "race to the bottom" in tax revenues as these remain stable'.[9]

[6] 'Offshore Financial Centres, The Assessment Program, A Progress Report', IMF, 25 February 2005, para. 16, p. 9.
[7] 'Pacific Centres Face Reputation Issues', *Offshore Red*, July/August 2002, p. 114.
[8] 'New Legislation to Replace Companies Act and IBC Act', *Offshore Red*, February 2005, p. 3.
[9] Mattias Levin, 'The Prospects for Offshore Financial Centres in Europe', CEPS Research Report, August 2002, p. i.

21.4 Stability and credibility

It is suggested that, for an 'Offshore Finance Centre' (howsoever described), success is only possible if an appropriate foundation has been laid. The foundation comprises two elements: stability and credibility.

Stable political, economic and financial environments are necessary. Stability means that the components of these environments are in equilibrium. This does not imply that there are no positive and negative movements within those environments but rather that the movements are incremental and not sufficiently large to lead to disequilibrium.

As a result of the general turbulence in the financial and economic sectors of the global environment – which includes events arising as a result of the OECD, FATF and FSF reports – there have been substantial legal and regulatory changes in most 'Offshore Finance Centres' around the world. On the one hand, this is inevitable as these changes have come about as the result of the centres involved responding to the demands of those organisations. If the OFCs had not made the required changes, they would have suffered the rebuke (and perhaps the punitive retaliation) of those organisations which had required the changes in the first place. However, the strategies for which 'Offshore Finance Centres' are used frequently cover lengthy timespans. Changes make individual users nervous because they fear that change may frustrate the strategies that they have implemented already or might do so in the future. This nervousness tends to lead to disequilibrium as investors manoeuvre to reposition themselves as a result of such changes. This repositioning may be a marginal activity, but, if investors become sufficiently nervous, they may move their business to another jurisdiction where there have been fewer changes. This is a further indication of the very fine balance that exists in many 'Offshore Finance Centres'. If business migrates, it may move to a 'lesser' centre – which negates the objectives of the changes in the first place and will mean that the centre must work even harder to reassure and comfort those users whose nervousness has reached problematic levels.

Credibility means that, in the eyes of the world at large, the centre is deemed to be a safe and acceptable place to transact business. One of the main principles used to assess the 'quality' of an OFC is the way in which the centre organises and conducts its affairs with the rest of the world. In assessing credibility, the following questions are often asked:

- Which global organisations are already located in the centre?
- Have there been any scandals in the financial services sector recently?

- If so, do the scandals indicate any weaknesses in the quality of regulation?
- How strong is regulation in the OFC?
- Who are the regulators and what is their previous experience?
- Does the centre have anti-money laundering legislation, and, if so, to what extent is it applied?
- Does the centre have a Financial Intelligence Unit?
- Do the regulatory authorities undertake compliance visits?
- What does the OECD, the FATF, the World Bank, the IMF and the FSF say about the centre?
- How many double taxation treaties does the centre have?

Stability and credibility combine to create reputation – which is the single most important criterion that must exist if any degree of success is to be achieved. In fact, this applies equally whether a finance centre is located 'Offshore' or 'Onshore'.

21.5 The components of a good reputation

How can a finance centre acquire a good reputation and, having done so, how can it be maintained? Both passive and active factors are involved.

First, the passive factors include the avoidance of any event or action that would diminish confidence if it happened. This ranges from adverse publicity to the failure of a financial services company – but especially a bank. It might be that the failure is slightly less significant in itself than the results it produces. For example, all parties in general, but external parties in particular (on the basis of their assessment of the centre), will be interested to know why the failure happened and whether it could have been avoided. In particular, people will want to know how safe their assets are and whether this problem indicates an innate weakness that puts or might put their assets at risk. Relevant questions include:

- Is there a compensation scheme?
- Is it triggered?
- Are there any systemic implications?
- How significant will this failure be for the financial services industry in that centre?
- Is this likely to affect the government?
- Are there any other significant implications?
- To what extent have ordinary investors/depositors lost money?

- How easily could this disaster have been prevented?
- Is there any fraud involved?

In matters of trust, perception equates with reality to a large extent. Thus, consumers will vote with their feet if their perception of a situation that affects (or might affect) the safety of their assets is negative.

The active factors comprise whatever measures are necessary to prevent the negative factors just described. In reality, this means regulation and supervision of the practitioners and of the markets in which they operate. In turn, regulation comprises both the attitude to regulation and also the regulatory mechanisms adopted. These are described in some detail in Chapters 6 and 7.

However, regulation and supervision do not guarantee anything – they merely attempt to protect consumers, systems and jurisdictions by managing exposure to risk.

21.6 The constitutents of success

Fundamentally, one must be able to determine what is meant by 'success'. Although this is not an easy question, the process for determining the answer is very instructive. The components of success for an 'Offshore Finance Centre' are illustrated in Figure 21.1.

In his review of the UK's 'Offshore' centres, Mr Edwards pointed out that: 'The Islands owe the success of their finance centres to their substantial constitutional independence in domestic affairs, their political stability and their continuing willingness, evident throughout their history, to adapt to changing world conditions. These are vital factors from which all else flows.'[10]

'Jersey and the Isle of Man remain touchstones for good practice. They have lit the way with their progressive approach to markets and regulation.'[11]

21.7 Three perspectives

Three interest groups were identified in Chapter 4. These comprise the jurisdiction itself, the service providers and consumers. In order to assess

[10] Michael Edwards, 'Review of Financial Regulation in the Crown Dependencies', Part 1, para. 2.7, 1998.
[11] Bob Reynolds, 'From the Editor', *Offshore Red*, February 2003 p. 241.

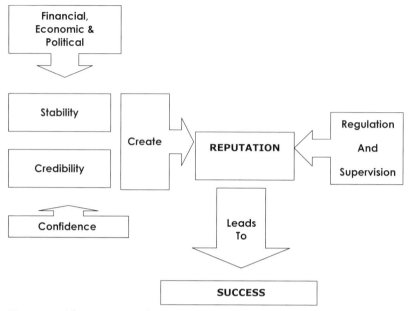

Figure 21.1. The success paradigm

whether the jurisdiction is appropriate, each interest group might consider the following factors.

21.7.1 The jurisdiction

In respect of financial services, the jurisdiction's objectives can be simply stated. The jurisdiction will want to create a financial environment that is conducive to an increasing amount of good business in order to create full employment and a continuous improvement in GDP. All policy decisions that the jurisdiction makes will be made on the basis of these two objectives.

21.7.2 The service providers

The following criteria (in random order) are amongst those that may be used by a service provider to assess the acceptability of an OFC:

● the stability of the political system;
● the extent to which the regulator is independent of government;

- the degree to which confidentiality is respected;
- language;
- time zone;
- the cost and sophistication of the telecommunications systems and hardware; and
- the quality of the professional infrastructure.

21.7.3 The consumer

The following criteria (in random order) are amongst those that may be used by a consumer to assess the acceptability of an OFC.

In making an assessment of an 'Offshore Finance Centre', there is always value in considering the views of others (always bearing in mind the weaknesses associated with relying only on perceptions). For example, one journal included the following comment: 'The Marshall Islands, Vanuatu, Nauru and Niue are regarded as poorly managed centres lacking the regulatory and financial expertise to respond to new market and political conditions.'[12] This report may or may not be true, so, if one was about to invest in one of these centres (or if an investment had been made already), there may be value in trying to corroborate such information. It is preferable to conduct wide research on a jurisdiction and not rely on one source of information exclusively.

Regrettably, there is relatively little published on 'Offshore' that is not advertising. Even what seems to be meaningful may be peppered with prompts encouraging readers to contact one or other practitioners advertising in the publication. That said, *Euromoney* publishes an *Offshore Finance Yearbook*. This provides a 'summary table' containing general information, tax regulations, trusts, and corporation law factors. These tables provide an overview. The journal more generally also includes articles of interest concerning 'Offshore' and some background on what is happening in those jurisdictions. Some journals publish surveys from time to time. For example, *Offshore Investment* published their 'Definitive Company Formation Survey' in March 2002. Certain books also include surveys on the main features of some of the 'Offshore Finance Centres'. It should be noted that while many features that apply to 'Offshore' are included, they are presented in the form of lists. Any tax planning carried out on the basis of such limited

---

[12] 'Pacific Centres Face Reputation Issues', *Offshore Red*, July/August 2002, p. 112.

information is done so entirely at the reader's risk. If one wants to know how to use all this information, the books encourage the reader to refer to one of the professional advisers/practitioners that they list in the text! The results of Financial Sector Action Programs (FSAPs) – which are normally published on the web – are an extremely helpful source of information.

The point made at the outset is emphasised again here. General information is available, but there is a substantial amount of advertising text that mixes opinions with facts. The number of meaningful, informative texts on 'Offshore' is limited.

21.8 Assessment criteria

The paradigm presented above might be used to make an assessment of an 'Offshore Finance Centre' by addressing questions such as the following.

21.8.1 Financial stability

- What trends can be identified in the balance of payments?
- If there are frequent balance of payments deficits, what is their extent and duration?
- Is there a satisfactory explanation?
- At what level are borrowings?
- Have there been any defaults?
- How effective is monetary control?
- What is the jurisdiction's credit rating now, and how has this changed historically?

21.8.2 Economic stability

- In respect of inflation, GDP and unemployment, what is the current level, and how has this changed historically?
- How stable are exchange rates?
- Are there currently any controls on the currency?
- What can be ascertained from the economic statistics that are available?
- To what extent does the economy rely on one or a few services, especially finance?

- Is the financial infrastructure (accounting, legal services and IT) developed to an acceptable extent?
- Assess fiscal policy.

21.8.3 Political stability

- What type of political system exists?
- Assess its effectiveness.
- What is the tenure of the existing government?
- What has it achieved?
- How effective is the opposition?
- What is the government's and the opposition's attitude towards the finance sector and its future?
- Are there currently any public policy matters that are likely to impinge upon the finance sector?
- Assess the judicial system.

21.8.4 Credibility

- Is there anti-money laundering and anti-terrorist financing legislation in place, and, if so, is it effective?
- Is there a Financial Intelligence Unit in the jurisdiction?
- To what extent are the FATF's recommendations applied in practice?
- Has an FSAP been carried out, and, if so, were the results generally satisfactory?
- What did the FSAP say concerning regulation, risks, the stock exchange and the central bank?
- Of which international organisations is this jurisdiction a member (e.g. the IAIS, IOSCO, the OGBS, the OGIS, etc.)?
- Is the jurisdiction a signatory to the Vienna Convention?
- Is there prevention of terrorism and prevention of corruption legislation?
- Assess relative effectiveness of current legislation in respect of the following: companies, trusts, securities, banking, NBFIs, insider dealing, insolvency etc.;
- Is the legislation that impinges upon financial affairs up to date?
- Are there meaningful penalties in respect of illegal financial activity?
- Is there an ombudsman and, if so, is he effective?
- Is the environment conducive to good business?

- Is there a legal requirement for licensees to adopt corporate governance principles?

21.8.5 Regulation

- Is there a regulatory authority, and, if so, is it separate from government?
- Is it effective? For example, does it require providers of financial services to be licensed and what is the rejection and revocation history? Does it conduct onsite compliance visits? Are wrongdoers punished? To what extent does form prevail over substance?
- When was the most recent problem with a licensed institution and to what extent did members of the public suffer?
- Are the regulatory rules published, and, if so, how often are they updated?
- Is the regulator sufficiently independent?
- Is regulation carried out separately from promotion?
- Are there any compensation schemes, and, if so, are they effective?
- Is the jurisdiction on any international 'black lists'?
- Is it fair to say that a 'compliance culture' prevails?
- Internationally, what is the reputation of the regulator?
- Does the regulator behave with integrity?

21.8.6 Supervision

- When was the most recent systemically significant failure?
- How was it resolved and was the outcome satisfactory?

21.8.7 Success

- In what ways has the jurisdiction been 'successful'?
- Has the jurisdiction the potential to become more 'successful'?
- Are the risks involved in investing in, working in or working with this jurisdiction reasonable?

21.9 In summary

It may not be possible to obtain (meaningful) answers to all the questions listed above, but, in fact, the amount of information available in most centres in respect of inflation, GDP and unemployment etc. in the public domain is constantly increasing. The results of the FSAP programme are a case in point. The FSF says that publication of the initial IMF assessment reports 'enables the position of individual OFCs to be evaluated by all concerned parties, is indicative of OFC jurisdictions' commitment to cooperate, and enhances transparency more generally . . . The FSF strongly encourages all jurisdictions to publish their IMF assessment reports.'[13] Jurisdictions themselves produce valuable information on their websites and in their own publications (such as annual reports). Frequently, the annual report of the regulatory authority is a good way to find out substantial information about a jurisdiction. (For example, the 2003 annual report of the Financial Services Commission in Mauritius ran to 150 pages.) Central banks often publish very detailed economic data.

Further, although there is only limited information available from books, substantially more is available from specific journals (such as those described above). The Internet is another useful information source and the websites of the FATF, the World Bank, the IMF, the FSF and the OECD are very much worth visiting, as are those of particular agencies (and licence-holding companies) operating from the jurisdiction itself. By way of example, as part of its OFC assessment programme, the IMF publishes very helpful information in its regular progress reports – the last of which was published on 25 February 2005. Table 1 of the IMF text sets out a summary of the status of jurisdictions contacted during the first phase of the programme. Tables 2 and 3 of the IMF's text provide summary analyses arising from assessments undertaken on those international and Offshore Financial Centres contacted so far. Table 2 of the IMF text deals with Module 2 Assessments, and Table 3 of the IMF text deals with FSAP assessments. These tables are most instructive. Table 3 of the IMF text contains a very enlightening summary on the numbers of jurisdictions that comply with the Principles and Recommendations related to cooperation and to information sharing. Finally, Table 4 of the IMF text contains a very detailed summary of the assessments so far undertaken on fifty-one jurisdictions, and includes relevant updates. This type of information is invaluable to anyone who really wants to find out what is happening 'Offshore'.

Often there is a great deal to be gained by conducting wide research as opposed to relying on only one source of information (e.g. that of a

---

[13] Press Release, 'FSF Reviews its Offshore Financial Centres (OFCs) Initiative', Financial Stability Forum, 5 April 2004, p. 2.

single 'gatekeeper' such as an accountant or lawyer). Perceptions need not be relied upon.

It is also useful to visit the jurisdiction (if that is possible) to see for oneself. This enables very focused one-to-one interviews with key people – and one advantage of using an 'Offshore' jurisdiction is that even the most senior people will (probably) be accessible. People to visit include not only practitioners but also the regulatory authority, the relevant ministry, the body responsible for promotion, lawyers, accountants, and maybe even the collector of taxes.

Finally, a comment on the media. On the face of it, press articles produced locally from any jurisdiction have substantial positive potential in describing the financial services environment of a financial services centre. Whether this potential is realised or not remains to be seen. Some care is required to ensure that the journalist knows what he is talking about.

22

Conclusion

The most important lesson to be learnt is that high ethical and professional standards must always be put before commercial advantage.[1]

22.1 A thumbnail sketch

The primary objective of this book is to provide information about the 'Offshore' environment. In doing so, an attempt has been made to describe the origins of 'Offshore', to place it in context and to define some terms that are considered relevant. However, since 'Offshore' does not exist in a vacuum, the text includes reference to other environments – alongside which 'Offshore' operates – including the 'Onshore' environment. Comparisons were made between 'Offshore' and jurisdictions, which, while not ordinarily referred to as OFCs, nevertheless offer similar services. Whether 'Offshore' or 'Onshore', the text identified taxation as one of the most significant factors in giving any finance centre a raison d'être.

Since taxation is a major component in economic global enterprise, so also is tax mitigation – and this explains why many financial centres benefit from being used by taxpayers (ranging from individuals to multinational companies) as components in tax mitigation strategies. No one is obliged to pay more tax than is due. Consequently, taxpayers are entitled to use finance centres to mitigate their tax if they so choose. Taxpayers are not entitled to evade tax. Perfect positive correlation between 'Offshore' finance centres and the evasion of tax has not been proved beyond reasonable doubt.

In attempting to explain why 'Offshore' has come under such public scrutiny in the recent past, reference was made to three important reports which were published in 2000. One report in particular classified

---

[1] 'Report of the Inspectors into the Collapse of Robert Maxwell's Business Empire'.

jurisdictions as 'tax havens' while a second report attempted to classify
the respective 'acceptability' of jurisdictions. Some of the implications of
these reports were considered – not least in connection with 'Offshore's'
future – because, even though the reports date back some years, their
influence remains extant.

Amongst the key concerns that engage those involved in 'Offshore'
activity, is what has been referred to as the 'level playing field'. In short,
the argument is that there are two teams competing for financial services
business. One team is the 'Onshore' team and the other is the 'Offshore'
team. The latter believes that, often, the playing field on which the teams
are required to compete is not level and the disequilibrium is to the
advantage of the 'Onshore' team. The OFCs have repeatedly expressed
their view that OECD countries must be forced to adopt the standards
that they are trying to impose on others. The core issues include national
sovereignty, alternative sources of income, confidentiality versus secrecy
and the right of individuals to a degree of privacy. The OECD is a
powerful organisation and has adequate influence to force many issues
but to achieve their purposes at the expense of the OFCs is not the
answer. That said, the analogy is perhaps not the most appropriate
since most playing fields are not level anyway – but nevertheless the
term is used widely, although not always accurately. The 'level playing
field' argument does not mean that everybody everywhere should be
doing everything the same way. Instead, it means that there should be no
finance centre – anywhere in the world – where it is easier than anywhere
else to operate illegally.

Regulation is the prime driver employed in ensuring that practitioners
behave properly. In light of its centrality in any debate that concerns the
bona fides of business 'Offshore', the text has devoted a substantial
amount of words and space to this topic.

22.2 Relative newness of regulation

Regulation is merely an imprecise tool that is used to assist supervisory
authorities to monitor financial services providers. Regulation is used to
identify and to manage the risks to which the providers of financial
services are exposed. Regulation has another part to play – in protecting
consumers and the financial services environment from those who would
try to abuse it. Regulation will not eradicate risk – it is only a tool used to
manage risk, not a panacea. That said, risk per se is not negative. The
tradeoff between risk and return is a core issue. The secret is in knowing,

in any circumstance, when the risk becomes too great. The next decision concerns what action is appropriate in the circumstances.

Regulation has come a long way, very quickly. For example, at one stage, the City of London was not subject to prescriptive regulation at all. In fact, the UK's first banking legislation was not enacted until 1979. Before that date, the City operated to a large extent on the basis of trust and on the basis of the integrity of market participants. This system proved to be effective for a very long time. It comprised certain elements that remain valid in the vastly different global marketplace in which financial business is transacted today.

What elements are common? One common element is the realisation that rules by themselves will not achieve the objectives of regulation. In this respect, Messrs McCarthy and Tiner, Chairman and Chief Executive, respectively, of the Financial Services Authority in the UK, recently 'signalled a move from policy development to policy implementation . . . placing the emphasis on management running their firms in accordance with the Principles'.[2] Rather, it is suggested that, in an ideal world, there should be little or no need for a rule-book because in such circumstances all participants would be operating according to a self-imposed code of conduct. That said, self-regulation has a chequered history: it has proved to be effective in some circumstances, but not all.

For example, so far as the UK is concerned, under the Financial Services Act 1986, self-regulation failed to meet the demands placed on it. So what is the alternative to creating more and more rules to prevent abuse? A proliferation of rules will merely produce an artificial financial environment that will stifle creativity and development.

Probably, the way forward is to adopt a different regulatory paradigm. Reference was made earlier to the reactive nature of regulation and to the factors involved in determining whether prevention was a more appropriate strategy than cure in all circumstances. It was suggested that, in respect of regulation, prevention was normally more effective than cure. The paradigm should now become more proactive and focus more on prevention than cure ex post facto. By definition, this means determining what factors constitute risk and how these can be measured and used as an indicator of likely future problems. Risk control becomes a critical function. This requires regulators to adopt a different perspective whereby they will become more sensitive to what might be a signal or

---

[2] 'Making Sense of It All', *Securities and Investment Review*, January–February 2004.

an indication of a future problem rather than responding to problems as they crystallise. To be effective, responses will probably also need to be novel. That is, existing regulatory methods may – or may not – produce the results required of a pro-active risk control environment. In *The Regulatory Craft*, the author presents many useful insights into the inherent difficulties and potential benefits of regulation. He adds that 'the failure to make the connection between lower-level activities and higher-level goals is never more apparent than in the context of performance measurement'.[3]

All this presupposes that respective 'Offshore' jurisdictions can clearly identify what constitutes 'success' for them.

22.3 A middle course

The answer lies somewhere between two extremes:

> The problems associated with 'Offshore Centres' are such that unilateral or bilateral actions by individual countries are close to meaningless. One single country cannot control its tax base in an economically integrated world. One single country cannot solve the problem of money laundering – it is a global phenomenon and requires concerted global action to deal with it. One single country cannot increase the stability of the financial system if other countries continue to endanger it.[4]

Having little or no rules is just as ineffective as having too many. Ideally, if practitioners were seriously to embrace the 'fit and proper' criteria responsibly (which include integrity, honesty and probity), the market would have much firmer foundations on which to develop. This theme is not new. For example, it was taken up by Eugene Ludwig, former Comptroller of the Currency in the USA, when he addressed Securities Institute practitioners in the UK at the Annual Ethics Lecture in January 2001. It remains extant today. Two articles in a recent edition of *The Economist* (17 February 2005) were entitled 'Are Business Schools Bad for Business?' and 'Is the MBA Responsible for Moral Turpitude at the Top?'. The articles refer to a forthcoming article based on the work of Sumantra Goshal, a respected business academic, who has suggested that what MBA students are taught, exonerates them from employing moral responsibility in their

---

[3] Malcolm Sparrow, *The Regulatory Craft*, Brookings Institution Press, 2000, p. 312.
[4] Mattias Levin, 'The Prospects for Offshore Financial Centres in Europe', CEPS Research Report, August 2002, p. 15.

future business careers. This approach is endorsed by Geoffrey Pfeffer from the Stanford University Graduate School of Business.

Replacing rules with sound ethical principles is not without inherent difficulties. For example, many people are comfortable with rules. Further, too strong an ethical culture may affect results – on which share price and performance bonuses are assessed. What price ethics? The idea might generate more support if the links between good corporate governance and improved performance could be established beyond doubt in the minds of practitioners. Mere verbal assent is inadequate. Much work has been carried out in this area already, and it is likely that more will follow as recognition spreads of the significant part that ethics and governance play in the regulatory process. That is not to say that the two are mutually exclusive – rather the suggestion is that practitioners need to adopt courses of action because they believe that it is in their best interests to do so and not merely because they have been required to do so. Corporate governance procedures contribute to the bottom line – and what is regulation all about if it is not good corporate governance procedures?

However, this means much more than splitting the role of the Chairman from that of the Chief Executive and recruiting good quality non-executive directors and establishing appropriate committees (such as for audit and remuneration). Accordingly, better performance does not automatically ensue from good corporate governance exclusively – the objective of which is not improved performance per se. Nevertheless, the recent corporate scandals in the USA indicate the growing need for meaningful corporate governance in financial services companies.

It has been said that '[f]ar from making the City a more honest place, the piling on of regulation has fostered a "letter of the law" compliance culture . . . [and that intelligent people] . . . have had their value systems completely warped by the "grab-it-all" environment in which they work'.[5] By way of example, the case of the mutual funds scam in the USA was cited – which the same writer said showed 'fundamental moral decay' and raised 'questions about the health of the entire system'. The author saw London as another example of the same thing. This sort of hypocrisy is rife. 'Offshore Finance Centres' must have none of it. The spirit of the law cannot be separated from the letter of the law without creating the sort of duplicity and lack of integrity that the 'fit and proper'

---

[5] Anthony Hilton, 'Thou Shalt Not Get Caught', *Securities and Investment Review*, January–February 2004, p. 9.

tests cannot tolerate. For their part, the OFCs must acknowledge that changes are necessary and that synergies can be exploited if those changes are made in an acceptable way. There is only one way forward if OFCs are to survive – and that is for each respective jurisdiction to focus on the need to demonstrate high levels of business ethics and morality in every aspect of their activity.

22.4 The 'Offshore' stigma

> [U]nhelpful selective value judgments – pursued by, on the one hand, some onshore jurisdictions who are too ready to take the view that such haven centres are the situs, not of intermediate economies as we have described them, but the international equivalent of the domestic 'black', 'informal', 'underground', 'hidden' economy sectors, the refuges of transnational moonlighters and tax evaders, which should be squeezed and, on the other hand, those extreme supporters of economic freedom at all costs, whose near anarchistic incivisime is unleashed against all bureaucracies and the impedimenta of government, may well cloud most discussions on this subject.[6]

Fraudsters, money launderers and other criminals are not going to stop wrongdoing because it is socially and morally dysfunctional. Therefore, the global financial system in general – and for the purposes of this discussion 'Offshore Finance Centres' in particular – will continue to face attempts to exploit them. This challenge is likely to increase. Although it is unfortunate, it is nevertheless the case that wrongdoing committed 'Offshore' frequently attracts much more attention than it would if committed 'Onshore'. It is simply a fact of life that OFCs must accept and factor into how they operate.

Naturally, all finance centres – whether 'Onshore' or 'Offshore' are at risk from fraudsters and other criminals who will seek out every opportunity to abuse the rules for illegitimate or illegal purposes. Recent reports on money transferred by Sani Abacha, the former Nigerian dictator, indicate that the Swiss Federal Banking Commission believes that more than half of the US$208 million deposited in Switzerland came from the UK and one-third from the USA. Of the US$514 million that was paid from Swiss banks, US$219 million went to the UK. There

[6] R. A. Johns, *Tax Havens and Offshore Finance: A Study of Transnational Economic Development*, Frances Pinter (Publishers) Ltd, 1983, p. 46.

appear to have been flaws in the due diligence checks and documenta-
tion.[7] So 'Onshore' centres do not get it right all the time either.
However, at the same time, 'Offshore' centres are far from blameless.
For example, 'Vanuatu was accused of draining about AU$295 million
(US$169 million) in potential tax revenues by providing tailored haven
services for Australians.'[8]

22.5 Is the stigma warranted?

It has already been pointed out that there is no consensus about the
meaning of 'Offshore', which in turn means there is confusion as to
which jurisdictions are really 'Offshore' centres and which are not. For
example, the IMF list started out with forty-four names (see Table 27 in
Appendix 1 below), the OECD identified thirty-seven tax havens and the
Offshore Group of Banking Supervisors (OGBS) has less than twenty
members. While it might reasonably be argued that this is not comparing
like with like, it demonstrates aptly why it is so difficult to say much
about 'Offshore' with any degree of certainty.

   The OGBS is the only grouping that provides some sort of solid basis
on which some sort of hypothesis might be built. OGBS members
have combined voluntarily into a definitive group and – as their name
suggests – members regard themselves as a part of the 'Offshore' environment. What can be said about the group? Section 9.21 above provides
some basic static data – but are there any features that might be super-
imposed on the wider 'Offshore' environment? Is the group a valid
sample of the whole population of 'Offshore' centres? Consider some
of the information already available, for example the results of the FSF's
work (despite its subjective and unscientific nature).

   Table 17 in Appendix 1 (below) shows that, while OGBS members
(nineteen) account for only 45 per cent of the global population of OFCs
(forty-two) – based on the FSF's analysis (which the FSF chose not to
restate until 2005), 63 per cent of those jurisdictions that were placed
in the upper category (1) are members of the OGBS and 67 per cent
of the middle category (2) were OGBS members. Only 32 per cent of
OGBS members were placed in category (3). Further, 58 per cent of
OGBS members were in either category (1) or (2).

---

[7] John Wilman and John Mason, 'UK Bankers Silent on Laundered Nigeria Cash', *Financial
   Times*, 5 September 2000.
[8] 'FSC Chairman Held by FBI over $14m', *Offshore Red*, February 2003, p. 238.

Table 19 shows that, of the thirty-five jurisdictions which the OECD identified as tax havens (which may or may not be the same as 'Offshore Finance Centres'), only eleven (30 per cent) are members of the OGBS.

Table 21 (below) shows that none of the jurisdictions that the OECD currently classifies as 'uncooperative tax havens' are members of the OGBS.

Table 23 (below) shows that, as at February 2005, none of the jurisdictions that the FATF currently classifies as 'non-cooperative countries and territories' are members of the OGBS.

Table 26 (below) shows that all but two of the OGBS members are also members of the Egmont Group.

Table 27 (below) shows those members of the OGBS that have published their IMF FSAP Module 2 reports.

Table 28 (below) shows the membership of IOSCO as at May 2005. Reference to Table 29 shows that fifteen out of the OGBS's nineteen members are 'Ordinary' members of IOSCO.

Table 29 (below) provides an overview of all these criteria and shows the status of members of the OGBS in respect of each.

These tables demonstrate the credibility of the 'Offshore' jurisdictions they describe – and, if the OGBS is a valid sample of the 'Offshore' environment as a whole, there may be more positive features about 'Offshore' than some people realise. Meanwhile, this has to be tempered with the ongoing criticism made by some of the world's larger countries which continue to regard 'Offshore' with a jaundiced eye. For example, Parmalat is often cited as a reason for concern in this respect, but is this because the 'Offshore' environment was responsible for the wrongdoing or because it was wrongly used to achieve the purposes of the wrong-doers? The suggestion seems to be that the fraud was only possible because the wrongdoers were able to conceal their wrongdoing 'Offshore'. Similarly, there is a suggestion that the financial excesses in Latin America and South East Asia in the recent past only arose because of the opportunities that presented themselves in the 'Offshore' environment. This type of reasoning is on a par with maligning light industry because people use metal to fabricate guns that are sometimes used to kill people. Does this warrant treating the industry with suspicion?

22.6 The rationale for 'Offshore'

The recent past has put 'Offshore' squarely in the spotlight; but, according to PriceWaterhouseCoopers, the 'Offshore' environment is losing business to 'Onshore'.[9] It has been suggested that this arises for a number of reasons which include the increasing difficulty involved in hiding wealth 'Offshore', but, also because of a newer trend for investors to be more involved in managing their own portfolios. Naturally, this is not good news for some advisers – but that is another story. Investors' expectations are rising, and this focuses attention on major markets, and away from tax mitigation strategies. 'Offshore Centres, characterised by anonymity, small size, small markets and limited services, and in light of ongoing international initiatives that threaten to tarnish their reputations, are finding it more difficult to grow in this environment.'[10]

'Offshore Finance Centres' are not in business to assist individuals or corporations to evade tax or to launder money. They are in business to promote their jurisdictions as credible places to transact business and the most effective way to do that is to ensure that regulatory standards are robust. Their strategy is not short term, so any damage to reputation is likely to have long-term repercussions.

While recognising that there are legitimate reasons for protecting customer confidentiality, it is also accepted that secrecy laws should not impede the ability of supervisors to ensure safety and soundness in the financial system by preventing the sharing of relevant information with other authorities. There is a balance to be achieved here. An effective regulatory system must balance the needs of high net worth individuals for confidentiality with the regulator's need to ensure that practitioners 'know their customers' and will report suspicious transactions. Confidentiality is a key issue. Practitioners must pay more than lip service to their regulatory responsibilities (including strict adherence to anti-money laundering rules) so that regulators can be more confident in them. However, with respect to anti-money laundering rules in particular, care must be taken to avoid confusing means with ends. Adherence to the detailed AML/CFT rules (compliance) is important but this should not be allowed to divert attention from where it should be concentrated – eradication of abuse in the first place – and removing dirty money from circulation in the second place.

Nevertheless, as one commentator has said,

---

[9] *European Private Banking/Wealth Management Survey 2000/01*, PriceWaterhouseCoopers, 2001, as reported by Mattias Levin, 'The Prospects for Offshore Financial Centres in Europe', CEPS Research Report, August 2002, p. 5.

[10] Mattias Levin, 'The Prospects for Offshore Financial Centres in Europe', CEPS Research Report, August 2002, p. 5.

> the regulatory spotlight is unlikely to deter financial institutions from
> setting up in offshore centres if they perceive an advantage in doing so.
> Indeed, a case in favour is overwhelming for those that aspire to offer a
> global service . . . But multinational financial services companies have
> reputations to protect. What is likely to happen is that they will shun those
> centres that have a bad name or are lacking in professional infrastructure
> (the two usually go together) in favour of well regulated, stable ones.[11]

While the 'Offshore' environment is alive and strong, its importance
has diminished and may in due course diminish further – but not for the
time being at least.

It is perverse yet true that the advantages provided by 'Offshore
Finance Centres' are simultaneously what gives rise to their potential
for success and their potential for exploitation.

In any event, it would be preferable if Member States of the EU and
members of the OECD dealt with their own harmful tax practices before
imposing any greater burdens on OFCs. OFCs must be given some
incentive to make the changes demanded of them. As it stands, they
receive no praise for making such changes. They only suffer damage to
their reputation if they do not.

22.7 Concluding remarks

International financial services centres (IFSCs) have reached a watershed
in their evolution – even their name has changed! Secrecy is no longer
acceptable. Transparency and higher ethical standards are the order of
the day. IFSCs must develop the quality and range of their services, and
adopt appropriate strategies to improve their image and credibility.
When he was Chairman of the Financial Services Authority in the UK
(September 2001), Mr Howard Davies said in a speech delivered in the
Isle of Man that:

> Those responsible for the governance of offshore centres would do well to
> be aware of the challenges they face. In short, offshore centres will need to
> do much more in the coming years to demonstrate that they can and do
> meet international standards of best practice. If that does not happen, then
> the future is bleak.[12]

---

[11] P. Gartland, 'Offshore Financial Centres', *Accountancy*, December 1992, p. 83.
[12] Press Release, 'FSA Warns Offshore Financial Centres', FSA, 26 September 2001.

These words were well understood, and much has now been done to meet international standards of best practice. The work is ongoing – continuous improvement is necessary. In this respect, 'renewed efforts will be required to ensure that financial centres which achieve high standards will not be put at a competitive disadvantage'.[13]

However, while IFSCs have amended their philosophy and improved their working practices by enhanced regulatory and supervisory regimes, their approach has not been emulated elsewhere. It seems that IFSCs have adopted a different paradigm than that adopted by some non-IFSCs. For example, with respect to internal governance, it has been said that the emphasis in such jurisdictions 'is consistent with the paradigm of modern financial supervision in which the supervisor relies increasingly on the internal governance and risk management procedures of the supervised entity and on market discipline and less on direct controls on the supervised entity'.[14] In this respect, the latest annual report of the Financial Services Authority in the UK said that 'our efforts have been devoted to finding means to restrict regulatory intervention to those areas where no market solution is possible'.[15] A recent article said that:

> In July 2005, the FSA is due to issue a consultation paper that will outline some far reaching changes to the Training and Competence Handbook. One proposed change is the removal of the mandatory requirement, for those working in the wholesale market, to take an appropriate examination, in order to demonstrate competence . . . As one seasoned practitioner observed, these proposals are not so much deregulation, as abdication by the FSA, since there is no change at all in the requirements for senior management to ensure that staff are, and remain, competent.[16]

If all this suggests that regulators will become less intrusive when they do not need to be more intrusive, this is a positive development. If this means eradicating unnecessary bureaucracy and limiting rules where it is safe and possible to do so, these also are positive developments. If this means focusing resources on risks that require additional resources and

---

[13] Jeffrey Owens, 'Global Financial Markets Need Global Rules', in *The 2005 Guide to International Financial Centres*, Euromoney Institutional Investor plc, February 2005, p. 9.
[14] White Paper on the Governance of CISs, Financial Market Trends, OECD, No. 88, March 2005, p. 140.
[15] Chairman's Statement, *Annual Report 2004/05*, Financial Services Authority (UK), p. 6.
[16] 'Competence: The Importance of Benchmarks', *Securities and Investment Review*, July–August 2005, p. 5.

lessening focus where there is little risk, then there is value in pursuing this route. What must be avoided is responding inappropriately when faced with complaints about costs. A proper balance must be struck – but not at the cost of adopting a softer, cheaper, more palatable approach – unless the circumstances are appropriate. There comes a point when, after all (or nearly all) the possible economies have been made, all that can be done to reduce costs further is to ease back on the actions that give rise to those costs. We must make sure that such action will not have a consequent negative effect on standards. We must ensure that the perceptible changes of emphasis – which are gaining momentum – are appropriate – because, shortly, IFSCs will follow the lead of their larger, mainland-based regulators.

There is one way, however, in which this new approach is entirely feasible – and that is to foster a new culture that relies more on ethical principles than on rules. Unless we can introduce a voluntary compliance culture – based on honesty, integrity and probity – we will continue to move forward but at an ever decreasing pace where risk-based supervision will degenerate into cost-based supervision. The adoption of basic corporate governance principles is the only feasible alternative to increasing bureaucracy and additional rules which in many centres are already prolific. Over-regulation (whatever that means) is just as dysfunctional as inadequate regulation.

If IFSCs continue to encourage an appropriate compliance culture in their respective environments, then, whenever the question is asked whether 'Offshore' has a future, the answer will not be that 'Offshore' is 'off course' – but rather the answer will be an affirmative 'of course'!

Appendix 1

Tables

Table 1 *Participation in the Information Framework*

Positive response	23
Positive response with proviso	1
Negative response	3
Total responses received	27
No response received	19
Total invitations sent	46

Table 2 *Services 'Offshore'*

Fiduciary	Banking	Insurance	Securities	Other
Trustee	Deposits	Life	Stock- broking	Movies
Corporate services	Loans	General	Asset management	Distribution of CISs
Estate planning	Trading inter-bank	Reinsurance	Fund management	Shipping registry
Formation of trusts	General banking	Captives	Discretionary portfolio management	IT
Provision of directors	Asset management	Unit-linked policies	Unit trusts	Special purpose vehicles
Company secretarial	Custodian	Pensions	Collective investment schemes	
Tax advice	Leasing			
Nominee	Registrar			

Table 3 *The medical paradigm*

Trait	Offshore	Society
Conducive environment	Prudential supervision	Health care
Ongoing needs	Regulatory framework	Preventive/reactive
Special circumstances	Ad hoc	Ad hoc
Vulnerable groups	Conduct of business	Focused attention
Mortality	Licence surrender	Anticipated event

Table 4 *Financial services regulatory tools*

Service	Consumer protection	Systemic risk?	Conduct of business	Compensation scheme?	Market integrity
Banking	Y	Y	Y	Y	N
Investment firm	Y	N	Y	N	N
Insurance	Y	N	Y	Y	N
Fund manager	Y	N	Y	N	N
Securities exchange	Y	N	N	Y	Y

Table 5 *Number of registered companies*

Jurisdiction	Number of companies
Bahamas[a]	47,000
British Virgin Islands[a]	635,000[c]
Cayman Islands[a]	30,000
Labuan[b]	4,281
Mauritius	24,000

Notes:

[a] Mark Wilson, 'Islands in the Sun', *Money Laundering Bulletin*, June 2004, p. 9.

[b] Registered offfshore companies, as cited in 'Malaysia's PM Renews Push for Labuan as a Strategic OFC', *Offshore Red*, October 2004, p. 151.

[c] Over the last twenty years. See Humphrey Leue, 'The British Virgin Islands', in *The 2005 Guide to International Financial Centres*, Euromoney Institutional Investor plc, February 2005, p. 4.

Table 6 *Regulatory structures worldwide*

No.	Model	Application
1	Separate regulators	The World Bank has identified 31 countries worldwide that have separate regulators for each group of institutions.
2	Mexican	Nine countries combine banking and securities regulation.
3	South African	Three countries combine securities and insurance regulation.
4	Canadian	Thirteen countries combine banking and insurance (and sometimes also pensions) in a regulatory authority other than the central bank.
5	UK	Ten countries combine all regulation (banking and otherwise) in one authority (not being the central bank).
6	Singapore	Three countries combine all regulation in the central bank.

Source: Jose de Luna Martinez and Thomas A. Rose, *International Survey of Integrated Supervision*, World Bank, 2003, as quoted in 'Overview of the Policy and Regulatory Framework for NBFIs', a presentation delivered by Dr Jeffrey Carmichael to a Regional Seminar on Non-Bank Financial Institutions Development in African Countries, 9–11 December 2003.

Table 7 *External factors versus regulatory factors*

External factors	Regulatory factors
Economy – global/local	Clear policies
Pace and extent of change	Consistent application of policy
Perception	Efficiency of operations
Integrity	Sensitivity
Competence	Adaptability
Solvency	
Prudential/regulatory action	

Table 8 *Examples of punitive measures that may be imposed by supervisory authorities*

No.	Measure	Description
1	Warnings	The progression is from polite to strong.
2	Direction	This is a direct order from the regulator.
3	Limitations	The regulator may apply conditions (or additional conditions) to a licence.
4	Monetary Fines	The application of a monetary penalty is simpler in theory than in practice.
5	Debarring	The regulator may bar an individual from acting as a shareholder, director, secretary or officer.
6	Public Notice	Where the regulator believes that it is in the interests of the public to be made aware of a situation, a notice may be issued in one or more newspapers.
7	Suspension	Where the regulator suspends a licence, no new business may be accepted. This is probably a 'death knell', because it is often accompanied with a Public Notice. This particular measure is administratively difficult to apply because account has to be taken of the licensee's clients who may suffer in this process. Usually, business may only continue to honour the ongoing obligations of existing clients, and all other business conduct must stop.
8	Revocation	The ultimate sanction, usually coupled with a press notice.

Table 9 *The evolutionary process describing the maturation of an international financial services centre*

Phase	Age of centre	Degree of regulation	Pace of change	Relationship with regulator	Pace of growth of business
1	New	Superficial	Rapid	Cooperative	Very rapid
2	Young	Growing	Very rapid	Aggressive	Rapid
3	Developed	Extensive	Fast	Persuasive	Incremental
4	Mature	Deep	Slow	Collaborative	Slow

Table 10 *Members of the Basel Committee*

No.	Country	Representative
1	Belgium	National Bank of Belgium
		Banking and Finance Commission
2	Canada	Bank of Canada
		Office of the Superintendent of Financial Institutions
3	France	Bank of France Banking Commission
4	Germany	Deutsche Bundesbank Federal Banking Supervisory Office
5	Italy	Bank of Italy
6	Luxembourg	Central Bank of Luxembourg
7	Netherlands	The Netherlands Bank
8	Spain	Banco de España
9	Sweden	Sveriges Riksbank
		Swedish Financial Supervisory Authority
10	Switzerland	Swiss National Bank
		Swiss Federal Banking Commission
11	United Kingdom	Bank of England
		Financial Services Authority
12	United States	Federal Reserve Board
		Federal Reserve Bank of New York
		Office of the Comptroller of the Currency
		Federal Deposit Insurance Corporation
	Secretariat	Bank for International Settlements

Table 11 *Analysis as at end 2003 of the number of jurisdictions assessed under the Financial Sector Assessment Program*

Criterion	No.
Jurisdictions contacted since start of assessments	44
Assessments	42
By Module 2	27
Completed	20
Published	9
Publication expected	6
Unpublished	5
Review	5
Underway	1
Scheduled for current year 2004	1
By FSAP	15
Of which underway	7
Expected in current year 2004	1

Table 12 *Analysis as at February 2005 showing the number of jurisdictions assessed under the Financial Sector Assessment Program*

Status	Total	FSAP	Module 2
Published	38	14	24
To be published	2	0	2
Considering publication	1	0	1
Total jurisdictions assessed	41	14	27
Scheduled in current year 2005	1	n/a	0
Training Assistance delivered in lieu of assessments in current year 2004	1	n/a	n/a
Training Assistance delivered in lieu of assessments in current year 2005	1	n/a	n/a
Total jurisdictions contacted	44		

Table 13 *The general framework of the Forty Recommendations*

Section	Recommendations	Theme
A	1–3	Specific requirements and roles of national legal systems regarding AML/CFT;
B	4–25	The roles and obligations imposed on the financial system, particularly banks and other financial institutions. Recommendations 10–29 focus on critical aspects of financial regulation and intermediation (i.e. the requirement for customer identification and record-keeping, increased due diligence by financial institutions and regulators, including NBFIs not otherwise subject to supervision).
C	26–34	Measures to strengthen international cooperation in AML/CFT.
D	35–40	International cooperation measures.

Table 14 *The general framework of the Nine Special Recommendations*

No.	Theme
1	Requirement to sign and implement the Terrorist Financing Convention and UN Security Council Resolutions 1267 (1999) and its successor, Resolution 1373 (2001).
2	Terrorist financing should be criminalised.
3	Countries should have effective laws and procedures to freeze terrorist funds and other assets.
4	Requires legislation imposing a duty to report suspicions of transactions related to terrorist financing.
5	Requires adherence to parts of Recommendations 36–40 in respect of terrorist financing.
6	Money or value transfer services should be licensed and adopt Forty Recommendations.
7	Wire transfers.
8	Non-profit organisations.
9	Physical cross-border transportation of currency and bearer negotiable instruments.

Table 15 *Population, land area and population density of selected OFCs*

No.	Jurisdiction	Population	Area (Sq Miles)	Area (Sq Kms)	Population density (per sq mile)
1	Brunei	280,000	2,227	5,765	126
2	Cayman Islands	37,716	100	260	377
3	Gibraltar	28,051	2.5	6.5	11,220
4	Guernsey	58,681	24.3	63	2,415
5	Isle of Man	76,000	221	572	344
6	Jersey	85,150	45	116	1,901
7	Malta	379,916	122	316	3,114
8	Mauritius	1,200,000	720	1,865	1,667

Table 16 *Global statistics: foreign direct investment, assets under management and world exports*

Category	Value (US$bn)
Global assets under management	7,500
World exports	4,200
Global foreign direct investment	644

Table 17 *The FSF's categorisation of OFCs (as at March 2000)*

OFC	OGBS	1	2	3
Andorra			Y	
Anguilla				Y
Antigua and Barbuda				Y
Aruba	Y			Y
Bahamas	Y			Y
Bahrain	Y		Y	
Barbados	Y		Y	
Belize				Y
Bermuda	Y		Y	
British Virgin Islands				Y

Table 17 (*cont.*)

OFC	OGBS	1	2	3
Cayman Islands	Y			Y
Cook Islands				Y
Costa Rica				Y
Cyprus	Y			Y
Gibraltar	Y		Y	
Guernsey	Y	Y		
Hong Kong	Y	Y		
Ireland		Y		
Isle of Man	Y	Y		
Jersey	Y	Y		
Lebanon				Y
Labuan	Y		Y	
Liechtenstein				Y
Luxembourg		Y		
Macau	Y		Y	
Malta			Y	
Marshall Islands				Y
Mauritius	Y			Y
Monaco			Y	
Nauru				Y
Niue				Y
Netherlands Antilles	Y			Y
Panama	Y			Y
Samoa				Y
Seychelles				Y
Singapore	Y	Y		
St Kitts and Nevis				Y
St Lucia				Y
St Vincent and the Grenadines				Y
Switzerland		Y		
Turks and Caicos Islands				Y
Vanuatu	Y			Y
Totals	19	8	9	25

Table 18 *FATF Members and Observers*

No.	Member country/institution
Members	
1	Argentina
2	Australia
3	Austria
4	Belgium
5	Brazil
6	Canada
7	Denmark
8	European Commission
9	Finland
10	France
11	Germany
12	Greece
13	Gulf Cooperation Council
14	Hong Kong
15	Iceland
16	Ireland
17	Italy
18	Japan
19	Luxembourg
20	Mexico
21	Netherlands
22	New Zealand
23	Norway
24	Portugal
25	Russian Federation (June 2003)
26	Singapore
27	South Africa (June 2003)
28	Spain
29	Sweden
30	Switzerland
31	Turkey
32	United Kingdom
33	United States
Observers	
1	African Development Bank
2	Asian Development Bank
3	Commonwealth Secretariat

Table 18 (*cont.*)

No.	Member country/institution
4	Egmont Group of Financial Intelligence Units
5	European Bank for Reconstruction and Development
6	European Central Bank
7	Europol
8	Inter-American Development Bank
9	Intergovernmental Action Group Against Money-Laundering in Africa (GIABA)
10	International Association of Insurance Supervisors
11	International Monetary Fund
12	International Organization of Securities Commissions (IOSCO)
13	Interpol
14	Offshore Group of Banking Supervisors
15	Organization for Economic Cooperation and Development
16	Organization of American States/Inter-American Committee Against Terrorism (OAS/CICTE)
17	Organization of American States/Inter-American Drug Abuse Control Commission (OAS/CICAD)
18	United Nations Office on Drugs and Crime
19	World Bank
20	World Customs Organization ('WCO')

Note:
The list of members was last updated on 27 July 2004 and remains unchanged as at 30 July 2005.

Table 19 *Tax havens, as defined by the OECD (as at June 2000)*

No.	Jurisdiction	OGBS
1	Andorra	0
2	Anguilla	0
3	Antigua and Barbuda	0
4	Aruba	1
5	Bahamas	1
6	Bahrain	1
7	Barbados	1
8	Belize	0
9	British Virgin Islands	0

Table 19 (*cont.*)

No.	Jurisdiction	OGBS
10	Cook Islands	0
11	Dominica	0
12	Gibraltar	1
13	Grenada	0
14	Guernsey	1
15	Isle of Man	1
16	Jersey	1
17	Liberia	0
18	Liechtenstein	0
19	Maldives	0
20	Marshall Islands	0
21	Monaco	0
22	Montserrat	0
23	Nauru	0
24	Netherlands Antilles	1
25	Niue	0
26	Panama	1
27	Samoa	0
28	Seychelles	0
29	St Kitts and Nevis	0
30	St Lucia	0
31	St Vincent and the Grenadines	0
32	Tonga	0
33	Turks and Caicos Islands	0
34	US Virgin Islands	0
35	Vanuatu	1
	Total	11

Note:
The OECD excluded the following eight members of the OGBS from their list of 'tax havens': Bermuda, Cayman Islands, Cyprus, Hong Kong, Labuan, Macau, Mauritius and Singapore.

Table 20 *The OECD's 'potentially uncooperative tax havens'*

Jurisdiction	06/00	12/00	08/01	02/02	04/02
Andorra					No
Anguilla					
Antigua and Barbuda				Yes	
Aruba			Yes		
Bahamas					
Bahrain			Yes		
Barbados					
Belize					
Bermuda	Yes	Yes	Yes	Yes	Yes
British Virgin Islands					
Cayman Islands	Yes				
Cook Islands					
Cyprus	Yes				
Dominica					
Gibraltar				Yes	
Grenada				Yes	
Guernsey				Yes	
Isle of Man		Yes			
Jersey				Yes	
Liberia					No
Liechtenstein					No
Maldives					
Malta	Yes				
Marshall Islands					No
Mauritius	Yes				
Monaco					No
Montserrat					
Nauru					No
Netherlands Antilles		Yes			
Niue					
Panama					
Samoa					
San Marino	Yes				
Seychelles			Yes		
St Kitts and Nevis					
St Lucia					
St Vincent and the Grenadines				Yes	
Tonga			Yes		
Turks and Caicos Islands					

Table 20 (*cont.*)

Jurisdiction	06/00	12/00	08/01	02/02	04/02
US Virgin Islands					
Vanuatu					No
Total cooperative	6				34
Total non-cooperative	35				7

Table 21 *The OECD's 'uncooperative tax havens'*

Jurisdiction	04/02	05/03	12/03	OGBS
Andorra	Y	Y	Y	0
Liberia	Y	Y	Y	0
Liechtenstein	Y	Y	Y	0
Marshall Islands	Y	Y	Y	0
Monaco	Y	Y	Y	0
Nauru	Y	Y		0
Vanuatu	Y			1
Total	7	6	5	1

Note:
Unchanged as at 30 July 2005.

Table 22 *The FATF's 'First Set of Jurisdictions'*

No.	OFC reviewed	Non-Cooperative Countries and Territories
1	Antigua and Barbuda	
2	Bahamas	Yes
3	Belize	
4	Bermuda	
5	British Virgin Islands	
6	Cayman Islands	Yes
7	Cook Islands	Yes
8	Cyprus	
9	Dominica	Yes
10	Gibraltar	

Table 22 (*cont.*)

No.	OFC reviewed	Non-Cooperative Countries and Territories
11	Guernsey	
12	Isle of Man	
13	Israel	Yes
14	Jersey	
15	Lebanon	Yes
16	Liechtenstein	Yes
17	Malta	
18	Marshall Islands	Yes
19	Mauritius	
20	Monaco	
21	Nauru	Yes
22	Niue	Yes
23	Panama	Yes
24	Philippines	Yes
25	Russia	Yes
26	Samoa	
27	St Kitts and Nevis	Yes
28	St Lucia	
29	St Vincent and the Grenadines	Yes
Total NCCTs		15

Table 23 *Ongoing changes to the FATF's List of Non-Co-operative Countries and Territories*

OFC	06/00	06/01	09/01	06/02	10/02	02/03	06/03	02/04	07/04	02/05	OGBS
Bahamas	Yes										
Cayman Islands	Yes										
Cook Islands	Yes	Yes	Yes	Yes	Yes	Yes	Yes	Yes	Yes		
Dominica	Yes	Yes	Yes	Yes							
Egypt		Yes	Yes	Yes	Yes	Yes	Yes				
Grenada			Yes	Yes	Yes						
Guatemala		Yes	Yes	Yes	Yes	Yes	Yes	Yes			
Hungary		Yes	Yes								
Indonesia		Yes	Yes	Yes	Yes	Yes	Yes	Yes	Yes		
Israel	Yes	Yes	Yes								
Lebanon	Yes	Yes	Yes								
Liechtenstein	Yes										
Marshall Islands	Yes	Yes	Yes	Yes							
Myanmar		Yes	Yes	Yes	Yes	Yes	Yes	Yes	Yes	Yes	0
Nauru	Yes	Yes	Yes	Yes	Yes	Yes	Yes	Yes	Yes	Yes	0

Nigeria	Yes									
Niue	Yes	Yes	Yes	Yes	Yes	Yes	Yes	Yes	Yes	Yes
Panama	Yes									
Philippines	Yes	Yes	Yes	Yes	Yes	Yes	Yes			
Russia	Yes	Yes	Yes							
St Kitts and Nevis	Yes									
St Vincent and the Grenadines	Yes	Yes	Yes	Yes	Yes	Yes				
Ukraine		Yes	Yes	Yes	Yes	Yes	Yes	Yes	Yes	Yes
Total	15	17	19	15	11	10	9	7	6	3	0

Note:
The FATF's current list of NCCTs was published on 11 February 2005, and remains unchanged as at 30 July 2005.

Table 24 *Members of the Egmont Group*

No.	Member	No.	Member	No.	Member
1	Albania	40	Greece	79	Qatar
2	Andorra	41	Grenada	80	Romania
3	Anguilla	42	Guatemala	81	Russia
4	Antigua and Barbuda	43	Guernsey	82	San Marino
5	Argentina	44	Honduras	83	Serbia and Montenegro
6	Aruba	45	Hong Kong	84	Singapore
7	Australia	46	Hungary	85	Slovakia
8	Austria	47	Iceland	86	Slovenia
9	Bahamas	48	Indonesia	87	South Africa
10	Bahrain	49	Ireland	88	Spain
11	Barbados	50	Isle of Man	89	St Kitts and Nevis
12	Belgium	51	Israel	90	St Vincent and the Grenadines
13	Belize	52	Italy	91	Sweden
14	Bermuda	53	Japan	92	Switzerland
15	Bolivia	54	Jersey	93	Taiwan
16	Bosnia and Herzegovina	55	Korea (South)	94	Thailand
17	Brazil	56	Latvia	95	Turkey
18	British Virgin Islands	57	Lebanon	96	Ukraine
19	Bulgaria	58	Liechtenstein	97	United Arab Emirates
20	Canada	59	Lithuania	98	United Kingdom
21	Cayman Islands	60	Luxembourg	99	United States
22	Chile	61	Macedonia	100	Vanuatu
23	Colombia	62	Malaysia	101	Venezuela
24	Cook Islands	63	Malta		
25	Costa Rica	64	Marshall Islands		
26	Croatia	65	Mauritius		
27	Cyprus	66	Mexico		
28	Czech Republic	67	Monaco		
29	Denmark	68	Montenegro		
30	Dominica	69	Netherlands		
31	Dominican Republic	70	Netherlands Antilles		
32	Egypt	71	New Zealand		
33	El Salvador	72	Norway		

Table 24 (*cont.*)

No.	Member	No.	Member	No.	Member
34	Estonia	73	Panama		
35	Finland	74	Paraguay		
36	France	75	Peru		
37	Georgia	76	Philippines		
38	Germany	77	Poland		
39	Gibraltar	78	Portugal		

Note: Unchanged as at 29 June 2005.

Table 25 *Members of the European Union*

No.	Country	Year of accession	Name of the Community
1	Germany	1951	European Coal and Steel Community
2	France	1951	
3	Italy	1951	
4	Netherlands	1951	
5	Belgium	1951	
6	Luxembourg	1951	
7	United Kingdom	1973	European Economic Community
8	Denmark	1973	
9	Ireland	1973	
10	Greece	1981	
11	Spain	1986	
12	Portugal	1986	
13	Sweden	1995	European Union
14	Austria	1995	
15	Finland	1995	
16	Cyprus	2004	
17	Czech Republic	2004	
18	Estonia	2004	
19	Hungary	2004	
20	Latvia	2004	
21	Lithuania	2004	
22	Malta	2004	
23	Poland	2004	
24	Slovakia	2004	
25	Slovenia	2004	

Table 26 OECD/FATF/FSF reports summarised

No.	Jurisdictions	OGBS	Egmont	OECD–tax havens	FATF–'Cooperative'	FATF–'Non-cooperative'	FSF I	FSF II	FSF III
1	Albania	0	★						
2	Alderney	0			★		★		
3	Andorra	0	★	★				★	
4	Anguilla	0	★	★					★
5	Antigua and Barbuda	0	★	★	★				★
6	Argentina	0	★						
7	Aruba	1	★	★					★
8	Australia	0	★						
9	Austria	0	★						
10	Bahamas	1	★	★		★			★
11	Bahrain	1	★	★				★	
12	Barbados	1	★	★				★	
13	Belgium	0	★						
14	Belize	0	★	★	★				
15	Bermuda	1	★		★			★	
16	Bolivia	0	★						
17	Bosnia and Herzegovina		★						
18	Brazil	0	★						
19	British Virgin Islands	0	★	★	★				★

#	Country	Cat 1	Cat 2	Cat 3	Cat 4	Cat 5	Cat 6	Cat 7	Value
20	Bulgaria							★	0
21	Canada	★			★			★	0
22	Cayman Islands							★	1
23	Chile							★	0
24	Colombia	★			★		★	★	0
25	Cook Islands	★						★	0
26	Costa Rica							★	0
27	Croatia	★				★		★	0
28	Cyprus							★	1
29	Czech Republic							★	0
30	Denmark				★		★	★	0
31	Dominica							★	0
32	Dominican Republic							★	0
33	Egypt							★	0
34	El Salvador							★	0
35	Estonia							★	0
36	Finland							★	0
37	France							★	0
38	Georgia							★	0
39	Germany							★	0
40	Gibraltar		★			★	★	★	1
41	Greece							★	0
42	Grenada						★	★	0
43	Guatemala							★	0
44	Guernsey			★		★	★	★	1

Table 26 (*cont.*)

No.	Jurisdictions	OGBS	Egmont	OECD–tax havens	FATF–'Cooperative'	FATF–'Non-cooperative'	FSF I	FSF II	FSF III
45	Honduras		★						
46	Hong Kong	1	★			★			
47	Hungary	0	★						
48	Iceland	0	★						
49	Indonesia	0	★						
50	Ireland	0	★				★		
51	Isle of Man	1	★	★	★		★		
52	Israel	0	★			★			
53	Italy	0	★						
54	Japan	0	★						
55	Jersey	1	★	★	★		★		
56	Korea (South)	0	★					★	
57	Labuan	1							
58	Latvia	0	★						
59	Lebanon	0	★			★			★
60	Liberia	0		★					
61	Liechtenstein	0	★	★		★			★
62	Lithuania	0	★						
63	Luxembourg	0	★				★		
64	Macau	1						★	
65	Macedonia	0	★						

#	Country									
66	Malaysia					★	0			
67	Maldives				★	★	0			
68	Malta				★	★	0	★		
69	Marshall Islands	★			★	★	0	★		
70	Mauritius	★				★	1			
71	Mexico			★		★	0			
72	Monaco			★	★	★	0	★		
73	Montenegro		★			★				
74	Montserrat	★			★		0	★		
75	Nauru				★		0			
76	Netherlands				★	★	0			
77	Netherlands Antilles	★		★	★	★	1	★		
78	New Zealand				★	★	0			
79	Niue	★			★	★	0			
80	Norway			★		★	0	★		
81	Panama	★		★	★	★	1			
82	Paraguay					★	0			
83	Peru					★				
84	Philippines			★		★	0			
85	Poland					★	0			
86	Portugal					★	0			
87	Qatar					★				
88	Romania					★	0	★		
89	Russia					★	0			
90	Samoa	★		★	★		0			

Table 26 (*cont.*)

No.	Jurisdictions	OGBS	Egmont	OECD–tax havens	FATF–'Cooperative'	FATF–'Non-cooperative'	FSF I	FSF II	FSF III
91	San Marino		★						
92	Sark	0			★		★		
93	Serbia	0	★						
94	Seychelles	0		★					★
95	Singapore	1	★				★		
96	Slovakia	0	★						
97	Slovenia	0	★						
98	South Africa	0	★						
99	Spain	0	★						
100	St Kitts and Nevis	0	★			★			★
101	St Lucia	0		★	★				★
102	St Vincent and the Grenadines	0	★	★		★			★
103	Sweden	0	★						
104	Switzerland	0	★				★		
105	Taiwan	0	★						
106	Thailand	0	★						
107	Tonga	0		★					
108	Turkey	0	★						
109	Turks and Caicos Islands	0		★					★
110	Ukraine	0	★						
111	United Arab Emirates	0	★						

		19	101	35	16	15	9	10	25
112	United Kingdom	0	★						
113	United States	0	★						
114	US Virgin Islands	0		★					
115	Vanuatu	1	★	★					★
116	Venezuela	0	★						
	Totals	19	101	35	16	15	9	10	25

Note:

In their Report entitled 'Towards Global Tax Co-operation: Progress in Identifying and Eliminating Harmful Tax Practices', the OECD treated Alderney and Sark as part of the entry for Guernsey.

Table 27 *Analysis of FSAP and Module 2 assessment reports (as at 12 March 2004)*

	Jurisdiction	OGBS	Published?	To be published?	Not expected to be published	Not publishing	NA	Unknown	Expected
1	Andorra	0	Y						
2	Anguilla	0	Y						
3	Antigua and Barbuda	0							Y
4	Aruba	1	Y						
5	Bahamas	1						Y	
6	Bahrain	1					Y		
7	Barbados	1	Y						
8	Belize	0							Y
9	Bermuda	1						Y	
10	British Virgin Islands	0		Y					
11	Cayman Islands	1							Y
12	Cook Islands	0		Y					
13	Costa Rica	0	Y						
14	Cyprus	1	Y						
15	Dominica	0							Y
16	Gibraltar	1	Y						
17	Grenada	0							Y
18	Guernsey	1	Y						
19	Hong Kong	1	Y						
20	Isle of Man	1	Y						
21	Jersey	1	Y						

22	Labuan	1			Y				
23	Liechtenstein	0	Y						
24	Luxembourg	0	Y						
25	Macau	1	Y						
26	Malta	0	Y						
27	Marshall Islands	0				Y			
28	Mauritius	1	Y						
29	Monaco	0	Y						
30	Montserrat	0	Y						
31	Nauru	0					Y		
32	Netherlands Antilles	1						Y	
33	Niue	0					Y	Y	
34	Palau	0		Y					
35	Panama	1	Y						
36	Samoa	0		Y					
37	Seychelles	0				Y			
38	Singapore	1		Y					
39	St Kitts and Nevis	0							Y
40	St Lucia	0							Y
41	St Vincent and the Grenadines	0							Y
42	Switzerland	0	Y						
43	Turks and Caicos Islands	0		Y					
44	Vanuatu	1	Y						
	Totals	19	21	6	1	2	3	2	9

Source: 'Offshore Financial Centres – The Assessment Program – An Update', IMF, 12 March 2004.

Table 28 *Members of IOSCO (as at 30 April 2005)*

No.	Member	Ordinary members	Associate members	Affiliated members
1	Albania	1		
2	Alberta	0	1	
3	Algeria	1		
4	Argentina	1		1
5	Armenia	1		
6	Australia	1		3
7	Austria	1		
8	Bahamas	1		1
9	Bahrain	1		
10	Bangladesh	1		
11	Barbados	1		
12	Belgium	1		
13	Bermuda	1		1
14	Bolivia	1		
15	Bosnia and Herzegovina	1		
16	Brazil	1		3
17	British Columbia	0	1	
18	Brunei	1		
19	Canada	0		2
20	Cayman Islands	0		1
21	Channel Islands	0		1
22	Chile	1		
23	China	1		2
24	Chinese Taipei	1		3
25	Colombia	1		
26	Costa Rica	1		
27	Croatia	1		
28	Cyprus	1		
29	Czech Republic	1		
30	Denmark	1		
31	Dominican Republic	1		
32	Dubai	0	1	
33	Ecuador	1		
34	Egypt	1		2
35	El Salvador	1		
36	Estonia	1		
37	Finland	1		
38	France	1		7

Table 28 (*cont.*)

No.	Member	Ordinary members	Associate members	Affiliated members
39	Germany	1		1
40	Ghana	1		
41	Gibraltar	1		
42	Greece	1		1
43	Guernsey	1		
44	Honduras	1		
45	Hong Kong	1		1
46	Hungary	1		
47	India	1		2
48	Indonesia	1		1
49	Ireland	1		
50	Isle of Man	1		
51	Israel	1		
52	Italy	1		1
53	Jamaica	1		
54	Japan	1	3	3
55	Jersey	1		
56	Jordan	1		2
57	Kazakhstan	1		
58	Kenya	1		
59	Korea (South)	1		2
60	Kyrgyz Republic	1		
61	Lithuania	1		
62	Luxembourg	1		1
63	Malawi	1		
64	Malaysia	1	1 (Lab)	1
65	Macedonia	1		
66	Malta	1		1
67	Mauritius	1		
68	Mexico	1		
69	Mongolia	1		
70	Montenegro	1		
71	Morocco	1		
72	Netherlands	1		1
73	New Zealand	1		
74	Nigeria	1		
75	Norway	1		
76	Oman	1		
77	Ontario	1		3

Table 28 (*cont.*)

No.	Member	Ordinary members	Associate members	Affiliated members
78	Pakistan	1		1
79	Panama	1		
80	Papua New Guinea	1		
81	Peru	1		
82	Philippines	1		6
83	Poland	1		1
84	Portugal	1		
85	Quebec	1		
86	Romania	1		
87	Russia	1		1
88	Serbia	1		
89	Singapore	1		1
90	Slovak Republic	1		
91	Slovenia	1		
92	South Africa	1		
93	Spain	1		1
94	Sri Lanka	1		
95	Srpska	1		
96	Sweden	1		
97	Switzerland	1		7
98	Tanzania	1		
99	Thailand	1		1
100	Trinidad and Tobago	1		
101	Tunisia	1		
102	Turkey	1		2
103	Uganda	1		
104	Ukraine	1		
105	United Arab Emirates	1		
106	United Kingdom	1		
107	United States	1	2	26
108	Uruguay	1		
109	Uzbekistan	1		
110	Venezuela	1		
111	Vietnam	1		
112	West African Monetary Union	1		
113	Zambia	107	9	95

Table 29 OFCs, summary status

No.	Jurisdiction	FSF3	FATF 'Non-Cooperative'	OECD 'Tax Haven'	OECD 'Uncooperative Tax Haven'	Egmont	OGBS	IOSCO
As at...->		March 2000	July 2004	June 2000	December 2003	June 2004	November 2004	May 2005
1	Alderney	0	0	1	0	0	0	0
2	Andorra	0	0	1	1	1	0	0
3	Anguilla	1	0	1	0	1	0	0
4	Antigua and Barbuda	1	0	1	0	1	0	0
5	Aruba	1	0	1	0	1	1	0
6	Bahamas	1	0	1	0	1	1	1
7	Bahrain	0	0	1	0	1	1	1
8	Barbados	0	0	1	0	1	1	1
9	Belize	1	0	1	0	1	0	0
10	Bermuda	0	0	0	0	1	1	1
11	British Virgin Islands	1	0	1	0	1	0	0
12	Cayman Islands	1	0	0	0	1	1	0
13	Cook Islands	1	1	1	0	1	0	0
14	Costa Rica	1	0	0	0	1	0	0
15	Cyprus	1	0	0	0	1	1	1
16	Dominica	0	0	1	0	1	0	0
17	Gibraltar	0	0	1	0	1	1	1

Table 29 (*cont.*)

No.	Jurisdiction	FSF3	FATF 'Non-Cooperative'	OECD 'Tax Haven'	OECD 'Uncooperative Tax Haven'	Egmont	OGBS	IOSCO
18	Grenada	0	0	1	0	1	0	0
19	Guernsey	0	0	1	0	1	1	1
20	Hong Kong	0	0	0	0	1	1	1
21	Indonesia	0	1	1	0	1	0	0
22	Isle of Man	0	0	1	0	1	1	1
23	Jersey	0	0	1	0	1	1	1
24	Labuan	0	0	0	0	0	1	0
25	Lebanon	1	0	0	0	1	0	0
26	Liberia	0	0	1	1	0	0	0
27	Liechtenstein	1	0	1	1	1	1	0
28	Macau	0	0	0	0	0	0	0
29	Maldives	0	0	1	0	0	0	0
30	Marshall Islands	1	0	1	1	1	1	1
31	Mauritius	1	0	0	0	1	0	0
32	Monaco	0	0	1	1	1	0	0
33	Montserrat	0	0	1	0	0	0	0
34	Myanamar	1	1			0	0	0
35	Nauru	1	1	1	0	0	0	0
36	Netherlands Antilles	1	0	1	0	1	1	1
37	Nigeria	1	1			0	0	0

#	Country							
38	Niue	1	0	1	0	0	0	0
39	Panama	1	0	1	0	1	1	1
40	Philippines	1	1	1	0	0	0	0
41	Samoa	0	0	1	0	0	0	0
42	Sark	0	0	1	0	0	0	0
43	Seychelles	0	0	1	0	0	0	0
44	Singapore	0	0	0	0	1	1	1
45	St Kitts and Nevis	0	0	1	0	1	0	0
46	St Lucia	1	0	1	0	0	0	0
47	St Vincent and the Grenadines	1	0	1	0	1	0	0
48	Tonga	0	0	1	0	0	0	0
49	Turks and Caicos Islands	1	0	1	0	0	0	0
50	US Virgin Is	0	0	1	0	0	0	0
51	Vanuatu	1	0	1	0	1	1	0
	Totals	25	6	37	5	34	19	15

Table 30 *IMF assessment status summarised*

No.	Jurisdiction	Assessed	Status	Published	Scope	Module 2/FSAP
1	Andorra	2002	Completed	Y	BCP, FATF	Module 2
2	Anguilla	2002	Completed	Y	BCP, FATF	Module 2
3	Antigua and Barbuda	2004	Completed	Y	BCP, FATF	FSAP
4	Aruba	2001	Completed	Y	BCP, ICP	Module 2
5	Bahamas	2002	Completed	Y	BCP, SCP, FATF	Module 2
6	Bahrain	2005	Scheduled	N	N	N
7	Barbados	2002	Completed	Y	BCP, ICP, SCP, FATF	FSAP
8	Belize	2003	Completed	Y	BCP, ICP, FATF	Module 2
9	Bermuda	2003	Completed	To be published	BCP, ICP, SCP, FATF	Module 2
10	British Virgin Islands	2002	Completed	Yes + Detailed assessment	BCP, ICP, SCP, FATF	Module 2
11	Cayman Islands	2003	Completed	To be published	BCP, ICP, SCP, FATF	Module 2
12	Cook Islands	2004	Completed	Yes + Detailed assessment	BCP, FATF	Module 2
13	Costa Rica	2001	Completed	Y	BCP	FSAP
14	Cyprus	2001	Completed	Yes + Detailed assessment	BCP	Module 2
15	Dominica	2003	Completed	Y	BCP, FATF	FSAP
16	Gibraltar	2001	Completed	Y	BCP, ICP, SCP	Module 2
17	Grenada	2003	Completed	Y	BCP, FATF	FSAP
18	Guernsey	2002	Completed	Yes + Detld Assmnt	BCP, ICP, SCP, FATF	Module 2
19	Hong Kong	2002	Completed	Y	BCP, ICP, SCP, FATF	FSAP
20	Ireland	2000	Completed	NA	NA	N
21	Isle of Man	2002	Completed	Yes + Detailed assessment	BCP, ICP, SCP, FATF	Module 2

22	Jersey	2002	Completed	Yes + Detailed assessment	BCP, ICP, SCP, FATF	Module 2
23	Lebanon	1999	Completed	NA	NA	N
24	Liechtenstein	2002	Completed	Yes + Detailed assessment	BCP, ICP, SCP, FATF	Module 2
25	Luxembourg	2001	Completed	Y	BCP, ICP, SCP, FATF AMLCFT	Y
		2003	Completed	Y		
26	Macau	2001	Completed	Y	BCP, ICP	Module 2
27	Malaysia (Labuan)	2002	Completed	Y	BCP, ICP, SCP, FATF	Module 2
28	Malta	2002	Completed	Y	BCP, ICP, SCP, FATF	FSAP
29	Marshall Islands	2002	Completed	Considering	BCP, FATF	Module 2
30	Mauritius	2002	Completed	Y	BCP, FATF	FSAP
31	Monaco	2002	Completed	Yes + Detailed assessment	BCP (partial) SCP, FATF	Module 2
32	Montserrat	2002	Completed	Y	BCP, FATF	Module 2
33	Nauru	2004	Completed	NA	Training in lieu of assessment	Module 2
34	Netherlands Antilles	2002	Completed	Yes + Detailed assessment	BCP, ICP, FATF	Module 2
35	Niue	2005	Scheduled	NA	Training in lieu of assessment	Module 2
36	Palau	2002	Completed	Yes + Detailed assessment	BCP, FATF	Module 2
37	Panama	2001	Completed	Y	BCP	Module 2
38	Samoa	2002	Completed	Y	BCP, FATF	Module 2
39	Seychelles	2002	Completed	Y	BCP, FATF	Module 2
40	Singapore	2002	Completed	Y	BCP, ICP, SCP, FATF	FSAP
41	St Kitts and Nevis	2003	Completed	Y	BCP, FATF	FSAP
42	St Lucia	2003	Completed	Y	BCP, FATF	FSAP
43	St Vincent and the Grenadines	2003	Completed	Y	BCP, FATF	FSAP
44	Switzerland	2001	Completed	Y	BCP, ICP, SCP, FATF	FSAP

Table 30 (*cont.*)

No.	Jurisdiction	Assessed	Status	Published	Scope	Module 2/FSAP
45	Turks and Caicos Islands	2003	Completed	Y	BCP, ICP, FATF	Module 2
46	Vanuatu	2002	Completed	Yes + Detailed assessment	BCP, ICP, FATF	Module 2

Note:

Both Lebanon and Ireland had FSAPs before the start of the OFC Program in the pilot phase of the FSAP. The Fund did not publish reports produced in the pilot. The FSAP for Lebanon, which is a regional financial centre, was updated in 2001.

Source: 'Offshore Financial Centres – The Assessment Program – A Progress Report', Appendix I, pp. 12–32, IMF, 25 February 2005.

Abbreviations: AML/CFT: Anti-money laundering and combating the financing of terrorism; Assessed: Calendar year of first mission; BCP: Basel Core Principles; Completed: Assessment, mission and review have been completed; FATF: FATF 40+9 Recommendations; FSAP: Financial Sector Assessment Program; ICP: IAIS Core Principles; Module 2: Module 2 Assessment; NA: Not applicable; Published: The Financial System Stability Assessment has been published; Scheduled: A date for the assessment has been agreed with the centre; SCO: IOSCO Objectives and Principles.

Table 31 *Analysis of total assets held in OFCs*

No.	Jurisdiction	Assessed	Published	Scope	Module 2/FSAP	Assets US$bn	Year
1	Andorra	2002	Y	BCP, FATF	Module 2	10.4	2001
2	Anguilla	2002	Y	BCP, FATF	Module 2	0.4	
3	Antigua and Barbuda	2004	Y	BCP, FATF	FSAP	4.0	2002
4	Aruba	2001	Y	BCP, ICP	Module 2	2.4	
5	Bahamas	2002	Y	BCP, SCP, FATF	Module 2	296.0	
6	Bahrain	2005	N	N	N	100.9	
7	Barbados	2002	Y	BCP, ICP, SCP, FATF	FSAP	38.5	2002
8	Belize	2003	Y	BCP, ICP, FATF	Module 2	0.7	
9	Bermuda	2003	To be published	BCP, ICP, SCP, FATF	Module 2	200.0	
10	Botswana	New				2.7	August 2003
11	British Virgin Islands	2002	Yes + Detailed assessment	BCP, ICP, SCP, FATF	Module 2	55.0	
12	Brunei	New				2.0	June 1998
13	Cayman Islands	2003	To be published	BCP, ICP, SCP, FATF	Module 2	1045.0	
14	Cook Islands	2004	Yes + Detailed assessment	BCP, FATF	Module 2	0.1	
15	Costa Rica	2001	Y	BCP	FSAP	8.7	
16	Cyprus	2001	Yes + Detailed assessment	BCP	Module 2	35.7	
17	Dominica	2003	Y	BCP, FATF	FSAP	0.3	
18	Dubai	New				NA	
19	Gibraltar	2001	Y	BCP, ICP, SCP	Module 2	8.7	
20	Grenada	2003	Y	BCP, FATF	FSAP	0.6	
21	Guernsey	2002	Yes + Detailed assessment	BCP, ICP, SCP, FATF	Module 2	130.0	

Table 31 (*cont.*)

No.	Jurisdiction	Assessed	Published	Scope	Module 2/FSAP	Assets US$bn	Year
22	Hong Kong	2002	Y	BCP, ICP, SCP, FATF	FSAP	838.1	
23	Ireland	2000	NA	NA	N	577.8	May 2003
24	Isle of Man	2002	Yes + Detailed assessment	BCP, ICP, SCP, FATF	Module 2	44.3	
25	Jersey	2002	Yes + Detailed assessment	BCP, ICP, SCP, FATF	Module 2	341.0	September 2003
26	Lebanon	1999	NA	NA	N	60.1	
27	Liechtenstein	2002	Yes + Detailed assessment	BCP, ICP, SCP, FATF	Module 2	30.7	
28	Luxembourg	2001	Y	BCP, ICP, SCP, FATF AML/CFT	Y	1083.8	
29	Macau	2003	Y	BCP, ICP	Module 2	19.5	
30	Malaysia (Labuan)	2001	Y	BCP, ICP, SCP, FATF	Module 2	18.7	June 2002
31	Malta	2002	Y	BCP, ICP, SCP, FATF	FSAP	21.1	
32	Marshall Islands	2002	Considering	BCP, FATF	Module 2	1.0	
33	Mauritius	2002	Y	BCP, FATF	FSAP	10.1	June 2003
34	Monaco	2002	Yes + Detailed assessment	BCP (partial) SCP, FATF	Module 2	75.7	
35	Montserrat	2002	Y	BCP, FATF	Module 2	1.1	June 2002
36	Nauru	2004	NA	Training in lieu of assessment	Module 2	NA	
37	Netherlands Antilles	2002	Yes + Detailed assessment	BCP, ICP, FATF	Module 2	43.7	

No.	Jurisdiction	2005		Training in lieu of assessment			
38	Niue		NA		Module 2	NA	June 2001
39	Palau	2002	Yes + Detailed assessment	BCP, FATF	Module 2	1.4	
40	Panama	2001	Y	BCP	Module 2	32.3	
41	Samoa	2002	Y	BCP, FATF	Module 2	0.5	2002
42	San Marino	New			Module 2	4.7	2000
43	Seychelles	2002	Y	BCP, FATF	Module 2	1.1	
44	Singapore	2002	Y	BCP, ICP, SCP, FATF	FSAP	213.3	
45	St Kitts and Nevis	2003	Y	BCP, FATF	FSAP	0.8	
46	St Lucia	2003	Y	BCP, FATF	FSAP	1.0	
47	St Vincent and the Grenadines	2003	Y	BCP, FATF	FSAP	0.6	June 2003
48	Switzerland	2001	Y	BCP, ICP, SCP, FATF	FSAP	1808.6	
49	Turks and Caicos Islands	2003	Y	BCP, ICP, FATF	Module 2	0.5	2002
50	Uruguay	New			Module 2	11.6	
51	Vanuatu	2002	Yes + Detailed assessment	BCP, ICP, FATF	Module 2	2.8	

Notes:

Both Lebanon and Ireland had FSAPs before the start of the OFC Program in the pilot phase of the FSAP. The [IMF] did not publish reports produced in the pilot. The FSAP for Lebanon, which is a regional financial centre, was updated in 2001.

Anguilla, Dominica, Grenada, St Kitts and Nevis, St Lucia: size denotes domestic banking sector assets.

Dominica, Grenada, St Kitts and Nevis, St Lucia: level of offshore activities not sufficiently significant to warrant an assessment. These jurisdictions have been invited to participate in the information dissemination and monitoring initiative.

Source: 'Offshore Financial Centres – The Assessment Program – A Progress Report', Appendix III, p. 34, IMF, 25 February 2005.

Abbreviations: AML/CFT: Anti-money laundering and combating the financing of terrorism; Assessed: Calendar year of first mission; assets: Total assets of the largest sector in the jurisdiction as at the end of 2003 (or as stated) based on national authorities' figures or IMF assessments; BCP: Basel Core Principles; Completed: Assessment, mission and review have been completed; FATF: FATF 40+9 Recommendations; FSAP: Financial Sector Assessment Program; ICP: IAIS Core Principles; Module 2: Module 2 Assessment; NA: Not applicable; New: Proposed new jurisdictions to be assessed; Published: The Financial System Stability Assessment has been published; Scheduled: A date for the assessment has been agreed with the centre; SCO: IOSCO Objectives and Principles.

Appendix 2

Some useful websites

Appendix 2

No.	Description	Web Site
1.	Annual Review of Non-Cooperative Countries and Territories, 20 June 2003	www.fatf-gafi.org/NCCT_en.htm
2.	Asia/Pacific Group on Money Laundering	http://www.apgml.org
3.	Bank for International Settlements	http://www.bis.org/index.htm
4.	Caribbean Financial Action Task Force	http://www.cfatf.org
5.	Cayman Islands Monetary Authority	http://www.cimoney.com.ky
6.	Coordinated Portfolio Investment Survey	www.imf.org/external/np/sta/pi/cpis.htm
7.	Council of Europe Select Committee of Experts on the Evaluation of Anti-Money Laundering Measures (Moneyval)	http://www.legal.coe.int/economiccrime
8.	Eastern and Southern Africa Anti-Money Laundering Group	www.esaamlg.org
9.	Edwards Review	www.officialdocuments.co.uk
10.	Egmont Group members	www.fatf-gafi.org/Ctry-orgpages/org-egmont_en.htm
11.	FATF, Criteria for defining NCCTs	www.oecd.org/fatf
12.	FATF, Forty Recommendations	www.oecd.org/fatf
13.	FATF members	www1.oecd.org/fatf/Members_en.htm
14.	FATF Specialist Recommendations on Terrorist Financing	www1.oecd.org/fatf/TerFinance_en.htm
15.	FATF List of NCCTs	www.fatf-gafi.org
16.	Financial Services Authority, UK	www.fsa.gov.uk
17.	Financial Stability Forum	www.fsforum.org

Appendix 2 (*cont.*)

No.	Description	Web Site
18.	GAFISUD, Financial Action Task Force on Money Laundering in South America	http://www.gafisud.org
19.	Gibraltar FSC	http://www.fsc.gi
20.	Guernsey FSC	www.gfsc.guernseyci.com
21.	International Association of Insurance Supervisors	www.iaisweb.org
22.	International Financial Services Centre, Dublin	www.ifsc.ie
23.	International Monetary Fund	www.imf.org
24.	International Monetary Fund, Background Paper on OFCs	www.imf.org/external/np/mae/oshore/2000/eng/back.htm
25.	International Money Laundering Information Network	www.imolin.org
26.	International Organization of Securities Commissions	www.iosco.org
27.	Isle of Man FSC	www.fsc.gov.im
28.	Jersey FSC	www.jerseyfsc.org
29.	KPMG Report	www.official-documents.co.uk/document/cm48/4855/4855.htm
30.	Malta FSA	www.mfsa.com.mt
31.	Mauritius FSC	www.fscmauritius.org
32.	National Criminal Intelligence Service, UK	www.ncis.co.uk
33.	OECD	www.oecd.org
34.	OECD, Advance Commitment Letters	www.oecd.org/daf/fa/harm_tax/advcom.htm
35.	Partnership for Progress and Prosperity: Britain and the Overseas Territories	http://files.fco.gov.uk/otd/wp/main.pdf
36.	Select Committee of Experts on the Evaluation of Anti-Money Laundering Measures	www.legal.coe.int
37.	Summaries of Mutual Evaluations undertaken by PC-R-EV	www.coe.fr/Press/Index.asp?Link=RpubE
38.	Underground Banking	http://www.fatf-gafi.org/FATDocs-en.htm#Trends

Appendix 2 (*cont.*)

No.	Description	Web Site
39.	UNSC Committee Monitoring Sanctions Against Al-Qaida and the Taliban	www.un.org/Docs/sc/committees/1267/tablelist.htm
40.	World Bank AML/CFT	www.amlctf.org

INDEX

References are to paragraph numbers.

Abacha, former Nigerian dictator, 346
accumulation and maintenance
    trusts, 68
advance commitments, 312
advisories, 289
Al-Qaeda, 406
alternative remittance systems, 217
Andersens, 157
Anguilla, 376
Anjouan, 448
anti-competitive behaviour, 117
anti-money laundering (UK), 395
arbitrage, regulatory, 45, 172
Article IV consultations, IMF, 269
Aruba, 376
assessment program, OFCs, IMF, 271
asset management, 64
asset protection trusts, 68
Assets Recover Agency, 228
asymmetry of information, 117, 466
auditors, 157
Australia, 179
avoidance of tax, *see* tax

back office, 76
Bahamas, 377
Bank for International Settlements,
    definition, 230
Bank of Ireland, 438
Banking Act 1979 (UK), 163
banking, 60
    parallel banks, 336
    shell banks/branches, 336
    underground banking, 217
Barbados, 377

Barings, 157
Basel 1, 142
Basel 2, 143
Basel Committee, definition, 230
    overview, 234
BCCI, 157, 165, 337
bearer shares, 357
Bermuda, 377
Best Practice Paper, OGBS, 61,
    154, 251
Bin Laden, 406
black market peso exchange
    mechanism, 217
boards, 191
British Virgin Islands, 378
business process outsourcing, 80

capital
    capital adequacy, 139
    capital flight, 56, 429
    long-term capital management, 64
Caribbean
    Caribbean Court of Justice, 453
    Caribbean Regional Technical
        Assistance Centre, 453
    Caribbean Securities Exchange, 453
    Caricom, 453
    single market and economy, 453
Cayman Islands, 379
Center for Freedom and Prosperity, 323
Centre for European Policy
    Studies, 358
Citigroup, 416
civil law, 404
code of conduct, 97

codes, 443
collective investment schemes, 64
  closed ended, 68
  open ended, 64
comitology, 236
commitments, specific, 93
Committee of European Securities
  Regulators, 180, 236
  definition, 236
Committee on Fiscal Affairs,
  OECD, 312
common law, 68, 404
companies
  controlled foreign companies, 113
  exempt companies, 61
  international business
    companies, 61
  numbers of, by jurisdiction, 155
  and trust service providers
    legislation, 155
  see also corporate vehicles; corporate
    veil; special purpose vehicles
competitive neutrality, 146
compliance, 163, 167
  offsite, 167
  onsite, 167
  voluntary, 45
components of a good reputation,
  469, 470
concordat, 232, 138
conduct of business, 117, 147
confidentiality, 46
conglomerates, 130
consolidated supervision, 161, 165
constituents of success, 471
consumers, 59, 80
  consumer protection, 117
  consumers' expectations, 78
contagion, 165
contractual collective investment
  scheme, 64
controlled foreign companies, 113
Cook Islands, 379
Coopers & Lybrand, 157
Coordinated Portfolio Investment
  Survey, 35
Core Principles for Effective Banking
  Supervision, 138, 234

corporate governance, 347
  Cadbury Report (UK), 347
  Combined Report on Corporate
    Governance (UK), 347
  Greenbury Report (UK), 347
  Hempel Report (UK), 347
corporate inversion, 85, 414
corporate service providers, Statement
  of Best Practice, OGBS, 61,
  154, 251
corporate vehicles, 325
  report on misuse for illicit
    purposes, 325
corporate veil, behind the
  corporate veil, 329
cost/benefit analysis, 123–4
crises and regulation, 148
critical mass, 359
critical success factor, 4, 170
cross-border cooperation, 423
Crown dependencies, 391
customer due diligence, 218, 251

definitions, 15
Delaware, 380, 408
dependent territories, 391
deposit interest example, 90
direction, 192
discretionary trusts, 68
domino effect, 130
dual criminality, 48

Edwards Report, 390
Egmont Group, 215
enforcement, 192
Enron, 78, 157, 340
Ernst & Young, 157
ethos, 451
EU
  and anti-money laundering, 222
  Capital Adequacy Directive, 141
  European Central Bank, 171
  European Investment Bank, 347
  European Parliament, 347
  First Banking Directive, 163
  Investment Services Directive, 139
  Money Laundering Directives,
    222, 395

EU (*cont.*)
  Savings Tax Directive
    agreement, 98
    background, 98
    summary, 99
    and Switzerland, 98
    and the USA, 102
  Securities Commission, 236
  UCIT Directive, 64
evasion of tax, *see* tax
exchange of information, 317
  on tax matters, 93
exempt companies, 61

FATF
  definition, 239
  Forty Recommendations, 239
    review, 306
  membership, 302
  negative comment, 294
  neutral comment, 296
  positive comment, 295
  role of, 287
  FATF-style regional bodies, 303
  and the USA, 406
Federal Deposit Insurance Corporation
    (USA), 402
Financial Action Task Force,
    see FATF
Financial Intelligence Units, 217
  definition, 240
Financial Sector Assessment
    Programs, 274
  results, 280
Financial Services and Markets Act
    2000 (UK), 163
Financial Services Authority (UK), 163
financial services, evolving, 178
Financial Stability Forum, *see* FSF
fiscal excuse, 239, 241
fishing expedition, 442
'fit and proper criterion', 136, 482
FIUs, *see* Financial Intelligence Units
flight capital, 56, 429
forced heirship, 73
foreign grantor trusts, 68
Forty Recommendations (FATF), 239
  review, 306

foundation, 6
France, parliamentary reports, 346
fraud
  examples of, 337
  Offshore, common features, 336
fraudulent conveyances, 68
fringe banks, 163
FSAPs, 274
  results, 280
FSF, 241
  report, reactions, 266
  role of, 261
FSRBs, 303
functional regulation, 130,
    153, 163
future, and supranational
    authorities, 447

G7/8, definition, 241
G20, definition, 242
Gibraltar, 380
global financial stability, 423
Global Forum Working Group on
    Effective Exchange of
    Information, 115, 317
governance, *see* corporate governance
Guernsey, 380
guidelines, 443

Hague Convention, 71
harmful tax competition, 308
Harmful Tax Initiative (OECD), and
    the USA, 410
hawala, 217
hedge funds, 64
home and host states, 89
Hungary, 448

IMF, 244
  Article IV consultations, 269
  assessment program, OFCs,
    271, 272
  background, 269
  Module 2 assessments, 272
  and OFCs, 272
independence, regulatory, 173
information sharing, 317
  information exchange treaties, 414

Ten Key Principles for the
    Improvement of International
    Cooperation Regarding Financial
    Crime and Regulatory Abuse, 317
institutional supervision, 130
insurance, 61
interest rates, negative, 178
International Accounting Standards
    Committee, definition, 243
International Association of Insurance
    Supervisors, 244
international business companies, 61
International Monetary Fund,
    see IMF
International Organization of
    Securities Commissions
    (IOSCO), 247
International Trade and Investment
    Organization, definition, 250
Ireland
    Bank of Ireland, 438
    Irish Financial Services Regulatory
        Authority, 179, 180
    not a tax haven, 15, 438
Isle of Man, 381

Jersey, 382
Johnson Matthey, 148, 163
Joint International Tax Shelter
    Information Centre, 85

'know your customer', 406
    criterion, 138
KPMG, report on Crown
    dependencies, 393

Lamfalussy, 180, 236
legislation
    primary legislation, 443
    secondary legislation, 443
legitimacy, 40
licensed deposit taker, 337
licensing, 133
Liechtenstein, 383
life interest trusts, 68
lifeboat, 163
limited liability company, 76
limited liability entity, 76

limited liability partnership, 76
logos, 451
London, as an OFC, 389
long-term capital management, 64
Luxembourg, 383

Malta, 383
managed banks, 60
market
    market misconduct, 117
    quantification of size of, 33
    marketplace, 37
Maxwell, 157
medical analogy, 125
memorandum of understanding,
    170, 303
Middle East and North African
    Financial Action Task Force, 306
minimum standards, 233
    Minimum Standards for the
        Supervision of International
        Banking Groups and Their
        Cross-Border Establishments, 165
misconduct, market misconduct, 117
Model Agreement on Exchange of
    Information on Tax Matters, 317
Module 2 assessments, IMF, 272
money laundering
    crime, 206
    jurisdictions at risk, 203
    laundered money,
        quantification, 205
    Offshore, 209
    preventive action, 210
    threat, 426
    and the USA, 405
Moneyval (PC-R-EV Committee),
    definition, 251
Montserrat, 385
moral hazard, 117
multilateral memorandum of
    understanding, 247
mutual evaluation, 210, 251
mutual funds, 418
mutual legal assistance, 48

name, significance, 465
Nauru, 385

Netherlands Antilles, 376
Nevada, 407
nominees, 74
non-bank financial institutions, 155
Non-Cooperative Countries and
    Territories, 289

OECD, 254
    Antigua and Barbuda
        withdrawal, 308
    Committee on Fiscal Affairs, 312
    Harmful Tax Initiative, and the
        USA, 410
    Model Tax Convention, 93
    report, harmful tax competition, 308
        reactions thereto, 308
    tax, 93
    uncooperative tax havens, 319
OFCs
    aspiring OFCs, 448
    assessment program, IMF, 271
    components of a good reputation,
        469, 470
    constituents of success, 471
    evolution, 194
    name, significance, 465
    particular OFCs, 341
    perspectives, 471
    reputation, 466
        components, 469, 470
        significance, 466
    services of OFCs in demand, 362
    stability and credibility, 469, 470
    success, constituents of, 471
    underlying principles, 335
    see also Offshore
Offshore Finance Centres, see OFCs
Offshore Group of Banking
    Supervisors, see OGBS
Offshore Group of Collective
    Investment Scheme
    Supervisors, 254
Offshore Group of Insurance
    Supervisors, 253
Offshore
    characteristics, 50
    comparatives in the USA, 407
    continued existence, 438

future projections, 433
issues, 422
meaning, 3, 12
money laundering, 209
v. onshore, 54
'Offshoring', 76, 80
origins and development, 18
prospects for the future, 433
rationale, 486
standards, 49
stigma, 484
and the zero tax option, 109
see also OFCs
offsite compliance, 167
OGBS, 251
    Best Practice Paper, 61, 154, 251
    corporate service providers,
        Statement of Best Practice, 61,
        154, 251
    Statement of Best Practice, corporate
        service providers, 61, 154, 251
onshore
    onshore finance centres,
        characteristics, 55
    problems onshore, 345
onsite compliance, 167
Organization for Economic
    Cooperation and Development,
    see OECD
outsourcing, business process
    outsourcing, 80
overseas territories, 391

Palermo UN Convention, 46, 206
parallel banks, 336
Parmalat, 351
Partnership for Progress and
    Prosperity: Britain and the
    Overseas Territories, 391
pathos, 451
PC-R-EV Committee, definition, 255
Peillon-Montebourg Commission, 346
perspectives, 471
Ponzi schemes, 337
practice notes, 443
PriceWaterhouseCoopers, 157
principal officers, 204
problem/impact analysis, 117

Proceeds of Crime Act 2002 (UK), 395
protection, 117, 147, 161
prudential regulation, 117, 161
prudential supervision, 130, 161
punitive measures, 192
purpose trusts, 68
pyramid schemes, 337

qualified intermediary status, 410

rationale for regulation, 117
regulation, 43, 130
    comments, 148
    constituent parts, 130
    and crises, 148
    Offshore, 154
    in practice, 149
    prudential regulation, 149
    rationale, 117
    relative newness, 480
    self-regulation, 151
regulator, role of the regulator, 125
regulatory arbitrage, 45, 172
regulatory capture, 173
regulatory cycle, 194
regulatory independence, 173
regulatory structures, 179
    Canadian model, 179
    Mexican model, 179
    separate regulators model, 179
    Singaporean model, 179
    South African model, 179
    UK model, 179
reports on the observance of standards
    and codes (ROSCs), 278
reputation, 466
    components of a good reputation,
        469, 470
    significance, 466
Review of Financial Regulation in the
    Crown Dependencies ('Edwards
    Report'), 390
Riggs Bank, 419
risk-based approach, 167
ROSCs, 278

Sarbanes–Oxley Act (USA), 347, 420
savings and loans institutions, 351

Savings Tax Directive, see EU Savings
    Tax Directive secrecy, 46
securitisation, 462
self-regulatory organisations
    (SROs), 151
September 11, 2001, 296, 413
Serious Fraud Office (UK), 203
service providers, 58
services, other, 76
Seychelles, 448
shell banks/branches, 336
shipping, 74
single passport, 146, 180
small islands
    concentration of business, 371
    conducive infrastructure, 363
    currency of advantages, 369
    dominance of finance, 367
    economic expedience, 359
    involvement of outsiders, 366
    lack of influence externally, 368
    natural good fit, 365
    uniqueness, 370
    value of business generated, 370
'smurfing', 337
Society of Trust and Estate
    Practitioners, 325
special purpose vehicles, 61
St Lucia, 385
stability and credibility, 469, 470
standards, 49, 278
    minimum standards, 233
Statute of Elizabeth, 74
success, constituents, 471
supervision, 161
    institutional supervision, 130
suspicious activity reports,
        217, 395
Switzerland, 385
    and the EU Savings Directive, 98
systemic instability, 117

tax
    amnesties, 111
    avoidance, 85
    competition, 91
    evasion, 89, 429, 443
    harmonisation, 92

tax (*cont.*)
    haven, 27
        identified by OECD, 479
        information sharing agreements with
            USA, 93
        and Offshore, 93
        territorial, 85, 402
        worldwide, 85
terrorist financing, 220, 239
Tournier v. *National Provincial Bank*, 46
training and experience, 183
transfer pricing, 115
Transparency International, 154, 395,
        397, 406
trust and corporate service providers,
        155, 251
trust, regulatory/external factors, 190
trusts, 68
    accumulation and maintenance
        trusts, 68
    asset protection, 68
    discretionary trusts, 68
    foreign grantor trusts, 68
    life interest trusts, 68
    purpose trusts, 68
    and tax planning, 68
    VISTA trusts, 68
Turks and Caicos Islands, 386
'Twin Peaks' model, 153

UBS AG, 419
UCITS, 65
UK government, White Paper, 391
UN
    Convention Against Corruption, 423
    Convention Against Illicit Traffic in
        Narcotic Drugs and Psychotropic
        Substances, 46, 204, 206

Convention for the Suppression and
        Financing of Terrorism, 413
    initiatives, 206
    Offshore Forum, 255
    Palermo UN Convention, 46, 206
uncooperative tax havens,
        OECD, 319
underground banking, 217
Undertakings for Collective
        Investment in Transferable
        Securities, 65
unit trusts, 64
USA
    banking regulation, 402
    comparatives to OFCs, 407
    and the EU Savings
        Tax Directive, 102
    and 'know your customer', 406
    legal system encourages OFCs, 404
    links to Offshore, 404
    as an OFC, 402
    tax, the new angle, 453
    USA Patriot Act, 206, 296, 413

Vanuatu, 387
Vienna Convention, 46, 204, 206
VISTA trust, 68

'Wise Men', 146, 236
Wolfsberg Anti-Money Laundering
        Principles, 218, 406
Working Group on Cross-Border
        Banking, 138, 218
World Bank, 255
    and OFCs, 274
    IMF, FATF, joint working, 301

zero tax, 109